SECURITIES
MARKETS

McGraw-Hill Series in Finance

Consulting Editor
Charles A. D'Ambrosio
University of Washington

McGraw-Hill Finance Guide Series

Consulting Editor
Charles A. D'Ambrosio
University of Washington

SECURITIES MARKETS

Kenneth Garbade

Professor of Economics and Finance
Graduate School of Business Administration
New York University

McGRAW-HILL BOOK COMPANY

New York St. Louis San Francisco Auckland Bogotá Hamburg
Johannesburg London Madrid Mexico Montreal New Delhi
Panama Paris São Paulo Singapore Sydney Tokyo Toronto

FOR ARTHUR AND LOUISE GARBADE
MY FIRST TEACHERS

This book was set in Times Roman by A Graphic Method Inc.
The editors were Bonnie E. Lieberman and James B. Armstrong;
the production supervisor was Phil Galea.
The drawings were done by VIP Graphics.
R. R. Donnelley & Sons Company was printer and binder.

SECURITIES MARKETS

1234567890 DODO 8987654321

ISBN 0-07-022780-2

Library of Congress Cataloging in Publication Data

Garbade, Kenneth D.
    Securities markets.

    (McGraw-Hill series in finance)
    Includes index.
    1. Capital market. 2. Securities. 3. Stock-
exchange. I. Title. II. Series.
HG4523.G37   332.63'2   81-5965
ISBN 0-07-022780-2   AACR2

CONTENTS

PREFACE

This text is the outgrowth of a set of lecture notes I used from 1973 to 1981 in teaching a course called "Financial Markets: Their Structure and Performance" at the Graduate School of Business Administration, New York University. The course, and this text, have two principal foci: (1) the pricing of securities and (2) the institutional characteristics of securities markets, including both the new issue and secondary markets.

The text is divided into eight parts. Part One provides a descriptive introduction to the major types of financial claims traded in American securities markets, including Treasury, municipal, and corporate debt and corporate stock. Part One also describes how issuers sell new issues in the primary markets through price auctions, subscription offerings, underwritten offerings, and tap offerings.

The analytical core of the text consists of the equilibrium valuation of common stock—separated into the analysis of investor demand (portfolio theory) in Part Three and the characterization of a stock market in equilibrium (the capital asset pricing model and the efficient markets hypothesis) in Part Four—and the equilibrium valuation of claims with a finite lifetime in Parts Five and Six. The latter includes the term structure of interest rates, the structure of settlement prices on futures contracts, the pricing of call option contracts, and the pricing of risky debt.

The text also includes, in Parts Seven and Eight, a description of the structure of a variety of secondary markets and an analysis of the behavior of transactions prices in those markets. These topics, which are given only cursory treatment in most finance texts, have become areas of active interest to researchers and regulators during the past decade. My own teaching experience suggests that the material in Parts Seven and Eight provides a useful point of intersection between the Walrasian auction markets assumed in most economic models (including those in Parts Four, Five, and Six of this text) and the acquaintance of students with real securities markets.

Despite its focus on securities markets, this text also discusses, in Part Two, the Federal Reserve System in order to establish the determinants of short-term interest rates in the Federal funds and repurchase agreement markets.

This reflects the crucial role played by those markets in determining the general level of yields on other financial instruments.

I should mention here that throughout the text the generic masculine pronoun has been used solely on account of the brevity it affords. "The investor ... he," for example, is far less cumbersome than "the investor ... he or she." Such use of the masculine pronoun should not be interpreted as a wish to exclude women from the use of this text or from the field in general.

In the course of teaching and writing about securities markets, I have had the good fortune to discuss analytical and institutional issues with many practitioners, including Kevin Baltazar, Steve Black, Dick Fisher, Bob Geiger, Irwin Guttag, Eric Gronningsater, David Harris, Joe Hunt, Kevin Kenny, Arlen Klinger, Martin Lipton, Frank McDermott, Andrew Melton III, Bill Melton, Jay Peake, Fred Siesel, Doug Skolnick, and Don Stone. I am particularly indebted to Richard Fieldhouse, Homer Kripke, Alan Lerner, Ken Marks, and Jay Pomrenze for numerous conversations over the past few years.

My greatest obligations are to my friend, coresearcher, and colleague, Bill Silber. His influence on this text, and on our research, is greatly appreciated and can hardly be overestimated, even if I do not heed his wise counsel as often as I should.

I thank Bob Kavesh and Larry Ritter for fostering a creative and enjoyable atmosphere in the Economics and Finance departments at the Graduate School of Business Administration.

I would also like to express my thanks for the many useful comments and suggestions provided by colleagues who reviewed this text during the course of its development, especially to J. Kimball Dietrich (University of Southern California) and Dale Osborne (Oklahoma State University).

Finally, I add the caveat that while the credit for this text must go to many, the errors are mine alone.

Kenneth Garbade
Hoboken, New Jersey

MARKETABLE FINANCIAL ASSETS

A financial asset represents a claim on the issuer for a stream of future payments. The claim may be for a fixed dollar amount, as with a debt security, or it may be a residual claim, as with common stock. The four chapters in this part present a descriptive introduction to some of the principal financial assets traded in American securities markets. These assets include issues of the United States Treasury, federal agency issues, municipal and corporate securities, and bank-related liabilities. One of the principal objectives of this part is to contrast the claims on future payment streams associated with each security.

New issues of financial assets are sold by issuers in what are called *primary markets*. It is in these markets that governments and corporations raise funds to finance their activities. Each of the chapters in Part One describes how issuers sell new issues. Along the way we note the differences among alternative selling methods, such as auction offerings, subscription offerings, and tap offerings.

Current holders of most of the financial assets described below can exchange their future claims for cash. These exchanges are accomplished by selling the assets in *secondary-market* transactions. Although such transactions do not yield any additional funds for issuers, the existence of secondary markets is quite important to both issuers and investors. The facility with which future claims can be converted to cash is one of the principal reasons investors are willing to buy and hold marketable financial assets.

The remaining chapters in this text are concerned with (1) the pricing of financial assets in secondary markets and (2) the organization of those markets. Part Two analyzes the determination of yields on a basic debt instrument: overnight credit. Equilibrium valuation of common stock is treated in Parts Three and Four. Valuation of debt securities with a maturity of more than 1 day is treated in Part Five. Part Six analyzes the valuation of options on risky securities and uses that analysis to investigate credit risk on debt instruments. The basic objective in each of these parts is analysis of the relative yields on different financial assets. For example, why should one stock be expected to appreciate at a greater rate than another stock, and why should yields on debt instruments differ as a function of the maturities of those instruments?

The last two parts of the text describe and analyze more closely the actual functioning of secondary markets. The institutional structures of secondary markets are described in Part Seven. Part Eight analyzes the transactional characteristics of secondary-market purchases and sales. The objective of these two parts is to study the processes by which buyers and sellers trade securities.

In summary, this text is concerned with the nature of securities, their valuation, and their exchange. We begin with the securities themselves.

CHAPTER 1

TREASURY AND FEDERAL AGENCY SECURITIES

From time to time the federal government issues debt securities to finance expenditures in excess of tax receipts or to refinance maturing debt. The cumulative size of the federal deficits carried over from World War II and the large deficits of the 1970s has fostered a central role for Treasury securities in American financial markets. Investors find those securities attractive because they are free of the risk of default: Treasury securities do not bear what is conventionally known as *credit risk*, or the risk that a debtor will not pay according to his promises. In addition, Treasury securities are usually outstanding in issue sizes which run to $5 billion or more. These large sizes ensure the existence of what is called a *liquid* secondary market, or one in which buyers and sellers can trade large quantities of a given security quickly without affecting the market price of the security. Many investors have a strong preference for Treasury securities because of their great liquidity. The first two sections of this chapter describe the characteristics of two types of Treasury debt: bills and coupon issues.

In addition to its regular tax and expenditure programs, the federal government also sponsors several financial intermediaries, commonly called *federal agencies*. These intermediaries issue debt securities and relend the proceeds of their borrowings for the benefit of selected interest groups, primarily farmers and home buyers. Although the activities of the federal credit agencies are not substantively different from those of private financial intermediaries like commercial banks and finance companies, discussions of federal agency debt are traditionally coupled with descriptions of Treasury debt. Moreover, the secondary markets for agency debt are closely associated with those for Treasury

3

debt, because the same investors are typically active in both markets. The third section of this chapter discusses some of the important characteristics of federal agency debt.

1.1 TREASURY BILLS

Treasury bills are promises of the United States Treasury to pay a stipulated amount (called the *face value* of the bill) on a stated maturity date. There are no intermediate payments such as semiannual coupons associated with the obligation. All Treasury bills have a maturity date no more than 1 year from their issue date; that is, they have original maturities of less than a year. Most bills currently issued have original maturities of 91 days (13 weeks), 182 days (26 weeks), or 364 days (52 weeks).

Price Conventions

One might think that because the holder of a Treasury bill receives only one future payment in return for his current investment outlay, the rate of return on a Treasury bill should be unambiguous and easy to express. This is not quite the case. In fact, market participants use one type of interest rate (the discount rate) when they are buying and selling bills and a different interest rate (the bond equivalent yield) when they are measuring rates of return. Moreover, analysts frequently use a third expression (the continuously compounded yield) for comparing returns on bills with different maturities. We now examine each of these interest rates.

The Discount Rate   Bills offered for sale and sought for purchase in the secondary market are quoted on a *discount rate* basis. Suppose a bill with n days to maturity is currently priced at P percent of its face value, that is, at $\$P$ per $\$100$ face value. That bill has a discount rate d defined as

$$d = \frac{360}{n} \frac{100 - P}{100} \tag{1.1}$$

The difference between face value and market price is the discount on the bill. It represents the dollar gain accruing to an investor who holds the bill to maturity. The discount rate is the annualized percentage discount from face value, assuming simple interest (no compounding) over a 360-day year. Market quotations for bills are conventionally made in terms of discount rates rather than dollar prices or percent of face value. The implied price can be computed readily by solving for P in Equation (1.1). Exhibit 1.1 shows an example of Treasury bill price and discount rate calculations.

The Bond Equivalent Yield   The discount rate is a poor measure of the rate of return on a Treasury bill, because it is based on face value rather than on the cost of the bill to the investor, and because it assumes a short (360-day) year. (It is important only because it is so widely used for quotation purposes.)

A more reasonable approximation of the return on a bill held to maturity is the bond equivalent yield. Letting P and n be as above, the bond equivalent yield i is defined[1] as

$$i = \frac{365}{n} \frac{100 - P}{P} \qquad (1.2)$$

The yield is the gain per dollar invested (rather than per dollar of face value), assuming simple interest over a 365-day year. The bond equivalent yield corrects for the two most glaring defects of the discount rate as a measure of the rate of return on a Treasury bill: the assumption of a short year and the use of face value as the base on which the gain is calculated. The bond equivalent yield on a Treasury bill is always greater than the discount rate on that bill, because the price of the bill is less than face value. Exhibit 1.1 shows how the bond equivalent yield is computed for a Treasury bill.

The Continuously Compounded Yield The bond equivalent yield on a Treasury bill does not correct the assumption of simple interest used to compute the discount rate. Comparing the yields on two bills with different maturities can, consequently, be misleading. Since there is no obvious choice for the compounding period on a bill, most analysts assume continuous compounding when they want standardized yields for comparative purposes.[2] For given values of P and n, the continuously compounded yield r is defined as

$$r = \frac{365}{n} \ln \left[\frac{100}{P} \right] \qquad (1.3)$$

where $\ln [x]$ is the natural logarithm of x. Readers unfamiliar with continuous compounding may wish to refer to the appendix to this chapter. Solving for P in Equation (1.3) gives

$$P = 100 \exp \left[-r \frac{n}{365} \right] \qquad (1.4)$$

where $\exp [x]$ is the base e of natural logarithms raised to the power x. Equation (1.4) shows that the price P is the present value of $100 to be received n days in the future, discounted at the continuously compounded annual rate r.

---

[1] When a Treasury bill has more than 182 days to run to maturity, the bond equivalent yield i is implicitly defined by the equation

$$100 = P(1 + \frac{1}{2}i) \left(1 + \frac{1}{2}i \frac{n - 182.5}{182.5}\right)$$

[2] The appendix to this chapter shows how rates of return can be computed for investment intervals of arbitrary length using continuously compounded yields.

Exhibit 1.1 shows the computation of continuously compounded yields for several different Treasury bill maturities.

New Issues

Treasury bills come to market through periodic public auctions open to all investors. The auctions are held by the twelve district Federal Reserve banks acting as fiscal agents for the United States Treasury. New supplies of 91- and

EXHIBIT 1.1
YIELDS ON TREASURY BILLS ON TUESDAY, MAY 16, 1978

Maturity date	Days to maturity (n)	Quoted discount rate (d), %	Price (P)	Bond equivalent yield (i), %	Continuously compounded yield (r), %
May 18	2	6.13	$99.966	6.22	6.21
June 15	30	5.99	99.501	6.10	6.09
July 13	58	6.00	99.033	6.14	6.11
August 17	93	6.41	98.344	6.61	6.55
September 14	121	6.59	97.785	6.83	6.76
October 12	149	6.82	97.177	7.12	7.01

Computations for bill maturing August 17:

To compute the price, solve for P in the equation for the discount rate [Equation (1.1)]:
$d = (360/n) [(100 - P)/100]$.

$$P = 100(1 - nd/360)$$
$$= 100(1 - 93(.0641)/360)$$
$$= 100(1 - .01656)$$
$$= 98.344$$

To compute the bond equivalent yield, use Equation (1.2):

$$i = \frac{365}{n} \frac{100 - P}{P}$$
$$= \frac{365}{93} \frac{100 - 98.344}{98.344}$$
$$= .0661, \text{ or } 6.61\%$$

To compute the continuously compounded yield, use Equation (1.3):

$$r = \frac{365}{n} \ln \left[\frac{100}{P} \right]$$
$$= \frac{365}{93} \ln \left[\frac{100}{98.344} \right]$$
$$= \frac{365}{93} \ln [1.01684]$$
$$= \frac{365}{93} (.01670)$$
$$= .0655, \text{ or } 6.55\%$$

182-day bills are auctioned once a week, and 52-week bills are auctioned once every 4 weeks. Except for conflicts with holiday schedules, auctions are held on a Monday and the new bills are issued and paid for the following Thursday.

There are two ways of participating in an auction of Treasury bills. The first is by submitting a competitive tender, on which a bidder states the amount he is willing to pay for the new bills (as a percent of face value) and the quantity of bills desired at that price. Exhibit 1.2 shows a tender for a 182-day bill. If the Treasury accepts an investor's competitive tender, the investor pays his bid price for the desired quantity of bills. If the Treasury rejects his tender, the investor pays nothing and gets nothing. Competitive bidders are uncertain whether they will get any bills, but they know exactly the price they will pay if their bid is accepted.

Some investors are not especially price-sensitive, possibly because they wish to purchase a relatively small amount of bills on which the dollar consequences of price variations of a few hundredths of a percent of face value are small. For the benefit of these investors, the Treasury also accepts noncompetitive tenders. As shown in Exhibit 1.2, a person submitting a noncompetitive tender states the face value of bills which he wishes to purchase and agrees to pay the average of the accepted competitive prices for those bills. Noncompetitive tenders are limited to a maximum of $500,000 per bidder. The Treasury guarantees to meet fully all noncompetitive demands, but at a price which is not known until the auction is completed. A noncompetitive tender sacrifices certainty of price in return for certainty of delivery. Individuals, small commercial banks, and small corporations account for the bulk of the noncompetitive demand for bills. Noncompetitive bids were introduced to allow these relatively unsophisticated investors the opportunity to acquire with certainty the small quantities of bills they typically demand. Larger banks and broker-dealer firms, especially those which make markets in Treasury issues, submit the bulk of the competitive bids.[3]

To determine which competitive bids will be satisfied, the Treasury first subtracts the face value of all noncompetitive tenders from the total face value of the bills it is offering. The difference must be sold to competitive bidders. Competitive tenders are then ordered by price, and the demands of the highest bidders are satisfied first. The lowest accepted competitive price is called the *stop-out* price. Once the accepted competitive bids have been determined, the average accepted competitive price is computed and applied to the noncompetitive bidders.[4] Exhibit 1.3 shows the results of the May 8, 1978, auction of 91-day Treasury bills.

The Treasury acts as a perfectly discriminating monopolist in bill auctions.[5]

[3] The behavior of government security dealers in bill auctions has been studied by Rieber (1965, 1967).

[4] Boatler (1975) has examined the determinants of the difference between the average accepted competitive price and the stop-out price in Treasury bill auctions.

[5] Friedman (1959, pp. 64–65) has argued that this auction procedure brings in less revenues than if all successful bidders were permitted to buy at the lowest accepted price. His claim was strongly disputed by Brimmer (1962), Goldstein (1962b), and Rieber (1964). Friedman has replied to his critics in Friedman (1963, 1964). See also Smith (1966, 1967).

That is, as the only, or monopolistic, seller of new Treasury bills, it can and does force each competitive bidder to pay exactly its bid price, thereby discriminating among different bidders by selling them identical securities at different prices. Two bidders may acquire the same quantity of bills yet pay different

EXHIBIT 1.2
Tender for 182-day Treasury bill.

(Closing date for receipt of this tender is Monday, September 29, 1975)

TENDER FOR 182-DAY TREASURY BILLS

Dated October 2, 1975   Maturing April 1, 1976

To FEDERAL RESERVE BANK OF NEW YORK,   Dated at ....
Fiscal Agent of the United States.   ...., 19___

Pursuant to the provisions of Treasury Department Circular No. 418 (current revision) and to the provisions of the public notice issued by the Treasury Department inviting tenders for the above-described Treasury bills, the undersigned hereby offers to purchase such Treasury bills in the amount indicated below, and agrees to make payment therefor at your Bank on or before the issue date at the price indicated below:

COMPETITIVE TENDER	*Do not fill in both Competitive and Noncompetitive tenders on one form*	**NONCOMPETITIVE TENDER**

$............................... (maturity value) $............................... (maturity value)
or any lesser amount that may be awarded.   *(Not to exceed $500,000 for one bidder through all sources)*

Price : .... per 100.   at the average price of accepted competitive bids.
(Price must be expressed with not more than three decimal places, for example, 99.925)

Subject to allotment, please issue, deliver, and accept payment for the bills as indicated below:

Pieces	Denomination	Maturity value			
	$ 10,000			□ 1. Deliver over the counter to the undersigned	Payment will be made as follows: □ By charge to our reserve account
	15,000			□ 2. Ship to the undersigned	□ By cash or check in *immediately available funds* on delivery
	50,000			□ 3. Hold in safekeeping (for member bank only) in—	*(Payment cannot be made through Treasury Tax and Loan Account)*
	100,000			□ Investment Account	
	500,000			□ General Account	□ 5. Special instructions:
	1,000,000			□ Trust Account	
	Totals			□ 4. Allotment transfer (see list attached) *(No changes in delivery instructions will be accepted)*	

The undersigned (member bank) hereby certifies that the Treasury bills which you are hereby instructed to dispose of in the manner indicated in item 3 above are owned solely by the undersigned.

Insert this tender in special envelope marked "Tender for Treasury Bills"

....
(Name of subscriber—please print or type)

....
(Address—incl. City and State)

....
(Tel. No.)   (Signature of subscriber or authorized signature)

....
(Title of authorized signer)

(Banking institutions submitting tenders for customer account must list customers' names on lines below or on an attached rider)

....
(Name of customer)   (Name of customer)

INSTRUCTIONS:

1. No tender for less than $10,000 will be considered, and each tender must be for an even multiple of $5,000 (maturity value).

2. Only banking institutions, and dealers who make primary markets in Government securities and report daily to this Bank their positions with respect to Government securities and borrowings thereon, may submit tenders for customer account; in doing so, they may consolidate competitive tenders *at the same price* and may consolidate noncompetitive tenders, provided a list is attached showing the name of each bidder and the amount bid for his account. Others will not be permitted to submit tenders except for their own account.

3. If the person making the tender is a corporation, the tender should be signed by an officer of the corporation authorized to make the tender, and the signing of the tender by an officer of the corporation will be construed as a representation by him that he has been so authorized. If the tender is made by a partnership, it should be signed by a member of the firm, who should sign in the form ".., a copartnership, by ...., a member of the firm."

4. Tenders will be received without deposit from incorporated banks and trust companies and from responsible and recognized dealers in investment securities. Tenders from others must be accompanied by payment of 2 percent of the face amount of Treasury bills applied for, unless the tenders are accompanied by an express guaranty of payment by an incorporated bank or trust company. All checks must be drawn to the order of the Federal Reserve Bank of New York; checks endorsed to this Bank will not be accepted.

5. If the language of this tender is changed in any respect, which, in the opinion of the Secretary of the Treasury, is material, the tender may be disregarded.

5/75   [40]

EXHIBIT 1.3

TREASURY BILLS AT ORIGINAL ISSUE

The Monday, May 8, 1978, auction of 91-day Treasury bills, deliverable May 11, 1978, and maturing August 10, 1978, had the following outcome:

	Price	Discount rate, %	Bond equivalent yield, %
High price	$98.370	6.448*	6.65†
Average price paid by noncompetitive bidders	98.366	6.464	6.66
Stop-out price	98.365	6.468	6.67

*Sample calculations:

$$d = \frac{360}{n} \frac{100 - P}{100}$$

$$= \frac{360}{91} \frac{100 - 98.370}{100}$$

$$= .06448, \text{ or } 6.448\%$$

†Sample calculations:

$$i = \frac{365}{n} \frac{100 - P}{100}$$

$$= \frac{365}{91} \frac{100 - 98.370}{98.370}$$

$$= .0665, \text{ or } 6.65\%$$

A total of $4.98 billion face value Treasury bills was applied for, of which $2.30 billion was accepted. Noncompetitive bidders accounted for $0.36 billion of the issue. Bids at the stop-out price were reduced to 79 percent of their tender size. All bids above that price were accepted in full, and all bids below that price were rejected.

---

prices for those bills. Moreover, since multiple competitive tenders at different bid prices may be submitted by a single investor, it is possible for a single bidder to have several of its tenders accepted at different prices.

The volume of tenders submitted by noncompetitive bidders can have a significant impact on the average price at which bills are sold in a given auction. For example, if noncompetitive demand is unexpectedly slack, the Treasury will have to sell a larger fraction of the issue to competitive bidders. This will lower the stop-out price and, in turn, lower the average accepted price. Conversely, unexpectedly strong noncompetitive demand will raise the stop-out price. The fraction of Treasury bills sold to noncompetitive bidders in a single auction has varied widely. It was 6.3 percent in the September 4, 1972, auction for 91-day bills, and 30.0 percent in the September 9, 1974, auction for bills of the same maturity.[6]

---

[6] Mullineaux (1973a, b) discusses the major reason for increased noncompetitive bidding when interest rates are high: the desire of small investors to get better rates than those available from savings accounts at commercial banks and savings and loan associations.

Bill auctions close at 1:30 P.M., New York time, and competitive bidders frequently wait until 1:20 or 1:25 before telephoning their bid prices to messengers at their local Federal Reserve bank. This gives them an opportunity to get the latest possible information on the prices at which outstanding bills are trading in the secondary market. A difference of 1 basis point ($\frac{1}{100}$ of a percent) in the discount rate on a 91-day $100 million bill is $2500.[7] Close attention to rapidly moving markets can mean the difference between acceptance or rejection of a bid, or paying a price close to or far above the stop-out price.

Denominations

Treasury bills come in a minimum face value of $10,000 and are available in $5000 increments above that amount. Until 1970 the Treasury offered bills in $1000 units. In that year high short-term interest rates led many small depositors to withdraw their funds from bank deposits (on which yields were limited by regulations of the Federal Reserve, the Federal Deposit Insurance Corporation, and the Federal Home Loan Bank Board) and invest directly in Treasury bills. The resulting outflow of deposits, so-called disintermediation, alarmed the officers of many thrift institutions. They petitioned the Treasury to raise the minimum size of a bill. The thrift institutions reasoned that while many savers might have a few thousand dollars to put into bills, there are significantly fewer investors who have $10,000 or more that they would be willing to tie up for 3 or 6 months. The Treasury consented and, in raising the minimum size of a bill to $10,000, created an indivisibility in Treasury bills that forced many small savers out of the market.[8]

Special Issues of Bills

Besides issuing the regular series of weekly 91- and 182-day bills and quadriweekly 52-week bills, the Treasury issues other bills on an irregular basis. It uses these special issues to bridge temporary cash flow problems. The first nonstandard bill was the *tax anticipation bill* (TAB), introduced in 1951. TABs have a maturity date approximately 1 week after corporate profit tax payment dates. They are, however, acceptable at face value in payment of such taxes when presented by a corporation. Corporate holders therefore get several days of "free interest" on TABs. This attractive feature leads corporations to bid up the price (and bid down the yield to stated maturity) on TABs relative to other bills with a similar stated maturity but without the tax anticipation feature.

A *strip issue* is a block of bills which mature on sequential maturity dates. Auctions of strip issues add to existing supplies of outstanding bills. Introduced

---

[7] This is, 1 percent of 100 million for a year is $1 million. Thus 1 basis point for a year is $\frac{1}{100}$ of that amount (or $10,000), and 1 basis point for a quarter of a year (or 91 days) is $2500.

[8] For an analysis and criticism of the Treasury action, see Kane (1970) and Mullineaux (1973a, b).

in 1961, strip issues are used when the Treasury needs cash and chooses to spread its borrowings out over several bill maturities rather than add a substantial amount to a single maturity. A strip of bills may also be issued if interest rates are particularly low in one segment of bill maturities, implying strong investor demand for those bills and providing the Treasury with an opportunity to borrow inexpensively.

When a strip issue is auctioned, investors must bid on a unit of the whole strip (typically $10,000 face value of each bill) and cannot pick and choose their preferred maturity. In the offering described in Exhibit 1.4, the Treasury offered a strip of fifteen bills and required bids for at least $150,000 face value of the block. Noncompetitive as well as competitive bidding was available, but noncompetitive bidders were limited to $20,000 of each of the fifteen bills.

EXHIBIT 1.4
AUCTION OFFERING OF A STRIP OF TREASURY BILLS
On February 24, 1972, the Treasury announced an offering of a strip of Treasury bills. The strip consisted of fifteen different outstanding bill maturities and had an aggregate face value of $3 billion. The bills included in the strip were as follows:

Maturity dates (1972)	Days from March 6, 1972, to maturity	Amount currently outstanding (in millions)	Amount of additional issues (in millions)
March 30	24	$3,903	$ 200
April 6	31	3,901	200
April 13	38	3,903	200
April 20	45	3,901	200
April 27	52	3,902	200
May 4	59	3,902	200
May 11	66	3,901	200
May 18	73	4,007	200
May 25	80	4,001	200
June 1	87	1,601	200
June 8	94	1,601	200
June 15	101	1,600	200
June 22	108	1,602	200
June 29	115	1,601	200
July 6	122	1,601	200
			$3000

The minimum size of a tender was set at $150,000 face value. Tenders for more than the minimum amount had to be in multiples of $75,000. A successful tender for, say, $300,000 face value of the strip would receive $20,000 face value of each bill in the strip.

The auction was held on Wednesday, March 1, 1972. The bills were issued, and paid for, on Monday, March 6, 1972. The average accepted competitive price was 99.3095. This means that a noncompetitive bidder paid $148,964 for $150,000 face amount of the strip ($148,964 is 99.3095 percent of $150,000).

Once a strip has been auctioned off, buyers are free to break up the strip as they desire; i.e., the strip is indivisible only through the auction. Because of their size, strip issues are sold mainly to professional investors and to dealer firms, who resell the component bills as individual maturities in the secondary market. Bidding on strips is more difficult than bidding on single bills, because

EXHIBIT 1.5
PRIMARY DEALERS IN UNITED STATES TREASURY SECURITIES
(AS OF FEBRUARY 1980)

Bank dealers

Bank of America N.T. & S.A.
Bankers Trust Company
The Chase Manhattan Bank, N.A.
Chemical Bank
Citibank, N.A.
Continental Illinois National Bank and Trust Company of Chicago
Crocker National Bank
First National Bank of Chicago
Harris Trust and Savings Bank
Morgan Guaranty Trust Company of New York
The Northern Trust Company
United California Bank

Nonbank dealers

ACLI Government Securities, Inc.
Bache Halsey Stuart Shields Inc.
A. G. Becker Incorporated
Briggs, Schaedle & Co., Inc.
Carroll McEntee & McGinley Incorporated
Discount Corporation of New York
Donaldson Lufkin & Jenrette Securities Corporation
The First Boston Corporation
First Pennco Securities, Inc.
Goldman, Sachs & Co.
E. F. Hutton & Company, Inc.
Kidder, Peabody & Co., Incorporated
Aubrey G. Lanston & Co., Inc.
Lehman Government Securities Incorporated
Merrill Lynch Government Securities Inc.
Morgan Stanley & Co., Inc.
Nuveen Government Securities, Inc.
Paine, Webber, Jackson & Curtis Incorporated
Wm. E. Pollock & Co., Inc.
Chas. E. Quincey & Co.
Salomon Brothers
Second District Securities Co., Inc.
Smith, Barney, Harris Upham & Co., Incorporated
Stuart Brothers N.Y. Hanseatic Division
Dean Witter Reynolds Incorporated

the secondary market places a different value on each of the component bills, yet the strip must be bid as a single block.

Cash management bills are a recent innovation in Treasury bill financing. Introduced in 1975, cash management bills usually have extremely short maturities (the first was 18 days) and are aimed at institutional rather than retail investors. The minimum tender for the first cash management bill was set at $10 million, with increments over the minimum of $1 million. Noncompetitive tenders were not permitted. Like strip issues, cash management bills are reopenings of existing maturities.

Secondary-Market Trading

Outstanding Treasury bills trade in an extremely efficient and highly liquid over-the-counter secondary market. More than thirty primary dealers, listed in Exhibit 1.5, make continuous bid and offer quotations at which they stand ready to buy and sell bills of most maturities for their own account. These dealers include both commercial banks, such as Morgan Guaranty Trust and Bankers Trust, which make markets in Treasury bills (that is, they are ready to buy and sell bills to accommodate their customers) as well as run their regular banking business; and nonbank dealers, such as Salomon Brothers and First Boston, which are dealers and brokers in a wide variety of negotiable securities. Dealers purchase and sell bills for their own inventory and at their own risk; i.e., a dealer is a principal in a transaction. This may be distinguished from, for example, a stock broker acting as agent for a customer in buying or selling common stock on the New York Stock Exchange.

When a dealer is asked for its market (or purchase and sale prices) in a particular bill, it quotes bid and offer discount rates. Suppose the bill that a customer is interested in has n days to go to maturity, and the dealer quotes bid discount rate d_b and offer rate d_o. The bid and offer prices at which the dealer is willing to buy and sell, denoted P_b and P_o, respectively, are then

$$P_o = 100 \left(1 - \frac{nd_o}{360}\right) \tag{1.5}$$

$$P_b = 100 \left(1 - \frac{nd_b}{360}\right) \tag{1.6}$$

For example, suppose a dealer quotes a market of 7.45 percent bid and 7.42 percent offered on a 60-day bill. Then its bid and offer prices are

$$P_o = 100 \left[1 - \frac{60(.0742)}{360}\right]$$
$$= 98.7633$$
$$P_b = 100 \left[1 - \frac{60(.0745)}{360}\right]$$
$$= 98.7583$$

The dealer's spread is 3 basis points, or $50 per $1 million face value of the bill. (Note that 98.7633 − 98.7583 = .0050 percent of face value.)

The most actively traded bills are those which were most recently auctioned, i.e., the latest 91- and 182-day bills and the latest 52-week bill. The spreads between the bid and offer discount rates on these bills are quite small, frequently no more than 1 or 2 basis points. Standard-size transactions in such new bills range from $5 million to $25 million, although transactions of up to $100 million are not infrequent and can usually be accomplished fairly easily. Seasoned bill maturities trade less actively and in a greater variety of face values, with large trades becoming less frequent as a bill approaches its maturity date.

The Treasury bill market is said to be the most liquid securities market in the world, because the size of a conventional transaction can run to as much as $25 million, and because the difference between the price a dealer is willing to pay for an issue and the price at which it is willing to sell the same issue is very small, sometimes as low as 1 basis point or $25 per $1 million face value on a 90-day bill. These characteristics of the bill market mean that investors do not have to spend much time looking for favorable quotations, nor do they have to incur much expense buying or selling large quantities of bills. This liquidity is quite different from the liquidity of the used-car market, for example, and it is a major reason investors view Treasury bills as a desirable store of wealth.

1.2   TREASURY COUPON ISSUES

Coupon issues are entitlements to a stream of multiple payments from the Treasury. The payment stream consists of two parts. First is the principal or maturity value of the issue, payable at a stated future date. The second is a regular sequence of semiannual interest or coupon payments. The ratio of the value of the coupon payments made in a single year to the principal value of the issue is called the *coupon rate*. The future payment stream associated with a coupon issue is fully specified by knowing its principal value, coupon rate, and maturity date. Each of these items is printed on the face of every issue.

Consider, for example, a 7 percent coupon issue which matures on May 15, 1987. That issue is *defined* by its coupon rate of 7 percent and its maturity date. An owner of $1 million principal value of the issue will receive $35,000 every May 15 and November 15 up to and including May 15, 1987. On that date he will also receive the $1 million principal value of the issue.

Price Conventions

Coupon issues are quoted in secondary-market trading on a price basis. The price is expressed as a percent of principal value or, equivalently, as the dollar price per $100 principal value. Price differences finer than 1 percent are conventionally quoted in 32nds of a percent, although coupon issues will occasionally trade on a 64th of a percent or even a 128th of a percent. Thus, an issue priced at 96.4375 percent of its principal value will be quoted as $96^{14}/_{32}$ percent. (Observe that .4375 = $^{14}/_{32}$.) Note the difference between the quotation of coupon instruments on a price basis and, as we discussed in the previous section, the quotation of Treasury bills on a discount rate basis.

There are two important yields used to measure the return on an investment in coupon issues. The first is the current yield, or the ratio of two coupon payments to current market value. The second is the yield to maturity, which is defined as that interest rate which makes the *present discounted value* of the future principal and coupon payments equal to the current market value of a coupon issue. The latter yield measure takes into account capital gains and losses at maturity as well as current coupon income.

Current Yield   The current yield is the rate of return derived from looking only at the coupon payments on a coupon issue. Let R_{cp} be the coupon rate on an issue, expressed as a fraction, and let P be the price of the issue. The dollar value of two semiannual coupon payments is then $\$(R_{cp})(100)$ per \$100 principal value. These coupon payments may also be expressed in terms of a rate of return on the market price P of the issue: $\$(R_{cr})(P)$, where R_{cr} is the implied current yield. Equating the two expressions for the coupon payments, we have

$$R_{cp}(100) = R_{cr}(P)$$

or
$$R_{cr} = R_{cp} \frac{100}{P} \qquad (1.7)$$

Exhibit 1.6 shows the current yields on some coupon issues on May 15, 1978. If an issue is priced at a discount ($P < 100$), the current yield is greater than the coupon rate. If the issue is at a premium ($P > 100$), the coupon rate overstates the current yield. Current yield is of interest to those investors primarily concerned with the intermediate cash payments offered by an issue prior to maturity.

Yield to Maturity   If a coupon issue is at a discount ($P < 100$), we can separate the stream of *net* future payments into two parts: the coupon payments and a capital gain of $100 - P$ at maturity. (The sum of the market price P and the capital gain $100 - P$ equals the principal returned at maturity.) Current yield ignores the capital gain component of the payment stream and hence understates the rate of return on an issue trading at a discount. (It also overstates the return on an issue selling at a premium, on which there will be a capital loss at maturity.) The yield to maturity attempts to correct for this omission.

The yield to maturity on a coupon issue is the internal rate of return on the issue. It is that interest rate which makes the present value of the future payment stream equal to the current market price of the issue.

To compute the yield to maturity on a coupon issue, we have to consider the nature of its payment stream. Suppose the issue is priced at P with a coupon rate R_{cp} and has n coupons remaining to be paid, one having just been paid. In

EXHIBIT 1.6
YIELDS ON TREASURY NOTES ON TUESDAY, MAY 16, 1978

Maturity date	Coupon rate (R_{cp}), %	Quoted price (P)	Current yield (R_{cr}), %	Yield to maturity (R_m), %	Continuously compounded yield to maturity (r), %
Nov. 15, 1978	6	$ 99^{10}/_{32}$	6.04	7.43	7.29
May 15, 1979	$7^7/_8$	$100^7/_{32}$	7.86	7.64	7.50
Nov. 15, 1979	$6^1/_4$	$97^{24}/_{32}$	6.39	7.87	7.72
May 15, 1980	$6^7/_8$	$98^7/_{32}$	7.00	7.85	7.70
Nov. 15, 1980	$7^1/_8$	$98^1/_{32}$	7.27	8.01	7.85
May 15, 1981	$7^1/_2$	$98^{18}/_{32}$	7.61	8.05	7.89

Computations for note maturing May 15, 1979:

The coupon rate is $7^7/_8$ percent, or $R_{cp} = .07875$. The price is $100^7/_{32}$, or $P = 100.2188$. To compute the current yield, use Equation (1.7):

$$R_{cr} = R_{cp} \frac{100}{P}$$

$$= .07875 \frac{100}{100.2188}$$

$$= .0786, \text{ or } 7.86\%$$

There is no way to compute directly the yield to maturity. However, we can use Equation (1.8) to check the asserted value of $R_m = .0764$. There are two coupons remaining to be paid on the May 15, 1979, $7^7/_8$ percent note. One will be paid in 6 months, on November 15, 1978, and the other will be paid at maturity. Thus, $n = 2$ in Equation (1.8). Using the equation, the quoted price P is

$$^1/_2 \frac{R_{cp}(100)}{1 + ^1/_2 R_m} + \frac{100 + ^1/_2 R_{cp}(100)}{(1 + ^1/_2 R_m)^2}$$

$$= ^1/_2 \frac{.07875(100)}{1 + ^1/_2(.0764)} + \frac{100 + ^1/_2(.07875)(100)}{[1 + ^1/_2(.0764)]^2}$$

$$= \frac{3.9375}{1.03820} + \frac{103.9375}{1.07786}$$

$$= 3.79 + 96.43$$

$$= 100.22, \text{ or } 100^7/_{32}$$

To compute the continuously compounded yield to maturity, use Equation (1.10):

$$1 + ^1/_2 R_m = \exp \left[\frac{r}{2} \right]$$

or

$$r = 2 \ln [1 + ^1/_2 R_m]$$

$$= 2 \ln [1 + ^1/_2(.0764)]$$

$$= 2 \ln [1.0382]$$

$$= .0750, \text{ or } 7.50\%$$

the United States a terminal coupon is conventionally paid at maturity on both public and private bond issues. For our example there are, then, $n - 1$ semiannual payments of $\frac{1}{2}R_{cp}(100)$ and a terminal payment of $100 + \frac{1}{2}R_{cp}(100)$ remaining on the issue. The yield to maturity is defined as the solution R_m to the equation

$$
\begin{aligned}
P = & \frac{\frac{1}{2}R_{cp}(100)}{1 + \frac{1}{2}R_m} \\
& + \frac{\frac{1}{2}R_{cp}(100)}{(1 + \frac{1}{2}R_m)^2} \\
& + \frac{\frac{1}{2}R_{cp}(100)}{(1 + \frac{1}{2}R_m)^3} \\
& \quad \cdots\cdots\cdots \\
& + \frac{\frac{1}{2}R_{cp}(100)}{(1 + \frac{1}{2}R_m)^{n-1}} \\
& + \frac{100 + \frac{1}{2}R_{cp}(100)}{(1 + \frac{1}{2}R_m)^n}
\end{aligned}
\tag{1.8}
$$

The current price P of the issue is equated to the sum of the discounted present values of the future payments from the issue. For some illustrative yields to maturity, see Exhibit 1.6.

The yield to maturity R_m in Equation (1.8) assumes, as is the convention for bond issues, a semiannual compounding period. (See the appendix to this chapter for a discussion of compounding conventions.) The *continuously compounded* yield to maturity r may be computed by solving for r in the equation

$$
\begin{aligned}
P = & \frac{1}{2}R_{cp}(100)\exp\left[-\frac{r}{2}\right] \\
& + \frac{1}{2}R_{cp}(100)\exp\left[-2\frac{r}{2}\right] \\
& + \frac{1}{2}R_{cp}(100)\exp\left[-3\frac{r}{2}\right] \\
& \quad \cdots\cdots\cdots\cdots \\
& + \frac{1}{2}R_{cp}(100)\exp\left[-(n-1)\frac{r}{2}\right] \\
& + [100 + \frac{1}{2}R_{cp}(100)]\exp\left[-n\frac{r}{2}\right]
\end{aligned}
\tag{1.9}
$$

Comparing Equations (1.8) and (1.9), we have that the semiannually and continuously compounded yields are related according to the equation

$$
1 + \frac{1}{2}R_m = \exp\left[\frac{r}{2}\right]
\tag{1.10}
$$

If r is small, exp $[r/2]$ is approximately equal to $1 + r/2$, so that R_m is approximately equal to r.

There is an equivalent way to write Equation (1.8) which is useful for analyzing the relation between coupon rates, current yields, and yields to maturity. It can be shown[9] that the price of a coupon issue can also be written as

$$P = 100 \left[\frac{R_{cp}}{R_m} + \frac{1 - R_{cp}/R_m}{(1 + \frac{1}{2}R_m)^n} \right] \tag{1.11}$$

To see why this formulation is useful, suppose we know that an issue has a yield to maturity equal to its coupon rate, so that $R_m = R_{cp}$. Then, from Equation (1.11) we have that $P = 100$. Thus, an issue with a price equal to its principal value has an identical coupon rate, current yield [see Equation (1.7)], and yield to maturity.

More generally, if at maturity we got back just the current market value of an issue, the yield to maturity would equal the current yield. For an issue at a discount, however, we get back more than the price P, and so the yield to maturity must be greater than the current yield, that is, $R_m > R_{cr} > R_{cp}$ when $P < 100$. Conversely, when an issue is at a premium, we suffer a capital loss at maturity, and so $R_m < R_{cr} < R_{cp}$ when $P > 100$. Exhibit 1.6 compares the current yield and yield to maturity on several coupon issues.

Accrued Interest   The dollar cost of buying a coupon issue is not exactly equal to the quoted price P if the purchase occurs at some date other than immediately after a coupon payment. In general, buyers must compensate sellers for the accrued interest since the last coupon payment. If a semiannual coupon was last paid, say, 4 months before a purchase date, a buyer will pay a seller the quoted price P plus accrued interest equal to $\frac{4}{6}$ of the next coupon payment. (If the buyer holds the issue to the next coupon payment date, he earns the entire coupon payment, thereby recouping his earlier payment.) Payment of accrued interest is a device for splitting up coupon income among those investors who hold an issue between coupon payment dates in proportion to the length of time they are holders.

New Issues

There are three types of coupon-bearing securities issued by the Treasury. The first is a *certificate of indebtedness* (CI), which has a maturity at original issue

---

[9] First note that Equation (1.8) may also be expressed as

$$\frac{P}{100} = \frac{1}{2} R_{cp}(x + x^2 + \cdots + x^n) + x^n$$

where $x = 1/(1 + \frac{1}{2}R_m)$. Now define $Q = x + x^2 + \cdots + x^n$, so that $xQ = x^2 + x^3 + \cdots x^{n+1}$. Subtracting xQ from Q gives $Q - xQ = x - x^{n+1}$. This implies that $Q = (x - x^{n+1})/(1 - x)$. Using this alternative expression for $x + x^2 + \cdots + x^n$, Equation (1.11) can be obtained after some reduction of terms.

of a year or less. CIs have not been issued since 1967, when they were replaced with the more convenient 1-year Treasury bills. The second coupon issue is a *note*, which has an original maturity of from 1 to 10 years. The third, a *bond*, may have any maturity, but conventionally matures in over 5 years, and typically matures in 25 to 30 years from its issue date.

Since the spring of 1975, the Treasury has adhered to a fairly regular program of sales of new coupon issues. It offers a 2-year note about the 20th of each month (usually for delivery and payment on the last business day of that month) and a 4-year note toward the end of the second month of each quarter (for delivery and payment in the first week of the next month). Exhibit 1.7 shows the offerings of 2- and 4-year notes during the first two quarters of 1977.

The Treasury also offers a set of three so-called refunding issues in the middle of each quarter. The issues include a 3-year note, either a 7- or a 10-year

EXHIBIT 1.7
TREASURY OFFERINGS OF COUPON DEBT IN THE FIRST
TWO QUARTERS OF 1977

Auction date	Delivery date	Maturity date	Coupon rate, %	Years to maturity
		2-year notes		
January 19	February 3	January 31, 1979	$5^7/_8$	2
February 17	February 28	February 28, 1979	$5^7/_8$	2
March 22	March 31	March 31, 1979	6	2
April 19	May 2	April 30, 1979	$5^7/_8$	2
May 18	May 31	May 31, 1979	$6^1/_8$	2
June 21	June 30	June 30, 1979	$6^1/_8$	2
		4-year notes		
February 23	March 8	March 31, 1981	$6^7/_8$	4
May 24	June 3	June 30, 1981	$6^3/_4$	4
		First quarter refunding issues		
February 1	February 15	February 15, 1980	$6^1/_2$	3
February 3	February 15	February 15, 1984	$7^1/_4$	7
February 4	February 15	February 15, 2002–2007	$7^5/_8$	30
		Second quarter refunding issues*		
May 3	May 16	February 15, 1984	$7^1/_4$	$6^3/_4$
May 4	May 16	February 15, 2002–2007	$7^5/_8$	$29^3/_4$
		End-of-quarter offerings		
March 29	April 4	May 15, 1982	7	5
June 28	July 8	August 15, 1992	$7^1/_4$	15

*Second quarter offerings were a reopening of two issues (quarterly refunding offerings) sold for the first time in the first quarter of 1977.

Source: Various issues of the *Treasury Bulletin.*

note, and a long-term 25- or 30-year bond. Exhibit 1.7 also shows the quarterly refunding issues offered during the first two quarters of 1977. Finally, at the end of each quarter the Treasury offers either a 5-year note or a 15-year bond (for delivery and payment in the first week of the following quarter).

There are three methods of selling new issues of notes and bonds. All three have been used since 1974. These methods include one nonauction technique, called subscription offerings, and two auction techniques, price auctions and yield auctions.

Subscription Offerings   In a *subscription offering* the Treasury specifies the coupon rate and maturity of the issue (thereby specifying the future payment stream completely) and also specifies the price at which it is willing to sell the issue. Investors tender subscriptions, telling the Treasury how much of the issue they want. The coupon rate is generally set to the 8th of a percent nearest the yield on outstanding Treasury issues of a comparable maturity. The offering price is then adjusted above or below the principal value to bring the yield to maturity on the issue into closer alignment with market yields.

When the Treasury is unsure of the extent of public demand for a new issue but wants to be sure to sell some minimum quantity of notes or bonds in a subscription offering, it may put the yield on a new issue somewhat above the level of yields prevailing in the secondary markets. A large premium will always guarantee a complete sale. Too much of a premium, however, can also result in a substantial oversubscription. For example, in February 1976 the Treasury offered $3.5 billion of 7-year notes at a premium of 25 basis points ($^1/_4$ percent) over prevailing market yields, and received more than $30 billion in tenders.

If the Treasury chooses not to sell as much of an issue as investors subscribe for, it reduces each tender on a proportional or pro rata basis. Usually it guarantees some minimum amount on each tender and reduces only the excess over that minimum. Such pro rata or nonprice rationing in subscription offerings indicates the Treasury is paying too much for its borrowings. If it had raised the offering price, some (but not all), of the subscribers would have dropped out or reduced their subscriptions. The same payment stream could have attracted adequate demand at a higher price or, equivalently, at a lower yield.[10]

Price Auctions   Criticism of subscription offerings led the Treasury to introduce *price auctions* in the late 1960s.[11] In a price auction the coupon rate and maturity are specified in advance. Investors submit tenders for desired quantities of the issue and specify the bid price they are willing to pay. Noncompetitive tenders, up to a specified limit per investor, are accepted for guaranteed delivery at the average accepted competitive bid price. Competitive

---

[10] See, for example, the behavior of prices on Treasury issues offered by subscription in Lang and Rasche (1977).

[11] Goldstein (1962a) discusses some of the points in the early 1960s debate over whether the Treasury should auction longer-term coupon issues.

tenders are accepted in order of decreasing bid price until the desired quantity of securities has been sold. Price auctions of coupon issues are essentially identical to Treasury bill auctions.

Dutch auctions are a special type of price auction. In this case everybody, including both noncompetitive and accepted competitive bidders, pays the stop-out price, i.e., the lowest accepted competitive bid price. Thus, the Treasury charges everyone the bid price of the marginal or last accepted bidder. If investors submitted the same bids whether an auction was regular or Dutch, the Treasury would clearly choose the former method. It has been argued, however, that since high bidders are not penalized in a Dutch auction, investors are more likely to bid up an issue and that Dutch auctions actually bring in more money for given promises of future payments.[12]

Yield Auctions   Price auctions require that the Treasury specify the coupon rate on the issues it is selling. In August 1974 an offering of 9 percent notes in minimum denominations of $1000 attracted substantial interest from small investors. Thrift institutions claimed the publicity given to the high coupon rate led to substantial withdrawals from savings accounts by small investors interested in acquiring the notes.

Following the August 1974 offering, the Treasury began to conduct *yield auctions*. In a yield auction only the maturity date of a new issue is specified prior to the auction. Investors submit competitive tenders stating the yield to maturity they are willing to accept on the quantity of notes or bonds they are bidding for. After segregating noncompetitive tenders, the Treasury accepts competitive tenders in order of increasing yield until it has exhausted the offering.

For any given coupon rate, the yield specified on each competitive tender implies a particular bid price. The coupon rate chosen is the highest rate which makes the average accepted bid price less than or equal to the principal value of the issue. Once the coupon rate is fixed, each accepted competitive bidder pays a price which gives him his specified bid yield. Noncompetitive tenders pay the average accepted bid price. With the exception of reopenings of outstanding issues, most coupon issues are now sold through yield auctions. Reopenings of existing issues have to be done by price auctions because the coupon rates on those issues are already specified.

Secondary-Market Trading

Treasury notes and bonds trade primarily in a dealer market. The same firms that buy and sell bills also deal in notes and bonds. Treasury coupon issues are

---

[12] This point has been investigated directly by Smith (1967) in a series of simulation experiments. See also Smith (1966). Vickrey (1961) analyzed several different auction processes. The relative desirability of Dutch auctions versus discriminatory price auctions was debated most completely when Friedman (1959) proposed introducing the former technique into Treasury bill auctions. His proposal was criticized by Brimmer (1962), Goldstein (1962b), and Rieber (1964). Friedman responded in Friedman (1963, 1964).

also listed on the New York Stock Exchange, in the so-called Bond Room. The American Stock Exchange has also introduced trading in Treasury coupon issues, with registered specialists making continuous markets in the issues. The latter market is designed primarily for small transactions, on the order of a few thousand dollars.

Coupon issues trade most actively in the first few weeks following their auction. During this time dealer bid-ask spreads are typically about a 32nd of a point for standard-size trades of $5 million principal value. After an issue has been outstanding for some time, it finds its way into the hands of long-term investors and becomes seasoned. Seasoned issues trade less frequently than new issues, receive wider bid-ask spreads, and trade in more irregular sizes.[13] At times it may become difficult to acquire more than a few million dollars of a seasoned issue in a single day without special efforts aimed at uncovering potential sellers. Conversely, dealers may require large price concessions to take on a position in an infrequently traded issue. Thus, the secondary market in Treasury coupon issues is less liquid than the Treasury bill market because dealer bid-ask spreads are larger and because it is harder to buy and sell in large blocks without affecting market prices.

1.3 ISSUES OF FEDERALLY SPONSORED FINANCIAL INTERMEDIARIES

Individuals who borrow relatively small amounts of money, i.e., on the order of a few tens of thousands of dollars, borrow from financial intermediaries such as commercial banks and savings and loan associations rather than issue marketable debt. The United States Congress determined that the cost of borrowing borne by some of these individuals, for some purposes, is a matter of national concern, and it created federally sponsored financial intermediaries to keep that cost as low as possible.[14] Federal agency intermediation is especially important to individuals borrowing for agricultural purposes and for the purchase of residential structures.

The basic idea of each of the federal agencies is the same: borrow by issuing marketable debt in large blocks and then relend the proceeds to numerous local intermediaries for the ultimate benefit of farmers and homeowners. Federal sponsorship assures a good reception for the agency debt. Borrowing costs are usually below the lowest yields on corporate debt, albeit somewhat above yields on Treasury issues. The large volume of outstanding agency issues means there is typically a good trading market and investors can buy and sell reasonably large amounts of the securities without disturbing the market. In this section several federal agencies acting as financial intermediaries are briefly described.

---

[13] The effect of seasoning on bid-ask spreads is described in the studies of Garbade and Silber (1976) and Garbade and Rosey (1977).

[14] The federal agencies and their securities are comprehensively described in Banks (1978). See also Webb (1980).

Agricultural Intermediaries

There are three networks of federally sponsored banks acting as agricultural intermediaries. The first two, the Federal Intermediate Credit Banks and the Banks for Cooperatives, lend primarily (but not exclusively) for short periods of time, such as a year or less. The third, the Federal Land Banks, do more long-term lending. The three networks are known collectively as the *Farm Credit Banks*. We will first discuss briefly what the banks in the three networks do and then discuss what types of securities they sell.

The Lending Functions of the Farm Credit Banks   The twelve regional Federal Intermediate Credit Banks (FICBs) borrow to finance the activities of production credit associations (PCAs). PCAs are local mutual associations of farmers which lend money to their members to finance seasonal crops and investments in capital equipment such as farm implements and tractors. Repayments on PCA loans are channeled back to the lending FICB.

The twelve Banks for Cooperatives (BCoops) and the Central Bank for Cooperatives borrow to finance the activities of agricultural cooperatives. These activities include inventorying farm supplies, marketing farm products, and providing business services to farmers. The individual BCoops lend within designated regions, and the Central Bank for Cooperatives makes loans to large cooperatives and to cooperatives that span more than one region.

The twelve Federal Land Banks (FLBs) borrow to finance the loan programs of local Land Bank Associations (LBAs). LBAs are mutual associations of farmers which service FLB loans to their members for construction of farm residences and outbuildings, purchase of farmland, and purchase of capital equipment. FLB loans typically have a longer maturity than either FICB or BCoop loans.

Farm Credit Banks Debt   Neither the individual Farm Credit Banks nor the three networks of Farm Credit Banks sell their own debt. Instead, debt of the agricultural intermediaries is sold as the "joint and several" obligation of the thirty-seven Farm Credit Banks. This means that each of the thirty-seven banks remains individually liable for the *full* amount of a Farm Credit Banks issue until that issue has been completely paid off.

Prior to 1979 the FICBs, the BCoops, and the FLBs each had their own debt series, but they were consolidated into debt of the Farm Credit Banks between the summer of 1977 and the winter of 1978–79. The consolidated securities allow the banks to raise funds with a smaller number of larger issues than was the case when each of the agencies sold its own debt.[15] With secondary-market trading more concentrated in relatively larger issues, the liquidity of the markets for Farm Credit Banks debt is enhanced. This makes investors more willing to hold that debt and reduces agency borrowing costs to something even closer to Treasury rates than was previously the case.

[15] Silber (1974) addressed the question of the optimum size of agency debt offering.

The thirty-seven Farm Credit Banks issue two types of consolidated securities. The first type is discount notes, which promise to pay specified face amounts at maturity dates ranging from 5 to 150 days after issue. Discount notes are available in a minimum denomination of $50,000.

In addition to the discount notes, there are currently three regular series of Farm Credit Banks coupon-bearing debt. Every month the banks offer a 6-month bond and a 9-month bond. The banks also offer a longer-term bond once every 3 months, in January, April, July, and October. Depending on the cash needs of the thirty-seven banks, the Farm Credit Banks will also offer additional longer-term bonds on an irregular basis. Exhibit 1.8 shows a public announcement of the February 1981 offering of the 6- and 9-month bonds.

Coupon issues of the Farm Credit Banks are not sold through public auctions the way Treasury securities are almost always sold. Instead, the banks use the subscription method of selling. After consultation with a national syndicate of commercial banks and broker-dealer firms, the banks place a coupon rate on a new issue and offer it to the members of the syndicate at a price equal to its principal value less a selling commission. Syndicate members then reoffer the issue to public investors at a price equal to principal value.

Farm Credit Banks discount notes are offered to investors continuously, on what is known as a *tap* basis. The Farm Credit Banks announce the rate at which they are willing to sell notes, and then satisfy all demands for the notes at that rate. When they want to sell more discount notes, they raise the rate, and when they want to sell fewer, they lower the rate. Thus, the notes are always on tap but at a rate which reflects the interest of the Farm Credit Banks in raising cash. Unlike Treasury bills, the maturity of new discount notes may be tailored to suit the convenience of a buyer. Notes of different maturities are generally offered at different rates.

Home Mortgage Intermediaries

Federally sponsored home mortgage intermediaries can be separated into two groups: those which lend on ordinary debt contracts against mortgage collateral and those which actually receive mortgage payments from homeowners. In the former category are the Federal Home Loan Banks. Their assets and liabilities are almost exclusively ordinary debt contracts. In the latter category is the Federal National Mortgage Association, which actually owns residential mortgages purchased with proceeds from the sale of ordinary debt. Two other intermediaries, the Federal Home Loan Mortgage Corporation and the Government National Mortgage Association, issue unique types of securities known as *pass-throughs*.

Federal Home Loan Banks   The twelve Federal Home Loan Banks (FHLBs) borrow funds by issuing debt securities and then relend the proceeds to savings and loan associations (S & Ls) which are members of the Federal Home Loan Bank System. In principle, the FHLBs and the S & Ls could operate exactly as the Farm Credit Banks, with the S & Ls relending their FHLB borrowings to howmeowners to finance residential mortgages. In practice, however, S & Ls borrow from the FHLBs not to extend new mortgage loans, but to finance depositor withdrawals at times of high interest rates.

When short-term interest rates are high, depositors at thrift institutions find

EXHIBIT 1.8
Announcement of Federal Farm Credit Banks 6-month and 9-month bonds.

New Issues   January 28, 1981

Federal Farm Credit Banks

The Thirteen Banks for Cooperatives
The Twelve Federal Intermediate Credit Banks
The Twelve Federal Land Banks

Consolidated Systemwide Bonds

15.65% $2,493,000,000
CUSIP NO. 313311 DP 4
Dated February 2, 1981   Due August 3, 1981

14.90% $1,545,000,000
CUSIP NO. 313311 DT 6
Dated February 2, 1981   Due November 2, 1981

Interest on the above issues payable at maturity

Price 100%

The Bonds are the secured joint and several obligations of The Thirty-seven Federal Farm Credit Banks and are issued under the authority of the Farm Credit Act of 1971.

**BONDS ARE AVAILABLE
IN BOOK-ENTRY FORM ONLY.**

Federal Farm Credit Banks

Fiscal Agency
90 William Street, New York, N. Y. 10038

Peter J. Carney   **Gerald F. Kierce**
Fiscal Agent   *Deputy Fiscal Agent*

This announcement appears as a matter of record only.

direct investments more rewarding than thrift deposits. Their deposit withdrawals would normally force the thrifts to liquidate part of their asset portfolios. Such liquidations, in a severely depressed mortgage market, could produce substantial losses and possibly bring on the insolvency of many S & Ls. To avoid these consequences, the Federal Home Loan Banks stand ready to advance funds to S & Ls on the strength of their mortgage holdings. FHLB loans are generally cyclical, peaking when interest rates are high and running off as interest rates fall and depositors redeposit at thrift institutions money from their maturing investments. This cyclical fluctuation in borrowing is, however, superimposed on a secular upward trend in FHLB debt.

The FHLBs sell bonds of short and intermediate maturities on an irregular basis, as dictated by demands for funds and repayments from member S & Ls. Exhibit 1.9 shows the announcement of a pair of FHLB offerings: a 14.0 percent 3-year 4-month issue and a 13.85 percent 4-year 11-month issue. Like agricultural agency bonds, FHLB bonds are sold by subscription to a national selling group of banks and broker-dealer firms and then reoffered to public investors.

The FHLBs also issue discount notes on a tap basis. Maturities on the discount notes range from 30 to 270 days at the discretion of the buyer, with the rates varied according to the cash needs of the banks. Both the bonds and discount notes are the joint and several obligations of the twelve banks.

Federal Home Loan Mortgage Corporation The Federal Home Loan Mortgage Corporation (FHLMC) is a wholly owned subsidiary of the twelve Federal Home Loan Banks. Congress created the FHLMC to enhance the liquidity of residential mortgage investments. The corporation accomplishes this end primarily by maintaining a secondary market in conventional mortgages, i.e., in mortgages not insured or guaranteed by the federal government. The FHLMC does not, however, resell individual mortgages which it has purchased. Instead, it issues obligations against itself which, because they are homogeneous and well known to investors, trade in an active secondary market. Individual mortgages are too heterogeneous to enjoy a good secondary market.

The principal FHLMC obligation is the guaranteed mortgage certificate. These certificates are claims to the payment stream given off by a specific pool of conventional mortgages. The payment stream includes interest at a stated rate on the unpaid principal, amortization of principal, and prepayments (if any) of principal. The certificates are not bonds because of the amortization of principal and because of fluctuating prepayments. The FHLMC guarantees payment of both principal and interest on all mortgages in a pool.

Guaranteed mortgage certificates are a "wrapper" for a pool of mortgages, with the added feature of risk reduction because of the FHLMC guarantee. These certificates are much more likely to enjoy a liquid secondary market than are the underlying mortgages, and hence the certificates attract the interest of investors.

Federal National Mortgage Association The Federal National Mortgage Association (FNMA) is a government-sponsored financial intermediary now wholly owned by private stockholders. Its principal function is to improve the liquidity of mortgage investments by buying and selling government-guaranteed or -insured mortgages. In practice the FNMA is primarily a buyer which finances its purchases by selling debentures and short-term discount notes. The debentures are sold through a national selling group on an irregular basis, according to the cash needs of FNMA. FNMA discount notes are available on a tap basis with maturities of from 30 to 270 days.

Government National Mortgage Association The Government National Mortgage Association (GNMA) is a federally chartered corporation wholly

EXHIBIT 1.9
Public announcement of two debt issues of the Federal Home Loan Banks.

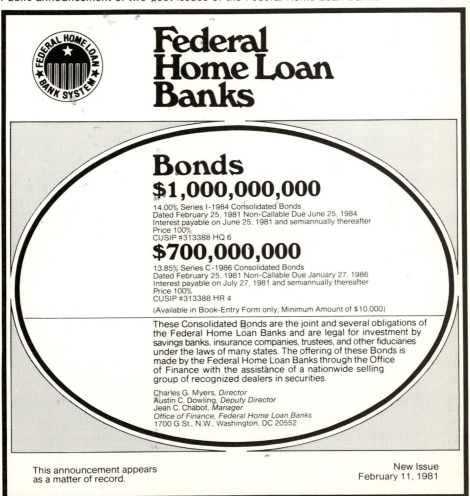

Federal Home Loan Banks

Bonds
$1,000,000,000

14.00% Series I-1984 Consolidated Bonds
Dated February 25, 1981 Non-Callable Due June 25, 1984
Interest payable on June 25, 1981 and semiannually thereafter
Price 100%
CUSIP #313388 HQ 6

$700,000,000

13.85% Series C-1986 Consolidated Bonds
Dated February 25, 1981 Non-Callable Due January 27, 1986
Interest payable on July 27, 1981 and semiannually thereafter
Price 100%
CUSIP #313388 HR 4

(Available in Book-Entry Form only; Minimum Amount of $10,000)

These Consolidated Bonds are the joint and several obligations of the Federal Home Loan Banks and are legal for investment by savings banks, insurance companies, trustees, and other fiduciaries under the laws of many states. The offering of these Bonds is made by the Federal Home Loan Banks through the Office of Finance with the assistance of a nationwide selling group of recognized dealers in securities.

Charles G. Myers, *Director*
Austin C. Dowling, *Deputy Director*
Jean C. Chabot, *Manager*
Office of Finance, Federal Home Loan Banks
1700 G St., N.W., Washington, DC 20552

This announcement appears as a matter of record.

New Issue
February 11, 1981

owned by the federal government. In addition to several special-assistance programs designed to reduce, by subsidy, the cost to homeowners of certain types of residential mortgages, it also sponsors a program of pass-through securities similar to the guaranteed mortgage certificates of the FHLMC.[16] GNMA pass-throughs are claims to the cash payments provided by a specific pool of government-insured and -guaranteed mortgages. The payments include interest at a stated rate on unpaid principal, amortization of principal, and prepayments (if any) of principal.

Secondary-Market Trading

Short-maturity coupon issues of the Farm Credit Banks and the Federal Home Loan Banks trade in a very liquid secondary market. Most of the banks and broker-dealer firms that deal in Treasury issues also deal in agency issues. Longer-maturity agency issues, and agency issues with a small volume outstanding, tend to be somewhat illiquid. Bid-ask spreads on those issues are wider than on Treasury issues of a comparable maturity, and it is difficult to purchase or sell more than a few million dollars of principal value of the issues without special efforts or without a substantial price concession.

One of the major factors contributing to the efficiency of the agency market has been the growth, since the mid-1960s, in the number and size of issues. Investors have become increasingly familiar with the securities, and increasingly willing to buy them, as they know a viable secondary market exists in which they can liquidate a position should their cash needs change.[17]

The pass-through securities of the FHLMC and GNMA trade in somewhat less liquid markets, primarily because of the heterogeneity of the issues. A pass-through that has been outstanding for some time may be quite different from other contemporaneously issued pass-throughs as a consequence of the prepayment experience on its underlying mortgages. Seasoned pass-throughs may not be very good substitutes for each other, even if they bear the same coupon rate and issue date. Their markets are, consequently, not especially active, and most transactions are done on a negotiated basis. Newly issued pass-throughs, on the other hand, are quite good substitutes (since they are too new to have distinguishing prepayment histories). They trade in moderately active markets.

CHAPTER SUMMARY

This chapter has provided an introduction to debt obligations of the United States Treasury and federally sponsored financial intermediaries. These obliga-

---

[16] GNMA securities, particularly pass-throughs, are described in GNMA Mortgage-Backed Securities Dealers Association (1978), Senft (1978), and Black, Garbade, and Silber (1981).

[17] Peskin (1971) analyzed the characteristics of the markets for federal agency debt.

tions can be divided into two broad classes: discount instruments (like Treasury bills, Farm Credit Banks discount notes, Federal Home Loan Bank discount notes, and Federal National Mortgage Association discount notes), which make only a single payment of face value at maturity; and notes and bonds, which make semiannual interest payments prior to maturity. Discount notes always have an original maturity of less than a year, while coupon-bearing securities generally have an original maturity of more than a year. (The 6- and 9-month coupon issues of the Farm Credit Banks are an exception.)

Treasury issues are generally sold in the primary market through competitive auctions open to all investors. The mechanics of the auctions differ slightly (e.g., price auctions compared with yield auctions), but competitive bidding is always present. In contrast, federal agency issues are sold through either subscription offerings or tap offerings. We will see in Chapter 2 that most private corporations also use either the tap method or the subscription method for selling their debt in the primary markets. On occasion, the Treasury has also used the subscription method to sell coupon-bearing securities.

Secondary-market transactions in Treasury and agency securities are usually accomplished through dealers who advertise purchase and sale quotations. Quotations on coupon-bearing issues are expressed in prices, as a percent of the principal value of an issue. Quotations on discount instruments are expressed as discount rates.

FURTHER READING

Lois Banks, "The Market for Agency Securities," Federal Reserve Bank of New York *Quarterly Review*, **3** (Spring 1978), 7–21.

Richard Lang and Robert Rasche, "Debt-Management Policy and the Own Price Elasticity of Demand for U.S. Government Notes and Bonds," Federal Reserve Bank of St. Louis *Review*, **59** (September 1977), 8–22.

Christopher McCurdy, "The Dealer Market for United States Government Securities," Federal Reserve Bank of New York *Quarterly Review*, **2** (Winter 1977–78), 35–47.

William Martin, chairman, *Joint Treasury-Federal Reserve Study of the U.S. Government Securities Market*, (Washington, D.C.: Board of Governors of the Federal Reserve System, 1969).

Allan Meltzer and Gert von der Linde, *A Study of the Dealer Market for Federal Government Securities*, Joint Economic Committee Print, 86th Cong., 2nd Sess. (1960).

Vernon Smith, "Bidding Theory and the Treasury Bill Auction: Does Price Discrimination Increase Bill Prices," *Review of Economics and Statistics*, **48** (May 1966), 141–146.

———, "Experimental Studies of Discrimination versus Competition in Sealed-Bid Auction Markets," *Journal of Business*, **40** (January 1967), 56–84.

Kerry Webb, "The Farm Credit System," Federal Reserve Bank of Kansas City *Economic Review*, **65** (June 1980), 16–30.

APPENDIX: Discrete and Continuous Compounding

The values of most financial assets change through time. When the value of an asset some time in the future differs from its present value, that asset is said to earn a return, either positive or negative. For investment purposes the only interesting questions about that return are the present and future values of the asset and the length of time required for the asset to appreciate or depreciate to its future value. For many analytical purposes, however, it is desirable to express these quantities in some standardized unit of measure, as a rate of return *per unit of time*. Precisely how a rate of return is expressed is not usually important, but it is important to recognize the differences among different expressions. In this appendix we summarize some alternative measures of a rate of return.

Returns are conventionally expressed on an annualized basis. Suppose an asset is *currently* valued at the present value PV and will have a future value FV at the end of exactly 1 year. The simple annual rate of return on that asset is the value of R which solves the present discounted value equation:

$$PV = \frac{FV}{1 + R} \qquad (A.1a)$$

or

$$R = \frac{FV}{PV} - 1 \qquad (A.1b)$$

If FV is 100 and PV is 95, the simple rate of return R will equal .0526, or 5.26 percent per annum.

In some cases, such as with coupon-bearing bonds, it is conventional to measure the rate of return over a 1-year investment interval assuming semiannual compounding. In this case the annualized rate of return on the asset described in the foregoing example is the value of R which solves the equation

$$PV = \frac{FV}{(1 + R/2)^2} \qquad (A.2a)$$

or

$$R = 2\left[\left(\frac{FV}{PV}\right)^{1/2} - 1\right] \qquad (A.2b)$$

Equation (A.2a) may be interpreted as implying that an asset worth PV at present will be worth $PV(1 + R/2)$ at the end of 6 months and will be worth $FV = PV(1 + R/2)^2$ at the end of 1 year. The rate of return, compounded semiannually, on an asset with present value $PV = 95$ and future value $FV = 100$ at the end of 1 year is 5.20 percent per annum. This return may be compared with the simple rate of return of 5.26 percent per annum on the same asset. These measured rates differ because of the assumed compounding convention, annual or semiannual, but not because of any difference in present or future values or the length of the investment interval.

The assumption on the number of compounding periods per year is arbitrary. In general, if the rate of return on the asset described above is measured assuming n discrete compounding periods per year, that rate will be the value of R which solves the equation

$$PV = \frac{FV}{(1 + R/n)^n} \tag{A.3a}$$

or

$$R = n\left[\left(\frac{FV}{PV}\right)^{1/n} - 1\right] \tag{A.3b}$$

If $n = 12$, $FV = 100$, and $PV = 95$, then R will be 5.14 percent per annum compounded monthly. Yields on corporate bonds are generally expressed with a semiannual compounding convention. Yields on GNMA pass-throughs, however, assume monthly compounding, so that $n = 12$. Some banks compound interest on deposits daily, in which case $n = 365$.

As the number of compounding periods per year increases, i.e., as the value of n in Equation (A.3b) goes to infinity, it can be shown that the measured rate of return on an asset currently worth PV and which will be worth FV at the end of 1 year converges to the value

$$r = \ln\left[\frac{FV}{PV}\right] \tag{A.4a}$$

where $\ln [x]$ is the natural logarithm of x. The continuously compounded return per annum on the asset is $\ln [FV/PV]$. From the definition of r in Equation (A.4a), the current value of the asset is

$$PV = FV \exp [-r] \tag{A.4b}$$

where $\exp [x]$ is the base e of natural logarithms raised to the power x. It follows that PV is the present value of a future payment FV, discounted at the continuously compounded rate r for 1 year. If $PV = 95$ and $FV = 100$, then, from Equation (A.4a), $r = 5.13$ percent per annum.

When the time between the present value and the future value of an asset is something other than 1 year, the above measures of annualized rates of return must be generalized. Assume there are n discrete compounding periods per year. If an asset currently worth PV dollars will be worth FV dollars at the end of k of those periods, the annualized rate of return is the value of R which solves the equation

$$PV = \frac{FV}{(1 + R/n)^k} \tag{A.5a}$$

or

$$R = n\left[\left(\frac{FV}{PV}\right)^{1/k} - 1\right] \tag{A.5b}$$

In particular, if $n = 2$ compounding periods per year, then

$$PV = \frac{FV}{(1 + R/2)^k}$$

This is the basis for the discounting factor used in Equation (1.8) to express the semiannually compounded yield to maturity on a bond.

In Equation (A.5) the investment interval is k/n years. This may be either greater or less than unity. Suppose now that the number n of compounding periods per year increases, but that the number k of investment periods also increases so that the investment interval k/n remains constant at t years. Then it can be shown that the measured annualized rate of return in Equation (A.5b) will converge to the continuously compounded value

$$r = \frac{\ln\ [FV/PV]}{t} \tag{A.6a}$$

Thus, as in Equation (1.3), the annualized rate of return, continuously compounded, on a Treasury bill currently worth $\$P$ and which will be worth $\$100$ at its maturity in n days is $\ln[100/P]/(n/365)$.

From the definition of r in Equation (A.6a) we have

$$PV = FV \ \exp[-rt] \tag{A.6b}$$

PV is the present value of a future payment *FV*, discounted for t years at the continuously compounded annual rate r. The investment interval t is measured in decimal years; for example, 6 months is $t = .5$ years. Equation (A.6b) provides the basis for the discount factor used in Equation (1.9) to compute the continuously compounded yield to maturity on a bond.

The term $\ln\ [FV/PV]$ is usually called the *log price relative* of an asset. From Equation (A.6a) any log price relative can be converted to a continuously compounded annualized rate of return by dividing the log price relative by the length of the investment period measured in years.

CHAPTER 2

CORPORATE SECURITIES

Corporations offer two principal types of securities to investors. Debt issues are contractual commitments to repay corporate borrowings. Equity issues are claims to the residual profits of an enterprise, after operating expenses and debt liabilities have been covered. Within each of these broad asset categories exist subclassifications, distinguished primarily by the priority in payment of one class of debt or equity relative to another class. The first three sections of this chapter describe several major types of corporate securities: a special type of marketable debt (commercial paper), other debt securities, and equities.

The fourth section examines securities issued by investment companies. An investment company is defined by the Investment Company Act of 1940 as any issuer engaged primarily in the business of investing or trading in securities. In the most common case the assets of an investment company consist exclusively of financial instruments and the company has only one class of securities outstanding. Ownership of those securities is, therefore, the economic equivalent of a fractional participation in the asset portfolio of the investment company. Investment company securities thus offer to investors with modest means important opportunities to acquire diversified portfolios.

2.1 COMMERCIAL PAPER

Commercial paper is unsecured short-term corporate debt.[1] Like Treasury bills, commercial paper is characterized by a single payment at maturity. Most

---

[1] Hurley (1977) provides a brief history of, and a discussion of recent developments in, the commercial paper market. Greef (1938) gives a history of the early years of the market. See also Cloos (1969), Schadrack (1970), Johnston (1971), Handal (1972), and Schweitzer (1975). Connelly (1978) discusses the relative costs of borrowing on bank loans and commercial paper.

commercial paper is sold in the same form as Treasury bills, promising to pay some stipulated face value at maturity. Such paper is called *discounted paper*, because it has a price prior to maturity which is at a discount from its face value.[2]

Almost all the commercial paper sold in the United States has less than 9 months to run at original issue. Longer-maturity corporate debt securities have to be registered with the Securities and Exchange Commission, in a process described in Section 2.2, before they can be offered for public sale. Most issuers find that the costs of preparing a registration statement make public borrowings economical only for maturities longer than a few years. Such longer-term liabilities are generally represented by coupon-bearing securities rather than single-payment securities.

Price Conventions

Commercial paper is most commonly quoted on a discount rate basis. As in the case of Treasury bills, the discount rate on commercial paper is computed on the assumption of a 360-day year and is based on the face value of the paper rather than on the purchase price.

Rates on commercial paper are also expressed on a yield basis, assuming a 360-day year. If an issue of commercial paper has n days to go to its maturity date and is priced at P per $100 face value, the yield on that issue will be

$$i = \frac{360}{n} \frac{100 - P}{P} \tag{2.1}$$

Thus, if an investor were to buy 60-day paper at a yield of 7.5 percent, his purchase cost could be found by solving Equation (2.1) for P:

$$P = \frac{100}{1 + (ni)/360}$$

Substituting the values of $n = 60$ and $i = .075$ gives

$$P = \frac{100}{1 + (60)(.075)/360}$$
$$= 98.7654$$

The cost of $1 million in face value would therefore be $987,654.

Note that the yield on commercial paper as defined by Equation (2.1) is quite similar to the bond equivalent yield on a Treasury bill as defined in Equation (1.2), *except* for the use of a 365-day year in the latter equation.

---

[2] Some commercial paper is sold in an interest-bearing form like bank certificates of deposit. Certificates of deposit are described in Section 4.1.

New Issues

There are two principal methods for offering commercial paper to investors. These methods differ according to whether the issuer sells its own paper (which it will do if it is sufficiently familiar with the needs of investors) or employs a securities firm to do the selling (which it will do if it can get better rates on its paper by letting a professional do the selling).

Directly Placed Paper   Paper which is issued directly to investors by large, well-known corporations who have a continuous need for substantial short-term borrowings is called *directly placed paper*. It is economical for these companies to maintain their own sales personnel to place paper directly with investors. Finance companies are the most important direct issuers and include, for example, General Motors Acceptance Corporation and Household Finance. These two companies use the proceeds of new issues to finance dealer car loans and consumer loans, respectively. Directly placed paper is continuously available on a tap basis, with the maturity of the paper at the discretion of the buyer. Rates on new offerings are adjusted to meet competitive pressures and to accommodate the cash needs of the issuer. Denominations are conventionally in units of $100,000.

Dealer-Placed Paper   Companies that do not need commercial paper loans on a daily basis or in large volume do not find it economical to maintain their own sales forces. Instead, they use the services of a broker-dealer firm to offer their occasional issues to investors. Goldman, Sachs & Co., The First Boston Corporation, and A. G. Becker & Co. are among the leading securities firms handling commercial paper placements.

There are two ways of selling paper through a dealer. When an issuer sells its paper directly to a securities dealer, the dealer acts as an underwriter. The dealer acquires the paper for its own inventory and at its own risk. It makes a profit from the underwriting if it can sell the paper to other investors at a higher price. Should market yields turn up while the dealer is in the middle of a distribution, the dealer will suffer a loss on its unsold inventory. Conversely, it will gain if yields fall.

When a company sells commercial paper to a broker-dealer firm on a "bought as sold" basis, the firm acts as a broker. In return for a commission fee the broker locates investors interested in purchasing the paper. When it finds an interested investor, the broker buys the paper from the issuer and immediately resells the same paper to the investor. In this case the dealer has no exposure to risk and can suffer no inventory losses (or gains). Dealer-placed paper, whether underwritten or brokered, is typically sold in $250,000 pieces.

Secondary-Market Trading

A secondary market for directly placed paper does not exist. As a substitute for the liquidity provided by a secondary market, direct issuers usually stand ready to buy back their own issues prior to maturity. Because direct issuers are in continuous contact with a wide variety of investors, they can readily replace repurchased paper with new issues.

The willingness of direct issuers to repurchase unmatured paper is a major factor in keeping their borrowing costs low. In the absence of such buy-back arrangements, investors would have reason to worry about the liquidity of their commercial paper positions. If an investor perceived the possibility that he might be forced to sell before maturity (because of an unexpected change in his cash needs) and that he might incur significant costs in locating a prospective buyer, he would doubtless demand a yield premium when originally buying commercial paper. By providing their commercial paper creditors with a ready source of liquidity, direct issuers avoid paying any yield premiums for illiquidity.

Dealer-placed paper does trade, albeit irregularly, in a secondary market. Most of the larger broker-dealer firms placing paper with investors either through an underwriting or as the agent of an issuer will, if requested, bid on paper which they sold at an earlier date. They make such bids only as a service to their own customers, however. In particular, they do not attempt to maintain bid quotations continuously on a wide variety of issues, as do Treasury bill dealers. Moreover, commercial paper dealers will rarely bid on paper which they did not originally sell. The bid rate on outstanding dealer-placed commercial paper is usually about 25 basis points over the offering rate on paper of a similar maturity from a comparable issuer. Thus, the effective bid-ask spread on paper is substantially wider than the spread of a couple of basis points which usually prevails on Treasury bills.

2.2 CORPORATE COUPON ISSUES

Corporate coupon issues are contractual claims to a stream of payments which include semiannual interest coupons and the return of principal at a stated maturity date. Such issues generally have maturities of from 5 to 30 or more years at original issue. The current yield and yield to maturity on corporate coupon issues are defined the same way they are defined for Treasury coupon issues. (See Section 1.2.)

Acceleration of Repayment of Principal

Corporate coupon issues are conventionally denominated in units with a principal value of $1000. Each unit of an issue carries a common stated coupon rate and maturity date. The holder of a particular unit may, however, be forced to accept (or entitled to demand) repayment of the principal amount of his unit prior to its stated maturity. Such early repayments arise from sinking fund, call, and put provisions.

Sinking Fund Repurchases   A sinking fund on a debt issue provides for the gradual retirement of part of the issue at dates before the final maturity date.

EXHIBIT 2.1
CALL PROVISIONS

On March 7, 1972, Chrysler Financial Corporation sold $60 million of debentures bearing a coupon rate of 7.70 percent per annum, dated March 1, 1972, and maturing March 1, 1992. The indenture prohibited Chrysler Financial from redeeming any part of the issue prior to March 1, 1982, that is, the debentures enjoyed 10-year call protection. Thereafter, Chrysler Financial could call all or part of the issue at the following prices (exclusive of accrued interest to the date of call):

March 1, 1982, to February 28, 1983	103.2% of principal value
March 1, 1983, to February 28, 1984	102.8%
March 1, 1984, to February 28, 1985	102.4%
March 1, 1985, to February 28, 1986	102.0%
March 1, 1986, to February 28, 1987	101.6%
March 1, 1987, to February 28, 1988	101.2%
March 1, 1988, to February 28, 1989	100.8%
March 1, 1989, to February 28, 1990	100.4%
March 1, 1990, to February 28, 1992	100.0%

Most sinking funds obligate the issuer to retire a specified number of units each year by buying those units from existing holders of the issue.[3] Purchases of debt units for sinking fund retirement may be made in ordinary secondary-market transactions or, if the price of an issue has increased to a substantial premium due to a fall in interest rates, the units may be purchased at their principal value. Units selected for involuntary retirement pursuant to a sinking fund provision are usually chosen randomly from among the outstanding units.

Call Provisions   In addition to sinking fund provisions, many debt issues also give the issuer an option to "call" all or part of the issue for early retirement at stated prices. Callable debt securities conventionally provide investors with a period of "call protection," usually 5 years from the date of issue for bonds of utility companies and 10 years for bonds of industrial companies. The call price is set to the principal value of a unit, plus a premium. The premium is greatest for calls exercised in the first year after the lapse of the call protection, and it declines toward zero as the issue approaches its maturity date.[4] If only part of an issue is called, the units to be retired are either chosen randomly or allocated pro rata among the existing bondholders.

Exhibit 2.1 shows the call provisions on a 1972 offering by Chrysler Financial Corporation of $60 million in 7.70 percent 20-year debentures. Chrysler Financial reserved to itself the right to buy back its debentures at prices ranging from 103.2 percent of principal value in 1982 to 100.4 percent in 1989 and at

---

[3] Sinking fund provisions on many utility bonds can be satisfied by the issuer purchasing additional real property, rather than repurchasing its own debt.

[4] Some debt securities also carry a special redemption schedule which allows an issuer to retire his debt early, usually at principal value, if a specified event occurs. Finance companies, for example, frequently retain the right to call their debt if their accounts receivable fall significantly below the level of receivables which existed at the time of the sale of the debt.

their principal value in 1990 and thereafter. Thus, the debentures had 10-year call protection and had call premiums ranging from 3.2 to 0 percent.

Sinking fund provisions and call options create uncertainty over the duration of the payment stream on a debt issue. A unit which nominally matures in 30 years may, possibly, be paid off only 5 or 10 years after its issue date. Nonetheless, most investors view mandatory sinking funds favorably, because they reduce the repayment obligations which issuers face at final maturity dates and hence reduce the probability that issuers will be unable to satisfy those obligations. Call options, however, create uncertainty in future payments without providing any similar benefits for investors. Issuers typically exercise call options when interest rates have declined and when investors do not have opportunities for reinvestment at the same yields they were earning on their called issues. Because call options work to the exclusive benefit of the issuer, investors are unwilling to acquire debt with such options except at relatively higher yields. That is, issuers have to pay for the availability of a call option by offering investors a yield premium over the rate at which they can sell noncallable debt.

Put Provisions A less common form of accelerated repayment arises from issues sold with put options. Put options allow debt *holders* to redeem their investments whenever they choose, usually at a price equal to the principal value of the issue. In 1976 Beneficial Corporation sold $150 million of 8 percent 25-year debentures. The debenture contract provided that a holder could sell his debentures back to Beneficial at their principal value on June 15, 1983, or on any subsequent June 15 prior to the June 15, 2001, maturity date.

Investors may be expected to exercise put options when interest rates have increased above the coupon rate on an issue and when an issuer can refinance its borrowings only at greater cost. Since put options work to the exclusive benefit of investors, the yield on debt with a put option should be lower than the yield on comparable debt without a put option.

New Issues

With some exceptions, corporations do not borrow in either the intermediate- or long-term credit markets on a continuous basis.[5] When they do borrow, they usually secure the assistance of broker-dealer firms familiar with the interests of investors in those markets. There are two types of primary-market sales of term debt issues: public offerings and private placements.

Publicly offered debt issues almost always come to market underwritten by a syndicate of broker-dealer firms.[6] The firms in an underwriting syndicate buy

---

[5] Unlike, for example, the continuous borrowings of many finance companies in the short-term credit markets through direct placements of their own commercial paper.

[6] Hayes (1971) and Robertson (1973) discussed the structure and composition of underwriting syndicates and the dramatic increase in the underwriting activity of some brokerage houses since the 1960s. See also Robertson (1978) for the response of the premier investment banking firm of

the new securities from the issuer for their own inventories and at their own risk; i.e., they act like dealers, and then reoffer the securities to interested investors. The terms of an underwritten offering may be negotiated between the issuer and a managing underwriter representing a particular syndicate, or an issue may be offered on a competitive basis to several syndicates. Privately placed debt issues are offered by securities firms to a limited number of investors on a brokered rather than on an underwritten basis.

Negotiated Underwriting of Public Offerings   The first step in a negotiated underwriting is setting the terms of the issue.[7] These terms, worked out between the issuer and the managing underwriter, include maturity, call, and sinking fund provisions; security covenants to restrict dividend payments; covenants to limit additional debt issues; and covenants to maintain a specified level of working capital.[8]

About 6 weeks before the proposed public offering date, the issuer files a registration statement with the Securities and Exchange Commission (SEC). This statement details the characteristics of the issue, the way in which the borrowing will be used, the financial health of the issuer, and the business of the issuer.[9] A preliminary prospectus, the so-called red herring, goes along with the registration statement, disclosing to potential investors all material information about the issue and issuer.[10]

At about the time the registration statement is filed, the managing under-

---

Morgan Stanley & Co. to that competition. The decision of Judge Harold Medina in *United States v. Morgan*, 118 F. Supp. 621 (S.D.N.Y. 1953), an antitrust case brought by the Justice Department against nineteen investment banking firms, provides a useful summary of the role and evolution of underwriting syndicates. See Steffen (1954, 1955), Whitney (1955a, b), and Carson (1956) for commentaries on that decision. The underwriting process is also discussed quite lucidly by Ruder (1972). The organization of underwriting syndicates in the 1920s is discussed in Galston (1928).

[7] West (1967) emphasizes the importance of the terms of an offering. A new issue which is a close substitute for existing issues will probably be easier to sell relative to issues with exotic features and (hence) limited substitutes. Moreover, underwriters may be less certain how to price an issue with exotic features. On the other hand, if novel features are responsive to genuine investor interests, they can make an issue easier to sell. See, for example, the description by Thackray (1974) of the first domestic American issue of floating rate notes by Citicorp in 1974.

[8] Smith and Warner (1979) have examined the economic basis for limitations on payment of dividends, restrictions on additional debt issues, and requirements for maintenance of working capital in debt contracts.

[9] The registration process is described in Jennings and Marsh (1972, chap. 3). See also Ruder (1972). New issues of some securities are exempted from registration by Section 3 of the Securities Act of 1933, including commercial paper with maturities not exceeding 9 months at original issue, and bank and savings and loan issues.

[10] Heller (1961) and Anderson (1974) provide excellent summaries of the disclosure requirements of the Securities Act of 1933, which is the principal federal legislation concerned with offerings of new issues. In a series of seminal articles, Kripke (1970, 1973, 1975, 1978) has argued that those disclosure requirements do not provide investors with the type of information necessary to make an informed decision about purchasing securities in a new offering, that they provide information already in the public domain, and that by being aimed at laymen they fail to disclose information which would be valuable to professional analysts. See also M. Cohen (1966). Schneider (1972), and Mann (1971) for similar reappraisals of the new issue disclosure requirements.

writer begins to form an *underwriting syndicate* and a *selling group* by offering to other broker-dealer firms tentative allotments in the proposed new issue. A firm which joins the underwriting syndicate places part of its capital at risk by agreeing to purchase, for its own inventory, some or all of its underwriting allotment in the event the issue cannot be sold quickly to final investors. A member of the selling group, on the other hand, simply agrees to use its best efforts to sell its allotment. In the event it cannot sell its entire allotment, it can return the unsold securities to the underwriting syndicate. Underwriters are usually members of the selling group, but the selling group may include securities firms which are not underwriters. The allotments of the new issue to members of the selling group are generally based on their ability to sell the issue to either institutional or retail customers.[11]

The day before the public offering, the members of the underwriting syndicate meet with the issuer to decide the coupon rate on the issue and the price which the issuer will receive. At this stage some syndicate members may drop out if they feel the coupon rate is too low and the issue will be hard to sell, and others may seek to increase their allotment if they think the issue will sell out quickly. An issuer may also withdraw its offering if it thinks it can raise funds at a lower cost some other time in the near future.

The process of setting the coupon on a new debt issue is somewhat like an auction, conducted by the managing underwriter, between the issuer and the members of the underwriting syndicate. If the managing underwriter places too high a tentative coupon rate on the issue, the issuer may threaten to withdraw its offering. As the managing underwriter lowers the coupon rate, however, the members of the underwriting syndicate become less willing to underwrite the issue because it will be harder to sell. Ideally, the coupon rate should be just high enough to induce the members of the syndicate to buy, in aggregate, all of the securities which the issuer wishes to sell.

After the price, coupon rate, and allotments to the underwriters are decided, a final prospectus reflecting that information is printed and the registration of the issue with the SEC becomes effective. The issuer and the underwriters bear the legal burden of ensuring that the final prospectus adequately discloses those facts concerning the issue and issuer which would be of material interest to investors.[12]

---

[11] The efforts which can be made by a securities firm seeking to sell a new issue differ substantially between the period before the filing of the registration statement, the waiting period between filing and the date the registration statement becomes effective, and the period after the registration statement becomes effective. See Jennings and Marsh (1972, pp. 54–137) and Ruder (1972). In particular, no sales effort may be made in the prefiling period. Offers to sell, but not sales, may be made in the waiting period. Sales are, of course, permitted once the registration statement becomes effective.

[12] The leading cases on fraud in the sale of a new securities issue due to incomplete or inadequate disclosure are *Escott v. Bar Chris Construction Corp.*, 283 F. Supp. 643 (S.D.N.Y. 1968); *Feit v. Leasco Data Processing Equipment Corp.*, 332 F. Supp. 544 (E.D.N.Y. 1971); and *Beecher v. Able*, 374 F. Supp. 341 (S.D.N.Y. 1974). Solmssen (1975) provides a fictional account of the disclosure problems which can be encountered in bringing a new issue to market.

On the day of the public offering each member of the selling group begins to sell his allotment of the new issue to public investors at a premium above what the underwriting syndicate agreed to pay the issuer.[13] The public offering price is set by the syndicate, and each member of the selling group quotes the same price to public investors.[14] Thus, the offering to the public is conducted on a subscription basis.

Exhibit 2.2 shows the cover page of the prospectus for a $25 million offering of 11 percent 30-year debt of the General Telephone Company of Michigan. The underwriters offered the securities to the public at 100 percent of principal value, but they bought the issue from South Central Bell at a price of 99.05 percent. Thus, the issue had a gross underwriting spread of $237,500. Exhibit 2.3 shows the distribution of the underwriting allotments on that issue. Paine, Webber, Jackson & Curtis received the largest allotment, because it was the managing underwriter.

If a new issue sells out completely, the gross underwriting spread is divided among the managing underwriter (for preparing the issue), the underwriters (for risking their capital), and the members of the selling group (as a commission for their sales efforts). A typical allocation is 20 percent to the managing underwriter, 25 percent to the underwriters in proportion to their underwriting allotments, and 55 percent to the members of the selling group in proportion to their completed sales.

If an issue does not sell out quickly, the underwriters take the unsold securities into their own inventories. They may continue to try to sell the issue at the original offering price, i.e., maintain the syndicate, or they may release the issue from syndication and get what they can for the remaining securities. An example of a debt offering which proved difficult to sell was a 1978 issue of $100 million in 30-year bonds of the Alabama Power Company. The bonds were first offered for public sale on Wednesday, January 25, 1978, at 100 percent of principal value. Only about $30 million of the bonds was sold that day. On the next day (Thursday, January 26) an additional $15 million of bonds was sold, leaving an unsold balance of $55 million in bonds. That balance remained approxi-

---

[13] Ederington (1975, 1976) found that underwriters' spreads, i.e., the difference between the price at which a new issue is offered to the public and the price paid to the issuer, vary directly with the underwriters' uncertainty about the price at which a new issue can be sold, and that the spreads vary inversely with the credit rating of an issue and with the size of an issue. The yield at which a new issue is offered to the public is generally in excess of yields on outstanding issues. Ederington (1974, 1976) found that the new issue yield premium on corporate debt can be attributed to longer call protection on new issues, to tax effects due to outstanding issues trading at premiums to or discounts from principal value, and to lags in the adjustment of secondary-market yields.

[14] The maintenance of a fixed offering price by all members of a selling group has antitrust implications and has been considered in *Matter of National Association of Securities Dealers*, 15 S.E.C. 577 (1944), 19 S.E.C. 424 (1945), and *Papilsky v. Berndt*, Fed. Sec. L. Rep. (CCH) ¶95,627 (S.D.N.Y. 1976). See also "Price Maintenance in the Distribution of Securities," *Yale Law Journal*, **56** (January 1947), 333–355 and Loomis (1979). Undercutting syndicate offering prices has been a problem of long standing to underwriters, as shown by Galston (1928, pp. 116–123); Bialkin et al. (1978, pp. 341–342); *Business Week*, June 20, 1977, p. 92; and *The Wall Street Journal*, March 3, 1978, p. 18, col. 3.

PROSPECTUS

GENERAL TELEPHONE COMPANY OF MICHIGAN

$25,000,000

First Mortgage Bonds, 11% Series Due 2004

The New Bonds will bear interest from October 1, 1974, payable semi-annually on April 1 and October 1 of each year to holders of record on March 15 or September 15 preceding such interest payment dates. The New Bonds are redeemable at the option of the Company at 111% of the principal amount prior to October 1, 1975 and at decreasing prices thereafter, but cannot be redeemed prior to October 1, 1984 through borrowings having an interest cost to the Company of less than 11.11% per annum.

	Price to Public(1)	Underwriting Discounts and Commissions(2)	Proceeds to Company(1)(3)
Per Unit	100.00%	.95%	99.05%
Total	$25,000,000	$237,500	$24,762,500

(1) Plus accrued interest from October 1, 1974 to date of delivery and payment.
(2) In the Purchase Agreement the Company has agreed to indemnify the Underwriters against certain liabilities, including liabilities under the Securities Act of 1933.
(3) Before expenses of the Company estimated at $100,000.

Concurrently with this offering of $25,000,000 of First Mortgage Bonds, 11% Series Due 2004 (the "New Bonds"), the Company is offering 180,000 Shares of $12.24 Cumulative Preferred Stock, $100 par value (the "New Preferred Stock"). The sales are separate transactions and are not contingent upon each other.

The New Bonds are offered by the several Underwriters when, as and if issued by the Company and accepted by the Underwriters and subject to their right to reject orders in whole or in part. The New Bonds will be issued only in registered form and may be transferred or exchanged without service charge. It is expected that definitive Bonds will be ready for delivery on or about October 16, 1974.

THESE SECURITIES HAVE NOT BEEN APPROVED OR DISAPPROVED BY THE SECURITIES AND EXCHANGE COMMISSION NOR HAS THE COMMISSION PASSED UPON THE ACCURACY OR ADEQUACY OF THIS PROSPECTUS. ANY REPRESENTATION TO THE CONTRARY IS A CRIMINAL OFFENSE.

PAINE, WEBBER, JACKSON & CURTIS
INCORPORATED

STONE & WEBSTER SECURITIES CORPORATION

The date of this Prospectus is September 26, 1974

EXHIBIT 2.2
Cover page of a prospectus for $25 million of first mortgage bonds of General Telephone Company of Michigan.

mately unchanged until Tuesday, January 31, when a rally in bond prices produced orders for an additional $35 million of the Alabama bonds. The last $20 million of bonds was sold over the following week, and the underwriting syndicate disbanded on Thursday, February 9. Thus, the bonds took almost 2 weeks to sell. This experience was, however, unusual. Most offerings sell out completely in 1 or 2 days.

EXHIBIT 2.3
UNDERWRITING ALLOTMENTS ON $25 MILLION OF FIRST MORTGAGE BONDS OF GEN-
ERAL TELEPHONE COMPANY OF MICHIGAN

	Principal amount
Paine, Webber, Jackson & Curtis Incorporated	$ 3,330,000
Stone & Webster Securities Corporation	2,220,000
Blyth Eastman Dillon & Co. Incorporated	700,000
The First Boston Corporation	700,000
Drexel Burnham & Co. Incorporated	700,000
Goldman, Sachs & Co	700,000
Halsey, Stuart & Co. Inc.	700,000
Hornblower & Weeks Hemphill, Noyes Incorporated	700,000
E. F. Hutton & Company Inc.	700,000
Kidder, Peabody & Co. Incorporated	700,000
Kuhn, Loeb & Co.	700,000
Lehman Brothers Incorporated	700,000
Loeb, Rhoades & Co.	700,000
Merrill Lynch, Pierce, Fenner & Smith Incorporated	700,000
Reynolds Securities Inc.	700,000
Salomon Brothers	700,000
Smith, Barney & Co. Incorporated	700,000
White, Weld & Co. Incorporated	700,000
Dean Witter & Co. Incorporated	700,000
Warburg Paribas Becker Inc.	700,000
Alex. Brown & Sons	400,000
Dominick & Dominick, Incorporated	400,000
Harris, Upham & Co. Incorporated	400,000
R. W. Pressprich & Co. Incorporated	400,000
L. F. Rothschild & Co.	400,000
Shields Model Roland Securities Incorporated	400,000
Thomson & McKinnon Auchincloss Kohlmeyer Inc.	400,000
Spencer Trask & Co. Incorporated	400,000
G. H. Walker, Laird Incorporated	400,000
Weeden & Co. Incorporated	400,000
Wood, Struthers & Winthrop Inc.	400,000
Abraham & Co. Inc.	200,000
Robert W. Baird & Co. Incorporated	200,000
First of Michigan Corporation	200,000
Freeman Securities Company, Inc.	200,000
McDonald & Company	200,000
The Milwaukee Company	200,000
Mitchum, Jones & Templeton, Inc.	200,000
Prescott, Ball & Turben	200,000
Stuart Brothers	200,000
Watling, Lerchen & Co. Incorporated	200,000
Hibbard & O'Connor Securities, Inc.	150,000
Hoppin, Watson Inc.	150,000
Manley, Bennett, McDonald & Co.	150,000
Total	$25,000,000

Competitive Underwriting of Public Offerings   Some debt issues, especially many issues of public utility companies, come to market through competitive rather than negotiated underwritings. In a competitive underwriting the *issuer* specifies the terms of the issue and prepares the registration statement. On the offering date the issuer puts the issue up for sale to competing underwriting syndicates in a sealed-bid auction. The highest-bidding syndicate wins the issue and immediately begins to reoffer it to public investors. The primary difference between a negotiated and a competitive underwriting is that in the former the members of the underwriting syndicate can explore and promote the purchase interest of public investors before they set the price of the issue. Extensive market exploration or sales promotion is usually not practical in competitive underwritings because a syndicate may not enter the highest bid and consequently may fail to win the issue.[15]

Issuers employ an underwriting syndicate to sell their public offerings for two reasons. First, the members of the syndicate are typically far more familiar than the issuer with the fixed-income market and with investors in that market. Second, the issuer avoids the risk of loss if the issue does not sell out at the offering price. Occasionally a firm will do its own underwriting and use a syndicate only in a brokerage capacity to market an issue. The American Telephone and Telegraph Company (AT&T) sold to public investors $1.57 billion of 8.75 percent 30-year debentures at its own risk in 1970. (This was the largest public sale of debt by a nongovernmental issuer in American history.) More rarely, a firm may even do its own selling if it thinks it knows the market well enough. General Motors Acceptance Corporation (GMAC) frequently offers registered 9-month to 5-year notes on a directly placed basis. It uses no brokers to assist in the offerings and does its own promotion. GMAC is, of course, familiar with the interests of institutional investors because of its direct sales of commercial paper.

Private Placements   Many corporate debt issues are never publicly offered for sale. An issuer may feel it can obtain sufficient funds at an attractive interest rate through direct negotiations with creditors. Successful negotiations result in a private placement rather than a public offering.

Private placements are attractive to issuers for two reasons. First, they do not have to be registered with the SEC, and so they neither require the frequently substantial public disclosures nor incur the preparation costs and delays of such registration.[16] Second, the terms of a private debt placement can

[15] Ederington (1976) analyzed some of the differences between negotiated and competitive underwritings. He found that underwriter spreads are more sensitive to uncertainty about investor demand in competitive offerings than in negotiated offerings, and he attributed that difference to the greater market exploration and sales promotion undertaken by underwriters in negotiated offerings.

[16] Section 4(2) of the Securities Act of 1933 permits an issuer to sell unregistered securities when the sale is not a public offering. Rule 146 of the Securities and Exchange Commission specifies sufficient requirements for an offering not to be construed as a public offering. In practice, private placements to institutional investors are largely ignored by the Commission, on the theory that those investors are sufficiently sophisticated to watch out for their own interests. Rule 146 is most important for private placements (especially of equity securities) to individual investors.

be tailored to the specific needs of the issuer and its creditors. Complex covenants and default provisions are usually avoided in publicly offered issues but
can be included easily in private placements.

An issuer making a private placement may secure the assistance of a securities firm in developing the terms of the issue and in locating interested buyers,
but it does not use the firm as an underwriter. The largest private placement in
American history was a 1975 sale of $1.75 billion in $10^5/_8$ percent 16- and
21-year debt. The proceeds were used by a subsidiary of Standard Oil Company (Ohio) and British Petroleum Company to help finance construction of
the Alaska pipeline. Morgan Stanley & Co. acted as adviser to the issuer and
played a major role in soliciting the interest of seventy-six institutional lenders,
including Prudential Life Insurance Company and public and private pension
funds.

Security Protection and Priorities in Payment

Investors have found that corporations do not always make good on their
promises to repay borrowings. The presence of credit or default risk is one of
the reasons why yields on corporate debt are greater than yields on United
States Treasury debt of the same maturity. The risk of default can be reduced,
however, by security clauses offering recourse to holders in the event of
default. These security clauses are a major distinguishing feature of different
classes of corporate debt.[17]

Mortgage bonds are the most highly secured class of corporate debt. They
are secured by a lien on specific property owned by the issuer. A mortgage
lien typically includes all real and tangible assets but excludes short-term
assets such as cash and accounts receivable.[18] In the event of default the collateral property may be sold and the proceeds applied to pay off the bonds.
Mortgage bonds may be further classified as senior, junior, etc., to reflect
whether a lien is a first lien, second lien, and so on.

Debentures are unsecured debt issues. Debenture holders are classed as general creditors of the issuer in the event of bankruptcy, along with commercial
paper holders and trade creditors. (In addition, mortgage bondholders are
usually classified as general creditors with respect to any residual claims they
may have on the issuer which are not satisfied by the sale of the assets collateralizing their bonds.) After the sale of property specifically pledged against
mortgage bonds, all the remaining assets of a bankrupt company may be sold to
pay off the general creditors. Thus, debentures are inferior to mortgage bonds

---

[17] The legal rights of bondholders in the event of default are discussed by Brudney and Chirelstein (1972, pp. 85–156).

[18] This is true of utility companies, which account for most issues of mortgage bonds. When an
industrial company wants to sell mortgage debt, it is more likely to sell equipment trust certificates
secured by specific property. Such trust certificates are commonly used by railroads to finance
rolling stock and, less frequently, by airlines to buy engines or airplanes. In 1976 The Flying Tiger
Line, Inc., sold $60 million of equipment trust certificates secured by three Boeing 747s and five
additional aircraft engines.

but superior to more junior classes of debt of the same issuer. Subordinated debentures are, as the name implies, unsecured debt issues ranking lower in priority than general creditor issues.

Although the presence of security protection clauses may reduce the risk of loss on some debt issues, it should be noted that they also increase that risk on other debt issues of the same firm. This follows because security protection clauses do not alter the aggregate riskiness of an issuer; they can only provide for particular allocations of whatever assets remain after a default has occurred. The presence of mortgage debt in a firm's capital structure means that general creditors will be worse off in a bankruptcy than if all of the issuer's debt had been unsecured. In the event of a default, the general creditors will be unable to reach those assets collateralizing the mortgage debt until the holders of that debt have been satisfied.

Although the priority of claims on different classes of debt would appear to guarantee that, for example, general creditors are paid fully before either subordinated creditors or stockholders get a nickel, in practice this is not always the case. A corporation is usually worth more as a going concern than as a firm in liquidation. Thus, general creditors may be willing to take 70 cents on the dollar (and let subordinated creditors have something) through a takeover or reorganization if the alternative is accepting 40 cents on the dollar in liquidation.

The settlement, in early 1978, of the Penn Central bankruptcy provides an excellent example of how different creditors can fare in a corporate reorganization. Penn Central Transportation Company had three major assets at the time of its reorganization: (1) ownership of the Pennsylvania Company, a holding company with interests in gas pipelines and real estate; (2) a large assortment of directly owned real estate, including some major New York City hotels; and (3) a suit against the federal government for undervaluation of the railroad properties that it turned over to the Consolidated Rail Corporation (Conrail) in 1976. In the reorganization of Penn Central the federal government and state and local governments received cash and notes in satisfaction of unpaid tax assessments. The notes were payable either from the proceeds of the sale of real estate or from judgments won in the Conrail suit. Secured creditors, such as mortgage bondholders, received a relatively smaller amount of cash, plus bonds and preferred and common stock in the reorganized Penn Central Transportation Company. The unsecured creditors, including commercial paper holders, received common stock in the reorganized company and a claim to any undistributed residual of the award from the Conrail suit. Finally, the holding company which held all the common stock of the original Penn Central Transportation Company received a smaller award of common stock in the reorganized company. It was estimated at the time of the settlement that the government tax claims would be fully satisfied in 10 years; it was also estimated that the secured creditors might ultimately recover their full claims, but that the unsecured creditors would probably take a loss, albeit not a total loss.

Secondary-Market Trading

The vast bulk of corporate coupon debt issues trade in a dealer market. Commercial banks are prohibited by federal law from acting as dealers in corporate securities. Thus, all dealers in corporate bonds are nonbank dealers; Salomon Brothers and Goldman, Sachs are among the largest. The formal structure of the corporate bond market is similar to that of the Treasury market. Investors contact dealers when they want to buy or sell an issue, and dealers generally transact with their customers as principals rather than as agents.

With the exception of new issues and issues of major corporations, trading in most issues of corporate debt is relatively infrequent. Weeks may pass between transactions in a particular security. However, since there are so many debt issues outstanding, it is usually possible to pick dozens of issues with similar maturities, coupons, and security protection clauses issued by companies of comparable credit risk. Thus, while a particular issue may be hard to buy, it is rarely difficult to find a close substitute. One of the most important aspects of trading corporate bonds is knowing which investors own what types of bonds, what they are willing to sell, and what they are looking to buy. Although the corporate bond market is formally a dealer market, in practice the dealers act very much like brokers. They need far more intimate knowledge of their customers than, for example, a dealer in Treasury or federal agency issues.

Debt issues originally sold through registered public offerings are eligible for unrestricted trading in the secondary markets. This is not the case with privately placed issues. Sellers of unregistered securities generally have to restrict their activities so as not to be construed as underwriters of those securities. These restrictions can reduce substantially the marketability of privately placed debt.[19] In practice, however, there is essentially unrestricted trading, among institutional investors, of unregistered debt securities issued by high-quality firms.[20] Some securities firms are active in this specialized market as brokers, undertaking to find buyers for an institution which wants to liquidate debt securities acquired through a private placement.

2.3 CORPORATE EQUITY ISSUES

Equity securities represent a claim on corporate earnings and assets subordinated to the claims of all creditors. The payment stream arising from an equity

---

[19] Rule 144 of the Securities and Exchange Commission details restrictions on the sale of unregistered securities which are sufficient to avoid violating the securities laws. See also Chapters 6 and 8 of Jennings and Marsh (1972), Ruder (1972), and, more generally, the 1972 supplement "A Guide to SEC Rule 144," *Northwestern University Law Review.*

[20] Section 4(1) of the Securities Act of 1933 exempts from the registration requirements of that Act sales of securities by persons other than an issuer, underwriter, or dealer. The Securities and Exchange Commission treats secondary-market transactions in registered securities, and in unregistered securities among institutional investors, as falling within that exemption. Transactions in unregistered securities among noninstitutional investors fall within the same exemption if they meet the requirements of Rule 144.

security can, therefore, be quite variable. Parts Three and Four will focus on how equity securities are valued in the secondary markets. In this section we describe briefly the nature of those securities.

As with corporate debt, equity issues are usually offered to public investors in primary-market sales by a syndicate of securities underwriters.[21] The offering must be registered with the SEC if it is to be available for unrestricted secondary-market trading.[22] This includes preparation of a prospectus describing the issue and issuer and detailing all material information necessary for an informed appraisal of the issue.

Classes of Equity Issues

There are two major classes of corporate stock, distinguished by their relative priorities in payment of dividends and in claims on the residual assets of a corporation in liquidation.

Preferred stock carries a stated dividend. This dividend must be fully paid before any dividends on common stock can be paid. The dividend does not, however, represent a *contractual* commitment of the issuing corporation. Omission of a preferred dividend is not an occasion of default. In most cases preferred dividends are cumulative, meaning that all arrearages must be paid prior to the payment of any dividends on common stock. Holders of preferred stock do not usually vote in the selection of corporate directors, but in some cases failure to pay preferred dividends may confer voting rights until the arrearages are satisfied.

When there is little likelihood that an issuer of preferred stock will fail to make its dividend payments, investors may be relatively indifferent between holding that preferred stock and holding debt from the same issuer. In that case it may be reasonable to measure the yield on preferred stock as if it were debt without a maturity date. (Some preferred stock does have a maturity, however, as noted in the next paragraph.) Examining Equations (1.7) and (1.11) shows

---

[21] There exist several studies of the behavior of prices on common stock following their first public offering. McDonald and Fisher (1972) found significantly positive returns (relative to the return on a broadly based market index) in the first week after issue but did not find any tendency for such "excess" returns to continue when the stocks began to trade in the secondary market. This finding, which has been confirmed in every subsequent study, implies that underwriters distribute rents to their customers. Logue (1973) found new issue premiums inversely related to the size of the offering and to the percent of the offering sold by existing insiders. These results appear to stem from differences in the bargaining strengths of underwriters and sellers at the time of the pricing decision on a new issue. Ibbotson (1975) found new issue premiums positively skewed, so that while the average premium is positive, there is a greater probability of loss than gain on a new issue. Ibbotson and Jaffe (1975) found new issue premiums positively serially correlated, implying the existence of "hot issue" and "cold issue" periods. Shaw (1971) and McDonald and Jacquillat (1974) report similar results for the Canadian and French new issue markets.

[22] Equity securities may also be sold in private placements. If a sale is made to other than institutional investors, it will be exempt from the registration requirements of the Securities Act of 1933 if it meets the requirements of Rule 146 of the Securities and Exchange Commission. Private placements of equity issues to institutional investors are, as with debt issues, largely unregulated in practice.

that the yield to maturity on a debt issue for which the number of remaining coupons is large is approximately equal to its current yield. Thus, the ratio of a year of dividend payments on preferred stock to the price per share of that stock measures the rate of return on an investment in that stock if it is held forever. Of course, this approach to measuring yield is inappropriate if there is a substantial likelihood that the issuer will omit some of the future dividends on the stock. In that case a high current yield may simply reflect the well-founded belief of buyers and sellers that some dividends are not going to be paid or are going to be deferred.

Preferred stock carries a *par value* (in some cases called a *liquidation value*). In the event of the liquidation of a corporation, holders of preferred stock have a claim on the assets of the corporation up to the stated par value of their stock holdings. This claim is subordinate to all claims of the creditors of the corporation but has priority over the claims of holders of common stock.[23] In some cases preferred stock also carries a *redemption value*. Should a corporation wish to retire an issue of preferred stock, it can call the stock in and pay the holders the stated redemption value. Finally, some issues of preferred stock have *mandatory* redemption provisions. Such issues are quite similar to debt securities, with the important exception that dividend payments on preferred stock are not contractual obligations of the issuer.

Common stock has the lowest priority in payment of dividends and in liquidation. However, dividends on common stock are not fixed and, if the company does well, may increase substantially. While common stock typically is the most volatile of corporate securities, it is also the security with the greatest expected return.

Ownership of common stock also carries management rights. In large corporations a small group of insiders and major stockholders typically control corporate affairs. In this case voting rights may be relatively unimportant to other stockholders. However, if a group of outsiders feel they can do a better job running the company, they can make a tender offer to buy enough of the outstanding common stock to get a voting majority with which they can remove the existing management.[24] Tender offers are usually extended at substantial premiums over secondary-market prices. These premiums represent the value of the management control associated with voting rights on common stock.

Secondary-Market Trading

The equity securities of most large American corporations trade on organized exchanges, such as the New York Stock Exchange, the American Stock

---

[23] The rights of holders of preferred stock (with respect to their claims to dividends and arrearages) in the event of corporate reorganization are discussed by Brudney and Chirelstein (1972, pp. 157–238).

[24] Purchases of stock to obtain control of the issuer, rather than simply as a financial investment, are not analyzed in this book, but are discussed by Manne (1965) and Posner (1972, chap. 12). See, especially, the comprehensive treatment of tender offers in Lipton and Steinberger (1978).

Exchange, and regional exchanges like the Midwest Stock Exchange. Exchange trading may be distinguished from dealer markets such as the corporate bond market in two ways.

First, all trading in a given stock occurs at a single place on an exchange floor. Brokers seeking to execute purchase and sale orders on behalf of their customers know exactly where to go to meet brokers representing other buyers and sellers. This feature of a unique trading location makes it quite cheap to acquire information on the prices at which other investors are willing to buy and sell. It is virtually impossible to sell securities on an exchange floor at a price greater than the offering price of another broker selling the same securities or to buy securities at a price lower than that which another broker is bidding. The ease of acquiring information on available purchase and sale interests, coupled with competition among brokers for the most favorable prices on their customers' transactions, leads to what is known as *price priority* in the execution of orders on a stock exchange. That is, high bidders always buy sooner than those with lower bids, and low offerers sell sooner than those with higher asking prices. This feature of exchange trading is the reason why the New York Stock Exchange is known as an *auction* market: securities are always bought by the highest bidders and sold by the lowest offerers. Price priority of execution may not be present in a dealer market if an investor (or a dealer) is ignorant of some existing trading opportunities. We will have more to say on this topic of information in dealer markets in Parts Seven and Eight.

The second distinguishing feature of exchange trading is that transactions prices are broadcast to the public over ticker tapes and similar devices. Investors not immediately interested in buying or selling can keep abreast of the market by watching the tape. If a security falls in price, they may decide to buy the security if they perceive the lower price as a bargain opportunity. The speedy flow of transaction price information tends to add liquidity to, and increase the efficiency of, exchange trading.

Stocks of smaller companies trade in a dealer market.[25] Prior to the innovation of electronic communication devices like the telegraph, the telephone, and the teletype (not to mention modern computer-based communication networks), securities which were not traded on an exchange floor were bought and sold "over the counter" in the front offices of securities firms. This led to the designation *over-the-counter*, or OTC, for trading which takes place in a dealer market. The term is applied in particular to stocks which are not listed for trading on an exchange, but it also applies in general to all dealer markets, including those for Treasury securities and corporate bonds.

2.4 INVESTMENT COMPANY SECURITIES

Securities issued by investment companies represent, directly or indirectly, participations in the earnings on the securities held in the portfolios of

---

[25] The dealer market is described by Bloomenthal (1960).

those companies. Investment company securities are important in a survey of financial instruments, because they provide a vehicle for the investment of relatively small sums of money in well-diversified portfolios of financial assets. There exist several types of investment companies, each of which provides diversification services in a slightly different way. The differences among various investment companies are worth noting, because we will be referring to those companies later, in Chapters 9, 10, and 13.

Classes of Investment Companies

The concept of a redeemable security is of fundamental importance when discussing investment companies. A security is said to be *redeemable* if a holder can, at his discretion, return it to the issuer for a proportional share of the net assets held by the issuer or for a comparable amount of cash. When an investment company issues only a single class of redeemable securities, the redemption value, or *net asset value*, of one unit of that security is equal to the total *net* market value of the company's portfolio divided by the number of outstanding units of the security. Having defined a redeemable security, we are now ready to categorize investment companies as unit investment trusts holding a fixed portfolio of assets or as managed investment companies holding portfolios which are reallocated from time to time.

Unit Investment Trusts   A unit investment trust is an investment company, organized under a trust indenture, which issues only redeemable securities (usually called *participation units*), each of which represents an undivided interest in a *fixed* portfolio of specified assets. Any cash payments made by the issuers of the assets in the trust, including interest and dividend payments and the return of principal at maturity, are distributed to holders of the participation units in proportion to their holdings of those units. Participation units are, therefore, similar to pass-through securities. However, because the units are redeemable, they can also be converted into cash at the current market value of a proportional share of the assets in the trust portfolio. Holding a participation in a unit investment trust is, therefore, equivalent to holding a portfolio diversified like the trust portfolio.

Participations in unit investment trusts have been offered in increasing numbers in recent years and with an increasing variety of assets in the trust portfolios. In almost all cases the assets have been either debt securities or preferred stock with a mandatory redemption date. (A trust expires when the last asset in its portfolio matures.) Among debt investment trusts there have been portfolios of commercial bank certificates of deposit, municipal bonds, corporate bonds, and Government National Mortgage Association pass-through securities. Some bond trusts have restricted their holdings to intermediate maturity issues, and others have chosen only longer-term issues. Thus, investors can invest in a variety of securities by choosing an appropriate unit investment trust.

Exhibit 2.4 shows the cover page from a prospectus offering units in an investment trust invested in certificates of deposit. The allocation of the portfolio of that trust is shown in Exhibit 2.5.

Trust units are generally offered in minimum denominations of $1000. The marketing of trust units has emphasized their appropriateness as a means of acquiring a portfolio of similar assets with greater diversification than many investors would be able to achieve through direct investments.

EXHIBIT 2.4
Cover page of a prospectus for $50 million of participations in a unit investment trust.

THE CORPORATE INCOME FUND

50,000 UNITS

EIGHTH SHORT TERM SERIES
(A Unit Investment Trust)
Prospectus dated November 20, 1974

THE CORPORATE INCOME FUND

The Corporate Income Fund, Eighth Short Term Series (A Unit Investment Trust) is formed for the purpose of obtaining a high level of current income through investment in a fixed portfolio of certificates of deposit with maturities of approximately six months issued by domestic banks insured by the Federal Deposit Insurance Corporation with assets of more than $250,000,000. The payment of interest and the preservation of principal is, of course, dependent upon the continuing ability of the issuers to meet such obligations.

PUBLIC OFFERING PRICE

The Public Offering Price of the Units is equal to the aggregate offering price of the underlying obligations (the price at which they could be directly purchased by the public assuming they are available) plus a sales charge of ¾% of the Public Offering Price for the first month and at a decreasing percentage thereafter; this results in a sales charge of .7556% of the net amount invested in the underlying obligations at the date of this Prospectus. Units are offered at the Public Offering Price plus net interest accrued at the annualized rate of 7.738% per Unit. Had the Units been available for sale on November 19, 1974, the Public Offering Price would have been $998.42 (see Public Sale of Units — Public Offering Price on p. 7).

FDIC COVERAGE

In the opinion of counsel, based upon an opinion dated September 11, 1974, as supplemented, which the Sponsor has received in writing from the Office of the General Counsel of the Federal Deposit Insurance Corporation, the undivided beneficial interest of each Certificateholder in the certificates of deposit (including interest accrued to the closing of the insured bank) issued by the same bank held by this and other short term series of The Corporate Income Fund for which the Trustee of this Series also acts as trustee, treated as a single interest, is insured by the Federal Deposit Insurance Corporation against loss in the event of the closing of the insured bank. The Units, as such, are not insured. See FDIC Insurance Coverage on page 5 for a more complete discussion of this insurance and certain limitations to which it is subject.

DISTRIBUTION AND TERMINATION OF THE FUND

A single distribution of interest will be made by the Fund on May 29, 1975 or shortly thereafter to holders of record on May 27, 1975. On May 29, 1975, the Fund will be liquidated and terminated, and a single final distribution of principal, which in certain circumstances may be less than the amount paid for a Unit, will be made on or shortly thereafter upon surrender of certificates (see Creation of the Fund — Principal Distribution After Six Months on p. 5 and Rights of Certificateholders — Interest Distribution on p. 11). **ESTIMATED CURRENT RETURN**
Estimated current return on a Unit is computed by dividing the net interest income per Unit after adding the discount under $1,000 per Unit ($1.58 per Unit, at November 19, 1974) by the Public Offering Price and expressing the result as an annualized percentage. The estimated current return thus determined was 8.07% on November 19, 1974. The net interest income per Unit will vary with changes in the fees and expenses of the Trustee and Evaluator and with the sale of underlying obligations; Public Offering Price will vary with changes in the offering price of the underlying obligations and with the decreasing sales charge; and therefore there is no assurance that the estimated current return will be realized in the future (see Creation of the Fund — Interest and Estimated Current Return on p. 4). The net interest income received by a Certificateholder is, of course, taxable.

Retain this prospectus for future reference (continued on following page)

SPONSOR:

Merrill Lynch Pierce Fenner & Smith Inc.

EXHIBIT 2.5
ALLOCATION ON NOVEMBER 20, 1974, OF THE PORTFOLIO OF A UNIT INVESTMENT
TRUST INVESTED IN BANK CERTIFICATES OF DEPOSIT

Issuer	Face amount of certificate	Maturity date	Yield to maturity, %
American Bank and Trust Company, Baton Rouge, La.	$5 million	May 29, 1975	9.55
First American National Bank, Nashville, Tenn.	$5 million	May 29, 1975	9.54
Industrial Valley Bank & Trust Co., Jenkintown, Pa.	$10 million	May 29, 1975	9.45
Liberty National Bank & Trust Co., Oklahoma, City, Okla.	$10 million	May 29, 1975	9.62
Sumitomo Bank of California, San Francisco, Calif.	$10 million	May 29, 1975	9.74
Bank of Tokyo of California, San Francisco, Calif.	$10 million	May 29, 1975	9.62

Managed Investment Companies   A different category of investment companies is that of managed companies. The trust indenture establishing a unit investment trust generally precludes, outside of unusual circumstances, the addition of new assets to the trust portfolio or the sale of assets prior to maturity. The portfolios of managed companies are not similarly frozen. Managed investment companies are corporations, chartered under state law, whose management can buy and sell securities for the account of the company, subject to the approval of the corporate directors. Managed companies which hold diversified portfolios and which distribute at least 90 percent of their ordinary income to stockholders in the form of dividends are exempt from federal taxes on that income.[26] Most managed companies qualify for the tax-exempt status by distributing all ordinary income and realized capital gains to their stockholders.

There are two subclassifications of managed investment companies, distinguished by whether the company does or does not issue redeemable securities.

Open-End Investment Companies   An *open-end* investment company is a managed investment company which issues only one class of redeemable security. Such a company is commonly called a *mutual fund*. Because mutual fund shares are redeemable, they are always worth the current market value of a proportionate share of the issuer's net assets. Unlike the value of a unit investment trust, however, the value of a mutual fund share may fluctuate not only because of changes in the market value of the assets in the fund's portfolio, but also because of changes in the composition of that portfolio.

Mutual fund shares are not simply a participation in a fixed portfolio of assets, but are also a participation in the investment skill of the managers of the

---

[26] See Subchapter M of the Internal Revenue Code of 1954.

investment company. At any point in time the value of a fund's shares is deter-mined by the value of its portfolio, but it is usually hoped that the value of that portfolio will grow more rapidly if the portfolio is actively managed than if it is left alone.[27]

Mutual funds have been a popular investment vehicle in the United States since shortly after World War II. There exists a wide variety of funds, including corporate bond funds emphasizing capital stability and certainty of income, speculative stock funds emphasizing opportunities for capital gains, and funds which invest only in equity securities issued by corporations in certain industry groups.

A recent innovation in mutual funds is the money-market funds, which in-vest in short-term debt such as Treasury bills, commercial paper, and commer-cial bank certificates of deposit. The minimum investment in these funds is usually $1000 or $5000, and so they offer investors an opportunity to hold par-ticipations in assets which are available through direct investment only in much larger minimum denominations. Exhibit 2.6 shows the cover page from a pros-pectus offering shares in a money-market fund.

Another new group of mutual funds is the municipal bond funds. In the fall of 1976, Congress revised the federal tax laws so that dividends paid by mutual funds from interest received on municipal bond holdings could be excluded from a recipient's income for federal tax purposes. Previously, all dividend in-come from mutual funds was taxed as ordinary income.

Closed-End Investment Companies If a managed investment company does not issue redeemable securities, it is called a *closed-end* company. Securities of closed-end companies can be liquidated only through sale in a secondary-market transaction. The issues of several closed-end companies, including Leh-man Corporation and Madison Fund, Inc., are listed on the New York Stock Exchange. Others trade in over-the-counter markets. Since the securities of closed-end companies are not redeemable, they may fluctuate in value above or, most commonly, below a proportionate value of the net assets of the is-suer.[28] Closed-end investment company securities, therefore, are not an eco-nomic substitute for holding directly the assets which appear in the company's portfolio.

New Issues

New issues of investment company securities come to market in quite different ways. In the case of a unit investment trust, a sponsor (typically one or more large brokerage firms) will arrange with a bank or trust company to act as trust-ee for the trust. The sponsor delivers to the trustee the securities to be placed in the trust portfolio and receives from the trustee the full issue of participation

---

[27] Empirical evidence, which we will consider in Section 13.4, suggests that active portfolio management does not contribute significantly to the return on mutual fund portfolios.

[28] Malkiel (1977) has considered the determinants of the discount below net asset value on closed-end investment company securities. See also Miller (1977).

units showing an interest in the trust. The sponsor then offers the units to investors at a price which reflects the current value of the trust portfolio. Unlike the case with syndicated corporate offerings, the issue price on investment trust units is not fixed during the offering period.

In contrast to investment trust units, shares of stock in open-end mutual funds are offered on a continuing basis directly by the issuer at a price propor-

EXHIBIT 2.6
Cover page of a prospectus for a money-market mutual fund.

PROSPECTUS   **MAY 1, 1979**

 Dreyfus Liquid Assets, Inc.

600 Madison Avenue, New York, N.Y. 10022—(Outside New York State—Toll Free—800-223-5525)
(In New York State Outside 212 Area—Call Collect—212-223-0303)
(In 212 Area—223-0303)

Dreyfus Liquid Assets, Inc. (the "Company") is a diversified, open-end investment company. Its objective is maximization of current income to the extent consistent with the preservation of capital. The Company pursues this objective by investing in money market obligations, including securities issued or guaranteed by the United States Government or its agencies and instrumentalities (whether or not subject to repurchase agreements), certificates of deposit ("CD's") issued by domestic banks or London branches of domestic banks, bankers' acceptances, and high grade commercial paper. At least 25% of the Company's assets will consist of bank CD's and bankers' acceptances. There can be no assurance that the objective of the Company will be realized. There is no sales or redemption charge.

It is the policy of the Company to attempt to maintain a net asset value of $1.00 per share for purposes of sales and redemptions by rounding its net asset value per share to the nearest cent. In order to effectuate this policy the Company follows certain investment, dividend and distribution policies. See "Investment Objective and Management Policies" and "Distributions of Net Investment Income, Realized Capital Gains and Taxes."

The Company was granted an exemptive order under the Investment Company Act of 1940 to the extent necessary to permit the Company's net asset value per share to be computed and maintained as set forth herein. There cannot be, however, any absolute assurance that the Company will at all times be able to maintain a continuous net asset value of $1.00 per share.

The Company has contracted to pay The Dreyfus Corporation, the Company's manager (the "Manager"), an annual management fee equal to ½ of 1% of the average market value of its daily net assets. See "Management of the Company—Management Fee." Dreyfus Service Corporation (the "Distributor") acts as distributor of the Company's shares. See "Purchase of Shares."

Funds used to purchase Company shares must be transmitted to The Bank of New York (the "Bank"), the Custodian and the Transfer and Dividend Agent for the Company. The minimum investment is $2,500, except that in the case of amounts forwarded by a securities dealer or an investment adviser the minimum investment is $1,000. Subsequent investments must be at least $100. Investments may be made in any amounts in excess of the above minimums. Securities dealers may charge a nominal transaction fee. Shares may be purchased directly from the Distributor at no charge. See "Purchase of Shares—Transactions through Securities Dealers." The Company reserves the right, upon not less than 30 days' notice, to redeem an account that has been reduced by an investor to 500 shares or less. See "Purchase of Shares—Reopening an Account."

An Application and Order Form is enclosed.

The investor is advised to retain this Prospectus for future reference.

THESE SECURITIES HAVE NOT BEEN APPROVED OR DISAPPROVED BY THE SECURITIES AND EXCHANGE COMMISSION NOR HAS THE COMMISSION PASSED UPON THE ACCURACY OR ADEQUACY OF THIS PROSPECTUS. ANY REPRESENTATION TO THE CONTRARY IS A CRIMINAL OFFENSE.

tionate to the net value of the assets and liabilities of the fund.[29] This type of continuous offering contrasts with the discrete offerings of syndicated corporate issues and investment trust units. Because mutual funds issue redeemable securities, and because they make continuous offerings of new issues, the aggregate number of outstanding shares of a given fund can grow or contract over time.

Closed-end investment companies make only a single offering of their securities, typically through an underwriting syndicate. After the initial offering, there are usually no further offerings and in particular no continuous offerings. Since there is no redemption option on the securities of closed-end funds, the number of outstanding securities issued by a closed-end company is constant over time.

New issues of investment company securities have to be registered with the SEC and can be publicly offered to investors only with a prospectus detailing the business of the issuer and the type of security offered. In the case of a unit investment trust the prospectus is fairly simple. The only important information is the identity of the securities in the trust portfolio.

For managed investment companies, the disclosure required in a prospectus is more complex. There must, of course, be a statement of the objective of the company, e.g., a bond fund, a short-term money-market fund, or a speculative stock fund.[30] There must also be a statement explaining how management expects to attain that objective, and there is always a disclaimer similar to the one in Exhibit 2.6 (near the end of the first paragraph) that says: "There can be no assurance that the objective of the Company will be realized." Because of the importance of portfolio management to the success of a managed investment company, a new issue prospectus will also disclose the identity of the investment advisers which the company has retained to make recommendations for purchases and sales.

Since mutual fund shares are offered continuously, those funds must constantly maintain a current prospectus. Participation units in investment trusts and closed-end company shares are usually sold within a short period of time, and so there is only a single prospectus associated with offerings of those issues.

CHAPTER SUMMARY

This chapter has described the characteristics of, and primary markets for, three types of corporate securities: commercial paper, coupon-bearing debt, and equity. The most important difference between debt and equity is that the former is a contractual commitment of the issuer to make specified payments,

---

[29] Some open-end companies offer their securities through brokers. The brokers charge a fee, called a *front-end load*, for their sales effort.

[30] See McDonald (1974) for an analysis of stated mutual fund objectives and the relation of those objectives to the risk and return experiences of the funds during the period 1960–1969.

while the latter is a residual claim on earnings and assets. Different types of debt (such as mortgage bonds, general credits, and subordinated credits) may be distinguished by their priorities in the event of bankruptcy, but they are all contractual claims. Similarly, preferred stock is distinguished from common stock by its more senior (but not contractual) claim to the payment of dividends and to the assets of a corporation in liquidation or reorganization.

Even though we have no more than scratched the surface of securities markets at this point, we can already ask three important questions. First, what forces determine relative prices on different stock issues? (This question is addressed in Parts Three and Four.) Second, ignoring the risk of default, what forces determine the yields on debt securities of different maturities? (The answer to this question is begun in Part Two and completed in Part Five.) Third, in view of the fact that corporate debt is not free of default risk, how is the yield on a corporate debt security determined? (This question is answered in Part Six.) These three questions are the *central* issues in the study of securities valuation.

Besides describing different types of corporate securities, this chapter has also explored the various methods used to sell those securities in the primary markets. The two most important methods for selling new issues of corporate securities are negotiated underwritings and private placements. In the former, broker-dealers buy a new issue for their own inventory and then reoffer the securities to public investors in a subscription offering. Although there is no formal auction, the issuer and the underwriters do bargain informally when setting the terms of the issue. In a private placement, an issuer bargains directly with final investors. Competitive underwritings are less common than either negotiated underwritings or private placements, although they are quite important for public utility issuers like power companies. The terms of a competitive underwriting are set through an explicit auction process rather than by bargaining. Given a choice, most corporations use the negotiated underwriting method rather than the competitive method, because they believe underwriters give better terms if they have an opportunity to explore and promote investor interest during the preoffering period.

Corporations sell commercial paper, or short-term debt liabilities, in a variety of ways, including directly to final investors, through underwritten offerings, and on a brokered basis. The decision to use a broker-dealer, either as an underwriter or as a broker, depends on the familiarity of the issuer with investor interests. Frequent issuers such as finance companies are more likely to maintain their own sales force instead of paying a broker-dealer to do the selling.

This chapter has also described three classes of investment companies: unit investment trusts, open-end managed companies, and closed-end managed companies. Companies in the first two classes issue redeemable securities; closed-end companies do not. The asset portfolio of a unit investment trust is usually not subject to substantial change during the lifetime of the trust (except for the retirement of assets reaching maturity), while the managements of both closed-end and open-end companies usually reallocate their assets on a frequent basis.

FURTHER READING

Alison Anderson, "The Disclosure Process in Federal Securities Regulation: A Brief Review," *Hastings Law Journal*, **25** (January 1974), 311–354.

Louis Ederington, "Negotiated versus Competitive Underwritings of Corporate Bonds," *Journal of Finance*, **31** (March 1976), 17–28.

Samuel Hayes, "Investment Banking: Power Structure in Flux," *Harvard Business Review*, **49** (March–April 1971), 136–152.

Evelyn Hurley, "The Commercial Paper Market," *Federal Reserve Bulletin*, **63** (June 1977), 525–536.

Henry Manne, "Mergers and the Market for Corporate Control," *Journal of Political Economy*, **73** (April 1965), 110–120.

David Ruder, "Federal Restrictions on the Sale of Securities," *Northwestern University Law Review*, **67** (Supplement, November 1972), 1–64.

John Thackray, "The Launching of Floating Rates," *Institutional Investor*, **8** (September 1974), 43.

CHAPTER 3

MUNICIPAL SECURITIES

Municipal securities are debt instruments issued by states and their political subdivisions, including counties, cities, and school districts. By law, the coupon interest income on a municipal security is not subject to federal income tax. This tax exemption is the most important feature distinguishing municipal issues from Treasury, federal agency, and corporate debt securities. The first section of this chapter shows how tax exemption affects the coupon rate and pricing of municipal debt. The following section describes several classes of municipal securities, including general obligation debt, revenue and authority securities, and pass-through securities. These classes are distinguished primarily by the sources of funds available to an issuer for meeting the interest and principal payments on its debt. The last section discusses the primary market for municipal securities, in which issuers sell their obligations to final investors, and the secondary market for trading in outstanding issues.

3.1 THE TAX-EXEMPTION FEATURE

Section 103 of the Internal Revenue Code specifies that gross income, for federal income tax purposes, does not include interest on "the obligations of a State, a Territory, or a possession of the United States, or any political subdivision of any of the foregoing." This exemption applies only to the interest or coupon income on municipal debt and does not extend to the capital gains realized when an investor sells a security for more than his original investment.

The Effect of Tax Exemption When All Investors Are Taxed at the Same Rate

The consequences of tax exemption for the coupon rate on municipal debt can be derived exactly in one simple case. Suppose all investors were liable for income taxes at the same marginal income tax rate, say, t, where $0 < t < 1$. Let R_{cp} be the annual coupon rate on a taxable bond selling at a price equal to its principal value, and let R_{cp}^e be the annual coupon rate on a tax-exempt municipal bond, also selling at principal value. Since the prices of the taxable and tax-exempt bonds are equal, their after-tax payments must be equivalent in the eyes of the investors. This equivalence allows us to establish the relation between R_{cp} and R_{cp}^e.

Ignoring any possibility of default, a holder of the municipal bond will get a coupon payment of $^{1}/_{2}R_{cp}^e$ every 6 months. Since he pays no tax on that interest, $^{1}/_{2}R_{cp}^e$ is also his after-tax income from the coupon. A holder of the taxable bond receives a semiannual coupon payment of $^{1}/_{2}R_{cp}$. Since he has to pay taxes on that payment at the rate t, his after-tax income from the taxable coupon is $(1 - t)\,^{1}/_{2}R_{cp}$. Because both bonds are priced at principal value, neither will show a capital gain or loss if held to maturity. Thus, the only possible difference between the bonds is the size of their respective semiannual after-tax coupon payments. Since the bonds have the same price, those after-tax payments must be equal, implying that

$$R_{cp}^e = (1 - t)R_{cp} \tag{3.1}$$

If the United States Treasury had to place an 8 percent annual coupon rate on 10-year notes to sell them to investors taxed at a rate of 60 percent, then Equation (3.1) says that a high-quality municipal issuer could sell its own 10-year notes to the same investors at a 3.2 percent annual coupon rate.

The Effect of Tax Exemption When Investors Are Taxed at Different Rates

When not all investors are taxed at the same marginal rate, the equilibrium relation between interest rates on taxable and municipal debt issues is not so easily derived. Because investors are in different tax brackets, they will not all be indifferent between holding municipal debt and corporate debt. Most will prefer one or the other type of issue. The debt markets will then be segmented by investor tax brackets, with the dividing tax rate determined by the relative yields on taxable and tax-exempt debt.

This segmentation of the debt markets can be illustrated for a given pair of yields on taxable and tax-exempt debt. Letting R_{cp} and R_{cp}^e be as above, we can solve Equation (3.1) for the tax rate t^* of an investor indifferent between the two types of securities:

$$t^* = \frac{R_{cp} - R_{cp}^e}{R_{cp}} \tag{3.2}$$

An investor taxed at the marginal rate t^* is indifferent between taxable and tax-exempt debt, because t^* satisfies the equation

$$R_{cp}^e = (1 - t^*)R_{cp}$$

If other factors are equal, investors taxed at marginal rates greater than t^* will prefer tax-exempt debt to taxable debt, because tax-exempt debt gives them a higher after-tax return. Investors taxed at marginal rates less than t^* will prefer taxable debt for comparable reasons. For example, suppose we observe a coupon rate on taxable debt of 9 percent and a coupon rate on tax-exempt debt of 5 percent. From Equation (3.2) we then have $t^* = .44$. Any investor subject to a tax rate greater than 44 percent would prefer to hold tax-exempt debt, because $5 > (1 - t)9$ when the tax rate t is greater than 44 percent. Conversely, any investor subject to a tax rate less than 44 percent would prefer to hold the taxable debt.

This segmentation of the taxable and tax-exempt debt markets between investors in different tax brackets shows why municipal securities are held mainly by wealthy individual investors; by fire, property, and casualty insurance companies; and by commercial banks. All of those investors are in relatively high tax brackets. Tax-exempt pension funds, on the other hand, are major holders of taxable debt.

Equation (3.2) suggests that when municipalities are heavy borrowers in the capital markets, the coupon rate on new issues of municipal debt will move up toward the coupon rate on new taxable issues. This rate movement will narrow the interest spread $R_{cp} - R_{cp}^e$ and hence lower t^*, making municipals attractive to a larger class of investors. Conversely, the relative spread will widen, and t^* will decline, when municipalities demand less credit. The spread between the coupon rates on new issues of taxable and nontaxable debt thus influences the decision of investors to hold one or the other class of debt instrument.

In practice, the equilibrium valuation of municipal debt issues and the comparative analysis of taxable and tax-exempt debt depends not only on federal tax law, but also on state and local income tax laws. For example, interest on debt of New York City is exempt from New York City, New York State, and federal income taxes. To a New York resident, however, interest on municipal debt of another state is exempt from only federal income taxes. Thus, the after-tax return on municipal debt depends both on the coupon rate of the issue and on whether the holder of the debt resides within the political boundaries of the issuer. This explains, in part, why municipal bonds tend to be held by residents of the issuing state or political subdivision.

3.2 TYPES OF MUNICIPAL SECURITIES

One of the most important uncertainties associated with any debt security is whether the issuer will fail to make good on its promised payments of interest and principal. This question is usually ignored for federal agency issues, and on

United States Treasury issues it is ignored completely. As the de facto 1975 default by New York City reminds us, however, the problem of credit risk on municipal debt cannot be ignored so easily.[1]

An important distinction among different types of municipal securities is the identity of the issuer. In some cases the issuer will be a state or a city and the security will be what is called a *general obligation* of that issuer. To evaluate the credit risk of such a general obligation security, we would want to know the revenues made available to the issuer through tax collections and other sources. In other cases the issuer may be a special authority organized to engage in a particular line of business, such as building and operating a turnpike. We then would want to know the actual or projected success of that business endeavor. Finally, the issuer may simply be acting as a financial intermediary, and so the credit risk on its debt will depend on the creditworthiness of its loans. In this section we describe in more detail each of these three types of municipal securities: general obligations, revenues, and pass-throughs.

General Obligation Securities

A general obligation security, or GO, is a municipal debt issue secured by a first lien, or priority claim, on all revenues received by the issuer.[2] In addition to this right of first claim, many GOs also provide that an issuer must, by law, levy taxes sufficient to pay its general obligations as they mature, including interest and principal. Other GOs, while creating a first lien on all revenues, specify a maximum rate at which an issuer can tax its residents. Unlike mortgage debt securities of corporate issuers, a GO does not provide a lien on any physical assets owned by the issuer. The lien created by a GO is on revenues and not on assets.

General obligation securities are typically sold by state governments and multipurpose political subdivisions with multiple revenue sources, such as counties and cities. Securities sold by single-purpose issuers, like water and sewer districts with limited taxing powers, are generally classified as revenue or authority securities and are described later in this section.

Bonds GO bonds may be of any maturity, and they range in practice from 1 to 30 or more years. Municipal issuers generally sell bonds to finance capital improvements—such as transit facilities, roads, or schools—that have a long useful life. Most state constitutions require a majority vote by residents before the state can create a lien on its tax revenues by selling GO bonds. Requirements for voter approval of GO bond issues are rare, however, at the local government level.

---

[1] Hillhouse (1936) surveys the default experience on municipal debt from the early nineteenth century to the middle of the Great Depression.

[2] The precise legal rights of a holder of general obligation debt may vary from this general statement, as many holders of New York City notes found out in 1975. See Securities and Exchange Commission (1977b).

Many GO issuers sell bonds in a serial form rather than offer an entire issue with a single maturity date. On June 22, 1977, for example, the state of Oregon sold $150 million of GO bonds. About $10 million of the issue bore a maturity date in 1989, and $20 million matured each year from 1990 to 1996, inclusive. Although any given bond in the issue had a unique specified maturity, the issue as a whole had a sequence of maturities and hence was designated a serial bond issue. Serial repayment of principal can also be accomplished by sinking fund repurchases, but in that case the date on which a given bond will be paid off is random.

Notes   General obligation notes of a municipal issuer typically have less than a year to run at original issue, although note issues occasionally come to market with 15- or 18-month maturities. Municipalities use note issues primarily to gain flexibility in their budgeting of cash receipts and expenditures and to obtain interim financing of projects which ultimately will be refinanced with longer-term issues. Since notes are of short duration and can be issued only for a limited number of purposes, issuers generally do not have to obtain voter approval before selling them.

Notes issued for budgetary reasons include tax anticipation notes (TANs) and revenue anticipation notes (RANs). TANs are issued against anticipated tax revenues, usually real estate property taxes, which have been levied but not collected. RANs are issued against other anticipated revenues, such as state and federal aid payments; reimbursements, such as Medicare payments; and projected sales and income tax revenues. Bond anticipation notes (BANs) are sold to provide temporary financing for capital projects. BANs are ultimately refunded through the sale of bonds already approved by voters.

Revenue and Authority Securities

From time to time a state or local government may decide that, for purposes of economic efficiency or political expediency, it should provide a particular service itself rather than rely on the private sector. Examples include transit services, such as turnpikes, airports, and parking facilities; water and other utilities; and public housing. These services are frequently provided through municipal authorities organized and run like private companies. In particular, a municipal authority will typically generate most of its revenues from user charges, such as turnpike tolls, landing fees, meter charges, and rents. It may, however, also receive a subsidy from its sponsoring government.

Like private businesses, municipal authorities sell debt obligations to finance capital improvement projects such as roads and buildings. These debt securities are obligations only of the issuing authority and, unless otherwise provided, are not general obligations of any sponsoring government. Thus, the creditworthiness of a municipal authority will depend on the level and stability of authority revenues and costs. To this extent municipal authority debt is closer to corporate debt than general obligation municipal debt.

When a municipal authority fails to earn enough from its user charges to meet its debt service obligations, it may default on its bonds. The best-known authority default of recent years is probably the temporary default of the New York State Urban Development Corporation in 1975. There are, however, many defaults which have been outstanding for far longer, including those of the West Virginia Turnpike Commission, the Calumet Skyway Toll Bridge in Chicago, and the Chesapeake Bay Bridge & Tunnel Commission. All of these authorities defaulted on their debt issues when they experienced automobile and truck volumes lower than anticipated.

In some cases an authority debt issue may be secured by limited taxing power granted to the authority, or the issue may be backed up by a general obligation pledge of the sponsoring government. In the latter case the security is, for all intents and purposes, a general obligation debt issue even though the issuer is a municipal authority.

Pass-Through Securities

In some cases the proceeds of debt securities sold by a political subdivision of a state are reloaned to some other ultimate borrower, such as a private, profit-making corporation. In return for the funds, the ultimate borrower agrees to provide the interest and principal payments needed to service the debt securities sold by the issuer. The issuer is then nothing more than a financial intermediary through which sale proceeds and interest and principal payments pass.

The purpose of pass-through municipal securities is to make credit available to business firms at interest rates lower than those firms could obtain on their own. For example, corporations routinely finance the purchase of large pollution-control systems by borrowing through pollution-control authorities instead of selling their own debt.

Pass-through securities may be issued directly by a municipality or, more conventionally, through a separate issuing authority. In either case, the ultimate borrower uses the proceeds to finance some designated capital project. In most cases the only credit guarantee standing behind a pass-through is the promise of the ultimate borrower to make scheduled payments to the issuer. Thus, the credit risk on a pass-through reflects primarily the creditworthiness of the ultimate borrower and not the creditworthiness of the issuer. In other cases the pass-through may also be secured either by a mortgage lien on property owned by the borrower or by some limited taxing power of the issuer.

Until 1968 corporations made active use of the opportunity to borrow funds at low cost by arranging pass-through financing with local municipal financing authorities. The most important category of that financing was through industrial development revenue bonds, or IDRs. The Internal Revenue Code defined an IDR as a municipal security whose proceeds are used in a business other than one conducted by a governmental unit or nonprofit organization and on which the payment of interest and principal is secured by or derived from a trade or business. In 1968 Congress amended the Internal Revenue Code to remove the tax-exemption feature on most IDR issues. The exemption was retained, however, on air- and water-pollution control, sewage and solid-waste disposal and sports facility issues, and several similar categories of IDRs. Since the passage of the Clean Air Act of 1970 and the Water Pollution Act of 1972, corporations have again become major borrowers through the tax-exempt IDR market.

3.3 PRIMARY AND SECONDARY MARKETS IN MUNICIPAL DEBT

Municipal securities come to market through a process which is a hybrid of the unrestricted competition among buyers characterizing Treasury auctions and the negotiated underwriting by a single syndicate of broker-dealers used in most corporate offerings. Issuers of general obligation municipal debt typically advertise for competitive bids for their offerings, just as the Treasury does. Unlike the Treasury, however, municipalities offer new issues on an "all or none" basis, so that bidders buy either an entire offering or nothing at all. In practice, this restricts the class of potential bidders to syndicates of broker-dealers and removes retail buyers from the bidding competition.[3] After a successful syndicate has obtained a new issue, it reoffers the securities on a fixed-price subscription basis just as in any corporate underwriting.

Municipal securities may also be sold to underwriters on a negotiated basis, where the issuer negotiates the terms of an issue directly with a single group of broker-dealers. Negotiated underwritings are rare with general obligation offerings but are more common with non-GO issues like revenue bonds and pass-through securities. This section discusses the characteristics of competitive underwriting.

Underwriting General Obligation Debt

Perhaps the most striking contrast between the corporate and GO debt markets is that commercial banks can underwrite and distribute the latter securities but are restricted (by the Banking Act of 1933) from underwriting corporate debt. It is not at all uncommon to see substantial commercial bank participation in underwriting syndicates bidding on GO debt, and most large syndicates are composed of both banks and nonbank broker-dealers. Banks may participate in a syndicate either for their own investment account or to obtain securities for resale. Bank underwriters are especially active in reselling municipal bonds to smaller correspondent banks and to fiduciary accounts managed by their trust departments.

Syndicate Bidding on Serial Bonds When municipal securities are offered as a serial issue (which is often the case with bonds), the rules for identifying the winning syndicate bid have a significant effect on the terms at which the issue is reoffered to the public. The purpose of the bidding is to minimize the

---

[3] Municipal securities are exempt from registration under the Securities Act of 1933, but underwriters nevertheless bear affirmative disclosure obligations. See Doty and Petersen (1976). The most notable failure of underwriter disclosure occurred in connection with some New York City offerings in 1974 and 1975. See Securities and Exchange Commission (1977b).

issuer's borrowing costs, but those costs for serial bonds are measured in a peculiar way.

Suppose an issuer wants to raise a total of A through a serial bond issue, with the principal amount A_i maturing i years in the future. If the longest maturity bond matures in I years, then

$$\sum_{i=1}^{I} A_i = A \qquad (3.3)$$

The issuer specifies the schedule $(A_1, A_2, \cdots, A_I)$ of serial maturities, but he will typically not specify a coupon rate on any of the issues. Instead, it has been the practice for an issuer to let underwriters submit proposed coupon rates and to judge different bids by their interest cost. This cost is computed as total interest, regardless of when particular payments are made.

To illustrate how the total interest cost of an issue is typically computed, we now suppose an underwriting syndicate bids a coupon rate of R_i on bonds maturing i years in the future. The total interest expense on those bonds over their lifetime will be iR_iA_i. The interest cost on the entire serial bond issue will be as follows:

$$\text{Interest cost} = \sum_{i=1}^{I} iR_iA_i \qquad (3.4)$$

For example, suppose an issue consists of $20 million each of 10-, 11-, and 12-year debt, and a syndicate bids coupon rates of 5, 5.2, and 5.5 percent, respectively. Then the total interest cost on the issue is found as follows:

10 years $\times$ .05   interest $\times$ \$20 million $= \$10$ million
11 years $\times$ .052 interest $\times$ \$20 million $= \$11.44$ million
12 years $\times$ .055 interest $\times$ \$20 million $= \underline{\$13.2 \text{ million}}$
Total $= \$34.640$ million

It has long been a convention among municipal bond issuers to judge bids on serial bond offerings by their interest cost as computed in Equation (3.4).[4]

The interest cost specified in Equation (3.4) implies the issuer cares only about the total dollar cost of his interest payments and is indifferent to the dates at which he makes those payments. Suppose, in an extreme case, some underwriting syndicate bids a huge coupon rate on the shortest-maturity bond in a serial issue and bids a zero coupon rate on longer-maturity bonds in the same issue, thus making them single-payment discount securities. As long as the aggregate interest cost [defined by Equation (3.4)] on that bid was less than the aggregate interest cost any other syndicate bid, the issue would be awarded to

---

[4] Hopewell and Kaufman (1974) have pointed out that this method of judging syndicate bids leads to inefficient coupon rates and increases "true" issuer borrowing costs.

EXHIBIT 3.1
TERMS OF A SERIAL BOND OFFERING
On September 27, 1972, a syndicate of two
nonbank broker-dealers underwrote a $25
million general obligation serial bond offering
of the state of Minnesota. The amount, coupon, and maturity of each bond in the offering
was as follows:

Maturity	Coupon, %	Amount
1973	50	$1.25 million
1974	50	1.25 million
1975	50	1.25 million
1976	50	1.25 million
1977	10	1.25 million
1978	10	1.25 million
1979	5	1.25 million
1980	5	1.25 million
1981	4.75	1.25 million
1982	4.75	1.25 million
1983	4.75	1.25 million
1984	4.75	1.25 million
1985	5	1.25 million
1986	.1	1.25 million
1987	.1	1.25 million
1988	.1	1.25 million
1989	.1	1.25 million
1990	.1	1.25 million
1991	.1	1.25 million
1992	.1	1.25 million

Note that the coupon rates are structured so that
the issuer pays his interest expenses sooner than he
would in a normal offering.

the first syndicate at the coupon rates bid by that syndicate.[5] After receiving the
bonds, the syndicate would break up the individual maturities for resale, with
the high-coupon–short-maturity issue being sold at a premium and the zero-
coupon–longer-maturity issues being sold at progressively deeper discounts.
Because issuers do not care exactly when they pay interest (at least for the purposes of judging syndicate bids on serial bonds), syndicates will enter bids with
interest payments loaded into the early maturities. This will be reflected in the
coupon rates and prices on bonds reoffered to public investors, with short-maturity obligations reoffered at premiums and longer-maturity obligations reoffered at discounts.

The incentive among underwriters to bid higher coupon rates on shorter-maturity issues is strikingly evident in the terms of a $25 million Minnesota GO
issue of 1972, shown in Exhibit 3.1. The first four maturities in that serial bond
issue bore coupon rates of 50 percent per annum, while the last seven maturi-

---

[5] Percus and Quinto (1956) have analyzed optimal syndicate bidding strategies.

ties bore coupon rates of .1 percent per annum. To prevent this extreme bidding behavior, many issuers restrict underwriting syndicates to bidding in a specified range of acceptable coupon rates.

Competition among Syndicates   An important topic in municipal finance is the effect of intersyndicate bidding competition on the outcome of an offering of municipal bonds.[6] There are three related areas where syndicate competition has an impact: the interest cost to the issuer, the spread earned by the winning underwriting syndicate, and the reoffering yield at which the syndicate sells bonds to ultimate investors.

In a 1966 study of GO offerings, Richard West[7] found that municipal issuers that received only a single bid on their offerings generally had to pay a net interest cost 23 basis points over prevailing market rates. When there were two competing syndicates, the premium fell to 8 basis points. The premium vanished when there were three or more competing underwriting syndicates. Thus, it appears that intersyndicate competition, at least for GO issues, is important for reducing an issuer's borrowing costs.

In a later study, West[8] found underwriting spreads inversely related to the number of bids submitted. This implies underwriters capture for themselves some of the greater interest expense paid by issuers on offerings which do not attract active competition. In particular, underwriters do not pass on to final investors all the premium yields paid by issuers.

The question of whether investors get any yield premium at all on issues with little or no intersyndicate bidding competition was addressed by West in a third study.[9] He found that issues which received only a single bid were generally reoffered at yields 12 basis points over prevailing market rates on comparable issues, while issues which received two bids were reoffered at a premium yield of 2 basis points. He found no reoffering premiums on issues receiving three or more bids. Thus, underwriters appear to share with investors at least some of the yield premiums on issues which attract little or no intersyndicate competition.

Underwriting Revenue, Authority, and Pass-Through Debt

There are two main distinctions between the primary markets in GO and non-GO municipal debt: commercial banks are prohibited by the Banking Act of 1933 from acting as underwriters of non-GO obligations, and negotiated underwritings of non-GOs are far more common than is the case with GO issues. The latter feature can probably be attributed to the greater need for preoffering

---

[6] There is some evidence of collusion among underwriters to limit competition in the late 1950s and early 1960s. This led to the so-called William Morris episode, when a small broker-dealer outbid a Bank of America syndicate for a $100 million California bond offering. See West (1965b).

[7] West (1966).

[8] West (1967). See also Kessel (1971).

[9] West (1965a). See also Kessel (1971).

market exploration and promotion of investor interest in many non-GO offerings. Compared with GOs, non-GO issues tend to be of longer maturity and lower creditworthiness and are typically sold in larger offerings. With the exception of the tax-exemption feature, pass-through debt and authority debt are quite similar to corporate debt, and so it is hardly surprising that their primary markets are also similar.

The exclusion of commercial banks from underwriting non-GO municipal debt has been a subject of intense dispute between banks and nonbank broker-dealers almost since the passage of the Banking Act of 1933. The dispute has become especially acrimonious during the post-World War II period, because non-GO financing has assumed a larger share of the municipal market. There are three elements in the debate:

- Would issuers save interest costs if commercial banks could underwrite non-GO issues?
- Would the primary municipal bond market become concentrated in the hands of a few large banks?
- Does underwriting subject a bank to important conflicts of interest?

Only the first question is susceptible to empirical examination, and it has been addressed in two studies.

In the first analysis of the differences between the primary markets in GO and non-GO debt, Kessel[10] found that offerings of non-GO bonds attract fewer bids and generally exhibit larger underwriting spreads and higher reoffering yields than GO issues with similar characteristics. These findings, however, do not directly support the argument that the differences between GO and non-GO offerings would disappear if banks could underwrite non-GO issues. It may be that the differences between the primary markets for the two types of securities are due to differences in the credit risk of the issues or the characteristics of buyers.

In a later study, Hopewell and Kaufman[11] concluded that making non-GO issues eligible for bank underwriting would probably not increase the *number* of competing syndicate bids, but it might decrease the interest expense borne by issuers. These two conclusions, while seemingly contradictory, would follow if banks joined existing syndicates and competed *within* those syndicates for a larger share of an offering. By bidding securities away from other syndicate members, bank underwriters could induce a syndicate as a whole to enter a lower bid.

Secondary-Market Trading

The market in outstanding municipal securities consists of several overlapping segments. One segment is the dealer activities of large banks (such as Chase

---

[10] Kessel (1971).
[11] Hopewell and Kaufman (1977). See also Silber (1979).

Manhattan Bank) and nonbank broker-dealers (such as Salomon Brothers). Recent offerings, and issues with large outstanding volumes, usually trade quite actively in this market. One step removed from the dealer market are a large number of broker-dealers which trade a wide variety of smaller issues. These broker-dealers may specialize in securities of issuers in particular geographic areas and often provide specialized financial advice to a limited customer base. Transactions in this market are generally smaller and more costly to complete than those which can be accommodated in the larger dealer market. Finally, there is an extremely thin market in small issues, such as school district bonds and debt of local governments. Transactions in this market may depend largely on word-of-mouth communication of available offerings.

Because of the large number of municipal bonds and wide assortment of coupon rates, most bonds are quoted on a yield basis rather than on a price basis. However, bonds with a large outstanding volume in a single maturity and a reasonably active secondary market do trade on a price basis. These are the so-called dollar bonds.

The bid-ask spread on a municipal bond may vary from $1/_4$ percent of principal value on an actively traded issue to 5 percent or more of principal value on inactive issues. Dealers do not usually make markets in securities in the latter class, and reported bid and offer prices are likely to be brokers' quotations reflecting the purchase and sale interests of investors who have no need to complete a trade expeditiously.

CHAPTER SUMMARY

This chapter has described the types of securities issued by states and their political subdivisions, and the way those securities reach final investors through primary-market offerings. The principal distinction between different municipal securities is whether they are (1) general obligations of an issuer with significant taxing powers or (2) obligations of an operating or pass-through authority with little or no taxing power. This distinction affects the sources of funds which the issuer can draw upon to meet its contractual obligations. The distinction between whether a municipal security is a general obligation or revenue issue also determines whether a commercial bank can act as an underwriter of the security.

The most important distinction between municipal securities and most other types of debt issues is that interest payments on municipal debt are exempt from federal income tax. This tax exemption means that coupon rates on municipal bonds are lower than coupon rates on comparable debt not eligible for such favorable tax treatment. In general, only investors above a threshold tax rate will find tax-exempt debt attractive. Investors in lower tax brackets will prefer taxable debt. The debt markets are, therefore, segmented, although marginal investors may move back and forth between taxable and tax-exempt debt as the yield spreads between the instruments change.

FURTHER READING

Michael Hopewell and George Kaufman, "Commercial Bank Bidding on Municipal Revenue Bonds: New Evidence," *Journal of Finance,* **32** (December 1977), 1647–1656.

Reuben Kessel, "A Study of the Effects of Competition in the Tax-Exempt Bond Market," *Journal of Political Economy,* **79** (July–August 1971), 706–738.

Richard West, "New Issue Concessions on Municipal Bonds: A Case of Monopsony Pricing," *Journal of Business,* **38** (April 1965), 135–148.

CHAPTER 4

COMMERCIAL BANK LIABILITIES

Commercial banks are corporations which issue a full range of corporate securities, including subordinated debentures and common and preferred stock. Banks also issue some unique types of short-term debt which play an important role in American financial markets. This chapter describes two bank-related liabilities: certificates of deposit and borrowings of Federal funds.

A *certificate of deposit*, commonly known as a *CD*, is a negotiable deposit liability of the issuing commercial bank. Because CDs are negotiable, they can be sold in a secondary-market transaction prior to maturity. A borrowing of Federal funds, on the other hand, is not evidenced by a negotiable instrument, but is a nonnegotiable, usually oral, loan contract between a creditor bank and the borrowing bank.

4.1 CERTIFICATES OF DEPOSIT

Since at least the 1920s, commercial banks have offered to investors interest-bearing deposit liabilities with a stated maturity date, or certificates of deposit. Until 1960, however, these CDs were generally nonnegotiable. A holder had to wait to maturity to get his money back. The absence of any possibility of selling the instruments before maturity meant they were attractive only to those investors who were extremely confident they would not need cash on short notice.

In 1961, First National City Bank (since renamed Citibank) began to offer certificates of deposit in a negotiable form. For the first time, investors had the opportunity to acquire an interest-bearing deposit liability of a commercial bank which could be liquidated prior to maturity in the event of a change in the holder's need for cash. To accommodate sellers of the First National CDs,

Discount Corporation (a New York broker-dealer firm) began to make a secondary market in those securities. That is, Discount quoted to customers bid prices at which it would buy outstanding CDs and offer prices at which it would sell First National CDs from its own inventory. Today, most of the largest American banks, and many smaller ones, offer negotiable CDs to investors, and several dozen banks and nonbank broker-dealers make secondary markets in the certificates.[1]

Price Conventions

The major differences between CDs and the other two short-term debt instruments which we have encountered (Treasury bills and commercial paper) is that the latter promise to pay only their face value at maturity while CDs promise to pay their face value *plus interest* at some stated rate. Certificates of deposit are called *interest-bearing* securities for this reason, while Treasury bills and commercial paper are called *discount* instruments. It is conventional to use face value to indicate the size of both interest-bearing and discount instruments, but it should be remembered that the market value of the former may exceed face value, while the market value of the latter will always be less than face value. For example, a $1 million face value CD is worth $1 million on the day it is issued, but it is worth a greater amount on its maturity date. A $1 million face value Treasury bill, on the other hand, is worth less than $1 million at all times prior to maturity.

The maturity value of a CD can be computed from (1) the number of days to maturity at the time it is issued and (2) the interest rate stated on the CD. Suppose a CD has a maturity date n_0 days after its issue date and a stated interest rate of i_o, expressed as a fraction per annum. The maturity value of that CD, as a percent of its face value, will be

$$V = 100 \left(1 + \frac{n_o}{360} i_o\right) \tag{4.1}$$

Note that interest is paid on the basis of a 360-day year. If an investor buys from an issuing bank a 45-day CD bearing a stated interest rate of 8 percent per annum, the maturity value of his investment will be

$$V = 100 \left(1 + \frac{n_o}{360} i_o\right)$$

$$= 100 \left(1 + \frac{45}{360} (.08)\right)$$

$$= 101.0$$

If the CD had a face value of $1,000,000, its maturity value would be $1,010,000.

---

[1] The CD market is described in Willis (1972a) and Melton (1977–78).

Quotations for the purchase and sale of outstanding CDs in the secondary market are given as yield rates. If a CD has a maturity value of V percent of its face value [where V is computed by Equation (4.1)], has n days remaining to maturity, and is quoted at a yield of i, the market price P of the CD, as a percent of face value, is

$$P = \frac{V}{1 + ni/360} \tag{4.2}$$

We saw above that an 8 percent CD with an original maturity of 45 days has a maturity value equal to 101 percent of its face value. If a holder of that CD wanted to sell it when it had 10 days remaining to maturity, and if the buyer quoted a bid yield of 7.5 percent, the bid price would be

$$
\begin{aligned}
P &= \frac{V}{1 + ni/360} \\
  &= \frac{101}{1 + 10(.075)/360} \\
  &= 100.79
\end{aligned}
$$

Thus, if the CD had a face value of $1,000,000, the bid price would be $1,007,900.

New Issues

Commercial banks generally sell new CDs on a tap basis. Rather than have a periodic offering of large quantities of the certificates (which is how the Treasury sells Treasury bills), banks continuously quote offer rates at which they are willing to sell deposit liabilities of various maturities. Thus, potential buyers know the CDs are always on tap. An issuing bank will raise or lower its offering rate (to stimulate or reduce sales) as a function of internal cash needs and in light of competitive pressure from other issuing banks.

Commercial banks also use nonbank broker-dealers to help sell their CDs. For example, if a regional bank wants to sell an unusually large volume of certificates, it may contact a broker-dealer to aid in its sales effort on a "bought-as-sold" basis. (See the discussion of commercial paper in Section 2.1 for a description of bought-as-sold brokerage.) The broker-dealer acts as an agent of the issuing bank and earns a commision on the CDs which it places. It does not, however, bear any underwriting risk. More infrequently, a bank may offer a block of CDs through a broker-dealer on an underwritten basis. Chase Manhattan Bank and Citibank used this device to sell $200 million of 4-year and $225 million of 5-year CDs, respectively, in December 1976. Salomon Brothers underwrote the Chase Manhattan offering, and Morgan Stanley & Co. underwrote the Citibank offering. Exhibit 4.1 shows an announcement of the Citibank offering. Exhibit 4.1 shows an announcement of the Chase offering.

We own and offer subject to prior sale or change in price:

$200,000,000
The Chase Manhattan Bank, N.A.
6½% Certificates of Deposit

($100,000 minimum denominations)
Interest payable June 15 and December 15
Dated: December 8, 1976 / Due: December 15, 1980

Price 100% and accrued interest

Salomon Brothers

One New York Plaza, New York, New York 10004
Atlanta, Boston, Chicago, Cleveland, Dallas, London, Los Angeles, Philadelphia, San Francisco
Members of Major Securities Exchanges.

EXHIBIT 4.1
Announcement of offering of Chase Manhattan Bank certificates of deposit.

Maturities on new CDs offered on a tap basis are at the option of the buyer, but must be at least 14 days at original issue. (Commercial banks are prohibited, by Regulation Q of the Federal Reserve System, from paying interest on time deposits with original maturities of less than 14 days.[2]) Shorter-maturity CDs can be purchased from dealers in the secondary market. Most CDs have a maturity of less than a year at original issue, and the majority have maturities of 6 months or less. The offerings of Chase and Citibank described above were novel, because they were the first major issues of intermediate-maturity CDs. Although there is no limitation on minimum size, most certificates are denominated in units of $1 million.

[2] Regulation Q generally prescribes maximum rates of interest which banks can pay on their deposits. The maximum rate on demand deposits is zero. The regulation also prescribes maximum rates for "small" certificates of deposit of different maturities (defined as CDs smaller than $100,000) but does not now limit rates on "large" CDs (defined as CDs greater than $100,000). For former uses of Regulation Q as a tool of monetary policy, see Tobin (1970), Friedman (1970), and Ruebling (1970).

Secondary-Market Trading

Dealers are responsible for most secondary-market transactions in unmatured CDs. The dealers include both bank and nonbank firms, with Salomon Brothers, First Boston Corporation, and Merrill Lynch, Pierce, Fenner & Smith among the largest. Federal Reserve regulations prohibit bank dealers from repurchasing their own certificates before maturity. They may, however, buy the unmatured CDs of other banks. The standard trading size in CDs is $5 million. Yields on outstanding CDs in the secondary market are generally slightly above yields on new issues from the same bank, because an investor can tailor a new issue to his exact maturity requirement. Dealers have to give their customers a yield incentive to induce them to buy a CD that may not fit their needs precisely.

Because there are a relatively large number of issuing banks and no standardized maturity conventions, one might expect that the CD market would exhibit little liquidity, with wide dealer bid-ask spreads and infrequent trading. Until the fall of 1975, however, dealers and institutional investors treated as perfect substitutes the CDs of several large New York banks, including Morgan Guaranty Trust, First National City Bank, Chase Manhattan Bank, Bankers Trust, and Chemical Bank. Sellers were obliged to disclose only that they were offering the CD of a "New York name," and buyers would accept a CD issued by any of the several banks. Market participants also treated the CDs of Bank of America in California as a perfect substitute for the CDs of the major New York issuers. Many market participants also regarded the CDs of the largest Chicago banks as perfect substitutes.

The market in CDs of New York names was far larger and more liquid than the market in any particular New York bank CD. In contrast, quotations for the purchase or sale of the CDs of regional banks, or the less-than-largest California and Chicago banks, were given only after the issuing bank was identified. Markets in those CDs were less liquid, and in the case of the regional banks substantially less liquid, than the market in New York names. As a consequence of this lack of liquidity, regional banks generally had to offer a yield premium over the New York CD rate to induce investors to buy their certificates.[3]

In the fall of 1975 the structure of the CD market underwent some change. Investors, concerned over the solvency of particular New York banks in light of bank holdings of New York City debt, began to make distinctions among New York names. Some investors even began to express a preference for non-New York issuers. New York names were no longer recognized as perfect substitutes by all investors, and regional banks were able to sell their CDs at yields close to, and in some cases below, the yields offered by New York City banks. By the spring of 1976, with the New York City crisis in abeyance if not resolved, yields on the CDs of even the larger regional banks again moved above the yields on prime New York bank CDs.

---

[3] See Crane (1975, 1976) and Melton (1977–78) for a discussion of rate levels or tiers in the CD market.

4.2 FEDERAL FUNDS

Federal funds are not a security at all. They are a form of money, and as such are part of the national payments mechanism. Reserve balances on deposit with Federal Reserve banks provide the basis for this form of money.

Federal law requires that depository institutions like commercial banks, savings and loan associations, mutual savings banks, and credit unions keep assets equal to a designated fraction of their demand and time deposit liabilities on reserve with a district Federal Reserve bank in the form of an interest-free deposit (see Section 5.1). These reserve balances appear as a liability of the Federal Reserve bank to the depository institution, and are known as *Federal funds*, or *Fed funds*.

Transfers of Federal Funds

A depository institution can transfer funds from its reserve account to the reserve account of another depository institution. Suppose, for example, Irving Trust in New York wants to send $5 million to Crocker National Bank in San Francisco, possibly at the request of a customer who has to make a payment in California. Irving would instruct the Federal Reserve Bank of New York to debit its reserve account and to send the funds to the Federal Reserve Bank of San Francisco, for the credit of Crocker. The latter Federal Reserve bank would then credit Crocker's reserve account by $5 million.

Transfers of reserve balances between depository institutions are book-entry operations; i.e., there is no movement of paper such as a check. If both institutions are in the same Federal Reserve district, the transfer is completed on the books of their common Federal Reserve bank. If the institutions are in different districts, as in the example above, the transfer will involve two Federal Reserve banks. Instructions on how the transfer is to be credited are then sent over a private wire network maintained by the Federal Reserve System. The principle of an *immediate* transfer of credit between the reserve accounts of the two depository institutions is, however, the same in either case.

Purchase and Sale of Federal Funds

The purchase and sale of Fed funds is the unsecured borrowing and lending of reserve balances.[4] A depository institution may find from time to time that it has more than the required amount of funds on deposit with its district Federal Reserve bank. Since reserve balances do not earn interest, the institution has an incentive to convert its excess reserves into earning assets. This conversion might take the form of extending a loan or making an investment in a negotiable financial instrument. Frequently, however, a depository institution will prefer to lend out its excess reserves on an overnight basis. This could happen, for ex-

---

[4] Nichols (1965), Willis (1972b), and Lucas, Jones, and Thurston (1977) provide extended discussions of the overnight market in Federal funds. Turner (1931) describes the origins and early years of the market.

ample, because the institution anticipates adverse check collections in the near future or because a corporate customer is expected to draw down shortly a substantial balance.

Suppose a depository institution with excess reserves locates another institution that needs funds the same day and is willing to repay the loan the following day. If the two institutions agree on a borrowing rate for an overnight loan, the lending institution directs its district Federal Reserve bank to transfer part of its excess reserves to the district Federal Reserve bank of the borrowing institution, for deposit to the reserve account of that institution. When the transfer is complete, usually in a matter of a few minutes, the lending institution will have "sold" some of its excess reserves, and the borrowing institution will have increased its reserve deposits with its district Federal Reserve bank by "buying" reserves. On the following day the borrowing institution reverses the transfer and sends along an additional sum for the interest on the overnight use of the funds.

The Fed funds market is a loan market in which the asset being lent is balances on deposit with a Federal Reserve bank. The deposit accounts and wire transfer facilities of the Federal Reserve System make possible the immediate crediting of the reserve account of the buying institution and the immediate debiting of the reserve account of the selling institution.

Commercial banks and other depository institutions use the overnight Fed funds market primarily to buffer short-run fluctuations in their reserve accounts. Thus, a bank may buy funds one day (when it has a deficiency) and sell funds the next day (when it has a surplus). Short-run reserve fluctuations can result from temporary imbalances between aggregate check collections and check payments, or from imbalances between repayments of outstanding loans and disbursements on new loans.

Depository institutions may also make loans or investments with the expectation of financing their new assets by repeated daily purchases of Fed funds. Although this use of the market is quantitatively not as important as the adjustment of reserve positions, about a dozen major banks do run chronic reserve deficiencies which they meet through daily purchases of Fed funds. These banks could as easily finance their assets by selling CDs as by buying Fed funds, but they evidently believe that the latter source of funds is cheaper in the long run.

Fed funds trade in a brokered market which is national in scope. Garvin-GuyButler (formerly Garvin Bantel), Mabon, Nugent, and Lasser Brothers are among the principal brokers. During the day these brokers receive bids for and offerings of overnight loans and report these tenders to inquiring institutions. If an institution needs funds and is willing to pay the current offering rate, it will take an existing offering shown on the books of one of the brokers. Conversely, if it has funds to sell, it can sell to an existing bidder. When a bid or an offer is accepted, the broker informs the selling (or lending) institution of the identity of the buying (or borrowing) institution and tells the buying institution to expect delivery of the amount agreed upon.

Fed funds conventionally trade in $5 million blocks, although more than half the trading is done in larger blocks. About 100 large commercial banks participate in the national market on a daily basis. These banks rely on the brokers to keep them informed about the going rate and changes in aggregate supply and demand conditions. Smaller banks and other depository institutions with irregular offerings and needs tend to deal directly with one or two larger commercial banks as part of a correspondent relationship, and they rarely enter the national market.

Line Limits in Fed Funds Transactions

Because selling Fed funds is no different from unsecured lending, sellers must be careful about the identity of buying institutions. Most selling banks have limitations, called *lines*, on how much they are willing to have out on loan to a particular institution at a given point in time. Before 1974, lines to the larger commercial banks were usually quite substantial and had little practical significance for the amount of funds which a large bank could buy in aggregate. Lines to most smaller and some intermediate-size banks were much smaller and in many cases zero. These line limitations served to exclude such banks from the national market.

After the collapse of Franklin National Bank in mid-1974, and in the midst of the specter of a default by New York City in the fall of 1975, many selling institutions substantially reduced their lines to individual buyers, especially to larger New York banks. It is not now an infrequent occurrence for a Fed funds broker to get two banks to agree on the rate and size of an overnight loan, but to be unable to complete the transaction because the selling bank has already reached the limits of its lines to the buyer. In such an event both buyer and seller have to wait until more compatible names appear in the market at some later time in the day.

The Fed funds market is a loan market between buyers and sellers and is not a market for the sale and purchase of a negotiable instrument, as is the Treasury bill market or the CD market. Thus, if bank B sells funds to bank C, it cannot subsequently buy funds from bank A in exchange for the claim which it holds on bank C. All it can do is borrow from bank A on its own credit. In view of what are now fairly restrictive lines, this means that transactions in Fed funds may not occur even when there are willing buyers and sellers at a given rate.

Term Federal Funds

In addition to overnight loans, transactions in Fed funds can be negotiated on a term basis, i.e., for several weeks or months.[5] Although the maturity of a term

---

[5] The term market in Federal funds is quite similar to the interbank Eurodollar deposit market. Eurodollar deposits are an offshore rather than domestic asset. Clendenning (1970) and Bell (1973) provide excellent discussions of the market. Friedman (1969) and Machlup (1971) offer very readable expository articles on the nature of Eurodollar deposits. Black (1971), Rich (1972), and Hewson and Sakabibara (1975) report on empirical studies of the market for Eurodollars.

funds borrowing is solely at the mutual discretion of the borrowing and lending institutions, most loans are negotiated for 1 week or for from 1 to 6 months. Because loans of Federal funds on a term basis are outstanding for more than a single day, line limitations are far more important in the term market than in the overnight market. A bank which has sold $25 million in term Fed funds to another bank for 2 months may be unwilling to extend any additional credit to that bank until the loan has matured and been repaid.

Unlike the case with the overnight Fed funds market, few depository institutions use the term funds market to effect temporary adjustments in their reserve positions. Rather, lenders view term funds as competing with other investments, such as Treasury bills, while borrowers view the purchase of term funds as an alternative to the sale of certificates of deposit. For creditors, term interbank loans offer a higher return than either Treasury bills or bank CDs and hence are an attractive, albeit nonmarketable, asset in which to place cash balances. Savings and loan associations are important creditors in the term funds market for this reason. For borrowers, term interbank loans can be a cheaper source of credit than selling CDs.

Repurchase Agreements

Repurchase agreements (RPs) are collateralized loan contracts.[6] A market participant borrowing on a repurchase agreement sells securities to a creditor and simultaneously agrees to buy back those same securities at a later date for the same price, plus interest to cover the use of the funds for the period of the agreement. Repurchase agreements can run from overnight to several months, just as in the case of uncollateralized purchases of Federal funds. Payment for securities involved in repurchase agreements is almost always in immediately transferable funds. As with the purchase and sale of Federal funds, RPs are completed by transfers of reserve balances.

Treasury and federal agency securities are most often used in repurchase agreements, although bank CDs are also used on occasion.[7] The securities are usually valued slightly below their current bid prices to give the creditor some margin of protection in the event market prices move down and the borrower defaults on his agreement. Longer-term RPs frequently have deeper discounts from the current bid on the collateral securities than do shorter-term agreements. This protects the lender from the greater risk on a long-term RP that the value of the collateral will depreciate below the amount of the loan while the loan is outstanding.

Rates on RPs are typically close to rates on Fed funds transactions of the same maturity, as the two loan contracts are quite close substitutes. Commercial banks, for example, can and do borrow on both types of contracts. RPs give a bank opportunities to borrow which it might not otherwise have because

---

[6] Lucas, Jones, and Thurston (1977) provide an excellent discussion of the RP market and the participants in that market. See also Smith (1978).

[7] Commercial banks cannot use CDs as collateral in a repurchase agreement unless the creditor is also a commercial bank. Nonbank institutions are not similarly restricted.

of line limitations. A holder of excess reserves which is not willing to lend funds to a bank on an unsecured basis in the Fed funds market is frequently less reluctant to make a loan if it can obtain collateral assets to guarantee repayment.

The RP market is not, however, limited to borrowings by depository institutions. In fact, the major borrowers on repurchase agreements are nonbank government securities dealers which finance their inventories in part with repurchase agreements.[8] Corporate and municipal treasurers with money to invest for short periods of time are major suppliers of funds on repurchase agreements.

Nondepository institutions participate in the RP market through their ability to effect transfers of immediately available funds through their commercial banks. If, for example, General Motors lends $5 million to Goldman, Sachs on a repurchase agreement, it will instruct a commercial bank at which it holds a deposit to transfer $5 million to a bank at which Goldman, Sachs has an account. GM's bank completes the transfer through the Federal Reserve System, exactly as if it had sold Fed funds itself to Goldman, Sachs's bank. The difference, of course, is that Goldman, Sachs obtains use of the funds and GM earns the interest on the loan. Comparing this RP transaction to a loan in the Federal funds market suggests that there is little to distinguish the two types of loans (except, of course, for the collateral protection on an RP). Thus, RPs provide nondepository institutions with a vehicle for participating as lenders in the market for immediately transferable funds, i.e., in the market for claims on reserve balances. All the nonbank institutions have to do is find a borrower with suitable collateral.

Treasury securities dealers which borrow money from corporate and municipal treasurers on repurchase agreements solicit potential lenders directly. In particular, they do not usually give bids for money to RP brokers, as is the practice of commercial banks in the Fed funds market. One reason for this different behavior is that dealers typically want to limit knowledge of the composition of their inventory as much as possible and frequently want to choose themselves which lenders will get what type of collateral.

In addition to soliciting funds on repurchase agreements for their own account, Treasury securities dealers also solicit RP funds for other borrowers with suitable collateral. This brokerage business is known as *matched book* brokerage, because the dealer enters into an ordinary RP with the lender and then executes a "reverse RP" of the same maturity, using the same collateral, with the ultimate borrower. (A reverse RP is a repurchase agreement viewed from the perspective of the lender of the funds.) The dealer thus has a lending position which matches its borrowing position, or a matched book.

CHAPTER SUMMARY

This chapter has described two bank-related liabilities which have become increasingly important in American securities markets during the past 15 years.

---

[8] See McCurdy (1977–78) and Monhollon (1977) for discussions of dealer financing.

A certificate of deposit is a deposit liability of the issuing bank. CDs under a year to maturity are functionally similar to Treasury bills and commercial paper, except that CDs are interest-bearing while Treasury bills and commercial paper simply promise to pay a specified face value at maturity. The secondary market in negotiable CDs has improved markedly since it first appeared in 1961, and is now as liquid as the Treasury bill market. This liquidity has encouraged corporate treasurers and other cash managers to invest in the instruments, even when they are not perfectly confident that they can wait until maturity for the return of their funds.

The second section of this chapter described the market in overnight purchases and sales of Federal funds, and the related markets in term funds and overnight and term repurchase agreements. The overnight Federal funds market is used primarily by commercial banks to adjust their holdings of reserve balances. Other participants who have indirect control over reserve balances could gain access to the market were it not for a Federal Reserve regulation prohibiting banks from paying interest to nondepository institutions on short-term nondeposit borrowings. For this reason participation in the Federal funds market is limited to depository institutions. Other institutions do, however, have access to the closely related market in repurchase agreements.

FURTHER READING

Dwight Crane, "Lessons from the 1974 CD Market," *Harvard Business Review*, **53** (November–December 1975), 73–79.

Charles Lucas, Marcos Jones, and Thom Thurston, "Federal Funds and Repurchase Agreements," Federal Reserve Bank of New York *Quarterly Review*, **2** (Summer 1977), 33–48.

William Melton, "The Market for Large Negotiable CDs," Federal Reserve Bank of New York *Quarterly Review*, **2** (Winter 1977–78), 22–34.

Jimmie Monhollon, "Dealer Loans and Repurchase Agreements," in *Instruments of the Money Market*, 4th ed., Timothy Cook, ed. (Richmond, Virginia: Federal Reserve Bank of Richmond, 1977).

Parker Willis, *The Federal Funds Market, Its Origin and Development*, 5th ed. (Boston: Federal Reserve Bank of Boston, 1972).

PART TWO

INTEREST RATES ON OVERNIGHT LOANS

CHAPTER 5   The Market for Overnight Credit

The single chapter in this part begins the analysis of equilibrium prices on financial assets, an analysis which continues with the pricing of common stock in Parts Three and Four and long-term debt securities in Part Five. Chapter 5 examines the determinants of the return on a basic financial asset: overnight credit.

The return on overnight credit is important to the structure of prices on other securities like stock and long-term debt, because it is the return which an investor can get if he postpones for 1 day his decision to buy other assets, and it is the return which an investor gives up by continuing to hold other assets for 1 more day. Thus, the decision to buy, sell, or hold other securities depends, in part, on the prevailing overnight credit rate. This implies that the prices of stocks and long-term debt securities are a function of the overnight rate. For example, we will see in Chapter 14 that debt contracts with maturities longer than a single day may be viewed as "bundles" of consecutive 1-day loans. The equilibrium yields on these long-term debt instruments depend, therefore, on the 1-day rates prevailing at present and expected to prevail in the future. Similarly, we will see in Chapters 9 and 12 that the demand for stock, and equilibrium stock prices, are functions of the level of short-term interest rates. Although much of the analysis in this book is concerned with the differences in yields on different financial instruments, the reader should not lose sight of the important role played by overnight interest rates in determining the general level of yields.

THE MARKET FOR OVERNIGHT CREDIT

Of all the investments described in Part One, the most basic are the contracts for overnight lending: sales of Federal funds and purchases of securities under agreements to resell. The 1-day duration of these loans makes them essentially pure credit agreements. In particular, there is no exposure to the risk of unanticipated fluctuations in the value of an unmatured loan, and there is little risk that a creditor will not get his funds back at the maturity of a loan.

The largest and most important component of the overnight credit market is the market in Federal funds, or loans of reserve balances. The four sections of this chapter examine the characteristics of demand and supply in the market for reserve balances, and examine how rates on overnight loans bring that market into equilibrium.

5.1 THE DEMAND FOR RESERVE BALANCES

Reserve balances are funds of a depository institution, such as a commercial bank, on deposit with a district Federal Reserve bank.[1] Although depository institutions would probably hold some of their assets in this form even in the absence of any specific requirement, federal law and regulations of the Federal Reserve System require that they maintain specified minimum balances. These *reserve requirements* create a direct demand by depository institutions for reserve balances and indirectly create a demand for overnight borrowings of

---

[1] There are twelve district Federal Reserve banks. The twelve banks are corporations chartered by Congress which operate under the supervision of the Board of Governors of the Federal Reserve System. The Board is an agency of the federal government.

those balances. This section examines the determinants of the demand for reserve balances by depository institutions. The derived demand for borrowings of reserve balances is considered in Section 5.3.

Computing and Satisfying Reserve Requirements

Depository institutions (including commercial banks, savings and loan associations, mutual savings banks, and branches and agencies of foreign banks) are subject to the reserve requirements specified in Regulation D of the Board of Governors of the Federal Reserve System.[2] Reserves must be held against two primary types of liabilities:

1 Transactions accounts, including demand deposits, negotiable order of withdrawal (NOW) accounts, automatic transfer service (ATS) accounts, and share draft accounts

2 Nonpersonal time deposits

A *nonpersonal time deposit* is an interest-bearing deposit with a maturity date at least 14 days after its date of issue which is either (1) transferable or (2) held by a depositor that is not a natural person. As a practical matter, this means that a nonpersonal time deposit is a time deposit which is issued to a corporation or which could be sold, i.e., transferred, to a corporation after its original issue.[3]

Table 5.1 shows the reserve requirement rates in effect on January 1, 1981.[4] A depository institution had to maintain reserve balances equal to (1) 3 percent of the first $25 million of its aggregate transaction account liabilities, plus (2) 12 percent of its aggregate transaction account liabilities in excess of $25 million. Thus, an institution would have had a reserve requirement of $9.75 million on aggregate transaction account liabilities of $100 million. This $9.75 million reserve requirement is equal to 3 percent of $25 million ($750,000), plus 12 percent of $75 million ($9 million). As shown in Table 5.1, the Board of Governors can vary the reserve requirement rate on aggregate transactions balances in excess of $25 million anywhere within the range of 8 to 14 percent. The Board cannot vary the reserve requirement rate on the first $25 million of the aggregate transactions liabilities of a depository institution.

On January 1, 1981, a depository institution also had to maintain reserves equal to 3 percent of nonpersonal time deposit liabilities which were issued

---

[2] Until 1980 only commercial banks which were members of the Federal Reserve System were subject to Federal Reserve reserve requirements. Broader imposition of reserve requirements was mandated by the Depository Institutions Deregulation and Monetary Control Act of 1980.

[3] The most important category of nonpersonal time deposits is negotiable certificates of deposit. See Section 4.1 for a description of negotiable CDs.

[4] The entries of Table 5.1 reflect the changes in reserve requirements which occurred following passage of the Depository Institutions Deregulation and Monetary Control Act of 1980. For expositional simplicity we ignore the differences in reserve requirements between (1) commercial banks which are members of the Federal Reserve System and (2) other depository institutions, during a transition period lasting until September 1987.

TABLE 5.1
RESERVE REQUIREMENT RATES IN EFFECT ON JANUARY 1, 1981

Deposit category	Current requirement, %	Statutory minimum, %	Statutory maximum, %
Aggregate balances in transactions accounts*†			
First $25 million	3	3	3
Amount in excess of $25 million	12	8	14
Aggregate balances in personal time deposits‡§	0		0
Aggregate balances in nonpersonal time deposits‡◖			
Original maturity less than 4 years	3	0	9
Original maturity of 4 years or more	0	0	9

*Includes demand deposits, negotiable order of withdrawal (NOW) accounts, automatic transfer service (ATS) accounts, and share draft accounts. A demand deposit is a deposit payable on demand or issued with an original maturity of less than 14 days.
†Net of cash items in process of collection and aggregate balances due from other depository institutions.
‡A time deposit is a deposit that the depositor does not have the right to withdraw for at least 14 days after the date of deposit.
§A personal time deposit is a time deposit which is not transferable and in which no beneficial interest is held by a depositor that is not a natural person.
◖A nonpersonal time deposit is a time deposit which is transferable or in which a beneficial interest is held by a depositor that is not a natural person.

with an original maturity of less than 4 years. As shown in Table 5.1, the Board of Governors can vary the reserve requirement rate on nonpersonal time deposits from 0 to 9 percent. On January 1, 1981, the Board did not require any reserves on nonpersonal time deposit liabilities which were issued with an original maturity of 4 years or more.

The accounting period for computing reserve requirements is a 7-day "computation period" beginning on Thursday and ending the following Wednesday. A depository institution must report its aggregate transaction account liabilities and nonpersonal time deposit liabilities as of the close of business each day of a computation period. The reserve requirement rates shown in Table 5.1 are applied to the *average* daily liabilities reported for the computation period. Example 5.1 illustrates the procedure.

The accounting period for satisfying reserve requirements is a 7-day "maintenance period" which begins 2 weeks after the Wednesday start of the computation period.[5] A depository institution must hold reserve balances during a

[5] Separating the computation period and the maintenance period is known as *lagged reserve accounting*. Prior to September 1968, the maintenance period was the same as the computation period. This was called *contemporaneous reserve accounting*. See Coats (1976) and Laufenberg (1976) for a comparative analysis of the two reserve accounting schemes. See Laurent (1979) for a proposal to lead, rather than lag, the maintenance period relative to the computation period. See Poole (1976) for an alternative reserve scheme designed to link deposits and reserve requirements more closely than is the case under lagged reserve accounting.

EXAMPLE 5.1
COMPUTING REQUIRED RESERVE BALANCES

Aggregate deposit liabilities and vault cash (in millions) in computation period:

Day	Transactions accounts	Nonpersonal time deposits*	Vault cash
Thursday	$750.00	$1590.00	$10.00
Friday†	730.00	1595.00	10.00
Saturday†	730.00	1595.00	10.00
Sunday†	730.00	1595.00	10.00
Monday	745.00	1575.00	8.00
Tuesday	760.00	1575.00	9.00
Wednesday	755.00	1575.00	8.00
7-day average	$742.86	$1585.71	$ 9.29

*With original maturity of less than 4 years.
†Deposits and vault cash held on Friday count for Saturday and Sunday.

Required reserve balances (in millions) in maintenance period:

Transactions accounts	
3% of $25 million	$ .75
12% of ($742.86 − 25) million	86.14
Nonpersonal time deposits*	
3% of $1585.71 million	47.57
Reserve requirement	$134.46
Vault cash	− 9.29
Required reserve balances	$125.17

*With original maturity of less than 4 years.

---

maintenance period with a daily average value not less than the difference between (1) the reserve requirements calculated in the earlier computation period, and (2) its daily average holdings of vault cash during that computation period.[6,7]

The foregoing summary of how reserve requirements are computed and satisfied is illustrated in Example 5.1. The depository institution in that example had, during a computation period, daily average transaction account liabilities of $742.86 million and daily average nonpersonal time deposit liabilities of $1585.71 million. Those liabilities imply a reserve requirement of $134.46

---

[6] A depository institution is permitted to carry over a deficiency or excess of reserve balances not greater than 2 percent of its reserve requirements into the next maintenance period. It cannot, however, carry over such deficiencies or excesses in two *consecutive* maintenance periods. If, after accounting for permissible carry-overs, a depository institution has a deficiency at the end of a maintenance period, its district Federal Reserve bank will move balances into its reserve account sufficient to eliminate the deficiency and will charge the institution interest on those balances at a rate equal to its lowest lending rate plus 2 percent.

[7] See Coats (1973) for a description of a game which bankers can play—shifting vault cash into balances on deposit with a Federal Reserve bank to meet current reserve requirements.

million. In addition, the institution had daily average holdings of vault cash equal to $9.29 million during the computation period. This led to a requirement for $125.17 million in reserve balances during the maintenance period 2 weeks after the computation period.

Deposit Liabilities and the Demand for Reserve Balances

The aggregate demand by depository institutions for reserve balances is a derived demand which depends on the volume of deposits at those institutions. The most important deposit category for our purposes is transactions accounts.[8] To understand the determinants of the demand by depository institutions for reserve balances, one must first understand the determinants of the demand by individuals and corporations for transactions balances. After the latter determinants have been established, the demand by depository institutions for reserve balances follows mechanically from the rules described above for computing and satisfying reserve requirements.

Public Demand for Transactions Balances   There are two primary determinants of public demand for transactions balances: the level of aggregate economic activity and the level of short-term interest rates.[9] Individuals and corporations maintain balances in transactions accounts to facilitate their purchases of goods and services. Everything else remaining the same, higher levels of economic activity are generally associated with greater public demand for transactions balances.

The second primary determinant of public demand for transactions balances is the level of short-term interest rates. Regulation Q of the Board of Governors prohibits or limits the payment of interest by depository institutions on transactions balances.[10] However, short-term loans like overnight repurchase agreements are a good substitute for balances in transactions accounts. This means that individuals and corporations have an increasing incentive to reduce their holdings of balances in transactions accounts, and to switch those balances into repurchase agreements, as the rate on repurchase agreements increases.[11] Everything else remaining the same, higher levels of short-term in-

---

[8] For expositional simplicity, the discussion in the text ignores the reserve requirement on nonpersonal time deposits with less than 4 years to maturity at original issue.

[9] The analysis of the demand for transactions balances is part of the analysis of the demand for money. See Ritter and Silber (1980) for a more complete analysis of the demand for money in the context of fluctuations in aggregate economic activity.

[10] More specifically, Regulation Q prohibits the payment of interest on deposit balances payable on demand or in less than 14 days after the date of deposit, and limits the payment of interest on balances subject to negotiable orders of withdrawal to $5\frac{1}{4}$ percent.

[11] Note that as individuals and corporations reduce their holdings of transactions balances, they have to turn over their remaining transactions balances more often in completing the same volume of transactions per unit time. The added cost of more frequent turnover must be weighed against the gains of earning interest on repurchase agreements when deciding to switch transactions balances into RPs. Note that advances in payment technologies, such as credit cards and electronic funds transfer systems, can be expected to lower the cost of completing transactions and hence can be expected to reduce public demand for transactions balances at any given level of short-term interest rates.

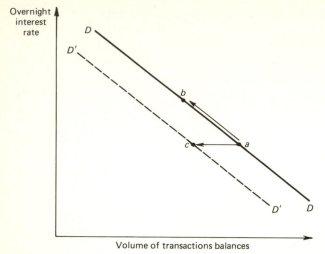

FIGURE 5.1
Public demand for balances in transactions accounts. *a* to *b*: reduction in demand due to an increase in overnight interest rates; *a* to *c*: reduction in demand due to a decrease in economic activity.

terest rates are generally associated with lower public demand for balances in transaction accounts.

Figure 5.1 shows the schedule of public demand for balances in transactions accounts as a function of the level of short-term interest rates. As short-term rates increase, individuals and corporations will reduce their demand for transaction balances. This reduction in demand implies a shift *along* the demand schedule *DD* shown in Figure 5.1, for example, from point *a* to point *b* in the figure.[12]

Public demand for balances in transactions accounts is also a function of the level of aggregate economic activity. A reduction in economic activity will lead to a reduced demand for transactions balances at any given level of short-term interest rates. This is illustrated in Figure 5.1 by the change in demand from point *a* to point *c*. The effect of decreases in economic activity is represented in Figure 5.1 by a horizontal shift *of* the demand schedule, for example, from *DD* to *D'D'* in the figure.

Demand for Reserve Balances by Depository Institutions   Since the volume of balances which individuals and corporations are willing to hold in transactions accounts is inversely related to the rate on short-term credit agreements, it follows that the demand by depository institutions for reserve balances (based on their reserve requirements and transactions account liabilities) is *also* an in-

---

[12] Several authors have reported that the interest sensitivity of the demand for money has declined during the period since the end of World War II. See Cagan and Schwartz (1975) and Garbade (1977). This means that the demand schedule in Figure 5.1 will be more nearly vertical.

verse function of the level of that rate. The inverse relationship can be illustrated by a simple example.

Suppose the XYZ Corporation has a demand deposit account at Large Bank. Now let XYZ convert, say, $5 million of its deposits to a loan to Large Bank on an overnight repurchase agreement. The reserves of Large Bank at its district Federal Reserve bank are unchanged, but its reserve requirements have become smaller because of its reduced deposit liabilities. In particular, if Large Bank had more than $25 million in transactions account liabilities and hence had a 12 percent marginal reserve requirement (see Table 5.1), its reserve requirements would fall by $600,000 (12 percent of $5 million reduction in aggregate transactions accounts).[13] Other things remaining the same, this reduction in reserve requirements reduces the demand by Large Bank for reserve balances.[14]

In general, the higher the rate on overnight repurchase agreements, the more likely are conversions like that described in the paragraph above. Although a bank may not always borrow on a repurchase agreement directly from one of its customers, the same effect can be achieved through a chain of repurchase agreements. The important point is that the demand for reserve balances is a declining function of the rate on overnight credit, because public demand for transactions balances is a declining function of that rate. Similarly, the demand for reserve balances is an increasing function of the level of aggregate economic activity, because public demand for transactions balances is an increasing function of the level of economic activity.

Figure 5.2 shows the relation between short-term interest rates, aggregate economic activity, and the demand for reserve balances by depository institutions. The figure follows the same form as Figure 5.1. The only novel feature is the observation that an increase in reserve requirement *rates* on transactions balances will lead to a proportional expansion in the demand for reserve balances at any given level of economic activity and short-term interest rates. This is illustrated in Figure 5.2 by the movement from point *a* to point *d*, or as the shift of the demand schedule from *DD* to *D"D"*.

5.2 THE SUPPLY OF RESERVE BALANCES

Reserve balances are an asset of the depository institutions which own them, but they are a liability of district Federal Reserve banks. To understand how the aggregate supply of reserve balances can vary, we have to consider how the Federal Reserve System can alter its aggregate indebtedness to depository institutions.

---

[13] In view of the lagged reserve accounting scheme presently in use, this reduction in reserve requirements would actually occur in the maintenance period 2 weeks later. Large Bank's contemporaneous requirements for reserve balances are fixed as a function of its deposit liabilities and vault cash holdings during the computation period 2 weeks earlier.

[14] Essentially the same result would occur if XYZ converted its demand deposit to a 15-day interest-bearing certificate of deposit. However, since CDs have a 3 percent reserve requirement, the reduction in the aggregate reserve requirements of Large Bank would then be $450,000 (12 percent of $5 million, less 3 percent of $5 million) instead of $600,000.

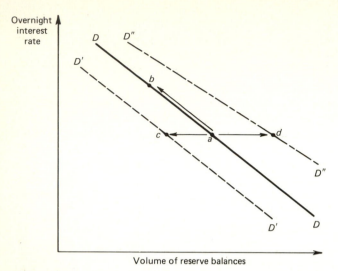

FIGURE 5.2
Demand by depository institutions for reverse balances. *a* to *b*: reduction in demand due to an increase in overnight interest rates; *a* to *c*: reduction in demand due to a decrease in economic activity; *a* to *d*: increase in demand due to an increase in reserve requirement rates

Exhibit 5.1 shows a simplified consolidated balance sheet of the twelve district Federal Reserve banks as of January 14, 1981. The assets include $130.3 billion in securities owned by the Reserve banks and $2.5 billion in loans and discounts made by Reserve banks to depository institutions. The liabilities include $121.4 billion of Federal Reserve currency held by the public and in the vaults of depository institutions, and $29.8 billion in reserve balances held by depository institutions.

The sum of Federal Reserve currency liabilities and Federal Reserve deposit liabilities is called the *monetary base*.[15] Demand for currency both by depository institutions and by members of the public is not especially sensitive to the level of short-term interest rates. As a first approximation we assume the aggregate demand for currency is fixed. This implies that the supply of reserve balances is equal to the size of the monetary base less the fixed demand for currency. More particularly, it implies that increases or decreases in the monetary base will cause the supply of reserve balances to increase or decrease by the same amount.

The size of the monetary base is directly affected by variations in (1) the volume of securities held by Federal Reserve banks and (2) the loans of Federal Reserve banks to depository institutions. These two asset categories correspond to two of the major tools of monetary policy: open market operations and discount operations.

[15]The monetary base is derived in Balbach and Burger (1976). See also Andersen and Jordan (1968) and Burger (1975).

EXHIBIT 5.1

CONSOLIDATED ASSETS AND LIABILITIES OF THE FEDERAL RESERVE BANKS,
JANUARY 14,1981 (BILLIONS OF DOLLARS)

Assets	
Discounts and advances to depository institutions	2.539
Securities	130.310
Other assets, including gold certificates, cash items in process of collection, and physical assets	33.405
Total	166.254
Liabilities and capital	
Federal Reserve currency outstanding*	121.413
Deposits of depository institutions*	29.807
Other liabilities, including deposits of the U.S. Treasury and deferred availability cash items	12.365
Capital	2.669
Total	166.254

*The monetary base consists of currency outstanding plus deposits of depository institutions.

Open Market Operations

Open market operations are the purchase and sale of securities, primarily Treasury and federal agency securities, by the Federal Reserve. These transactions are executed by the Federal Reserve Bank of New York at the direction of the Federal Open Market Committee, a committee of the seven members of the Board of Governors of the Federal Reserve System and the presidents of five of the district Federal Reserve banks.[16]

Open market *purchases* of securities *increase* the amount of assets owned by the Federal Reserve banks and also increase the monetary base. For example, if the Federal Reserve Bank of New York buys $25 million of Treasury bills from Citibank in New York, that Reserve bank increases its bill position by $25 million and pays for those bills by crediting Citibank's reserve account, thereby increasing the monetary base. Citibank may leave the additional credits in its reserve account, or it may order the credits transferred to the reserve account of another bank, or it may convert the credits to currency either for holding in its own vaults or for paying out to its customers. All these actions, however, leave the monetary base unchanged at a new higher level.[17] Conversely, if the Federal Reserve Bank of New York sells $25 million of bills to Citibank, it will collect payment by debiting the reserve account of that commercial bank, thereby decreasing the monetary base.

[16] Open market operations are described in Meek (1978).
[17] Essentially the same result would occur if the Federal Reserve Bank of New York bought $25 million of Treasury bills from a nonbank broker-dealer such as Goldman Sachs. It would then credit the reserve account of Goldman Sach's commercial bank. The only difference is that Goldman Sachs would have the right to transfer the $25 million credit.

Discount Operations

Federal Reserve banks can also make reserve balances available to depository institutions by lending funds through the "discount window."[18] If an institution needs cash, it can request a loan from its district Reserve bank. The rate on the loan is called the *discount rate*.[19] If the Federal Reserve bank agrees to make the loan, it credits the reserve account of the borrower for the principal of the loan, thereby increasing the monetary base. When the loan is terminated, the borrower's reserve account is debited for the principal of the loan plus interest charges.

Let us summarize the results of this section. The supply of reserve balances available to depository institutions can be altered by policy actions of the Federal Reserve System. The two policy tools for changing the supply of reserve balances are open market operations (or purchases and sales of Treasury and federal agency securities) and loans to depository institutions. An increase in loans or in securitities held by the Federal Reserve System will increase the assets of the Federal Reserve System and hence must increase the liabilities of the System. The increase in liabilities appears as an increase in the monetary base and, under our assumption of a fixed demand for currency, as an increase in the stock of reserve balances held by depository institutions.[20]

5.3 EQUILIBRIUM IN THE MARKET FOR RESERVE BALANCES

Thus far we have shown how reserve requirements lead to a demand by depository institutions for reserve balances and how Federal Reserve open market operations and loans to depository institutions affect the supply of those balances. To understand how the supply of and demand for reserve balances comes to affect the rate on overnight credit, we will find it useful to analyze first an economy with only a single commercial bank. The analysis can then be extended readily to an economy with multiple depository institutions.

[18] Credit from a Federal Reserve bank is available to a depository institution on a short-term basis to assist in an orderly adjustment of the institution's assets and liabilities, and on an extended basis to meet regular seasonal movements of assets and liabilities or in exceptional cases. See, generally, Regulation A of the Board of Governors of the Federal Reserve System. Federal Reserve loans are described and analyzed in *Reappraisal of the Federal Reserve Discount Mechanism* (Board of Governors of the Federal Reserve System, 1971). See also Hackley (1973) for a history of Federal Reserve discount operations.

[19] Each district Federal Reserve bank sets its own discount rate, subject to approval by the Board of Governors. Usually all twelve banks set a common rate, although differences can exist for short intervals of time. The discount rate on extended-term loans to depository institutions in exceptional cases typically exceeds the discount rate on short-term loans and the discount rate on extended-term loans to meet seasonal needs.

[20] Increases in public demand for currency will drain vault cash and/or reserve balances from the banking system if the monetary base remains unchanged. This means that the Federal Reserve System has to undertake "defensive" open market operations if it is trying to keep the sum of vault cash and reserve balances constant in the face of changes in public demand for currency. See, similarly, the discussion of the effect of changes in Federal Reserve "float" in Hoel (1975).

Analysis of an Economy with a Single Commercial Bank

When there is only a single commercial bank, that bank must, by definition, absorb all the reserve balances supplied by the Federal Reserve System. On the other hand, the quantity of reserve balances which the bank *wants* to hold is a function of reserve requirement rates and its deposit liabilities. If it holds more than the required quantity of reserve balances, the bank is carrying nonearning assets needlessly. If it has less than the required quantity of reserve balances, the bank is failing to meet its reserve requirements. In equilibrium the bank will want to hold exactly the quantity of reserve balances which the Federal Reserve makes available. The question is: What brings about such a happy circumstance?

The market for reserve balances is in equilibrium when the demand for reserve balances equals the supply of those balances. In Section 5.1 we saw that the demand by a bank for reserve balances is inversely related to the level of short-term interest rates, because the level of public demand for balances in transactions accounts is inversely related to the level of those rates.[21] Variations in the interest rate on overnight credit thus brings the demand for reserve balances into equilibrium with the supply of those balances.

If, in our simple single-bank model, there is an excess demand for reserves at some level of the overnight interest rate, i.e., if the bank has deficient reserves, then, as shown in Figure 5.3, that interest rate must rise to bring about an equilibrium. The increase in the rate will induce depositors to reduce their holdings of balances in transactions accounts in favor of short-term nondeposit bank debt like repurchase agreements. This reduction in deposits will lead to a reduction in the reserve requirements levied on the bank.

In the simplest case, the bank, facing a shortfall in reserve balances, could increase the rate it is paying on overnight repurchase agreements. Some depositors will then reduce their transactions balances by converting them to a loan to the bank on a repurchase agreement. The bank will continue to raise the RP rate until it has induced a sufficient runoff of deposits and conversion to repurchase agreements to allow it to meet its reserve requirements.[22] A similar line of analysis shows that an excess supply of reserves will lead to a fall in the level of short-term interest rates.

---

[21] It should be noted that under a lagged reserve accounting scheme, the demand for reserve balances within a maintenance period is fixed because that demand depends on deposit liabilities 2 weeks earlier. Within a maintenance period, the Federal Reserve *must* make available reserves sufficient to satisfy the fixed demand. The discussion in the text is, strictly speaking, correct only for intervals longer than 2 weeks or for a contemporaneous reserve accounting scheme. Feige and McGee (1977) have argued that under a lagged reserve accounting scheme, the monetary base should be viewed as determined endogenously in the economy rather than as an instrument of central bank policy.

[22] Note that deposits and reserve requirements will fall only if a depositor lends his transactions balances to the bank on a repurchase agreement. If he lends to a nonbank, the only change will be the identity of the holder of the transaction balance; i.e., the transaction balance will not be extinguished.

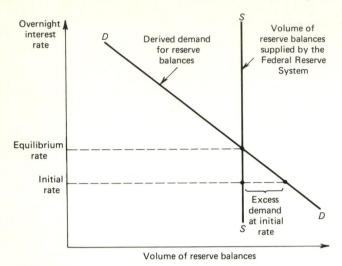

FIGURE 5.3
Supply of and demand for reserve balances.

Analysis of an Economy with Multiple Depository Institutions

Although over 15,000 depository institutions are subject to reserve requirements, instead of only a single bank, the concept of a single bank is a useful
stylization for understanding the determinants of the rate on overnight credit.
This follows because, even where there are multiple depository institutions,
only the Federal Reserve can change the size of the monetary base through policy actions like open market operations and discount window loans. However,
from the point of view of one of the thousands of depository institutions, what
matters is not the total size of the monetary base but rather the reserve balances held by that institution. In an economy with many depository institutions
there has to be a mechanism by which institutions can obtain the reserve balances needed to satisfy their *individual* reserve requirements.

Our previous analysis of reserve balances in an economy with a single bank
can be interpreted as an analysis of a *consolidated* banking system. The only
wrinkle added by an explicit recognition of multiple depository institutions is
that we have to be sure that the distribution of reserve balances among institutions is somehow consistent with equilibrium in the consolidated banking system. The need for a mechanism to distribute reserves is especially important in
view of the fluidity of ownership of reserve balances.

Fluctuations in the Distribution of Reserve Balances On a day-to-day basis
the volume of reserve balances owned by an individual depository institution
can be quite volatile. This volatility results from check clearings and other
transfers of balances in transactions accounts. When, for example, a bank customer writes a check to a depositor at another bank, the depository bank

typically collects the check through the Federal Reserve System and thereby sets in motion a transfer of reserve balances.

Consider the transfer of reserve balances induced by the transaction shown in Figure 5.4. As shown in Figure 5.4*a*, person A writes a $100 check, drawn on his demand deposit account at Chase Manhattan Bank, to person B. Person B then deposits the check in step (1) to his demand deposit account at Bankers

FIGURE 5.4
Collection of a $100 check written by A to B. *(a)* Movement of the check; *(b)* movement of credit balances.

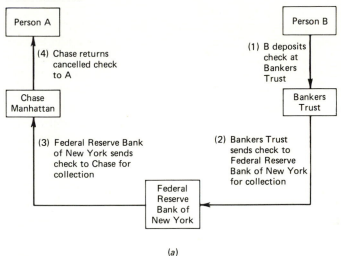

(a)

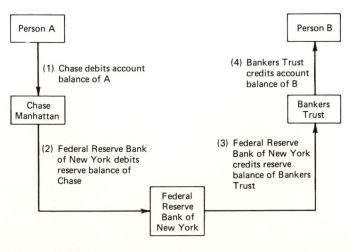

(b)

Trust Company. To collect the check, Bankers Trust sends the item to the Federal Reserve Bank of New York in step (2) which in turn sends it to Chase in step (3).

Assuming Chase has no objection to paying the check (such as insufficient funds in the deposit account of person A), the Federal Reserve Bank of New York will deduct $100 from the reserve account of Chase and will credit the reserve account of Bankers Trust by the same amount. This transfer of reserve balances is shown in Figure 5.4*b*. At the completion of the collection process, Chase will show $100 less in demand deposit liabilities and $100 less in reserve balances, and Bankers Trust will show $100 more in each category. The important point of the example is that Chase has lost $100 in reserve balances and Bankers Trust has gained an identical amount.

Loans by bank depositors on repurchase agreements (to institutions other than the depository bank) have an effect similar to that of check collections on the reserve position of the depository bank. The lender typically directs his bank to transfer funds to the commecial bank account of the borrower. This transfer of bank credit is accomplished through a transfer of reserve balances essentially identical to that used to pay the checks written by bank depositors.

On any given day the reserve account of a depository institution may be credited for hundreds of thousands of transfers and checks collected *from* other banks, and debited for a similar magnitude of transfers and checks collected *by* other banks. Over a long period of time the net gain or loss from these credits and debits may be nearly zero, but on any particular day the institution can experience net favorable or unfavorable clearings of a substantial magnitude. Even if the Federal Reserve System has supplied a volume of reserves sufficient to satisfy *aggregate* reserve requirements, there may nevertheless exist depository institutions with a surplus of reserve balances (because of temporarily favorable clearings) and institutions with deficient reserves (because of temporarily unfavorable clearings). The former institutions have an incentive to convert their surplus reserve balances into an earning asset, and the latter institutions have an incentive to acquire reserve balances to eliminate their deficiencies.

Correction of Reserve Deficiencies by a Single Depository Institution   A depository institution can do one of two things when faced with a deficient reserve balance. First, it can hope the situation corrects itself within the current maintenance period. Since reserve requirements are satisfied by *average* reserve balances, a deficient balance early in a maintenance period can be offset by an excess balance later in the same period. If, however, an institution finds that its reserve deficiency is too large to expect the situation to correct itself by the end of the maintenance period, the institution will have to take some more direct action.

One possible course of action for a depository institution with a reserve deficiency is to borrow from its district Federal Reserve bank. If the institution has no alternative source of reserves, its loan request will usually be accommodated. In general, however, the Federal Reserve System has taken the position that institutions should diligently seek out alternative sources of reserves, such as borrowing from another institution, before applying for a loan.[23] The reason for this policy is that loans from district Federal Reserve banks increase the monetary base, while borrowings from other institutions simply redistribute an existing stock of reserve balances. Thus, if the Federal Reserve is trying to control the size of the monetary base, large volumes of loans to depository institutions will force it to execute offsetting open market sales of securities.

Individual depository institutions can usually acquire reserve balances quite easily from other institutions. These balances are "bought" in the Federal funds market.[24] An institution with an excess reserve balance has an incentive to lend the excess portion of that balance, because reserve balances do not earn interest. Similarly, an institution with a reserve deficiency has an incentive to buy balances to meet its reserve requirements. The Federal funds market provides a vehicle for the efficient distribution of an existing stock of reserve balances.

With well-developed and efficient markets for the distribution of reserve balances among depository institutions and for the purchase and sale of government securities, the Federal Reserve System can direct its attention to controlling the size of the monetary base and the aggregate supply of reserve balances with open market operations, and it can leave the distribution of those balances among depository institutions to market forces.[25] Open market purchases and sales of securities are the major policy instrument for effecting change in the monetary base. Loans to member banks are used primarily to assist individual banks in meeting unusually severe reserve deficiencies.

Equilibrium in a Market with Multiple Depository Institutions   When there are multiple depository institutions, an individual institution can obtain reserve balances by borrowing those balances from another institution either in the Federal funds market or in the RP market. Suppose, for example, there is a net deficiency of reserve balances in the banking system at some initial level of the rates on repurchase agreements and borrowings of Federal funds. The existence of such a net deficiency means that the number of depository institutions trying to buy Federal funds will exceed the number of depository institutions seeking to sell Federal funds. The existence of an excess demand for reserve balances in the Federal funds market will begin to put upward pressure on the Federal funds rate. As the Federal funds rate increases, some depository insti-

---

[23] See Shull (1971).

[24] The Federal funds market is described in Section 4.2. See also the descriptions of the mechanics of the overnight and term Federal funds markets in Section 22.1 and Section 23.1, respectively.

[25] In countries where there is not a liquid market in government securities, monetary authorities use discount window operations instead of open market operations to change the size of the monetary base. If, in addition, there is no well-developed interbank market in reserve balances, the proper distribution of reserve balances among depository institutions must also be accomplished through discount window operations. See Garvy (1971).

tutions will switch and seek to borrow on repurchase agreements, thereby putting comparable upward pressure on the overnight RP rate. Increases in the overnight RP rate will induce holders of balances in transactions accounts to reduce those balances and to lend to depository institutions on repurchase agreements. As they reduce their holdings of transactions balances, the reserve requirements of some depository institutions will fall, thereby eliminating part of the net reserve deficiency in the banking system. The Federal funds rate and the RP rate will continue to rise until the banking system as a whole, and each individual depository institution, holds reserve balances which just equal its reserve requirements. Thus, the RP market and the Federal funds market operate in tandem to equate the supply of and demand for reserve balances at individual depository institutions and in the banking system as a whole.

5.4 DETERMINANTS OF OVERNIGHT INTEREST RATES

The preceding sections of this chapter described the determinants of the demand for reserve balances and the supply of reserve balances, and described how the rate on overnight credit moves to bring the market for reserve balances into equilibrium. This section uses those results to examine the effect on overnight interest rates of:

1 Changes in the level of aggregate economic activity
2 Federal Reserve open market operations
3 Changes in reserve requirement rates

These analyses will illustrate some of the important dimensions of monetary policy and its effect on interest rates, and will also provide practice in applying the concepts presented earlier in the chapter.

Changes in Aggregate Economic Activity

The supply and demand curves denoted by SS and DD, respectively, in Figure 5.5 show the initial schedules of supply and demand for reserve balances. The initial equilibrium rate on overnight credit is R_0. This discussion examines how that equilibrium rate of interest changes in response to an expansion in the level of aggregate economic activity.

As described in Section 5.1 above, an increase in the level of economic activity will lead to an expansion in public demand for transactions balances at any given level of short-term interest rates. This increase in public demand for transactions balances will precipitate a comparable increase in the demand for reserve balances by depository institutions as a result of the reserve requirements imposed on their transactions account liabilities. This shift in the demand for reserve balances is illustrated as a movement of the demand schedule in Figure 5.5 from DD to $D'D'$.

As a result of the shift in the demand for reserve balances by depository institutions, R_0 will no longer be the equilibrium rate of interest on overnight

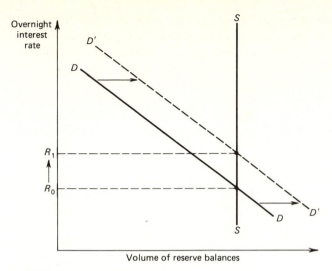

FIGURE 5.5
Effect on overnight interest rates of an expansion in aggregate economic activity.

credit. As shown in Figure 5.5, the overnight rate must rise from R_0 to R_1 to re-establish equilibrium in the market for reserve balances. Thus, we can conclude that increases in the level of economic activity will be accompanied by an increase in the level of short-term interest rates. This increase in rates has the effect of reducing the demand of depository institutions for reserve balances down to the level of the supply of those balances made available by the Federal Reserve System. In particular, it offsets the increase in demand for reserve balances which would have appeared at the old equilibrium rate R_0 as a result of the expansion in economic activity.

It should be noted that the increase in short-term interest rates caused by an expansion in economic activity is not a consequence of Federal Reserve policy actions. As shown in Figure 5.5, the Federal Reserve did not "cause" the higher interest rates by altering either the supply of reserve balances or the reserve requirement rates. This implies that, contrary to popular impression, rising interest rates are not always a signal of "tighter" monetary policy. They may be, as in the present case, a consequence of changes in aggregate economic conditions.

Open Market Operations

The second case considered in this section is the effect on short-term interest rates of Federal Reserve open market operations. As noted in Section 5.2, purchases of Treasury or federal agency securities by the Federal Reserve System increase the monetary base and, given that depository institutions and the public wish to hold a fixed quantity of currency, increase the supply of reserve balances.

Figure 5.6 illustrates the effect on interest rates of purchases of Treasury and federal agency securities by the Federal Reserve. Those purchases expand the supply of reserve balances from SS to $S'S'$. As a result of this expansion in reserves, the equilibrium level of the overnight rate falls from R_0 to R_1. The fall in interest rates stimulates public willingness to hold transactions balances and, as a result of an increase in public demand for those balances, increases the demand of depository institutions for reserve balances. The rate must fall far enough to make depository institutions want to hold all the additional reserves made available by the Federal Reserve System.

Changes in the level of interest rates caused by Federal Reserve open market operations are a genuine signal of the direction of monetary policy. Interest rates fell in Figure 5.6 only because the Federal Reserve was pursuing an "easier" policy and was making more reserves available to the banking system.

In some cases interest rates can remain unchanged even while the Federal Reserve is pursuing an active monetary policy. For example, suppose the Federal Open Market Committee believed that the level of aggregate economic activity was expanding, but it did not want interest rates to rise as a consequence of that expansion. If the Federal Reserve does nothing then, as shown in Figure 5.5, short-term interest rates will rise as a consequence of greater economic activity. Suppose, however, the Federal Reserve expands the supply of reserve balances through open market purchases of securities concurrently with the increase in economic activity. The net effect on the level of interest rates will then be a combination of Figure 5.5 and Figure 5.6.

FIGURE 5.6
Effect on overnight interest rates of Federal Reserve purchases of securities in open market operations.

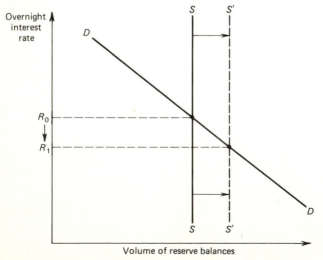

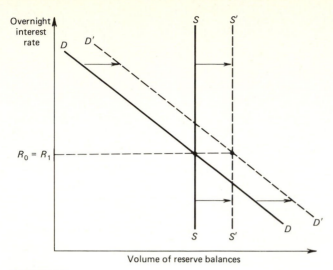

FIGURE 5.7
Federal Reserve open market purchases of securities accommodating an expansion in
aggregate economic activity.

Figure 5.7 illustrates the net effect in a case when interest rates on overnight
credit remain unchanged. In that figure the Federal Reserve has "accommodated" the increased demand for reserve balances (caused by an expansion in
aggregate economic activity) by increasing the supply of those balances. Essentially, the Federal Reserve has "sterilized" the normal effect of greater economic activity on the level of interest rates by pursuing an expansionary monetary
policy. This is true even though market participants do not observe any change
at all in the level of short-term rates.[26]

Changes in Reserve Requirement Rates

The third case examined in this section is the effect of a change in reserve
requirement rates on the level of overnight interest rates. Suppose, for example, the Board of Governors decides to increase the reserve requirements on
transactions account liabilities in excess of $25 million from 12 percent to 14
percent. As described in Section 5.1 and as illustrated in Figure 5.8, this would
shift the schedule of demand for reserve balances by depository institutions to

---

[26] Until October 1979, the Federal Reserve generally pursued a policy of maintaining short-
term interest rates within a narrow target band. In October 1979 it announced a new policy of maintaining reserve balances within a target band. See Lang (1980) and *Federal Reserve Bulletin*, October 1979, p. 830. Under the old policy the Federal Reserve sterilized, through open market operations, the effect on interest rates of short-run fluctuations in aggregate economic activity and resulting short-run fluctuations in public demand for transactions balances. Under the new policy the
Federal Reserve will allow short-term interest rates to move in a broader band in response to
changes in aggregate economic activity. See Wallich and Keir (1979) for a historical review of Federal Reserve monetary policy operations.

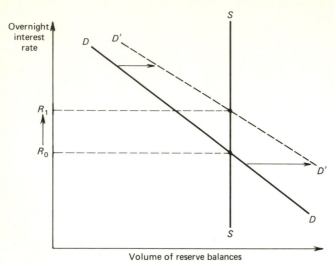

FIGURE 5.8
Effect on overnight interest rates of an increase in reserve requirement rates.

the right and would lead to a higher equilibrium level of short-term interest rates.

It should be noted that the shift in the demand schedule shown in Figure 5.8 is not comparable to the shift shown in Figure 5.5. The latter shift occurred because of a shift in public demand for transactions balances as a result of an increase in aggregate economic activity. In the present case, the schedule of public demand for transactions balances is unchanged. However, the higher reserve requirement rates imply a greater demand for reserve balances by depository institutions at any given level of public demand for transactions balances. This shows that the shift in the demand schedule shown in Figure 5.8 was a consequence of the Federal Reserve pursuing a tighter monetary policy.

Thus far we have seen two ways in which the Federal Reserve can pursue a tighter monetary policy: draining reserves from the banking system by executing open market sales of securities, and absorbing reserves by raising reserve requirements rates. These instruments of monetary policy would appear to be close substitutes. However, as a practical matter, the Federal Reserve nearly always chooses to work through open market operations rather than change reserve requirements. The reason is largely a matter of the profitability of depository institutions. Higher reserve requirements would force those institutions to maintain a relatively larger percentage of their assets in the form of non-interest-earning reserve balances. Open market operations, on the other hand, do not similarly force unprofitable changes in the balance sheets of depository institutions.

CHAPTER SUMMARY

This chapter has described how the rate on overnight credit is determined in the market for reserve balances. The Federal Reserve System controls the *supply* of reserve balances primarily through open market operations and, to a smaller extent, through loans to depository institutions. The *demand* for reserve balances is a derived demand which depends on the level of public deposits at depository institutions and on reserve requirement rates.

Transactions balances are the most important class of deposits for reserve purposes, because they have the highest reserve requirement. The willingness of depositors to keep a part of their assets in transactions balances is an inverse function of the level of short-term interest rates in general, and of the rate on overnight credit in particular. As the overnight credit rate rises, public demand for transactions balances falls, and so does the demand for reserve balances by depository institutions. The market for reserve balances is in equilibrium when the overnight rate is such that the derived demand for reserve balances equals the supply of those balances made available by the Federal Reserve System.

If there were only one commercial bank in the United States, there would be no need for a market in Federal funds. The rate on overnight credit would then be the rate on repurchase agreements between the single bank and members of the public. Since there are multiple depository institutions in the economy, a single institution can obtain credit by borrowing from another institution as well as through a repurchase agreement with a member of the public. The Federal funds market provides a mechanism for the efficient distribution of reserve balances among depository institutions. Because each institution is unlikely to care whether it borrows on an RP or in the Federal funds market, the rates on the two instruments will be quite similar. Although there are important institutional differences between the RP and Fed funds markets, the substantive differences are small.

The last section of this chapter examined how changes in aggregate economic activity and in Federal Reserve monetary policy come to affect the rate on overnight credit. Aggregate economic activity affects overnight interest rates by shifting the schedule of public demand for transactions balances and hence inducing a shift in the demand for reserve balances by depository institutions. Federal Reserve policy actions can change either the supply of reserve balances (through open market and discount window operations) or the demand for reserve balances (through changes in reserve requirement rates).

FURTHER READING

Anatol Balbach, and Albert Burger, "Derivation of the Monetary Base," Federal Reserve Bank of St. Louis *Review*, **58** (November 1976), 2–8.

Warren Coats, "Lagged Reserve Accounting and the Money Supply Mechanism," *Journal of Money, Credit, and Banking*, **8** (May 1976), 167–180.

Richard Lang, "The FOMC in 1979: Introducing Reserve Targeting," Federal Reserve Bank of St. Louis *Review*, **62** (March 1980), 2–25.

Paul Meek, *Open Market Operations* (New York: Federal Reserve Bank of New York, 1978).

William Poole, "A Proposal for Reforming Bank Reserve Requirements in the United States," *Journal of Money, Credit, and Banking*, **8** (May 1976), 137–147.

Lawrence Ritter and William Silber, *Principles of Money, Banking, and Financial Markets*, 3d ed. (New York: Basic Books, Inc., Publishers, 1980).

Henry Wallich and Peter Keir, "The Role of Operating Guides in U.S. Monetary Policy: A Historical Review," *Federal Reserve Bulletin*, **65** (September 1979), 679–691.

THREE

PORTFOLIO THEORY IN A SINGLE-PERIOD CONTEXT

The equilibrium prices of financial assets are those prices which lead to a balancing of supply and demand for every asset simultaneously. Since issuers sell new securities (and retire existing securities) relatively infrequently, we can assume asset supplies are fixed in the short run. Thus, at any given time, equilibrium prices depend upon balancing investor demands with a fixed stock of assets. To analyze the characteristics of equilibrium prices we first need a theory of investor demand for financial assets.

Portfolio theory is a theory of the demand for financial assets as a function of the risks and returns on those assets. One of the major objectives of portfolio theory is to suggest why people hold diversified portfolios, instead of concentrating all their wealth in a single security. The answer necessarily involves an analysis of risk in financial investments. If investors cared only about return, they would allocate all their resources to the single asset which they expected to yield the greatest return.

One of the central aspects of the portfolio theory presented in this part is that all investors are assumed to have a common "investment planning horizon." Investors care only about the return on their portfolios over the interval which begins when the portfolios are initially allocated and which ends when the planning horizon ends. Investors are assumed to be indifferent to fluctuations in the value of their portfolios prior to the end of the planning horizon and indifferent to asset values following the end of the horizon. This is why the portfolio theory presented here is called a *single-period* theory.

In practice the dates at which investors contemplate the *ultimate* liquidation of their portfolios may differ widely. Some investors may plan to liquidate their investments at relatively distant dates, e.g., at retirement, while others might contemplate ultimate liquidation much sooner. Whatever their ultimate liquidation horizons, however, all investors can consider rebalancing or reallocating portfolios of marketable assets at intermediate dates. In particular, the planning horizon which an investor uses in deciding upon his current allocation may be quite short, even if his liquidation horizon is relatively far in the future.

Mossin (1968) has shown that in some cases investment decisions oriented toward distant liquidation dates may be decomposed into a consecutive sequence of portfolio allocations and reallocations over shorter investment planning intervals.[1] Mossin's argument is valid if security returns over successive nonoverlapping intervals of time are statistically independent. Section 13.1 presents evidence that returns on common stock follow such a model. Thus, the assumption of a single-period planning horizon is not inappropriate for the analysis of investments in common stock.[2] In the limit, the length of a planning period may become as small as a day or less.[3]

The portfolio theory developed in this part depends on several assumptions in addition to that of a single-period investment planning horizon. We assume there are no taxes either on cash distributions (like dividends) or on capital gains. This assumption permits a substantial simplification of the analysis. To account realistically for the presence of taxes on cash distributions, we would have to recognize that not all investors are in the same tax bracket and that two investors can derive different after-tax returns on the same stock. Taxes on capital gains lead to a difference between the liquidated and unliquidated values of a portfolio, since those taxes are levied only on realized gains.[4]

We also assume that all securities are infinitely divisible so that an investor can hold fractional equity shares in a corporation. We assume there are no transactions costs so the cash value of a portfolio is identical to its value computed from current market prices.[5] Finally, we assume financial markets are perfectly competitive, so that a single investor's demands for stocks are not large enough (relative to available supplies) to affect market prices. How the

[1] See the more general analysis of Stapleton and Subrahmanyam (1978) and the works cited therein.

[2] The introduction to Part Five shows that debt securities do not exhibit serially independent returns over successive investment intervals. Because they do not, the analysis of equilibrium prices on debt securities is separated from the analysis of equilibrium prices on common stock.

[3] The derivation in the appendix to chapter 18 of the equilibrium value of option contracts on common stock assumes an arbitrarily short planning horizon, which could well be a matter of hours or minutes.

[4] The problem of portfolio choice and market equilibrium when dividends and capital gains are taxed at different rates and when investors are in different tax brackets has been studied by Brennan (1970) and Long (1977). Black and Scholes (1974b) were unable to find any effect of high versus low dividend yields on total pretax stock returns, suggesting the absence of any significant tax effects, but Litzenberger and Ramaswamy (1979) found contrary results.

[5] Evans (1970) has observed that taxes on realized capital gains, and transactions costs on purchases and sales, reduce the optimal frequency of portfolio reallocation and alter the optimal level of portfolio diversification. In particular, higher tax rates will lead to less frequent reallocation but broader diversification, while lower tax rates induce more frequent reallocation with narrower diversification. Lower transactions costs induce more frequent reallocation and broader diversification.

aggregate demands of individual investors come to affect market prices is the topic of Part Four.

The assumptions of portfolio theory as outlined in the preceding paragraphs are:

1 Single-period investment planning horizon
2 No taxes
3 Infinite divisibility of securities
4 No transactions costs
5 Perfectly competitive markets

These assumptions may seem exceedingly restrictive and likely to render the theory unusable. This appears not to be the case, however. The single-period horizon is, for common stock, an analytical device which does not alter any substantive results. The existing indivisibilities of securities are hardly significant to institutional investors, who now play a central role in American securities markets. Although taxes may have a significant effect on individual portfolio allocations, Black and Scholes (1974b) were unable to find any tax effects on the *equilibrium values* of securities. Since it is the latter which is of ultimate interest, we will avoid the complications which taxes would create for the analysis. Finally, as we will see in Parts Seven and Eight, transactions costs and departures from perfect competition can be ascribed to the trading characteristics of a market. They can be ignored in a theory of portfolio allocation, because they can often be avoided in actual investment situations. Even with the restrictive assumptions which we have made, the predictions of the theory do not seem to be in serious conflict with what we observe about the behavior of stock prices.

Chapter 6 begins the development of portfolio theory by introducing definitions of risk and return for a single stock. To formalize the notion of risk, we assume investors perceive the actual return on a risky investment as a random variable. Chapter 7 expands the definitions of risk and return to portfolios allocated between two risky stocks. The major theme of Chapter 7 is the effect of portfolio composition on portfolio risk and portfolio return. We will see that this effect depends not only on the risk/return characteristics of the individual securities in a portfolio but also on the correlation between the uncertain returns on pairs of risky stocks. Chapter 8 introduces investor indifference curves as a descriptive representation of preferences for return and distaste for exposure to risk, and it solves the problem of choosing an optimal portfolio. This solution depends on what risk/return combinations are available to the investor and how the investor judges the relative attractiveness of those combinations. Chapter 9 extends portfolio analysis to multiple-stock portfolios, introduces a risk-free asset into the theory, and develops the separation theorem of portfolio theory. Chapter 10 considers the solution to the portfolio selection problem for the special case where all investors share a common probability description of future stock returns. The principal result of this chapter is the identification of the market portfolio as a particularly important portfolio of risky assets. This key result will carry us over to the analysis of market equilibrium in Part Four.

CHAPTER 6

RISK AND RETURN
FOR A SINGLE ASSET

The purpose of portfolio theory is to suggest why and how investors allocate their wealth among different securities. As stated in the introduction to Part Three, investor demand must depend on the risks and returns on different portfolio allocations. Thus, portfolio theory requires a formal definition of "risk" and "return" and a description of how alternative portfolio allocations affect that risk and return.

If we start with the case of a single asset, we do not have an allocation problem at all. An investor can hold only the single available security. We can, however, ask how the investor perceives the risk and return on that security. This allows us to develop appropriate measures of those two concepts in the simplest possible setting.

In elaborating a theory of portfolio allocation, we begin with the concept of risk and return for individual assets considered in isolation. This chapter addresses that topic. In subsequent chapters we extend the analysis to portfolio risk and portfolio return, and to the consequences of alternative portfolio allocations.

6.1 MEASURING REALIZED RETURNS

Before we can analyze the anticipated risk and the anticipated return on an investment in a single asset, we first have to know how the return is measured after it has occurred. In light of the assumptions outlined in the introduction to Part Three, we are interested in the return on a security over the interval from the beginning to the end of an investor's planning period, and we will ignore taxes and transactions costs in measuring that return.

Suppose that the market price per share of some issue of common stock is P at the beginning of the planning period, that the price of a share at the end of the planning period is P', and that the issuer of the stock pays to each holder an amount D per share at the end of the period. (D may be zero.) The return on the stock over the period is then

$$R = \frac{P' - P + D}{P} \tag{6.1}$$

The return occurs in two forms. The quantity $P' - P$ is the capital appreciation or depreciation of the asset. D represents cash and noncash distributions.

The distribution D will generally be a cash dividend payment. It could also include the market value of rights, spin-offs of other securities, or distributions of assets by a firm in reorganization or partial liquidation. Rights are securities which allow the holder to buy other securities from the issuer at some fixed price; i.e., they are "rights to purchase." In 1970 American Telephone and Telegraph sold $1.6 billion in debentures by offering the new debt securities to AT&T stockholders through a rights offering. Each stockholder received, free, one right for each share of AT&T common stock which he owned. For $100 and 35 rights a stockholder could buy, between April 14 and May 18, 1970, a $100 principal value 8.75 percent debenture maturing in the year 2000. The rights had a market value of 70 cents the first day they were traded. They were, consequently, valuable distributions, just as cash dividends are valuable distributions.

The end-of-period price P' must be adjusted for intraperiod stock splits, reverse stock splits, and stock dividends. If an issuer splits its stock 2 for 1 during the period, 2 end-of-period shares are equivalent to each beginning-of-period share. If the market price per share at the end of the period is $25, P' will be the value of 2 of those end-of-period shares, or $50. A reverse stock split is similar to a stock split, except that the issuer makes 1 share of the new stock equal to, say, 5 shares of the old stock. If the market price of the new stock is $100 at the end of the period, P' would be one-fifth of $100, or $20. A stock dividend is like a small stock split. For example, a 5 percent stock dividend is similar to a 21 for 20 stock split. If an issuer declares a 5 percent stock dividend payable during the period, and the stock is priced at $80 at the end of the period, P' would be set to $80 \times 1.05 = \$84$, since each old share has become 1.05 new shares.

6.2   UNCERTAIN RETURNS AS RANDOM VARIABLES

At the beginning of the planning period the price P is directly observable and known with certainty. However, neither the end-of-period price P' nor the payment D is known with certainty in most cases. This uncertainty creates risk in the investment.

The only security for which the rate of return over the planning period is known with certainty is a Treasury issue which matures at the end of the period and which makes no intermediate coupon payments (which would have to be reinvested at uncertain yields when they are paid during the period). For planning periods less than a year, a Treasury bill maturing at the end of the period is a risk-free investment.[1] For planning periods of 1 or 2 days, a loan on a repurchase agreement is risk-free for all practical purposes.

The presence of uncertainty with respect to P' and D induces uncertainty in the return R defined in Equation (6.1). This uncertainty can be represented by treating the return R as a random variable.

Suppose R can occur in any of n discrete states, denoted by $(R_1, R_2, \ldots, R_n)$. Let $p(R_i) \geq 0$ be the probability that the ith state will occur. $p(R_i)$ is the probability that the realized return will equal R_i. Since one of the n states must occur, the sum of the probabilities of all states must equal unity, or[2]

$$\sum_{i=1}^{n} p(R_i) = 1 \qquad (6.2)$$

Example 6.1 shows a random return which can occur in any of three discrete states: 0 percent (the state designated as $i = 1$), 10 percent (state $i = 2$), and 20 percent (state $i = 3$). Note that the sum of the three probabilities is unity ($.10 + .50 + .40 = 1$).

All our information about the uncertainty in the return is carried in the $p(R_i)$ probabilities. However, those probabilities are not convenient to work with directly. We prefer simple summary measures of the return which is expected (that is, a mean or expected return) and of the dispersion of possible returns around the expected return. The latter will serve as our measure of risk.

Expected Return

We define the expected return μ on an investment in the single security as

$$\mu = \text{Exp } [R] = \sum_{i=1}^{n} R_i p(R_i) \qquad (6.3)$$

The notation Exp $[R]$ is read as "the expected value of R."[3] μ is a weighted-average combination of all the possible returns, where the weight on the return

---

[1] For longer periods, a risk-free instrument can be constructed by buying a coupon-bearing Treasury note or bond, stripping off the intermediate coupons, and then selling the stripped coupons for cash. We will discuss such coupon sales more extensively in section 14.4.

[2] The notation $\sum_{i=1}^{n} x_i$ means the sum of the x_i series, or the sum $x_1 + x_2 + \cdots + x_n$. It can be read as "the summation of the x_i's, from i equal to 1 to i equal to n." i is called the *index*, and 1 and n are the lower and upper limits of the summation, respectively.

[3] This is *not* the same as exp $[x]$, which means e^x. We will consistently use "Exp" to mean the expectation of a random variable.

EXAMPLE 6.1

RISK AND RETURN ON A SINGLE ASSET

Assume the return on an asset can occur in any of three discrete states, R_1, R_2, or R_3, with the probability that $R = R_i$ given by the following table:

i	1	2	3
R_i	.0	.10	.20
$p(R_i)$	.10	.50	.40

From Equation (6.3) we have that the expected return on the asset is

$$\mu = R_1 p(R_1) + R_2 p(R_2) + R_3 p(R_3)$$
$$= .0(10) + 10(.50) + .20(.40)$$
$$= .13$$

From Equation (6.4) we have that the variance of return on the asset is

$$\sigma^2 = (R_1 - \mu)^2 p(R_1) + (R_2 - \mu)^2 p(R_2) + (R_3 - \mu)^2 p(R_3)$$
$$= (-.13)^2(.10) + (-.03)^2(.50) + (.07)^2(.40)$$
$$= .0041$$

so that $\sigma = .064$.

R_i is the probability $p(R_i)$ that the return will equal R_i. We use μ as a measure of the central tendency of the random return on a risky security.

Example 6.1 shows how the expected return on a hypothetical security is found to be $\mu = .13$, or 13 percent. An investor could not actually earn 13 percent on the security (he can only earn 0, 10, or 20 percent, because those are the only possible realizations of the return). However, he would *expect* to earn an *average* return of 13 percent if he could make repeated investments in the same security. This is what most people mean when they talk about an "expected" return.

Variance of Return

Having defined a measure of central tendency, we now have to define a measure of how *different* an actual return might be from the expected return. That is, we need to define a measure of the dispersion of possible returns around the expected return. For that measure we use the variance of return, denoted by σ^2 and defined as

$$\sigma^2 = \text{Var }[R] = \sum_{i=1}^{n} (R_i - \mu)^2 p(R_i) \tag{6.4}$$

The notation Var $[R]$ is read as "the variance of R." σ^2 is a weighted-average combination of the squared deviations of the possible returns from the expected return, where the weight on the squared deviation $(R_i - \mu)^2$ is the probability $p(R_i)$ that the actual return will equal R_i. Example 6.1 shows how the variance of the return on a hypothetical security is found to be .0041.

Since $(R_i - \mu)^2 \geq 0$, a variance of return is always nonnegative. Moreover, $\sigma^2 = 0$ if and only if there is only one possible return, i.e., if there is no uncertainty or risk to the security. We use variance of return as a measure of the riskiness of a single asset considered in isolation. Greater dispersion of returns implies a larger variance, and a smaller dispersion of returns around the mean return implies a smaller variance. A risk-free security is one which has zero dispersion or zero variance of return.

The square root of the variance is called the *standard deviation* and is denoted by σ. Since the variance and standard deviation are uniquely related (if we know one we automatically know the other), we can use either as a measure of risk.

At this stage of the analysis we need not assume that all investors perceive similar probability distributions for the future returns on risky assets. The distributions could be subjective and may differ among investors. For example, suppose an investor has access to important information on the affairs of an issuer not yet available to other investors. His expectation of the future return on the issuer's securities could differ substantially from the expectations held by other investors.

6.3 UNCERTAIN RETURNS AS NORMALLY DISTRIBUTED RANDOM VARIABLES

In the previous section it was suggested that the uncertain return on a risky asset can be treated as a random variable with expected value μ and variance σ^2. Although these simple descriptive parameters are adequate for the development of portfolio theory, in some applications it is important to inquire more closely into the statistical characteristics of the returns on financial assets.

One of the most frequently used models of return is the assumption of a normal or gaussian random variable. A normally distributed random variable is fully described by its mean and variance. Thus, nothing other than μ and σ^2 needs to be specified to obtain the complete structure of the possible returns on an asset.

Regardless of whether one agrees or disagrees with the mean and variance as the appropriate measures of the return and risk on a security, those two parameters convey all the available information about possible future returns if the return has a normal distribution. This means that regardless of how risk and return are measured, those measures must be functions of the mean and variance of the return. It follows that investor preference for return and distaste for risk can be phrased in terms of μ and σ^2. Chapter 8 does exactly that.

Normal distributions have another desirable characteristic. Weighted-average combinations of normal random variables are themselves normal random variables. This feature is convenient when we speak of the return on a portfolio of several stocks, as we will do in Chapters 7 and 9.

A more extensive treatment of the normality of returns on common stock is given in the appendix to this chapter. It is shown there that the normality assumption is most useful over periods longer than a few days but not as long as a year or more, and that the assumption may be unjustified for either shorter or longer periods.

CHAPTER SUMMARY

This chapter has discussed the measurement of returns on common stock and the representation of uncertain future returns. A return is measured by the end-of-period value of a security relative to its beginning-of-period value. The end-of-period value includes any valuable distributions made by the issuer, including both cash and noncash distributions, as well as the market value of the security. The latter is adjusted for intraperiod stock splits, reverse stock splits, and stock dividends.

Uncertain future returns are represented as random variables. The risk and return on a security are then measured as the variance (or standard deviation) of return and the expected return, respectively. The expected return is a measure of central tendency. The variance of return is a measure of the dispersion of possible returns around the expected return. In the case where the return is normally distributed, these two parameters summarize completely the entire probability distribution of possible returns.

FURTHER READING

Robert Blattberg and Nicholas Gonedes, "A Comparison of the Stable and Student Distributions as Statistical Models for Stock Prices," *Journal of Business*, **47** (April 1974), 244–280.

Paul Cootner, ed., *The Random Character of Stock Market Prices* (Cambridge, Mass.: The M.I.T. Press, 1964).

Eugene Fama, "Mandelbrot and the Stable Paretian Hypothesis," *Journal of Business*, **36** (October 1963), 420–429.

———, "The Behavior of Stock Market Prices," *Journal of Business*, **38** (January 1965), 34–105.

Benoit Mandelbrot, "The Variation of Certain Speculative Prices," *Journal of Business*, **36** (October 1963), 394–419.

APPENDIX: The Normality of the Return on Common Stock

This appendix discusses why, and under what circumstances, we can model the return on common stock as a normally distributed random variable. The reader may wish to review the discussion of compounding, especially continuous compounding, presented in the appendix to Chapter 1 before continuing with this appendix. There are extensive references in what follows to continuously compounded returns.

In Equation (6.1) we defined the simple return R on a security over a period of arbitrary length. One can also define the log price relative or log return r per period as

$$r = \ln \left[\frac{P' + D}{P} \right] \tag{A.1}$$

Noting that $P/P = 1$, we have

$$r = \ln \left[1 + \frac{P' - P + D}{P} \right]$$

$$= \ln [1 + R] \tag{A.2}$$

If the absolute value of R is less than about .15, or less than 15 percent, $\ln [1 + R]$ (and therefore r), will be approximately equal to R. For purposes of analyzing the normality of returns, however, it is more convenient to work with log returns rather than simple returns.

Compound Returns and Multiple-Day Log Returns

Consider the behavior of the return on a security over investment periods of 1 day, 2 days, and so on. Let $R_t(1)$ be the simple 1-day return from day t to day $t + 1$, and let $r_t(1)$ be the analogous log return, so that $r_t(1) = \ln [1 + R_t(1)]$. Assuming cash and non-cash distributions are immediately reinvested in the security at its current market price, we can define a *compound n-day return* $R_t(n)$ from day t to day $t + n$ as the product of a consecutive sequence of simple 1-day returns:

$$1 + R_t(n) = [1 + R_t(1)] [1 + R_{t+1}(1)] \cdots [1 + R_{t+n-1}(1)]$$

If there are no distributions *during* the n-day investment period, the compound return $R_t(n)$ will be identical to the simple return defined in Equation (6.1) over the n-day period. [When we specified that the cash and noncash distributions represented by D in Equation (6.1) were paid at the end of the investment period, we were avoiding the problem of how to treat the reinvestment of intraperiod distributions.] Our objective in this appendix is to develop some results on the normality, or near normality, of the distribution of $R_t(n)$.

The log return $r_t(n)$ analogous to $R_t(n)$ is defined as $r_t(n) = \ln [1 + R_t(n)]$. Since $\ln [xy] = \ln [x] + \ln [y]$, we have[4]

$$\ln [1 + R_t(n)] = \ln \left[\prod_{k=0}^{n-1} (1 + R_{t+k}(1)) \right]$$

$$= \sum_{k=0}^{n-1} \ln [1 + R_{t+k}(1)]$$

or

$$r_t(n) = \sum_{k=0}^{n-1} r_{t+k}(1) \tag{A.3}$$

---

[4] The notation $\prod_{i=1}^{n} x_i$ means the product of the x_i series, or the product $(x_1) \cdot (x_2) \cdots (x_n)$. It may be read as "the product of the x_i's, from i equal to 1 to i equal to n."

That is, the n-day log return is the sum of the n daily log returns realized over the n-day investment interval.

Normal Multiple-Day Log Returns

Now suppose that the 1-day log returns are independently and identically distributed random variables with some mean m and some finite variance s^2.[5] Under fairly general conditions on the distribution of these 1-day log returns, the central-limit theorem asserts that the n-day log return defined in Equation (A.3) will converge to a normal or gaussian distribution with mean nm and variance ns^2 as n grows large.[6]

As long as the 1-day log returns are statistically independent random variables with finite variance, the distribution of log returns over longer intervals will converge to a normal probability distribution as the length of the investment period increases. Empirical evidence suggests that convergence is attained in about a week or a month.[7] This result is important to the analysis of the behavior of stock prices, because there exists a substantial body of literature from probability and statistics dealing with normal distributions. The literature can be applied to the study of stock prices if log returns are asymptotically normally distributed.

In one special case the distribution of log returns will be exactly normally distributed for any investment period. If the 1-day log returns $r_t(1)$ are themselves normally distributed, then the n-day log returns $r_t(n)$ will also be normally distributed for all $n \geq 1$. $r_t(n)$ is then a sum of normally distributed random variables, as shown by Equation (A.3). In this case we do not have to appeal to the central-limit theorem to obtain the normality of $r_t(n)$.

Early investigations of the distribution of returns on common stock found that the sample variance of log returns increases approximately linearly with the length of the investment period.[8] That evidence supported, albeit weakly, the hypothesis that log returns on common stock are asymptotically normally distributed with a finite variance on the distribution of daily returns. Those investigations also found, however, that there are more extreme positive and negative observations on returns measured over short intervals of time than would be expected were those short-interval returns normally distributed.[9] This finding of so-called fat tails in the distribution of the daily log returns contradicts the hypothesis that those returns are themselves normally distributed, and suggests that the normality of log returns over longer intervals is, at best, an asymptotic result.

Stable Paretian Log Returns

To account for the phenomenon of fat tails in the distribution of daily log returns, Mandelbrot (1963) advanced the idea that log returns are distributed according to a stable Paretian probability density function.[10] There exists a family of such density functions characterized by a parameter, usually denoted by α, which lies in the interval

---

[5] This is the assumption that security prices follow a random walk. See Section 13.2.

[6] The central-limit theorem is stated in Gnedenko and Kolmogorov (1954).

[7] See Blattberg and Gonedes (1974).

[8] See Kendall (1953), Moore (1962), and Osborne (1959). See also the articles reprinted in Cootner (1964).

[9] See Mandelbrot (1963, fn. 3).

[10] Fama (1963) presents a highly readable introduction to Mandelbrot's hypothesis.

$0 < \alpha \leq 2$. If $\alpha = 2$, the distribution is normal. If $\alpha < 2$, however, the distribution is more peaked near the mean and has fatter tails than is the case with a normal distribution. This is exactly the observed empirical characteristic of daily log returns. Estimates of α from daily stock price returns suggest that those returns have a value of α between 1.65 and 1.8.[11]

An important characteristic of all stable Paretian distributions is that sums of independent stable Paretian random variables, all with a common value of α, are also distributed as stable Paretian random variables with the same α. (In the special case of $\alpha = 2$, this is the familiar statement that sums of normally distributed variables are themselves normally distributed.) Thus, if daily log returns are stable Paretian with $\alpha = 1.8$, then weekly and monthly log returns will also be stable Paretian with $\alpha = 1.8$.[12]

The problem introduced by the assertion that daily returns are stable Paretian with $\alpha < 2$ is that the variances of returns over all investment intervals are then infinite. This feature renders infeasible the construction of a theory of portfolio allocation which relies on the notion of a finite variance of returns.[13] Moreover, it implies that a large body of statistical tools used in empirical analyses, such as the use of the t statistic in hypothesis testing, may be inappropriate for the analysis of stock returns.

Tests of the stable Paretian hypothesis proceeded by estimating a value of α from data on daily log returns. Those tests assumed the distribution of log returns belonged to a stable Paretian class and sought to discover whether $\alpha = 2$ (implying normality of the log returns) or whether $\alpha < 2$. Blattberg and Gonedes (1974) discussed whether daily log returns are stable Paretian or are from a class of probability distributions with finite variance but with fatter tails than is the case for normal distributions. (They used Student's t distribution.[14]) The authors found the stable Paretian model provided an inferior description of their data. Their results imply that daily log returns have a finite variance but that the distribution of those returns have fatter tails than would be the case for a normal distribution. Because of the finite variance on the daily returns, the distributions of log returns over longer investment intervals converge to normal distributions as the length of the intervals increase.[15]

---

[11] Fama (1965a) presented the first empirical evidence supporting the stable Paretian hypothesis using data on daily stock returns. Fama and Roll (1968, 1971) developed new techniques for estimating the parameters of stable distributions. Roll (1970) applied the stable Paretian model to the structure of yields on United States Treasury bills. Blattberg and Gonedes (1974) also presented estimates of the α parameter using daily returns on common stock.

[12] Several studies have suggested that the α parameters of common stock are not stable under either cross-sectional or longitudinal aggregation. See Officer (1972); Barnea and Downes (1973); and Hsu, Miller, and Wichern (1974). This evidence casts doubt on the validity of the stable Paretian hypothesis.

[13] Fama (1965b) and Samuelson (1967) have proposed an approach to portfolio theory appropriate to the case of stable Paretian returns on securities.

[14] See also Praetz (1972) using Student's t distribution for related work.

[15] The distribution of stock returns generated by stock prices following a subordinated stochastic process will also exhibit "fat tails" (relative to a normal distribution) yet have a finite variance over fixed intervals of time. Subordinated stochastic processes presume that stock returns are normally distributed in "transaction time" but that the number of transaction time units in a fixed interval of chronological time is a random variable. This means that stock returns over a fixed interval of chronological time are drawn from a mixture of normally distributed random variables. In most cases transaction time is measured by trading volume. See Press (1967), Mandelbrot and Taylor (1967), Clark (1973), Epps and Epps (1976), Morgan (1976), and Westerfield (1977).

The Normality of Compound Returns

The compound return $R_t(n)$ and the log return $r_t(n)$ over an n-day investment period are related as $r_t(n) = \ln [1 + R_t(n)]$, or $R_t(n) = \exp [r_t(n)] - 1$. If the 1-day log returns are independent random variables with expected value m and finite variance s^2, the distribution of n-day log returns, as was mentioned above, will converge to a normal distribution with mean nm and variance ns^2 as n increases. This result allows us to compute the asymptotic mean and variance of $R_t(n)$.

If x is a normally distributed random variable with mean K_1 and variance K_2, it is not hard to show[16] that the first and second moments of $\exp [x]$ are

$$\text{Exp } [\exp [x]] = \exp [K_1 + \tfrac{1}{2}K_2] \qquad (A.4a)$$
$$\text{Exp } [\exp^2 [x]] = \exp [2K_1 + 2K_2] \qquad (A.4b)$$

The variance of any random variable may be computed as the difference between the second moment and the squared value of the mean. Thus, the variance of $\exp [x]$ is given by

$$\text{Var } [exp [x]] = \exp [2K_1 + 2K_2] - \exp [2K_1 + K_2] \qquad (A.4c)$$

Assume n is sufficiently large so that $r_t(n)$ may be considered normally distributed with mean nm and variance ns^2. Since $R_t(n) = \exp [r_t(n)] - 1$, it follows that $R_t(n)$ has a mean and variance given by

$$\mu = \text{Exp } [R_t(n)] = \exp [nm + \tfrac{1}{2}ns^2] - 1 \qquad (A.5a)$$
$$\sigma^2 = \text{Var } [R_t(n)] = \exp [2nm + 2ns^2] - \exp [2nm + ns^2] \qquad (A.5b)$$

The mean and variance given by Equations (A.5) are exact when $r_t(n)$ is normally distributed. Since $r_t(n)$ converges to a normal distribution as n grows large, the expectation and variance of $)_t(n)$ similarly coverage to the values given by Equations (A.5).

If n is small enough so that the inequality $2n(m + s^2) < .15$ is satisfied, and if s^2 is small relative to m, then to a first-order approximation Equations (A.5) may be written as

$$\mu = nm \qquad (A.6a)$$
$$\sigma^2 = ns^2 \qquad (A.6b)$$

For values of n large enough so that the asymptotic normality of $r_t(n)$ holds, but small enough so that $2n(m + s^2) < .15$, the mean and variance of the compound return $R_t(n)$ will grow approximately linearly with n.

This result on the behavior of μ and σ^2 as a function of n can be obtained another way. If n is such that $-.15 < nm - 3ns$ and $nm + 3ns < .15$, then 99.74 percent of the random realizations of $r_t(n)$ will be less than .15 in absolute value. Thus, the approximation of $r_t(n)$ by $\exp [r_t(n)] - 1$ will be reasonable. Since $r_t(n)$ is normally distributed with mean nm and variance ns^2, so is its approximation. But $R_t(n)$ is equal to $\exp [r_t(n)] - 1$ by definition, and so $R_t(n)$ is approximately normally distributed with mean $\mu = nm$ and variance $\sigma^2 = ns^2$. This is the same result for the moments of

---

[16] See Aitchison and Brown (1957).

$R_t(n)$ given by Equation (A.6), but here we have the additional result that $R_t(n)$ is approximately normally distributed.

The assumption that the compound return $R_t(n)$ is normally distributed results in important simplifications for many aspects of portfolio analysis, as we will see in the appendix to Chapter 8. This assumption is not, however, justified over short investment intervals such as 1 or 2 days (when the log return is itself not normally distributed), nor is it justified over long investment periods such as a year or more (when the approximation of the log return by the compound return is not justified). For intermediate periods such as a month, however, the approximation can be quite convenient for empirical analysis.

CHAPTER 7

RISK AND RETURN FOR A PORTFOLIO OF TWO ASSETS

The previous chapter developed summary statistical measures of the risk and return on a single asset considered in isolation. Suppose, however, an investor chooses to invest in a portfolio of two assets. He should then be concerned with the risk and return on the portfolio as a whole, rather than with the risk and return on the individual assets in the portfolio.

In this chapter we will see how the expected return and variance of return on a portfolio of two assets are related to (1) the risk/return characteristics of the assets in the portfolio and (2) the composition of the portfolio.[1] From the point of view of an investor, the risk/return characteristics of individual assets are fixed. The composition of the portfolio is, however, a matter of investor choice. By altering the composition of his portfolio, an investor can change the expected return and risk exposure of that portfolio. The effect of portfolio composition on portfolio risk and return is what makes the problem of portfolio selection interesting.

7.1 PORTFOLIO COMBINATIONS

Suppose we have two assets, labeled 1 and 2, with current prices P_1 and P_2, respectively, and suppose those assets will be valued at P_1' and P_2' at the end of one period. Proceeding analogously with Chapter 6, we can define the returns earned on the assets over the period as

[1] The mean-variance portfolio selection criterion developed in Chapters 7 to 10 has been criticized by Feldstein (1969) and Borch (1968, 1969). Tobin (1969) has replied to these criticisms, and Samuelson (1970) has shown that a mean-variance criterion may be viewed as an approximation to a fuller solution of the portfolio selection problem.

$$R_1 = \frac{P_1' - P_1 + D_1}{P_1} \tag{7.1a}$$

$$R_2 = \frac{P_2' - P_2 + D_2}{P_2} \tag{7.1b}$$

where $P_i' - P_i$ is the (uncertain) capital gain or loss on asset i, and D_i is the (uncertain) value of any distribution from the issuer of asset i.

R_i is the net return on an investment in security i. If the investor has initial wealth[2] W which he allocates as W_1 to asset 1 and W_2 to asset 2, his end-of-period wealth W' will be

$$W' = W + W_1 R_1 + W_2 R_2$$

Since we are ignoring indivisibilities in securities, W_1 and W_2 may assume any values as long as $W_1 + W_2 = W$.

The return on the portfolio as a whole, denoted as R, is defined as $R = (W' - W)/W$, and so we have

$$R = \frac{W_1 R_1 + W_2 R_2}{W}$$

or
$$R = x_1 R_1 + x_2 R_2 \tag{7.2}$$

where $x_i = W_i/W$ is the fraction of initial wealth allocated to the ith asset.

Observe that the sum of x_i and x_2 must equal unity. This just says that all the investor's wealth *must* be allocated either to the first asset or to the second asset. For the present we assume $x_1 \geq 0$ and $x_2 \geq 0$. (We will see in Section 7.4 how an investor can hold negative amounts of an asset by short selling.) Since we are ignoring indivisibilities in securities, x_1 and x_2 can take on any value between zero and unity as long as $x_1 + x_2 = 1$.

Equation (7.2) says that the realized return on the portfolio is a weighted combination of the realized returns on the assets in the portfolio, where the weights are the fractional allocations of the investor's initial wealth. If an investor allocated 75 percent of his wealth to the first asset (and 25 percent to the second), and R_1 was 10 percent and R_2 was 15 percent, then

$$\begin{aligned}
R &= x_1 R_1 + x_2 R_2 \\
&= .75(.10) + .25(.15) \\
&= .1125, \text{ or } 11.25\%
\end{aligned}$$

---

[2] If an investor enters the market with cash, his initial wealth is simply his cash holdings. If he enters the market with some portfolio of assets, his initial wealth is the value of that portfolio computed from current market prices. Since we are assuming a competitive market and are ignoring taxes and transactions costs, the liquidated and unliquidated values of a portfolio are identical. Initial wealth may then be measured by either value. This will not be true if an investor incurs tax liabilities on his realized capital gains, or if he incurs transactions costs in converting financial assets to cash, or if his liquidation of securities leads to a change in market prices.

The returns R_1 and R_2 on the individual assets in the portfolio are uncertain events. These uncertainties lead to uncertainty in the return on the portfolio.

To represent the uncertainty in the return on the portfolio, we will model that return as a random process. This leads us to compute the expected return and variance of return on the portfolio. However, rather than ascribe some probability distribution to R directly, we will begin with probability distributions on the R_i's and then ask what those distributions imply for the distribution of the portfolio return.[3] By starting our analysis with the distributions of returns on the individual assets, we can derive explicitly the consequences, for the return on the portfolio, of changing the portfolio allocation.

Before beginning the analysis, consider briefly two simple polar cases. Suppose the investor places all his wealth in the first asset. Then by Equation (7.2) we have $R = R_1$. If R_1 has mean μ_1 and variance σ_1^2, it follows that the expected return on the portfolio is μ_1 and that the variance of return on the portfolio is σ_1^2. Similarly, if the investor places all his wealth in the second asset, then $R = R_2$, so that the expected return on the portfolio is μ_2 and the variance of return is σ_2^2. We are interested here in deriving the expected return and variance of return on the portfolio for portfolio allocations *between* these two polar cases, i.e., when positive amounts of *both* assets are held. For simplicity in this chapter we assume neither of the two assets is risk-free. Portfolio analysis when a risk-free asset is present is considered in Chapter 9.

7.2   RISK AND RETURN ON A PORTFOLIO

Chapter 6 suggested that the return and risk on a single asset can be measured by the mean and variance of the return on the asset. When we consider a portfolio of two assets, we are interested in the mean and variance of the return on the portfolio. This section shows how those parameters are computed.

Return Probabilities for a Pair of Assets

We begin the analysis by postulating what is known as a *joint probability distribution* for the returns on a pair of assets. Suppose R_1 can occur in any of n discrete states $(R_{1,1}, R_{1,2}, \cdots R_{1,n})$, and that R_2 can occur in any of m discrete states $(R_{2,1}, R_{2,2}, \cdots R_{2,m})$. (It is not necessary that $n = m$.) Let $p(R_{1,i}, R_{2,j})$ be the probability of the event where the first asset returns $R_{1,i}$ and the second asset returns $R_{2,j}$. There will be nm such events, or pairs of returns. The table in the beginning of Example 7.1 shows a set of probabilities for the returns on a pair of assets. In that table the probability that R_1 will be 10 percent (state $i = 2$) *and* that R_2 will be 40 percent (state $j = 3$) is 15 percent, or .15. The particular combination of $R_1 = .0$ and $R_2 = .4$ (state $i = 1$ and $j = 3$)

---

[3] Although Equation (7.2) always holds as a matter of definition, the probability distribution of R will belong to the same class as the distributions of R_1 and R_2 only if those distributions are in the stable Paretian class with the same characteristic parameter α. See Jensen (1969, p. 173, fn. 16). The only stable Paretian distribution with finite variance is the normal or gaussian distribution.

is impossible in the example, because the probability is 0 that those returns will occur simultaneously.

The collection of nm probabilities $p(R_{1,i}, R_{2,j})$ for $i = 1, \cdots, n$ and $j = 1, \cdots, m$ is the joint probability distribution of the returns on the first and second assets. It is called a *joint* distribution because the definition of an event is a pair of returns rather than the return on a single asset. That is, we specify the probability that a particular value of R_1 *and* a particular value of R_2 will occur simultaneously. Since one of the nm possible pairs of returns must occur, we require[4]

$$\sum_{i=1}^{n} \sum_{j=1}^{m} p(R_{1,i}, R_{2,j}) = 1 \qquad (7.3)$$

This equation just says that the sum of the probabilities, taken over all possible events, is unity. Observe that the sum of the nine probabilities in Example 7.1 is indeed unity.

In some cases the joint probability distribution of returns is separable into probability distributions for the two assets individually, so that the probability of the event $R_1 = R_{1,i}$ and $R_2 = R_{2,j}$ can be written as the probability that $R_1 = R_{1,i}$ times the probability that $R_2 = R_{2,j}$. In this case the returns of the two assets are called *statistically independent events*.[5] Such cases are rare in practice, because the prices of common stocks generally move up or down together. It is therefore necessary to state the probabilities as joint probabilities.

The Expected Return on a Portfolio

Having specified the probability that a given pair of returns will occur, we are now ready to derive the expected return on a portfolio of two assets. The expected portfolio return is a weighted average of the expected returns on the individual assets. We need to define those individual expected returns.

Given the joint probability of pairs of asset returns, we define the expected return on the individual assets as

$$\mu_1 = \text{Exp } [R_1] = \sum_{i=1}^{n} \sum_{j=1}^{m} R_{1,i} p(R_{1,i}, R_{2,j}) \qquad (7.4a)$$

$$\mu_2 = \text{Exp } [R_2] = \sum_{i=1}^{n} \sum_{j=1}^{m} R_{2,j} p(R_{1,i}, R_{2,j}) \qquad (7.4b)$$

Equation (7.4a) says that to compute the expected return μ_1 or Exp $[R_1]$ on the first asset, we should take a probability-weighted average of a number as-

---

[4] The notation $\sum_{i=1}^{n} \sum_{j=1}^{m} x_{ij}$ means the sum of the x_{ij} series over all possible combinations of i and j, for i equal to 1 to i equal to n, and from j equal to 1 to j equal to m.

[5] See Mood, Graybill, and Boes (1974, p. 150).

EXAMPLE 7.1

RISK AND RETURN FOR A PORTFOLIO OF TWO ASSETS

Consider two assets, labeled 1 and 2, such that the return on asset 1 can take on $n = 3$ values and the return on asset 2 can take on $m = 3$ values. The $p(R_{1,i}, R_{2,j})$ probabilities in the joint probability distribution of the returns are given by the entries in the following table:

	j	1	2	3
	$R_{2,j}$	.0	.20	.40
i	$R_{1,i}$			
1	.0	.05	.05	.00
2	.10	.05	.30	.15
3	.20	.05	.15	.20

Thus, for example, the probability that $R_1 = .10$ and $R_2 = .20$ is .30, or 30 percent. This figure is located where $i = 2$ and $j = 2$ in the table.

From Equation (7.4a) we have as the expected return on the first asset

$$\mu_1 = R_{1,1} \sum_{j=1}^{m} p(R_{1,1}, R_{2,j})$$

$$+ R_{1,2} \sum_{j=1}^{m} p(R_{1,2}, R_{2,j})$$

$$+ R_{1,3} \sum_{j=1}^{m} p(R_{1,3}, R_{2,j})$$

$$= .00(.05 + .05 + .00)$$

$$+ .10(.05 + .30 + .15)$$

$$+ .20(.05 + .15 + .20)$$

$$= .13$$

and similarly, $\mu_2 = .24$.

From Equation (7.7a) we have as the variance of return on the first asset

$$\sigma_1^2 = (R_{1,1} - \mu_1)^2 \sum_{j=1}^{m} p(R_{1,1}, R_{2,j})$$

$$+ (R_{1,2} - \mu_1)^2 \sum_{j=1}^{m} p(R_{1,2}, R_{2,j})$$

$$+ (R_{1,3} - \mu_1)^2 \sum_{j=1}^{m} p(R_{1,3}, R_{2,j})$$

$$= (-.13)^2(.05 + .05 + .00)$$

$$+ (-.03)^2(.05 + .30 + .15)$$

$$+ (.07)^2(.05 + .15 + .20)$$

$$= .0041$$

so that $\sigma_1 = .064$. Similarly, $\sigma_2^2 = .0184$ and $\sigma_2 = .136$. Note that $\mu_1 < \mu_2$, so that asset 2 has a greater expected return, but $\sigma_1 < \sigma_2$, so that the return on asset 2 is relatively more uncertain.

EXAMPLE 7.1 *(Continued)*

From Equation (7.8) we have as the covariance of returns on the two assets

$$\text{Cov}\ [R_1,\ R_2] = \sum_{i=1}^{n} \sum_{j=1}^{m} (R_{1,i} - \mu_1)(R_{2,j} - \mu_2)p(R_{1,i},\ R_{2,j})$$

$$= -.13(-.24)(.05) + -.13(-.04)(.05) + -.13(.16)(.00)$$
$$+ -.03(-.24)(.05) + -.03(-.04)(.30) + -.03(.16)(.15)$$
$$+ .07(-.24)(.05) + .07(-.04)(.15) + .07(.16)(.20)$$
$$= .0028$$

For a portfolio composed of assets 1 and 2, the relation between portfolio composition and portfolio risk and return is described by the pair of equations

$$\mu = x_1\mu_1 + x_2\mu_2$$
$$= x_1(.13) + x_2(.24)$$
$$\sigma^2 = x_1^2\sigma_1^2 + x_2^2\sigma_2^2 + 2x_1x_2\ \text{Cov}\ [R_1,\ R_2]$$
$$= x_1^2(.0041) + x_2^2(.0184) + 2x_1x_2(.0028)$$

If we consider eleven different portfolio allocations, given by $x_2 = .0, .1, .2, \ldots, .9, 1.0$ and $x_1 = 1 - x_2$, we can compute the (μ, σ) pairs as follows:

x_1	x_2	μ	σ
1.0	.0	.130	.0640
.9	.1	.141	.0633
.8	.2	.152	.0652
.7	.3	.163	.0696
.6	.4	.174	.0759
.5	.5	.185	.0838
.4	.6	.196	.0929
.3	.7	.207	.1028
.2	.8	.218	.1133
.1	.9	.229	.1243
.0	1.0	.240	.1360

This table shows explicitly the trade-off between portfolio risk and portfolio return as the composition of the portfolio is varied.

sociated with each of the nm events. For the event where $R_1 = R_{1,i}$ and $R_2 = R_{2,j}$, the number is $R_{1,i}$, the realized return on the first asset. In computing μ_2, the number associated with the same event is $R_{2,j}$, the realized return on the second asset. Example 7.1 shows how Equation (7.4) is used to compute the expected return on an asset from a given probability distribution of pairs of returns.

We can also define the expected return on the portfolio as a whole. If the fractional portfolio allocation is (x_1, x_2), then the portfolio return which occurs from a realization of the event where $R_1 = R_{1,i}$ and $R_2 = R_{2,j}$ is $x_1R_{1,i} + x_2R_{2,j}$.

The expected return on the portfolio is thus

$$\mu = \text{Exp } [R] = \sum_{i=1}^{n} \sum_{j=1}^{m} (x_1 R_{1,i} + x_2 R_{2,j}) p(R_{1,i}, R_{2,j}) \tag{7.5}$$

This expression shows that the expected return on the portfolio depends on (1) the joint probability distribution of the returns on the individual assets and (2) the allocation of the portfolio.

Equation (7.5) can be reduced to a simpler form by using the definitions of μ_1 and μ_2 given in Equation (7.4). It can be shown[6] that

$$\mu = x_1 \mu_1 + x_2 \mu_2 \tag{7.6}$$

The expected return μ on the portfolio is now seen to be a weighted-average combination of the expected returns on the individual assets, where the weights are the fractional allocations of the portfolio to the respective assets.

Note the similarity between Equations (7.2) and (7.6). The former is a statement of the relation between the realized returns on the assets and the realized return on the portfolio. The latter, however, is a statement of the relation between expected returns. Equation (7.6) shows how a change in the composition of the portfolio affects the expected return on the portfolio.

The Variance of the Return on a Portfolio

We next see how the risk of a portfolio is related to the risk on the assets in the portfolio. This relation involves the correlation of the uncertain returns, as well as the variances of the returns on the individual assets.

The correlation of the returns on a pair of assets is extremely important to the variance of the return on a portfolio of those assets. Consider, for example, the pairs of returns shown in Figure 7.1. Since each of those pairs has an equal probability of occurring, we would say that the return on the first asset varies inversely with the return on the second asset. When one happens to be high, the other is likely to be low. The return on a portfolio evenly divided between those two assets may be relatively stable, because we would make up on one asset what we would lose on the other. On the other hand, if the returns are positively related (so that they are likely to be either both high or both low), we either win big or lose big. This is shown in Figure 7.2. In this case the return associated with almost any portfolio allocation is likely to be quite uncertain.

---

[6] From Equation (7.5) we have

$$\mu = \sum_{i=1}^{n} \sum_{j=1}^{m} x_1 R_{1,i} p(R_{1,i}, R_{2,j}) + \sum_{i=1}^{n} \sum_{j=1}^{m} x_2 R_{2,j} p(R_{1,i}, R_{2,j})$$

$$= x_1 \sum_{i=1}^{n} \sum_{j=1}^{m} R_{1,i} p(R_{1,i}, R_{2,j}) + x_2 \sum_{i=1}^{n} \sum_{j=1}^{m} R_{2,j} p(R_{1,i}, R_{2,j})$$

Identifying the double sums from Equation (7.4) gives Equation (7.6).

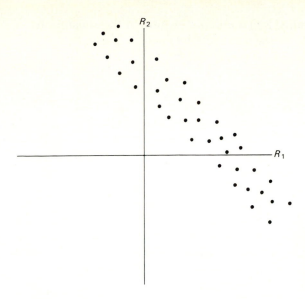

FIGURE 7.1
Two assets with inversely
correlated returns. Each point
has an equal probability of
occurring.

To obtain the variance of the return on a portfolio, we first specify the variances of the returns on the individual assets in the portfolio and a third parameter related to the correlation of the asset returns. Given the joint probability of pairs of asset returns, we define the *variance* of return on each of the assets individually as

$$\sigma_1^2 = \text{Var } [R_1] = \sum_{i=1}^{n} \sum_{j=1}^{m} (R_{1,i} - \mu_1)^2 p(R_{1,i}, R_{2,j}) \qquad (7.7a)$$

$$\sigma_2^2 = \text{Var } [R_2] = \sum_{i=1}^{n} \sum_{j=1}^{m} (R_{2,j} - \mu_2)^2 p(R_{1,i}, R_{2,j}) \qquad (7.7b)$$

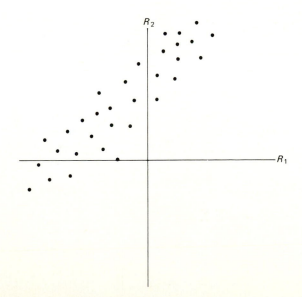

FIGURE 7.2
Two assets with positively
correlated returns. Each point has
an equal probability of occurring.

These variances are a probability-weighted combination of the squared deviations of the realized returns from their expected values.

We can also define the *covariance* of the returns:

$$\text{Cov } [R_1, R_2] = \sum_{i=1}^{n} \sum_{j=1}^{m} (R_{1,i} - \mu_1)(R_{2,j} - \mu_2)p(R_{1,i}, R_{2,j}) \qquad (7.8)$$

The covariance will be positive if R_1 and R_2 are likely to be either higher or lower than their expected values simultaneously. It will be negative if R_1 is likely to be higher than its expected value when R_2 is lower, or vice versa. The covariance of the returns shown in Figure 7.1 is negative, because R_1 and R_2 vary inversely with each other. The covariance of the returns shown in Figure 7.2 is positive, because there the returns are either higher or lower than average simultaneously. The covariance parameter is our summary measure of the correlation between pairs of asset returns. It can be shown that a sufficient, although not necessary, condition for a zero covariance is that the returns on the assets are statistically independent of each other.[7]

Example 7.1 shows how Equation (7.7) is used to compute the variance of the return on an asset and how Equation (7.8) is used to compute the covariance of the returns on a pair of assets.

With the definitions of Equations (7.7) and (7.8) we are ready to derive an expression for the variance of the return on a portfolio. That variance is the probability-weighted average of the squared differences between the realized returns on the portfolio and the expected return on the portfolio:

$$\sigma^2 = \text{Var } [R] = \sum_{i=1}^{n} \sum_{j=1}^{m} (x_1 R_{1,i} + x_2 R_{2,j} - x_1 \mu_1 - x_2 \mu_2)^2 p(R_{1,i}, R_{2,j}) \quad (7.9)$$

Using Equations (7.7) and (7.8) it can be shown[8] that this definition of σ^2 reduces to

[7] Statistical independence is both necessary and sufficient for a zero covariance when the asset returns are normally distributed.

[8]
$$\sigma^2 = \text{Var } [R] = \sum_{i=1}^{n} \sum_{j=1}^{m} (x_1 R_{1,i} + x_2 R_{2,j} - x_1 \mu_1 - x_2 \mu_2)^2 p(R_{1,i}, R_{2,j})$$

$$= \sum_{i=1}^{n} \sum_{j=1}^{m} [x_1(R_{1,i} - \mu_1) + x_2(R_{2,j} - \mu^2)]^2 p(R_{1,i}, R_{2,j})$$

$$= \sum_{i=1}^{n} \sum_{j=1}^{m} [x_1^2(R_{1,i} - \mu_1)^2 + x_2^2(R_{2,j} - \mu_2)^2 + 2x_1 x_2(R_{1,i} - \mu_1)(R_{2,j} - \mu_2)] p(R_{1,i}, R_{2,j})$$

$$= x_1^2 \sum_{i=1}^{n} \sum_{j=1}^{m} (R_{1,i} - \mu_1)^2 p(R_{1,i}, R_{2,j}) + x_2^2 \sum_{i=1}^{n} \sum_{j=1}^{m} (R_{2,j} - \mu_2)^2 p(R_{1,i}, R_{2,j})$$

$$+ 2x_1 x_2 \sum_{i=1}^{n} \sum_{j=1}^{m} (R_{1,i} - \mu_1)(R_{2,j} - \mu_2) p(R_{1,i}, R_{2,j})$$

Using Equation (7.7) to identify the first two terms of the above equation for σ^2 and using Equation (7.8) to identify the last term gives Equation (7.10).

$$\sigma^2 = x_1^2\sigma_1^2 + x_2^2\sigma_2^2 + 2x_1x_2 \text{ Cov } [R_1, R_2] \tag{7.10}$$

Equation (7.10) shows how the risk exposure of a portfolio, as measured by its variance of return, varies as a function of (1) the composition of the portfolio and (2) the variances and the covariance of returns on the assets in the portfolio. Asset variances are appropriate measures of risk when individual assets are considered in isolation from each other. When assets are mixed in a portfolio, however, attention should be focused on the variance of the return on the portfolio as a whole, which depends on the correlation of the uncertain asset returns as well as on the individual variances of those returns.

We have now derived two equations, one for the expected return on a portfolio of two assets and another for the variance of the return on a portfolio of two assets:

$$\mu = x_1\mu_1 + x_2\mu_2$$
$$\sigma^2 = x_1^2\sigma_1^2 + x_2^2\sigma_2^2 + 2x_1x_2 \text{ Cov } [R_1, R_2]$$

For given values of μ_1, μ_2, σ_1, σ_2, and Cov $[R_1, R_2]$, these two equations show how the expected return μ and variance of return σ^2 vary as the allocation (x_1, x_2) of the portfolio is altered. The concluding part of Example 7.1 shows how the equations are used to compute a set of possible μ-σ combinations. In the next section we analyze some special cases of the general equations for μ and σ^2.

7.3   ANALYSIS OF SOME SPECIAL CASES

In this section we consider some special cases of the risk/return structure of portfolios allocated between two assets. We assume throughout that $\mu_1 < \mu_2$, so that the first asset has an expected return lower than the second, and that $0 < \sigma_1 < \sigma_2$, so that the return on the second asset is more uncertain than the return on the first asset and the first asset is not riskless. We also assume the investor holds nonnegative amounts of both assets, so that $x_1 \geq 0$ and $x_2 \geq 0$. The requirement that $x_1 + x_2 = 1$ continues to apply.

The Correlation Coefficient

The analyses in this section will be easier to understand if we introduce a new number to replace the covariance. When $\sigma_1 > 0$ and $\sigma_2 > 0$, the *correlation coefficient* ρ is defined as

$$\rho = \frac{\text{Cov } [R_1, R_2]}{\sigma_1\sigma_2} \tag{7.11}$$

It can be shown that ρ must lie within the interval between -1 and $+1$, including possibly one of the boundary values of -1 or $+1$.

The reason for introducing the correlation coefficient is that it provides a simple way to scale the covariance. We can get an idea of the "size" of the covariance if we write it as $\rho\sigma_1\sigma_2$. A value of $\rho = 0$ implies the covariance of returns is zero, so that the return on one asset is unrelated to the return on the other asset. An example of two uncorrelated events is flipping a pair of coins. The outcome of the toss of the first coin (heads or tails) has no effect on the outcome of the toss of the second coin. A value of $\rho = +1$ implies the two returns move in a perfectly synchronous fashion. For example, the return on one Treasury bill is exactly the same as the return on another Treasury bill if both have the same maturity date. If $\rho = -1$, the two returns move in lock-step, but inversely.

Using the coefficient of correlation, we can write the equations for the risk and return on a portfolio as

$$\mu = x_1\mu_1 + x_2\mu_2 \tag{7.12a}$$
$$\sigma^2 = x_1^2\sigma_1^2 + x_2^2\sigma_2^2 + 2x_1x_2\rho\sigma_1\sigma_2 \tag{7.12b}$$

We investigate in this section the behavior of these two equations for the special cases where $\rho = +1$, $\rho = -1$, and $\rho = 0$. Our objective is demonstrating how the coefficient of correlation (and hence the covariance) between the random returns on the two assets affects the opportunity of an investor to trade off risk against return by altering the composition of his portfolio.

Perfect Positive Correlation, $\rho = 1$

Consider Equation (7.12b) when the returns on the two assets are perfectly correlated. We have

$$\sigma^2 = x_1^2\sigma_1^2 + x_2^2\sigma_2^2 + 2x_1x_2\sigma_1\sigma_2$$
$$= (x_1\sigma_1 + x_2\sigma_2)^2$$

Since the term inside the parentheses cannot be negative when x_1 and x_2 are both nonnegative, the standard deviation of the return on the portfolio is

$$\sigma = x_1\sigma_1 + x_2\sigma_2 \tag{7.13}$$

Equation (7.13) shows how the standard deviation of the return on the portfolio varies as a function of the composition of the portfolio. Equation (7.12a), which does not include ρ as an argument, shows how the expected return of the portfolio varies as a function of the composition of the portfolio.

If we compute the μ and σ of many portfolio allocations and plot those pairs of points, we obtain Figure 7.3. This figure shows we can increase the expected return on a portfolio only by increasing the risk exposure of the portfolio. The cost of additional expected return, in terms of increased risk, is constant at all

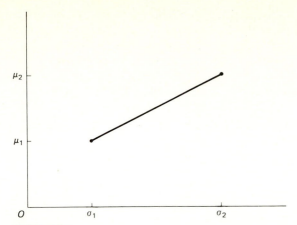

FIGURE 7.3
Portfolio possibility locus for $\rho = -1$.

risk levels since the plot is a straight line. Figure 7.3 is called a *portfolio possibility locus*. It shows all the μ-σ combinations attainable from different portfolio allocations.

Perfect Negative Correlation, $\rho = -1$

Consider next Equation (7.12*b*) for the case when the returns on the two assets are perfectly negatively correlated. We then have

$$\sigma^2 = x_1^2\sigma_1^2 + x_2^2\sigma_2^2 - 2x_1x_2\sigma_1\sigma_2$$
$$= (x_1\sigma_1 - x_2\sigma_2)^2$$
or
$$\sigma = |x_1\sigma_1 - x_2\sigma_2| \qquad (7.14)$$

The vertical bars denote absolute value and are used because the standard deviation is always taken as the positive square root of the variance. Equation (7.14) shows how the standard deviation of the return on the portfolio varies as a function of the composition of the portfolio. Equation (7.12*a*) does the same for the expected return on the portfolio.

If we selected many portfolio allocations, computed the μ and σ values associated with each allocation, and plotted those values, we would obtain the portfolio possibility locus shown in Figure 7.4. Suppose we started with a portfolio devoted entirely to asset 1 and then sold off some of that asset to diversify into asset 2. This reallocation would move us along the lower branch of the locus, increasing our expected return and simultaneously decreasing our risk exposure. This, clearly, is a favorable course of conduct.

There is one portfolio which drives risk to zero in the case of $\rho = -1$. Consider the allocation

$$x_1^* = \frac{\sigma_2}{\sigma_1 + \sigma_2} \tag{7.15a}$$

$$x_2^* = \frac{\sigma_1}{\sigma_1 + \sigma_2} \tag{7.15b}$$

This is a feasible allocation because $x_1^* + x_2^* = 1$. If we evaluate the standard deviation of the return on this portfolio by Equation (7.14), we find $\sigma = 0$. Thus, portfolio (7.15) has zero risk. This is true in spite of the fact that each of the assets individually are risky.

By mixing the assets in an appropriate combination we can eliminate completely any uncertainty about the return on a portfolio of two assets whose returns are perfectly negatively correlated. This illustrates why the covariance cannot be neglected in determining the variance of the return on a portfolio.

Once the fraction of the portfolio allocated to the second asset exceeds x_2^*, the portfolio possibility locus bends back onto the upper branch shown in Figure 7.4. Greater expected return can be obtained only at the cost of greater exposure to risk on this upper branch.

Zero Correlation, $\rho = 0$

Suppose the returns on the two assets are uncorrelated. From Equation (7.12b) we see that the variance of the return on a portfolio is

$$\sigma^2 = x_1^2 \sigma_1^2 + x_2^2 \sigma_2^2 \tag{7.16}$$

In view of our assumption that both assets are risky, so that $\sigma_1 > 0$ and $\sigma_2 > 0$, Equation (7.16) shows that risk cannot be eliminated from the portfolio, since

FIGURE 7.4
Portfolio possibility locus for $\rho = -1$.

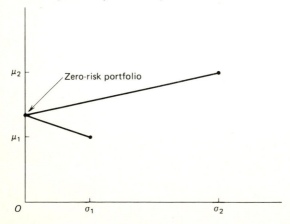

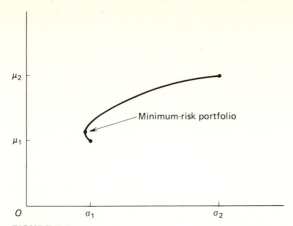

FIGURE 7.5
Portfolio possibility locus for $\rho = 0$.

x_1 and x_2 cannot both be zero simultaneously. Figure 7.5 shows the portfolio possibility locus for the case $\rho = 0$.

Although risk can never be eliminated completely from a portfolio of two assets with uncorrelated returns, it can be reduced to a value less than the risk on either of the individual assets in the portfolio. Consider the portfolio allocation

$$x_1^* = \frac{\sigma_2^2}{\sigma_1^2 + \sigma_2^2} \qquad (7.17a)$$

$$x_2^* = \frac{\sigma_1^2}{\sigma_1^2 + \sigma_2^2} \qquad (7.17b)$$

If we evaluate σ^2 by Equation (7.16) for this portfolio, we have

$$\sigma^2 = \frac{\sigma_1^2 \sigma_2^2}{\sigma_1^2 + \sigma_2^2}$$

or $$\sigma^2 = \sigma_1^2 \frac{\sigma_2^2}{\sigma_1^2 + \sigma_2^2} \qquad (7.18a)$$

Equation (7.18a) implies $\sigma^2 < \sigma_1^2$. We also have

$$\sigma^2 = \sigma_2^2 \frac{\sigma_1^2}{\sigma_1^2 + \sigma_2^2} \qquad (7.18b)$$

which implies $\sigma^2 < \sigma_2^2$ as well. Portfolio (7.17) thus has less uncertainty of return than either of its constituent assets. In fact, it turns out that portfolio (7.17) is the minimum-risk portfolio.[9]

Arbitrary Correlation

Thus far we have developed portfolio possibility loci for the special cases of $\rho = -1$, $\rho = 0$, and $\rho = +1$. When ρ is unspecified, the relation between the portfolio allocation and the risk/return characteristics of the portfolio is given by the general equations

$$\mu = x_1\mu_1 + x_2\mu_2 \tag{7.19a}$$
$$\sigma^2 = x_1^2\sigma_1^2 + x_2^2\sigma_2^2 + 2x_1x_2\rho\sigma_1\sigma_2 \tag{7.19b}$$

As shown in Figure 7.6, the portfolio possibility locus will be some intermediate case of the special loci analyzed above.

When $\rho > -1$, it is impossible to eliminate risk completely from a portfolio of two assets when both assets are held in nonnegative amounts. To see this, observe that Equation (7.19b) can be expressed as

$$\sigma^2 = (x_1\sigma_1 - x_2\sigma_2)^2 + 2(1 + \rho)x_1x_2\sigma_1\sigma_2 \tag{7.20}$$

Since we require the holding of nonnegative amounts of each asset, the first and second terms in Equation (7.20) will both be nonnegative for all portfolio allocations. Thus, σ^2 can be zero only if both terms are zero simultaneously. However, since $\rho > -1$ by hypothesis, the second term is zero only if either x_1 or x_2 is zero, in which case the first term is strictly positive. Thus, $\sigma^2 > 0$ for all possible portfolios when $\rho > -1$, $x_1 \geq 0$, and $x_2 \leq 0$.

---

[9] Using $x_1 = 1 - x_2$ in Equation (7.16) gives

$$\sigma^2 = (1-x_2)^2\sigma_1^2 + x_2^2\sigma_2^2$$

Minimizing σ with respect to x_2 requires $d\sigma/dx_2 = 0$. Computing that derivative by the chain rule, we have

$$\frac{d\sigma}{dx_2} = \frac{d(\sigma^2)/dx_2}{d(\sigma^2)/d\sigma}$$
$$= \frac{-2(1 - x_2)\sigma_1^2 + 2x_2\sigma_2^2}{2\sigma}$$

Since $\sigma > 0$ for all allocations, the minimum-risk portfolio is found by solving the equation

$$0 = -2(1-x_2^*)\sigma_1^2 + 2x_2^*\sigma_2^2$$

which has the solution

$$x_2^* = \frac{\sigma_1^2}{\sigma_1^2 + \sigma_2^2}$$

This corresponds with portfolio (7.17), showing that that portfolio is, in fact, the minimum-risk portfolio.

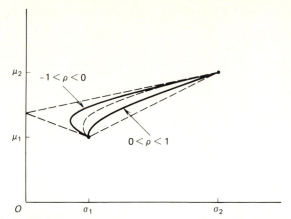

FIGURE 7.6
Portfolio possibility locus for arbitrary ρ. Dashed
lines show the special cases of Figures 7.3, 7.4,
and 7.5.

7.4   SHORT SELLING

In the preceding sections of this chapter we assumed an investor held positive
amounts of two assets or else allocated all his wealth to a single asset. This
implies x_1 and x_2 are both nonnegative. In this section we consider the
consequences of allowing an investor to hold *negative* amounts of an asset
through a device known as *short selling*. Short selling is a sale of securities not
owned by the seller, i.e., of securities which must be borrowed to effect
delivery to the buyer.

Portfolio Combinations with Short Selling

As in Section 7.1, assume an investor has initial wealth W. Suppose at the
beginning of the period the investor goes to a current holder of the first asset
and borrows an amount B of that asset, where the amount B of the borrowing is
calculated as the number of units of the asset borrowed valued at the current
market price per unit. The borrower stipulates to the lender of the securities
that he will return the *same number of units* of the borrowed asset at the end of
the period. Note that his liability to the lender is denominated in units of the
first asset and not in dollars.

 If the investor sells the borrowed securities for cash, he can use that cash,
plus his own initial wealth, to buy a position in the second asset. At this point
the investor has wealth $W_2 = W + B$ committed to the second asset and wealth
$W_1 = -B$ committed to the first asset. The total value of his investments equals
his initial wealth, that is, $W_1 + W_2 = W$.

 If the net return on the first asset over the period is R_1, the *value* of the investor's liability to the lender will be $(1 + R_1)B$ at the end of the period. For ex-

EXAMPLE 7.2

SHORT SELLING

Over the course of an investment period the prices of two stocks increased as follows:

Stock	Beginning-of-period price	End-of-period price
ABC	$30/share	$60/share
XYZ	$90/share	$100/share

Suppose an investor initially had $30,000 in cash, sold 100 shares of XYZ short, and used the proceeds of the short sale plus his cash to buy ABC. The proceeds on the short sale would be $9000 (that is, $90 per share × 100 shares). Adding the $30,000 cash to these proceeds, he could buy 1300 shares of ABC ($39,000 = $30 per share × 1300 shares). His position at the beginning of the period was as follows:

Stock	Position	Value
ABC	long 1300	$39,000
XYZ	short 100	−9,000
		Net worth = $30,000

At the end of the period the investor's position was as follows:

Stock	Position	Value
ABC	long 1300	$78,000
XYZ	short 100	−10,000
		Net worth = $68,000

The return on the investor's initial net worth was

$$R = \frac{68{,}000 - 30{,}000}{30{,}000}$$
$$= 1.26, \text{ or } 126\%$$

This return can also be computed from the returns on the individual stocks and the investor's initial allocation of wealth. The returns on the stocks were

$$R_{ABC} = \frac{60 - 30}{30}$$
$$= 1.00, \text{ or } 100\%$$
$$R_{XYZ} = \frac{100 - 90}{90}$$
$$= .111, \text{ or } 11.1\%$$

EXAMPLE 7.2 *(Continued)*

The investor's initial allocation of wealth was

$$x_{ABC} = \frac{\$39{,}000}{\$30{,}000}$$

$$= 1.30$$

$$x_{XYZ} = \frac{-\$9000}{\$30{,}000}$$

$$= -.30$$

Using Equation (7.21) gives

$$R = x_{ABC}R_{ABC} + x_{XYZ}R_{XYZ}$$
$$= 1.30(1.00) + (-.30)(.111)$$
$$= 1.26, \text{ or } 126\%$$

ample, if the investor borrowed 200 shares of a stock valued at \$50 a share at the beginning of the period, we would have $B = \$10{,}000$. If the return on the stock over the period was 10 percent, so that $R_1 = .10$, then the investor's liability to the lender of the stock would be \$11,000 [that is, $(1 + .10) \times \$10{,}000$] at the end of the period. The *net* change in the investor's liability to the lender of the stock would be $R_1B = .10 \times \$10{,}000 = \$1000$. It follows that the net change in the wealth of the investor due to his borrowing of the first asset is $-R_1B = R_1W_1$. His net change in wealth due to his investment in the second asset is $R_2(W + B) = R_2W_2$. His end-of-period wealth is therefore

$$W' = W - R_1B + R_2(W + B)$$
$$= W + R_1W_1 + R_2W_2$$

The net return over the period on his portfolio is $R = (W' - W)/W$, or

$$R = \frac{W_1R_1 + W_2R_2}{W}$$

Letting $x_i = W_i/W$, this becomes

$$R = x_1R_1 + x_2R_2 \tag{7.21}$$

This equation is the same as Equation (7.2), except that we now have $x_1 < 0$ because $x_1 = W_1/W = -B/W$. In addition, $x_2 > 1$ because $x_2 = W_2/W = (W + B)/W$. Note that $x_1 + x_2 = 1$ as before. Example 7.2 gives a numerical illustration of Equation (7.21).

The practice described above is known as short selling. In Example 7.2 the investor short sold the second asset. Short selling is the sale of securities which the seller does not actually own. In borrowing securities for delivery on the short sale, the short seller agrees to return them to the lender either at a specific future date or, most commonly, at his discretion or upon demand by the lender. The short seller also agrees to pay the lender any cash and noncash distributions made by the issuer of the securities during the borrowing period. Thus, the lender does not suffer a loss of such distributions during the period of the loan, and he is made whole when the loan is terminated.[10]

Those who lend securities to short sellers demand and receive collateral on their loans. Loans of stock are usually collateralized by an amount of cash equal to the market value of the borrowed stock. The lender of the securities is free to invest this cash but must return it when he gets back his securities. Use of the cash compensates the lender for his willingness to lend securities.

Loans of government securities, including Treasury and federal agency issues, are usually collateralized with comparable securities rather than with cash. To induce a lender to loan his securities, the borrower, by convention in the government debt markets, pays the lender of securities a fee at the rate of $1/2$ percent per annum on the principal value of the borrowed issues, prorated over the duration of the borrowing.[11]

The Effect of Short Selling on Portfolio Possibility Loci

In Section 7.2 we developed two equations relating the risk and return on a portfolio to (1) the allocation of the portfolio and (2) the statistical characteristics of the returns on the assets in the portfolio. Nothing in that development relied on the assumption that the investor held nonnegative amounts of both assets. Thus, the equations

$$\mu = x_1\mu_1 + x_2\mu_2 \tag{7.22a}$$
$$\sigma^2 = x_1^2\sigma_1^2 + x_2^2\sigma_2^2 + 2x_1x_2\rho\sigma_1\sigma_2 \tag{7.22b}$$

remain valid as long as $x_1 + x_2 = 1$, even if $x_1 < 0$ or if $x_2 < 0$.

In Section 7.3 we analyzed three special cases of Equation (7.22): when the correlation coefficient ρ was +1, when it was 0, and when it was −1. The only change in those analyses is that Equation (7.13), giving the value of σ for the case of $\rho = +1$, must now be written

$$\sigma = |x_1\sigma_1 + x_2\sigma_2| \tag{7.23}$$

---

[10] Short sales of most securities, including especially stock listed on national securities exchanges, are limited by the margin requirements of Regulation T of the Federal Reserve System. Rule 431 of the New York Stock Exchange also prescribes margin requirements for the maintenance of short positions by customers of member firms. These margin requirements exist to protect the lender of securities in the event of price rises and to control the amount of credit available from short selling. The computational aspects of margin requirements are described by Kerekes (1970), Ritteureiser (1977), and Meeker (1932).

[11] Securities to cover short sales can also be obtained, in the Treasury securities markets, by entering into reverse repurchase agreements. See Lucas, Jones, and Thurston (1977).

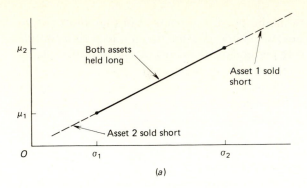

(a)

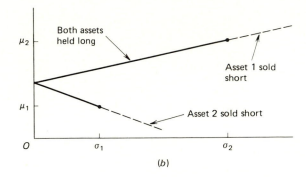

(b)

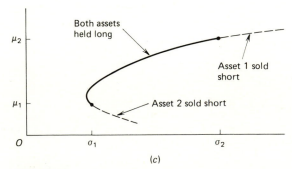

(c)

FIGURE 7.7
Portfolio possibility loci with short setting.

Observe that for the case of perfect positive correlation, the portfolio allocation

$$x_1^* = \frac{-\sigma_2}{\sigma_1 - \sigma_2} \qquad (7.24a)$$

$$x_2^* = \frac{\sigma_1}{\sigma_1 - \sigma_2} \qquad (7.24b)$$

will bear no risk. This may be verified by evaluating, with Equation (7.23), the standard deviation of the return on the portfolio specified in Equations (7.24). x_1^* will be negative if $\sigma_1 > \sigma_2$. Thus, while it is possible to eliminate risk entirely from a portfolio of two assets with perfectly positively correlated returns, to do so requires the short sale of the more volatile asset.

In the discussion following Equation (7.20) we observed that it is impossible to eliminate risk entirely from a portfolio of two assets when $\rho > -1$ and both assets are held in nonnegative amounts. We have just seen that risk can also be eliminated by short selling when $\rho = +1$. These two polar cases are, however, unique. As long as $|\rho| < 1$, it is impossible to eliminate risk from a portfolio of two assets either with or without short selling.

When we introduce the possibility of short selling, the portfolio possibility locus expands. Figure 7.7 shows the portfolio possibility loci for the three values of the correlation coefficient ($\rho = +1$, $\rho = -1$, and $\rho = 0$) analyzed in Section 7.3. The μ-σ combinations obtained from a portfolio with one asset sold short lie on the dashed parts of the loci. The μ-σ combinations from portfolios consisting of nonnegative amounts of both assets lie on the solid parts of the loci.

CHAPTER SUMMARY

This chapter has extended the concepts of risk and return from the single asset analyzed in Chapter 6 to portfolios of two assets. The three principal results were (1) an equation for the realized return on a portfolio:

$$R = x_1 R_1 + x_2 R_2 \tag{7.25a}$$

(2) an equation for the expected return on a portfolio:

$$\mu = x_1 \mu_1 + x_2 \mu_2 \tag{7.25b}$$

and (3) an equation for the variance of the return on a portfolio:

$$\sigma^2 = x_1^2 \sigma_1^2 + x_2^2 \sigma_2^2 + 2 x_1 x_2 \, \text{Cov} \, [R_1, R_2] \tag{7.25c}$$

The realized return, the expected return, and the variance of return all depend on the allocation of the portfolio.

The fractions x_1 and x_2 are the fractional allocations of initial wealth to the first and second assets, respectively. The sum $x_1 + x_2$ must equal unity, because an investor must allocate his entire wealth to one or the other of the assets. (If he did not want to allocate all his wealth to the two assets, he would have to find some other way to "store" his residual wealth, e.g., a demand deposit account or cash in his mattress. This would put him in a three-asset world, a case considered in Chapter 9.)

Equation (7.25a) for the realized return on the portfolio is no more than an accounting identity. The substantive results are the equations for the mean and variance of the return on the portfolio. The key step for deriving Equations (7.25b) and (7.25c) was the assumption of a joint probability distribution describing the likelihood of different *pairs* of returns on the first and second assets.

The risk exposure of a particular portfolio, as measured by the variance of return on that portfolio, is not a function only of the variances of the returns on the constituent assets. Portfolio risk is also a function of the covariance of asset returns. This was illustrated by analyzing the quite different portfolio possibility loci which result from different correlation coefficients. To say that the return on an asset is highly uncertain is not to say that the asset is risky *in a portfolio context*. The asset may be negatively correlated with the return on some other asset and hence may tend to stabilize the return on a portfolio consisting of both assets.

Portfolios of two assets can also be constructed by short selling one or the other of the assets. Short sales are accomplished by borrowing an asset in order to sell it. The ability to undertake short sales extends an investor's portfolio possibility locus beyond the μ-σ combinations which can be obtained by holding only nonnegative amounts of the two assets.

CHAPTER 8

SELECTION OF AN OPTIMAL PORTFOLIO

The previous chapter showed how risk and return on a portfolio of two assets depends on the composition of the portfolio and on the joint probability distribution of the returns on the assets in the portfolio. The problem for the investor is to choose that portfolio allocation which leads to the best, or optimal, combination of risk and return.

This chapter describes what is meant by an optimal portfolio allocation and offers a framework for analyzing the problem of portfolio choice. The first section introduces the concept of efficient portfolios. Efficient portfolios can be identified without knowing the preference for return or the aversion to risk of particular investors. Efficient portfolios are of interest because *any* optimal portfolio is also an efficient portfolio. To narrow the problem of portfolio choice beyond efficiency, we require specific information about the preferences of an investor. The second section develops investor preferences as indifference curves defined over risk and expected return. In the third section we combine indifference curves with the set of portfolio possibilities to identify an optimal portfolio. The appendix derives investor indifference curves from the more fundamental perspective of maximizing the expected value of a utility function.

8.1 EFFICIENT PORTFOLIOS

We assume that investors prefer larger expectations of return to smaller expectations and that they prefer lower exposure to risk to greater exposure. Even in the absence of any knowledge of how an individual investor judges greater exposure to risk relative to increased expectations of return, we can use the principle of preference for return and aversion to risk to analyze the comparative desirability of some (but not all) portfolio allocations.

Our measure of comparative desirability is expressed through the concept of *dominance*. One portfolio allocation is said to dominate another if (1) it is characterized by at least as large an expected return *and* no greater uncertainty of return and (2) it has *either* strictly greater expected return *or* strictly lower exposure to risk.

Intuitively, one portfolio dominates another if it is not less preferable in both the risk and return dimensions and if it is strictly preferable in at least one of those dimensions. The statement that one portfolio allocation dominates another allocation does not depend on a risk versus return analysis. Instead, it is a consequence of independent comparisons of risk and return.

The concept of dominance can be illustrated with some simple examples. Suppose an investor can choose between two portfolio allocations, labeled *a* and *b*, where the risk/return characteristics of the portfolios, as shown in Figure 8.1, are such that

$$\mu_a = \mu_b$$
$$\sigma_a < \sigma_b$$

Portfolio *a* is clearly superior to portfolio *b* since it offers the same expected return with less risk. Portfolio *a* dominates portfolio *b*.

Now suppose the investor can also choose between portfolio *a* and some other portfolio, labeled *c*, where the risk/return relations (in Figure 8.1) are

$$\mu_a > \mu_c$$
$$\sigma_a = \sigma_c$$

FIGURE 8.1
A dominant portfolio. Portfolio *a* dominates portfolio *b* and portfolio *c*.

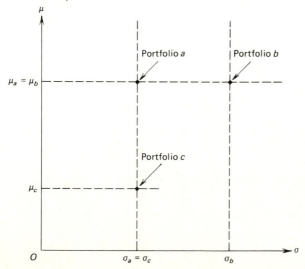

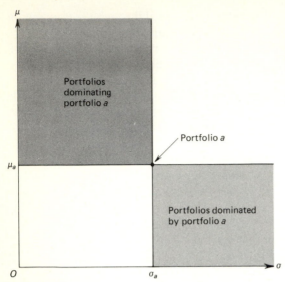

FIGURE 8.2
Portfolios dominating, and dominated by, portfolio a.

Again portfolio a is clearly superior, because it offers greater expected return but bears the same risk as portfolio c. Thus it also dominates portfolio c.

The process of comparing portfolios with some initial portfolio to determine which is dominant can be extended to all possible pairs of μ-σ combinations. As shown in Figure 8.2, the choice of an initial portfolio, say, portfolio a, divides the μ-σ plane into three regions: the set of μ-σ pairs dominated by portfolio a (this is the light gray area to the "southeast" of a), the set of μ-σ pairs which dominate portfolio a (this is the dark gray area to the "northwest" of a), and all of the other μ-σ pairs, which neither dominate nor are dominated by portfolio a.

A portfolio is *efficient* if it is not dominated by any other *available* portfolio. An efficient portfolio has the greatest expected return among the set of all available portfolios with the same level of risk, *and* it has the lowest risk among the set of all available portfolios with the same expected return. Figure 8.3 shows the efficient portfolios for several different portfolio possibility loci in the two-asset case. These loci were derived in Section 7.3 and correspond to the cases where the coefficient of correlation is $\rho = +1$ (Figure 8.3a), $\rho = -1$ (Figure 8.3b), and $\rho = 0$ (Figure 8.3c).

Assuming that investors prefer increased expected return but are averse to greater exposure to risk, any portfolio which is optimal for some investor must be efficient. If an optimal portfolio were inefficient, there would exist either another portfolio with the same or lower risk as the optimal portfolio but with greater expected return, or another portfolio with the same or greater expected return but with lower risk. In either case the existence of such an alternative portfolio would contradict the notion of optimality ascribed to the original

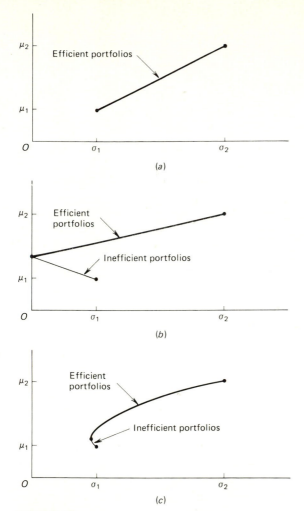

FIGURE 8.3
Efficient portfolios in the two-asset case. (a) Perfect positive correlation, $\rho = -1$; (b) perfect negative correlation, $\rho = -1$; (c) zero correlation, $\pi = 0$.

portfolio. It follows that an investor trying to decide on what portfolio allocation is best, or optimal, need not examine every possible allocation. He can restrict his search to the set of efficient allocations.

All optimal portfolios are efficient, but it does not follow that an investor will view two efficient portfolios as equally desirable. Suppose, for example, that portfolios a and d are both efficient, but that their risk/return characteristics are related as

$$\mu_a < \mu_d$$
$$\sigma_a < \sigma_d$$

One investor may decide the extra expected return on portfolio d is adequate compensation for the additional uncertainty in return on that portfolio, and thus prefer d to a. Another investor, presumably more risk-averse, may prefer a to d. An optimal portfolio selection thus requires information on the preferences of the investor who will hold the portfolio.

8.2 INVESTOR PREFERENCES

In the previous section it was suggested that two portfolios can be ranked in order of their desirability if one portfolio has at least as much expected return and no more risk than the other. It was also suggested that two portfolios cannot be so ranked if one has both more risk and more return. The desirability of one or the other will then depend on the preferences of the investor.

Investor preferences can be represented as *sets of equivalent portfolios.* These sets are constructed so that an investor is indifferent among portfolios in the same equivalence set but ranks any member of one set as either better or worse than any member of another set. The sets of equivalent portfolios for one investor need not be identical to the sets for another investor, since the sets represent the preferences of the investors.

A single set of equivalent portfolios can be constructed by an iterative process of choice. In describing this process, it will be convenient to denote a portfolio by its expected return and risk, i.e., by (μ, σ).

Suppose an investor can choose between a portfolio with expected return μ_a and zero risk, i.e., portfolio $(\mu_a, 0)$, and some other portfolio $(\mu_a, \sigma_a(1))$ where $\sigma_a(1) > 0$. As shown in Figure 8.4, portfolio $(\mu_a, 0)$ is clearly preferred. In

FIGURE 8.4
Portfolios more desirable, equally desirable, and less desirable than a specified zero-risk portfolio.

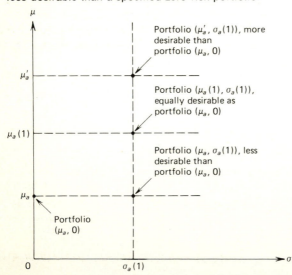

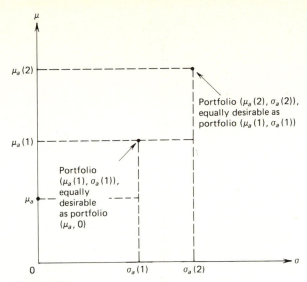

FIGURE 8.5
Triplet of equally desirable portfolios.

moving from portfolio $(\mu_a, 0)$ to portfolio $(\mu_a, \sigma_a(1))$, the investor would assume greater exposure to risk yet expect to earn no greater return.

Now suppose the choice is between portfolio $(\mu_a, 0)$ and portfolio $(\mu'_a(\sigma_a, 1))$ where $\mu'_a > \mu_a$. If μ'_a is sufficiently large, the investor will prefer the second portfolio, because the additional return will provide more than enough compensation for the extra risk.

For some level of expected return, denoted by $\mu_a(1)$, between μ_a and μ'_a, the investor will be *indifferent* between portfolio $(\mu_a, 0)$ and portfolio $(\mu_a(1), \sigma_a(1))$. These two portfolios are equivalent in the eyes of the investor. As shown in Figure 8.4, the increase in expected return from μ_a to $\mu_a(1)$ is just sufficient to compensate the investor for the increase in risk from zero to $\sigma_a(1)$.

Similarly, for risk $\sigma_a(2) > \sigma_a(1)$ there will exist a portfolio $(\mu_a(2), \sigma_a(2))$ with expected return $\mu_a(2) > \mu_a(1)$ such that the investor is indifferent between $(\mu_a(1), \sigma_a(1))$ and $(\mu_a(2), \sigma_a(2))$. In this case, as shown in Figure 8.5, the increase in expected return from $\mu_a(1)$ to $\mu_a(2)$ is just sufficient to compensate the investor for bearing the increase in risk from $\sigma_a(1)$ to $\sigma_a(2)$. Note that because the investor is indifferent between portfolios $(\mu_a(2), \sigma_a(2))$ and $(\mu_a(1), \sigma_a(1))$, and because he is also indifferent between portfolios $(\mu_a(1), \sigma_a(1))$ and $(\mu_a, 0)$, he is indifferent between portfolios $(\mu_a(2), \sigma_a(2))$ and $(\mu_a, 0)$. This is summarized in the statement that all three portfolios are in the same equivalence set; i.e., they are all equivalent to each other in the eyes of the investor.

This process can be repeated at successively higher risk levels $\sigma_a(i) > \sigma_a(i-1)$ such that the portfolios $(\mu_a(i), \sigma_a(i))$ and $(\mu_a(i-1), \sigma_a(i-1))$ are equivalent portfolios, implying $(\mu_a(i), \sigma_a(i))$ is equivalent to $(\mu_a, 0)$. The set of all portfolios equivalent to $(\mu_a, 0)$ is the equivalence set of that portfolio.

Figure 8.6 illustrates a set of equivalent portfolios. That figure is a combina-

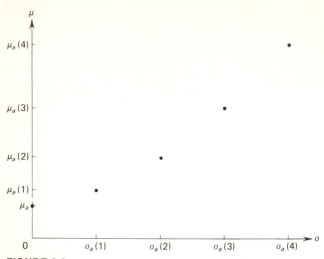

FIGURE 8.6
Set of five equivalent portfolios. Given $\sigma_a(i)$, the expected return
$\mu_a(i)$ is chosen so that the investor is indifferent between portfolio
$(\mu_a, 0)$ and portfolio $(\mu_a(i), \sigma_a(i))$.

tion and extension of Figures 8.4 and 8.5, and shows μ-σ combinations which
an investor considers equivalent to the original combination of $(\mu_a, 0)$. That is,
the investor is indifferent between $(\mu_a, 0)$ and any of the other portfolios shown
in Figure 8.6.

An *indifference curve* is a graph in the risk/return space of all the μ-σ combinations in a single set of equivalent portfolios. The investor is, by definition,
indifferent between any two portfolios whose expected return and standard
deviation of return lie on the same indifference curve.

Having derived the set of portfolios equivalent to $(\mu_a, 0)$, we can do the same
for $(\mu_b, 0)$, where $\mu_b > \mu_a$. This leads to the formation of a family of indifference curves, as shown in Figure 8.7. *Any* member of one equivalence set is
preferred to any member of another set if the indifference curve of the former
set lies above or to the left of the indifference curve of the latter. The indifference curves represent the preferences of a particular investor in trading off risk
against return.[1]

8.3   SELECTION OF AN OPTIMAL PORTFOLIO

The allocation of an optimal portfolio depends upon two pieces of information:
first, what expected returns and variances of return are associated with alternative portfolio allocations (this is the portfolio possibility set or opportunity set),

---

[1] Borch (1968) has shown that it is impossible to assert the existence of indifference curves
defined in the μ-σ space unless the probability distributions of the returns are limited to some class.
Tobin (1958) shows that normal distributions are one such class.

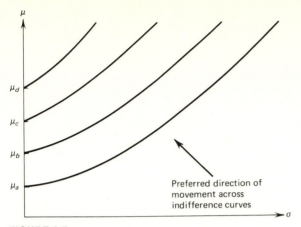

FIGURE 8.7
Investor indifference curves.

and second, the preference structure of the investor. Figure 8.8 combines a portfolio possibility set and the indifference curves of an investor. The investor prefers that portfolio whose expected return and risk lies on the "highest" attainable indifference curve.[2] In Figure 8.8 this optimal portfolio is located at a point of tangency between an indifference curve and the efficiency locus.

Different preference structures lead to different optimal portfolios. Figure 8.9 shows that as we consider increasingly risk-averse investors with increasingly steep indifference curves, the optimal portfolios chosen by those investors exhibit declining risk and declining expected return. Portfolio selection depends on how the available alternatives are judged by particular investors. In the absence of knowledge of such preferences, a selection cannot be made.[3]

Preference Functions and Indifference Curves

Portfolio selection can be placed in a more formal structure which will be useful in subsequent chapters. Let G be a preference function defined over the expected return and variance of return on a portfolio. That is, G is a function of μ and σ^2. We write this function as $G(\mu, \sigma^2)$, with μ as the first argument of G and σ^2 as the second argument.

The function G is a quantitative representation of the preference structure of an investor. We will say that if $G(\mu_a, \sigma_a^2) > G(\mu_b, \sigma_b^2)$ for two portfolios a and b,

---

[2] Sharpe (1966) has suggested a decomposition of the portfolio allocation problem which follows the institution organization of the investment community: securities analysts provide predictions of the performance of individual securities (including their interrelationships) and hence define the portfolio possibility locus, portfolio analysts identify efficient portfolio allocations, and individual investors pick an optimal portfolio from the efficient set.

[3] It is interesting to note that federal securities law imposes a duty on brokers and dealers to abstain from making "unsuitable" recommendations to their customers, in light of the financial resources, age, and other characteristics of those customers. See Wolfson, Phillips, and Russo (1977, chap. 2) and Jacobs (1972).

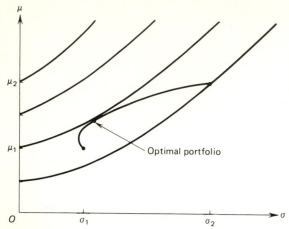

FIGURE 8.8
The optimal portfolio as a function of investor
preferences and portfolio possibilities.

then the investor prefers portfolio a to portfolio b. If $G(\mu_a, \sigma_a^2) = G(\mu_b, \sigma_b^2)$, the investor is indifferent between a and b. The level sets of G, i.e., all the μ-σ combinations which lead to common values of G, are the investor's indifference curves.

An illustrative example of the function G may be useful. Suppose we set $G(\mu, \sigma^2) = \mu - 8\sigma^2$. For a risk-free portfolio with an expected return of 8 percent ($\mu = .08$), the preference function would have the value

$$G(\mu, \sigma^2) = G(.08, 0)$$
$$= .08 - 8(0)$$
$$= .08$$

For a portfolio with an expected return of 10 percent and a standard deviation of return of 5 percent ($\sigma = .05$, or $\sigma^2 = .0035$), we would have

$$G(\mu, \sigma^2) = G(.10, .0025)$$
$$= .10 - 8(.0025)$$
$$= .08$$

Comparing these results, we have $G(.08, 0) = G(.10, .0025)$, and so the two portfolios lie on the same indifference curve. On the other hand, a portfolio with an expected return of 13 percent and a standard deviation of return of 7.07 percent has a preference function value of

$$G(\mu, \sigma^2) = G(.13, .005)$$
$$= .13 - 8(.005)$$
$$= .09$$

Since this value is greater than .08, the third portfolio is preferred to either of the first two portfolios.

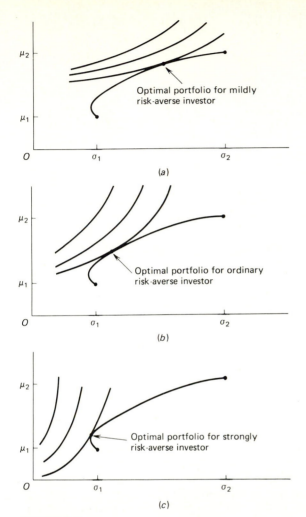

FIGURE 8.9
Risk aversion and optimal portfolios.

Figure 8.10 shows some graphs of the level sets of the function $G(\mu, \sigma^2) = \mu - 8\sigma^2$. As we asserted, portfolios with higher values of the function are preferred to portfolios with lower values. In general, of course, a preference function could have any of a wide variety of specifications [for example, $G(\mu, \sigma^2) = \mu/\sigma$ or $G(\mu, \sigma^2) = \mu - 1/\sigma$], but in all cases the function simply reflects the indifference curves of a particular investor.

Using the preference function G we can write the portfolio selection problem for a two-asset porfolio as

$$\text{maximize } G(x_1\mu_1 + x_2\mu_2, \ x_1^2\sigma_1^2 + x_2^2\sigma_2^2 + 2x_1x_2\rho\sigma_1\sigma_2) \qquad (8.1)$$
$$\text{over all alternative choices of } x_1 \text{ and } x_2$$
$$\text{subject to the constraint that } x_1 + x_2 = 1$$

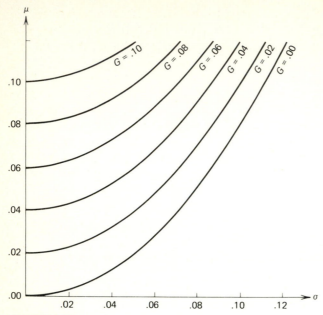

FIGURE 8.10
Level sets of the preference function $G(\mu,\sigma^2) = \mu - 8\sigma^2$.

The investor whose preferences are represented by G wants to maximize the value of that function by choosing optimal values for x_1 and x_2. The expected return on a portfolio as a function of x_1 and x_2 is the first argument of G. The variance of return on a portfolio as a function of x_1 and x_2 is the second argument of G. x_1 and x_2 cannot be chosen independently, however, since they must sum to unity. The maximization of G is subject to that constraint. If short selling is not permitted, we would add to the maximization problem of (8.1) the additional constraints that x_1 and x_2 must be chosen so that $x_1 \geq 0$ and $x_2 \geq 0$.

CHAPTER SUMMARY

This chapter has described how an investor selects an optimal portfolio allocation as a function of his personal tastes and the opportunities which are available to him for trading off risk against return. An initial analysis of the problem of portfolio choice suggested that any optimal allocation must be efficient; i.e., it must not be dominated by any other available μ-σ combination. To select a single optimal portfolio from the set of efficient portfolios, however, requires information on investor preferences beyond the assertion that an investor likes greater expected return and dislikes exposure to risk.

Investor preferences are represented by indifference curves in the μ-σ plane. If two portfolios lie on the same indifference curve, the investor has no basis for preferring one portfolio over the other. If two portfolios lie on different indifference curves, the investor will have a strict preference for one of those two portfolios. The problem of selecting an optimal portfolio is thus one of choosing an allocation which leads to a μ-σ combination on as "high" an indifference curve as possible.

An optimal portfolio allocation depends on (1) the statistical characteristics of the returns on the individual assets, (2) the way in which different portfolio allocations lead to different portfolio risks and portfolio returns, and (3) the preferences of the investor choosing the portfolio. These three elements have been the topics of this chapter and the two preceding chapters. We have, therefore, already described the conceptual foundations of portfolio theory. In the next chapter we generalize the analysis to portfolios of more than two assets.

FURTHER READING

Karl Borch, "Indifference Curves and Uncertainty," *Swedish Journal of Economics*, **70** (March 1968), 19–24.

Martin Feldstein, "Mean-Variance Analysis in the Theory of Liquidity Preference and Portfolio Selection," *Review of Economic Studies*, **36** (January 1969), 5–12.

Harry Markowitz, *Portfolio Selection* (New York: John Wiley & Sons, Inc., 1959).

Jan Mossin, "Optimal Multiperiod Portfolio Policies," *Journal of Business*, **41** (April 1968), 215–229.

APPENDIX: Utility Functions and Preference Functions

In Section 8.3 we observed that the indifference curves of an investor can be represented by a preference function G defined over the expected return μ and the variance of return σ^2 on a portfolio. Two portfolios are equivalent if they lead to a common value of the preference function. Two portfolios are strictly ordered according to the preferences of the investor if they yield different values of the preference function. Although one can postulate the existence of preference functions from the indifference curves described in Section 8.3, preference functions can also be derived from a more fundamental concept: maximization of the expected utility of terminal wealth.

As in Section 7.1, let W represent the initial wealth of an investor, W' his end-of-period or terminal wealth, and $R = (W' - W)/W$ the return on his portfolio over the holding period. It follows that $W' = (1 + R)W$. Now suppose the investor evaluates his end-of-period wealth by a utility function $U(W')$ defined over that wealth. Larger values of the utility function are preferred to smaller values.

Utility functions are usually assumed to possess several important properties. We certainly expect that $U(W'_a) > U(W'_b)$ if $W'_a > W'_b$, so that utility is an increasing function of wealth. This may be expressed equivalently by the assertion that the *marginal* utility of wealth is positive, or that the first derivative of the utility function, denoted U', is positive at all wealth levels.

In addition it is frequently assumed that utility functions exhibit decreasing marginal utility of wealth; i.e., that $U'(W_a') > U'(W_b') > 0$ if $W_a' < W_b'$. This implies that a marginal increase in wealth leads to greater additional utility at low wealth levels than at high wealth levels. Decreasing marginal utility of wealth is equivalent to the assertion that the second derivative of the utility function, denoted U'', is negative at all wealth levels. The statements $U'(W') > 0$ and $U''(W') < 0$ for all $W' > 0$ together imply that utility is a *concave* function of end-of-period wealth.

The end-of-period utility for an investor with initial wealth W will have the random value $U(W(1 + R))$, where R is the random return on the investor's portfolio. As we demonstrated in Chapter 7, an investor can change the distribution of R, i.e., change the mean and variance of R, by altering the composition of his portfolio. We assume he judges the preferability of different distributions by the *expected value* of $U(W(1 + R))$. That is, he wants to select the portfolio allocation which maximizes the expectation of $U(W(1 + R))$.[4]

In some cases the expected value of end-of-period utility will induce a preference function defined over the mean μ and variance σ^2 of the random return R. Suppose, for example, the utility function has a quadratic form:

$$U_q(W') = W' + b(W')^2 \qquad b < 0 \tag{A.1}$$

b is a parameter which may vary from one investor to another. From the utility function of Equation (A.1) it follows that $U_q(W')$ has an expected value given by

$$
\begin{aligned}
\text{Exp } [U_q(W')] &= \text{Exp } [W(1 + R) + bW^2(1 + R)^2] \\
&= W \text{ Exp } [1 + R] + bW^2 \text{ Exp } [(1 + R)^2] \\
&= W(1 + \mu) + bW^2 [(1 + \mu)^2 + \sigma^2]
\end{aligned}
$$

The expected value of utility thus defines a preference function G_q on μ and σ^2:

$$G_q(\mu, \sigma^2) = \mu + bW[(1 + \mu)^2 + \sigma^2] \tag{A.2}$$

Since higher values of expected utility are preferred to lower values, higher values of G_q will be preferred to lower values of G_q. That is, maximizing the expectation of $U_q(W')$ in (A.1) is equivalent to maximizing $G_q(\mu, \sigma^2)$ in Equation (A.2). Moreover,

$$\frac{\partial G_1}{\partial \mu} = 1 + 2bW(1 + \mu) > 0 \qquad \text{if } 1 + 2bW(1 + \mu) > 0 \tag{A.3a}$$

$$\frac{\partial G_q}{\partial \sigma} = 2bW\sigma < 0 \tag{A.3b}$$

Thus, both increased expected return and decreased risk lead to greater expected utility. The former holds, however, only if the initial wealth of the investor is small enough so that $W < [-2b(1 + \mu)]^{-1}$. This peculiarity of the quadratic utility function stems from the fact that the marginal utility of wealth is negative at high wealth levels. Specifically, $U_q'(W') < 0$ if $W' > (-2b)^{-1}$.

The shape of the indifference curves along which G_q, and hence Exp $[U_q(W')]$, is

---

[4] Von Neumann and Morgenstern (1947) provided the first full analysis of decision making based on maximization of expected utility. For an early application of this principle to portfolio selection see Markowitz (1959, chaps. 10–13).

constant is not hard to determine. If the value of G_q is held constant in Equation (A.2), it can be shown that

$$\frac{d\sigma}{d\mu}\bigg|_{G_q \text{ constant}} = - [1 + 2(1 + \mu)bW](2bW\sigma)^{-1} > 0$$
$$\text{if } 1 + 2bW(1 + \mu) > 0 \quad \text{(A.4}a\text{)}$$

$$\frac{d^2\sigma}{d\mu^2}\bigg|_{G_q \text{ constant}} = \frac{- [1 + 2(1 + \mu)bW]^2(2bW)^{-2}\sigma^{-3} - \sigma^1 < 0}{\text{if } 1 + 2bW(1 + \mu) > 0 \quad \text{(A.4}b\text{)}}$$

Thus, the indifference curves of G_q are upward-sloping and convex, following the general shape shown in Figure 8.7.

Other classes of utility functions lead to preference functions with similar properties. The exponential utility function is defined as

$$U_e(W') = -\exp [-\lambda W'] \qquad \lambda > 0 \qquad \text{(A.5)}$$

λ is a parameter of the utility function whose value may vary from one investor to another. If the return R is normally distributed with mean μ and variance σ^2, then

$$\text{Exp } [U_e(W')] = \text{Exp } [-\exp [-\lambda(1 + R)W]]$$
$$= -\exp [-\lambda W(1 + \mu) + \tfrac{1}{2}\lambda^2 W^2\sigma^2]$$

The preference function G_e corresponding to an exponential utility function may be defined as

$$G_e(\mu, \sigma^2) = \mu - \tfrac{1}{2}\lambda W\sigma^2 \qquad \text{(A.6)}$$

Maximizing the value of $G_e(\mu,\sigma^2)$ in (A.6) is equivalent to maximizing the expected value of $U_e(W')$ in (A.5).

As with the quadratic utility function, the indifference curves for G_e in Equation (A.6) are upward-sloping and convex, that is,

$$\frac{d\sigma}{d\mu}\bigg|_{G_e \text{ constant}} = (\lambda W\sigma)^{-1} > 0 \qquad \text{(A.7}a\text{)}$$

$$\frac{d^2\sigma}{d\mu^2}\bigg|_{G_e \text{ constant}} = -(\lambda W)^{-2}\sigma^{-3} < 0 \qquad \text{(A.7}b\text{)}$$

Tobin (1958) has demonstrated that for a variety of distributions of the random return R on a portfolio (including especially normal distributions), any investor with a concave utility function, that is, $U' > 0$ and $U'' < 0$, will have convex indifference curves, that is, $d\sigma/d\mu > 0$ and $d^2\sigma/d\mu^2 < 0$ along an indifference curve. This result justifies, in part, our assumption of convex indifference curves. Feldstein (1969), however, has shown that Tobin's result does not extend to all distributions of R and in particular does not include the case where the log return $\ln [1 + R]$ is normally distributed.[5]

Observe, in Equations (A.2) and (A.6), that the shape of the indifference curves in

---

[5] The indifference curves of an investor will, however, be convex if he has a concave *quadratic* utility function, regardless of the distribution of R. This is shown by Equations (A.1) to (A.4).

the risk/return space depends upon the level of initial wealth in both the quadratic and exponential utility cases.[6] In the present analysis this is not too important because we are assuming the wealth of an investor is fixed while he is making his choice of an optimal portfolio allocation. If, for example, he comes to the market with some endowment of securities rather than with cash, we assume he can liquidate those securities at prevailing market prices and redistribute the proceeds according to his preferences. This follows from our assumptions of a competitive market and the absence of taxes and transactions costs. When analyzing in Chapters 11 and 12 the properties of a market equilibrium, where the prices of different securities are determined simultaneously with optimal investor portfolio allocations, we must bear in mind that investor preference functions may depend upon the values of the endowments of the investors.

[6] Mossin (1968) shows that the only cases where indifference curves, and hence optimal portfolio allocations, are independent of initial wealth are when the utility function exhibits constant relative risk aversion, that is $-U''(W)W/U'(W)$ is constant for all W. This requires that $U(W) = \ln [W]$, or $U(W) = -W^{1-k}$ for $k - 1$ or $U(W) = W^{1-k}$ for $0 < k < 1$.

CHAPTER 9

MULTIPLE-ASSET
PORTFOLIOS

This chapter extends portfolio theory to the case where an investor allocates wealth among more than two assets. Our primary interest is exploring the relation between the allocation of a portfolio and the risk and return characteristics of the portfolio. As in the two-asset case, the analysis leads to the construction of a portfolio possibility set, or set of attainable μ-σ combinations. After identifying the efficient μ-σ combinations, we locate the optimal portfolio allocation for a given investor from the specification of his indifference curves.

The first section treats the case where only risky assets are available. We will see in that section that an investor can hold a diversified portfolio either by direct investment or by an indirect participation in the asset holdings of another investor. Securities issued by investment companies are examples of such indirect participations. (See Section 2.4 for a description of the major types of investment companies.)

The remaining sections of the chapter describe the consequences of adding a risk-free asset to the set of available investments. In the second section we consider the case where an investor can hold only nonnegative amounts of such an asset. The resulting changes in the portfolio possibility set and the set of efficient portfolios are developed. The third section shows how borrowing at the risk-free rate, or short selling the risk-free asset, induces further change in both the portfolio possibility set and the set of efficient portfolios. The fourth section presents an analysis of the relation between risk premiums on risky assets and the contribution of an individual asset to the risk exposure of an efficiently allocated portfolio. The results of that section are important for the analysis in Chapter 12 of equilibrium yields on risky assets.

9.1 PORTFOLIOS OF SEVERAL RISKY ASSETS

In Chapter 7 we saw how the allocation of wealth between two risky assets affects the risk and return characteristics of an investor's portfolio. The principal results from that chapter were the equations for the realized return on a portfolio, the expected return on a portfolio, and the variance of return on a portfolio. The equations are

$$R = x_1 R_1 + x_2 R_2 \tag{9.1a}$$
$$\mu = x_1 \mu_1 + x_2 \mu_2 \tag{9.1b}$$
$$\sigma^2 = x_1^2 \sigma_1^2 + x_2^2 \sigma_2^2 + 2x_1 x_2 \, \text{Cov} \, [R_1, R_2] \tag{9.1c}$$

When an investor can allocate wealth among multiple risky assets, a similar set of equations exists relating the realized return R on the portfolio to the realized returns on the assets in the portfolio, and relating the risk σ^2 and expected return μ on the portfolio to the statistical characteristics of the constituent assets.

Suppose there are I risky assets and that an investor chooses the portfolio allocation $(x_1, x, \ldots, x_I)$. x_i is the fractional allocation of wealth to the ith asset. Since the portfolio must be fully allocated, we require $x_1 + x_2 + \cdots + x_I = 1$. The realized return on the portfolio will then be

$$R = \sum_{i=1}^{I} x_i R_i \tag{9.2a}$$

The expected return on the portfolio is

$$\mu = \sum_{i=1}^{I} x_i \mu_i \tag{9.2b}$$

and the variance of return on the portfolio is[1]

$$\sigma^2 = \sum_{i=1}^{I} \sum_{j=1}^{I} x_i x_j C_{ij} \tag{9.2c}$$

C_{ij} is the covariance of the returns on the ith and jth assets:

$$C_{ij} = \text{Cov} \, [R_i, R_j] = \text{Cov} \, [R_j, R_i] = C_{ji}$$

In the special case where $i = j$, we have $C_{ii} = \text{Cov} \, [R_i, R_i] = \text{Var} \, [R_i] = \sigma_i^2$.

The interpretation of Equations (9.2b) and (9.2c) is analogous to the interpretation of Equations (9.1b) and (9.1c) in the two-asset case. The expected

---

[1] The double summation $\sum_{i=1}^{I} \sum_{j=1}^{I} w_{ij}$ means the summation of the w_{ij} terms over all possible combinations of i and j, from $i = 1$ to $i = n$ and from $j = 1$ to $j = m$.

EXAMPLE 9.1

COMPUTING THE EXPECTED RETURN AND STANDARD DEVIATION OF RETURN FOR A THREE-ASSET PORTFOLIO

Suppose the expected returns over the course of a month on three assets are

$$\mu_1 = 2.0\% \qquad \mu_2 = 1.78\% \qquad \mu_3 = 1.50\%$$

and suppose the variances and covariances of returns over the same interval are

$$
\begin{array}{lll}
C_{11} = 4.0 & C_{12} = 1.0 & C_{13} = 1.0 \\
C_{21} = 1.0 & C_{22} = 1.0 & C_{23} = .5 \\
C_{31} = 1.0 & C_{32} = .5 & C_{33} = 1.0
\end{array}
$$

An investor allocates 4 percent of his wealth to the first asset, 76 percent of his wealth to the second asset, and 20 percent of his wealth to the third asset. This means that $x_1 = .04$, $x_2 = .76$, and $x_3 = .20$.

The expected return μ on the the investor's portfolio can be calculated from Equation (9.2b):

$$
\begin{aligned}
\mu &= \sum_{i=1}^{3} x_i \mu_i \\
&= x_1 \mu_1 + x_2 \mu_2 + x_3 \mu_3 \\
&= .04(2.0) + .76(1.78) + .20(1.50) \\
&= 1.73\%
\end{aligned}
$$

The variance of return σ^2 on the investor's portfolio can be calculated from Equation (9.2c):

$$
\begin{aligned}
\sigma^2 &= \sum_{i=1}^{3} \sum_{j=1}^{3} x_i x_j C_{ij} \\
&= x_1 x_1 C_{11} + x_1 x_2 C_{12} + x_1 x_3 C_{13} \\
&\quad + x_2 x_1 C_{21} + x_2 x_2 C_{22} + x_2 x_3 C_{23} \\
&\quad + x_3 x_1 C_{31} + x_3 x_2 C_{32} + x_3 x_3 C_{33} \\
&= .04(.04)(4.0) + .04(.76)(1.0) + .04(.20)(1.0) \\
&\quad + .76(.04)(1.0) + .76(.76)(1.0) + .76(.20)(.5) \\
&\quad + .20(.04)(1.0) + .20(.76)(.5) + .20(.20)(1.0) \\
&= .0064 + .0304 + .0080 \\
&\quad + .0304 + .5776 + .0760 \\
&\quad + .0080 + .0760 + .0400 \\
&= .8528
\end{aligned}
$$

The standard deviation of the return on the portfolio is $\sigma = (.8528)^{1/2} = .92$ percent.

The foregoing computation of μ and σ can be repeated for any portfolio allocation. Figure 9.1 shows the resulting portfolio possibility set and efficiency frontier.

---

return μ and the variance of return σ^2 depend on (1) the allocation of the portfolio and (2) the expected returns and variances and covariances of returns on the assets in the portfolio.

As the allocation of a multiple-asset portfolio varies over the set of all possi-

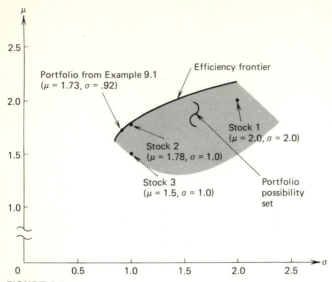

FIGURE 9.1
Portfolio possibility set and efficiency frontier for a three-asset portfolio.

ble allocations, Equations (9.2b) and (9.2c) describe the risk and return associated with each allocation.[2] The portfolio possibility set for multiple-asset portfolios is constructed by computing μ and σ for every possible allocation $(x_1, x_2, \ldots, x_I)$. Example 9.1 illustrates the computation of risk and return for a particular portfolio of three assets. Figure 9.1 is a graph of the portfolio possibility set for all portfolios constructed from those three assets. The locus, or frontier, of efficient portfolios is the *upper-left* boundary of the portfolio possibility set in the μ-σ space.[3] (See Section 8.1 for a discussion of efficient portfolios.)

[2] As stipulated in Equations (9.2b) and (9.2c), construction of the portfolio possibility set requires I expected returns, I variances, and $^1/_2 I(I - 1)$ covariances, or a total of $^1/_2(I^2 + 3I)$ parameters. If I is on the order of 1000 (which is not unreasonable since there are well over 1000 stocks listed on the New York Stock Exchange and thousands more traded over-the-counter), an investor would have to know 501,500 parameters, which is clearly an unwieldy number. Sharpe (1963) suggested an approximation to the structure of securities returns with a single-index model, using the return on the market as a whole, which vastly reduces the required amount of data. King (1966) extended Sharpe's single-index approach to a multiple-index model using market and industry returns. Fama (1965b) and Samuelson (1967) have shown how Sharpe's model can be applied when securities returns follow a stable Paretian distribution. Blume (1970) compares the prediction properties of the single-index approach when returns are assumed to be distributed normally or stable Paretian with characteristic values less than 2. Elton and Gruber (1973) have examined empirically the ability of the single- and multiple-index models to predict interasset correlation structures in future periods. Elton and Gruber (1974) have also considered the problem of multiple-asset portfolio theory when securities returns are log normally distributed.
[3] Since all optimal portfolios must lie on the efficiency frontier, identification of efficient portfolio allocations is quite important. Sharpe (1970) suggests a quadratic programming algorithm for computing those allocations when the full covariance structure of returns is known. That algorithm also shows that each efficient μ-σ combination can be identified with a unique portfolio allocation when there are no linear dependencies among the returns on the securities, i.e., when the covariance matrix is positive definite. Cohen and Pogue (1967) have examined empirically the ability of single- and multiple-index models to forecast the efficiency frontier in future periods.

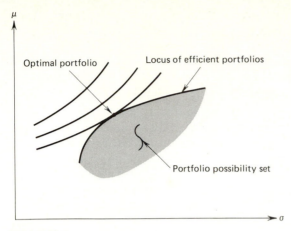

FIGURE 9.2
Multiple-asset portfolios.

The Optimal Allocation Problem

When an investor can allocate wealth among multiple risky assets, the optimal portfolio problem is not substantively different from the same problem in the two-asset case. The investor wants to select that allocation which will place him on as desirable an indifference curve as possible. In Figure 9.2 the optimal portfolio is located as a point of tangency between the efficiency frontier and an indifference curve.[4]

The portfolio selection problem in the multiple-asset case can be represented by the problem of maximizing the value of an investor's preference function,[5] denoted by G, over all alternative portfolio allocations:

$$\text{Maximize } G\left(\sum_{i=1}^{I} x_i \mu_i, \sum_{i=1}^{I}\sum_{j=1}^{I} x_i x_j C_{ij}\right) \tag{9.3}$$

over all alternative choices of $(x_1, x_2 \ldots, x_I)$

subject to the constraint that $\sum_{i=1}^{I} x_i = 1$

When $I = 2$, this is identical to the two-asset problem of Equation (8.1).

In general, an optimal allocation of wealth among risky assets will depend on the indifference curves, or preference function, of the investor. Different investors can be expected to hold different optimal allocations, even when they perceive common values for the expected returns and covariances of returns on

[4] The expected values and covariance structure of the uncertain returns are parameters from the point of view of an investor trading in a competitive market. As these parameters change, the portfolio allocation which an investor finds optimal also changes. Royama and Hamada (1966) have characterized portfolio reallocations, resulting from changes in the exogenous parameters, from the perspective of the microeconomic notions of substitutes and complements. Bierwag and Grove (1968) present a similar analysis.

[5] Preference functions are described in Section 8.3 and in the appendix to Chapter 8.

the available securities. If short selling is prohibited, the maximization of the preference function in (9.3) is subject to the additional constraints that $x_i \geq 0$ for $i = 1, \ldots, I$.

Returns on Investment Company Securities

The expressions for the realized return, the mean return, and the variance of return given in Equation (9.2) were stated in terms of direct investments in risky securities. Those equations also apply to the structure of returns on a security which represents a participating interest in a portfolio of direct investments. Suppose, for example, the portfolio of a unit investment trust[6] denoted by r is allocated in the proportions $(x_1(r), x_2(r), \ldots, x_I(r))$, where $x_1(r) + x_2(r) + \cdots + x_I(r) = 1$. The expected return μ_r on a participation unit in trust r will then be

$$\mu_r = \sum_{i=1}^{I} x_i(r)\, \mu_i \tag{9.4a}$$

and the variance of return σ_r^2 on a participation unit will be

$$\sigma_r^2 = \sum_{i=1}^{I} \sum_{j=1}^{I} x_i(r)\, x_j(r)\, C_{ij} \tag{9.4b}$$

An investor can allocate his wealth in the proportions $(x_1(r), x_2(r), \ldots, x_I(r))$ either by direct investment or by purchasing units of the investment trust r. *In the absence of transactions costs and indivisibilities*, the two strategies yield identical results. This equivalence is illustrated in Example 9.2. It follows that investment company securities do not create any new investment opportunities and therefore do not expand the portfolio possibility set. In particular, the location of the efficiency frontier is not changed by the existence of investment company securities.

Some investors, of course, cannot ignore either transactions costs or indivisibilities when they choose a portfolio allocation. Brokerage commissions on purchases and sales of odd lots of stock (usually less than 100 shares) are greater than commissions on round lots when measured on a per share basis. If an investor of limited means were to attempt to hold a portfolio diversified over many stocks, he might find a substantial portion of his wealth consumed in commission charges. The availability of investment company securities, representing participations in well-diversified portfolios, can benefit such an investor. Similarly, securities like Treasury bills and commercial paper are available in minimum denominations that either preclude purchase or limit opportunities

---

[6] Unit investment trusts are described in Section 2.4. In practice, trusts generally hold securities with a finite life, e.g., debt or preferred stock with a mandatory redemption date. A trust could also hold common stock and provide for a liquidation of assets and distribution of proceeds after a fixed interval of time.

for diversification by many investors. As we noted in Section 2.4, money-market mutual funds were innovated because many short-term debt instruments are issued only in relatively large units. To investors of modest means, the availability of participations in such funds created genuinely new investment opportunities.

9.2 PORTFOLIOS WHICH INCLUDE A RISK-FREE ASSET

Suppose an investor can allocate his initial wealth to a risk-free asset as well as among I risky assets. The effect on the portfolio possibility set of introducing the new asset is represented, formally, by changing the upper limits of the summations in Equations (9.2) to $I + 1$, where asset $I + 1$ is the risk-free security.

A simpler representation of the relation between the portfolio allocation (x_1, $x_2, \ldots, x_I, x_{I+1}$) and the risk and return on a portfolio which includes a risk-free asset is possible. Since asset $I + 1$ is risk-free, its return can assume only one value, denoted by R_f. This implies that the variance $\sigma_{I+1}^2 = C_{I+1,I+1}$ is zero and that the covariances $C_{j,I+1}$ and $C_{I+1,j}$ are also zero for $j = 1, \ldots, I$. The relation between a given portfolio allocation and the risk/return characteristics of the portfolio is therefore

$$\mu = \sum_{i=1}^{I} x_i \mu_i + x_{I+1} R_f \tag{9.5a}$$

$$\sigma^2 = \sum_{i=1}^{I} \sum_{j=1}^{I} x_i x_j C_{ij} \tag{9.5b}$$

where $x_1 + x_2 + \cdots + x_I + x_{I+1} = 1$.

In this section we consider the nature of the portfolio possibility set and efficiency frontier implied by Equations (9.5) when the risk-free asset cannot be sold short, i.e., when we require $x_{I+1} \geq 0$ for all portfolios. In the following section we relax this nonnegativity constraint on x_{I+1}.

Risk-Free Assets and Participations in Risky Portfolios

When studying the effect on the portfolio possibility set of adding a risk-free security to the set of available investments, we will find it instructive to consider first the consequences of allocating wealth between a risk-free security and participation units in a trust portfolio of strictly risky assets. Suppose there exists a unit investment trust, denoted by r, with a trust portfolio consisting entirely of risky assets, allocated as ($x_1(r), x_2(r), \ldots, x_I(r), 0$). (The zero in the last position of the allocation means the trust portfolio does *not* include the risk-free asset.) Participation units in trust r have the expected return μ_r and the variance of return σ_r^2 shown in Equations (9.4). One possible investment strategy is to allocate wealth between the risk-free asset and the trust r. The portfolio possibility set associated with this strategy has an exceedingly simple form.

EXAMPLE 9.2

THE EQUIVALENCE OF DIRECT INVESTMENTS IN RISKY ASSETS AND
INVESTMENTS IN UNIT INVESTMENT TRUSTS

Over the course of a month, three stocks changed in price and exhibited the following
returns:

Stock	Beginning-of-month price	End-of-month price	Return, %
1	$ 50	$ 55	10
2	40	38	−5
3	100	103	3

Suppose a unit investment trust r owned 10,000 shares of stock 1, 15,000 shares of
stock 2, and 8000 shares of stock 3, and had no liabilities. (Unit investment trusts are
described in Section 2.4 above.) The value of the trust's assets at the beginning of the
month would have been $1,900,000, computed thus:

Stock 1: 10,000 shares × $ 50 = $500,000
Stock 2: 15,000 shares ×   40 = 600,000
Stock 3: 8,000 shares ×   100 = 800,000
                 Total assets = $1,900,000

Assuming the trust neither bought nor sold any stock during the month, the value
of its assets at the end of the month would have been $1,944,000, computed thus:

Stock 1: 10,000 shares × $ 55 = $550,000
Stock 2: 15,000 shares ×   38 = 570,000
Stock 3: 8,000 shares ×   103 = 824,000
                 Total assets = $1,944,000

If the investment trust had 100,000 participation units outstanding, those units
would have had a value of $19 per unit at the beginning of the month ($19 = $1,900,000
net asset value ÷ 100,000 units issued) and $19.44 at the end of the month.

If an investor had bought 1000 participation units at the beginning of the month (for
$19,000), he would have earned a return of 2.32 percent over the course of the month.

- Beginning-of-month wealth:

$$1000 \text{ units} \times \$19.00 = \$19,000$$

- End-of-month wealth:

$$1000 \text{ units} \times \$19.44 = \$19,440$$

- Return during the month:

$$\frac{19,440 - 19,000}{19,000} = .0232$$

EXAMPLE 9.2 (*Continued*)

Suppose instead that the investor used his $19,000 to buy stocks 1, 2, and 3 directly, in the same proportions as the allocation of the investment trust portfolio. At the beginning of the month the trust's asset portfolio would have been allocated in the proportions

$$x_1(r) = \frac{500,000}{1,900,000} = .2632, \text{ or } 26.32\%$$

$$x_2(r) = \frac{600,000}{1,900,000} = .3158, \text{ or } 31.58\%$$

$$x_3(r) = \frac{800,000}{1,900,000} = .4210, \text{ or } 42.10\%$$

Note that $x_1(r) + x_2(r) + x_3(r) = 1$. The investor would have committed 26.32 percent of his wealth to stock 1, or $5000 (that is, $.2632 \times \$19,000$), and would therefore have purchased 100 shares of that stock ($5000 = 100 shares $\times$ \$50 per share). He would have committed 31.58 percent of his wealth to stock 2, or $6000 (that is, $.3158 \times \$19,000$), and would therefore have purchased 150 shares of that stock ($6000 = 150 shares $\times$ \$40 per share). Finally, he would have committed 42.10 percent of his wealth to stock 3, or $8000 (that is, $.4210 \times \$19,000$), and would therefore have purchased 80 shares of that stock ($8000 = 80 shares $\times$ \$100 per share).

The wealth of the investor at the end of the month would have been $19,440, computed thus:

Stock 1:	100 shares $\times$	$	55 =	$5,500
Stock 2:	150 shares $\times$		38 =	5,700
Stock 3:	80 shares $\times$		103 =	8,240
		Total assets =		$19,440

The investor's return over the month would have been 2.32 percent [$.0232 = (19,440 - 19,000) \div 19,000$]. This is the same as the return on the investment trust participation units.

Regardless of whether the investor put money in trust participation units or directly in stocks, his return over the month could be computed as

$$R = x_1(r)R_1 + x_2(r)R_2 + x_3(r)R_3$$
$$= .2632(10) + .3158(-5) + .4210(3)$$
$$= 2.32\%$$

Equations (9.4*a*) and (9.4*b*) give the expected return and variance of return for both the participation units and a direct investment in a comparably allocated portfolio.

Derivation of the Portfolio Possibility Set The analysis of a portfolio allocated between participation units of trust *r* and the risk-free asset is just a special case of the analysis from Chapter 7 of two-asset portfolios. Let x_r be the fraction of wealth allocated to the trust participation units, and let x_f be the fraction of wealth allocated to the risk-free asset, where $x_r + x_f = 1$. The expected return on the portfolio is

$$\mu = x_r \mu_r + x_f R_f \tag{9.6a}$$

and the variance of return is

$$\sigma^2 = x_r^2 \sigma_r^2 + x_f^2 \sigma_f^2 + 2x_r x_f \, \text{Cov} \, [R_r, R_f]$$

Since $\sigma_f = 0$ and $\text{Cov} \, [R_r, R_f] = 0$, the value of σ^2 will be

$$\sigma^2 = x_r^2 \sigma_r^2$$

so that the standard deviation of return on the portfolio is

$$\sigma = x_r \sigma_r \qquad\qquad\qquad (9.6b)$$

Equations (9.6a) and (9.6b) describe the μ-σ combinations which result from allocating wealth between the risk-free asset and units of the trust r. Since, from Equation (9.6b), $x_r = \sigma/\sigma_r$, and since $x_f = 1 - x_r = 1 - (\sigma/\sigma_r)$, Equation (9.6a) may be expressed in the form

$$\mu = R_f + \frac{\mu_r - R_f}{\sigma_r} \sigma \qquad \sigma \le \sigma_r \qquad (9.7)$$

σ is the standard deviation of the return on a portfolio allocated between the risk-free asset and the investment trust. As we increase the proportion of wealth allocated to the trust, we increase the value of σ [see Equation (9.6b)] and, as shown in Equation (9.7), we also increase the value of μ. Equation (9.7) shows that the expected return on the portfolio increases linearly with the risk exposure of the portfolio. We will see Equation (9.7) several more times. It occupies a place of central importance in portfolio theory.

Equation (9.7) is the equation of the portfolio possibility locus for allocations of wealth between the risk-free asset and trust r, as shown in Figure 9.3. The constraint $\sigma \le \sigma_r$ appears because the fraction of wealth allocated to the risk-free asset must be nonnegative in the present analysis, so that $x_f \ge 0$. This implies $x_r \le 1$ or, from Equation (9.6b), $\sigma \le \sigma_r$ for any feasible allocation.

Participations in Risky Portfolios and Direct Investments in Risky Assets

The preceding discussion considered the allocation of wealth (x_r, x_f) between the risk-free asset and a unit investment trust r. [The trust portfolio was assumed to be allocated as $(x_1(r), x_2(r), \ldots, x_I(r), 0)$.] An investor could obtain the same portfolio allocation by a direct investment in the ith risky asset of the fraction $x_i = x_r x_i(r)$ of his initial wealth and an investment in the risk-free asset of the fraction $x_{I+1} = x_f$ of his initial wealth. This equivalence is illustrated in Example 9.3. The existence of the trust participation units does not afford the investor any new investment opportunities (ignoring transactions costs and indivisibilities), but simply provides a convenient vehicle for his investment in risky assets.

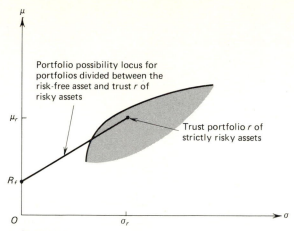

FIGURE 9.3
Mixture of a risk-free asset with a participation in
a trust portfolio of risky assets.

A converse argument shows that any direct allocation of wealth among the I risky assets and the risk-free asset can be treated as an allocation between some trust portfolio of strictly risky assets and the risk-free asset.[7] Thus, all the portfolio possibilities implicit in Equations (9.5) can be obtained as combinations of the risk-free asset and different trust portfolios of strictly risky assets.

The Efficiency Frontier for Portfolios of Risk-Free and Risky Assets

Since the composition of a trust portfolio is arbitrary, the foregoing analysis can be replicated for any allocation of risky assets. This will yield an expanded portfolio possibility set and a new efficiency frontier, as shown in Figure 9.4. The portfolio denoted by m in that figure is a portfolio of strictly risky assets. The portfolio possibility locus for allocations between the risk-free asset and m is tangent to the old efficiency frontier of strictly risky assets. The point of tangency is (μ_m, σ_m).

When investors can hold a risk-free asset as well as risky assets in their portfolios, the efficiency frontier will have two segments. As shown in Figure 9.4, the first segment is a straight line extending from $(R_f, 0)$ to (μ_m, σ_m). m is a portfolio consisting only of risky assets, say $(x_1(m), \ldots, x_I(m), 0)$. Any μ-σ combination on the linear segment of the efficiency frontier can be obtained by mixing the risk-free asset with the portfolio m. Portfolio m is just a special case

---

[7] Suppose an investor divided his wealth directly among the $I + 1$ assets in a portfolio allocated as $(x_1, x_2, \ldots, x_I, x_{I+1})$. This is equivalent to investing a fraction $x_f = x_{I+1}$ of his wealth in the risk-free asset and a fraction $x_r = 1 - x_{I+1}$ in a trust portfolio r of risky assets, where that portfolio has the allocation $(x_1(r), x_2(r), \ldots, x_I(r))$ with $x_i(r) = x_i/(1 - x_{I+1})$ for $i = 1, 2, \ldots, I$. It follows that any direct allocation of wealth among the $I + 1$ assets may be viewed as an allocation of wealth between the risk-free asset and a particular trust portfolio of strictly risky assets.

EXAMPLE 9.3

THE EQUIVALENCE OF DIVERSIFYING BETWEEN A RISK-FREE ASSET AND A UNIT INVESTMENT TRUST AND DIVERSIFYING BETWEEN A RISK-FREE ASSET AND DIRECT INVESTMENTS IN RISKY ASSETS

Example 9.2 described three stocks and participation units in an investment trust r which held only those stocks in its portfolio. Over the course of a month the stocks and the participation units changed in price and exhibited the following returns:

Security	Beginning-of-month price	End-of-month price	Return, %
Stock 1	$ 50	$ 55	10
Stock 2	40	38	−5
Stock 3	100	103	3
Trust units	19	19.44	2.32

At the beginning of the month the trust portfolio was allocated among the three stocks in the allocation $x_1(r) = .2632$, $x_2(r) = .3158$, and $x_3(r) = .4210$.

Suppose an investor allocated 30 percent of his wealth to a risk-free asset bearing a known return $R_f = 1$ percent over the month and allocated 70 percent of his wealth to participation units in the investment trust. His return over the month would have been

$$R = x_r R_r + x_f R_f$$
$$= .70(2.32) + .30(1.0)$$
$$= 1.92\%$$

Since the investor allocated 70 percent of his wealth to risky assets (through his purchase of the trust participation units), and since 26.32 percent of the trust's assets were invested in stock 1, the investor implicitly allocated 18.42 percent of his wealth to stock 1 ($.1842 = .70 \times .2632$). Similarly, since 31.58 percent of the trust's assets were invested in stock 2, the investor implicitly allocated 22.11 percent of his wealth to stock 2 ($.2211 = .70 \times .3158$). Finally, since 42.10 percent of the trust's assets were invested in stock 3, the investor implicitly allocated 29.47 percent of his wealth to stock 3 ($.2947 = .70 \times .4210$). The investor therefore had the implicit allocation

$$x_1 = x_r x_1(r) = .70(.2632) = .1842$$
$$x_2 = x_r x_2(r) = .70(.3158) = .2211$$
$$x_3 = x_r x_3(r) = .70(.4210) = .2947$$

In addition to owning the three stocks, the investor also had wealth allocated to the risk-free asset (denoted as security 4):

$$x_4 = x_f = .30$$

Note that $x_1 + x_2 + x_3 + x_4 = 1$.

If the investor had diversified his wealth between the risk-free asset and the three stocks directly, in the allocation computed above, his return would have been

$$R = x_1 R_1 + x_2 R_2 + x_3 R_3 + x_4 R_4$$
$$= .1842(10) + .2211(-5) + .2947(3) + .30(1)$$
$$= 1.92\%$$

This is the same return which he would have earned by allocating 70 percent of his wealth to the trust participation units and 30 percent to the risk-free asset.

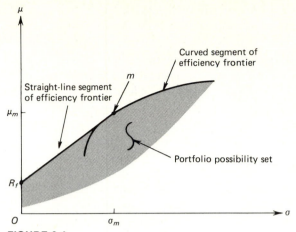

FIGURE 9.4
The efficiency frontier with a risk-free asset.

of the arbitrary trust portfolio r considered above, and so Equation (9.7) continues to apply. The relation between risk and return for efficient portfolios with risk less than σ_m is therefore given by

$$\mu = R_f + \frac{\mu_m - R_f}{\sigma_m}\sigma \qquad \sigma \leq \sigma_m \tag{9.8}$$

This equation is important because it gives the relation between risk and return over the straight-line segment of the efficiency frontier shown in Figure 9.4.

If an investor wants a portfolio allocation with an expected return greater than μ_m, and if he is willing to pay the price of additional risk exposure, he must choose a portfolio on the curved segment of the efficiency frontier which lies beyond m. Portfolios on this segment contain only risky securities, in allocations different from m.

9.3 EFFICIENT PORTFOLIOS WHEN BORROWING IS PERMITTED

In the previous section we saw that if an investor is satisfied with an expected return between R_f and μ_m, he will allocate his wealth between the portfolio consisting only of the risk-free asset

$$(0, 0, \ldots, 0, 1)$$

and some portfolio m of risky assets

$$(x_1(m), x_2(m), \ldots, x_I(m), 0)$$

If he wants an expected return greater than μ_m, he will hold a portfolio of risky assets other than m.

Suppose we now allow the investor to borrow at the risk-free rate R_f and to invest the proceeds of his loan in risky assets. This new opportunity, usually called *leveraging* or *buying on margin*, is represented by relaxing the constraint $x_f \geq 0$. With borrowing permitted, x_f may take on negative values, which is equivalent to saying that the investor can issue debt obligations against himself which are free of the risk of default. In practice, a lender insures himself against borrower default by insisting that his loan be collateralized with the securities which the borrower purchases with the proceeds of his borrowing. Moreover, lenders will lend only a fraction of the market value of the collateral securities.[8] The less volatile the prices of the collateral securities, the greater this fraction. A loan against short-term Treasury issues may approximate the market value of those issues, while a loan against corporate stock might be for between 20 and 70 percent of the market value of the stock. Borrowing at the risk-free rate R_f is also equivalent to selling the risk-free security short for one period, i.e., borrowing risk-free securities and then selling them for cash.[9]

With the ability to buy on margin, an investor can allocate a fraction $x_r > 1$ of his initial wealth to units of a trust portfolio r by holding a fraction $x_f < 0$ of his initial wealth in the risk-free asset. The analysis which led to Equations (9.6a) and (9.6b) remains unchanged, but now we no longer require $x_f \geq 0$. This added flexibility in the construction of a portfolio expands the portfolio possibility set from that shown in Figure 9.4 to the set shown in Figure 9.5.

Because of the expanded opportunity set, efficient portfolios with an expected return greater than μ_m will no longer be constructed by allocating wealth solely among risky assets. It will now be more efficient to borrow at the risk-free rate and invest the proceeds of the loan in portfolio m.

When borrowing at the risk-free rate (or short selling the risk-free asset) is permitted, the trade-off between risk and return on efficient portfolio allocations has an especially simple form. Equation (9.8) will be valid for all levels of

---

[8] The lending of funds for the purpose of purchasing or carrying securities is limited by several regulations of the Board of Governors of the Federal Reserve System, adopted pursuant to Section 7 of the Securities Exchange Act of 1934. Regulation T prohibits broker-dealers from lending to their customers more than the "loan value" of the assets collateralizing a loan. This loan value is set by the Board from time to time and is currently 50 percent for stock and convertible bonds. Loans for the purchase of Treasury and municipal securities and corporate bonds are exempt from Federal Reserve margin requirements. Rule 431 of the New York Stock Exchange prescribes maintenance margin requirements for loans by member firms. Rittereiser (1977) and Geelan and Fay (1977) describe the computational aspects of margin requirements. Kelly and Webb (1969) and Karmel (1970) wrote good introductory articles describing Federal Reserve margin requirements. See Lipton (1971); Solomon and Hart (1971, 1974); and Hart and Homer (1974) for more recent developments. Wolfson, Phillips, and Russo (1977, chap. 9) present a general overview of the margin rules. Several studies, including those of J. Cohen (1966); Moore (1966); Largay (1973); Largay and West (1973); Eckardt and Rogoff (1976); and Grube, Joy, and Panton (1979) have failed to find any effect of margin requirements on stock price behavior.

[9] The ability of investors to borrow, as well as lend, at a risk-free rate may be questioned. Securities dealers, however, frequently borrow funds through overnight or term repurchase agreements (see Section 4.2) at rates quite close to Federal funds and Treasury bill rates. See also Black and Scholes (1974a).

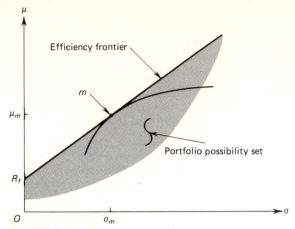

FIGURE 9.5
The efficiency frontier with a
risk-free asset when borrowing is
permitted.

risk $\sigma \geq 0$. The expected return on *any* efficient portfolio, as a function of the risk exposure of that portfolio, will then be

$$\mu = R_f + \frac{\mu_m - R_f}{\sigma_m} \sigma \tag{9.9}$$

This is the equation of the efficiency frontier shown in Figure 9.5.

When funds may be either invested *or* borrowed at the risk-free rate, and when risky assets may be held long or short, the optimal portfolio allocation problem is to

$$\text{Maximize } G\left(\sum_{i=1}^{I} x_i\mu_i + x_{I+1}R_f, \sum_{i=1}^{I}\sum_{j=1}^{I} x_ix_jC_{ij}\right) \tag{9.10}$$

over all alternative choices of $(x_1, x_2, \ldots, x_I, x_{I+1})$

subject to the constraint that $\sum_{i=1}^{I+1} x_i = 1$

Since any of the $I + 1$ assets may be sold short, there are no nonnegativity constraints on the x_i's. The maximization problem of (9.10) may be compared to the equivalent problem of (9.3), where only risky assets are available.

The Separation Theorem

Although it does not appear that the solution to (9.10) would be any simpler than that of (9.3), this is not the case. Inspection of Figure 9.5 shows that *all* efficient portfolios, and hence *any* optimal portfolio, can be constructed by combining portfolio m with the risk-free asset. The latter may be held in either negative or positive amounts. Thus, the portfolio allocation problem in (9.10) can be reduced to the problem

$$\text{Maximize } G(x_m\mu_m + x_fR_f, \, x_m^2\sigma_m^2) \tag{9.11}$$

over all alternative choices of x_m and x_f
subject to the constraint that $x_m + x_f = 1$

x_m is the fraction of wealth allocated to portfolio m, and x_f is the fraction of wealth allocated to the risk-free asset.

The allocation problem in (9.11) is the problem of choosing how much wealth to allocate to risky assets as a group, and how much wealth to allocate to the risk-free asset. If the allocation (x_m^*, x_f^*) solves problem (9.11), then the solution $(x_1^*, x_2^*, \ldots, x_I^*, x_{I+1}^*)$ to problem (9.10) *must* be

$$x_i^* = x_m^* x_i(m) \qquad i = 1, \ldots, I \tag{9.12a}$$
$$x_{I+1}^* = x_f^* \tag{9.12b}$$

Once the allocation $(x_1(m), \ldots, x_I(m), \, 0)$ of portfolio m has been identified, we need only decide on x_f and x_m, that is, how much of the risk-free asset and how much of m we want to hold. No other allocations need be considered. This important property is known as the *separation theorem* of portfolio theory.[10] The theorem states that when an investor can borrow and lend at the risk-free rate, he can separate the problem of allocating wealth *between* the risk-free asset and all risky assets from the problem of how to allocate wealth *among* risky assets. In the next chapter we will consider a special case where the composition of portfolio m is easily identified.

9.4   PREMIUM RETURNS ON EFFICIENT PORTFOLIOS AND ON INDIVIDUAL ASSETS IN AN EFFICIENT PORTFOLIO

Equation (9.9), describing μ-σ combinations on the efficiency frontier, may be written in a form which has an interesting interpretation. Specifically, for *all* efficient portfolios the difference between the expected return on a portfolio and the risk-free rate is a linear function of the risk exposure of the portfolio:

$$\mu - R_f = \frac{\mu_m - R_f}{\sigma_m} \, \sigma \tag{9.13}$$

Any reallocation of wealth from one efficient portfolio to another efficient portfolio that increases the risk exposure of an investor, i.e., that increases σ, will lead to a proportional increase in the *premium* expected return $\mu - R_f$ on

[10] The separation theorem was first stated by Tobin (1958). Black (1972) has shown there is a similar separation theorem even when there is no risk-free asset and only risky assets are available to investors. See also the exposition in Jensen (1972). In an unpublished paper whose results are reported by Jensen (1972), Vasicek (1971) shows there is a bifurcated separation theorem when investors can lend, but not borrow, at the risk-free rate.

the portfolio. The term $(\mu_m - R_f)/\sigma_m$ is commonly labeled the *price of risk.*[11] Equation (9.13) says that the premium expected return on an efficient portfolio is equal to the risk exposure of the portfolio times the price of risk.

The foregoing results apply to the relation between risks and premium returns on *efficient portfolios*. In this section we stipulate the existence of a similar relation for individual assets. This relation is important because it permits us to identify the correct measure of the risk of individual assets.

The relation of interest is summarized by the statement that the premium return on an asset is, in an optimal portfolio, equal to the price of risk times a risk-free term which depends on the allocation of the portfolio. The premium return on the *i*th asset is $\mu_i - R_f$, which is shown in the appendix to satisfy the equation

$$\mu_i - R_f = \frac{\mu_m - R_f}{\sigma_m}\,\sigma^{-1}\sum_{j=1}^{I} x_j C_{ij} \tag{9.14}$$

This relation holds for the individual premium returns $\mu_i - R_f$ on all risky assets, i.e., for $i = 1, \ldots, I$, in an optimal portfolio.

The last term in (9.14) can be given a more concrete interpretation. From the definition of σ^2 given by Equation (9.5b), we have[12]

$$\frac{\partial\sigma}{\partial x_i} = \sigma^{-1}\sum_{j=1}^{I} x_j C_{ij} \tag{9.15}$$

Equation (9.15) thus becomes

$$\mu_i - R_f = \frac{\mu_m - R_f}{\sigma_m}\frac{\partial\sigma}{\partial x_i} \tag{9.16}$$

Equation (9.16) is the analog to Equation (9.13) for the individual assets in an optimal portfolio. $\partial\sigma/\partial x_i$ is the *marginal* or incremental change in the risk ex-

---

[11] The price of soup is expressed as dollars per can of soup. Similarly, the price of risk is expressed as units of premium expected return $(\mu_m - R_f)$ per unit of risk (σ_m).

[12] The term $\partial\sigma/\partial x_i$ means the partial derivative of σ with respect to changes in x_i. Equation (9.15) follows because

$$\frac{\partial\sigma}{\partial x_i} = \frac{\partial\sigma}{\partial\sigma^2}\frac{\partial\sigma^2}{\partial x_i} = \frac{1}{2\sigma}\frac{\partial}{\partial x_i}\left(\sum_{k=1}^{I}\sum_{j=1}^{I} x_k x_j C_{kj}\right)$$

$$= \frac{1}{2\sigma}\frac{\partial}{\partial x_i}\left(x_i^2 C_{ii} + \sum_{\substack{k=1\\k\neq i}}^{I} x_k x_i C_{ki} + \sum_{\substack{j=1\\j\neq i}}^{I} x_i x_j C_{ij} + \sum_{\substack{k=1\\k\neq i}}^{I}\sum_{\substack{j=1\\j\neq i}}^{I} x_k x_j C_{kj}\right)$$

$$= \frac{1}{2\sigma}\left(2 x_i C_{ii} + \sum_{\substack{k=1\\k\neq i}}^{I} x_k C_{ki} + \sum_{\substack{j=1\\j\neq i}}^{I} x_j C_{ij}\right)$$

$$= \sigma^{-1}\sum_{j=1}^{I} x_j C_{ij}$$

posure of a portfolio with respect to changes in the proportion of security i in the portfolio. It is the marginal contribution of security i to portfolio risk. Equation (9.16) says that an investor will reallocate his portfolio until the marginal contribution of security i to the total risk on the portfolio, times the price of risk, just equals the premium return on security i. This suggests that $\partial\sigma/\partial x_i$, and not σ_i, is the correct measure of the risk of the ith asset in a portfolio context.

Equation (9.16) holds for any optimal portfolio. However, since any efficient portfolio may be an optimal portfolio for an investor with a suitable preference function, the equation must be satisfied by all efficient portfolio allocations.

CHAPTER SUMMARY

This chapter has extended portfolio theory to multiple-asset portfolios and to the case where one asset is risk-free. The extension proceeded in three stages.

We first considered the problem of allocating wealth among multiple risky assets. The equations for the risk and return on a multiple-asset portfolio were exhibited and compared with the same equations for the two-asset case. We pointed out that investment company securities, which provide a participation in a given asset portfolio, neither expand the portfolio possibility set nor shift the efficiency frontier.

The second stage of the extension of portfolio theory showed the effect of allowing investors to hold positive amounts of a risk-free asset. This new investment opportunity expanded the portfolio possibility set and, more importantly, shifted part of the efficiency frontier.

The third stage analyzed the consequences of allowing investors to margin their holdings of risky assets, or to borrow at the risk-free rate, or to short sell the risk-free asset. When borrowing and lending at the risk-free rate is permitted, any efficient portfolio will be allocated between the risk-free asset and some portfolio of strictly risky assets which we designated m. This property is known as the separation theorem of portfolio theory. We also showed that the efficiency frontier is a straight line in the μ-σ space when it is possible to borrow and lend at the risk-free rate. The slope of that line is the price of risk.

The premium return on an efficient portfolio is equal to the risk exposure of that portfolio (measured by the standard deviation of its return) times the price of risk. This relation is important, because it provides a direct link between risk and return for efficient portfolios. A similar, and equally important, result was shown to hold for the individual assets in an efficient portfolio. In particular, the premium return on an asset is equal to the marginal contribution of that asset to portfolio risk times the price of risk. In Chapter 12 we will use this result to show how premium returns on stock are established in a market equilibrium.

FURTHER READING

Fischer Black, "Capital Market Equilibrium with Restricted Borrowing," *Journal of Business*, **45** (July 1972), 444–454.

Eugene Fama, "Portfolio Analysis in a Stable Paretian Market," *Management Science*, **11** (January 1965), 404–419.

Robert Rittereiser, *Margin Regulations and Practice* (New York: New York Institute of Finance, 1977).

Shoichi Royama and Koichi Hamada, "Substitution and Complementarity in the Choice of Risky Assets," in *Risk Aversion and Portfolio Choice*, D. Hester and J. Tobin, eds. (New York: John Wiley & Sons, Inc., 1966).

William Sharpe, "A Simplified Model for Portfolio Analysis," *Management Science*, **9** (January 1963), 277–293.

——, *Portfolio Theory and Capital Markets* (New York: McGraw-Hill Book Company, 1970).

APPENDIX: Derivation of Equation (9.14)

In the multiple-asset case with a risk-free security available, the portfolio selection problem is the following:

$$\text{Maximize } G\left(\sum_{i=1}^{I} x_i\mu_i + x_{I+1}R_f, \sum_{i=1}^{I}\sum_{j=1}^{I} x_i x_j C_{ij}\right) \tag{A.1}$$

over all alternative choices of $(x_1, x_2, \ldots, x_I, x_{I+1})$

subject to the constraint that $\sum_{i=1}^{I+1} x_i = 1$

A solution to this optimization problem may be characterized by introducing the lagrangian for the constrained maximization

$$L = G\left(\sum_{i=1}^{I} x_i\mu_i + x_{I+1}R_f, \sum_{i=1}^{I}\sum_{j=1}^{I} x_i x_j C_{ij}\right) + \lambda\left[\sum_{i=1}^{I+1} x_i - 1\right] \tag{A.2}$$

where λ is the lagrangian multiplier.[13] At an optimal allocation, i.e., at an allocation which solves (A.1), the partial derivatives of L with respect to x_i have value zero for $i = 1, \ldots, I + 1$. Thus, we have

$$\frac{\partial L}{\partial x_i} = G_1\mu_i + 2G_2\sum_{j=1}^{I} x_j C_{ij} + \lambda = 0 \qquad i = 1, \ldots, I \tag{A.3a}$$

$$\frac{\partial L}{\partial x_{I+1}} = G_1 R_f + \lambda = 0 \tag{A.3b}$$

where $G_1 = \partial G/\partial\mu$ and $G_2 = \partial G/\partial\sigma^2$. Equation (A.3b) implies $\lambda = -G_1 R_f$. Using this value for λ in (A.3a) gives

---

[13] An introduction to lagrangian multipliers and constrained optimization may be found in Koo (1977, chap. 3).

$$0 = G_1(\mu_i - R_f) + 2G_2 \sum_{j=1}^{I} x_j C_{ij} \qquad i = 1, \ldots, I \tag{A.4}$$

or

$$\frac{-G_1}{2G_2} = (\mu_i - R_f)^{-1} \sum_{j=1}^{I} x_j C_{ij} \qquad i = 1, \ldots, I \tag{A.5}$$

The left-hand side of (A.5) does not depend on the value of the index i, and so the equation must hold for every one of the risky securities. If we pick some pair of securities, say, k and i, we must have

$$(\mu_k - R_f)^{-1} \sum_{j=1}^{I} x_j C_{kj} = (\mu_i - R_f)^{-1} \sum_{j=1}^{I} x_j C_{ij}$$

or

$$\sum_{j=1}^{I} x_j C_{kj} = \frac{\mu_k - R_f}{\mu_i - R_f} \sum_{j=1}^{I} x_j C_{ij} \tag{A.6}$$

Multiplying both sides of Equation (A.6) by x_k, summing both sides from $k = 1$ to $k = I$, and using Equation (9.5b) gives

$$\sigma^2 = \sum_{k=1}^{I} x_k \frac{\mu_k - R_f}{\mu_i - R_f} \sum_{j=1}^{I} x_j C_{ij} \tag{A.7}$$

Using Equation (9.5a) and the constraint that $x_1 + x_2 + \cdots + x_{I+1} = 1$ gives

$$\sigma^2 = \frac{\mu - x_{I+1}R_f - (1 - x_{I+1})R_f}{\mu_i - R_f} \sum_{j=1}^{I} x_j C_{ij}$$

or

$$\mu_i - R_f = \frac{\mu - R_f}{\sigma^2} \sum_{j=1}^{I} x_j C_{ij} \tag{A.8}$$

From Equation (9.9) we have that $(\mu - R_f)/\sigma = (\mu_m - R_f)/\sigma_m$, and so Equation (A.8) can be rewritten as

$$\mu_i - R_f = \frac{\mu_m - R_f}{\sigma_m} \sigma^{-1} \sum_{j=1}^{I} x_j C_{ij} \tag{A.9}$$

Equation (A.9) is the same as Equation (9.14), completing the derivation.

CHAPTER 10

HOMOGENEOUS EXPECTATIONS AND THE MARKET PORTFOLIO

The theory of portfolio selection developed in the preceding four chapters was primarily descriptive and offered no practical method for constructing the joint probability distribution of the returns on risky assets.[1] The theory certainly suggests some important aspects of the problem of allocating wealth among capital assets, but there is no simple method of application. In this chapter we impose one additional assumption on how investors solve their portfolio allocation problems; by doing so we bring the theory of portfolio choice into a concrete setting.

10.1 HOMOGENEOUS EXPECTATIONS

An investor's optimal portfolio allocation depends on (1) his preferences and (2) his beliefs about the statistical structure of future returns on risky assets. The latter is a reflection of information known to the investor. If, for example, two healthy companies of approximately equal size are both active in the same competitive industry, an investor may believe that the returns on the common stock of those companies will be highly correlated. If the industry expands, both companies will do well. If it contracts, both companies will suffer.

Information about issuers of financial assets plays a significant role in the formation of investor expectations of future security returns. The process of

---

[1] The single-index model of Sharpe (1963) and the multiple-index model of King (1966) may be used to estimate future expected returns and covariance relations from past data. Cohen and Pogue (1967), Elton and Gruber (1973), and Blume (1975) have investigated the stability of such forecasting techniques.

acquiring, interpreting, and disseminating investment information is a major business in the United States.[2] Investors pay substantial sums to obtain new information, and interpretations of new information, as rapidly as possible. Wire services like Dow Jones communicate developments in commerce and finance to their subscribers within minutes. Newspapers report the same events in more detail with a day's delay. Trade journals report specialized information with somewhat more delay, but they offer extensive analyses. Securities analysts and other commentators expend substantial efforts interpreting the impact of unforeseen developments on the earnings prospects of large and medium-size corporations. The upshot of such a vast system of information collection, processing, and dissemination is that, to a good approximation, most investors possess (or have access to) essentially identical information.

If investors interpret information in approximately comparable ways,[3] then, given that they share the same information, it follows that they should arrive at a common probability description of the prospective returns on risky assets. The assumption of *homogeneous expectations* formalizes this conclusion. To say that investors have homogeneous expectations is to say they share a common perception of the expected returns and variances and covariances of returns on risky securities.[4]

10.2 THE MARKET PORTFOLIO

If all investors have the same probability description of the returns on risky securities, it follows immediately that the portfolio m identified in the preceding chapter and shown in Figure 9.5 is the same portfolio for all investors. This observation allows us to identify the allocation of m.

We have already established that each investor allocates his wealth between the risk-free asset and some portfolio m of strictly risky assets. If m is the same for every investor, then the wealth which any *individual* investor does not allocate to the risk-free asset must be allocated to risky assets in the proportions of m. This means the collective portfolio of risky assets held by *all* investors is in the proportions of m. Example 10.1 illustrates this principle.

If investors collectively hold m as their portfolio of risky assets, then m must be the portfolio allocation of the market. If it were not, investors would collectively hold more than the available amount of some assets and less of others. This contradicts the observation that the collective holdings of all investors is

---

[2] A convenient summary of the disclosure process (including the roles of securities issuers, news media, security analysts, and portfolio managers) appears in Securities and Exchange Commission (1977a).

[3] Results reported by Lloyd-Davies and Canes (1978) imply that analyst recommendations, which are based on publicly available information, have value to market participants. This seems to imply that the way in which professional analysts process or interpret information is superior to the interpretative efforts of others. The consequences of this difference, however, appear to be small.

[4] It would be preferable to call this assumption *homogeneous perceptions*, since it includes variances and covariances as well as expectations, and can be extended to higher moments of the probability distribution of returns. The term *homogeneous expectations* has, however, become ingrained in the literature of financial markets.

the market. Under homogeneous expectations, m is therefore the market allocation of risky assets.

The composition of the market portfolio is easy to compute. Suppose that security i has a unit price of P_i and that there are N_i units of that security outstanding. If there are I risky assets in the market, the total value V_m of all risky securities is

$$V_m = \sum_{i=1}^{I} N_i P_i \tag{10.1}$$

Security i accounts for the fraction $x_i(m)$ of the total market value of all assets, where

$$x_i(m) = \frac{N_i P_i}{V_m} \qquad i = 1, \ldots, I \tag{10.2}$$

The market allocation $(x_1(m), \ldots, x_I(m))$ is a permissible portfolio allocation of strictly risky assets, because its elements sum to unity by definition. Note that computing the allocation of portfolio m by Equations (10.1) and (10.2) does not require any information on investor preferences or expectations.

Investing in the Market Portfolio and the Risk-Free Asset

The separation theorem discussed in Section 9.3 states that an investor can first decide the proportions in which to allocate wealth among risky assets, and then decide how he should allocate his wealth between (1) the risk-free asset and (2) all risky assets collectively. Under the assumption of homogeneous expectations, the allocation of that part of an investor's wealth devoted to risky assets should be in the market allocation specified by Equation (10.2).[5] This allocation does not depend on the preferences of the investor and is the same for all investors. Preferences enter the portfolio selection problem only when an investor has to decide how much of his wealth should be allocated to the risk-free asset and how much should be allocated to risky assets. In general, more risk-averse investors will hold a greater proportion of their wealth in the risk-free asset. Less risk-averse investors will hold a smaller proportion of their wealth in the risk-free asset or may borrow at the risk-free rate, or short sell the risk-free asset, to lever the market portfolio.

It should be borne in mind that identification of the market portfolio as the only efficient portfolio of strictly risky assets depends on the validity of the assumption of homogeneous expectations. If investors have heterogeneous perceptions of the statistical structure of the future returns on risky assets, there

---

[5] The return on stock portfolios (from the mid-1920s to the mid-1960s) with very large numbers of issues, approximating the return on the market as a whole, has been studied by Fisher and Lorie (1964, 1968, 1970) and Fisher (1966). Ibbotson and Sinquefield (1976) compared the returns on stock and bond portfolios and Treasury bills from 1926 to 1974.

EXAMPLE 10.1

INDIVIDUAL AND AGGREGATE ALLOCATIONS TO RISKY ASSETS WHEN INVESTORS HAVE HOMOGENEOUS EXPECTATIONS

This example illustrates the fact that when investors have homogeneous expectations, they will allocate their wealth between the risk-free asset and the market portfolio of risky assets.

Suppose that there are only three investors in the market and that investor A has a net worth of $100,000, investor B has a net worth of $40,000, and investor C has a net worth of $10,000. These investors will allocate their wealth between the risk-free asset and some portfolio m of strictly risky assets. Since the investors have homogeneous expectations, the allocation of portfolio m must be the same for all three investors. Suppose that there are only three stocks in the market, and that the allocation of portfolio m is

$$x_1(m) = .30 \qquad x_2(m) = .60 \qquad x_3(m) = .10$$

Suppose also that investor A is moderately risk-averse, that investor B is less risk-averse, and that investor C is even less risk-averse. The allocations of the three investors between the risk-free asset and portfolio m might then be as follows:

| | Fraction of wealth allocated | |
Investor	To portfolio m, %	To risk-free asset, %
A	50	50
B	80	20
C	130	−30

Note that a less risk-averse investor holds relatively less of the risk-free asset and relatively more of portfolio m and that investor C has purchased portfolio m on margin; i.e., he has sold the risk-free asset short.

From the net worths and portfolio allocations of the three investors, we can compute the dollar amount which each allocates to risky assets, i.e., to portfolio m:

Investor	Value of holdings of risky assets
A	.50 × $100,000 = $50,000
B	.80 × $ 40,000 = 32,000
C	1.30 × $ 10,000 = 13,000
Total	$95,000

The dollar value of the individual stock holdings of each of the three investors can be calculated from the dollar values of their holdings of risky assets and the allocation of portfolio m:

| | Value | | | |
Investor	Of stock 1	Of stock 2	Of stock 3	Of all stocks
A	$15,000	$30,000	$5,000	$50,000
B	9,600	19,200	3,200	32,000
C	3,900	7,800	1,300	13,000
Total	$28,500	$57,000	$9,500	$95,000

EXAMPLE 10.1 *(Continued)*

In the foregoing table, the dollar value of stock 1 held by investor A is the product of the dollar value of his wealth allocated to portfolio *m* ($50,000) and the fraction of stock 1 in portfolio *m* (30 percent), or $15,000 (that is, .30 × $50,000). Note that each investor individually allocated 30 percent of that portion of his wealth which he did not allocate to the risk-free asset to stock 1, 60 percent to stock 2, and 10 percent to stock 3.

In aggregate, the three investors allocated $95,000 to risky assets. They placed 30 percent of this aggregate amount in stock 1 ($28,500), 60 percent in stock 2 ($57,000), and 10 percent in stock 3 ($9500). Thus, the collective portfolio of risky assets held by *all* investors is in the proportions of portfolio *m*.

The allocation of portfolio *m* is clearly the allocation of the market portfolio, because we have accounted for all the issues and all the investors in the market. Thus, each investor has allocated his wealth between the risk-free asset and the market portfolio of risky assets.

---

may be no reason to ascribe any significance to the market portfolio. More importantly, our analysis does *not* suggest that all investors *should*, as a normative proposition, simply divide their wealth between the market allocation of risky assets and the risk-free asset. Our analysis does show that, as a positive proposition, investors *will* make such a division if they share homogeneous expectations.

The Capital Market Line and the Market Price of Risk

Under homogeneous expectations, the allocation of portfolio *m* can be determined by Equation (10.2) without specifically knowing the expectations which investors share about future security returns. Since portfolio *m* is the same portfolio for all investors, it becomes convenient to give more specific names to some of the concepts introduced in Chapter 9.

When investors share homogeneous expectations, all efficient portfolios consist of the risk-free asset (held long or short) and the market portfolio of risky assets. The resulting efficiency frontier, shown in Figure 10.1, is called the *capital market line*. Over the period from January 1960 to December 1969, the average premium return on stocks listed on the New York Stock Exchange, i.e., the return in excess of the rate of return on high-quality commercial paper, was .510 percent per month, or 6.3 percent per year.[6] The variance of return on the same stocks was 14.67 percent squared per month, or $\sigma_m^2 = (3.83)^2$. The capital market line which results from assuming $\mu_m - R_f = .51$ and $\sigma_m = 3.83$ over a 1-month planning period is shown in Figure 10.1.

The price of risk has previously been defined as the ratio of the premium expected return to the standard deviation of return on a particular portfolio *m*, or as $(\mu_m - R_f)/\sigma_m$. Since we have now identified portfolio *m* as the market portfolio, it is convenient to call the ratio $(\mu_m - R_f)/\sigma_m$ the *market price of risk*. That ratio is the premium return available on an *efficient* portfolio per unit of

---

[6] See McDonald (1974, p. 319).

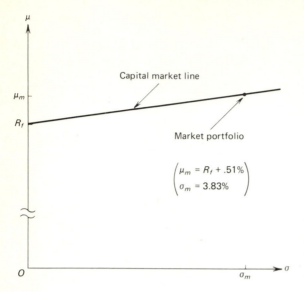

FIGURE 10.1
Efficiency frontier for a 1-month period when investors have homogeneous expectations, estimated from the average behavior of stock prices from 1960 to 1969. *Source:* McDonald, (1974, p. 319).

risk of that portfolio. That is, the market price of risk is the slope of the capital market line. (The intercept of the capital market line is the risk-free rate.)

10.3 MARKET INDEXES

Under the assumption of homogeneous expectations, the return on the market portfolio of risky assets plays a uniquely important role in capital market theory. Any efficient portfolio must be allocated only between the risk-free asset and the market portfolio of risky assets. The return on an efficient portfolio is, therefore, a weighted average of the predictable return on the risk-free asset and the random return on the market portfolio of risky assets. We will further see, in Chapter 12, that the *covariance* between the return on an individual security and the return on the market portfolio is a parameter of great importance to the structure of expected risk premiums in a market equilibrium. Because of the importance of the return on the market, it is worthwhile to consider several measures of that return.

In this section we describe four commonly used market indexes: Standard & Poor's Composite Index of 500 Stocks (the S&P 500), the New York Stock Exchange Composite Index (the NYSE index), the Dow Jones Average of 30 Industrial Stocks (the Dow average), and an index constructed by Lawrence Fisher (Fisher's index) which has been used in several empirical studies of the structure of returns on financial assets and which is described at greater length in Fisher (1966). These indexes primarily cover common stocks listed on the New York Stock Exchange,[7] but because the equity securities of most major

---

[7] The S&P 500 includes about a dozen stocks, mainly of financial corporations, which are traded over-the-counter and are not listed on the NYSE. The NYSE index includes preferred as well as common stock.

American corporations are listed on the NYSE, the failure to include equity issues traded only in other market centers is not too important.

Before describing the construction of the specific indexes, let us consider how the return on the market might best be measured. Suppose at time t there are $I(t)$ securities in the market, with security i having price $P_i(t)$ and $N_i(t)$ shares outstanding. The market allocation to the ith security at time t, denoted by $x_i(m, t)$, is then

$$x_i(m, t) = \frac{N_i(t)P_i(t)}{\sum\limits_{j=1}^{I(t)} N_j(t)P_j(t)} \tag{10.3}$$

If an investor purchased one unit of security i at time t, his investment in that security would grow (or shrink) to some future value at time $t + 1$. In the simplest case the future value would be the price $P_i(t + 1)$ of security i at time $t + 1$, adjusted for stock splits and stock dividends. The future value should also include any cash dividends $D_i(t + 1)$ paid to those who held the security between time t and time $t + 1$. In addition, it should include the value of any rights, spin-offs of other securities, or distributions of assets in reorganization or partial liquidation.[8] If we denote the value of these extraordinary distributions as $E_i(t + 1)$, the return on security i from time t to time $t + 1$ is

$$R_i(t) = \left[\frac{P_i(t + 1) + D_i(t + 1) + E_i(t + 1)}{P_i(t)} \right] - 1 \tag{10.4}$$

The total return on the market over the interval from time t to time $t + 1$ is a market-weighted average of the returns on the individual securities in the market:

$$R_m(t) = \sum\limits_{i=1}^{I(t)} x_i(m, t)R_i(t) \tag{10.5}$$

From the definitions of (10.3) and (10.4), the return on the market can also be written as

$$R_m(t) = \frac{\sum\limits_{i=1}^{I(t)} N_i(t)[P_i(t + 1) + D_i(t + 1) + E_i(t + 1)]}{\sum\limits_{j=1}^{I(t)} N_j(t)P_j(t)} - 1 \tag{10.6}$$

Equation (10.6) expresses the return on the market as the change in the aggregate value of all securities existing at time t. Fisher's index comes closest to the form of (10.5). The other indexes can more easily be related to the expression of Equation (10.6).

---

[8] Descriptions and examples of rights distributions, stock splits, and stock dividends are given in Section 6.1.

Fisher's Index

The construction of Fisher's index begins by calculating the return over a chosen holding period on every issue of common stock listed on the NYSE, as in Equation (10.4). In Fisher's original work the holding period was 1 month. Fisher then computes a simple arithmetic average gross return

$$L_a(t) = \sum_{i=1}^{I(t)} \frac{1 + R_i(t)}{I(t)} \tag{10.7}$$

In addition to this arithmetic average return, Fisher also computes a modified geometric average gross return, defined as

$$L_g(t) = \frac{1 + U(t)}{1 - U(t)} \tag{10.8}$$

where
$$U(t) = \sum_{i=1}^{I(t)} \frac{R_i(t)}{[2 + R_i(t)]I(t)} \tag{10.9}$$

The composite gross return is defined as

$$L(t) = .56\,L_a(t) + .44\,L_g(t) \tag{10.10}$$

The net return on the market from time t to time $t + 1$ is defined as

$$R_{\text{Fisher}}(t) = L(t) - 1 \tag{10.11}$$

The technical details justifying the use of a composite return based on both arithmetic and geometric averages are given in Fisher (1966).

The important aspect of Fisher's index is that it includes in the calculation of the return on the market not only capital gains and losses but also cash dividends and other extraordinary distributions. However, unlike the definition of the market return given by Equation (10.5), Fisher's index is based on a simple average of the returns on individual securities rather than on a market-weighted average.

The NYSE Index

Since 1966 the New York Stock Exchange has computed a composite index of the value of all listed common stock issues. For time t the index is defined as

$$\text{NYSE}(t) = \frac{\displaystyle\sum_{i=1}^{I(t)} N_i(t)P_i(t)}{\text{BASE}(t)} \tag{10.12}$$

The variable $\text{BASE}(t)$ is a *divisor* whose value is changed from time to time to reflect the effect of changes in listings and new stock issues by listed companies. The value of the divisor is revised, when necessary, according to the equation

$$\frac{\text{New BASE}}{\text{Old BASE}} = \frac{\sum_{i=1}^{I'} N'_i P_i}{\sum_{i=1}^{I} N_i P_i} \qquad (10.13)$$

where P_i is the prevailing market price of the ith security at the time the divisor is revised, N'_i is the revised number of units of security i, and N_i is the former number of units of that security and where there were formerly I securities and there are now I' securities. An example of how the divisor is revised is given in Example 10.2.

The return on the market from time t to time $t + 1$ may be computed from the NYSE index as

$$R_{\text{NYSE}}(t) = \frac{\text{NYSE}(t + 1)}{\text{NYSE}(t)} - 1 \qquad (10.14)$$

EXAMPLE 10.2
REVISING THE DIVISOR OF THE NEW YORK STOCK EXCHANGE INDEX

This example illustrates the use of Equation (10.13) in revising the divisor of the New York Stock Exchange index as a result of a new stock listing on that exchange.

Suppose that at the close of trading on some Tuesday the value of the divisor was BASE = 15 billion and that the aggregate market value of all listed common stock was $765 billion. The NYSE index would then have the value $51 = $765/15.

Suppose a new company is to be added to the NYSE listings for initial trading on the following Wednesday morning. As of the close of trading Tuesday night the new company had 10 million shares of common stock outstanding, valued at $40 per share. The total value of the new company's common stock was, therefore, $400 million. Solely as a result of the new listing, the aggregate market value of all listed common stock would increase from $765 billion to $765.4 billion. The revised value of the divisor can be computed from Equation (10.13) as

$$\text{New BASE} = \text{Old BASE}\ \frac{\Sigma N'_i P_i}{\Sigma N_i P_i}$$

$$= (15\ \text{billion})\ \frac{\$765.4}{\$765.0}$$

$$= 15.00784\ \text{billion}$$

The value of the index on Tuesday night would be unchanged by this revision of the divisor, because $51 = $765.4/15.00784. The new divisor of 15.00784 billion would be used to deflate the aggregate market value of listed common stock until it had to be changed because of a subsequent listing or delisting or for some other reason.

EXAMPLE 10.3
USING THE NEW YORK STOCK EXCHANGE INDEX TO MEASURE THE RETURN ON
THE MARKET

This example illustrates the use of Equation (10.14) to measure the return on the
market using the New York Stock Exchange index.

The table below shows the aggregate market value of all listed common stock, the
divisor BASE, and the NYSE index at the close of trading on 3 consecutive days. Note
that the divisor is revised at the close of trading on Tuesday as described in Example
10.2 above.

Day	Aggregate value of listed stock	Divisor (BASE)	NYSE index
Monday	$750 billion	15 billion	$50
Tuesday (original)	765 billion	15 billion	51
Tuesday (revised)	765.4 billion	15.00784 billion	51
Wednesday	775 billion	15.00784 billion	51.6397

Using Equation (10.14) to compute the return on the market gives the returns shown
below for three different intervals:

• Monday–Tuesday:

$$\text{Return} = \frac{51}{50} - 1$$
$$= .02, \text{ or } 2\%$$

• Tuesday–Wednesday:

$$\text{Return} = \frac{51.6397}{51} - 1$$
$$= .0125, \text{ or } 1.25\%$$

• Monday–Wednesday:

$$\text{Return} = \frac{51.6397}{50} - 1$$
$$= .0328, \text{ or } 3.28\%$$

If we used the raw aggregate market value data, we would have computed the following returns:

• Monday–Tuesday:

$$\text{Return} = \frac{765}{750} - 1$$
$$= .02, \text{ or } 2\%$$

• Tuesday–Wednesday:

$$\text{Return} = \frac{775}{765.4} - 1$$
$$= .125, \text{ or } 1.25\%$$

EXAMPLE 10.3 *(Continued)*

These returns agree with the returns on the market computed from the NYSE index. It is not, however, clear how to measure the return on the market from Monday to Wednesday using the raw aggregate market data. We clearly cannot compute that return as (775/750) − 1, because a new listing was added between the close of trading on Monday and the close of trading on Wednesday. The most natural way of computing the 2-day return is to note that if we had started with $1.00 invested in the market as a whole on Monday night, we would have had $1.02 on Tuesday night. This could have then been reinvested to give $1.0328 on Wednesday night ($1.0328 = $1.02 × 1.0125 increase from Tuesday to Wednesday). Thus, the return on the market from Monday night to Wednesday night was 3.28 percent, after accounting for the new listing. Note that this also agrees with the return from Monday to Wednesday computed above using the NYSE index. (This illustrates that the revision in the divisor on Tuesday was necessary.)

   It should be noted that the foregoing returns do *not* include the value of any cash dividends or distributions of securities.

If the divisor is unchanged from time t to time $t + 1$, this becomes

$$R_{\text{NYSE}}(t) = \frac{\displaystyle\sum_{i=1}^{I(t+1)} N_i(t+1)P_i(t+1)}{\displaystyle\sum_{i=1}^{I(t)} N_i(t)P_i(t)} - 1$$

$$= \frac{\displaystyle\sum_{i=1}^{I(t)} N_i(t)P_i(t+1)}{\displaystyle\sum_{i=1}^{I(t)} N_i(t)P_i(t)} - 1 \tag{10.15}$$

This measure of the return on the market can be compared with Equation (10.6). Example 10.3 illustrates the use of the NYSE index in measuring the return on the market.

   The NYSE index measures the change in the market value of all listed securities *exclusive* of cash and noncash distributions. Like Fisher's index, the NYSE index covers all listed issues but employs a market-weighted average rather than a simple average.

The S&P 500 Index

The design of the S&P 500 index is similar to that of the NYSE index except that it covers only 500 selected common stocks. The issues included in the index change from time to time as a result of mergers and consolidations, bankruptcies, and other changes in coverage.

   The value of the S&P 500 index at time t[call it S&P(t)] is defined as in Equation (10.12) but with the summation running over only 500 selected stocks. The divisor of the S&P 500 index differs from that of the NYSE index, but it is adjusted in a similar fashion for new stock issues and changes in the identity of the 500 stocks included in the index. The return on the market from time t to time $t + 1$ is defined as

$$R_{S\&P}(t) = \frac{S\&P(t+1)}{S\&P(t)} - 1 \tag{10.16}$$

This return measures the net change in the total value of the 500 covered securities *exclusive* of cash and noncash distributions. The returns on the 500 individual issues are weighted according to what their market weights would be if they were the only securities in the market.

The Dow Average

Unlike the three preceding indexes, the Dow average is a simple price average which is not adjusted for change in the outstanding volume of the thirty stock issues which appear in the average, nor is it adjusted for stock dividends smaller than 10 percent. The Dow average at time t is defined as

$$\text{DOW}(t) = \sum_{i=1}^{30} \frac{P_i(t)}{\text{BASE}(t)} \tag{10.17}$$

$\text{BASE}(t)$ is a divisor which is changed from time to time to reflect the effect of stock splits and stock dividends in excess of 10 percent.

Suppose the holder of one share of security i becomes the holder of g_i shares due to a stock split or stock dividend. For example, $g_i = 2$ if a split is 2 for 1, and $g_i = 1.25$ for a 25 percent stock dividend. The divisor is then revised according to the equation

$$\frac{\text{New BASE}}{\text{Old BASE}} = \frac{\sum\limits_{i=1}^{30} P_i/g_i}{\sum\limits_{i=1}^{30} P_i} \tag{10.18}$$

where P_i is the market price of the ith security at the time of the revision.

If the return on the market between time t and time $t + 1$ is defined as

$$R_{\text{DOW}}(t) = \frac{\text{DOW}(t+1)}{\text{DOW}(t)} - 1 \tag{10.19}$$

and if the divisor is unchanged during that interval, then the return is

$$R_{\text{DOW}}(t) = \frac{\sum\limits_{i=1}^{30} P_i(t+1)}{\sum\limits_{i=1}^{30} P_1(t)} - 1 \tag{10.20}$$

As a measure of the return on the market over some interval of time, the Dow average has several major deficiencies. The average ignores returns due to cash dividends and noncash distributions. It also ignores changes in the price of a stock that result from stock dividends of less than 10 percent. Of the four indexes which we have discussed, however, it is the most widely reported in the financial press.

Correlations among Market Indexes

Although the four market indexes discussed above are constructed in quite different ways and cover different securities, they nevertheless tend to be highly correlated with each other. Figure 10.2 shows monthly values of the NYSE index, the S&P 500 index, and the Dow average during the 1970s. Exhibit 10.1 shows the correlation coefficients among returns measured by the different indexes.

Most empirical studies have used either the S&P 500 index or Fisher's index to measure the return on the market portfolio, but it seems likely that the NYSE index or the Dow average would often give substantially similar results.

10.4 INDEX FUNDS

In the second section of this chapter we saw that if each investor's perception of the expected returns and of the covariances of returns on risky assets is identical to the perceptions of all other investors, then each investor will hold only two basic assets: the risk-free asset and the market portfolio of risky assets.

Most casual observers and many market participants reject this view of the investment process. They argue that market prices frequently fail to reflect the "intrinsic" value of a security and that professional investment advisers can discriminate between overvalued and undervalued securities by careful analysis of available information about the issuers of those securities. Expectations

---

EXHIBIT 10.1
CORRELATIONS AMONG RETURNS ON THE MARKET MEASURED WITH ALTERNATIVE INDEXES
(Returns Measured over 1-Month Intervals, January 1970 to December 1979)

Correlation between return measured with New York Stock Exchange Composite Index and return measured with Standard & Poor's Composite Index of 500 Stocks: .996

Correlation between return measured with New York Stock Exchange Composite Index and return measured with Dow Jones Average of 30 Industrial Stocks: .946

Correlation between return measured with Standard & Poor's Composite Index of 500 Stocks and return measured with Dow Jones Average of 30 Industrial Stocks: .953

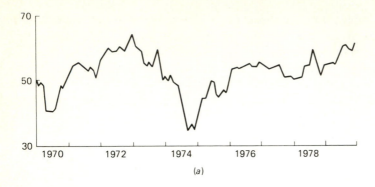

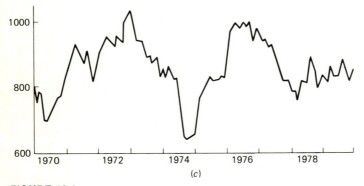

FIGURE 10.2
(a) The New York Stock Exchange Composite Index, (b) Standard &
Poor's Composite Index of 500 Stocks, and (c) the Dow Jones Average
of 30 Industrial Stocks, 1970–1979.

derived from such analyses would presumably be more accurate predictors of
future values than the expectations held by other market participants. Moreover, a portfolio allocated on the basis of such superior expectations should exhibit more desirable risk/return characteristics than one constructed simply by
combining the risk-free asset and the market portfolio of risky assets. Most in-

stitutional investments are, consequently, managed on the principle that research and analysis can produce superior performance and are worth paying for. Such managed investments include almost all mutual funds, pension funds, and personal trusts.

The problem with the proposition that research and analysis pays is that a large and growing literature, reviewed in Chapter 13, suggests that the prices at which securities can be bought and sold reflect all information which is publicly available about the issuers of the securities. If this is true, then purchases and sales of securities on the basis of analyses of public information cannot be expected to lead to measurably superior investment performance.[9] Only investors possessing and trading on undisclosed "inside" information can expect to make abnormally large profits from their investments. Thus, from a pragmatic viewpoint, there may be some justification for accepting the notion that all efficient portfolios can be constructed by mixing the market portfolio with a risk-free asset. The arguments for such an investment strategy have not gone wholly unappreciated by institutional investors.

Several large professional money managers, including Wells Fargo Bank in San Francisco, American National Bank & Trust Company of Chicago, Batterymarch Financial Management Corporation in Boston, Bankers Trust Company in New York, and The Vanguard Group of Investment Companies in Valley Forge, Pennsylvania, have recently begun to offer their clients the opportunity of participating in so-called index funds.[10] The precise structure of these funds varies,[11] but they are generally constructed with a view to duplicating the return on the Standard & Poor's Composite Index of 500 Stocks. (Exhibit 10.2 shows the cover page of the prospectus for a publicly offered index fund.) Thus, the funds offer a close approximation to an investment in the market portfolio of risky assets, at least if one is willing to restrict the concept of the market to the 500 common stock issues in the S&P 500 index.

Although some commentators argue that the abandonment of any effort to

---

[9] Several commentators have recently taken to heart these findings about the informational efficiency of the markets. Salmanowitz (1977, p. 1101, n. 121) proposed that purchase and sale confirmation notices from brokerage houses should carry this legend:

"Empirical evidence indicates that security prices fully reflect all publicly available information. . . . The evidence . . . implies that above average gains cannot be expected from the analysis of historical prices or from the analysis of publicly available accounting and nonaccounting information. . . . The empirical evidence also suggests that at any risk level diversification of portfolio risk in light of the investor's needs, resources and desires yields the best possible expected returns after transaction costs."

Pozen (1976) proposed that money managers, including pension fund trustees and investment advisors to mutual funds and pension funds, be prohibited from purchasing research on securities based on past price movements or publicly available information without the specific consent of their clients.

[10] Black and Scholes (1974a) discuss some of the considerations which went into the development of the Wells Fargo index fund, as well as some of the difficulties encountered in selling the concept of an index fund to investors. See also Belliveau (1976). Langbein and Posner (1976) discuss the legal implications of fiduciary investments in index funds.

[11] Ehrbar (1976, p. 152) discusses the details of the management policies of three index funds. See also Gray (1976) and Shapiro (1976).

FIRST INDEX
INVESTMENT TRUST
Post Office Box 1100
Valley Forge, PA 19482
(800) 523-7910 (Toll Free)
(215) 293-1100 (Call Collect in
　　　　　　　　　Pennsylvania)

Distributor
Wellington Management Company
28 State Street
Boston, MA 02109
Post Office Box 823
Valley Forge, PA 19482

Transfer Agent
The Vanguard Group, Inc.
P. O. Box 1100
Valley Forge, PA 19482

Contents

First Index
INVESTMENT TRUST

A NO-LOAD MUTUAL FUND

First Index Investment Trust (the "Trust") is a no-load open-end investment trust designed as an "index fund," and is the first of its kind to be offered to the public. The Trust's investment objective is to provide investment results that correspond to the price and yield performance of publicly-traded common stocks in the aggregate, as represented by the Standard & Poor's 500 Composite Stock Price Index (the "Index"). The Trust is neither sponsored by, nor affiliated with, Standard & Poor's Corporation. See page 6.

The Trust is a member of The Vanguard Group of Investment Companies, which provides for its own administrative services on a non-profit basis. Since the Trust's portfolio will not be "managed," the Trust has no investment adviser, pays no advisory fee and is expected to have a relatively low annual operating expense ratio, estimated at approximately 3/10 of 1% of net assets. In addition, each shareholder will be charged a quarterly account maintenance fee of $1.50 ($6 per year). See page 8.

You may purchase shares of the Trust at net asset value without a sales commission. The minimum initial investment is $1,500; $50 minimum for subsequent investments. You may at any time redeem (sell back to the Trust) all or a portion of your shares at net asset value, without sales charge. The Trust reserves the right, on thirty days' notice, to redeem accounts having a value of less than $250 as a result of shareholder redemptions.

Please retain this prospectus for future reference.

───────────────

THESE SECURITIES HAVE NOT BEEN APPROVED OR DISAPPROVED BY THE SECURITIES AND EXCHANGE COMMISSION NOR HAS THE COMMISSION PASSED UPON THE ACCURACY OR ADEQUACY OF THIS PROSPECTUS. ANY REPRESENTATION TO THE CONTRARY IS A CRIMINAL OFFENSE.

No dealer, salesman or any other person has been authorized to give any information or to make any representations other than those contained in this Prospectus, and if given or made, such information must not be relied upon as having been authorized by the Trust. This Prospectus does not constitute an offer to sell or a solicitation of an offer to buy any of the securities offered hereby in any state to any person to whom it is unlawful to make such offer in such state.

PROSPECTUS—May 2, 1977

1

EXHIBIT 10.2
Cover page of a prospectus for an index fund.

"outperform" the market is defeatist, the new index funds have attracted a modest but growing following from corporate pension funds. By 1976, the first three money managers cited above (Wells Fargo, American National, and Batterymarch Financial Management) had more than $500 million of assets under management in index funds. Their clients included Samsonite, Greyhound, Asarco, and several affiliates of AT&T. In addition, Ford Motor Company and Exxon Corporation had a total of $100 million invested in index funds which they managed themselves.[12] In the spring of 1977 three pension funds of the City of New York reallocated 20 percent of their assets, worth about $250 million, to an index fund managed by Bankers Trust Company.[13]

One of the more attractive features of index-fund investments is that management fees on such investments are substantially lower than those on conventionally managed portfolios. Langbein and Posner (1976, p. 16) report that management fees on index funds may be only about one-tenth as large as the fees charged by managers of conventional portfolios. Although the fees going to those managers might be well spent if their research efforts actually produced superior returns, empirical evidence suggests that they do not.[14] As one index-fund client succinctly stated, "Whatever you're paying for professional management, it just isn't worth it."[15] Index funds can charge smaller management fees, because they make little or no effort to acquire and interpret information which might allow them to discriminate between overvalued and undervalued securities. The only difference between the gross return on the S&P 500 index and the net return on an index fund is the cost of executing transactions to reinvest dividends, rebalance the portfolio of the fund when the market weights attached to different securities have changed, or accommodate net cash inflows from and outflows to the clients of the fund.

CHAPTER SUMMARY

When investors have homogeneous expectations, they will allocate their wealth between the risk-free asset and a particular portfolio of risky assets. Since the collective holdings of all investors is, by definition, the market portfolio, that portion of wealth not invested in the risk-free asset must be allocated like the market portfolio. This positive proposition simplifies portfolio theory considerably, because it permits an objective identification of the two assets (the market portfolio and the risk-free asset) which make up all efficient portfolios.

Although the market portfolio of common stocks should include all stocks, errors from failing to recognize any but the largest 500 or 1500 issuers are not large. The return on the market portfolio is closely approximated by Fisher's index or by the change in value of the NYSE index, the S&P 500 index, or even the Dow average.

Since the early 1970s, market participants have become increasingly cognizant of the efficiency characteristics of the market portfolio. This has led to the development of index funds to provide convenient access to portfolios as well diversified as the market as a whole. Sponsors of index funds typically charge lower fees than do sponsors of actively managed funds, because they do not seek to acquire and act on any information other than past changes in the values of securities.

---

[12] Ehrbar (1976, p. 150).
[13] *The New York Times*, March 24, 1977, p. 53, col. 4, and March 26, 1977, p. 26, col. 3.
[14] Jensen (1968). Jensen's analysis is discussed in Section 13.4.
[15] Quoted in Ehrbar (1976, p. 150).

FURTHER READING

A. F. Ehrbar, "Index Funds—An Idea Whose Time Is Coming," *Fortune*, **93** (June 1976), 145–154.

John Langbein and Richard Posner, "Mutual Funds and Trust-Investment Law," *American Bar Association Research Journal*, (1976), 1–34.

Peter Lloyd-Davies and Michael Canes, "Stock Prices and the Publication of Second-Hand Information," *Journal of Business*, **51** (January 1978), 43–56.

Robert Pozen, "Money Managers and Securities Research," *New York University Law Review*, **51** (1976), 923–980.

John Salmanowitz, "Broker Investment Recommendations and the Efficient Capital Market Hypothesis: A Proposal Cautionary Legend," *Stanford Law Review*, **29** (1977), 1077–1114.

Securities and Exchange Commission, *Report of the Advisory Committee on Corporate Disclosure to the Securities and Exchange Commission*, (1977).

Harvey Shapiro, "How Do You Really Run One of Those Index Funds?" *Institutional Investor*, **10** (February 1976), 24.

PART FOUR

CAPITAL MARKET EQUILIBRIUM IN A SINGLE-PERIOD CONTEXT

The five chapters of Part Three analyzed the behavior of an individual investor in a competitive securities market. Because the market was assumed competitive, we treated both securities prices and the statistical structure of returns as fixed. While this may be acceptable for purposes of analyzing individual investors, it clearly cannot be true for all investors collectively, because prices are determined by the aggregate purchase and sale interests of all market participants. In the following three chapters we broaden our analysis to consider how prices are determined in a competitive securities market.

Chapter 11 describes a financial market reduced to its barest essentials: communication of prices to market participants and establishment of equilibrium prices at which the total demand for each asset equals the available supply of that asset. We assume in that chapter that all investors make their portfolio choices according to the single-period risk and return criteria presented in Part Three.

Chapter 12 develops the cross-sectional characteristics of equilibrium expected asset returns for a market where participants have homogeneous expectations, i.e., a common probability description of end-of-period asset values. We have already seen, in Chapter 10, that the assumption of homogeneous expectations implies a uniquely important role for the market-weighted portfolio of risky assets. In Chapter 12 we extend that analysis to demonstrate the importance of the covariance of the return on an individual asset with the return on the market portfolio. The model of equilibrium asset pricing presented in Chapters 11 and 12 is commonly called the *capital asset pricing model.*[1]

Chapter 13 discusses the efficiency of capital markets and addresses the question of whether securities prices reflect all available information concerning the future prospects of securities issuers. This question is important, because if market participants ignore relevant information in deciding on their purchase and sale interests, prices which lead to a clearing of aggregate supply and demand cannot be said to be equilibrium prices in a broader sense of the word.

---

[1] The capital asset pricing model was developed in a series of approximately contemporaneous papers by Sharpe (1964), Lintner (1965a, b), and Mossin (1966). See also the expository comments by Fama (1968, 1971, 1973) and Beja (1972). S. Ross (1976) has recently proposed a competitor to the capital asset pricing model for explaining the cross-sectional structure of expected asset returns. His "arbitrage pricing theory" is examined empirically in Roll and Ross (1980).

CAPITAL MARKET EQUILIBRIUM

This chapter sets forth the basic ideas underlying the analysis of a market in equilibrium. Our principal objectives are to describe the structure of a competitive auction market and to explore the notion of market equilibrium.

The description of any financial market requires specification of three elements: (1) the framework or rules of the game within which individual market participants make their portfolio choices, (2) the process by which participants make their choices, and (3) a procedure for enforcing consistency in the collective choice of all participants. The last element provides the mechanism by which aggregate demand expands or contracts to equal the available supply of each asset.

The Market Framework

The framework for individual choice assumed here is that of a competitive auction market. Purchase and sale prices for all securities are announced by an auctioneer. Each investor, knowing the market is competitive, believes he can buy or sell as much of any security as he desires at the announced price for that security. The first section develops further the implications of this type of market.[1]

---

[1] This is not the only conceivable type of market framework. Another possibility is a bilateral barter market, in which an investor may exchange one security for a different security held by some other investor as long as both investors want to complete the exchange. See Beja and Hakanson (1977) for a description of a bilateral barter market.

Investor Demand

Given the prices announced by the auctioneer, individuals are assumed to make their choices among alternative financial assets according to the single-period portfolio selection criteria developed in Part Three. The second section of this chapter extends portfolio analysis to show explicitly the role of securities prices in portfolio selection. The demand functions of an investor for the securities in the marketplace are derived in that section.

Market Equilibrium

The third section of this chapter discusses the consistency requirement, or equilibrium condition, that the total demand for each asset equals the available supply of that asset. If this requirement is satisfied for *every* asset at some set of announced asset prices, the market is in equilibrium and the announced prices are equilibrium prices. When a market is in equilibrium, an investor will be able to satisfy his demand for each security since, by definition of an equilibrium, the collective demand for each security by all investors equals the available supply of that security. In this sense the choices of individual participants are collectively consistent when a market is in equilibrium.[2]

The Risk-Free Return

The market for capital assets which we will consider in this chapter is not complete. In particular, we assume that the return R_f on the risk-free asset is determined outside of the market for risky assets. For the case where the length of an investment period is 1 day, the risk-free rate will be the rate on repurchase agreements and purchases and sales of Federal funds. That rate will be determined by the supply of and demand for reserve balances, as discussed in Chapter 5. Only the equilibrium prices of risky assets are determined in the market discussed in this chapter.

11.1   THE MARKET FRAMEWORK

Individual investors do not play a direct role in setting asset prices in a competitive auction market. Prices are, instead, set by an auctioneer in a manner designed to lead to equilibrium prices for every security simultaneously. Auction markets differ in this respect from most real securities markets. In a dealer market, for example, inventory specialists quote bid and offer prices at which they stand ready to purchase and sell securities for their own account. The abstraction of a competitive auction market has the important advantage, howev-

---

[2] A market equilibrium can also be achieved by rationing. For example, the auctioneer could announce a set of prices and then administratively allocate the available supply of each security for which there was an excess demand. This technique has been used in subscription offerings of Treasury coupon issues, as noted in Section 1.2.

er, of allowing us to distinguish the trading interests of individual investors from the process by which the market comes into equilibrium.

A market is *competitive* if each participant believes he can buy or sell an arbitrarily large amount of any asset at the price which the auctioneer has announced for that asset. This is not an unrealistic assumption as long as individual investors neither own nor demand more than a negligible fraction of each of the assets traded in the market. In a competitive market, investors view the price of each asset as being determined by impersonal market forces, upon which their own particular purchase and sale interests cannot exert any influence.

We ignore the element of time in this chapter by treating a market auction as a discrete event completed in a timeless world and at no expense to any participant. We assume that all investors know the prices of securities as they are announced by the auctioneer and that no investor receives new information which would lead him to reconsider the value of any security while the auctioneer is trying to bring the market to equilibrium. The former assumption is not unrealistic in view of the extensive quotation and transaction price reporting systems associated with most active markets. The latter assumption, that investors do not receive new information during a market auction, is primarily a matter of convenience. We do not specify the frequency of successive auction meetings. It may be, for example, that equilibrium prices are reestablished at frequent intervals, so that information flows can be treated as changes in information between discrete auction meetings.[3]

An important element in the specification of an auction market is that participants cannot exchange securities until the auctioneer has established the equilibrium price of every asset. During the course of an auction, investors indicate to the auctioneer their current demands for each asset. They do not, however, try to fill those demands by trading with other investors until an equilibrium has been reached. This assumption is tantamount to a prohibition against trading at "false" or disequilibrium prices.

An Example of a Competitive Auction Market

The foregoing description of a competitive auction may seem unrealistic to those familiar with the stock market on the floor of the NYSE or the over-the-counter market in Treasury securities. Nonetheless, there does exist a market, of global importance, which operates almost exactly like a competitive auction. That market is the twice-daily "fixing" of gold bullion prices in London.[4]

---

[3] Garbade and Silber (1979a) analyze the determinants of the frequency of market meetings.

[4] The description of the London gold fixings market is taken from Jarecki (1976) and Robards (1974). The Tel-Aviv Stock Exchange, described by Silber (1975), also operates very much like a competitive auction market, as did the New York Stock Exchange until 1871 [Securities and Exchange Commission (1963, pt. 2, p. 61)]. See also the description of the San Francisco Stock Exchange during the 1870s given by King (1910, pp. 43–44) and the description of European stock exchanges in Schmidt (1977).

The fixings market for gold has remained essentially unchanged since its beginnings in 1919. Shortly before 10:30 A.M. and 3 P.M. London time each business day, representatives of four London gold dealers [Mocatta and Goldsmid; Samuel Montagu & Co.; Sharps, Pixley; and Johnson Matthey Bankers] meet at the offices of a fifth gold dealer, N. M. Rothschild & Sons. A Rothschild representative acts as the auctioneer and starts the auction by announcing a tentative price for purchases and sales of gold bullion. Each of the five representatives then declares whether he (actually, his firm) is a buyer or seller *at that price*, and states the size of his purchase or sale interest. If the total demand for gold bullion by the buyers exceeds the amount the sellers are willing to supply, the Rothschild representative will announce a new, higher price for bullion and will resolicit the other four representatives for their purchase and sale interests *at the new price*. As the successive prices announced by the Rothschild auctioneer approach a market clearing price, the changes in the auctioneer's announced prices become smaller and smaller. Finally, when the purchase interests among the five dealers just balance the sale interests, the Rothschild auctioneer announces that the price of gold bullion has been "fixed," i.e., located or determined. The sellers are obligated to deliver to the buyers the quantities of gold which they previously specified to the auctioneer, at the fixed or equilibrium price. No trading takes place at any prices which preceded the fixed price, because those earlier prices were disequilibrium prices, nor are there any further *auction* transactions after an equilibrium has been reached. (The dealers are, of course, free to trade among themselves at mutually agreeable prices after the auction.)

Although the London gold fixings market would be important even if participation was strictly limited to the five dealers, the fixings market is, in fact, far larger. Each of the five representatives remains in continuous contact by telephone with employees at his own firm while the auction is in progress. As the Rothschild representative varies the announced price in the course of searching for a market clearing price, all five representatives communicate the most recently announced price back to their firms. Their firms are similarly in touch (via telephone or cable) with customers throughout the world, informing them of changes in the auction price. As the auctioneer announces each price, a customer can indicate to the firm he is in contact with how much he wants to buy or sell at that price. Each firm nets out the purchase and sale interests of its customers, adds its own trading interest, and communicates the sum to its representative at the auction. It is this aggregate figure which a representative discloses in the fixings market as the purchase or sale interest of his firm. Thus, in a way precisely analogous to our competitive auction model, supply and demand in the fixings market is based on the price last announced by the auctioneer, whether or not that price is later established as an equilibrium price. Should the auctioneer find that he has to revise the announced price, customers have an opportunity to similarly revise their trading interests. Because of the continuous communications maintained during the auction, the extent of the London gold fixings market is worldwide, although all auction orders must ultimately go through one of the five participating firms.

The London fixings market is a discrete auction. The five firms must deliver or receive gold according to the trading interest they showed in the auction, but they are *not* obligated to either purchase or sell any additional gold at the fixed price following the auction. The auction price is binding only for transactions completed *within* the auction.

Although the London fixings market is not, strictly speaking, a timeless process, the equilibrium price is usually attained quite quickly, on average within 15 or 20 minutes and occasionally within 3 to 5 minutes. When the price of gold has been changing rapidly, however, it may take up to an hour to establish an equilibrium in the auction. This happens when new information arrives *while* the auction is in progress, leading some transactors to alter their purchase and sale interests. This is reflected in a change in the trading interests of one or more of the five participating firms, and necessitates further search for an equilibrium price. (We ignore this problem in our model of an auction and assume the equilibrium price can be located instantly by the auctioneer.)

The London fixings market brings together worldwide purchase and sale interests in gold prevailing at a single time and leads to an equilibrium transaction price which balances the supply and demand for gold at that moment. Our use of a competitive auction market as the locus of price determination similarly focuses attention on the *equilibrium* character of transactions prices. In Parts Seven and Eight we will consider the determination of transactions prices in other markets, such as dealer markets and brokered markets.

11.2 INVESTOR DEMAND

In this section we consider how investors arrive at their demands for financial assets as a function of an announced set of securities prices. The structure of investor demand is the end result of a three-part process. First, given the endowment of securities which an investor brings to the marketplace, his current wealth is computed at the prices announced by the auctioneer. Then, from a joint probability distribution describing the investor's uncertainty about the prices at which securities will be valued in the next auction, the implied joint probability distribution of returns is derived. From the investor's wealth and joint distribution of returns, the portfolio allocation problem is solved for his demand for each asset.

Endowments and Investor Wealth

Let Q_i^e be the "endowment" of some investor in the ith asset. This endowment is measured in arbitrary units of account, such as shares of common stock. An endowment is the bundle of assets which the investor took away from the last auction and which he is prepared to liquidate in the present auction.

Suppose, as in Part Three, there are I risky assets and a risk-free asset denoted by the index number $I + 1$. If the auctioneer has tentatively announced the prices $(P_1, P_2, \ldots, P_I, P_{I+1})$, the wealth of the investor is

$$W = \sum_{i=1}^{I+1} P_i Q_i^e \qquad (11.1)$$

His wealth is his endowment valued at the announced securities prices and is a function of those prices.

Return Distribution

Given the value of his endowments as specified in Equation (11.1), the investor has to decide how to allocate, or reallocate, his portfolio. This allocation will depend, in part, upon the risk/return structure of alternative assets.

Let P_i' be the price of the ith asset in the next auction, i.e., at the end of the holding period which begins with the current auction. For simplicity we assume the value of all prospective cash and noncash distributions are included in P_i'. With the exception of the risk-free asset, labeled $I + 1$, P_i' is not currently known with certainty. We assume that the investor, on the basis of available information, believes P_i' has an expected value Exp $[P_i']$ and a variance Var $[P_i']$, and that P_i' and P_j' have a covariance Cov $[P_i', P_j']$. In this chapter we do not need to assume that all investors share a common statistical description of the uncertain future prices of risky assets, although we will make that assumption in the next chapter.

Given the joint probability distribution of future asset prices, we may compute the joint distribution of returns over the holding period. By definition, the return on security i is

$$
\begin{aligned}
R_i &= \frac{P_i' - P_i}{P_i} \\
&= \frac{P_i'}{P_i} - 1 \qquad (11.2)
\end{aligned}
$$

where P_i is the announced price of security i in the current auction. The expected return on security i is

$$\mu_i = \text{Exp } [R_i] = \text{Exp } \left[\frac{P_i'}{P_i} - 1\right] = \frac{\text{Exp } [P_i']}{P_i} - 1 \qquad (11.3a)$$

The variance of return on security i is

$$C_{ii} = \sigma_i^2 = \text{Var } [R_i] = \frac{\text{Var } [P_i']}{P_i^2} \qquad (11.3b)$$

The covariance of the returns on security i and security j is

$$C_{ij} = \text{Cov } [R_i, R_j] = \frac{\text{Cov } [P_i', P_j']}{P_i P_j} \qquad (11.3c)$$

The $(I + 1)$th asset is a risk-free investment, and so we have $\mu_{I+1} = R_f = (P'_{I+1}/P_{I+1}) - 1$, $\sigma^2_{I+1} = 0$, and $C_{i,I+1} = 0$ for $i = 1, \ldots, I$. These results are a consequence of the fact that, by definition, P'_{I+1} is known with certainty.

As we noted in the introduction to this chapter, the return on the risk-free asset is determined outside the auction for risky assets. The current price P_{I+1} of the risk-free asset, and the return R_f on that asset, is therefore fixed while the auctioneer brings the demand for risky assets into equilibrium with the supplies of those assets.

Once the current prices of the risky assets are announced by the auctioneer, Equations (11.3) can be used to compute the distribution of the returns on those assets from the distribution of their end-of-period prices. The distribution of returns depends upon current prices. If, for example, the auctioneer were to reduce the announced price on security i during the auction, investors would perceive an increase in the expected return on that security. This increased return would probably lead them to want to increase their investment in that asset, leading to greater aggregate demand for the asset at the lower price.[5] Example 11.1 illustrates the dependence of expected asset returns on announced prices.

With the exception of the risk-free asset, securities prices announced by the auctioneer are subject to change while the market is coming into equilibrium. On the other hand, the probability distribution of prices in the next auction is invariant with respect to prices announced during the current auction. This separation of the distribution of future prices from the level of current prices is important to the analysis of a market equilibrium. It implies that investors do not change their perception of *future* securities prices in response to changes in *current* prices while a market is coming into equilibrium. The separation of the distribution of future prices from current prices is justified by the assumption that all market participants share the same information on the future prospects of issuers of securities and that they do not receive any additional information while the auction is in progress.[6]

Portfolio Selection

The demand of an investor for a particular asset is determined by the investor's optimal solution to his portfolio allocation problem. This solution depends on

---

[5] The effect (on investor demand) of changes in expected returns and covariances of returns has been considered by Royama and Hamada (1966) and by Bierwag and Grove (1968) in terms of the microeconomic notions of substitutes and complements.

[6] Grossman (1976) and Grossman and Stiglitz (1976) have analyzed markets wherein some ill-informed investors can extract information from equilibrium prices. The present analysis abstracts from the possibility of such learning behavior by assuming all investors have the same information; i.e., there are no ill-informed market participants. Kryzanowski (1978b) and Garbade, Pomrenze, and Silber (1979) report empirical studies supporting the proposition that current prices affect expectations of future prices.

EXAMPLE 11.1
DEPENDENCE OF EXPECTED SECURITY RETURNS, AND THE VARIANCES OF RETURNS, ON ANNOUNCED ASSET PRICES

To illustrate how change in the prices announced by an auctioneer can alter the expected return and variance of return on a security, consider the analysis of two risky assets, labeled 1 and 2. The expected prices of the assets in the next auction are known to be

$$\text{Exp } [P'_1] = 50.000 \qquad \text{Exp } [P'_2] = 100.00$$

The variances and covariance of the prices in the next auction are

$$\text{Var } [P'_1] = (2.83)^2 \qquad \text{Var } [P'_2] = (10.97)^2$$
$$\text{Cov } [P'_1, P'_2] = 9.99$$

These price expectations and variances do not depend on the asset prices announced by the auctioneer in the current auction.

Now suppose the auctioneer announces tentative prices on the two assets of $P_1 = 42.00$ and $P_2 = 85.00$. Using Equations (11.3) we can compute the expected return and variance of return on the first asset given the announced value of P_1:

$$\mu_1 = \frac{\text{Exp } [P_1]}{P_1} - 1$$
$$= \frac{50.00}{42.00} - 1$$
$$= .19$$

and

$$\sigma_1^2 = \frac{\text{Var } [P'_1]}{P_1^2}$$
$$= \frac{(2.82)^2}{(42.00)^2}$$
$$= (.067)^2$$

his preference for return and his aversion to risk as well as on the joint return distribution derived above.

In Part Three we used the function G to represent investor preferences. (See Equation 8.1.) Let $G(\mu, \sigma^2, W)$ be the preference function of an investor for a given portfolio allocation. The value of G depends upon the expected return μ on the portfolio, the variance of return σ^2 on the portfolio, and the investor's wealth W. (This last argument, which did not appear in the analyses of Part Three, is necessary in the present analysis because we can no longer assume market prices, and hence wealth, are fixed.[7])

---

[7] See the discussion in the appendix to Chapter 8 for comments concerning the effect of wealth on an investor's preference function.

EXAMPLE 11.1 *(Continued)*

Similarly, $\mu_2 = (100.00/85.00) - 1 = .18$ and $\sigma_2^2 = (10.97)^2/(85.00)^2 = (.129)^2$. The covariance of asset returns is computed as follows:

$$
\begin{aligned}
\text{Cov } [R_1, R_2] &= \frac{\text{Cov } [P_1', P_2']}{P_1 P_2} \\
&= \frac{9.99}{42.00(85.00)} \\
&= .0028
\end{aligned}
$$

Now suppose the auctioneer finds that at $P_1 = 42.00$ and $P_2 = 85.00$, there is an excess demand for the first asset (so that he has to raise P_1), and an excess supply of the second asset (so that he has to lower P_2). If he raises P_1 from 42.00 to 44.25, the new expected return and variance of return on the first asset will be

$$
\begin{aligned}
\mu_1 &= \frac{\text{Exp } [P_1']}{P_1} - 1 \\
&= \frac{50.00}{44.25} - 1 \\
&= .13
\end{aligned}
$$

and

$$
\begin{aligned}
\sigma_1^2 &= \frac{\text{Var } [P_1']}{P_1^2} \\
&= \frac{(2.83)^2}{(44.25)^2} \\
&= (.064)^2
\end{aligned}
$$

Observe that μ_1 has fallen from .19 to .13 as a result of the increase in P_1, and that σ_1 has declined from .067 to .064 for the same reason. If P_2 is lowered to 80.65, we have $\mu_2 = (100.00/80.65) - 1 = .24$, an increase from .18, and $\sigma_2^2 = (10.97)^2/(80.65)^2 = (.136)^2$, an increase from $(.129)^2$. Thus, the reduction in P_2 raises both the expected return and variance of return on the second asset.

The optimal portfolio allocation is the solution to the following problem:

$$
\text{maximize } G \left(\sum_{i=1}^{I} x_i \mu_i + x_{I+1} R_f, \sum_{i=1}^{I} \sum_{j=1}^{I} x_i x_j C_{ij}, W \right) \tag{11.4}
$$

over all alternative choices of $(x_1, x_2, \ldots, x_I, x_{I+1})$
subject to the constraint that $x_1 + x_2 + \cdots + x_I + x_{I+1} = 1$

The expected returns μ_i and the covariances of returns C_{ij} as a function of announced prices are derived from Equations (11.3). The wealth W of the investor as a function of announced prices is derived from Equation (11.1). The optimal portfolio allocation can therefore be solved for any set of prices announced by the auctioneer.

Investor Demands for Financial Assets

Suppose the investor finds that the solution to problem (11.4) for some set of announced prices is $(x_1^*, \ldots, x_{I+1}^*)$. Since his wealth is W and since he chooses to allocate the fraction x_i^* of that wealth to the ith asset, he will demand the quantity $Q_i = x_i^* W / P_i$ of that asset. For any set of announced prices the investor will demand some quantity (possibly zero or a negative amount) of each asset. Note that the demand for any asset will, in general, depend upon the entire set of prices announced by the auctioneer.[8]

The demand schedules of the investor, as a function of his endowments Q_i^e and the announced prices P_i, may be written

$$Q_i = D_i(P_1, \ldots, P_{I+1}; Q_1^e, \ldots, Q_{I+1}^e) \qquad i = 1, 2, \ldots, I, I+1 \quad (11.5)$$

These schedules are derived from the information available to the investor, i.e., from his probability description of future asset values, as well as from his preferences for risk and return.

As a consequence of the portfolio allocation constraint of problem (11.4) we must have

$$\sum_{i=1}^{I+1} P_i Q_i^e = \sum_{i=1}^{I+1} P_i D_i(P_1, \ldots, P_{I+1}; Q_1^e, \ldots, Q_{I+1}^e) \qquad (11.6)$$

for all announced prices $(P_1, \ldots, P_{I+1})$ and all initial endowments $(Q_1^e, \ldots, Q_{I+1}^e)$. Equation (11.6) is a consistency or wealth constraint on each investor individually. It says that the aggregate value of an investor's endowment, shown on the left-hand side of (11.6), must equal the aggregate value of his demands, shown on the right-hand side of (11.6), at every announced set of securities prices. Nothing, however, says that an investor must have a positive demand for every asset. Some of the demand functions could have negative values at particular prices. In fact, this would be likely if P_i were larger than Exp $[P_i']$, so that the investor expected the price of the ith asset to fall in the future. In this case a short position may well be favorable. Equation (11.6) only says that the *net* value of the demand of an investor for all available securities must equal the investor's *net* worth. This equality must hold at *all* prices, whether or not the market is in equilibrium.

11.3 MARKET EQUILIBRIUM

A securities market is in equilibrium when, at some set of prices, the aggregate demand by all investors for each security equals the available supply of that security.

The total supply TS_i of the ith security is the sum of the endowments of all investors in that security. Specializing the notation of Equation (11.1), let $Q_i^e(k)$

---

[8] This follows because W depends on *all* the announced prices and because x_i^* depends on *all* the expected returns and variances and covariances of returns.

be the endowment of the kth investor in the ith security. Suppose there are a total of K investors in the market. (K will typically be in either the thousands or the tens of thousands.) Then we have that the total supply of the ith security is

$$TS_i = \sum_{k=1}^{K} Q_i^e(k) \qquad i = 1, 2, \ldots, I, I+1 \tag{11.7}$$

The total demand TD_i for the ith security is the summation of the demands of the individual investors. Specializing Equation (11.5), let $D_i(P_1, \ldots, P_{I+1}; Q_1^e(k), \ldots, Q_{I+1}^e(k); k)$ be the demand of the kth investor for the ith asset when the prices $(P_1, \ldots, P_{I+1})$ have been announced and when that investor has an endowment $(Q_i^e(k), \ldots, Q_{I+1}^e(k))$. The total demand by all investors for the ith asset is therefore

$$TD_i = \sum_{k=1}^{K} D_i(P_1, \ldots, P_{I+1}; Q_1^e(k), \ldots, Q_{I+1}^e(k); k) \qquad i = 1, 2, \ldots, I, I+1 \tag{11.8}$$

A set of announced prices are equilibrium prices if the total demand TD_i for the ith asset, as given by (11.8), equals the total supply TS_i of that asset, as given by (11.7), and if the equality between TD_i and TS_i holds for each of the $I+1$ assets *simultaneously*.

Supply and Demand in an Equilibrium

In equilibrium the total demand for each of the I risky assets equals the available supplies of those assets, and the total demand for the risk-free asset equal the supply of that asset. Although this would seem to imply there are $I + 1$ supply and demand equalities which must be satisfied by a set of equilibrium prices, it is shown in the appendix to this chapter that one of those $I + 1$ conditions is redundant. The key step in the demonstration is showing that the value of the total excess demand for the risk-free asset equals the value of the total excess supply of all risky assets at *any* set of announced prices, even at disequilibrium prices. This implies that if the markets for *each* of the risky assets are in equilibrium, so that there is no excess supply or demand for any of those assets, then there can *not* be any excess supply of or demand for the risk-free asset arising from capital market participants. Thus, a capital market equilibrium requires solving I equations (the supply and demand equalities for each risky asset) for I unknowns (the equilibrium prices of the risky assets).

Function of an Auctioneer in Establishing an Equilibrium

The role of the auctioneer is to find the equilibrium prices of the I risky assets. We can picture his search for those equilibrium prices as an iterative process like that followed by the Rothschild representative in the London gold fixings. The auctioneer begins by announcing a set of tentative prices. From these prices each investor computes his demand for each security and informs the auctioneer of those demands. The auctioneer then cumulates investor demands. If the aggregate demand for asset i is greater than the supply of that asset, he will raise the price of asset i in the next round to reduce demand. If supply exceeds demand, he will reduce the price to stimulate demand. If, after a series of tentative announcements, the auctioneer finds that supply equals demand for each risky asset, he will announce that an equilibrium has been attained. Once equilibrium prices have been established, investors may trade with each other to establish the portfolio allocations which are optimal at those prices.[9] Since the transactions prices are equilibrium prices, total supply equals total demand for each security and every investor will obtain the quantity of each security which he desires.[10] A market in equilibrium is a consistent market; i.e., there are neither unsatisfied demands nor excess (unwanted) supplies of assets.

CHAPTER SUMMARY

This chapter has begun our analysis of capital market equilibrium by outlining the nature of an equilibrium in the simple framework of a competitive auction market. Our model of an auction market has been patterned closely on the twice-daily fixings of gold bullion prices in London. An auctioneer first announces a tentative price for each risky asset. Market participants next compute the value of their endowments, the statistical structure of returns over the interval to the next auction, and the optimal allocation of their wealth. They then indicate to the auctioneer their demand for each security. The auctioneer cumulates the individual demands. If the aggregate demand for a security exceeds the aggregate supply of that security, he will announce a revised higher price. Conversely, if supply exceeds demand, he will revise the price downward. If the demand for every security equals the supply, the auctioneer will announce that an equilibrium has been reached, just as the Rothschild representative announces that the price of gold has been fixed. Investors then trade with each other to establish the portfolio allocations which they found optimal at the equilibrium prices.

We analyzed an auction market equilibrium at some length for two reasons. First, we must understand exactly what is meant by the term *equilibrium price*. This is important because we will be examining the characteristics of equilib-

---

[9] Beja and Hakansson (1977) have pointed out that this grouping toward equilibrium prices may be impractical in real markets because it is time-consuming. They consider alternative market processes for the conversion of purchase and sale orders into transactions.

[10] The process by which individual buyers and sellers eventually come to exchange their assets is not specified in auction models. Transactions are assumed to occur in a timeless exchange process, the mechanics of which neither consume real resources nor impose any costs on market participants. Parts Seven and Eight discuss the transactional characteristics of real markets.

rium prices in the next two chapters and we should know where they come from. Second, the idea of an auction market provides a standard against which we can compare the functioning of other markets, like brokered markets and dealer markets. It is usually advantageous to analyze fully the characteristics of a simple market first, and then analyze more complex markets by asking how they differ from the simple market and what the consequences of those differences are.

FURTHER READING

Avraham Beja and Nils Hakansson, "Dynamic Market Processes and the Rewards to Up-to-Date Information," *Journal of Finance*, **32** (May 1977), 291–304.

Kenneth Garbade, Jay Pomrenze, and William Silber, "On the Information Content of Prices," *American Economic Review*, **69** (March 1979), 50–59.

Kenneth Garbade and William Silber, "Structural Organization of Secondary Markets: Clearing Frequency, Dealer Activity and Liquidity Risk," *Journal of Finance*, **34** (June 1979), 577–593.

Sanford Grossman, "On the Efficiency of Competitive Stock Markets Where Trades Have Diverse Information," *Journal of Finance*, **31** (May 1976), 573–585.

———— and Joseph Stiglitz, "Information and Competitive Price Systems," *American Economic Review*, **66** (May 1976), 246–253.

Henry Jarecki, "Bullion Dealing, Commodity Exchange Trading and the London Gold Fixing: Three Forms of Commodity Auctions," in *Bidding and Auctioning for Procurement and Allocation*, Y. Amihud, ed. (New York: New York University Press, 1976).

Lawrence Kryzanowski, "Misinformation and Regulatory Actions in the Canadian Capital Markets: Some Empirical Evidence," *Bell Journal of Economics*, **9** (Autumn 1978), 355–368.

APPENDIX: On the Redundancy of an Equilibrium Requirement for the Risk-Free Asset

This appendix demonstrates that if the markets in each of I risky assets are in equilibrium, then there cannot be any excess supply of or demand for the risk-free asset stemming from capital market participants. To demonstrate that proposition, we have to consider the values of the aggregate excess demands for risk-free and risky assets.

From Equation (11.6) we have that at any set of announced prices, the value of the excess demand for the risk-free asset by any individual investor (denoted by k) must equal the total value of his excess supplies of risky assets:

$$P_{I+1}[D_{I+1}(k) - Q^e_{I+1}(k)] = -\sum_{i=1}^{I} P_i[D_i(k) - Q^e_i(k)] \tag{A.1}$$

In Equation (A.1) we have deleted the price and endowment arguments of the demand functions D_i for notational simplicity.

From (A.1) it follows that the aggregate value of the excess demand for the risk-free asset by *all* investors ($k = 1, \ldots, K$) must equal the aggregate value of the total excess supplies of risky assets:

$$\sum_{k=1}^{K} P_{I+1}[D_{I+1}(k) - Q_{I+1}^{e}(k)] = -\sum_{k=1}^{K} \left\{ \sum_{i=1}^{I} P_i[D_i(k) - Q_i^e(k)] \right\} \qquad \text{(A.2)}$$

The equality of Equation (A.2) will be true for any set of prices announced by the auctioneer, whether or not the prices are equilibrium prices.

Now suppose that at some set of prices the total demand for each *risky* asset equals the supply of that asset. Then we must have

$$\sum_{k=1}^{K} [D_i(k) - Q_i^e(k)] = 0 \qquad i = 1, 2, \ldots, I \qquad \text{(A.3)}$$

Since the excess demand for each risky asset is zero, the value of the total excess demands for all risky assets is also zero:

$$\sum_{i=1}^{I} P_i \left\{ \sum_{k=1}^{K} [D_i(k) - Q_i^e(k)] \right\} = 0 \qquad \text{(A.4)}$$

If Equation (A.4) holds, however, the right-hand side of Equation (A.2) must equal zero. This means that the left-hand side of (A.2) must also be zero, or that

$$\sum_{k=1}^{K} [D_{I+1}(k) - Q_{I+1}^{e}(k)] = 0 \qquad \text{(A.5)}$$

Equation (A.5) says that the excess demand for the risk-free asset is zero, or that the aggregate demand for that asset equals its supply. We have therefore demonstrated that if the excess demand for *each* of the *I* risky assets equals zero at some set of announced prices, then the excess demand for the risk-free asset must also equal zero at those prices. Thus, the market for the risk-free asset will be in balance if the markets for each of the risky assets are in balance.[11]

---

[11] This result occurs frequently in general equilibrium models and is called Walras' law. See Henderson and Quandt (1971, chap. 5).

CHAPTER 12

CAPITAL MARKET EQUILIBRIUM WITH HOMOGENEOUS EXPECTATIONS – BETA AND THE CAPITAL ASSET PRICING MODEL

This chapter derives the structure of equilibrium expected returns on risky assets when all investors perceive the same probability distribution of end-of-period asset values.[1] The principal result is an explicit relationship between risk (appropriately defined) and return for individual securities and for portfolios of securities.

The first section derives the *beta* parameter of a security. This coefficient, which appears frequently in the academic and practical literature on financial markets, is grounded in the theory of market equilibrium and optimal portfolio selection. The concepts of diversifiable risk and undiversifiable risk for individual securities are treated in the second section. The third section extends the concept of beta to portfolios of securites and discusses the concepts of diversifiable risk and undiversifiable risk for portfolios.

12.1 BETA AND THE CROSS-SECTIONAL STRUCTURE OF EQUILIBRIUM EXPECTED RETURNS

Consider a capital market in equilibrium when investors have homogeneous expectations. From the analysis of Chapter 9, we know that every investor will allocate his wealth between the risk-free asset and some portfolio of strictly risky assets denoted m (see Section 9.3). Since expectations are homogeneous,

---

[1] The case of heterogeneous expectations has been addressed by Lintner (1965b, 1969), Figlewski (1978), and Gonedes (1976). See also Miller (1977) for a discussion of the effect of heterogeneous expectations on the pricing of risky assets.

the allocation of m will be the same for every investor. Since the market is in equilibrium, m must be the market portfolio of risky assets (see Section 10.2).

In this section we derive a remarkably simple relation between the equilibrium expected return on individual risky assets and the equilibrium expected return on the market portfolio. This relation provides a description of the *cross-sectional* structure of expected asset returns, i.e., the relation among the expected returns on different assets at a specific time.

Defining the Coefficient of Correlation between the Return on an Asset and the Return on the Market Portfolio

To establish our main results we first need some mathematical preliminaries. Let $x_i(m)$ be the fractional value of the ith asset in the market portfolio m as computed by Equation (10.2). The return on the market as a whole, denoted R_m, is a market-weighted average of the returns on the I risky assets in the market:

$$R_m = \sum_{i=1}^{I} x_i(m)R_i \qquad \text{where } \sum_{i=1}^{I} x_i(m) = 1$$

The covariance of the return on the ith asset with the return on the market is

$$\text{Cov } [R_i, R_m] = \text{Cov } \left[R_i, \sum_{j=1}^{I} x_j(m)R_j \right]$$

$$= \sum_{j=1}^{I} x_j(m) \text{ Cov } [R_i, R_j]$$

or
$$\text{Cov } [R_i, R_m] = \sum_{j=1}^{I} x_j(m)C_{ij} \qquad (12.1)$$

The covariance between two random variables can always be written as the product of a coefficient of correlation and the standard deviations of each of the variables. We can therefore define the coefficient of correlation between the random return on asset i and the random return on the market portfolio m as the value of λ_i which solves the equation

$$\text{Cov } [R_i, R_m] = \lambda_i \sigma_i \sigma_m$$

It can be shown that λ_i cannot be less than -1 nor greater than $+1$ for any asset. Using Equation (12.1) for Cov $[R_i, R_m]$ we then have

$$\sum_{j=1}^{I} x_j(m)C_{ij} = \lambda_i \sigma_i \sigma_m \qquad (12.2)$$

We are now ready to proceed with our substantive derivation.

The Cross-Sectional Structure of Equilibrium Expected Returns

Recall, from Section 9.4, the cross-sectional relation given by Equation (9.14) between the premium return on the ith asset and the contribution of that asset to portfolio risk. Although we developed the results of that section for an investor making an optimal portfolio allocation in a competitive market, the results did not depend explicitly on the preferences of a particular investor. Suppose an investor's preferences were such that he decided to invest only in the portfolio m of risky assets and not at all in the risk-free asset. Then the standard deviation of the return on his portfolio would be σ_m, and Equation (9.14) becomes

$$\mu_i - R_f = \frac{\mu_m - R_f}{\sigma_m^2} \sum_{j=1}^{I} x_j(m) C_{ij} \qquad i = 1, 2, \ldots, I$$

which, using Equation (12.2), is

$$\mu_i - R_f = \frac{\mu_m - R_f}{\sigma_m} \lambda_i \sigma_i \qquad i = 1, 2, \ldots, I \qquad (12.3)$$

Since this result holds for an investor facing any competitive market, it must hold for a market in equilibrium when investors have homogeneous expectations and m is the market portfolio.

Equation (12.3) characterizes the expected premium return on the ith asset as the product of the market price of risk, $(\mu_m - R_f)/\sigma_m$, and the term $\lambda_i \sigma_i$. The market price of risk is the premium expected return on the market portfolio per unit of risk. It is therefore appropriate to identify $\lambda_i \sigma_i$ as the "risk" of the ith asset. More specifically, $\lambda_i \sigma_i$ is the marginal contribution of the ith asset to the risk of the market portfolio, because $\partial \sigma_m / \partial x_i(m) = \lambda_i \sigma_i$.[2]

Equation (12.3) shows that in a capital market in equilibrium, the expected return on an asset exceeds the risk-free return R_f only as a function of its marginal contribution to market risk. If the return on asset i is uncorrelated with the return on the market as a whole, so that $\lambda_i = 0$, then that asset adds nothing to the risk of the market portfolio and $\mu_i = R_f$. Such an asset has an expected return equal to the return on the risk-free asset, *even though it has an uncertain return*. On the other hand, if $\lambda_i > 0$, so that the return on asset i and the return on the market are positively correlated, then the asset adds to market risk and that asset is expected to earn a risk premium, that is, $\mu_i > R_f$.

Figure 12.1 shows the relation between the expected return μ_k, the standard deviation of return σ_k, and the marginal risk $\lambda_k \sigma_k$ of some asset labeled k. In that figure the point (μ_k, σ_k) will lie in the interior of the portfolio possibility

---

[2] This follows because

$$\sigma_m^2 = \sum_{i=1}^{I} \sum_{j=1}^{I} x_i(m) x_j(m) C_{ij}$$

so that $\partial \sigma_m / \partial x_i(m) = \sigma_m^{-1} \sum_{j=1}^{I} x_j(m) C_{ij} = \lambda_i \sigma_i$. (See also footnote 12 in Chapter 9.)

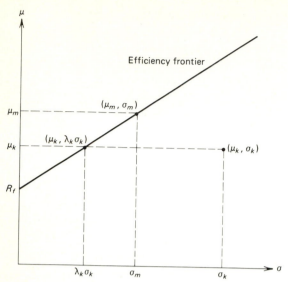

FIGURE 12.1

Marginal risk, expected return, and the standard deviation of return. μ_k = expected return on security k; σ_k = standard deviation of return on security k; $\lambda_k\sigma_k$ = marginal risk of security k. Note that the $(\mu_k, \lambda_k\sigma_k)$ pair must lie on the efficiency frontier, and that the (μ_k, σ_k) pair will lie in the interior of the portfolio possibility set if $\lambda_k < 1$.

set if $\lambda_k < 1$. The point $(\mu_k, \lambda_k\sigma_k)$, however, must lie *on* the efficiency frontier. This follows because all μ-σ combinations which lie on the efficiency frontier satisfy the equation $\mu = R_f + [(\mu_m - R_f)/\sigma_m]\sigma$. The μ-σ combination $\mu = \mu_k$ and $\sigma = \lambda_k\sigma_k$ satisfies that equation, as shown by Equation (12.3), and so the point $(\mu_k, \lambda_k\sigma_k)$ lies on the efficiency frontier.

The Beta of a Risky Security

Equation (12.3) is commonly written in the form

$$\mu_i - R_f = \beta_i(\mu_m - R_f) \qquad i = 1, 2, \ldots, I \tag{12.4}$$

where β_i is defined as the ratio $\lambda_i\sigma_i/\sigma_m$. Equation (12.4) is the so-called beta model of capital market equilibrium.[3] The beta coefficient of security i is

[3] Cross-sectional pricing relationships similar to Equation (12.4) exist under a variety of alternative portfolio models. See Jensen (1972) and Ross (1978) for general discussions. Black (1972) has demonstrated the existence of a similar relation when there is no risk-free security and no opportunities for risk-free borrowing and lending. Jensen (1972) reports a similar relation derived by Vasicek (1971) where a risk-free asset exists but borrowing at the risk-free rate is prohibited. Brennan (1971) has demonstrated the existence of a similar relation when borrowing is possible only at a rate greater than that available on investments in the risk-free asset. Cross-sectional pricing relationships have also been derived by Mayers (1972) for the case where some assets are nonmarketable, such as human capital. Brennan (1970) analyzes the case where dividends and capital gains are both taxed, at possibly different marginal rates across investors.

defined as the ratio of the marginal risk $\lambda_i \sigma_i$ of security i to the risk σ_m of the market.[4]

Equation (12.4) shows that the premium return on a security is proportional to the premium return on the market, where the factor of proportionality is the beta of the security.[5] Figure 12.2 illustrates the relation between beta and the expected return on a security. A beta of zero implies a zero covariance with the market and, as discussed above, the absence of any premium expected return in excess of the risk-free rate. As the beta of a security increases, so does the expected return on the security. At a beta of unity, the expected return is equal to the expected return on the market portfolio. Thus, beta is a convenient index for measuring the premium return which can be expected on a security.

Beta is also an index to the riskiness of a security. β_i is the ratio of the marginal risk of the ith asset (in an efficiently diversified portfolio of strictly risky assets) to the risk of the market. Thus, as illustrated by Figure 12.3, the marginal risk on an asset is proportional to the beta of that asset. If $\beta_i = 1$, the marginal risk of the ith asset is equal to the risk on the market portfolio. If $\beta_i > 1$, the ith asset bears relatively more risk than the market as a whole (and consequently is expected to earn at a greater rate than the market portfolio).

---

[4] Crowell (1973) discusses some uses of beta, including the control of portfolio risk (see also Section 12.3), performance measurement (see also Section 13.4), and the allocation of security research efforts. The beta of a security may be estimated from the linear regression model $R_i - R_f = \beta_i(R_m - R_f) + u_i$, where u_i is a random variable [see Equations (A.10) in the appendix to this chapter]. Roll (1969) discusses some of the problems which may be encountered in such an estimation procedure. Vasicek (1973) has proposed the use of bayesian estimation to estimate betas, and Klemkosky and Martin (1975) report empirical results from the use of Bayes' estimators. Blume (1975) and Schaefer, Brealey, Hodges, and Thomas (1975) present empirical results showing that the beta of a security may vary through time, a finding which can complicate any estimation procedure. Kantor (1971) has suggested applying Kalman filtering to estimate evolving betas, and Szeto (1973) reports some empirical results of such an application. Beta coefficients may also vary as the result of special events. Bar-Yosef and Brown (1977) have shown that the beta of a stock may vary at the time of a stock split, and Sunder (1975) shows that beta may vary when a firm changes its inventory valuation accounting from FIFO (first-in–first-out) to LIFO (last-in–first-out) accounting. Fabozzi and Francis (1977) report results showing that beta is not dependent on whether the general market is rising or falling.

[5] See Welles (1971) for a description of the impact of this seemingly benign observation on the investment community. Whether the expected premium return on a stock is an increasing linear function only of the beta of the stock is a problem that has been investigated by several authors. Black, Jensen, and Scholes (1972) find that the average returns on low-beta stocks are higher, and the average returns on high-beta stocks are lower, than the theory suggests. They find more satisfactory the pricing model proposed by Black (1972), which assumes investors cannot borrow or lend at the risk-free rate. Fama and MacBeth (1973) find that the expected return on a stock is an increasing linear function of its beta, but they also find that a zero-beta stock has an expected return greater than the risk-free rate. Miller and Scholes (1972) point out some of the statistical problems encountered in testing the capital asset pricing model. Jensen (1972) summarizes the foregoing studies. More recently, Roll (1977a) raised some important questions about the power of the foregoing studies to discriminate between alternative models of asset pricing. See also Ross (1978). Black and Scholes (1974b) have found that total security returns are not significantly affected by the division of those returns between dividends and capital gains, suggesting the absence of any "tax effect" on stock prices due to differential taxation of ordinary income and capital gains. Contrary results, however, have been obtained by Litzenberger and Ramaswamy (1979). See also Elton and Gruber (1970).

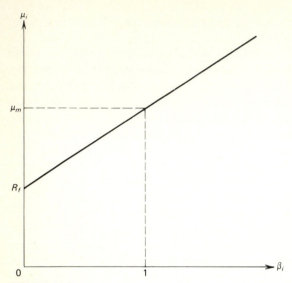

FIGURE 12.2
β and the expected return on a security.

Example 12.1 shows a numerical example of the computational aspects of a market equilibrium.

Equation (12.4) and the beta parameter of a risky asset are consequences of several specific assumptions. First, the market for capital assets must be competitive, so that no investor perceives his own trading as affecting the prices at which he transacts. Second, each investor must allocate his wealth optimally according to a single-period risk/return criterion. Third, borrowing and lending at the risk-free rate must be possible. Finally, investors must share homogen-

FIGURE 12.3
β and the marginal risk of a security.

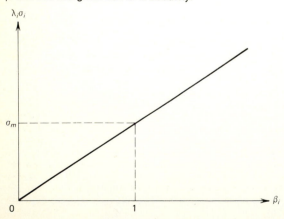

eous expectations about the future prices of risky securities. Besides implying the cross-sectional pricing relationship of Equation (12.4), these assumptions also imply that each investor will divide his wealth between the risk-free asset and the market portfolio of risky assets. (The exact division will vary according to the preferences of individual investors.) The concept of beta and the central importance of the market portfolio arise out of the same set of assumptions.

The cross-sectional structure of expected returns on risky assets, the cross-sectional structure of beta values, and the level of the expected return and variance of return on the market portfolio of risky assets are characteristics of a capital market in equilibrium. They are determined as a function of the allocation of endowments to market participants, the information available to investors, and the preferences of investors. There is no theoretical reason to believe that either the market price of risk or the beta of any security is invariant with respect to alternative endowment patterns, information structures, and investor preferences.[6] For example, suppose the market has come into equilibrium contingent upon some distribution of endowments among investors. Before trading begins, imagine that the endowments are reallocated in some different distribution. Since the wealth of each investor is his endowments valued at the equilibrium prices, the reallocation of endowments is equivalent to a reallocation of initial wealth (at the original equilibrium prices). The new endowment distribution may lead to a change in the demand functions of the investors. The new demand functions may be such that the original equilibrium prices no longer clear the market of excess demands, so that a new set of equilibrium prices must be established. This new equilibrium may be characterized by different beta values for each asset and by a different equilibrium expected return on the market portfolio. Indeed the weights given to the risky assets in the market portfolio may change. Similarly, the demand functions of investors depend on available information concerning future asset prices and on investor preferences for risk and return. A change in information or preferences can also lead to a different market equilibrium.[7]

12.2 DIVERSIFIABLE AND UNDIVERSIFIABLE RISK

One of the most important analytical results of the capital asset pricing model is the distinction between diversifiable and undiversifiable risks. For an individual security or portfolio considered in isolation, the appropriate measure of risk is the standard deviation of return. Thus, the risk on the market portfolio of risky

---

[6] Several authors have analyzed the cross-sectional determinants of the betas of the common stock of different corporate issuers. The first were Beaver, Kettler, and Scholes (1970), who found a high degree of association between beta and accounting measures of issuer risk. Subsequent studies by Breen and Lerner (1973) and Rosenberg and McKibben (1973) were less encouraging, because they found a lack of a statistically significant relation between betas and issuer characteristics. Hamada (1972) and Ben-Zion and Shalit (1975) focused on a narrower list of characteristics and found, in particular, a positive relation between beta and the leverage of an issuer.

[7] The related problem of the effect of intergrating two previously segmented markets has been studied by Subrahmanyam (1975a, b).

EXAMPLE 12.1

COMPUTATIONAL ASPECTS OF A MARKET EQUILIBRIUM

Suppose there are three stocks in the market, labeled 1, 2, and 3. After the market has come into equilibrium, the expected returns on the stocks over a 1-month period are

$$\mu_1 = 2.0\% \qquad \mu_2 = 1.78\% \qquad \mu_3 = 1.5\%$$

The variances and covariances of return are

$$\begin{array}{lll}
C_{11} = 4.0 & C_{12} = 1.0 & C_{13} = 1.0 \\
C_{21} = 1.0 & C_{22} = 1.0 & C_{23} = .5 \\
C_{31} = 1.0 & C_{32} = .5 & C_{33} = 1.0
\end{array}$$

The allocations of the three stocks in the market portfolio are

$$x_1(m) = .04 \qquad x_2(m) = .76 \qquad x_3(m) = .20$$

The return on the risk-free asset over the 1-month period is .80 percent, or about 9.6 percent per annum.

From the foregoing data we can compute several characteristics of the market equilibrium. The expected return on the market portfolio is

$$\begin{aligned}
\mu_m &= \sum_{i=1}^{3} x_i(m)\mu_i \\
&= x_1(m)\mu_1 + x_2(m)\mu_2 + x_3(m)\mu_3 \\
&= (.04)(2.0) + (.76)(1.78) + (.20)(1.5) \\
&= 1.73\%
\end{aligned}$$

The variance of return on the market portfolio is

$$\begin{aligned}
\sigma_m^2 &= \sum_{i=1}^{3}\sum_{j=1}^{3} x_i(m)x_j(m)C_{ij} \\
&= x_1(m)x_1(m)C_{11} + x_1(m)x_2(m)C_{12} + x_1(m)x_3(m)C_{13} \\
&\quad + x_2(m)x_1(m)C_{21} + x_2(m)x_2(m)C_{22} + x_2(m)x_3(m)C_{23} \\
&\quad + x_3(m)x_1(m)C_{31} + x_3(m)x_2(m)C_{32} + x_3(m)x_3(m)C_{33} \\[4pt]
&= (.04)(.04)(4.0) + (.04)(.76)(1.0) + (.04)(.20)(1.0) \\
&\quad + (.76)(.04)(1.0) + (.76)(.76)(1.0) + (.76)(.20)(.5) \\
&\quad + (.20)(.04)(1.0) + (.20)(.76)(.5) + (.20)(.20)(1.0) \\[4pt]
&= .0064 + .0304 + .0080 \\
&\quad + .0304 + .5776 + .0760 \\
&\quad + .0080 + .0760 + .0400 \\[4pt]
&= .8528
\end{aligned}$$

The standard deviation of the return on the portfolio is $\sigma_m = (.8528)^{1/2} = .92$ percent.

The covariance of the return on stock 1 with the return on the market can be computed using Equation (12.1) with $i = 1$:

$$\begin{aligned}
\text{Cov }[R_1, R_m] &= \sum_{j=1}^{3} x_j(m)C_{1j} \\
&= x_1(m)C_{11} + x_2(m)C_{12} + x_3(m)C_{13} \\
&= (.04)(4.0) + (.76)(1.0) + (.20)(1.0) \\
&= .16 + .76 + .20 \\
&= 1.12
\end{aligned}$$

EXAMPLE 12.1 (*Continued*)

The marginal risk of stock 1 is

$$\lambda_1 \sigma_1 = \frac{\text{Cov } [R_1, R_m]}{\sigma_m}$$

$$= \frac{1.12}{.92}$$

$$= 1.22\%$$

Note that this marginal risk is much less than the total uncertainty of return on stock 1 $[\sigma_1 = (C_{11})^{1/2} = 2.0 \text{ percent}]$.

The beta of stock 1 is

$$\beta_1 = \frac{\lambda_1 \sigma_1}{\sigma_m}$$

$$= \frac{1.22}{.92}$$

$$= 1.31$$

This says that stock 1 has a marginal risk which is about 30 percent greater than the risk of the market as a whole.

The covariance with the market, the marginal risk, and the beta for stocks 2 and 3 can be computed in a similar way:

	Stock 2 $(i = 2)$	Stock 3 $(i = 3)$
Cov $[R_i, R_m]$	.90	.62
$\lambda_i \sigma_i$	.97	.67
β_i	1.06	.73

Equation (12.4) says that the premium expected return on a stock equals the product of the beta of that stock and the premium expected return on the market:

$$\mu_i - R_f = \beta_i(\mu_m - R_f)$$

This assertion can be verified by substituting numerical values for μ_i, β_i, μ_m, and R_f. For example, when $i = 1$, we have

$$\mu_1 - R_f = \beta_1(\mu_m - R_f)$$
$$2.00 - .80 = (1.31)(1.73 - .80)$$
$$1.20 = (1.31)(.93)$$
$$1.20 = 1.20$$

assets is clearly σ_m, since the market portfolio includes all risky assets. We cannot, however, aggregate in any simple way the standard deviations of the returns on individual assets to obtain the risk on the market portfolio, because, in general,

$$\sigma_m \neq \sum_{i=1}^{I} x_i(m)\sigma_i \tag{12.5}$$

It turns out, however, that a relation not unlike Equation (12.5) is valid. We need only replace the standard deviation σ_i with the marginal risk $\lambda_i\sigma_i$. This procedure opens the way for the identification of diversifiable risk and undiversifiable risk on individual assets.

Recall, from Equation (12.2), that

$$\lambda_i\sigma_i\sigma_m = \sum_{j=1}^{I} x_j(m)C_{ij}$$

Multiplying both sides by $x_i(m)$ and summing from $i = 1$ to $i = I$, we obtain

$$\sum_{i=1}^{I} x_i(m)\lambda_i\sigma_i\sigma_m = \sum_{i=1}^{I}\sum_{j=1}^{I} x_i(m)x_j(m)C_{ij} \tag{12.6}$$

By definition, the right-hand side of Equation (12.6) equals σ_m^2 and so we have

$$\sigma_m = \sum_{i=1}^{I} x_i(m)\lambda_i\sigma_i \tag{12.7}$$

Equation (12.7) says that the market-weighted sum of the marginal risks $\lambda_i\sigma_i$ equals the risk of the market portfolio. Thus, if we use the risk measure $\lambda_i\sigma_i$ instead of σ_i, we find that the market-weighted average of the risks on the individual assets in the market equals the risk of the market as a whole. Since $\beta_i\sigma_m = \lambda_i\sigma_i$ by definition of β_i, Equation (12.7) may also be written

$$\sigma_m = \sum_{i=1}^{I} x_i(m)\beta_i\sigma_m \tag{12.8}$$

The term $\beta_i\sigma_m$ or $\lambda_i\sigma_i$ is conventionally labeled the *systematic risk* or *undiversifiable risk* of the ith asset. $\lambda_i\sigma_i$ is the risk on the ith asset which remains even in an optimally diversified portfolio of strictly risky assets. The market-weighted average of the undiversifiable risks on the I risky assets equals the risk of the market portfolio. This is shown by Equations (12.7) and (12.8). Example 12.2 gives a numerical illustration of this aggregation property.

EXAMPLE 12.2

AGGREGATION OF THE MARGINAL RISKS ON THE INDIVIDUAL ASSETS IN THE MARKET PORTFOLIO

This example illustrates the proposition set forth by Equation (12.7) in the text: that the market-weighted sum of the marginal risks on the individual assets in the market equals the risk of the market as a whole.

Example 12.1 set forth the characteristics of an equilibrium over a 1-month period in a market of three stocks. The allocation of each of the stocks in the market porfolio and the marginal risks of those stocks were

Stock	$x_i(m)$	$\lambda_i\sigma_i$
1 ($i=1$)	.04	1.22%
2 ($i=2$)	.76	.97%
3 ($i=3$)	.20	.67%

From these data we have

$$\sum_{i=1}^{3} x_i(m)\lambda_i\sigma_i = x_1(m)\lambda_1\sigma_1 + x_2(m)\lambda_2\sigma_2 + x_3(m)\lambda_3\sigma_3$$

$$= (.04)(1.22) + (.76)(.97) + (.20)(.67)$$
$$= .92\%$$

This result agrees with the direct computation of $\sigma_m = .92$ percent shown in Example 12.1.

Separation of Total Variance into Diversifiable and Undiversifiable Components

The variance of return on the ith asset is σ_i^2. This total variance can be separated into an undiversifiable variance, $\beta_i^2\sigma_m^2 = \lambda_i^2\sigma_i^2 \leq \sigma_i^2$, and a diversifiable variance, $\sigma_i^2 - \beta_i^2\sigma_m^2 = \sigma_i^2(1 - \lambda_i^2) \geq 0$. The covariance of the returns on the ith and jth assets is C_{ij}. This total covariance may also be separated into an undiversifiable covariance $\beta_i\beta_j\sigma_m^2$ and a diversifiable covariance $C_{ij} - \beta_i\beta_j\sigma_m^2$.

The formal justification for the interpretation of $\beta_i\beta_j\sigma_m^2$ as an undiversifiable variance or covariance is technical and is considered in the appendix to this chapter. We can, however, suggest the origin of the interpretation with a short exercise. By definition, the variance of the return on the market portfolio is

$$\sigma_m^2 = \sum_{i=1}^{I} \sum_{j=1}^{I} x_i(m)x_j(m)C_{ij}$$

If we separate C_{ij} into its undiversifiable component $\beta_i\beta_j\sigma_m^2$ and its diversifiable component $C_{ij} - \beta_i \beta_j \sigma_m^2$, we have

$$
\begin{aligned}
\sigma_m^2 &= \sum_{i=1}^{I} \sum_{j=1}^{I} x_i(m) x_j(m) (\beta_i \beta_j \sigma_m^2) + \sum_{i=1}^{I} \sum_{j=1}^{I} x_i(m) x_j(m) (C_{ij} - \beta_i \beta_j \sigma_m^2) \\
&= \left[\sum_{i=1}^{I} x_i(m) \beta_i \sigma_m \right]^2 + \sum_{i=1}^{I} \sum_{j=1}^{I} x_i(m) x_j(m) (C_{ij} - \beta_i \beta_j \sigma_m^2)
\end{aligned}
$$

Identifying [from Equation (12.8)] the term inside the brackets as σ_m, this implies that

$$
0 = \sum_{i=1}^{I} \sum_{j=1}^{I} x_i(m) x_j(m) (C_{ij} - \beta_i \beta_j \sigma_m^2)
$$

This result shows that what we have identified as the diversifiable variances and covariances of the returns on the I risky assets contribute *nothing* to the variance of return on the market portfolio; i.e., they are diversified away in a market allocation. Since the only contribution to the uncertainty of return on any efficient portfolio allocation is through the market portfolio, the same comment applies as well to all efficient portfolios.

Example 12.3 illustrates the separation of the total variance of the return on an asset into diversifiable and undiversifiable components.

We can view the construction of an optimal portfolio as the process of allocating wealth among alternative assets to reduce the risk on each asset to its undiversifiable minimum, or as the process of eliminating all diversifiable variance of return on the portfolio. In a capital market equilibrium with homogeneous expectations, assets are expected to earn premium returns only as a function of their undiversifiable risks, as shown by Equation (12.3). If an investor holds an inefficient portfolio, he has not completely eliminated all diversifiable variance of return and hence must be bearing risk for which he cannot expect to earn a compensating premium return. This analysis of diversifiable risk in a portfolio context is considered at greater length in the next section.

12.3 PORTFOLIO BETAS AND PORTFOLIO RISK

The concept of beta and expected premium returns can be extended from single assets to portfolios of assets. Suppose an investor held the portfolio allocation $(x_i, x_2, \ldots, x_I, x_{I+1})$ where x_{I+1} is the fraction of his wealth allocated to the risk-free asset. The realized return R_p on his portfolio would then be

$$
R_p = \sum_{i=1}^{I} x_i R_i + x_{I+1} R_f \tag{12.9}
$$

If the investor is a minor factor in the market, we can assume the equilibrium conditions of Equation (12.4) hold, even if the investor's portfolio is not strictly allocated between the risk-free asset and the market portfolio of risky assets.

EXAMPLE 12.3
SEPARATION OF THE VARIANCE OF THE RETURN ON A STOCK INTO DIVERSIFIABLE
AND UNDIVERSIFIABLE COMPONENTS

Example 12.1 set forth the characteristics of an equilibrium in a market of three stocks. The variance of the return on the market over a 1-month period was $\sigma_m^2 = .8528$. The betas and variances of return on the individual stocks were as follows:

Stock	β_i	$\sigma_i^2 = C_{ii}$
1 ($i = 1$)	1.31	4.0
2 ($i = 2$)	1.06	1.0
3 ($i = 3$)	.73	1.0

The total variance of the return on a stock can be separated into an undiversifiable component $\beta_i^2 \sigma_m^2$ and a diversifiable component $\sigma_i^2 - \beta_i^2 \sigma_m^2$. These components may be computed:

Stock	$\beta_i^2 \sigma_m^2$	$\sigma_i^2 - \beta_i^2 \sigma_m^2$
1 ($i = 1$)	1.46	2.54
2 ($i = 2$)	.96	.04
3 ($i = 3$)	.45	.55

Note that stocks 1 and 3 have a substantial diversifiable variance of return, but that the variance of return on stock 2 is largely undiversifiable. This is because the total risk on stock 2 ($\sigma_2 = 1.0$ percent) is largely systematic or undiversifiable risk ($\lambda_2 \sigma_2 = \beta_2 \sigma_m = .97$ percent).

Using those equilibrium conditions allows us to identify the expected return on the portfolio as a function of a beta for the portfolio and to identify the diversifiable and undiversifiable risks borne by the portfolio.

Portfolio Beta

The expected return on the investor's portfolio is, from Equation (9.5a),

$$\mu_p = \sum_{i=1}^{I} x_i \mu_i + x_{I+1} R_f \qquad (12.10)$$

Assuming Equation (12.4) holds, we can replace μ_i in Equation (12.10) by the expression $R_f + \beta_i(\mu_m - R_f)$. This replacement gives

$$\mu_p = \sum_{i=1}^{I} x_i [R_f + \beta_i(\mu_m - R_f)] + x_{I+1} R_f \qquad (12.11)$$

Since $x_1 + x_2 + \cdots + x_I + x_{I+1} = 1$, we have

$$\mu_p = R_f + \left(\sum_{i=1}^{I} x_i \beta_i \right) (\mu_m - R_f)$$

or
$$\mu_p = R_f + \beta_p(\mu_m - R_f) \qquad (12.12)$$

where β_p is defined as

$$\beta_p = \sum_{i=1}^{I} x_i \beta_i \qquad (12.13)$$

β_p is the beta of the investor's portfolio. A single asset is expected to earn a premium return as a function of its beta. Equation (12.12) shows that a portfolio of assets is also expected to earn a premium return as a function of its beta.[8]

It is possible to show that $\beta_p = \lambda_p \sigma_p / \sigma_m$, where λ_p is the coefficient of correlation between the return on the market and the return on the portfolio and σ_p is the standard deviation of the return on the portfolio. The weighted-average definition of a portfolio beta given in Equation (12.13) is therefore consistent with the definition of beta as a risk ratio parameter for a single security.[9]

The Beta of the Market Portfolio

The beta of the market portfolio of risky assets is easily computed. From Equation (12.13) that beta is

$$\beta_m = \sum_{i=1}^{I} x_i(m)\beta_i$$

Since $\beta_i = \lambda_i \sigma_i / \sigma_m$, this implies

$$\beta_m = \sum_{i=1}^{I} x_i(m) \frac{\lambda_i \sigma_i}{\sigma_m}$$

Using the result of Equation (12.7), that the risk on the market equals the market-weighted sum of undiversifiable risks, we have

$$\beta_m = \frac{\sigma_m}{\sigma_m} = 1 \qquad (12.14)$$

---

[8] This would suggest that the beta of a mutual fund should be of great interest to an investor in that fund. McDonald (1974, p. 315, fn. 5) points out that services measuring mutual fund performance began to report beta values about 1972.

[9] Fama (1968) has commented on the relationship between the single-index portfolio model of Sharpe (1963) and the capital asset pricing model derived in this chapter. His discussion is particularly relevant to the interpretation of portfolio betas derived from regression estimates of betas for individual securities. Beja (1972) pointed out some errors in Fama's analysis of the single-index model, with which Fama (1973) agreed.

The market portfolio therefore has a beta of exactly unity.

The Beta of an Efficient Portfolio

Equation (12.13) can also be specialized to derive the beta of any efficient portfolio. Efficient portfolios are formed by combining the risk-free asset, which has a beta of $\beta_f = 0$, with the market portfolio of risky assets, which has a beta of $\beta_m = 1$. Let x_f denote the fraction of wealth allocated to the risk-free asset, and let x_m denote the fraction of wealth allocated to the market portfolio. The beta of an efficient portfolio, denoted β_e, is then

$$\begin{aligned}
\beta_e &= x_f \beta_f + x_m \beta_m \\
&= x_f(0) + x_m(1) \\
&= x_m
\end{aligned}$$

(12.15)

The beta of an efficient portfolio equals the fraction of wealth allocated to the market portfolio of risky assets. This fraction will exceed unity if the investor margins his investment in the market portfolio.

Undiversifiable Portfolio Risk

The undiversifiable risk on the ith asset has been identified as $\beta_i \sigma_i$. From the definition of β_p in Equation (12.13), the weighted sum of undiversifiable risks in an arbitrary portfolio is therefore

$$\sum_{i=1}^{I} x_i \beta_i \sigma_m = \beta_p \sigma_m \qquad (12.16)$$

$\beta_p \sigma_m$ is the undiversifiable risk on the portfolio as a whole. A comparison of this risk with the premium expected return on the portfolio, as given in Equation (12.12), shows that the premium return on an arbitrary portfolio is a function only of the undiversifiable risk of that portfolio, that is, $\mu_p - R_f = [(\mu_m - R_f)/\sigma_m]\beta_p \sigma_m$. This follows a similar result for individual assets.

Separation of the Variance of Return on a Portfolio into Diversifiable and Undiversifiable Components

The variance of return on an arbitrary portfolio allocated as $(x_1, x_2, \ldots, x_I, x_{I+1})$ is, from Equation (9.5b),

$$\sigma_p^2 = \sum_{i=1}^{I} \sum_{j=1}^{I} x_i x_j C_{ij} \qquad (12.17)$$

This variance can be decomposed into an undiversifiable variance and a diversifiable variance. The decomposition is similar to the decomposition of a single security.

$\beta_p^2 \sigma_m^2$ is the undiversifiable variance of the return on an arbitrary portfolio. (This result is demonstrated in the appendix to this chapter.) Subtracting the undiversifiable variance $\beta_p^2 \sigma_m^2$ from the total variance σ_p^2 gives the diversifiable variance $\sigma_p^2 - \beta_p^2 \sigma_m^2$. In an inefficient portfolio this diversifiable variance of return will be greater than zero; i.e., the portfolio will bear risk for which no compensating premium return can be expected. In an efficient portfolio the diversifiable variance of return will be zero.

Example 12.4 illustrates the computation of the beta of a portfolio and shows the decomposition of the total variance of return on the portfolio into a diversifiable component and an undiversifiable component.

The claim that the diversifiable variance of the return on any efficient portfolio must be zero is easily demonstrated. If the portfolio is efficient, the allocation of wealth to the ith risky asset must be $x_i = x_m x_i(m)$, where $x_i(m)$ is the allocation of the ith asset in the market portfolio and x_m is the fraction of wealth which the investor has allocated to all risky assets collectively. The total variance of return on the portfolio will then be

$$
\begin{aligned}
\sigma_p^2 &= \sum_{i=1}^{I} \sum_{j=1}^{I} x_i x_j C_{ij} \\
&= \sum_{i=1}^{I} \sum_{j=1}^{I} x_m x_i(m) x_m x_j(m) C_{ij} \\
&= x_m^2 \sum_{i=1}^{I} \sum_{j=1}^{I} x_i(m) x_j(m) C_{ij} \\
&= x_m^2 \sigma_m^2
\end{aligned}
\tag{12.18}
$$

The undiversifiable variance of return will be

$$
\begin{aligned}
\beta_p^2 \sigma_m^2 &= \left(\sum_{i=1}^{I} x_i \beta_i \right)^2 \sigma_m^2 \\
&= \left[\sum_{i=1}^{I} x_m x_i(m) \beta_i \right]^2 \sigma_m^2 \\
&= x_m^2 \sigma_m^2 \left[\sum_{i=1}^{I} x_i(m) \beta_i \right]^2
\end{aligned}
$$

The term inside the brackets is the beta of the market portfolio of risky assets. Since this beta is unity [see Equation (12.14)], we have

$$
\beta_p^2 \sigma_m^2 = x_m^2 \sigma_m^2
\tag{12.19}
$$

Since the total variance in (12.18) and the undiversifiable variance in (12.19)

EXAMPLE 12.4
COMPUTING THE BETA AND UNDIVERSIFIABLE VARIANCE OF RETURN ON AN
ARBITRARY PORTFOLIO

Suppose a market consisting of three stocks is in equilibrium as described in Example
12.1, and suppose an investor has allocated his portfolio as $x_1 = .25$, $x_2 = .40$, and
$x_3 = .35$.

The beta of the investor's portfolio is calculated from Equation (12.13):

$$\beta_p = \sum_{i=1}^{I} x_i \beta_i$$
$$= x_1\beta_1 + x_2\beta_2 + x_3\beta_3$$
$$= (.25)(1.31) + (.40)(1.06) + (.35)(.73)$$
$$= 1.007$$

The expected return on the portfolio is calculated from Equation (12.12):

$$\mu_p = R_f + \beta_p(\mu_m - R_f)$$
$$= .80 + (1.007)(1.73 - .80)$$
$$= 1.74\%$$

The variance of return on the portfolio is calculated from Equation (12.16):

$$\sigma_p^2 = \sum_{i=1}^{3} \sum_{j=1}^{3} x_i x_j C_{ij}$$
$$= x_1 x_1 C_{11} + x_1 x_2 C_{12} + x_1 x_3 C_{13}$$
$$\quad + x_2 x_1 C_{21} + x_2 x_2 C_{22} + x_2 x_3 C_{23}$$
$$\quad + x_3 x_1 C_{31} + x_3 x_2 C_{32} + x_3 x_3 C_{33}$$
$$= (.25)(.25)(4.0) + (.25)(.40)(1.0) + (.25)(.35)(1.0)$$
$$\quad + (.40)(.25)(1.0) + (.40)(.40)(1.0) + (.40)(.35)(.5)$$
$$\quad + (.35)(.25)(1.0) + (.35)(.40)(.5) + (.35)(.35)(1.0)$$
$$= .2500 + .1000 + .0875$$
$$\quad + .1000 + .1600 + .0700$$
$$\quad + .0875 + .0700 + .1225$$
$$= 1.0475$$

The undiversifiable variance of return on the portfolio is

$$\beta_p^2 \sigma_m^2 = (1.007)^2(.92)^2$$
$$= .8583$$

so that the diversifiable variance of return is

$$\sigma_p^2 - \beta_p^2 \sigma_m^2 = 1.0475 - .8583$$
$$= .1892$$

Note that this diversifiable variance would be zero if the portfolio had been efficiently
allocated by leveraging the market portfolio to get a beta of 1.007.

are equal, the diversifiable variance of return, $\sigma_p^2 - \beta_p^2 \sigma_m^2$, must be zero. Thus, as asserted in Section 12.2, *efficient portfolios do not bear diversifiable risk*; i.e., they bear no risk which is not compensated by a premium expected return.

A given expected return on a portfolio can be achieved in two ways. One way is mixing the market portfolio with the risk-free asset (either long or short). Under the assumptions of our model this is the only efficient method. A second way is selecting some other portfolio allocation such that the resulting portfolio beta, as defined in Equation (12.13), leads to the desired level of expected return, as given in Equation (12.12). Under our assumptions this method unambiguously results in greater variance of return on the portfolio, because it is inefficient and the portfolio will bear diversifiable risk. If, however, an investor cannot ignore transactions costs (brokerage commissions, transfer taxes, etc.), this method may be a cheaper way to achieve a desired expected return.[10] For example, if the investor is risk-averse, he might select only a few low-beta assets, so that $\mu_p < \mu_m$. If he tried to attain the same expected return by investing partly in the risk-free asset and partly in the market portfolio, he might find that, net of transactions costs, his expected return is negative. Although inefficient portfolio strategies are formally ruled out in our model as irrational, we certainly observe them in real life. Few investors actually hold risky assets in anything like the market allocation. This may be attributable partly to the barriers to diversification raised by transactions costs.

CHAPTER SUMMARY

This chapter has answered one of the three main questions about the equilibrium valuation of financial assets: how the expected returns on different issues of common stock are related to each other. (The other two questions are the relation among yields on debt instruments of different maturities and the effect of default risk on the yield of a debt instrument.) We found that the expected *premium* return on an asset is equal to the product of the expected *premium* return on the market portfolio and the beta parameter of the asset. The beta parameter is defined as the ratio of the marginal risk or undiversifiable risk of the asset to the risk of the market portfolio. Thus, beta is an index to both undiversifiable risk and expected return. We observed that beta parameters come from the same analytical framework that suggests an important role for the market portfolio in efficient portfolio allocations.

This chapter has also analyzed the separation of the variances and covariances of security returns into diversifiable and undiversifiable components. The diversifiable components are so named because they contribute nothing to the variance of the return on the market portfolio. The square root of an undiversifiable variance of return is what we have called the undiversifiable risk of an asset. The market-weighted sum of undiversifiable risks equals the

---

[10] See, for example, Evan's (1970) analysis of portfolio rebalancing in the presence of transactions costs. The recent development of index funds suggests that even small investors no longer have to pursue such suboptimal strategies. See Section 10.4.

risk of the market portfolio. This aggregation property is analogous to the observation that the market-weighted sum of expected returns equals the expected return on the market portfolio.

The concepts of diversifiable and undiversifiable variances of return, and the relation between an expected premium return and undiversifiable risk, can be extended from individual assets to portfolios of assets. We saw that efficient portfolios bear only undiversifiable risks. An investor holding an efficient portfolio bears no risk which is not compensated by a premium expected return.

FURTHER READING

Michael Brennan, "Taxes, Market Valuation and Corporate Financial Policy," *National Tax Journal*, **23** (December 1970), 417–427.

Eugene Fama and James MacBeth, "Risk, Return and Equilibrium: Empirical Tests," *Journal of Political Economy*, **81** (May–June 1973), 607–636.

Michael Jensen, "Capital Markets, Theory and Evidence," *Bell Journal of Economics and Management Science*, **3** (Autumn 1972), 357–398.

Edward Miller, "Risk, Uncertainty, and Divergence of Opinion," *Journal of Finance*, **32** (September 1977), 1151–1168.

Chris Welles, "The Beta Revolution: Learning to Live with Risk," *Institutional Investor*, **5** (September 1971), 21.

APPENDIX: Identification of Diversifiable and Undiversifiable Risk

This appendix discusses technical aspects of the identification of diversifiable and undiversifiable risk.[11] We will see that the random return on any of I risky assets can be written as a linear combination of two random variables: the return on the market and the return on a second variable, called the *independent* component, which is uncorrelated with the return on the market. Following the notation of Section 12.2, we will also see that the variance of the market component for the ith asset is $\beta_i^2 \sigma_m^2$ and that the variance of the independent component is $\sigma_i^2 - \beta_i^2 \sigma_m^2$. Finally, we will see that all uncertainty in return due to the independent components is diversified away in a market-weighted portfolio. We therefore identify the diversifiable risk of the ith asset with its independent component and the undiversifiable risk of that asset with its market component.

The discussion proceeds in two stages. First we separate the random return on an asset into two components, and then we consider the implications of that separation. For notational convenience we use the expression $z \sim N(\mu, \Sigma)$ to mean that the random column vector z is normally distributed with mean column vector μ and covariance matrix Σ.

---

[11] The analysis in this appendix makes use of matrix notation, joint probability distributions, and conditional probability theory. The results derived here follow the line of analysis suggested in Fama (1973).

Separation of the Components of a Random Return

Let R be the I-dimensional column vector of random returns on the risky assets in the market. R is assumed to be distributed as

$$R \sim N(\mu, C) \tag{A.1}$$

The $i - j$ element of the covariance matrix C is $C_{ij} = \text{Cov}\ [R_i, R_j]$ and $C_{ii} = \sigma_i^2$.

Let x_m be the I-dimensional column vector of fractional allocations in the market portfolio of risky assets. The random return on the market is then $R_m = x_m'R$. From (A.1), R_m is distributed as

$$R_m \sim N(\mu_m, \sigma_m^2) \tag{A.2}$$

where

$$\mu_m = x_m'\mu \tag{A.3a}$$

$$\sigma_m^2 = x_m'Cx_m \tag{A.3b}$$

Having defined the distribution of R and derived the distribution of R_m, we now state the joint distribution of R and R_m and derive the distribution of R conditional on an arbitrary realization of R_m. This conditional distribution will lead to the separation of each element of R into a market component and an independent component.

From Equations (A.1) and (A.2) and the definition of R_m, we have for the joint distribution of R and R_m

$$\begin{bmatrix} R \\ R_m \end{bmatrix} \sim N\left(\begin{bmatrix} \mu \\ \mu_m \end{bmatrix}, \begin{bmatrix} C & Cx_m \\ x_m'C & \sigma_m^2 \end{bmatrix} \right) \tag{A.4}$$

Applying conditional probability theory to the joint distribution of (A.4) gives the conditional distribution of R. From Astrom (1970, p. 219) the distribution of R conditional on an arbitrary realization of R_m is

$$(R|R_m) \sim N(\mu + Cx_m\ \sigma_m^{-2}(R_m - \mu_m),\ C - Cx_mx_m'C\sigma_m^{-2}) \tag{A.5}$$

This distribution can be expressed in terms of the betas of the risky assets.

Let β be the I-dimensional column vector of beta coefficients for the I risky assets. Recalling that $\beta_i = \text{Cov}\ [R_m, R_i]/\sigma_m^2$, we have

$$\beta = \frac{\text{Cov}\ [R, R_m]}{\sigma_m^2}$$

$$= \frac{\text{Cov}\ [R, R'x_m]}{\sigma_m^2}$$

$$= \frac{\text{Cov}\ [R, R]x_m}{\sigma_m^2}$$

$$= \frac{Cx_m}{\sigma_m^2} \tag{A.6}$$

Substituting β into (A.5) for the expression on the right-hand side of (A.6) gives the alternative expression for the conditional distribution of R

$$(R|R_m) \sim N\ (\mu + \beta(R_m - \mu_m),\ C_1' - \beta\beta'\ \sigma_m^2) \tag{A.7}$$

The distribution in (A.7) contains the expected values μ and μ_m. These expectations can be eliminated by using the equilibrium conditions of the capital asset pricing model.

Let ι be an I-dimensional column vector with unity in each element. The capital asset pricing model asserts that for a market in equilibrium, $\mu_i = R_f + \beta_i(\mu_m - R_f)$ for $i = 1$, ..., I, or, in vector form,

$$\mu = R_f\iota + \beta(\mu_m - R_f) \tag{A.8}$$

Substituting the right-hand side of (A.8) for μ in the distribution of (A.7) gives

$$(R|R_m) \sim N(R_f\iota + \beta(R_m - R_f), C - \beta\beta'\sigma_m^2) \tag{A.9}$$

The distribution shown in (A.9) is the central result needed to separate the market and independent components of the random return on a risky asset. From the distribution of (A.9) it follows that the realized return on the ith asset, conditional on R_m, can be written as

$$R_i = R_f + \beta_i(R_m - R_f) + u_i \tag{A.10a}$$
$$u_i \sim N(0, \sigma_i^2 - \beta_i^2\sigma_m^2) \tag{A.10b}$$
$$\text{Cov } [u_i, u_j] = C_{ij} - \beta_i\beta_j\sigma_m^2 \tag{A.10c}$$
$$\text{Cov } [u_i, R_m] = 0 \tag{A.10d}$$

Equation (A.10a) says that R_i may be expressed as a linear combination of two random variables: the return on the market R_m and an independent component u_i which, by (A.10d), is uncorrelated with R_m. Equations (A.10b) and (A.10c) give the covariance structure of the independent components.[12]

Interpretation of the Separation

Having separated R_i into a market component and an independent component, we next consider the relation between the variances of each of those components and the total variance of R_i. The variance of R_i is

$$\text{Var } [R_i] = \text{Var } [R_f + \beta_i(R_m - R_f) + u_i]$$
$$= \beta_i^2\text{Var } [R_m] + \text{Var } [u_i] + 2\beta_i \text{ Cov } [R_m, u_i] \tag{A.11}$$

From (A.2) we have Var $[R_m] = \sigma_m^2$, from (A.10b) we have Var $[u_i] = \sigma_i^2 - \beta_i^2\sigma_m^2$, and from (A.10d) we have Cov $[u_i, R_m] = 0$. Using these values in (A.11) gives Var $[R_i]$ $= \sigma_i^2$. The total variance of the return on the ith asset is thus the sum of the variance of the market component $\beta_i R_m$ and the variance of the independent component u_i. The standard deviation of the market component is $\beta_i\sigma_m$, which we identified in Section 12.2 as the undiversifiable risk on the ith asset. The variance of u_i is $\sigma_i^2 - \beta_i^2\sigma_m^2$, which we identified in Section 12.2 as the diversifiable variance of R_i. It remains to be shown that the diversifiable variance of the return on a portfolio of risky assets is eliminated in a market portfolio.

---

[12] Equations (A.10) had a prolonged gestation in the literature. See Fama (1968, 1973) and Beja (1972).

Let $(x_1, \ldots, x_I)$ be an arbitrary portfolio allocation of risky assets. The random return on the portfolio is

$$R_p = \sum_{i=1}^{I} x_i R_i \qquad \text{where } \sum_{i=1}^{I} x_i = 1 \tag{A.12}$$

The return R_p can be separated into a market component and an independent component by substituting the expression for R_i given in Equation (A.10a) into (A.12). This substitution gives

$$R_p = \sum_{i=1}^{I} x_i [R_f + \beta_i (R_m - R_f) + u_i]$$

or

$$R_p = R_f + \beta_p (R_m - R_f) + u_p \tag{A.13a}$$

$$u_p \sim N(0, \sigma_p^2 - \beta_p^2 \sigma_m^2) \tag{A.13b}$$

$$\text{Cov } [R_m, u_p] = 0 \tag{A.13c}$$

where

$$\beta_p = \sum_{i=1}^{I} x_i \beta_i \tag{A.14a}$$

$$u_p = \sum_{i=1}^{I} x_i u_i \tag{A.14b}$$

$$\sigma_p^2 = \sum_{i=1}^{I} \sum_{j=1}^{I} x_i x_j C_{ij} \tag{A.14c}$$

The variance of R_p is σ_p^2, which may be separated into the undiversifiable variance $\beta_p^2 \sigma_m^2$ of the market component $\beta_p R_m$ and diversifiable variance $\sigma_p^2 - \beta_p^2 \sigma_m^2$ of the independent component u_p.

For the special portfolio allocation where x_i is the fractional allocation of the ith asset in the market portfolio, we have from (A.14c) $\sigma_p^2 = \sigma_m^2$ and from (A.14a) $\beta_p = 1$. From (A.13b) it follows that Var $[u_p] = 0$ for the market-weighted portfolio. The variance of the independent component of the return on the portfolio R_p is zero when the portfolio is allocated like the market. This justifies both the identification of the u_i's with the diversifiable uncertainty in return on the ith asset and the identification of the variance $\sigma_i^2 - \beta_i^2 \sigma_m^2$ of u_i as the diversifiable variance of return on the ith asset.

CHAPTER 13

CAPITAL MARKET EFFICIENCY

The prices which bring a securities market into equilibrium depend, in part, on the information investors use in forming their expectations of future asset values. It has long been argued that financial markets are "inefficient" in the sense that investors do not make use of all relevant information in forming their expectations, and that equilibrium prices do not, therefore, fully reflect all relevant information. If this is true, investors who exploit information ignored by others should be able to earn abnormally high returns. More specifically, by buying "undervalued" stock and by selling (or short selling) "overvalued" stock, investors should expect to earn a return in excess of the sum of (1) the risk-free return and (2) a premium return for bearing systematic or undiversifiable risk.

This chapter explores the meaning of an "efficient" stock market and presents empirical evidence on the efficiency of the market. The first section considers an intuitive notion of efficiency and then presents a more precise analytical definition. The following three sections describe the results of several empirical investigations of stock market efficiency, including the efficiency of the market with respect to the following:

1 Information contained in past stock prices
2 Publicly available information
3 All information[1]

The results suggest that the stock market is, in fact, quite efficient, and that in-

---

[1] This categorization of the information with respect to which the efficiency of the market is in doubt appears in Fama (1970). See also the expository note by Fama (1976a).

vestors therefore can expect to earn returns in excess of the risk-free return only by bearing systematic or undiversifiable risk.[2]

13.1   A DEFINITION OF CAPITAL MARKET EFFICIENCY

Capital market efficiency is comparable to "stale" news. Consider, for example, how much an investor would pay for knowledge of (1) the earnings which International Business Machines Corporation (IBM) announced *last* year, compared to (2) the earnings which IBM will announce *this* year.

The earnings which IBM announced last year is a number well known to many market participants and readily and cheaply available to all participants in back issues of newspapers and financial news magazines and in IBM's annual report. Whatever significance that number might originally have had for the price of IBM stock is likely to be already "reflected" in the stock price. Certainly no investor would believe that he could make substantial excess profits by buying or selling IBM stock *now* on the basis of last year's earnings announcement, which is just another way of saying that the price at which he can buy or sell IBM stock already reflects that announcement. Widespread dissemination and cheap and easy access mean the earnings number has become stale information and is no longer of substantial value to investors.

The situation is quite different with respect to *this* year's earnings announcement. Many investors and securities analysts devote substantial efforts trying to forecast future corporate earnings, but their forecasts are inaccurate. Earnings announcements replace faulty forecasts with firm numbers and resolve uncertainty. The quantitative difference between announced earnings and previously expected earnings is new information which, if it is large, may be expected to affect investor expectations and stock prices. If the announced earnings of IBM turn out to be greater than expected, and provide the market with a pleasant surprise, the price of IBM stock will rise. If announced earnings are less than anticipated, the price of IBM stock will fall. An investor who knows the forthcoming earnings announcement can, therefore, expect to make money, perhaps a lot of money, by buying or selling IBM stock before the announcement. If earnings are stronger than expected, he would buy IBM stock, wait until its price went up following the announcement, and then sell the stock for a profit. If earnings are weaker than expected, he would short sell the stock, wait until its price fell following the announcement, and then cover his short position for a profit. Regardless of whether the announcement is good news or bad news, the investor can profitably use his superior information about earnings, because he can trade at prices which do not yet reflect those earnings. This year's earnings announcement is not yet stale news. An investor would, therefore, pay a substantial sum for advance knowledge of that announcement.

The stock market is *efficient* with respect to a piece of information if that information is stale. More specifically, the market is efficient with respect to a

---

[2] Welles (1977) describes the reactions of money managers to the two concepts of an efficient market and a market which rewards investors only for their assumption of systematic risk.

piece of information if an investor cannot make a profit by buying or selling on the basis of that information. Conversely, the market is *inefficient* with respect to a piece of information if securities prices do not reflect that information and if an investor can earn excess returns by trading on the basis of that information.

The remainder of this section sets forth a more precise definition of market efficiency in terms of investor expectations. The definition is based on the idea that stale news will not lead an investor to change his expectation of the future price of a security. News which is not stale, however, may be a surprise and may cause an investor to reevaluate the prospects of a securities issuer. The market is efficient if investors do not ignore any information which would affect their expectations of future securities prices, i.e., if all relevant information becomes stale very quickly.

A More Precise Definition of Efficiency

Suppose investors form their expectations of future stock prices as a function of observations from some information set Φ. This information set could include, for example, the price behavior of the market or of particular stocks over the last 5 years; the data contained in recent corporate annual reports; the prices of the last ten reported trades in every security; or anything else that seems relevant.[3] An observation from Φ is denoted by ϕ. If, for example, a company earned \$10 million in its last fiscal year, that information would constitute a particular observation on earnings. If it lost \$15 million, we would have a different observation on last year's earnings. The issue of market efficiency is whether there exists any information not already included in the observation ϕ which would lead investors to change their current expectations of future stock prices.

Let Exp $[P'|\phi]$ denote the current expectation of the price at which a securi-

---

[3] Information emanating from issuers of securities reaches market participants through several channels. See *Report of the Advisory Committee on Corporate Disclosure to the Securities and Exchange Commission*, Securities and Exchange Commission (1977a), for a general discussion. Almost all large and medium-size corporations are required to file annual and quarterly reports (the 10-K and 10-Q filings) and to register new public offerings of securities with the SEC; this is the *official* channel of disseminating information. See Heller (1961), M. Cohen (1966), Kripke (1970), and Anderson (1974) for a discussion of this channel. Critical evaluations of the SEC disclosure requirements appear in Stigler (1964), Benston (1969, 1973), Mann (1971), Schneider (1972), and Kripke (1979). See also Collins (1975) and Horwitz and Kolodny (1977). Information also reaches investors through corporate documents such as annual and quarterly reports to shareholders and press releases and informal conversations with securities analysts [on the latter, see Beaver (1978) and Kripke (1976)]. Although SEC policy has generally been to permit the dissemination of only "hard" or verifiable information through the official channel [see Heller (1961)], several commentators have argued that disclosure of "soft" information such as earnings forecasts should also be permitted [see Kripke (1970), Mann (1971), and Schneider (1972)]. How investors obtain the observations on which they base their expectations is a topic in the economics of information; see Gonedes (1975); Gonedes, Dopouch, and Penman (1976); Demetz (1969, 1970); Fama and Laffer (1971), Hirschleifer (1971, 1973); Arrow (1974); and Sarri (1977).

ty will trade in the next auction, conditional on the observation ϕ from the information set Φ. This expected future price is a function of what investors currently know and choose to recognize; that is, it is a function of the observation ϕ.[4]

Consider now another information set, denoted by U. If investors recognized observations from U as well as observations from Φ, the expected future price of the asset would be Exp $[P'|u, \phi]$, where u is an observation from U.

The market is said to be efficient with respect to the information set U if

$$\text{Exp } [P'|u, \phi] = \text{Exp } [P'|\phi] \qquad \text{for all } u \text{ in } U \text{ and for all } \phi \text{ in } \Phi \quad (13.1)$$

If the market is efficient with respect to U, adding an observation from U to an observation from the information set which investors already recognize will not alter the expected future price of the asset. In an efficient market the implications of an observation from U are already included in Φ, at least in the expected value sense.[5]

A sufficient, but not necessary, condition for a market to be efficient with respect to some information set U is that U be a subset of Φ.[6] In this case, as a matter of definition, investors recognize observations from U in forming their expectations.[7] Another sufficient condition is that observations from U provide irrelevant information. An investor might doubt, for example, that the market would be affected by whether or not he had a stomachache that morning.[8] More generally, a market can be efficient with respect to an information set U if the observation ϕ recognized by the market provides sufficient information to infer the observation u from U. A sharp fall in the price of a security, or the sudden appearance of substantial selling, may lead market participants to infer the exis-

---

[4] Our discussion assumes that all investors will have a common expected future price given the observation ϕ. If market participants interpret the same data differently, this assumption will not be justified and the market could be inefficient in the sense that securities prices will not reflect a concensus expectation. See Miller (1977). The empirical tests of market efficiency reported below are valid even in the absence of this assumption of homogeneous expectations because they are phrased in terms of unexploited profit opportunities.

[5] The definition of efficiency could be extended to the second moment of P' or, indeed, to the complete probability distribution of future prices. See Fama (1975). Tests of such an extended definition have not yet appeared in the literature.

[6] A sufficient condition is one which will guarantee efficiency; i.e., it logically precludes inefficiency. A *necessary condition* is one which is implied by efficiency, so that the *absence* of a necessary condition logically precludes efficiency.

[7] Kripke (1970) and Sarri (1977), for example, have argued that much of the information disclosed in a new issue prospectus is redundant and already available to investors. For an example to the contrary, see the reaction of the market to the release by Chemical New York Corporation of its final prospectus in a March 1975 offering of convertible debentures (*The New York Times*, March 25, 1975, p. 45, col. 5, and April 1, 1975, p. 49, col. 4; and *The Wall Street Journal*, March 25, 1975, p. 3, col. 2, and March 31, 1975, p. 3, col. 2.

[8] The occurrence of some illnesses may be important information for the market, as demonstrated by the reaction of stock prices to President Eisenhower's heart attack in 1955. The Dow Jones Industrial Average dropped 6.5 percent on September 26, 1955, the first trading day after the President's attack.

tence of adverse information about the issuer of that security even though they do not have firsthand knowledge of such information.[9]

In general, we cannot test directly whether observations from an information set have already been taken into account by the market or whether they are useless, but we can develop some testable implications of Equation (13.1). The tests typically seek to discover whether there exists unexploited information whose recognition would lead to superior investment performance.

The return on a security over the interval from the current auction to the next auction is defined as

$$R = \frac{P' - P}{P} \tag{13.2}$$

where P is the equilibrium price in the current auction and P' is the price in the next auction.[10] It follows that the expected return on the security, conditional on the observation ϕ from the information set Φ, is

$$\mu(\phi) = \frac{\text{Exp }[P'|\phi] - P}{P} \tag{13.3}$$

The current equilibrium price of the asset is thus its expected future value discounted at the rate $\mu(\phi)$:

$$P = \frac{\text{Exp }[P'|\phi]}{1 + \mu(\phi)} \tag{13.4}$$

If the market is efficient, in the sense of Equation (13.1), it follows that

$$P = \frac{\text{Exp }[P'|u, \phi]}{1 + \mu(\phi)} \qquad \text{for all } u \text{ in } U \text{ and for all } \phi \text{ in } \Phi \tag{13.5}$$

Equation (13.5) says the current market price P "fully reflects" the discounted value of observations from U as well as from Φ. The discount rate $\mu(\phi)$ is dependent upon only those observations which the market chooses to recognize. If P fully reflects observations from U, then those observations are impounded in the equilibrium price P. Intuitively, it should be clear that if Equation (13.5) is true, then buying or selling stock *solely* on the basis of an observa-

---

[9] Grossman (1976) and Grossman and Stiglitz (1976) have observed that information can be obtained through observation of securities prices as well as by direct acquisition. They point out that this can complicate the analysis of market efficiency when information cannot be acquired directly at zero cost. See Garbade, Pomrenze, and Silber (1979) for empirical evidence on their conjecture. See also the analyses by Kryzanowski (1978a, b), suggesting that manipulation of stock prices can communicate "misinformation," i.e., false information.

[10] Any distributions such as dividends are assumed to be included in P' for simplicity.

tion from U is a waste of time. The price at which an investor can buy or sell the asset already reflects whatever implications the observation may have for the future price of the asset.

From Equation (13.2) we can define the expected return on the security, conditional on the observations ϕ and u, as

$$\mu(u, \phi) = \frac{\text{Exp}\,[P'|u, \phi] - P}{P} \tag{13.6}$$

If the market is efficient with respect to observations from U, so that Equation (13.1) holds, it follows from the definitions of $\mu(\phi)$ in Equation (13.3) and $\mu(u, \phi)$ in Equation (13.6) that

$$\mu(u, \phi) = \mu(\phi) \qquad \text{for all } u \text{ in } U \text{ and for all } \phi \text{ in } \Phi \tag{13.7}$$

Thus, if the market is efficient with respect to the information set U, knowledge of observations from U will not alter the expected return on the security. Equation (13.7) is the statement of market efficiency most frequently tested in empirical studies.

Testing the Efficient Market Hypothesis

Equation (13.7) asserts that the expected return on a security is unaffected by an observation u from an information set U if the market is efficient with respect to U. Given an information set U we would, therefore, like to test the hypothesis that $\mu(u, \phi) = \mu(\phi)$. Such tests begin by first assuming some model for $\mu(\phi)$, the return expected by the market. The realized return on a security is then compared to $\mu(\phi)$, and the question is asked whether adding an observation from U would have afforded a superior ex ante prediction of the realized return. If an observation from U does not lead to improved predictions, we can conclude that the market is efficient with respect to U.

There are two reasons why we might reject the efficient market hypothesis. First, of course, the market may be genuinely inefficient. Second, our model of $\mu(\phi)$ may be so poor that we are not describing accurately the return on the security expected by the market. Thus, the test of market efficiency described above is a joint test of efficiency and the quality of our model for $\mu(\phi)$.

Even if a market is deemed inefficient with respect to U, it may nevertheless be the case that investors cannot use observations from U to engage in transactions with expected returns greater than $\mu(\phi)$. Securities transactions incur both pecuniary costs (such as brokerage commissions) and nonpecuniary costs (such as time spent searching for an acceptable trading partner). It may be that $\mu(u, \phi)$ and $\mu(\phi)$ are different, but unless the difference is large enough, it may not be profitable to incur the transactions costs required to trade on observations from the information set U.[11] If this is the case, the market is said to be efficient with respect to U *within the limitations imposed by transactions costs.* That is, U does not contain any information with *net* positive value.

13.2 WEAK-FORM EFFICIENCY

A stock market is weak-form efficient if knowledge of the past pattern of securities prices does not improve an investor's ability to forecast future stock returns.[12] In the language of the preceding section, the past pattern of prices is treated as an observation from U. The weak form of the efficient market hypothesis has been tested by correlation studies and by filter rules.

Correlation Analysis

Correlation analysis begins with the assumption that the expected return on a stock, conditional on information recognized by the market, is constant through time, so that $\mu(\phi) = \mu$. This assumes spot prices adjust, as a function of ϕ, to maintain a constant expected return.

Let R_t be the realized return on a stock over an interval from time t to some later time $t + 1$. The empirical results cited later in this chapter used a daily interval, but the elapsed time between t and $t + 1$ is arbitrary.[13] Consider now a model of the behavior of successive values of R_t given by the equation

$$R_t - \mu = \rho_k(R_{t-k} - \mu) + e_t \qquad \rho_k \neq 0 \qquad (13.8)$$

e_t is a random variable with mean zero. If this model describes the behavior of R_t through time, then those returns are said to be "serially correlated." If ρ_k is greater than zero, than above-average price changes will tend to follow above-average price changes, and below-average price changes will tend to follow below-average price changes. This is called *positive serial correlation.* If ρ_k is less than zero, then above-average price changes will tend to follow below-

---

[11] Studies reporting such results include Basu (1977); Garbade and Hunt (1978); Black and Scholes (1972); Dann, Mayers, and Raab (1977); Jaffee (1974b); Gould and Galai (1974), and Lloyd-Davies and Canes (1978). The latter study is of special interest because it shows that the market may not be efficient with respect to purchase and sale recommendations by securities analysts which are not publicly available but which are based on publicly available information.

[12] There exist several studies of weak-form efficiency in addition to those cited here. Schwert (1977) tested the weak-form efficiency of the market for seats on the New York Stock Exchange. Garbade and Hunt (1978) tested the weak-form efficiency of the markets for federal agency debt issues. Black (1971a) discussed the implications of weak-form market efficiency for portfolio managers. The sifting of price movements for predictive information is known as *technical analysis;* see Ehrbar (1975). See also Jennergren and Korsvold (1975).

[13] Niederhoffer and Osborne (1966), Simmons (1971), and Garbade and Lieber (1977) consider the special problem of the behavior of transactions prices over short intervals of time within a single day.

average price changes, and vice versa, This is called *negative serial correlation.*

In a market where stock returns are serially correlated, observation of a past value of R_{t-k} different from μ would lead us to expect, at time t, a value of R_t which is also different from μ. The expected value of R_t would be $\mu + \rho_k(R_{t-k} - \mu)$. Since the expected value of R_t, conditional on the observed value of R_{t-k}, is not equal to μ, R_{t-k} provides information not already included in μ and hence not included in the price of the asset at time $\overset{\cdot}{t}$. Because R_{t-k} can be computed from observations on past stock prices, a market where returns are serially correlated would be weak-form inefficient.

If $\rho_k = 0$ for all values of k in Equation (13.8), then

$$R_t - \mu = e_t \tag{13.9}$$

In this case the expected value of R_t is μ regardless of the observed pattern of past securities prices. The information set U would not be valuable for predicting future stock returns.

The hypothesis of weak-form efficiency should be rejected if stock returns are serially correlated. For any lag interval of k periods we can estimate the correlation of R_t with R_{t-k} and determine whether ρ_k is significantly different from zero. Table 13.1 shows correlation coefficients on daily returns for values of k equal to 1 to 10 days for the thirty stocks included in the Dow Jones Industrial Average, computed from daily closing prices from about January 1958 to September 1962. The correlations shown in that table are too small to be of interest for profitable trading strategies. For example, the largest value of ρ_k is .111 for American Tobacco for $k = 1$ day. This means that if the price of American Tobacco stock rose 10 percent in excess of the expected return on that stock on one day, it could be expected to rise at an excess of 1.1 percent over the expected return on the next day. Even a large price move of 10 percent thus shifts the expected price change on the next day by a comparatively small amount. The expected excess increase of 1.1 percent becomes insignificant when we subtract brokerage commissions on purchases and sales of .5 percent to 1.5 percent. Consequently, we cannot reject the hypothesis that the market is weak-form efficient up to the limitations imposed by transactions costs.

The evidence from Table 13.1 suggests that there are no significant correlations in stock returns which can be exploited profitably by investors. To see why this result is reasonable, suppose stock returns were positively correlated. A stock return above its expected value some time in the past would imply that the return during the current period is also likely to be above its expected value. Some alert investor would quickly catch on to this pattern and invest more heavily in securities with a greater-than-average expected return. If his investment was modest, he could profit from his knowledge of the correlation pattern. However, if he invests aggressively, or if other investors catch on to the pattern and increase their own demands for the asset, the current price of the asset will

TABLE 13.1
ESTIMATED VALUES OF ρ_k FOR THIRTY STOCKS

| Stock | \multicolumn{10}{c}{Lag K} | | | | | | | | | |
	1	2	3	4	5	6	7	8	9	10
Allied Chemical	.017	−.042	.007	−.001	.027	.004	−.017	−.026	−.017	−.007
Alcoa	.118*	.038	−.014	.022	−.022	.009	.017	.007	−.001	−.033
American Can	−.087*	−.024	.034	−.065*	−.017	−.006	.015	.025	−.047	−.040
AT&T	−.039	−.097*	.000	.026	.005	−.005	.002	.027	−.014	.007
American Tobacco	.111*	−.109*	−.060*	−.065*	.007	−.010	.011	.046	.039	.041
Anaconda	.067*	−.061*	−.047	−.002	.000	−.038	.009	.016	−.014	−.056
Bethlehem Steel	.013	−.065*	.009	.021	−.053	−.098*	−.010	.004	−.002	−.021
Chrysler	.012	−.066*	−.016	−.007	−.015	.009	.037	.056*	−.044	.021
Du Pont	.013	−.033	.060*	.027	−.002	−.047	.020	.011	−.034	.001
Eastman Kodak	.025	.014	−.031	.005	−.022	.012	.007	.006	.008	.002
General Electric	.011	−.038	−.021	.031	−.001	.000	−.008	.014	−.002	.010
General Foods	.061*	−.003	.045	.002	−.015	−.052	−.006	−.014	−.024	−.017
General Motors	−.004	−.056*	−.037	−.008	−.038	−.006	.019	.006	−.016	.009
Goodyear	−.123*	.017	−.044	.043	−.002	−.003	.035	.014	−.015	.007
International Harvester	−.017	−.029	−.031	.037	−.052	−.021	−.001	.003	−.046	−.016
International Nickel	.096*	−.033	−.019	.020	.027	.059*	−.038	−.008	−.016	.034
International Paper	.046	−.011	−.058*	.053*	.049	−.003	−.025	−.019	−.003	−.021
Johns Manville	.006	−.038	−.027	−.023	−.029	−.080*	.040	.018	−.037	.029
Owens Illinois	−.021	−.084*	−.047	.068*	.086*	−.040	.011	−.040	.067*	−.043
Procter & Gamble	.099*	−.009	−.008	.009	−.015	.022	.012	−.012	−.022	−.021
Sears	.097*	.026	.028	.025	.005	−.054	−.006	−.010	−.008	−.009
Standard Oil (Calif.)	.025	−.030	−.051*	−.025	−.047	−.034	−.010	.072*	−.049*	−.035
Standard Oil (N.J.)	.008	−.116*	.016	.014	−.047	−.018	−.022	−.026	−.073*	.081*
Swift & Co.	−.004	−.015	−.010	.012	.057*	.012	−.043	.014	.012	.001
Texaco	.094*	−.049	−.024	−.018	−.017	−.009	.031	.032	−.013	.008
Union Carbide	.107*	−.012	.040	.046	−.036	−.034	.003	−.008	−.054	.008
United Aircraft	.014	−.033	−.022	−.047	−.067*	−.053	.046	.037	.015	−.037
U.S. Steel	.040	−.074*	.014	.011	−.012	−.021	.041	.037	−.021	−.019
Westinghouse	−.027	−.022	−.036	−.003	.000	−.054*	−.020	.013	−.014	−.044
Woolworth	.028	−.016	.015	.014	.007	−.039	−.013	.003	−.008*	−.008

*Coefficient is twice its computed standard error. *Source:* From Fama (1965), Table 10.

be driven up. As the price goes up, the realized return over the next period falls. This process of bidding up the price when the expected return is greater than average, and the converse process of selling off the asset when the expected return is less than average, will destroy the correlation pattern. When the existing correlation pattern is exploited, that pattern is destroyed and information on past prices is rendered useless.[14]

The Random-Walk Model of Securities Prices

The foregoing section observed that stock returns do not appear to be serially correlated through time. This property has been used to justify an important model of stock price behavior: the random-walk model. Although the random-walk model appears often in the academic literature on financial markets, it cannot be derived as a *necessary* consequence of an efficient market.[15] The model is useful primarily because it is simple and leads to testable implications (see Section 18.3 on option pricing).

The most frequently posited form of the random-walk model asserts that the natural log of the price of a security evolves *continuously* through time as a random walk.[16] Let $P(t)$ be the price of a security at time t. The model assumes that the price at some later time $t + \Delta t$ is related to the price at time t by the equation

$$\ln [P(t + \Delta t)] = \ln [P(t)] + m \, \Delta t + v(\Delta t)^{1/2}z \qquad (13.10)$$

m and v are constants and z is a random variable with mean zero and a variance of unity. Equation (13.10) says that the log of the price at time $t + \Delta t$ equals the log of the price at time t plus a drift term $m \, \Delta t$, which gets larger with the differencing interval, plus a random term. In most versions of the random-walk model it is also assumed that z has a normal or gaussian distribution.

The implications of Equation (13.10) become clear if we note that the continuously compounded rate of return per unit time on the security from time t to time $t + \Delta t$ is

$$r(t, t + \Delta t) = \frac{\ln [P(t + \Delta t)/P(t)]}{\Delta t}$$

$$= \frac{\ln [P(t + \Delta t)] - \ln [P(t)]}{\Delta t}$$

$$= m + v(\Delta t)^{-1/2}z \qquad (13.11)$$

---

[14] Fama (1965a) presents a fuller discussion of why we should not expect to observe serial dependence of price changes in an efficient market.

[15] See Mandelbrot (1966) and Roll (1970, pp. 4 and 9–13).

[16] As shown in the appendix to Chapter 1, the return on an asset over an arbitrary differencing interval is most easily measured by the log price relative [see Equation (A.6a) in the appendix to Chapter 1]. This leads to the use of log prices instead of prices in most models of price behavior.

EXAMPLE 13.1
THE RANDOM-WALK MODEL OF SECURITIES PRICES

Assume it has been determined that the expected change in the log of the price of a security is 12 percent over the course of a year, and that the standard deviation of the log of the price is 15 percent over the same interval. The change in log prices may then be written as

$$\ln[P(t + 1.0)] - \ln[P(t)] = .12 + .15z$$

where z is a random variable with mean zero and a variance of unity. In this equation time is measured in units of years, so that time $t + 1.0$ is 1 year later than time t. Comparing this equation with Equation (13.10) in the text, and using $\Delta t = 1$ in the later equation, we see that $m = .12$ and $v = .15$.

Using the foregoing values of m and v, the change in the log of the security price over any arbitrary interval of length Δt may be written as

$$\ln[P(t + \Delta t)] - \ln[P(t)] = .12\,\Delta t + .15(\Delta t)^{1/2}z$$

If, for example, we wanted the change over a 1-month interval, where $\Delta t = \frac{1}{12} = .083$, we would have

$$\ln[P(t + .083)] - \ln[P(t)] = .12(.083) + .15(.083)^{1/2}z$$
or
$$\ln[P(t + .083)] - \ln[P(t)] = .01 + .0433z$$

This equation shows that the expected log price change over the course of a month is .01, or 1 percent, and that the standard deviation over the course of a month is .0433, or 4.33 percent.

[The continuously compounded rate of return is defined in Equation (A.6a) in the appendix to Chapter 1.] Equation (13.11) says that the continuously compounded rate of return is equal to the sum of the drift term m and a random term. It follows from Equation (13.11) that the rate of return has the expected value[17]

$$\text{Exp}\,[r(t, t + \Delta t)] = m \tag{13.12}$$

Thus m is the expected value of the continuously compounded rate of return. Example 13.1 illustrates a random-walk process.

Observe in Equation (13.11) that the value of $r(t, t + \Delta t)$ does not depend on any past prices, and so those prices would not provide any information useful for predicting, at time t, the value of $r(t, t + \Delta t)$. The random-walk model is therefore consistent with weak-form market efficiency.

The random-walk model asserts that Equation (13.10) holds for all values of t and Δt. It can be shown that this implies that the rates of return on a security

---

[17] This follows because $\text{Exp}\,[m + v(\Delta t)^{-1/2}z] = m + v(\Delta t)^{-1/2}\text{Exp}\,[z]$ and $\text{Exp}\,[z] = 0$.

over two disjoint intervals of time are uncorrelated. In particular, for any times t_1, t_2, and t_3,

$$\text{Cov } [r(t_1, t_2), r(t_2, t_3)] = 0 \qquad \text{where } t_1 < t_2 < t_3 \qquad (13.13)$$

Equation (13.13) says that the rate of return over the interval from time t_1 to time t_2 has a zero covariance with the rate of return over the interval from time t_2 to time t_3. It follows immediately that $r(t_1, t_2)$ is uncorrelated with $r(t_2, t_3)$.[18] By definition of the rate of return, Equation (13.13) can also be written

$$\text{Cov } \{\ln [P(t_2)] - \ln [P(t_1)], \ln [P(t_3)] - \ln [P(t_2)]\} = 0$$

This shows that, under the random-walk model, the log of the price of a security evolves through time as a random process with uncorrelated *increments*. Given the whole sequence of past prices up to time t, the only element of that information set useful for predicting the price at time $t + \Delta t$ is the current price $P(t)$.

The random-walk model of securities prices is frequently confused with a weak-form efficient market. We have just demonstrated that *if* stock prices follow a random walk, then the market will be weak-form efficient. This says that the random-walk model is a *sufficient* condition for weak-form efficiency. We have *not* shown, however, that if the market is weak-form efficient, then stock prices must follow a random walk. This second statement would imply that the random-walk model is a *necessary* consequence of weak-form efficiency. There exist models of price behavior which are consistent with weak-form efficiency but are not random-walk models. However, the random-walk model retains great popularity as a simple analytical model.

Security Returns over a Fixed Time Interval   Although the random-walk model has been developed for continuous observations on prices, it can be specialized to the case where price observations are made only at regular intervals, such as in successive auctions separated by fixed intervals of time. In the latter case the return on a security is more conventionally measured by the gain or loss over one interval per unit investment cost. That is, the return on a security from time t to time $t + \Delta t$ is defined as

$$R = \frac{P(t + \Delta t) - P(t)}{P(t)}$$
$$= \exp [m \, \Delta t + v(\Delta t)^{1/2}z] - 1$$

For small values of Δt, we can approximate R by

---

[18] Rosenberg and Ohlson (1976) have pointed out that the assumption of serially independent returns with a stationary probability distribution may be inconsistent with the endogenous determination of expected returns and variances and covariances of returns in a capital market equilibrium.

$$R = m \Delta t + v(\Delta t)^{1/2}z \qquad (13.14)$$

In Part Three and in Chapters 11 and 12 we designated the expected return on a security over an arbitrary interval as μ, and we designated the variance of return over that interval as σ^2. Suppose the length of the interval is T time units. From Equation (13.14) we have that the return R over that interval has the statistical properties

$$\text{Exp }[R] = mT$$
$$\text{Var }[R] = v^2T$$

Thus, we can identify $\mu = mT$ and $\sigma^2 = v^2T$. m and v^2 are the mean and variance (respectively) of the return *per unit time*. μ and σ^2 are the mean and variance (respectively) of the return over an interval of length T. T, of course, must be measured in the same units of time as those used to express m and v^2, for example, hours, days, or years. Example 13.2 illustrates the measurement of security returns in continuous time and between discrete points in time.

Filter Rules

The supposition that a market is weak-form inefficient because returns are serially correlated is quite strong in view of the ease of exploiting correlations. It is hardly surprising that correlation studies do not allow us to reject the hypothesis of market efficiency. Consequently, researchers have also investigated more modest models of weak-form inefficiency.

It is possible to imagine that returns are uncorrelated most of the time but that transient patterns of positive correlation do appear occasionally. For example, research analysts and institutional investors are usually the first to learn when issuers disclose new information. Suppose some disclosure is favorable and alert investors begin to buy stock issued by the company at temporarily "cheap" prices. As time goes on, other investors learn the news and they too buy the stock. As more and more investors learn the news and revise their expectations of the future value of the company, they bid up the price of the stock issued by the company. Eventually, following a sequence of transactions at higher and higher prices, a new equilibrium price is reached. While the information is disseminating through the market, a transient correlation pattern may be established.[19]

Gradual dissemination of news such as that described above was excluded as a matter of definition from the auction market developed in the two preceding chapters. All participants in a given auction shared the same information, and no new information reached the market while an auction was in progress. In real markets it is, of course, possible that news travels so slowly that transient price trends develop, only to disappear after a disclosure is fully dissemi-

---

[19] Copeland (1976) presents a model of price behavior while information is disseminating through a market. See also Copeland (1977).

EXAMPLE 13.2
MEASURING RETURNS IN CONTINUOUS TIME AND BETWEEN DISCRETE POINTS IN TIME

Assume, as in Example 13.1, that time is measured in units of years and that $m = .12$ and $v = .15$ in those units. If the interval between observations of securities prices is 1 month, the length T of the holding period is $T = \frac{1}{12} = .083$ year. The expected return over a 1-month holding period is approximately

$$\mu = mT$$
$$= .12(.083)$$
$$= .01, \text{ or } 1\%$$

The variance of return over a 1-month holding period is

$$\sigma^2 = v^2 T$$
$$= (.15)^2(.083)$$
$$= (.0433)^2$$

Thus, the standard deviation of return over a 1-month holding period is 4.33 percent. Similar results hold for weekly and daily holding periods:

Holding period	T	μ, %	σ, %
1 week	$\frac{1}{52} = .01923$	.23	2.08
1 day	$\frac{1}{365} = .00274$	.04	.79

Note that over very short holding periods the distribution of the return is only slightly affected by the expected value of the return. That is, μ is very small relative to σ when T is small.

---

nated. Doubtless such trends do exist, but the critical question is how long they last. Phrased another way, if investors quickly recognize and act on new information, prices will move to reflect that information quite rapidly and correlation patterns will not last long enough to be of any value.

One test of whether transient correlation patterns persist long enough to be useful is to govern purchases and sales of securities by a "filter rule." A filter is a device used to recognize price trends likely to persist in the future. An x percent filter is defined by the following trading rule:

If the daily closing price of a particular stock moves up at least x percent, buy and hold the stock until its price moves down at least x percent from a subsequent high, at which time simultaneously sell and go short. The short position is maintained until the price rises at least x percent above a subsequent low, at which time one covers and buys. Price moves of less than x percent in either direction are ignored.

The idea behind a filter rule is that a price change of x percent is *prima facie* evidence that a price trend has been established and is likely to continue.

Fama and Blume (1966) applied filters ranging in size from .5 to 50 percent

TABLE 13.2
AVERAGE RATES OF RETURN BY SIZE OF FILTER

Filter size, %	Returns based on filter rule			Returns based on buy and hold strategy, %†
	Before commissions, %*	After commissions, %*	Number of transactions	
.5	11.52	−103.59	12,514	10.4
1.0	5.47	−74.94	8,660	10.3
1.5	2.77	−56.14	6,270	10.2
2.0	.23	−45.15	4,784	10.3
2.5	−1.56	−37.32	3,750	10.3
5.0	−1.88	−16.62	1,484	10.0
10.0	2.98	−1.43	435	9.3
20.0	4.28	2.98	110	9.8
30.0	−.54	−1.42	51	6.4
40.0	−2.73	−3.47	21	4.4
50.0	−21.42	−22.95	4	12.1

*Average for 30 stocks, percent per annum.
†Average for 30 stocks, percent per annum. Assumes stock was held long during intervals when stock was held *either* long *or* short according to filter rule.
Source: From Fama and Blume (1966), Tables 1 and 3.

to decide the timing of purchases and sales of the 30 stocks in the Dow Jones Industrial Average.[20] The data were daily closing prices from late 1957 to September 1962. To obtain a basis for comparison, the authors also evaluated the return on a "buy and hold" strategy. In that strategy they bought a stock the first time it was either bought or sold by a filter rule and continued to hold the stock until the end of the sample period. A buy and hold strategy does not involve purchases or sales based on past price behavior. A summary of their results, shown in Table 13.2, indicates that the buy and hold strategy dominated the filter rule for every size filter they examined. It does not appear that price changes of from .5 to 50 percent were indicative of persistent trends.

Correlation analysis and filter rules test only two ways in which a market can be weak-form inefficient. Although weak-form efficiency cannot be rejected by either test, it is possible that there exists some other way of using past price data to improve investment performance. Market efficiency is only a hypothesis subject to refutation, which no experiment can ever "prove."

13.3 SEMISTRONG-FORM EFFICIENCY

A market is semistrong-form efficient if the information which investors recognize in forming their expectations of future prices includes *all* information in

---

[20] The use of a filter rule to test dependencies in the price behavior of financial assets was first proposed by Alexander (1961). Mandelbrot (1963), however, pointed out a flaw in Alexander's computations. A second paper by Alexander (1964) is discussed by Fama (1965a). Fama and Blume (1966) developed the empirical evidence reviewed here. Praetz (1976) has noted that the rate of return from trading with a filter rule may be difficult to interpret. See also Jennergren (1975) and Jensen and Bennington (1970).

the public domain. In terms of the definition of efficiency given in Section 13.1, the information set U with respect to which the market is efficient extends over all publicly available information.[21]

The hypothesis of semistrong-form efficiency is not tested directly. Instead, researchers choose an event which occurs fairly frequently, such as a stock split or block trade, and test whether the distribution of stock returns *following* the time when the public first becomes aware of the occurrence of the event is significantly different from the normal structure of returns. If it is, then investors must have ignored, at least for some time, the information communicated by the occurrence of the event.[22] This section discusses two tests of the semistrong form of the efficient market hypothesis.[23]

---

[21] Corporate financial statements are believed to be one of the most important sources of publicly available information on securities issuers. Beaver (1968) has found that reports of annual earnings do contain information. Ball and Brown (1968) estimate that about 50 percent of the new information on a firm which becomes public during a year is captured in the annual earnings figure but that 85 percent of the difference between announced income and the net income expected at the beginning of the year is anticipated by the time of the year-end announcement. This anticipation is due in part to quarterly earnings announcements. Brown and Niederhoffer (1968) and Brown and Kennelly (1972) have shown that those quarterly announcements have value for predicting annual earnings. Several studies have shown that investors are not "fooled" by different accounting reporting policies, including Kaplan and Roll (1972), who considered accelerated vs. straight-line depreciation and flow-through vs. deferred recognition of investment tax credits, and Sunder (1973, 1975), who considered LIFO versus FIFO inventory valuation policies.

[22] Several studies of the behavior of prices of stock sold in underwritten offerings by first-time issuers have shown those offerings to be priced, on average, below their equilibrium values. See McDonald and Fisher (1972), Logue (1973), Ibbotson (1975), and Ibbotson and Jaffe (1975). Similar results for Canada and France are reported by Shaw (1971) and McDonald and Jacquillat (1974), respectively. These results imply that underwriters distribute economic rents to their customers. The same studies provide no evidence of inefficiency in subsequent secondary-market trading of new issues.

[23] Other studies of semistrong-form efficiency include the study by Waud (1970) of the reaction of stock prices to changes in discount rates at Federal Reserve banks; Schwert (1977) on the value of seats on the New York Stock Exchange; and Fama (1975) on the inclusion of expected rates of future inflation in Treasury bill yields. On the latter topic see also Garbade and Wachtel (1978). Basu (1977) presents evidence that stocks with low (or high) price-earnings ratios may be underpriced (or overpriced), but that the inefficiency cannot be exploited profitably unless an investor is trading, and hence bearing transactions costs, for some other reason. Latane, Joy, and Jones (1970) report similar evidence on price-earnings ratios but do not consider the effect of transactions costs on portfolio returns. Black (1973) has reported that the Value Line stock ranking system has positive value, but he did not treat fully the effect of transactions costs in his conclusions. Jaffe (1974b) reports results which suggest that profit opportunities net of transactions costs persist after publication of insider transactions, but it is not clear how long these opportunites last. Klemkosky (1978) reports that stock prices fall by a significant amount preceding option expiration dates, but does not consider whether profits net of transactions costs exist. Kryzanowski (1978b, 1979) has suggested that the prices of stocks which have been suspended from trading on an exchange because of manipulation or some other unfavorable reason do not fully reflect the bad news communicated by the suspension when they resume trading. Ying, Lewellen, Schlarbaum, and Lease (1977) find that stock prices appreciate significantly after listing on a stock exchange, but they too do not consider whether an investor can exploit that price appreciation net of transactions costs. In an innovative paper, Figlewski (1979) showed that horse race handicapper predictions have positive value but that those predictions are fully reflected in track betting odds. In particular, knowledge of handicapper predictions permits a bettor to make a forecast of race results which is superior to assuming an equal probability of each horse winning but does not permit him to expect to earn positive amounts from betting on the basis of those superior predictions.

Stock Splits

Market analysts have observed that managers of publicly held corporations are loath to reduce regular dividend payments. [See, for example, Lintner (1956).] Conversely, a company will normally increase its regular dividend only when it feels confident that it can maintain a higher level of payments for the foreseeable future. Thus, an increase in dividends communicates to market participants the expectation of the management that earnings have stabilized at a higher level than was previously the case. Analysts have also observed that dividend increases frequently accompany stock splits, either at the time of the split or shortly thereafter. Based on these observations, a firm which splits its stock may reasonably be viewed as being confident that its future earnings are going to be higher than previously expected. Thus, stock splits provide a favorable signal to market participants.[24]

Stock splits are well-publicized events which clearly lie within the realm of publicly available information. Suppose the market was inefficient with respect to the occurrence of a stock split. We would then anticipate that the price of a stock should, on average, rise in months following a split, as investors gradually come to appreciate the improved earnings outlook of the issuer. If the market is efficient, however, all the information communicated by a stock split should be recognized at the time of the split, and subsequent stock prices should not show any unusual tendency to rise.

Fama, Fisher, Jensen, and Roll (1969) investigated whether there were abnormally large increases in stock prices following stock splits. They looked at 940 splits occurring between January 1927 and December 1959 in 622 issues of common stock listed on the New York Stock Exchange.

From the capital asset pricing model, the return $\mu_{j,t}(\phi_t)$ expected by the market on security j over the interval between time t and time $t + 1$ is

$$\mu_{j,t}(\phi_t) = R_{f,t} + \beta_{j,t}[\mu_{m,t}(\phi_t) - R_{f,t}] \tag{13.15}$$

ϕ_t is the observation from the information set Φ recognized by the market at time t. $\mu_{m,t}(\phi_t)$ is the expected return on the market portfolio over the interval from time t to time $t + 1$, and $R_{f,t}$ is the risk-free return over the same interval. $\beta_{j,t}$ is the beta coefficient of security j over the interval.

Fama, Fisher, Jensen, and Roll (FFJR hereafter) used the equilibrium model of Equation (13.15) to test the efficiency of the market with respect to stock splits. They first had to define the residual return on a security, i.e., the realized return in excess of the return which would be expected given the behavior of the market as a whole. Let $R_{j,t}$ and $R_{m,t}$ be the realized return on security j and on the market portfolio, respectively, over the interval from time t to time $t + 1$. Define the residual return $e_{j,t}$ as

---

[24] In addition to the Fama, Fisher, Jensen, and Roll (1969) study discussed below, stock splits have also been studied by Bellemore and Blucher (1956); Hausman, West, and Largay (1971); Copeland (1979); and Bar-Yosef and Brown (1977).

$$e_{j,t} = R_{j,t} - R_{f,t} - \beta_{j,t}(R_{m,t} - R_{f,t}) \qquad (13.16)$$

The expectation of $e_{j,t}$, conditional on information recognized by the market at time t, is

$$\begin{aligned}
\text{Exp } [e_{j,t}|\phi_t] &= \text{Exp } [R_{j,t} - R_{f,t} - \beta_{j,t}(R_{m,t} - R_{f,t})|\phi_t] \\
&= \text{Exp } [R_{j,t}|\phi_t] - R_{f,t} - \beta_{j,t}(\text{Exp } [R_{m,t}|\phi_t] - R_{f,t}) \\
&= \mu_{j,t}(\phi_t) - R_{f,t} - \beta_{j,t}[\mu_{m,t}(\phi_t) - R_{f,t}]
\end{aligned}$$

or, from Equation (13.15),

$$\text{Exp } [e_{j,t}|\phi_t] = 0 \qquad (13.17)$$

This equation says that at time t the market does not *expect* a positive residual return on security j. If the market is *inefficient* with respect to stock splits, this zero expectation will be biased in months following a split; i.e., the market will fail to anticipate the forthcoming appreciation in the price of a split stock. In particular, the excess returns in an *inefficient* market should be positive, on average, during months following a stock split.

The second step in the analysis of stock splits by FFJR was reducing Equation (13.16) to a more convenient form. FFJR assumed the beta coefficient of a stock is stationary through time, so that $\beta_{j,t} = \beta_j$ for all t, and they assumed the term $R_{f,t}(1 - \beta_{j,t})$ could be approximated by a constant α_j. In view of their assumption of stationary betas, this second approximation is equivalent to assuming a constant risk-free return. FFJR then dated all their observations of the monthly returns on a stock *relative* to the month in which the stock split. Let $t = 0$ denote the month of the split. $t > 0$ denotes months after the split and $t < 0$ denotes months prior to the split. Using all the returns data available on a stock [with the exception of the 16 returns observed (1) during the 15 months prior to a split and (2) during the month of a split], FFJR estimated α_j and β_j for security j from the regression model:

$$R_{j,t} = \alpha_j + \beta_j R_{m,t} + e_{j,t} \qquad (13.18)$$

$R_{m,t}$ is Fisher's return on the market in month t [see Fisher (1965) and Section 10.3 above]. Let $\hat{\alpha}_j$ and $\hat{\beta}_j$ denote the regression estimates of α_j and β_j. From these estimates FFJR defined the estimated residual monthly return $\hat{e}_{j,t}$ on a stock during the 60 months around the month in which the stock was split:

$$\hat{e}_{j,t} = R_{j,t} - \hat{\alpha}_j - \hat{\beta}_j R_{m,t} \qquad -29 \le t \le 30 \qquad (13.19)$$

Equation (13.19) is the empirical analog to the conceptual model of Equation (13.16). From Equation (13.17) and the estimates of α_j and β_j we have that the expected value of $\hat{e}_{j,t}$ is zero.

To test whether the average value of $\hat{e}_{j,t}$ is zero, FFJR computed an average residual return across all the stocks in their sample set. Let N_t denote the number of observations on stocks which split t months earlier (or t months later if $t < 0$). The *average residual return* for month t is defined as

$$u_t = \sum_{j=1}^{N_t} \frac{\hat{e}_{j,t}}{N_t} \qquad -29 \le t \le 30 \qquad (13.20)$$

If all the $\hat{e}_{j,t}$'s have an expected value of zero, then u_t, the average residual return, should be approximately equal to zero.

The values of u_t found by FFJR are recorded in Table 13.3 and graphed in

TABLE 13.3
AVERAGE RESIDUAL
RETURNS AND CUMULATIVE
AVERAGE NET CHANGE IN
VALUE RELATIVE TO MONTH
OF STOCK SPLIT

t	u_t*	S_t†
−29	.54	.54
−25	.56	2.41
−20	.33	4.76
−15	1.25	9.00
−10	.97	14.85
−9	1.63	16.47
−8	1.57	18.04
−7	1.38	19.42
−6	1.69	21.11
−5	1.67	22.78
−4	2.16	24.94
−3	2.89	27.83
−2	3.63	31.47
−1	1.92	33.39
0	.68	34.07
1	−.14	33.93
2	.31	34.24
3	−.08	34.16
4	.00	34.16
5	.33	34.49
6	−.02	34.47
7	−.24	34.23
8	−.12	34.11
9	.09	34.20
10	−.08	34.12
15	−.19	34.16
20	.06	34.09
25	−.02	33.74
30	−.31	33.21

*Percent during month t.
†Percent change in value from base date 30 months prior to split.
Source: From Fama, Fisher, Jensen, and Roll (1969), Table 2.

Figure 13.1. In months after a split the values of u_t are approximately equal to zero and are not consistently greater or less than zero. Thus, the average behavior of the returns on the securities in the sample set, in months after the months in which those securities split, does not appear to be different from their behavior over the periods from which the α_j's and β_j's were estimated. In particular, there was no tendency, on average, for the price of a stock to appreciate by an usual amount *after* it had split. This implies that whatever favorable information is communicated by the occurrence of a stock split is, on average, imbedded in the price of the stock by the end of the month in which the split occurred. The behavior of u_t for $t > 0$ does not merit rejecting the semistrong form of the efficient market hypothesis.

Table 13.3 and Figure 13.1 show that the average residual returns are positive for $t \leq 0$. FFJR suggested a reason for this behavior. Companies which split their stock frequently enjoy higher-than-average earnings prior to the split. Public disclosure of those higher earnings provides *new* information which leads market participants to bid up the prices of the stocks, so that stockholders earn at an average rate greater than what would be expected given the normal relation of the return on the stocks to the return on the market as a whole.

Table 13.3 shows that the largest values of the average residual return occurred 2, 3, and 4 months prior to a split. This corresponds to the usual lead time between the announcement of a split and the actual split. Once a split is announced, investors can reasonably anticipate that the split will actually occur and hence will bid up the price of the stock, again resulting in abnormally high

FIGURE 13.1
Average residual returns around the month of a stock split.

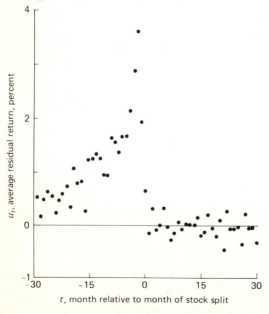

t, month relative to month of stock split

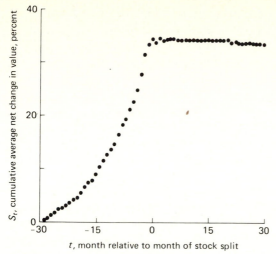

FIGURE 13.2
Cumulative average net change in value around the month of a stock split.

yields.[25] Announcement of a split provides confirmation to the market that management expects the higher earnings of the recent past to continue in the future, and is a signal that it feels capable of paying a larger dividend. By the time the split takes place, however, the market has repriced the stock to reflect the new information.

Another measure of the price behavior of split stock is the cumulative average change in value of such stock, net of contemporaneous movements in the market as a whole. If we choose a base date 30 months prior to the month of a split, the cumulative average net change in the value of split stock up to month t may be defined as

$$S_t = \sum_{k=-29}^{t} u_k \qquad t \geq -29 \qquad (13.21)$$

S_t measures the cumulative average change in value after abstracting from price movements in the market as a whole. Table 13.3 shows selected values of S_t for $t = -29$ to $t = 30$. The S_t series is plotted in Figure 13.2. Figure 13.2 shows that, on average, split stocks experience a positive net appreciation in value throughout the $2^{1}/_{2}$ years prior to their splitting. By the time a stock actually splits, it is worth, on average, about 34 percent more than would be expected given the behavior of the market during the preceding $2^{1}/_{2}$ years. This net excess change in value represents the effects of disclosure of higher earnings

---

[25] Hausman, West, and Largay (1971) argue that most of the price appreciation occurs immediately *before* the announcement of the stock split. They suggest that this results from news leaks and insider trading.

and the announcement of a pending stock split. After the occurrence of the split, however, there are no further average net changes in value. This is another way of saying that split stocks appreciate at abnormally high rates *before* they are split, but do not earn abnormal returns *after* being split.

Block Transactions

The purchase or sale of stock in large block transactions is another publicly reported event believed to convey information to investors. *Block* transactions involve trades of anywhere from 10,000 shares of stock to 250,000 shares and more. (The largest single block trade on the New York Stock Exchange occurred on March 14, 1972, and involved 5,245,000 shares of American Motors common stock.) Block trades are notable, because (as described below and in Section 23.2) they require special handling (i.e., they cannot be executed like an ordinary purchase or sale of 100 or 200 shares of stock) and because they are frequently triggered by new information or revised appraisals of existing information.

In a semistrong-form efficient market, securities prices reflect all publicly available information. The mere trading of a block, unaccompanied by any other new information, would not provide any reason for a stock price change. Available evidence indicates, however, that block transactions initiated by sellers frequently occur at prices lower than prices on preceding transactions of a more modest size, and that block transactions initiated by buyers occur at relatively higher prices. There are two possible explanations for this phenomenon:

1 Since block transactions are typically initiated by sophisticated institutional investors, they can be expected to occur when those investors acquire new information. That is, the sale (or purchase) of a block of stock may be triggered by incompletely disseminated unfavorable (or favorable) information. In an efficient market we would expect the prices of subsequent transactions in the stock to remain stable, on average, at the price at which the block transaction occurred, since that price should reflect the new information. If the market is inefficient, we would expect that any price trend established before the block trade would continue after the trade until the information which motivated the trade is fully disseminated.

2 The market for large blocks of stock is thin and characterized by relatively high liquidity costs. Block transactions require the liquidity services of a securities dealer, and those services command a higher price than the liquidity services provided in standard-size transactions. (See the discussion of block trading in Section 23.2.) Thus, sales of blocks may be accomplished only at lower prices, or purchases of blocks only at higher prices, relative to normal sale and purchase prices (see Chapter 24). In this case we would expect the prices of subsequent transactions to return toward the prices which prevailed before a block trade.

Kraus and Stoll (1972) inspected the characteristics of 1565 block trades executed between July 1, 1968, and September 30, 1969, in the common stock of 402 companies listed on the New York Stock Exchange.[26] Each transaction involved at least 10,000 shares valued at not less than $1 million. Kraus and Stoll divided their sample into transactions occurring at a price greater than the previous trade (plus ticks) and transactions occurring at a price less than the previous trade (minus ticks). They ignored zero-tick trades. Kraus and Stoll pointed out that plus-tick block trades are generally initiated by buyers and that minus-tick blocks are initiated by sellers. This identification is important to the interpretation of their results.

The first result presented by the authors is the behavior of the price of a stock during the day of a block trade in that stock. They define two measures of return:

$$E_1 = 100 \frac{P_b + D_{-1} - P_{-1}}{P_{-1}} \qquad (13.22a)$$

$$E_2 = 100 \frac{P_o - P_b}{P_b} \qquad (13.22b)$$

where P_{-1} = closing price on the day prior to the block trade
P_b = price at which the block is traded
P_o = closing price on the day of the block trade
D_{-1} = dividend paid to holders of record at the close of trading on the day preceding the block trade
E_1 = percent change in stock price from the previous day's closing transaction to the time of the block trade
E_2 = percent change in price from the block trade to the closing transaction on the same day

Averaging over 1199 blocks trade on minus ticks and 366 blocks traded on plus ticks, the authors computed the average values of E_1 (denoted by $\bar{E}_1$) and E_2 (denoted by $\bar{E}_2$) as follows:

	Minus ticks, %*	Plus ticks, %*
$\bar{E}_1$	−1.861	1.501
	(.068)	(.127)
$\bar{E}_2$	.713	−.091
	(.047)	(.099)

*Standard error of estimate in parentheses.

[26] In addition to the study of block trading by Kraus and Stoll (1972), the topic has been considered by Radcliffe (1973); Grier and Albin (1973); Close (1975); Dann, Mayers, and Raab (1977); and Carey (1977). Reback (1974) comments on the study by Grier and Albin (1973), and Grier replies in Grier (1974). Scholes (1972) considers the closely related topic of the behavior of stock prices around the time of a secondary distribution. Fiske (1969) and West (1971) describe the relation between the block market and the round-lot market on the New York Stock Exchange.

These results confirm the hypothesis that block trades initiated by sellers (those which trade on minus ticks) occur at relatively lower prices than the prices which prevailed at the close of trading on the preceding day; that is, $\bar{E}_1 < 0$. Conversely, $\bar{E}_1 > 0$ for block trades initiated by buyers. The market is efficient or inefficient, depending on whether these price changes represented trends which continued after a block was traded. $\bar{E}_2$ has an algebraic sign opposite to that on $\bar{E}_1$ for both plus-tick and minus-tick blocks. It thus appears that the price trend established by a block trade does not continue after the trade. This evidence does not merit rejecting the hypothesis that the market is efficient with respect to block trades.

Observe that the closing price following a block trade on a minus tick represents, on average, a substantial recovery from the price of the block trade itself, while the closing price following a block trade on a plus tick shows only minimal average recovery. This disparate behavior can be explained by an institutional characteristic of block trading. Securities dealers provide liquidity services in large block transactions by buying stock for their own inventories to accommodate sales initiated by customers. The inducement to provide such a liquidity service is the opportunity to buy stock at an unusually low price. The same dealers will less frequently short sell an issue to accommodate the purchase of a customer. Thus, there is no basis for compensating a dealer for any liquidity services on a block bought by a customer, and no price recovery should be expected on that account. On sales, however, where dealers do provide liquidity services, there is a significant price recovery. This suggests that part of the lower price in the sale of a block of stock represents an implicit payment to securities dealers. (See also Section 23.2.)

The results of Kraus and Stoll indicate that there are liquidity costs incorporated in transactions prices on *sold* blocks of stock and that an investor who can buy a piece of a block can anticipate a return on his participation in the block transaction. The authors also point out, however, that the small size of the average price recovery following a block trade, .71 percent on average, makes participation uneconomic for investors who have to pay substantial brokerage commissions. In a further study of *sales* of blocks of stock, Dann, Mayers, and Raab (1977) found no statistically significant profit opportunities unless an investor could obtain execution of his purchase order within 15 minutes after a block had traded, ignoring brokerage commissions. When commissions were included, only participation in the block trade itself allowed positive expected returns. Carey (1977) reports similar results. Thus, it appears that while liquidity costs affect transactions prices on block sales, their effects dissipate rapidly.

Kraus and Stoll also investigated the relation between block trades and stock returns on days preceding and following those trades. Let $R_{j,t}$ be the return on stock j during day t (measured by the percent change in the value of the stock from the close of the market on day $t-1$ to the close of the market on day t). Let $R_{m,t}$ be the return on the market portfolio during day t (measured by the percent change in Standard & Poor's Composite Index of 500 Stocks; see Section 10.3). Kraus and Stoll computed the residual daily returns $\hat{e}_{j,t}$ as follows:

$$\hat{e}_{j,t} = R_{j,t} - R_{m,t} \qquad -20 \le t \le 20 \qquad (13.23)$$

This residual daily return was computed for 20 days preceding and 20 days following a block trade in security j. In Equation (13.23) $t = 0$ for the day of the trade, $t > 0$ for days following the trade, and $t < 0$ for days prior to the trade. This model is similar to that used by FFJR, with $\hat{\alpha}_j = 0$ and $\hat{\beta}_j = 1$. [See Equation (13.19).] Kraus and Stoll then defined the average residual return during day t as

$$u_t = \sum_{j=1}^{N_t} \frac{\hat{e}_{j,t}}{N_t} \qquad (13.24)$$

where N_t is the number of observations for that day. They also defined the cumulative average net change in value up to day t as

$$S_t = \sum_{k=-20}^{t} u_k \qquad t \ge -20 \qquad (13.25)$$

S_t uses the price of the stock 21 days prior to the block trade as a base value. Table 13.4 and Figure 13.3 show the values of u_t and S_t.

Observe that S_t is quite stable for $t > 0$ for both plus-tick and minus-tick block trades. There is no tendency for market-adjusted stock prices to change in days following the day of a block trade. Whatever liquidity costs were present in the sale of a block have, on average, vanished by the end of the day in which the block trade occurred. Any information which motivated either a block purchase or a block sale is, on average, fully incorporated in the price of the stock at the end of that trading day.

Note that stock returns are relatively high in the days preceding the purchase of a block of stock. That is, S_t rises as the date of a block trade (initiated by a buyer) approaches. This may be due to gradual dissemination of the information that someone is trying to buy a large block of stock and the implication that there exists incompletely disseminated favorable information about the issuer. By the time the block trade occurs, however, the market has, on average, completely priced out the new information. The converse of this is demonstrated for block sales, but the decline occurs over a relatively shorter time span, because block sales are generally easier to complete than block purchases.

13.4 STRONG-FORM EFFICIENCY

If there exists *no* information which would make the market inefficient (in the sense of the definition given in Section 13.1), then the market is said to be strong-form efficient. A sufficient condition for strong-form efficiency is that the

TABLE 13.4
AVERAGE RESIDUAL RETURNS AND
CUMULATIVE AVERAGE NET CHANGE IN VALUE
RELATIVE TO DAY OF BLOCK TRADE

t	Blocks traded on a minus tick		Blocks traded on a plus tick	
	u_t*	S_t†	u_t*	S_t†
−20	−.06	−.06	.05	.05
−15	.01	−.11	.26	.72
−10	−.05	−.37	.09	1.20
−5	.02	−.24	.45	2.01
−4	.02	−.20	.07	2.10
−3	−.21	−.39	.30	2.43
−2	−.29	−.65	.36	2.84
−1	−.33	−.95	.72	3.64
0	−1.15	−2.04	1.29	5.01
1	−.01	−2.05	.23	5.31
2	−.07	−2.10	−.03	5.31
3	.10	−1.99	.02	5.34
4	.04	−1.94	.10	5.42
5	.04	−1.89	−.07	5.35
10	.02	−1.68	−.12	5.37
15	−.01	−1.53	.15	5.62
20	.02	−1.57	−.10	5.37

*Percent during day t.
†Percent change in value from base date 21 days prior to block trade.
Source: Adapted from Kraus and Stoll (1972), Tables 2 and 3.

information set Φ which investors recognize includes all information, public and private. The hypothesis of strong-form efficiency is the most difficult to test, because it is framed with respect to all information. One way to test the hypothesis is to consider the earnings performance of investors who might be expected to have an edge in acquiring new information or who might be expected to be exceptionally competent in their ability to discriminate between overpriced and underpriced securities: institutional investors and corporate insiders.

Returns on Managed Portfolios

Jensen (1968) analyzed whether professionally managed open-end equity mutual funds earned exceptional rates of return over the period 1945–1964.[27] Jensen assumed that each of 115 mutual funds in his sample had a stationary

---

[27] The problem of how to evaluate the performance of mutual funds is also considered in Treynor (1965), Sharpe (1966), Jensen (1968), Williamson (1972), Friend and Blume (1970), Campanella (1972), McDonald (1974), and Kim (1978).

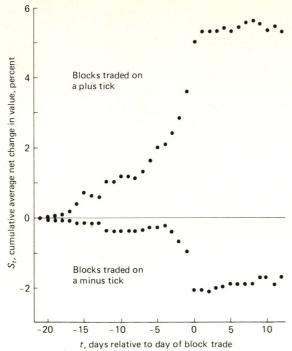

FIGURE 13.3
Cumulative average net change in value around the day of a block trade.

portfolio beta over the sample period.[28] The capital asset pricing model would then suggest that the expected return on portfolio p in year t is

$$\mu_{p,t} = R_{f,t} + \beta_p(\mu_{m,t} - R_{f,t}) \qquad t = 1945, \dots, 1964 \qquad (13.26)$$

where β_p is the beta of the portfolio of the fund. In that case, the expected value of the estimate of α_p will be zero in the model

$$R_{p,t} - R_{f,t} = \alpha_p + \beta_p(R_{m,t} - R_{f,t}) + e_{p,t} \qquad (13.27)$$

$R_{p,t}$ is the realized return on portfolio p; $R_{m,t}$ is the realized return on the market (measured by the relative change in value of Standard & Poor's Composite Index of 500 stocks during the year); and $e_{p,t}$ is a random term with mean zero. If the managers of the fund were consistently superior stock analysts, α_p should be positive.

Jensen estimated values for α_p for the cases where the return on a mutual fund portfolio was measured before deductions for research expenses, manage-

[28] McDonald (1974) has analyzed the relation between the objectives of 123 mutual funds (stated in terms of maximum capital gains, growth, income, and stability), and the betas, standard deviations of return and premium returns on those funds.

ment fees, and brokerage commissions, and where the return excluded those charges. In the former case the average value of α_p over the 115 funds was $-.4$ percent per annum, and in the latter case it was -1.1 percent per annum.[29] It appears that, on average, mutual funds cannot earn a premium return sufficient to cover their operating expenses, after adjusting for the risk exposure of the funds, and that participants in those funds lose about 1 percent of their wealth per year after deducting such expenses, in relation to the risk-adjusted expected returns on the fund portfolios.[30]

While this evidence suggests that mutual funds are unable to earn exceptional rates of return, it does not mean that mutual funds serve no useful economic role in financial markets. As we pointed out in Sections 2.4 and 9.1, mutual funds provide important diversification services to small investors.

Returns on Insider Portfolios

In at least one circumstance the strong form of the efficient market hypothesis must be wrong almost as a matter of definition. New information about securities issuers comes into existence constantly. At an early stage in the process of disseminating new information, some investors may learn a particular piece of news and may trade on the basis of that news ahead of all other investors. The prices at which they trade cannot possibly fully reflect the news. The market must therefore be strong-form inefficient with respect to the news which motivated their trading.[31]

Corporate insiders are likely to learn new information in advance of other in-

---

[29] McDonald (1974) found an average positive value of α_p equal to about .6 percent per annum from a sample of 123 mutual funds over the period 1960–1969. Fund returns did not exclude transactions costs in that study. McDonald (1973) found that French mutual fund managers were able to outperform other French investors during the period 1964–1969, but he attributed this result to access to nonpublic information.

[30] The role of security analysis in light of the efficient market hypothesis has been discussed by Black (1971a), Vasicek and McQuown (1972), Treynor (1974), and Bernstein (1975). Some early studies by Ferber (1958) and Ruff (1963) suggest that the purchase and sale recommendations of securities analysts have a significant, but small, impact on the price of a stock. This would imply that those recommendations do contain information but [as Ferber (1958) showed] not enough to justify trading. More recently, Lloyd-Davies and Canes (1978) have reported that analyst recommendations may have more substantial value than was previously believed. See also *SEC v. Capital Gains Research Bureau*, 375 U.S. 180 (1963), for an example of an analyst "scalping," or trading before his clients.

[31] Lloyd-Davis and Canes (1978) show that the market does not fully reflect the recommendations of security analysts until those recommendations are widely available, even though the recommendations may have been available for some time on a more restricted basis. This suggests that the market is not efficient with respect to information which is very difficult to acquire because it is not publicly available. Kryzanowski (1978b, 1979) shows that regulators who suspend trading in a stock because of suspected price manipulation or incomplete disclosure of new information possess information not available to the market which could have been exploited by manipulators or insiders prior to suspension. He also suggests that the information which led to the suspension is fully reflected in stock prices after resumption of trading if the information was favorable to the issuer, but not if the information was unfavorable to the issuer.

vestors, in some cases months before it is disclosed to the public.[32] Analysis of the returns on portfolios constructed from the purchases and sales of corporate insiders should be a powerful test of the hypothesis of strong-form market efficiency.[33]

Section 16(a) of the Securities Exchange Act of 1934 provides that corporate insiders (defined as officers, directors, and beneficial owners of 10 percent or more of a class of equity security) must report monthly to the Securities and Exchange Commission their purchases and sales of securities issued by corporations in which they are insiders. In *each* of the 36 months from January 1969 to December 1971, Finnerty (1976) constructed two portfolios, one divided equally among all securities bought by insiders during the month (the "buy" portfolio), and the other divided equally among all securities sold by insiders during the month (the "sell" portfolio). Finnerty analyzed the returns on these portfolios relative to contemporaneous returns on the market as a whole, both in the months the portfolios were formed and in subsequent months as well.

Let $R_{t,t+\tau}$ be the return on the buy or sell portfolio *formed* in month t ($t = 1$, $2, \ldots, 36$) and *realized* during month $t + \tau$ ($\tau = 0, 1, \ldots, 11$). Let $R_{m,t+\tau}$ be the return on Fisher's market index in month $t + \tau$ [see Fisher (1965) and Section 10.3]. Define the average residual return u_τ earned on an insider portfolio τ months after it is formed, for either buy or sell portfolios, as

$$u_\tau = \sum_{t=1}^{36} \frac{(R_{t,t+\tau} - R_{m,t+\tau})}{36} \qquad \tau = 0, 1, \ldots, 11 \qquad (13.28)$$

If insiders do not have superior access to new information, they should not be able to outperform the market, and hence u_τ should not be significantly different from zero for any τ. If, on the other hand, insiders do enjoy superior access to new information, then u_τ should be significantly greater than zero for buy portfolios and u_τ should be significantly less than zero for sell portfolios. Intuitively, if insiders learn of and act on news early, the securities which they buy should subsequently change in value at a rate greater than the market as a whole and the securities which they sell should subsequently change in value at a rate less than the market as a whole.

Table 13.5 shows value of u_τ for $\tau = 0, 1, \ldots, 11$ months for both buy and sell portfolios. We can easily reject the null hypothesis that the excess returns on insider portfolios are zero, in favor of the alternative hypotheses of positive residual returns on buy portfolios and negative residual returns on sell portfolios. u_τ is significantly greater than zero for buy portfolios in 6 of the 7

---

[32] Sarri (1977) has argued that the disclosure laws of the Securities Act of 1933 and the Securities Exchange Act of 1934 exacerbate the problem of slow dissemination of information, especially of so-called soft information. See also Schneider (1972).

[33] Returns to insider trading have been studied by Lorie and Niederhoffer (1968), Jaffe (1974a, 1974b), and Finnerty (1976).

TABLE 13.5
AVERAGE RESIDUAL RETURNS ON
INSIDER PORTFOLIOS

	u_τ*	
τ	Buy portfolios	Sell portfolios
0	3.68†	−.90†
1	1.01	−.45†
2	.85†	−.43†
3	.37†	−.42†
4	.53†	−.47†
5	.26†	−.33
6	.49†	−.31†
7	.16	−.26
8	.18	−.37†
9	.21	−.34†
10	.40†	−.28†
11	.20	−.26†

*Percent during month τ.
†Significantly different from zero at a confidence level in excess of 95 percent.
Source: From Finnerty (1976), Table 1.

months with $\tau \leq 6$, and it is significantly less than zero for sell portfolios in 6 of the 7 months with $\tau \leq 6$. Insider transactions appear to be a better guide to near-term price behavior than distant price behavior, because $|u_j| > |u_k|$ if $j < k$, although even the u_τ's for τ greater than 6 months are not negligible.[34]

This evidence suggests that if insiders have preferential access to new information, then they trade on the basis of that information at prices which do not fully reflect the information. Their transactions certainly appear unusually well timed relative to the transactions of other investors. In view of the great likelihood that insiders do have preferential access to new information, we are led to reject the strong form of the efficient market hypothesis.

CHAPTER SUMMARY

This chapter has analyzed whether, and to what degree, stock prices reflect information. The first step in the analysis was to clarify the meaning of "reflect information." We assumed market participants use observations from an information set Φ to form their expectations of future stock prices. The components of Φ were never elaborated explicitly. Instead, we asked whether observations

[34] Lorie and Niederhoffer (1968) note that reports of insider trading become publicly available about 2 months after the month of the trading. Jaffee (1974b) suggests that this information may not be impounded quickly into securities prices and has persistent positive value net of transactions costs.

from a specific information set U would alter the expectations of the market. If observations from U do not alter the market's expectations, then the market is efficient with respect to U. If observations from U do alter the market's expectations, then the market is inefficient with respect to U. The information set U then contains information not previously recognized by the market.

Three broad classes of information were examined in the analysis of market efficiency: past stock prices, publicly available information (which includes past stock prices as a special case), and all information (which includes public information as a special case). It appears that abnormal returns cannot be earned from trading on the basis of the past price behavior of a security, or from trading on the basis of publicly available information. Nor can consistently abnormal returns be earned from the efforts of professional analysts.[35] This implies that the prices at which securities can be bought and sold fully reflect all publicly available information, and in particular reflect whatever information is communicated by past price fluctuations.

In contrast, abnormal returns *can* be earned from preferential access to new information.[36] The purchases and sales of securities by corporate insiders appear unusually well timed, on average, relative to the transactions of other market participants.

FURTHER READING

S. Basu, "Investment Performance of Common Stocks in Relation to Their Price-Earnings Ratios: A Test of the Efficient Market Hypothesis," *Journal of Finance*, **32** (June 1977), 663–682.

Eugene Fama, "Efficient Capital Markets: A Review of Theory and Empirical Work," *Journal of Finance*, **25** (May 1970), 383–417.

Arthur Fleischer, Robert Mundheim, and John Murphy, "An Initial Inquiry into the Responsibility to Disclose Market Information,"*University of Pennsylvania Law Review*, **121** (1973), 798–859.

Sanford Grossman, "On the Efficiency of Competitive Stock Markets Where Trades Have Diverse Information," *Journal of Finance*, **31** (May 1976), 573–585.

——— and Joseph Stiglitz, "Information and Competitive Price Systems," *American Economic Review*, **66** (May 1976), 246–253.

[35] See Pozen (1976) and Salmanowitz (1977) for policy recommendations concerning the regulation of institutional money managers and broker-customer relationship which follow from the semistrong-form efficiency of the markets. The notion of semistrong-form efficient markets also casts doubts on the doctrine of the SEC that brokers and dealers should have a "reasonable basis" for their sale and purchase recommendations; see Wolfson, Phillips, and Russo (1977, Chap. 2).

[36] An interesting special case of investors trading on the basis of incompletely disseminated information is the so-called market facts problem. A market fact is information which may affect the price of a security but which does not directly concern the profitability of the issuer, e.g., tender offers and block trades. The seminal article on market facts is Fleischer, Mundheim, and Murphy (1973). See also Lipton (1974) and Note, "The Downstairs Insider: The Specialist and Rule 10b-5," *New York University Law Review*, **42** (1967), 695–715.

John Salmanowitz, "Broker Investment Recommendations and the Efficient Capital Market Hypothesis: A Proposed Cautionary Legend," *Stanford Law Review*, **29** (1977), 1077–1114.

Christopher Sarri, "The Efficient Capital Market Hypothesis, Economic Theory and the Regulation of the Securities Industry," *Stanford Law Review*, **29** (1977), 1031–1076.

Chris Welles, "Reprogramming the Money Manager," *Institutional Investor*, **11** (April 1977), 35.

DEBT SECURITIES
AND FUTURES MARKETS

The discussions of portfolio theory in Part Three and capital market equilibrium in Part Four focused on investors with a planning horizon of a single period. This focus is appropriate if the return on an asset in one period is uncorrelated with the return in the next period. Investors will then behave as if they had one-period horizons, even if they do not plan to liquidate their portfolios for several periods.[1] Because the returns on common stock are uncorrelated through time,[2] a single-period framework was appropriate for the analysis of stock investments and stock market equilibrium.

The structure of returns on debt securities is significantly different from the structure of returns on common stock. The principal difference can be illustrated by examining the structure of returns on a 1-year Treasury bill. During the first 6 months following its purchase, the return on the bill is uncertain, because of uncertainty about its market price at the end of those 6 months. Nonetheless, a holder knows with certainty his return over the full year, because the maturity value of the bill is known with certainty. Whatever unexpected loss is experienced in the first 6-month interval *must* be made up before the bill matures. Since the average return over the 12-month lifetime of the bill is known, the returns over the two consecutive 6-month intervals between purchase and maturity must be inversely correlated.[3] This means that a single-

---

[1] See Mossin (1968).

[2] Section 13.2 pointed out that returns on common stock appear to be serially independent over nonoverlapping intervals of time.

[3] If the holder experiences an unexpected loss during the first 6 months, he must experience an unexpected gain during the second 6 months. Conversely, if he experiences an unexpected gain during the first 6 months, he must experience an unexpected loss during the second 6 months. Taken together, these observations mean that the unexpected return in the first 6 months is inversely correlated with the unexpected return in the second 6 months.

267

period framework is *not* appropriate for the analysis of 1-year Treasury bills or, more generally, for the analysis of debt securities and debt market equilibrium.

A debt security is different from common stock, because it has a perfectly predictable value at a specific future date: at maturity it will be worth its face value (assuming the issuer is not in default). This predictability of future value can be quite attractive to some investors. For example, portfolio managers at life insurance companies have to be concerned with the predictability of the value of their asset holdings at relatively distant dates in the future, because their liabilities (in the form of life insurance contracts) have distant maturities. However, it should also be clear that different debt holders may be concerned about the predictability of their investments at different future dates. While portfolio managers at life insurance companies have long investment planning horizons, corporate treasurers managing cash balance positions have very short horizons, possibly only a few days or a few weeks. This means that there may be significant differences, based on institutional considerations, in the debt investment planning horizons of different investors.[4] Thus, there are both analytical and institutional reasons why the assumption of a common single-period planning horizon is inappropriate for the analysis of debt securities and debt market equilibrium.

The three chapters in this part examine two related financial instruments: debt securities and futures contracts to purchase or sell an asset for deferred delivery. In the simplest cases, debt securities can be viewed as instruments which fix the future value of a present investment of cash. Chapter 14 discusses why investors find predictability of value on a specific future date an attractive feature of a financial instrument, and it analyzes the determinants of yields on debt instruments of different maturities.

Futures contracts can be viewed as financial instruments which fix the future values of assets other than cash, such as grain, pork bellies, and unmatured debt securities. Chapter 15 describes the structure and organization of futures markets and shows how futures contracts can be used to hedge against the risk inherent in uncertain future asset prices.

Chapter 16 analyzes the determinants of settlement prices on futures contracts. It is observed in that chapter that, in some cases, there exists a very close relation between the structure of settlement prices on futures contracts and yields on debt securities. This result is reasonable, because both types of instruments fix the future values of particular assets: debt securities fix the future value of cash, and futures contracts fix the future values of noncash assets.

---

[4] Bierwag and Kaufman (1978) have made this point in criticizing several studies of risk and return on debt securities.

CHAPTER 14

THE TERM STRUCTURE OF INTEREST RATES

The term structure of interest rates is the structure of yields on debt instruments which differ only in the time remaining to their maturity dates. There are many factors which can cause one debt security to offer a yield different from that of another, including maturity, tax treatment, creditworthiness of the issuer, and the existence of early redemption schedules such as call or sinking-fund provisions. When we consider variations in yield as a function only of time to maturity, however, we are concerned specifically with term structure.

Figure 14.1 shows two yield curves, or graphs of yields versus maturity dates, for United States Treasury securities. In the curve from August 30, 1974, short-term yields are high, but interest rates decline as term to maturity increases. In the curve for February 27, 1976, the reverse holds: short-term yields are low, and yields rise with term to maturity. Term structure theory seeks to suggest the reasons for such disparate behavior.

The first four sections of this chapter present four theories of the term structure of interest rates.[1] The theories all involve concepts of risk due to uncertainty and expectations of return. The theories are developed for discount debt instruments which offer a single payment of funds at a specified maturity date. The fifth section shows that the theories apply equally well to instruments which make intermediate coupon payments.

We assume the following throughout this chapter:

---

[1] In addition to the other references cited in this chapter, see the texts on term structure by Kessel (1965), Malkiel (1966), Meiselman (1962), Nelson (1972a), and Roll (1970), and see also the survey article by Telser (1967).

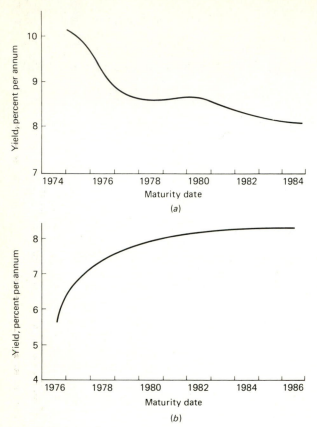

FIGURE 14.1
Yield curves from (a) August 30, 1974, and (b) February 27, 1976.

1 Transactions are costless.
2 There are no taxes of any kind.[2]
3 Investors have homogeneous expectations of future yields.[3]
4 No debt instrument bears any default risk.

The last assumption implies the theories developed in this chapter are appropriate only for Treasury securities. In Chapter 19 we will extend the analysis of yields on debt instruments to include the structure of risk premiums on debt issues which bear credit risk.

There are two basic elements to any theory of term structure. First is a *portfolio theory* of investor demand for debt instruments of different maturities. Part Three developed a theory of stock allocation for an investor with a single-period investment planning horizon. In this chapter we present more

---

[2] The effect of taxes on debt yields has been studied by Pye (1969), Robichek and Niebuhr (1970), and McCulloch (1975b).

[3] See Kane and Malkiel (1967) for evidence on the heterogeneity of expectations of future interest rates.

descriptive theories of investments in debt securities of different maturities. The second element of term structure theory is deriving the characteristics of a *market equilibrium*. In Chapter 12 we found that the expected premium return on a stock was related to the beta of that stock. As we will see, no such general results are available for debt securities.

14.1 SEGMENTED-MARKETS THEORY

The first theory of term structure relies heavily on the concept of risk aversion. The theory is important, because it clarifies the notion of an investment horizon, and because it suggests why different investors have preferences for debt of different maturities.

Introducing the Segmented-Markets Theory

The segmented-markets theory of term structure is grounded in the observation that many creditors invest in debt securities of particular maturities and are seemingly insensitive to yields on debt of other maturities.[4] The resulting "segmentation" of the debt markets is a consequence of the desire of investors to minimize their exposure to risk.

Life insurance companies sell long-term liabilities against themselves in the form of insurance contracts. Because most policyholders can be expected to live for some time, the liabilities represented by their insurance contracts will typically mature at relatively distant dates. Life insurance companies have to be concerned with the value of their investments at comparably distant dates in the future.[5] That is, life insurance companies have long investment planning horizons.

The price of a life insurance policy reflects an assumption made by the issuer of the policy about the rate of return which can be earned on the policy premiums received between the date of sale and the ultimate maturity of the policy. If an insurance company buys long-term debt, it can substantially reduce its uncertainty over future earnings on its investment portfolio. If, on the other hand, it invests and reinvests in short-term debt, it must bear the "reinvestment risk" that at some date in the future its portfolio will not be earning at the rate originally anticipated, because of an unexpected fall in the level of short-term interest rates. Holding long-term debt is, therefore, a hedged investment strategy for life insurers, and risk-averse insurance companies have a preference for such debt. Similar comments apply to the investment horizons and asset preferences of many pension funds.

An example of asset perferences at the other end of the maturity spectrum can be found by examining corporate cash management policies. Many corporations actively manage what in past decades were called *idle cash balances*.

---

[4] Culbertson (1957) provides a comprehensive exposition of the segmented-markets theory.

[5] A life insurance company will also have to be concerned with the value of its assets over a short horizon if there is some probability that it will have to sell some of those assets to fund requests for loans by policyholders against their policies.

Corporations come to hold these balances as a result of a temporary excess of receipts over disbursements. For example, several large oil companies make royalty payments to member nations of OPEC (Organization of Petroleum Exporting Countries) on the 15th of each month. These oil companies begin to accumulate funds immediately after one payment in anticipation of the next payment. By the second week of a month, the balances accumulated by the companies amount to hundreds of millions of dollars.

Oil companies employ cash managers to invest balances accumulated in anticipation of OPEC payments. Cash managers have extremely short planning horizons for investing these balances. If they were to buy debt securities with a maturity date later than a scheduled OPEC payment date, they would face the "market risk" that an unexpected change in the market value of their holdings might wipe out any anticipated returns, or might even reduce the principal value of their investments. A hedged investment strategy for the cash manager of an oil company is to allocate his portfolio only to debt instruments with maturities matched to his investment planning horizon. Risk-averse cash managers therefore have a decided preference for short-term debt.

These two illustrations of investor preferences for debt of a particular maturity can be extended to other maturities. The important point is that it is often possible to identify the investment planning horizon of an investor holding debt instruments. Assuming the investor is risk-averse, he will have a preference for debt with a maturity matched to that horizon. If he invests in shorter-maturity debt, he will bear the *reinvestment risk* of being uncertain about the yield at which he can reinvest funds from investments which mature before the end of his horizon. If he invests in longer-maturity debt, he will bear the *market risk* of being uncertain about the price at which he can sell unmatured debt. In either case he will be uncertain about his wealth at the end of his investment planning horizon. He can eliminate this uncertainty by investing in debt which matures exactly at the end of that horizon.[6]

Portfolio Allocation under the Segmented-Markets Theory

The segmented-markets theory of the term structure of interest rates asserts that investors will hold *only* those debt instruments whose maturities match their investment horizon. This portfolio policy results from the assumption that investors are *completely risk-averse* and will never mismatch the maturities of their investments relative to their horizons, regardless of the yield incentives which may exist for mismatches.

Debt Market Equilibrium under the Segmented-Markets Theory

If investors are indifferent to yields on alternative maturity debt assets, the markets for debt of different maturities will be segmented. A premium yield on

---

[6] Many investment managers will actually have multiple horizons. Life insurers, for example, will have short-term investment horizons for policies written long ago, and longer-term horizons for more recently written policies. Similarly, cash managers may be investing in anticipation of multiple future payments at different dates, rather than a single payment at a single date.

debt of one maturity will not attract the interest of investors with longer or shorter investment horizons. As a consequence of this segmentation of the debt markets, the segmented-markets theory of term structure implies that the equilibrium yield on debt of a given maturity is determined only by the conditions of supply and demand in the market for that debt. Long-term yields will be at whatever level is required to induce investors with long horizons to hold the existing stock of long-term debt. Similar comments apply to the equilibrium level of yields in markets for debt of other maturities.

One essential problem with the segmented-markets theory is that it fails to explain why high short-term yields are usually associated with a declining yield curve, and why low short-term yields are usually associated with a rising yield curve. In addition, it is difficult to believe that investors are unwilling to accept any risk, however small, to achieve a higher expected return on their investments in debt instruments. To see how investor expectations might affect investment decisions, we consider next a theory of term structure completely congruent to segmented markets.

14.2   PURE-EXPECTATIONS THEORY

The pure-expectations theory of the term structure of interest rates assumes that investors are *indifferent* to risk and that they will buy and sell debt assets of different maturities until the expected yields on all assets are equal over all planning periods.[7]

To introduce some notational conventions, suppose at time t a debt instrument which pays \$100 n periods later, at time $t + n$, is priced at $P_{n,t}$. The yield *per period* on that instrument is defined as the value of $R_{n,t}$ which solves the equation[8]

$$P_{n,t} = 100 \cdot \exp\left[-n \cdot R_{n,t}\right] \tag{14.1}$$

where $\exp[x] = e^x$. Solving Equation (14.1) for $R_{n,t}$ gives

$$R_{n,t} = \frac{\ln\left[100/P_{n,t}\right]}{n}$$

where $\ln[x]$ is the natural logarithm of x. This definition of the yield on a debt instrument assumes continuous compounding from time t to time $t + n$.[9] If $n = 2$ and $P_{2,t} = \$86.94$, then $R_{2,t} = \ln[100/86.94]/2 = \ln[1.1502]/2 = .07$, or 7 percent per period, compounded continuously for two periods.

Equation (14.1) is an important equation which is used repeatedly in the analysis of the term structure of interest rates. $P_{n,t}$ is the present value at time t

---

[7] The pure-expectations theory was first proposed by Irving Fisher (1930). Roll (1970) presents convincing evidence for its rejection as an explanation of the behavior of yields on Treasury bills.

[8] The chronological duration of a period may be assumed to be a day for the sake of convenience. The yield per period can be converted into the yield per annum by multiplying it by the number of periods in a year, as shown in the appendix to Chapter 1.

[9] Discrete and continuous compounding is explained in the appendix to Chapter 1.

of an asset which matures in n periods, or at time $t + n$. The maturity value 100 is the future value of the asset. The term $\exp[-n \cdot R_{n,t}]$ is called the *discount factor* for the n-period asset, where the discount rate is the continuously compounded yield $R_{n,t}$ per period. In words, Equation (14.1) says that

$$\text{Present value} = \text{future value} \times \text{discount factor}$$

In computing the discount factor, note that we take the yield *per period* [$R_{n,t}$ in Equation (14.1)] and multiply it by the *number of periods* [n in Equation (14.1)].

Equation (14.1) can also be written in the form

$$100 = P_{n,t} \cdot \exp[n \cdot R_{n,t}] \tag{14.2}$$

The term $\exp[n \cdot R_{n,t}]$ in Equation (14.2) is called the *compounding factor* for the n-period asset. In words, Equation (14.2) says that

$$\text{Future value} = \text{present value} \times \text{compounding factor}$$

Note that the compounding factor is the reciprocal of the discount factor: $\exp[n \cdot R_{n,t}] = 1/\exp[-n \cdot R_{n,t}]$. Equation (14.2) says that the present value $P_{n,t}$ of the asset will grow to the future value of 100 over n periods at the continuously compounded growth rate of $R_{n,t}$ per period.

Introducing the Pure-Expectations Theory

The foundations of the pure-expectations theory are readily apparent in the simple case where there exist only one-period and two-period debt instruments and where there are only two types of investors: those with a one-period planning horizon and those with a two-period planning horizon.

Investment Alternatives for an Investor with a Two-Period Horizon Consider first the investment alternatives available to an investor with a two-period horizon. If he invests at time t in a two-period instrument, he will earn at the known rate $R_{2,t}$ over his investment horizon. For example, if the investor starts with $1000 and if $R_{2,t} = .075$ (or 7.5 percent per period), then he will have $1161.83 at time $t + 2$ ($1161.83 = $1000 \cdot \exp[2 \cdot R_{2,t}]$ when $R_{2,t} = .075$).

The same two-period investor could also invest in a one-period instrument and then reinvest the proceeds of that investment for another period. This is called a *rollover* strategy. If he starts with $1000 at time t, he will have $1000 \cdot \exp[R_{1,t}]$ at time $t + 1$. If the yield on one-period debt at time $t + 1$ is $R_{1,t+1}$, the investor can reinvest his wealth and obtain $1000 \cdot \exp[R_{1,t}] \cdot \exp[R_{1,t+1}]$ at the end of the second period. For example, if $R_{1,t} = .09$ (or 9 percent), the investor would have $1094.17 at the end of the first period ($1094.17 = $1000 \cdot \exp[.09]$). If $R_{1,t+1} = .06$ (or 6 percent), the investor would reinvest that $1094.17 and would have $1161.83 at the end of the second period ($1161.83 = $1094.17 · exp [.06]).

The average yield per period over the two-period investment horizon earned by an investor pursuing a rollover strategy will be the value of E_2 which solves the equation

$$1000 = \{1000 \cdot \exp [R_{1,t} + R_{1,t+1}]\} \cdot \exp [-2 \cdot E_2]$$

That is, E_2 is the discount rate which equates the present value of the investor's future wealth to the investor's present wealth. Solving for E_2, we have

$$E_2 = {}^1\!/_2(R_{1,t} + R_{1,t+1})$$

In the case where $R_{1,t} = 9$ percent and $R_{1,t+1} = 6$ percent, we have $E_2 = 7.5$ percent $[{}^1\!/_2(9 + 6)]$. This can be verified by noting that the investor's present wealth ($1000) is equal to his future wealth ($1161.83) discounted for 2 periods at 7.5 percent per period, or

$$\$1000 = \$1161.83 \cdot \exp [-2 \cdot .075]$$

Thus, the investor earned 7.5 percent per period for 2 periods.

The realized yield E_2 is the average of the current one-period yield $R_{1,t}$ and the one-period yield $R_{1,t+1}$ prevailing in the next period. $R_{1,t+1}$ is unknown at time t. The investor, however, has an expectation of what that yield will be; call it $r_{1,t+1}$. It follows that the expected yield per period on a sequence of two consecutive one-period investments, i.e., the expected value of E_2, is

$$\text{Exp } [E_2] = {}^1\!/_2(R_{1,t} + r_{1,t+1}) \tag{14.3}$$

In deciding whether to buy one-period debt (with the intent of rolling over the investment) or two-period debt, an investor with a two-period horizon should compare Exp $[E_2]$ with $R_{2,t}$. That is, he should compare the *expected* yield per period from the rollover strategy with the *known* yield per period from an investment in two-period debt.

Investment Alternatives for an Investor with a One-Period Horizon We can also consider the alternatives available to an investor with a one-period horizon. If that investor buys one-period debt, he will earn at the known rate $R_{1,t}$ over his holding period. Alternatively, the investor can buy a two-period debt instrument at time t and liquidate that investment at time $t + 1$ in a secondary-market sale. If the two-period instrument promised to pay $100 at maturity, its purchase cost at time t would be $100 \cdot \exp [-2 \cdot R_{2,t}]$ and its liquidation value at time $t + 1$ would be $100 \cdot \exp [-R_{1,t+1}]$. (Note that at time $t + 1$ the instrument has become a one-period asset.) For example, if $R_{2,t} = .075$ (or 7.5 percent), then a debt instrument promising to pay $100 at time $t + 2$ is worth $86.07 at time t ($86.07 = $100 \cdot \exp [-2 \cdot .075]$). If that debt instrument is sold at time $t + 1$ when $R_{1,t+1} = .06$ (or 6 percent), then it will be sold at a price of \$94.18 (\$100 · exp $[-.06]$).

The return over the interval from time t to time $t + 1$ is the value of E_1 which solves the equation

$$\{100 \cdot \exp\,[-2 \cdot R_{2,t}]\} = \{100 \cdot \exp\,[-R_{1,t+1}]\} \cdot \exp\,[-E_1]$$

or
$$E_1 = 2 \cdot R_{2,t} - R_{1,t+1}$$

In the case where $R_{2,t} = 7.5$ percent and $R_{1,t+1} = 6$ percent, we have $E_1 = 9$ percent. This can be verified by noting that an investment which costs \$86.07 at time t and which can be sold for \$94.18 at time $t + 1$ will have earned interest at the continuously compounded rate of 9 percent per period for one period:

$$\$86.07 = \$94.18 \cdot \exp\,[-.09]$$

The realized yield E_1 depends on the value of $R_{1,t+1}$. This future yield is not known with certainty at time t. If the investor expects $R_{1,t+1}$ to have the value $r_{1,t+1}$, then the expected yield on holding two-period debt for one period will be

$$\text{Exp}\,[E_1] = 2 \cdot R_{2,t} - r_{1,t+1} \tag{14.4}$$

In deciding whether to buy one-period debt or two-period debt (with the intent of selling that debt at the end of one period), an investor with a one-period horizon should compare $R_{1,t}$ with Exp $[E_1]$. That is, he should compare the *known* yield on one-period debt with the yield *expected* from buying two-period debt and then liquidating that investment at the end of one period.

Summary In summary, a one-period investor can (1) buy one-period debt with the *known* rate of return $R_{1,t}$ or (2) buy two-period debt and sell that debt at the end of one period. He would then *expect* to earn at the rate Exp $[E_1] = 2 \cdot R_{2,t} - r_{1,t+1}$ over his one-period investment horizon. A two-period investor can (1) buy two-period debt with the *known* rate of return $R_{2,t}$ or (2) buy one-period debt and roll over that investment at the end of the period. He would then *expect* to earn at the rate $\frac{1}{2}(R_{1,t} + r_{1,t+1})$ over his two-period investment horizon. The question is this: How does either investor decide whether to hold one-period debt or two-period debt? The answer requires a theory of portfolio allocation.[10]

Portfolio Allocation under the Pure-Expectations Theory

The portfolio allocation model underlying the pure-expectations theory of term structure is exceedingly simple. Because investors are assumed indifferent to

---

[10] Note that the segmented-markets theory of term structure would say that the investor with a one-period horizon will buy one-period debt regardless of the value of Exp $[E_1]$, and that the investor with a two-period horizon will buy two-period debt regardless of the value of Exp $[E_2]$.

risk, they will hold that debt instrument which maximizes their expected return over their investment horizon.[11]

An investor with a two-period horizon will hold two-period debt if $R_{2,t} >$ Exp $[E_2]$.[12] He will hold one-period debt if the inequality runs in the opposite direction. In the latter case the investor holds one-period debt with the intention of rolling over into another investment in one-period debt at the end of the first period.

Similarly, an investor with a one-period horizon will hold one-period debt if $R_{1,t} >$ Exp $[E_1]$. He will hold two-period debt if the inequality is reversed.[13] In the latter case the investor holds two-period debt with the intention of liquidating his investment at the end of the first period.

Debt Market Equilibrium under the Pure-Expectations Theory

From the preceding analysis of portfolio choice, we have that an investor with a one-period horizon *and* an investor with a two-period horizon will hold two-period debt if $R_{2,t} > \frac{1}{2}(R_{1,t} + r_{1,t+1})$.[14] Conversely, they will each hold one-period debt if $R_{2,t} < \frac{1}{2}(R_{1,t} + r_{1,t+1})$. This result is crucial to the characterization of a market equilibrium under the pure-expectations theory.

Pure-expectations theory argues that, in equilibrium, the yield on a two-period debt investment must equal the expected yield on two sequential one-period debt investments:

$$R_{2,t} = \text{Exp } [E_2] = \frac{1}{2}(R_{1,t} + r_{1,t+1})$$

or
$$2 \cdot R_{2,t} = R_{1,t} + r_{1,t+1} \qquad (14.5)$$

If $2 \cdot R_{2,t} > R_{1,t} + r_{1,t+1}$, investors with one-period horizons and investors with two-period horizons will both want to hold two-period debt. Neither type of investor will be willing to hold one-period debt. This contradicts the requirement that all existing one-period and two-period debt securities must be held by somebody in an equilibrium. If $2 \cdot R_{2,t} < R_{1,t} + r_{1,t+1}$, both types of investors will want to hold one-period debt and neither will be willing to hold two-period debt, resulting in a similar contradiction. Thus, the equality of Equation (14.5) must hold in an equilibrium.[15]

---

[11] Observe the difference between portfolio allocation under the segmented-markets theory—where investors are assumed completely risk-averse and hence only buy debt that matures at the end of their investment horizon—and under the pure-expectations theory—where investors are indifferent to risk and will prefer debt of whatever maturity maximizes the expected rate of return over their investment horizon.

[12] This means a two-period investor will hold two-period debt if $R_{2,t} > \frac{1}{2}(R_{1,t} + r_{1,t+1})$. This follows from the definition of Exp $[E_2]$ in Equation (14.3).

[13] From the definition of Exp $[E_1]$ given by Equation (14.4), this means a one-period investor will hold two-period debt if $R_{1,t} < 2 \cdot R_{2,t} - r_{1,t+1}$, or if $R_{2,t} > \frac{1}{2}(R_{1,t} + r_{1,t+1})$.

[14] See footnotes 12 and 13 above.

[15] If Equation (14.5) is true, then we also have that Exp $[E_1] = R_{1,t}$. This follows from Equation (14.5) and the definition of Equation (14.4) that Exp $[E_1] = 2 \cdot R_{2,t} - r_{1,t+1}$. It means the expected yield on an investment in two-period debt for one period is the same as the yield on an investment in one-period debt for one period.

Equation (14.5) says that the yield on two-period debt depends on the current yield on one-period debt and the yield on one-period debt *expected* to prevail one period in the future. This is the key implication of the pure-expectations theory of the term structure of interest rates: yields on debt with a maturity greater than a single period depend on the current one-period yield and on one-period yields expected to prevail in the future.[16] For example, if the current one-period rate is 8 percent, and if investors expect that the one-period rate will increase to 9 percent in the next period, then the current two-period rate must, in equilibrium, be 8.5 percent. In terms of Equation (14.5) this is

$$2 \cdot R_{2,t} = R_{1,t} + r_{1,t+1}$$
$$2 \cdot 8.5 = 8.0 + 9.0$$

If $R_{2,t}$ were less than 8.5 percent, *all* investors would want to hold one-period debt. If $R_{2,t}$ were more than 8.5 percent, *all* investors would want to hold two-period debt.

Equilibrium with Multiperiod Debt Assets

Equation (14.5) says that if investors are indifferent to risk, then in equilibrium, the current two-period yield is an average of the current one-period yield and the one-period yield presently expected to prevail in the next period. The argument which led to this result can be extended to debt instruments with maturities of one, two, and three periods. In that case we have the additional result that the yield on three-period debt must, in equilibrium, satisfy the equality

$$3 \cdot R_{3,t} = R_{1,t} + r_{1,t+1} + r_{1,t+2} \tag{14.6}$$

Equation (14.6) implies that an investor with a three-period horizon who is indifferent to risk will also be indifferent between (1) investing directly in three-period debt and (2) investing in one-period debt and rolling over the investment for the following two periods.

In the general case, where there exist debt instruments with arbitrary maturities, the yield on k-period debt must satisfy the equilibrium condition

$$k \cdot R_{k,t} = R_{1,t} + r_{1,t+1} + \cdots + r_{1,t+k-1} \tag{14.7}$$

In the pure-expectations theory of the term structure, equilibrium yields on multiperiod debt instruments are averages of the *current* one-period yield and the *expected future* one-period yields.

---

[16] Unlike the segmented-markets theory, there is no role for risk aversion in the determination of yields on long-term debt in the pure-expectations theory of the term structure of interest rates. Yields depend *only* on expectations.

Expectations and the Shape of the Yield Curve. In a market characterized by pure expectations, expectations of future yields determine current yields on debt instruments of maturities longer than one period. Example 14.1 shows three cases of future expectations and the yield curves which result from each. The yield curves are graphed in Figure 14.2. In case A the current one-

---

EXAMPLE 14.1
TERM STRUCTURE UNDER PURE EXPECTATIONS

	Case A, %	Case B, %	Case C, %
One-period yield at time t, $R_{1,t}$			
	3.0	7.0	11.0

Expected future one-period yields, $r_{1,t+k}$

	Case A, %	Case B, %	Case C, %
$k = 1$	4.0	7.0	10.0
2	4.5	7.0	9.5
3	5.0	7.0	9.0
4	5.5	7.0	8.5
5	6.0	7.0	8.0
6	6.5	7.0	7.5
7	7.0	7.0	7.0
8	7.0	7.0	7.0
9	7.0	7.0	7.0

Term yields at time t, $R_{n,t}$

	Case A, %	Case B, %	Case C, %
$n = 1$	3.00	7.0	11.00
2	3.50	7.0	10.50
3	3.83	7.0	10.17
4	4.13	7.0	9.88
5	4.40	7.0	9.60
6	4.67	7.0	9.33
7	4.93	7.0	9.07
8	5.19	7.0	8.81
9	5.39	7.0	8.61
10	5.55	7.0	8.45

Sample computation (for case A, $n = 3$):

$$R_{3,t} = \frac{R_{1,t} + r_{1,t+1} + r_{1,t+2}}{3}$$

$$= \frac{3.0 + 4.0 + 4.5}{3}$$

$$= 3.83\%$$

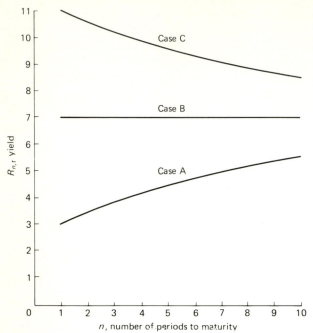

FIGURE 14.2
Yield curves under pure-expectations theory (data from Example 14.1).

period yield is 3 percent per period but the one-period yield is expected to rise to 7 percent in the future. As a result, the yield curve is low and rising. In case B the one-period yield is currently 7 percent per period and is expected to remain at that level in the future. The yield curve for case B is flat. In case C the current one-period yield is 11 percent per period but one-period yields are expected to decline to 7 percent in the future. The yield curve is high and falling for that case.

The relationship between current yields and expectations of future yields implied by pure-expectations theory offers an explanation of the yield curve behavior noted in the introduction to this chapter. When economic activity is strong, short-term interest rates are usually high but most investors expect them to fall as time goes on and the economy cools off. Thus, high short-term yields would be associated with falling expectations and a falling yield curve, as in case C in Figure 14.2. Conversely, when the economy is in a recession, short-term rates are relatively low. As economic activity expands, those rates will rise. Low short-term rates would be associated with rising future expectations and a rising yield curve, as in case A in Figure 14.2.

Forward Rates and Expected Future Rates

If the pure-expectations theory is correct, we can compute the market's expectation of future yields quite easily. The first step is to define what are known as *forward rates*.

The k-period forward rate at time t is defined[17] as

$$f_{k,t} = (k+1) \cdot R_{k+1,t} - k \cdot R_{k,t} \qquad k = 1, 2, 3, \ldots \qquad (14.8)$$

For example, if the yield on 5-period debt is 8 percent per period ($R_{5,t} = 8.0$ percent) and if the yield on 4-period debt is 9 percent per period ($R_{4,t} = 9.0$ percent), then the 4-period forward rate is 4 percent. This is computed from Equation (14.8) with $k = 4$:

$$
\begin{aligned}
f_{4,t} &= 5 \cdot R_{5,t} - 4 \cdot R_{4,t} \\
&= 5 \cdot 8.0 - 4 \cdot 9.0 \\
&= 4.0
\end{aligned}
$$

Example 14.2 illustrates the computation of forward rates using Treasury bills with maturities spaced 3 months apart. Figure 14.3 shows 3-month forward rates from 1970 to 1979.

Under the pure-expectations theory of the term structure of interest rates, forward rates are exactly equal to expected future rates. This equivalence can be demonstrated by expressing the yields on k-period and $(k+1)$-period debt with Equation (14.7):

$$k \cdot R_{k,t} = R_{1,t} + r_{1,t+1} + \cdots + r_{1,t+k-1}$$

$$(k+1) \cdot R_{k+1,t} = R_{1,t} + r_{1,t+1} + \cdots + r_{1,t+k-1} + r_{1,t+k}$$

It follows that

$$(k+1) \cdot R_{k+1,t} = k \cdot R_{k,t} + r_{1,t+k}$$

or
$$r_{1,t+k} = (k+1) \cdot R_{k+1,t} - k \cdot R_{k,t} \qquad (14.9)$$

Comparing Equations (14.8) and (14.9) we have

$$f_{k,t} = r_{1,t+k} \qquad k = 1, 2, 3, \ldots \qquad (14.10)$$

Under the pure-expectations theory of the term structure of interest rates, forward rates are identified as expected future rates. For example, if $f_{4,t} = 4$ percent, then at time t the market expects that a one-period rate of 4 percent will prevail at time $t + 4$.

An obvious question is how the forward rate $f_{k,t}$ compares with the one-period rate $R_{1,t+k}$ which ultimately prevails at time $t + k$. These two rates need not be equal, because there is no reason to expect that market participants make perfect forecasts of future interest rates. We should not, however, find $f_{k,t}$ greater or less than $R_{1,t+k}$ on average. Nonetheless, forward rates do appear to provide upward-biased forecasts of future spot rates. Research reported by

---

[17] The first appendix to Chapter 16 shows that the k-period forward rate $f_{k,t}$ is the yield on a one-period loan which begins at time $t + k$ and which is paid off at time $t + k + 1$ when the commitment for that loan is made at time t.

EXAMPLE 14.2
COMPUTATION OF FORWARD RATES

In June 1977, the discount rates on 3-month and 6-month Treasury bills were 4.75 percent and 5.23 percent per annum, respectively. Assume the length of a period is 3 months, so that a 3-month bill matures in $n = 1$ periods and a 6-month bill matures in $n = 2$ periods.

The price of the 3-month bill, as a percent of face value, can be computed from Equation (1.1) as

$$P_{1,t} = 100 \left[1 - \frac{91}{360} (.0475) \right]$$

$$= 98.7993$$

Using Equation (14.1) we can compute the continuously compounded yield (per 3-month period) on the 3-month bill as

$$R_{1,t} = \ln \left[\frac{100}{P_{1,t}} \right]$$

$$= \ln \left[\frac{100}{98.7993} \right]$$

$$= \ln [1.012153]$$

$$= .01208, \text{ or } 1.208\% \text{ per period.}$$

The price of the 6-month bill can be computed as

$$P_{2,t} = 100 \left[1 - \frac{182}{360} (.0523) \right]$$

$$= 97.3559$$

and the continuously compounded yield (per 3-month period) on that bill is

$$R_{2,t} = \frac{1}{2} \ln \left[\frac{100}{P_{2,t}} \right]$$

$$= \frac{1}{2} \ln \left[\frac{100}{97.3559} \right]$$

$$= \frac{1}{2} \ln [1.027159]$$

$$= .01340, \text{ or } 1.340\% \text{ per period.}$$

The one-period forward rate can be computed from the definition of that rate in Equation (14.8):

$$f_{1,t} = 2 \cdot R_{2,t} - R_{1,t}$$

$$= 2(1.340) - 1.208$$

$$= 1.472\%$$

Figure 14.3 shows the yield per 3-month period on 3-month and 6-month Treasury bills over the interval from January 1970 to December 1979. The figure also shows each of the one-period forward rates computed from those yields.

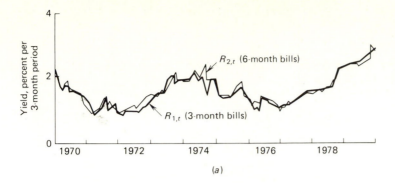

(a)

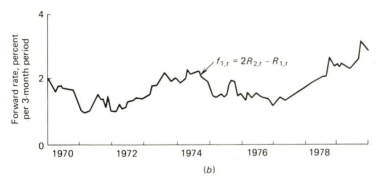

(b)

FIGURE 14.3
Yields and forward rates on Treasury bills, 1970–1979.

Roll (1970, p. 99) and McCulloch (1975b) has found the forecasting error $f_{k,t} - R_{1,t+k}$ significantly greater than zero.[18] This type of result is illustrated in Example 14.3. The results suggest that pure-expectations theory does not provide a complete explanation of term structure. It is unreasonable to believe the market makes biased forecasts of future interest rates. There must, therefore, be a component to forward rates other than the market's expectation of future one-period yields.

14.3 LIQUIDITY-PREFERENCE THEORY

Pure-expectations theory assumes that investors undertake different investment strategies until the expected yields for a given holding period are equal across all alternative strategies.[19] The theory allows no room for risk aversion

---

[18] See also Fama (1976b).
[19] For example, Equation (14.5) says that the yield on an investment in two-period debt for two periods is equal to the expected yield on two consecutive investments in one-period debt. See also footnote 15 of this chapter.

EXAMPLE 14.3
ESTIMATING THE FORECASTING BIAS IN FORWARD RATES

The existence of bias in forward rates as predictors of future interest rates can be illustrated with the data shown in Figure 14.3. That figure shows yields (per 3-month period) on 3-month Treasury bills from January 1970 to December 1979. Those yields are denoted as $R_{1,t}$. Figure 14.3 also shows 3-month forward rates, denoted $f_{1,t}$, over the same interval.

Forward rates are biased predictors of future interest rates if $f_{1,t} - R_{1,t+1}$ is, on average, significantly greater than zero. In that case the forward rate $f_{1,t}$ would, on average, exceed the future interest rate $R_{1,t+1}$, and so it would be a biased predictor of that future interest rate. Using the data from Figure 14.3 from $t =$ January 1970 to $t =$ November 1979, the average value of $f_{1,t} - R_{1,t+1}$ is found to be .14 percent per 3-month period. Thus, on average, the yield per 3-month period on a 3-month Treasury bill was .14 percent less than the forward rate which prevailed 3 months earlier. This confirms the presence of bias in the forward rates shown in Figure 14.3.

---

or for risk premiums. Liquidity-preference theory redresses, in part, this omission.[20]

Portfolio Allocation under the Liquidity-Preference Theory

Consider again the position of an investor with a one-period horizon, but this time assume that he is averse to bearing risk. If that investor holds a one-period debt security, he can predict with certainty the value of his investment at the end of his investment horizon. If he holds a two-period debt security, he will have to liquidate his investment in a secondary-market sale at the end of the first period. The price at which this sale can be completed is uncertain at the time he makes his original investment. This uncertainty means that holding two-period debt is risky for an investor with a one-period horizon.[21]

In the discussion of pure-expectations theory we saw that the return to an investor holding two-period debt for one period is

$$E_1 = 2 \cdot R_{2,t} - R_{1,t+1}$$

At time t this return is uncertain, because the future value of $R_{1,t+1}$ is not known with certainty. The expected value of the uncertain return E_1 is

$$\text{Exp}\ [E_1] = 2 \cdot R_{2,t} - r_{1,t+1}$$

[20] Liquidity preference was suggested by Keynes (1930) and developed at greater length by Hicks (1946). Meiselman (1962) reported the first major test of the theory, although Wood (1963) and Kessel (1965) pointed out an error in his interpretation of his results. Buse (1967), Wallace (1969), Nelson (1972c), and Findlay and Kleinschmidt (1975) have also contributed to the literature on Meiselman's tests. The forecasting power of forward rates was tested directly by Fama (1976b). Nelson (1972b) and McCulloch (1975a) report direct estimates of risk premiums.

[21] Bodie and Friedman (1978) have advanced a technique for measuring investor uncertainty about future interest rates based on the yield premium on callable debt issues.

If an investor with a one-period horizon holds two-period debt, he bears the "market risk" that the one-period rate $R_{1,t+1}$ prevailing at time $t + 1$ will differ from its expected value $r_{1,t+1}$. This means he bears the risk that his actual one-period return E_1 will differ from the expected value Exp $[E_1]$. For example, if the one-period rate at time $t + 1$ is greater than previously expected $(R_{1,t+1} > r_{1,t+1})$, then the investor will not earn at as high a rate of return as he originally expected $(E_1 < \text{Exp } [E_1])$.[22] Conversely, if the one-period rate at time $t + 1$ is less than previously expected $(R_{1,t+1} < r_{1,t+1})$, then the investor will earn at a higher rate than he previously anticipated $(E_1 > \text{Exp } [E_1])$.

A risk-averse investor with a one-period horizon will be unwilling to bear risk by holding two-period debt unless he can expect to earn a risk premium by doing so. If Exp $[E_1] = R_{1,t}$, there is no risk premium available from holding the longer-maturity instrument. In that case a risk-averse investor with a one-period horizon will *not* be indifferent between holding one-period debt and two-period debt. He will prefer to hold one-period debt, because he knows he will earn as much on that investment as he can expect to earn on an investment in two-period debt, and because the shorter-maturity debt does not leave him exposed to market risk.

A similar analysis can be developed for an investor with a k-period horizon contemplating an investment in $(k + 1)$-period debt. An investor buying a $(k + 1)$ period asset at time t will pay a price of $\$100 \cdot \exp [-(k + 1) \cdot R_{k+1,t}]$ per $100 maturity value of the asset [see Equation (14.1)], and he will receive $\$100 \cdot \exp [-R_{1,t+k}]$ if he sells that asset at time $t + k$, that is, at the end of k periods. His realized yield per period over the k periods is the value of E_k which solves the equation

$$\{100 \cdot \exp [-(k + 1) \cdot R_{k+1,t}]\} = \{100 \cdot \exp [-R_{1,t+k}]\} \cdot \exp [-k \cdot E_k]$$

or

$$E_k = \frac{(k + 1) \cdot R_{k+1,t} - R_{1,t+k}}{k}$$

At time t the expected value of $R_{1,t+k}$ is $r_{1,t+k}$, and so the expected yield per period from holding a $(k + 1)$-period asset for k periods is

$$\text{Exp } [E_k] = \frac{(k + 1) \cdot R_{k+1,t} - r_{1,t+k}}{k} \tag{14.11}$$

This expected yield can be compared to the known yield $R_{k,t}$ on k-period debt. If Exp $[E_k] = R_{k,t}$, the investor cannot expect to earn any more by buying $(k + 1)$-period debt and liquidating it after k periods than by buying k-period debt directly. He will then prefer to hold k-period debt, because holding $(k + 1)$-period debt leaves him exposed to market risk.

The foregoing discussion can be summarized with the observation that a risk-averse investor will not extend the maturity of his debt investments

---

[22] A higher-than-expected one-period rate at time $t + 1$ means that the sale price of one-period debt will be lower than expected at that time. This leads to a lower-than-expected return over the interval from time t to time $t + 1$.

beyond his planning horizon unless he can expect to earn a risk premium. If current yields on long-term debt are averages of the current one-period yield and the one-period yields expected to prevail in the future (as is implied by pure-expectations theory), then an investor cannot expect to earn a risk premium by extending the maturity of his investments beyond his planning horizon. The absence of a premium return will make him unwilling to bear market risk.

Debt Market Equilibrium under the Liquidity-Preference Theory

Liquidity-preference theory asserts that investors are averse to bearing the market risk which results from holding debt issues with maturities longer than their investment horizons. This assertion by itself does not have any implications for the term structure of interest rates. However, the theory also asserts that the supply of debt instruments with maturities greater than one period exceeds the demand for such instruments by investors with multiperiod horizons. In particular, the supply of k-period debt is greater than the demand for that debt *from investors with k-period horizons*. Moreover, this "excess supply" of longer-maturity debt is asserted to be a nondecreasing function of maturity. In combination with investor aversion to market risk, this fundamental disparity between the supply of and demand for multiperiod debt by investors with multiperiod horizons has direct implications for the term structure of interest rates.

For a market to be in equilibrium, the aggregate demand for debt of *each* maturity must equal the available supply of that debt. Absent any risk premiums in the yields on longer-maturity debt, however, there would be an excess supply of such debt given the assumptions of the preceding paragraph. Therefore, for the debt markets to be in equilibrium there must be a risk premium on multiperiod debt assets. In particular, investors with a one-period horizon will be willing to hold two-period instruments only if Exp $[E_1] > R_{1,t}$. This inequality will be satisfied if

$$2 \cdot R_{2,t} > R_{1,t} + r_{1,t+1} \tag{14.12}$$

If the inequality of (14.12) holds, the expected yield from holding two-period debt for one period, which we saw is Exp $[E_1] = 2 \cdot R_{2,t} - r_{1,t+1}$, will exceed the yield $R_{1,t}$ on one-period debt. The difference in yields must be large enough to entice one-period investors to extend the maturity of their debt portfolio to two periods in an amount sufficient to raise the demand for two-period debt to the level of the existing supply.

As a matter of convention it is usually assumed that there exists a positive risk premium L_1 which, in equilibrium, restores the inequality of (14.12) to an equality:

$$2 \cdot R_{2,t} = R_{1,t} + r_{1,t+1} + L_1 \tag{14.13}$$

L_1 is the risk premium expected to be earned for one period by extending the maturity of a debt investment from one period to two periods. This can be seen by noting that Equations (14.4) and (14.13) together imply $\text{Exp}\ [E_1] = R_{1,t} + L_1$.

The arguments which led to the inequality of Equation (14.12) extend to the general case of comparing k-period and $(k + 1)$-period assets. Equation (14.12) generalizes to

$$(k + 1) \cdot R_{k+1,t} > k \cdot R_{k,t} + r_{1,t+k} \tag{14.14}$$

The equality is restored by adding a risk premium L_k:

$$(k + 1) \cdot R_{k+1,t} = k \cdot R_{k,t} + r_{1,t+k} + L_k \tag{14.15}$$

L_k is the risk premium expected to be earned over k periods by extending the maturity of a debt investment from k to $k + 1$ periods. This can be seen by noting that Equations (14.11) and (14.15) together imply that $\text{Exp}\ [E_k] = R_{k,t} + L_k/k$.

Because the supply of multiperiod debt, over and above the demand for such debt by investors with matching investment horizons, is a nondecreasing function of maturity, liquidity-preference theory implies that the risk premiums on multiperiod debt will have the structure $0 < L_1 \leq L_2 \leq L_3 \leq \cdots$. Increasing amounts of capital from shorter-horizon investors must be attracted into longer-maturity debt assets as a direct function of maturity. This is possible only with nondecreasing risk premiums.

Risk Premiums and the Shape of the Yield Curve   The existence of risk premiums affects the shape of the yield curve for any given set of investor expectations about future interest rates. Equations (14.13) and (14.15) can be combined to express the equilibrium yield on multiperiod debt as a function of risk premiums and expectations of future one-period yields:

$$k \cdot R_{k,t} = R_{1,t} + r_{1,t+1} + \cdots + r_{1,t+k-1} \\ + L_1 + L_2 + \cdots + L_{k-1} \tag{14.16}$$

This expression may be compared with Equation (14.7) for the comparable result from pure-expectations theory. For given expectations of future one-period yields, the yields on longer-maturity assets will be greater in liquidity-preference theory, because of the presence of the positive risk premiums.

Example 14.4 and Figure 14.4 show the yield curves which result from the three cases of expectations shown in Example 14.1 when risk premiums are factored into the computations. The yield curves either rise more sharply or fall more gently.

Forward Rates and Expected Future Rates

The presence of risk premiums in term yields alters the identification of forward rates. Those rates were defined in Equation (14.8) as

$$f_{k,t} = (k + 1) \cdot R_{k+1,t} - k \cdot R_{k,t} \qquad k = 1, 2, 3, \ldots$$

Using Equation (14.15) we find that

$$f_{k,t} = r_{1,t+k} + L_k \qquad k = 1, 2, 3, \ldots \qquad (14.17)$$

EXAMPLE 14.4
TERM STRUCTURE UNDER LIQUIDITY PREFERENCE

The one-period yield and expected future one-period yields at time t are the same as in Example 14.1.

Risk premiums, L_K (in percent):

K	L_K
1	.5
2	.75
3	.875
4	1.0
5	1.0
6	1.0
7	1.0
8	1.0
9	1.0

Term yields at time t, $R_{n,t}$:

n	Case A, %	Case B, %	Case C, %
1	3.00	7.00	11.00
2	3.75	7.25	10.75
3	4.25	7.42	10.58
4	4.66	7.53	10.41
5	5.03	7.63	10.23
6	5.35	7.69	10.02
7	5.66	7.73	9.80
8	5.95	7.77	9.58
9	6.18	7.79	9.40
10	6.36	7.81	9.26

Sample computation (for case A, $n = 3$):

$$R_{3,t} = \frac{R_{1,t} + (r_{1,t+1} + L_1) + (r_{1,t+2} + L_2)}{3}$$

$$= \frac{3.0 + (4.0 + .5) + (4.5 + .75)}{3}$$

$$= 4.25\%$$

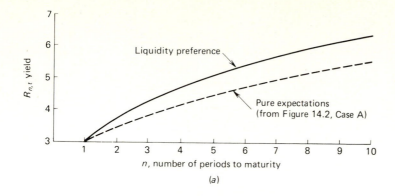

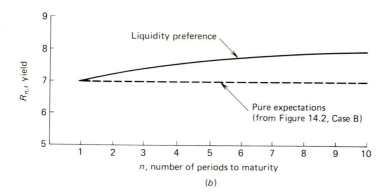

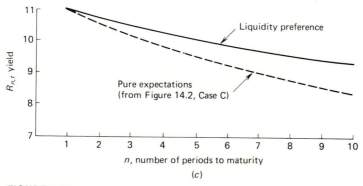

FIGURE 14.4
Yield curves under liquidity-preference theory compared with pure-expectations theory (data from Examples 14.1 and 14.4).

The forward rate $f_{k,t}$ is now seen to be the one-period rate expected to prevail k periods in the future *plus* a risk premium. The presence of risk premiums thus explains why forward rates are upward-biased predictors of future one-period rates.

The risk premiums added by liquidity-preference theory would seem to correct the deficiencies of the pure-expectations theory. Unfortunately, this may not be the case. Empirical evidence suggests the L_k's do not necessarily rise monotonically as a function of k.[23] Moreover, there may well be investors who hold assets with maturities shorter than their investment horizons. Liquidity-preference theory rules out such behavior by assumption, and so it is not too useful for understanding the effect of that behavior on equilibrium yields. To round out our discussion of term structure we next consider a theory which recognizes the possibility that investors can bear reinvestment risk as well as market risk.

14.4 PREFERRED-HABITAT THEORY

The preferred-habitat theory of term structure parallels liquidity-preference theory in the assumption that risk-averse investors will not extend the maturity of their debt portfolios beyond their investment horizon unless they can expect to earn a risk premium by so doing. Preferred-habitat theory assumes in addition that risk premiums are needed to induce investors to *contract* the maturity of their debt portfolios to intervals *shorter* than their investment horizon. The primary distinction between the two theories is that the preferred-habitat theory does not assume that a market equilibrium always requires shorter-horizon investors to hold longer-maturity debt.[24] There may be an excess demand for long-term debt by investors with long horizons, so that those investors must hold some shorter-maturity assets in equilibrium. We will see that the incentive to hold shorter-maturity assets stems from the existence of risk premiums with negative values.

Portfolio Allocation under the Preferred-Habitat Theory

The discussion of liquidity-preference theory showed that a positive value for the risk premium L_1 will encourage an investor with a one-period horizon to bear market risk by holding two-period debt. Let us now consider what would encourage an investor with a two-period horizon to hold one-period debt.

If an investor buys one-period debt at time t and rolls over his investment at time $t + 1$ into another investment in one-period debt, his yield per period over the two periods will be

$$E_2 = \frac{1}{2}(R_{1,t} + R_{1,t+1})$$

---

[23] See Roll (1970, p. 99) and Lee, Maness, and Tuttle (1980). McCulloch's (1975a) research suggests that the premiums do rise monotonically but come to within a couple of basis points of their maximum value at surprisingly short maturities.

[24] Modigliani and Sutch (1966, 1967) were the first to advance the preferred-habitat theory. Variants of the theory are presented in Roll (1970) and Lee, Maness, and Tuttle (1980). McCallum (1975), Lee, Maness, and Tuttle (1980), and Elliot and Echols (1976) have tested the theory. *Inter alia*, preferred-habitat implies that exogenous variation in the maturity composition of debt can alter the term structure of interest rates. I. Scott (1965), Modigliani and Sutch (1967), Wallace (1967), Hamburger and Silber (1971), and Lang and Rasche (1977) have investigated the effect of federal debt management policies on the term structure.

The value of $R_{1,t+1}$ is not known at time t, and so E_2 is uncertain. The expected yield on the rollover strategy will be

$$\text{Exp } [E_2] = {}^1\!/_2 \, (R_{1,t} + r_{1,t+1}) \qquad (14.18)$$

An investor with a two-period horizon bears "reinvestment risk" when he buys one-period debt. In particular, if the one-period rate at time $t + 1$ turns out to be less than expected ($R_{1,t+1} < r_{1,t+1}$), then the investor will earn less than he expected over his two-period horizon ($E_2 < \text{Exp } [E_2]$). Conversely, if the one-period rate at time $t + 1$ is greater than expected ($R_{1,t+1} > r_{1,t+1}$), then the investor will earn more than he anticipated ($E_2 > \text{Exp } [E_2]$). Thus, an investor with a two-period horizon will not buy one-period debt unless he can expect to earn a risk premium by so doing.

A two-period investor can expect to earn a risk premium on an investment in one-period debt if

$$\text{Exp } [E_2] > R_{2,t}$$

or, using Equation (14.18), if

$${}^1\!/_2(R_{1,t} + r_{1,t+1}) > R_{2,t}$$

Rearranging the terms in the above equation, we can conclude that an investor with a two-period horizon will have an incentive to hold one-period debt if

$$2 \cdot R_{2,t} < R_{1,t} + r_{1,t+1} \qquad (14.19)$$

The risk premium L_1 has been defined as that premium which, in equilibrium, satisfies the equation

$$2 \cdot R_{2,t} = R_{1,t} + r_{1,t+1} + L_1$$

If the inequality of Equation (14.19) is true, then L_1 must be negative.

The foregoing analysis shows that a *negative* value of L_1 will attract an investor with a two-period horizon into holding one-period debt. This is the opposite side of the argument that a *positive* value of L_1 will attract an investor with a one-period horizon into holding two-period debt. In general, if L_1 is positive, all two-period investors will hold two-period debt (they certainly have no incentive to contract the maturity of their investments, because they would then bear reinvestment risk *and* expect to earn at a rate less than $R_{2,t}$), and some one-period investors will also hold two-period debt. However, if L_1 is negative, all one-period investors will hold one-period debt (they certainly have no incentive to extend the maturity of their investments, because they would then bear market risk *and* expect to earn at a rate less than $R_{1,t}$), and some two-period investors will also hold one-period debt. A negative value for the risk premium L_1 creates an incentive for two-period investors to *contract* the maturity of their investments, just as a positive value for the risk premium creates an incentive for one-period investors to *extend* the maturity of their investments.

These results extend readily to yields on multiperiod debt. A positive value of L_k creates an incentive for an investor with a k-period horizon to hold $(k + 1)$-period debt and to bear what he perceives as the market risk of that position. A negative value of L_k creates an incentive for an investor with a $(k + 1)$-period horizon to hold k-period debt and to bear what he perceives as the reinvestment risk of that position.

Debt Market Equilibrium under the Preferred-Habitat Theory

Once we remove the assumptions (of liquidity-preference theory) that the supply of multiperiod debt exceeds the demand for that debt from investors with matching multiperiod investment horizons, and that that excess supply is a nondecreasing function of maturity, we can no longer assert that equilibrium risk premiums are positive and nondecreasing. If the supply of long-term debt is less than the demand of long-term investors for that debt, the L_k premiums may be negative for large values of k, because there would otherwise be an excess demand for long-term debt.

Preferred-habitat theory asserts that investors will not hold debt securities outside of their preferred habitats, i.e., debt-securities with maturities longer *or* shorter than their investment horizons, without the incentive of premium expected yields. Holding longer-maturity assets exposes them to market risk, and holding shorter-maturity assets exposes them to reinvestment risk. Unlike segmented-markets theory, however, preferred-habitat theory also provides that investors *will* shift the allocation of their portfolios *in response to* expectations of premium yields. In particular, preferred-habitat theory does not assume investors are completely risk-averse. The implications of such shifts in portfolio allocations for the characteristics of a market equilibrium are not easily determined. An L_k risk premium will be positive if an equilibrium requires that k-period investors hold some $(k + 1)$-period assets. L_k will be negative if an equilibrium requires that some k-period assets be held by investors with $(k + 1)$-period horizons. The sign of L_k will depend on the supply and demand imbalances in k-period and $(k + 1)$-period debt and, more generally, on imbalances throughout all maturity segments of the debt markets.

There does not appear to be any unique characterization of the magnitude of the risk premium on debt as a function of some beta-like parameter such as we found for stock.[25] The reason is that debt of a given maturity will be risk-free for an investor with a matching investment horizon but will expose an investor with a longer horizon to reinvestment risk and will expose an investor with a shorter horizon to market risk. In the single-period analysis of stock returns we enjoyed that luxury of knowing that all investors perceived the risk of a particular stock in the same way.

---

[25] See, however, the analysis in Roll (1971).

14.5 COUPON ISSUES AND TERM STRUCTURE THEORY

The four theories of term structure presented in the previous sections applied to single-payment discount instruments. Many debt issues, however, make multiple payments prior to maturity in the form of semiannual coupons. The market prices of such coupon-bearing issues can be established within the context of the preceding sections by treating those issues as "bundles" of discount instruments.[26]

Let $R_{k,t}$ be the continuously compounded yield per period at time t on a k-period discount debt instrument. The present value of a promise to pay 100 k periods in the future is then $100 \cdot \exp [-k \cdot R_{k,t}]$. Consider now a bond promising (1) periodic coupon payments in the amount $\$C$ per coupon (n coupons remaining) and (2) a return of principal at maturity of 100. The present value of the coupon that is to be paid k periods in the future is $C \cdot \exp [-k \cdot R_{k,t}]$. The present value of the principal to be paid in n periods is $100 \cdot \exp [-n \cdot R_{n,t}]$. The market price of the bond is the sum of the present values of these future payments. Thus, the price P of the bond is

$$P = \sum_{k=1}^{n} C \cdot \exp [-k \cdot R_{k,t}] + 100 \cdot \exp [-n \cdot R_{n,t}] \qquad (14.20)$$

This equation views the bond as a bundle of single-payment securities. The market price of each future payment is the product of the amount of that payment [C or 100 in Equation (14.20)] and the discount factor for the payment. Each discount factor is computed from the yield on a single-payment instrument of a corresponding maturity. The market price of the bond as a whole is the sum of the market prices of its component payments.

The bond pricing rule shown in Equation (14.20) can be illustrated with a simple example. Suppose a bond promises to pay $5 every 6 months and promises to pay $100 at maturity in 18 months. Suppose also that the length of a period is 6 months, and that there exist discount instruments with 6-, 12-, and 18-month maturities, and that those instruments have yields of $R_{1,t} = .05$, $R_{2,t} = .045$, and $R_{3,t} = .04$, respectively. The present value of the first coupon on the bond is then $\$4.76 = C \cdot \exp [-R_{1,t}] = \$5.00 \cdot \exp [-.05]$. The present value of the second coupon, payable in 2 periods, or 12 months, is $\$4.57 = C \cdot \exp [-2 \cdot R_{2,t}] = \$5.00 \cdot \exp [-2 \cdot .045]$. The present value of the third coupon, which is payable in 3 periods, or 18 months, is $\$4.43 = C \cdot \exp [-3 \cdot R_{3,t}] = \$5.00 \cdot \exp [-3 \cdot .04]$. The present value of the $100 principal, payable in 18 months, is $\$88.69 = \$100 \cdot \exp [-3 \cdot R_{3,t}] =$

---

[26] Streams of multiple payments can also be analyzed as a whole. Duration, or the average lifetime of a multiple-payment stream, is an important concept in that analysis; see Weil (1973) for a general discussion. Hopewell and Kaufman (1973) and Yawitz (1977) show that the price volatility of fixed-income securities is a function of their duration. See also Weil (1973) and Haugen and Wichern (1974). Fisher and Weil (1971) show that matching duration to the investment horizon of an investor is, in some cases, a hedged investment strategy. Their analysis has been extended by Bierwag and Kaufman (1977), Bierwag (1977), and Cooper (1977).

$100.00 \cdot \exp [-3 \cdot .04]$. The sum of the present values of the three coupon payments plus the present value of the principal payment is $102.45 ($4.76 + $4.57 + $4.43 + $88.69). Thus, the bond will be priced at $102.45.

The importance of Equation (14.20) lies in the fact that if we have yields on discount instruments of different maturities, then we can compute the market price of a debt instrument that makes more than one payment. We only have to compute the present values of each of the future payments and then sum up those present values.

Yield to Maturity

It is conventional to express the yield on a multiple-payment debt security as a *yield to maturity*. If a bond pays $C every period for n periods and pays $100 at maturity, then the continuously compounded yield to maturity per period on that bond is defined as the value of R_m which solves the equation

$$P = \sum_{k=1}^{n} C \cdot \exp[-k \cdot R_m] + 100 \cdot \exp[-n \cdot R_m] \qquad (14.21)$$

Equation (14.21) says that the yield on a bond is that yield which makes the present discounted values of the bond's future payments equal to the bond's market price.[27]

If a bond is priced at $102.45, pays $5 every 6 months for 18 months, and pays $100 at maturity, then the yield on the bond is $R_m = .0403$, or 4.03 percent per 6-month period. This follows because $R_m = .0403$ solves the equation

$$102.45 = \sum_{k=1}^{3} 5.00 \cdot \exp [-k \cdot R_m] + 100 \cdot \exp [-3 \cdot R_m]$$

Comparing Equations (14.20) and (14.21) shows that the yield on a bond is a complicated "average" of the yields on discount instruments with maturities less than and equal to the maturity of the bond. Thus, in the preceding numerical example, we had yields on discount instruments of $R_{1,t} = .05$, $R_{2,t} = .045$, and $R_{3,t} = .04$, and we found that the yield on a bond which pays $5 every 6 months was $R_m = .0403$. If we had started with different values for the yields on the discount instruments, i.e., with a different term structure, we would have computed a different price on the bond with Equation (14.20) and we would have computed a different yield to maturity on the bond with Equation (14.21). Similarly, the price and yield of the bond also depend on the size of the bond's coupon payments.[28]

A yield curve based on the yields to maturity of bonds of different maturities

---

[27] A similar expression appears in Equation (1.9), except that that equation defines yield per annum on a bond that has two coupon payments per year. Equation (14.21) defines yield per period on a bond that has one coupon payment per period.

[28] Higher coupon payments will give a greater "weight" to yields on short-term debt.

will differ from a yield curve based on the yields of discount instruments. Example 14.5 and Figure 14.5 show the yields to maturity on a sequence of coupon issues priced at principal value for each of the three cases of Example 14.4. Note that when the yield curve is rising, as in case A, a yield curve based on coupon-bearing debt will rise less rapidly than a yield curve based on dis-

FIGURE 14.5
Yield curves using discount debt securities and coupon-bearing debt securities (data from Example 14.5).

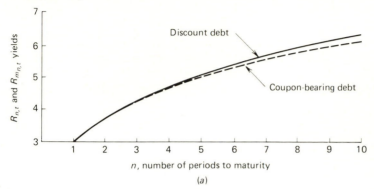

(a)

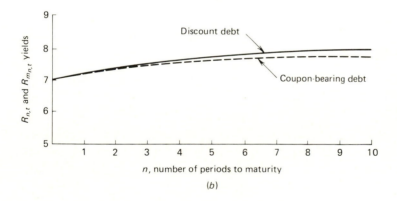

(b)

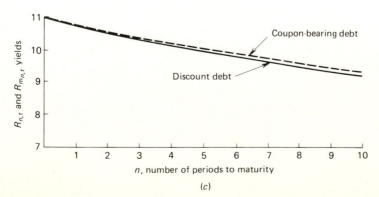

(c)

EXAMPLE 14.5

YIELD TO MATURITY ON COUPON DEBT PRICED AT PRINCIPAL VALUE

In these three examples we assume the current price and principal value of each issue is 100. Given the values of $R_{k,t}$ from Example 14.4 we computed from Equation (14.20) the periodic coupon payments C_n which must be paid on an n-period issue priced at principal value:

$$C_n = \frac{100 \cdot (1 - \exp\,[-n \cdot R_{n,t}])}{\sum\limits_{k=1}^{n} \exp\,[-k \cdot R_{k,t}]}$$

Since the bonds are priced at principal valve, the continuously compounded yield to maturity on an n-period issue is that value of $R_{m\,n,t}$ which solves

$$100 = \sum\limits_{k=1}^{n} C_n \cdot \exp\,[-k \cdot R_{mn,t}] \cdot 100 + \exp\,[-n \cdot R_{mn,t}]$$

Yield to maturity at time t:

	Case A		Case B		Case C	
n	Discount debt, %*	Coupon debt, %†	Discount debt, %*	Coupon debt, %†	Discount debt, %*	Coupon debt, %†
1	3.00	3.00	7.00	7.00	11.00	11.00
2	3.75	3.75	7.25	7.24	10.75	10.76
3	4.25	4.22	7.42	7.40	10.58	10.61
4	4.66	4.60	7.53	7.50	10.41	10.45
5	5.03	4.94	7.63	7.58	10.23	10.30
6	5.35	5.24	7.69	7.64	10.02	10.13
7	5.66	5.51	7.73	769	9.80	9.96
8	5.95	5.75	7.77	7.71	9.58	9.79
9	6.18	5.93	7.79	7.73	9.40	9.65
10	6.36	6.08	7.81	7.75	9.26	9.54

*These are the $R_{k,t}$'s and are taken from Example 14.4 and shown for purposes of comparison.
†These are the $R_{mn,t}$'s.

Sample computation (for case A, $n = 3$):

$$P = C_3 \cdot \exp\,[-R_{1,t}] + C_3 \cdot \exp\,[-2 \cdot R_{2,t}]$$
$$+ C_3 \cdot \exp\,[-3 \cdot R_{3,t}] + 100 \cdot \exp\,[-3 \cdot R_{3,t}]$$
$$100 = C_3\{\exp\,[-.03] + \exp\,[-2(.0375)\,]$$
$$+ \exp\,[-3(.0425)]\} + 100 \cdot \exp\,[-3(.0425)]$$
$$C_3 = \$4.31$$

Now observe that $R_{m\,3,t} = .0422$ solves the equation

$$100 = C_3\{\exp\,[-R_{m3,t}] + \exp\,[-2 \cdot R_{m3,t}]$$
$$+ \exp\,[-3 \cdot R_{m3,t}]\} + 100 \cdot \exp\,[-3 \cdot R_{m3,t}]$$
$$100 = 4.31\{\exp\,[-.0422] + \exp\,[-2(.0422)\,]$$
$$+ \exp\,[-3(.0422)]\} + 100 \cdot \exp\,[-3(.0422)]$$

count debt. This is because, for example, the 6.08 percent yield on 10-period coupon debt is an "average" of the 6.36 percent yield on 10-period discount debt and the lower yields on shorter-maturity discount debt. Case C shows that when the yield curve is falling, a yield curve based on coupon-bearing debt will fall less rapidly than a yield curve based on discount debt. This is because, for example, the 9.54 percent yield on 10-period coupon debt is an "average" of the 9.26 percent yield on 10-period discount debt and the higher yields on shorter-maturity discount debt.

The preceding paragraph showed that the yield on 10-period coupon-bearing debt may overstate or understate the yield on 10-period discount debt, depending on the shape of the yield curve. It is, therefore, important to use true discount yields in term structure analysis, rather than yields on coupon debt.[29] We next see how yields on discount debt securities can be computed from the prices and coupons on coupon-bearing debt securities.

"Unbundling" Coupon-Bearing Debt Issues

Since most long-term debt is sold in coupon-bearing form, it is reasonable to inquire whether we can compute the discount yields implied by the prices and coupons on coupon-bearing issues of different maturities. It turns out that we can, and so it makes sense to discuss the term structure of interest rates as if there were only discount issues in the market.

Consider a sequence of coupon-bearing issues where the issue with j coupons remaining to maturity is priced at $P_{j,t}$ at time t and where the payment value of each of the coupons on that issue is C_j. To compute the one-period discount yield $R_{1,t}$ we need only solve for $R_{1,t}$ in the equation

$$P_{1,t} = (100 + C_1) \cdot \exp\left[-R_{1,t}\right] \tag{14.22}$$

Suppose we have found $R_{i,t}$ for $i = 1, \ldots, n-1$. For an n-period issue we know from Equation (14.20) that

$$P_{n,t} = \sum_{k=1}^{n} C_n \cdot \exp\left[-k \cdot R_{k,t}\right] + 100 \cdot \exp\left[-n \cdot R_{n,t}\right]$$

so that

$$P_{n,t} - \sum_{k=1}^{n-1} C_n \cdot \exp\left[-k \cdot R_{k,t}\right] = (100 + C_n) \cdot \exp\left[-n \cdot R_{n,t}\right] \tag{14.23}$$

Since all the elements on the left-hand side of Equation (14.23) are known, we can compute the n-period discount yield $R_{n,t}$ directly. It follows that since we can compute $R_{1,t}$ by Equation (14.22) and since we can compute $R_{n,t}$ if we know $R_{1,t}$ to $R_{n-1,t}$ by Equation (14.23), we can compute all the discount yields implied by a sequence of coupon-bearing issues, regardless of whether

---

[29] See Carr, Halpern, and McCallum (1974) for a further analysis of the distinction between the yield on a discount instrument and the yield to maturity on a coupon-bearing instrument.

those issues have high, low, or mixed coupon rates. Example 14.6 illustrates the computations. A yield curve expressed in terms of the yield to maturity on discount issues can therefore be obtained even if there are no multiperiod discount issues in the market.

Equation (14.23) has a concrete interpretation. $P_{n,t}$ is the total present value of the future coupon payments and the principal payment promised by a bond with n coupons remaining. Suppose we removed the coupon payable in k periods and sold that coupon for cash. This would reduce the market value of the bond by $C_n \cdot \exp[-k \cdot R_{k,t}]$. If we removed all of the $n-1$ coupons payable before maturity and sold them for cash, the market value of the stripped instrument would equal the left-hand side of Equation (14.23). That would leave us with an instrument which promises to make a single payment of $100 + \$C_n$ at the end of n periods; i.e., we would be left with a simple n-period discount instrument whose present value is the left-hand side of Equation (14.23). The yield on that discount instrument could then be computed by solving for $R_{n,t}$ in Equation (14.23). This shows that coupon-bearing debt can be converted to discount debt by stripping the intermediate coupon obligations from the issue and selling them for cash.

EXAMPLE 14.6
COMPUTING YIELDS ON DISCOUNT DEBT INSTRUMENTS FROM COUPON-BEARING DEBT INSTRUMENTS

Suppose there are coupon-bearing debt securities with maturities of one, two, and three periods, and you wish to compute the yields on discount debt securities with comparable maturities. Assume the coupon-bearing securities have the following charactertistics:

Number of periods to maturity, n	Current market price, $P_{n,t}$	Coupon payment per period, C_n
1	$ 99.50	$6.00
2	101.00	7.00
3	100.25	6.25

The first coupon-bearing security promises to pay $106.00 in one period: a $6.00 coupon and $100.00 principal. The yield on one-period discount debt can be computed from Equation (14.22) by solving for $R_{1,t}$:

$$P_{1,t} = (100 + C_1) \cdot \exp[-R_{1,t}]$$
$$99.50 = (106.00) \cdot \exp[-R_{1,t}]$$

or

$$R_{1,t} = \ln\left[\frac{106.00}{99.50}\right]$$

$$= .0633, \text{ or } 6.33\% \text{ per period}$$

EXAMPLE 14.6 (*Continued*)

The second coupon-bearing security promises to pay $7.00 in one period—the first $7.00 coupon—and $107.00 in two periods—the second $7.00 coupon and $100.00 principal. The present value of the first coupon is $6.57 = $C_2 \cdot \exp[-R_{1,t}] = \$7.00 \cdot \exp[-.0633]$. Subtracting this $6.57 from the market price of the two-period bond gives $94.43 ($101.00 − $6.57). This is the present value of $107.00 payable in two periods. The yield on two-period discount debt can be computed from Equation (14.23) with $n = 2$ by solving for $R_{2,t}$:

$$P_{2,t} - C_2 \cdot \exp[-R_{1,t}] = (100 + C_2) \cdot \exp[-2 \cdot R_{2,t}]$$
$$94.43 = (107.00) \cdot \exp[-2 \cdot R_{2,t}]$$

or
$$R_{2,t} = \frac{\ln[107.00/94.43]}{2}$$
$$= .0625, \text{ or } 6.25\% \text{ per period}$$

The third coupon-bearing security promises to pay $6.25 in one period, $6.25 in two periods, and $106.25 in three periods. The present value of the first coupon is $5.87 = $C_3 \cdot \exp[-R_{1,t}] = \$6.25 \cdot \exp[-.0633]$. The present value of the second coupon is $5.52 = $C_3 \cdot \exp[-2 \cdot R_{2,t}] = \$6.25 \cdot \exp[-2(.0625)]$. Subtracting the present values of these two intermediate coupons from the total price of the three-period bond gives $88.86 ($100.25 − $5.87 − $5.52). This is the present value of a $106.25 payment in three periods. The yield on three-period discount debt can be computed from Equation (14.23) with $n = 3$ by solving for $R_{3,t}$:

$$P_{3,t} - C_3 \cdot \exp[-R_{1,t}] - C_3 \cdot \exp[-2 \cdot R_{2,t}] = (100 + C_3) \cdot \exp[-3 \cdot R_{3,t}]$$
$$88.86 = (106.25) \cdot \exp[-3 \cdot R_{3,t}]$$

or
$$R_{3,t} = \frac{\ln[106.25/88.86]}{3}$$
$$= .0596, \text{ or } 5.96\% \text{ per period}$$

CHAPTER SUMMARY

This chapter has examined why yields differ on debt securities of different maturities. The answer is (1) investor expectations of higher or lower future short-term interest rates and (2) investor aversion to bearing risk.

As expressed by the pure-expectations theory of term structure, yields on long-term debt depend *only* on investor expectations of future short-term interest rates if investors are indifferent to risk. In that case, the yield on long-term debt is a simple average of the current short-term yield and expected future short-term yields. More particularly, long-term yields will not depend on the relative supplies of short-, intermediate-, or long-term debt, or on differences in investor planning horizons. Empirical evidence refutes the hypothesis that pure expectations is an appropriate theory of the term structure of interest rates, because forward rates computed from yields on term debt securities appear to contain risk premiums as well as reflect investor expectations of future short-term yields.

The preferred-habitat theory of term structure says that investors will prefer to hold debt securities with maturities matched to their investment planning horizons, but that they will hold longer-maturity debt or shorter-maturity debt if they can expect to earn a risk premium. (Pure-expectations theory is a special case of preferred-habitat theory, where no risk premium is required to induce an investor to mismatch the maturity of his debt holdings and his planning horizon.) The risk premium on long-term debt is conventionally defined as the difference between the yield on that debt and the yield expected from rolling over short-term debt securities for a comparable interval. If that risk premium is positive, investors will have an incentive to bear market risk by investing in debt with a maturity longer than their planning horizons. If the risk premium is negative, investors will have an incentive to bear reinvestment risk by investing in debt with a maturity shorter than their planning horizons.

Preferred-habitat theory does not predict whether the risk premium on debt of a particular maturity will be positive or negative. The answer depends on the imbalance between the supply of that debt and the level of demand by investors with a comparable planning horizon and on similar imbalances in other maturities.

Liquidity-preference theory is a special case of preferred-habitat theory, which asserts that the supply of long-term debt is always greater than the demand for that debt by investors with long planning horizons. This imbalance means that risk premiums on long-term debt must be positive, because investors with short planning horizons must be induced to hold long-term debt.

The segmented-markets theory of term structure is also a special case of the preferred-habitat theory. The segmented-markets theory asserts that investors are completely risk-averse and that they will always match the maturities of their debt investments with their planning horizons. No risk premium, however large, will induce them to bear either market risk or reinvestment risk. In this case the yield on debt of a particular maturity will depend only on the supply of that debt and on the demand for that debt by investors with a comparable planning horizon. It will not depend on supply and demand conditions in any other segment of the debt market.

Empirical evidence refutes the segmented-markets theory of term structure, because long-term yields do reflect investor expectations of future short-term interest rates. When short-term yields are high and expected to fall, long-term yields will be lower than short-term yields. Conversely, when short-term interest rates are low and expected to rise, long-term yields will be greater than short-term yields. The segmented-markets theory gives no reason to anticipate such regular behavior of the yield curve.

The theories of term structure developed in the first four sections of this chapter assumed that debt securities were discount instruments which paid a stipulated amount at maturity but which made no intermediate coupon payments. The last section showed that this assumption is not necessary. A coupon-bearing security can be viewed as a bundle of discount instruments, and claims to intermediate payments can be eliminated by stripping the coupons and selling them for cash. This would leave a debt security which promises only a single payment at its maturity date.

FURTHER READING

Richard Lang and Robert Rasche, "Debt-Management Policy and the Own Price Elasticity of Demand for U.S. Government Notes and Bonds," Federal Reserve Bank of St. Louis *Review*, **59** (September 1977), 8–22.

Wayne Lee, Terry Maness, and Donald Tuttle, "Nonspeculative Behavior and the Term Structure," *Journal of Financial and Quantitative Analysis*, **15** (March 1980), 53–83.

J. Huston McCulloch, "An Estimate of the Liquidity Premium," *Journal of Political Economy*, **83** (February, 1975), 95–119.

Burton Malkiel, *The Term Structure of Interest Rates* (Princeton, N.J.: Princeton University Press, 1966).

Richard Roll, *The Behavior of Interest Rates* (New York: Basic Books, 1970).

CHAPTER 15

DEFERRED DELIVERY CONTRACTS AND FUTURES MARKETS

Up to now we have focused on securities prices in markets for immediate exchange, or on prices in so-called spot markets. Such markets allow investors to purchase and sell securities for immediate delivery and immediate payment. In some cases, however, an investor may be concerned with the price at which he will be able to transact in the future. For example, a bank may know in January that it will have to sell some of its Treasury bonds to finance a customer who has notified the bank of his intention to draw down an existing line of credit in June. If the bank has to wait until June to sell its bonds, it cannot know in January what price it will be able to get on the sale. Thus, as of January the bank perceives its continued investment in Treasury bonds as uncertain and risky.

One way to eliminate the risk on a transaction that will not be completed until some future date is to enter into a *deferred delivery contract*. In the preceding example the bank would know the exact revenues from the future bond sale if it could fix in January a price for Treasury bonds to be delivered in June. Instead of waiting until June to sell bonds for immediate delivery, it would then be selling bonds in January for deferred delivery and deferred payment.[1]

Deferred delivery contracts between buyers and sellers are quite common in commerce and finance. Foreign exchange and agricultural commodities, for example, have been bought and sold for deferred delivery since before the turn of

---

[1] The bank could also eliminate the risk on its continued investment in Treasury bonds by selling those bonds in a spot market transaction in January and investing the proceeds in Treasury bills that mature in June. Either way, the bank would establish with certainty the value of its securities holdings *as of June*, when it will need to meet the customer's loan demand.

the century.[2] There also exist two closely related, but nonetheless distinct, types of markets for deferred delivery transactions in securities.

A *forward contract* is a bilateral contract between a purchaser and a seller. The asset to be exchanged and the settlement price and settlement date of the exchange is whatever is mutually agreeable to the two transactors. When the settlement date arrives, the buyer tenders cash equal to the previously agreed upon settlement price to the seller, and the seller delivers the previously agreed upon asset to the buyer. Government National Mortgage Association (GNMA) pass-throughs provide the most important example of an interest-bearing asset traded in a forward delivery market.[3] Several dozen securities firms, many of them primary dealers in government securities, purchase and sell GNMAs for forward delivery. As in the spot GNMA market, these dealers trade with individual and institutional investors and among themselves.

For some assets, buying and selling for deferred delivery can be facilitated by the organization of a formal exchange market. One of the principal characteristics of exchange trading for deferred delivery is the establishment of conventional settlement dates, usually monthly or quarterly, at which time buyers and sellers tender payment and delivery, respectively, against their open obligations. (Settlement dates in dealer markets for forward contracts typically vary from contract to contract, according to the mutual interests of the buyer and seller.) Standardized settlement dates make for more homogeneous contracts and thereby improve the liquidity of the market.

Purchase and sale contracts for deferred delivery entered into on organized exchanges are called *futures* to distinguish them from the forward contracts of dealer markets. Since 1975 it has become possible to trade in commercial paper futures, Treasury bill and Treasury coupon futures, and GNMA futures.[4] The GNMA futures market supplemented the dealer market in GNMA forward contracts, while the other three markets provided new opportunities for deferred delivery transactions.

This chapter describes the organization of futures markets and the use of futures contracts for hedging or reducing risk. The first section provides a general outline of futures markets. Futures in Treasury bills and GNMAs are described more fully in the second section. The third section shows how futures can be used to eliminate risk completely on some types of transactions, and the fourth section shows how futures can be used to reduce (but not eliminate) risk on transactions in assets which do not trade in a futures market.

---

[2] See Stevens (1974) for a discussion of futures markets in farm commodities. See Kubarych (1978) for a description of markets in foreign exchange.

[3] GNMA pass-throughs are described in Section 1.3. See also Senft (1978); Sivesind (1979); and Black, Garbade, and Silber (1981). There are other securities traded for forward delivery besides GNMA pass-throughs. Issuers of long-maturity debt who wish to fix an interest rate on a future sale of securities use forward contracting of private placements. See Fleuriet (1975). Repurchase agreements, which are described in Section 4.2, are also similar to forward delivery contracts, in the sense that the seller's agreement to repurchase is a forward contract to buy at a fixed price.

[4] See Arak and McCurdy (1979–80) for an overview of futures markets on debt securities.

15.1 FUTURES MARKETS

Spot markets provide investors with opportunities for the purchase and sale of assets for immediate delivery and immediate payment. Futures markets provide investors with opportunities for transactions for deferred delivery and deferred payment. A buyer who wants to take immediate title to an asset should look for a seller of that asset in the spot market. If, however, the buyer wants to take title at some later time, he will look for a seller in a futures market. Upon finding such a seller, the buyer enters into a futures contract, whereby he agrees (1) to accept delivery of the asset on the specified settlement date and (2) to make payment at the agreed upon settlement price on that settlement date. The seller agrees (1) to accept payment and (2) to make delivery of the asset on the settlement date.

For every trransaction in a spot market there is a buyer and a seller. Similarly, every time somebody enters into a sale contract for deferred delivery of an asset in a futures market, there must be somebody else agreeing to accept delivery on that contract. Investors who have agreed to buy an asset sometime in the future are said to be *long* a futures contract. Investors who have agreed to sell an asset in the future are *short* a futures contract[5] Since there must be a buyer for every seller, the *net* long and short positions of all investors in a given futures contract must be zero.

Clearing Corporations

One of the major disincentives to entering into a forward contract for deferred delivery is the possibility that the party on the other side of the contract will renege on his commitment.[6] Suppose, for example, an investor bought 3-month Treasury bills in January for delivery in June at a settlement price of 98 percent of face value, or at a yield of about 8 percent per annum. When June comes around, 3-month bills might be trading at a price of 98.5 percent of face value in the spot market, and the seller might refuse to honor his forward delivery contract so that he can sell his bills at the higher spot market price. Conversely, if the bills are trading at a price of 97.5 percent of face value in the spot market in June, the buyer would have an incentive to renege on his forward contract.

Organized futures exchanges standardize the reliability of purchasers and sellers by requiring that a well-capitalized *clearing corporation*, usually owned

---

[5] The terms *long* and *short* refer to contracts for delivery when applied to a futures market. A long investor holds a contract for delivery; i.e., he has agreed to accept delivery. A short investor holds a negative amount of a contract for delivery; i.e., he has agreed to make delivery. When an investor is long in the spot market, he owns the asset itself rather than a contract for future delivery. Similarly, an investor who is short in the spot market has borrowed the asset from some holder and has an obligation to repay that borrowing; i.e., he holds a negative quantity of the asset.

[6] Default on a forward contract is more than a theoretical possibility, as shown by the bankruptcies of Winters Government Securities, Inc. (see *The Wall Street Journal*, May 17, 1977, p. 15, col. 1, and October 28, 1977, p. 1, col. 6; *Forbes*, June 1, 1977, p. 27), Hibbard & O'Connor, Government Securities (see *Securities Week*, January 14, 1980, p. 7), and Sheridan Associates (see *Securities Week*, December 3, 1979, p. 2, and January 14, 1980, p. 4).

by the members of the exchange, participate on the other side of every futures contract.[7] When a buyer and seller enter into a futures contract, they do not agree to a bilateral deferred delivery transaction. Instead, the seller agrees to deliver the stated assets to a clearing corporation on the settlement date in return for the agreed upon settlement price. The buyer agrees to pay the clearing corporation the same amount on the settlement date in return for delivery of the same assets.[8] The buyer and seller look to the clearing corporation as the other party to their contract instead of looking to each other. As long as the clearing corporation is well capitalized, each participant can be confident he will be able to complete his transaction as specified in his contract at the designated settlement price. Even if one or several transactors default on their contracts, other transactors are unaffected as long as the clearing corporation fulfills its responsibilities.[9] The expense of any recourse to the courts to force a defaulting transactor to fulfill his contractual obligations is borne by the clearing corporation and not by other transactors.

The use of a clearing corporation in matching future purchases with future sales means that every futures market participant faces the same transactor (the clearing corporation) on the other side of every futures contract. This makes futures contracts homogeneous across participants and simplifies the execution of transactions. An investor who has decided to go long in a futures contract can ask a broker to contract for the deferred purchase without having to pass on the acceptability or reliability of the seller who is going short in that contract.

Clearing corporations do not negotiate the settlement prices on futures contracts. Suppose in January two parties (Buyer and Seller) want to buy and sell, respectively, 3-month Treasury bills for March delivery, and they agree on a settlement price of $980,000 for $1 million face amount of bills.[10] As a result of

---

[7] See Telser and Higinbotham (1977) for a discussion of the importance of a reliable clearing corporation. In some cases the clearing corporation of a futures exchange may be organized as a division of the exchange rather than as a separate corporation. For example, the clearing corporation of the Chicago Mercantile Exchange is a division of that exchange, while the clearing corporation of the Chicago Board of Trade (CBT) is a separately capitalized corporation wholly owned by CBT members.

[8] If, after a buyer and seller have fixed a mutually acceptable settlement price on a futures contract, another buyer and seller enter into a futures contract for the same asset and for the same settlement date at a *different* settlement price, the settlement price on the old contract will be changed to the settlement price on the more recent contract. That change in price will be settled by an *immediate* cash transfer between the original transactors through the clearing corporation. This is known as *marking-to-market*. The appendix to this chapter explains marking-to-market in more detail. Forward contracts are not usually marked-to-market prior to settlement.

[9] A clearing corporation default on a futures contract can occur if the supply of the deliverable asset is small or nonexistent. In that case the shorts may not own enough of the asset to settle with the clearing corporation, and the clearing corporation may not be able to obtain enough of the asset from other sources to settle with the longs. This happened in 1976 in Maine potato futures contracts traded on the New York Mercantile Exchange, and it nearly happened in 1979 in 1-year Treasury bills (see *The Wall Street Journal*, March 28, 1979, p. 35, col. 6, and April 3, 1979, p. 38, col. 4).

[10] This agreement would be reached on the floor of a futures exchange, such as the International Monetary Market of the Chicago Mercantile Exchange.

this bargaining Buyer acquires a long position with a clearing corporation. He agrees to accept $1 million face value of 3-month Treasury bills from that clearing corporation in March and to pay $980,000 upon delivery. Seller acquires a short position with the same clearing corporation. He agrees to deliver $1 million face amount of 3-month Treasury bills to that clearing corporation in March upon receipt of $980,000.[11] The role of the clearing corporation is strictly limited to acting as an intermediary in the settlement of the bill futures contract. It has no economic interest in the settlement price of that contract.

The clearing corporation of a futures exchange runs a *balanced book* of long and short futures positions. For every futures contract on which it is obligated to deliver an asset, it will have a matching contract to receive that same asset. The aggregate amount of futures contracts on which it is obligated to deliver (or receive) an asset on a given settlement date is called the *open interest* in that contract.

The existence of clearing corporations also makes it possible for market participants to liquidate their futures positions with offsetting transactions before a settlement date. This endows futures contracts with a kind of negotiability, in the sense that buyers and sellers can avoid settlement by transferring their contractual rights and obligations to another party. An investor who is long a contract for June delivery of 3-month Treasury bills, and who in April decides he does not want to take actual delivery of those bills, can enter into an offsetting contract for sale of bills in June. Since his long and short positions are with the same clearing corporation, his net position is zero.[12] If the same deferred delivery transactions were executed by forward contracting with dealers, the investor would have to accept delivery of bills on his initial long contract and then redeliver the same bills to the dealer on the other side of his short contract. Clearing corporations save investors the trouble and expense of such redeliveries by keeping their books on a net basis against each participant.

15.2 TREASURY BILL AND GNMA FUTURES

Organized trading of futures contracts on interest-bearing financial assets is relatively new in the United States.[13] Trading in debt futures began in October 1975 when GNMA pass-through certificates began to trade for future delivery on the Chicago Board of Trade (CBT).[14] This was followed by the opening of trading in 3-month Treasury bill futures on the International Monetary Market (IMM) of the Chicago Mercantile Exchange in January 1976.[15] This section

---

[11] See, however, the description of marking an old futures contract to a new settlement price in the appendix to this chapter.

[12] See the appendix to this chapter for a description of the cash settlement which follows a liquidating transaction.

[13] See Arak and McCurdy (1979–80) for a general discussion.

[14] The GNMA futures market has been discussed by Sandor (1975), Stevens (1976), Rattner (1977), and Froewiss (1978).

[15] The IMM is a division of the Chicago Mercantile Exchange. Duncan (1977), Burger, Lang and Rasche (1977), and Poole (1978) discuss the Treasury bill futures market. See also U.S. Treasury, *Treasury/Federal Reserve Study of Treasury Futures Markets* (May, 1979).

describes futures on 3-month Treasury bills and GNMA pass-throughs in detail, and then summarizes the characteristics of other financial futures.

3-Month Treasury Bill Futures

The standard contract in 3-month Treasury bill futures traded on the IMM is $1 million face value of 90-day bills. There are four settlement dates each year: on the third business day following the auction of 13-week bills in the third week of March, June, September, and December. In most cases this means that settlement occurs on a Thursday,[16] which is also the usual day for delivery of newly auctioned 13-week bills.[17] Transactors can make purchase and sale commitments for any of the next eight settlement dates, so that settlement of futures contracts on 3-month Treasury bills can be deferred for as long as 2 years. Exhibit 15.1 shows a summary of trading in bill futures on Friday, May 9, 1980. Note that it was possible to buy and sell bills for delivery and payment in June, September, and December 1980; in March, June, September, and December 1981; and in March 1982.[18]

The settlement price on a bill futures contract on the IMM is quoted in units of 100 percent minus the discount rate (in percent) to be applied to bills delivered on the settlement date. Thus, a quoted price of 94 means a discount rate of 6 percent (100 minus quoted price of 94). Exhibit 15.1 shows that on May 9, 1980, Treasury bill futures closed at quoted prices ranging from 91.01 (8.99 percent discount rate) for March 1982 settlements to 91.48 (8.52 percent discount rate) for December 1980 settlements.

A seller settling a Treasury bill futures contract can deliver to the IMM's clearing corporation Treasury bills with remaining maturities of 90, 91, or 92 days.[19] If he delivers a 90-day Treasury bill against a futures contract bearing the quoted price P, he will receive payment of $100 - (100 - P)(90/360)$ percent of the face value of the bill. Thus, if the quoted price is 94 (implying a discount rate of 6 percent), the settlement price on a futures contract for $1 million of 90-day bills will be 98.5 percent of the face value of the bills $[98.5 = 100 - (100 - P)(90/360)$ when $P = 94]$. This corresponds to the con-

---

[16] The 13-week Treasury bills are normally auctioned on a Monday and delivered and paid for the following Thursday. See Section 1.1.

[17] There are at least two sources of Treasury bills deliverable against a 3-month bill futures contract: the 3-month Treasury bills auctioned 3 days earlier, and the 6-month Treasury bills auctioned 3 months earlier. Note that both classes of bills have the same ultimate maturity date and hence are indistinguishable.

[18] Note that a Treasury bill deliverable on, e.g., a March futures contract is not deliverable on any other 3-month bill futures contract, because a deliverable bill must have 3 months to run to maturity on the settlement date. Thus, 3-month Treasury bill futures with different settlement dates are futures contracts on different assets, i.e., on Treasury bills with different maturity dates.

[19] Except for holidays, contracts in Treasury bill futures are always settled on a Thursday with 91-day Treasury bills. A holiday on a normal settlement day will result in a Friday settlement with 90-day Treasury bills. A holiday 91 days after a regular Thursday settlement day will result in a Thursday settlement with 92-day Treasury bills, because in that case the Treasury will set the maturity of the deliverable Treasury bills at the day after the Thursday holiday, i.e., on a Friday. Thus, there is really only a single bill deliverable on a given 3-month Treasury bill futures contract, but that bill could have a maturity of 90, 91, or 92 days.

EXHIBIT 15.1
TRADING IN 3-MONTH TREASURY BILL FUTURES ON THE INTERNATIONAL MONETARY MARKET ON FRIDAY, MAY 9, 1980

Settlement date	Open interest (contracts)*	Quoted price	Implied discount rate, %†	Implied settlement prices, % of face value‡		
				For 90-day bills	For 91-day bills	For 92-day bills
June 1980	7359	91.14	8.86	97.785	97.760	97.736
Sept. 1980	6030	91.36	8.64	97.840	97.816	97.792
Dec. 1980	4459	91.48	8.52	97.870	97.846	97.823
March 1981	3661	91.37	8.63	97.843	97.819	97.795
June 1981	1945	91.24	8.76	97.810	97.786	97.761
Sept. 1981	1093	91.11	8.89	97.778	97.753	97.728
Dec. 1981	455	91.09	8.91	97.773	97.748	97.723
March 1982	353	91.01	8.99	97.753	97.728	97.703

*A contract is for $1 million face value of 90-, 91-, or 92-day Treasury bills.
†The discount rate is 100 minus the quoted price.
‡The settlement price is $100 - nd/360$, where d is the discount rate (percent) and n is the number of days to maturity on the bill as of the settlement date.

vention in the spot Treasury bill market that a 90-day bill quoted at a 6 percent discount rate has a price equal to 98.5 percent of its face value.[20] Exhibit 15.1 shows that on May 9, 1980, the settlement prices on Treasury bill futures on the IMM ranged from 97.753 percent of face value for March 1982 settlements to 97.870 percent of face value for December 1982 settlements, assuming those contracts are settled with 90-day Treasury bills.

A seller who settles a short Treasury bill futures contract with 91- or 92-day bills will receive less than if he had settled the same contract with 90-day bills, because some buyer will then receive Treasury bills which mature at a relatively later date. If a seller delivers a 91-day bill against a futures contract bearing the quoted price P, he will receive payment equal to $100 - (100 - P)$ $(91/360)$ percent of the face value of the bill. Thus, if the quoted price is 94 (implying a discount rate of 6 percent), the settlement price on a 91-day bill will be 98.4833 percent of its face value $[98.4833 = 100 - (100 - P) (91/360)$ when $P = 94]$. This corresponds to the convention in the spot Treasury bill market that a 91-day bill quoted at a 6 percent discount rate has a price equal to 98.4833 percent of its face value.

A buyer who is long a Treasury bill futures contract on the settlement date of that contract will receive either 90-, 91-, or 92-day Treasury bills from the IMM's clearing corporation, depending on what that clearing corporation receives from sellers settling short positions. The price paid by buyers to the clearing corporation for those bills is equal to the price paid by the clearing corporation to the sellers of the same bills.

GNMA Pass-Through Futures

The standard futures contract in GNMAs traded on the CBT is $100,000 principal value of a GNMA pass-through certificate bearing an 8 percent interest rate. There are four settlement months for GNMA futures each year: in March, June, September, and December. Settlement can be made *any time* during a settlement month (at the option of the seller) but must be completed by the last business day of the month.[21] At any point in time the CBT sponsors GNMA futures contracts for settlement in at least the next 10 settlement months, so that purchases and sales of GNMAs can be deferred up to $2^1/_2$ years into the future.

Settlement prices for GNMA futures are quoted in units of percent of principal value of a standard futures contract, with fractions of a percent expressed in 32nds. This follows the quotation convention used by traders in the dealer market in GNMA forward contracts. Exhibit 15.2 shows a summary of trading in GNMA futures on Friday, May 9, 1980. GNMAs for settlement in September 1982 were quoted at a price of 78 percent of principal value.

During a settlement month, sellers of GNMA futures can fulfill their con-

---

[20] See the discussion of Equation (1.1) in Chapter 1.

[21] This differs from the settlement practice on the IMM for bill futures, where all contracts are settled on a specific day in a settlement month.

EXHIBIT 15.2
TRADING IN GNMA PASS-THROUGH FUTURES ON
THE CHICAGO BOARD OF TRADE ON FRIDAY,
MAY 9, 1980

Settlement month	Open interest (contracts)*	Settlement price, % of principal value
June 1980	8,374	$79^{14}/_{32}$
Sept. 1980	11,555	$79^{12}/_{32}$
Dec 1980	8,812	$79^{11}/_{32}$
March 1981	7,838	$79^{6}/_{32}$
June 1981	5,412	$79^{1}/_{32}$
Sept. 1981	5,483	$78^{27}/_{32}$
Dec. 1981	5,549	$78^{20}/_{32}$
March 1982	4,499	$78^{13}/_{32}$
June 1982	2,404	$78^{6}/_{32}$
Sept. 1982	961	78
Dec. 1982	97	$77^{26}/_{32}$

*A contract is for $100,000 principal value of a GNMA
pass-through with an 8 percent interest rate, or some other
GNMA in a principal value such that it would have a price
of $100, 000 if it had a yield of 8 percent.

tractual obligations in either of two ways. First, they can tender to the clearing corporation of the CBT $100,000 principal value of 8 percent GNMAs for each contract they are short.[22] Second, sellers can tender GNMA certificates with other interest rates as long as the market price of the GNMA would be $100,000 if that GNMA had a yield to maturity of 8 percent. For example, a seller can deliver $96,502 of a GNMA pass-through which pays interest at a rate of 8.5 percent per annum or $103,806 of a 7.5 percent GNMA pass-through.[23] Holders of long positions in GNMA futures contracts may receive delivery in either of the two modes outlined above, at the option of the clearing corporation of the CBT.

According to the settlement prices shown in Exhibit 15.2, a seller of GNMA futures for September 1982 settlement would receive $78,000 if he delivered $100,000 principal value of GNMAs bearing an 8 percent interest rate. He could also deliver $96,502 principal value of GNMAs bearing an 8.5 percent interest rate, or $103,806 principal value of GNMAs bearing a 7.5 percent interest rate, for the same $78,000.[24]

---

[22] A seller will actually tender a due bill rather than a pass-through certificate. A due bill is a claim on a depository commercial bank for the stated pass-through. Due bills are used because GNMA certificates are registered instruments and changes in title take time to record.

[23] A $96,502 principal value of an 8.5 percent GNMA would have a market price of $100,000 if the yield on that GNMA were 8 percent. Similarly, $103,806 principal value of a 7.5 percent GNMA would have a market price of $100,000 if the yield on that GNMA were 8 percent.

[24] When there are several alternative deliverable assets, shorts will deliver the "cheapest" asset. For example, they will compare the dollar prices of a $96,502 principal value 8.5 percent GNMA, a $100,000 principal value 8.0 percent GNMA, and a $103,806 principal value 7.5 percent GNMA, and deliver the one with the lowest dollar price. See Ederington (1979, p. 167).

The ability to deliver any of several alternative GNMA certificates is an important advantage enjoyed by sellers of GNMA futures on the CBT, and it is a disadvantage to buyers. An investor who is long a GNMA futures contract on the CBT has no guarantee that he will actually receive a certificate bearing an 8 percent interest rate when his contract is settled.[25]

The ability to settle a deferred delivery contract with a variety of alternative assets is not present in the dealer market for GNMA forwards. Contracts in that market specify a particular certificate rate as well as a settlement date and price. Thus, a buyer of GNMAs for deferred delivery who is looking for a specific certificate rate has to contract with a dealer. The opportunity for specific performance which the forward market offers has been important to the survival of that market even in the face of strong competition from the GNMA futures market on the CBT.

Other Futures Contracts

Exhibit 15.3 summarizes the characteristics of the 3-month Treasury bill futures contract and the GNMA pass-through futures contract described above, as well as some of the other major financial futures contracts presently traded in the United States. These other contracts include futures on:

- 1-year Treasury bills
- 4-year Treasury notes
- 15-year Treasury bonds
- Commercial paper

The key aspects of each of the contracts are (1) specification of the standard contract and (2) specification of alternative assets that can be delivered to satisfy a short position on a settlement date.[26]

15.3 PERFECT HEDGES

Futures markets owe their existence to the desire of investors to eliminate or reduce the risk which stems from uncertainty about future asset prices. This section shows how short and long positions in futures contracts can be used to eliminate that risk. For purposes of illustration we use GNMA futures contracts.

---

[25] One of the important elements of a futures contract is the defined breadth of alternative deliverable assets. See Sandor (1973). If the definition of the deliverable assets is too narrow, the market may be subject to "corners" and "squeezes." See footnote 26 below. If the definition is too broad, the contract may not meet the needs of long hedgers and those hedgers may abandon the market. See the discussion of Kansas City wheat futures in Working (1954).

[26] Note that the 3-month and 1-year Treasury bill contracts provide for only a single deliverable asset, but that the Treasury note, Treasury bond, commercial paper, and GNMA contracts provide for an array of alternative deliverable assets. The United States Treasury and the Federal Reserve have expressed concern that the absence of alternative deliverable assets on the bill contracts could facilitate a market corner or squeeze on a deliverable Treasury bill. See U.S. Treasury, *Treasury/Federal Reserve Study of Treasury Futures Markets*, vol. I, pp. 13, 15, and 22–27 (May 1979).

EXHIBIT 15.3
SUMMARY OF FUTURES ON FINANCIAL INSTRUMENTS

Instrument	Standard contract	Other deliverable assets	Where traded*	Settlement months
3-month Treasury bills	$1 million face amount of 90-day Treasury bills	$1 million face amount of 91- or 92-day bills	IMM	March, June, Sept., Dec.
1-year Treasury bills	$250,000 face amount of 364-day Treasury bills	None	IMM	March, June, Sept., Dec.
4-year Treasury notes	$100,000 principal amount of 4-year Treasury notes with a 7% coupon rate	$100,000 principal amount of $3^1/_2$- to $4^1/_2$-year Treasury notes†	IMM	Feb., May, Aug., Nov.
15-year Treasury bonds	$100,000 principal amount of 15-year Treasury bonds with an 8% coupon rate	$100,000, principal amount of Treasury bonds with a maturity not less than 15 years‡	CBT	March, June, Sept., Dec.
GNMA pass-throughs	$100,000 principal amount of a GNMA pass-through with an 8% interest rate	GNMA pass-throughs in a principal amount such that they would have a price of $100,000 if they had a yield to maturity (assuming retirement of a 30-year mortgage at the end of 12 years) of 8% given their interest rate	CBT	March, June, Sept., Dec.
90-day commercial paper	$1 million face amount of 90-day commercial paper rated A-1 by Standard & Poor's and rated P-1 by Moody's	$1 million face amount of commercial paper maturing not more than 90-days after settlement date	CBT	March, June, Sept., Dec.

*IMM: International Monetary Market (a division of the Chicago Mercantile Exchange); CBT: Chicago Board of Trade.
† Invoice price equal to settlement price of 4-year 7% note times value (as a fraction of principal value) of delivered note when computed assuming a yield to maturity of 7%.
‡ Invoice price equal to settlement price of 15-year 8% bond times value (as a fraction of principal value) of delivered bond when computed assuming a yield to maturity of 8%.

Short Hedges

Consider a mortgage banker who, at time t, commits himself to making funds available for residential mortgages k quarters in the future. For simplicity we will assume that the mortgages can be placed in a GNMA pool when they are originated and that they will all pay 8 percent to holders of pass-through certificates on that pool. At time $t + k$ the price per $100 principal value of the mortgages will be P_{t+k} in the spot market. This is how much the mortgage banker will receive if he sells his mortgages to an investor after they have been taken down by new homeowners. If at time t the mortgage banker commits himself to making the mortgage funds available at a commitment price of P^c per $100 principal value, his profit will be $P_{t+k} - P^c$. That is, his profit is the price he gets for selling the mortgages at time $t + k$ (P_{t+k}), less the cost of acquiring those mortgages from home buyers (P^c).

When the mortgage banker sets the commitment price P^c at time t, his profit is uncertain, because he cannot know with certainty the price at which he will be able to sell the mortgages at time $t + k$. That is, he does not know P_{t+k} at time t. Thus, a mortgage banker bears risk when he commits himself to the future availability of funds at a fixed interest rate. If long-term interest rates, and mortgage rates in particular, are volatile, the future value of the mortgages could be quite uncertain and the mortgage banker's risk exposure could be substantial.

As an alternative to waiting until the mortgages are actually taken down to sell them in the spot market, suppose the mortgage banker sells them for deferred delivery. He can do this by taking a short position in a GNMA futures contract on which settlement is due k quarters in the future. Suppose, at time t, the settlement price of k-quarter forward GNMA futures is $P_t(k)$. At time $t + k$ the banker will fund his mortgage commitments at a cost of P^c per $100 principal value of the mortgages, receive the mortgage contracts, place those contracts in a GNMA pool for which he will receive a pass-through certificate, and then deliver the certificate in settlement of his short futures position, for which he is paid $P_t(k)$. His profit per $100 principal value is $P_t(k) - P^c$. *At time t* this profit is perfectly predictable and riskless to the mortgage banker. By taking a short position in GNMA futures he is able to sell for deferred delivery the mortgages which he originates and can thereby avoid the risk of waiting until time $t + k$ to sell the mortgages in the spot market.[27]

Long Hedges

As an illustration of the use of a long position in a futures contract to reduce risk, consider a pension fund which decides at time t to buy GNMA pass-throughs when funds become available in k quarters. Since the pension fund cannot predict with certainty what mortgage yields will be at time $t + k$, it cannot know, at time t, the cost of the desired pass-throughs.

[27] The same transaction can also be completed by forward contracting with a GNMA dealer. See GNMA Mortgage-Backed Securities Dealers Association (1978, pp. 25–26 and 33–34).

As an alternative to waiting until funds are actually available, the pension fund can take a long position in a GNMA futures contract due to be settled at time $t + k$. The fund will then know exactly what it will cost to buy the desired pass-throughs.[28] By taking a long position in GNMA futures, the fund can establish, at time t, the price which it will pay for pass-throughs which will not be delivered or paid for until time $t + k$.[29]

Futures Contracts and Social Risk Reduction

The two preceding examples illustrate how investors can use futures contracts to reduce their risk exposure. In the first example a mortgage banker reduced his risk by taking a short position in a futures contract. In the second example a pension fund accomplished the same end by taking a long position.

Besides allowing individuals and institutions to reduce their own exposure to risk, futures markets permit reduction in the risk borne by society as a whole. In the preceding examples the risk perceived by the mortgage banker was uncertainty over the future sale price of mortgages. He sold mortgages for future delivery to reduce that risk. The risk perceived by the pension fund, on the other hand, was uncertainty over the future purchase price of mortgages, and so it bought mortgages for future delivery. If the mortgage banker and the pension fund had been able to get together, they might well have agreed, bilaterally, to a forward exchange contract.[30] By so agreeing, each would have perceived a reduction in risk and each would have been better off. The risk of each of the transactors would have been transferred to somebody better able to bear it or, more precisely, to somebody who didn't perceive it as a risk at all.

Organized futures markets facilitate the meeting of market participants with congruent risk perceptions. By matching future buyers with future sellers, those markets reduce the risk exposure of each and, in consequence, the total risk borne by society.

15.4 IMPERFECT CROSS HEDGES

Futures contracts can be used to reduce risk even when investors cannot arrange purchases and sales for future delivery in every asset. As an illustration of such imperfect hedges, we will see how Treasury bill futures can be used to hedge a commitment in short-term commercial lending.

---

[28] The pension fund can also fix the price it will pay for mortgages to be delivered at time $t + k$ by entering into a forward contract with a GNMA dealer.

[29] This long position is a true hedge only if it reduces the uncertainty of the pension fund's future net worth. That is, absent the futures position the assets and liabilities of the pension fund must be such that an increase in interest rates would increase the fund's net worth and a decrease in interest rates would decrease the fund's net worth. This could be the case if the duration of the fund's liabilities exceeded the duration of the fund's assets. See the articles cited in footnote 26 in Chapter 14. A long futures position would then reduce the sensitivity of the fund's net worth to changes in the general level of interest rates.

[30] Alternatively, the banker and the fund could have established short and long positions, respectively, in forward contracts with a GNMA dealer. See footnotes 27 and 28 above.

Suppose a commercial bank has to commit itself at time t to the price on a 3-month loan scheduled to begin k quarters in the future, i.e., at time $t + k$. Assume the loan is on a discount basis with a maturity value of $1 million, and that the bank commits itself to pay out at time $t + k$ the amount $\$\pi^c$ per $100 maturity value of the loan, where $\pi^c < 100$. The bank plans to fund the loan by selling its own CDs, and it can get $\$\pi_{t+k}$ per $100 maturity value of a 3-month CD at time $t+k$.

If the bank waits until the borrower takes down his funds to sell CDs, its profit will be $\$(\pi_{t+k} - \pi^c)$ per $100 maturity value of the loan. This profit is uncertain at time t (when the bank sets the price of the loan), and, in consequence, the loan is a risky commitment.

The bank may be able to hedge its risk on the loan commitment by taking a short position at time t in a 3-month Treasury bill futures contract having a settlement date k quarters in the future. When the settlement date arrives, the bank settles its futures contract by buying bills in the spot market and delivering those bills to the clearing corporation of the IMM. Let $P_t(k)$ be the settlement price prevailing at time t on a Treasury bill futures contract due to be settled at time $t + k$, and let P_{t+k} be the price of bills in the spot market at time $t + k$. The net profit to the bank from the combined loan commitment and futures contract will then be

$$\text{Profit} = \pi_{t+k} - \pi^c + P_t(k) - P_{t+k} \tag{15.1}$$

This profit is composed of two parts. The first part is the proceeds from the sale of the CDs minus the amount of money loaned out: $\pi_{t+k} - \pi^c$. The second part is the proceeds received from settling the short Treasury bill futures contract minus the cost of buying the bills needed to settle that contract: $P_t(k) - P_{t+k}$.

At time t the expected value of the actual profit based on information to time t is

$$\text{Exp}_t\,[\text{profit}] = \text{Exp}_t\,[\pi_{t+k}] - \pi^c + P_t(k) - \text{Exp}_t\,[P_{t+k}] \tag{15.2}$$

where $\text{Exp}_t\,[x]$ represents the expected value of the random variable x as of time t. In Equation (15.2) the values of π^c and $P_t(k)$ are both known and perfectly certain at time t. The variance or uncertainty of the profit as of time t is

$$\begin{aligned}
\text{Var}_t\,[\text{profit}] &= \text{Var}_t\,[\pi_{t+k} - P_{t+k}] \\
&= \text{Var}_t\,[\pi_{t+k}] + \text{Var}_t\,[P_{t+k}] - 2\rho\{\text{Var}_t\,[\pi_{t+k}]\text{Var}_t\,[P_{t+k}]\}^{1/2}
\end{aligned} \tag{15.3}$$

where ρ is the coefficient of correlation between π_{t+k} and P_{t+k} as it is perceived at time t.

Equation (15.3) shows that if the uncertainty over the future spot market prices of CDs and Treasury bills is comparable, so that $\text{Var}_t\,[\pi_{t+k}]$ is approximately equal to $\text{Var}_t\,[P_{t+k}]$, and if the spot market prices of 90-day bills and 90-day CDs are highly correlated, so that ρ is approximately equal to unity, the bank can reduce its risk exposure on a loan commitment by short selling Treasury bill futures. More precisely, if

$$\text{Var}_t\ [\pi_{t+k}] = \text{Var}_t\ [P_{t+k}] \qquad (15.4a)$$

and if
$$\rho = 1 \qquad (15.4b)$$

then $\quad \text{Var}_t\ [\pi_{t+k}] + \text{Var}_t\ [P_{t+k}] - 2\rho\{\text{Var}_t\ [\pi_{t+k}]\ \text{Var}_t\ [P_{t+k}]\}^{1/2} = 0 \quad (15.5)$

In fact, bill prices and CD prices usually do move together, so that ρ is approximately unity, and the price variances of the two instruments are comparable. Thus, even though the bank cannot sell its own CDs for future delivery,[31] it can reduce its risk by selling Treasury bills for future delivery. This so-called cross hedge is not perfect, however, because the spread between bills and CDs can change over time, implying that the coefficient of correlation is somewhat less than unity.[32]

The key element in cross hedging is the existence of an asset which trades in a futures market and whose spot market price is highly correlated with the spot market price of the asset which an investor wants to hedge. Treasury bill futures can hedge positions in short-term instruments like CDs or commercial paper or short-term federal agency debt. They would be less useful for hedging a position in intermediate- or long-maturity debt instruments or in stock. GNMA futures, on the other hand, can be used to hedge positions in intermediate-term debt, but not in stock or short-term debt.[33]

CHAPTER SUMMARY

This chapter has explored how contracts for deferred delivery can be used to fix the purchase or sale price of an asset on some future date. There are two types of deferred delivery contracts: forward contracts and futures contracts.

A forward contract is an ordinary contract between a buyer and a seller. The settlement price and settlement date, and the asset being exchanged, are whatever is mutually acceptable to the two parties.

A futures contract is a contract for deferred purchase or deferred sale with the clearing corporation of a futures exchange. The exchange specifies what

---

[31] In late 1976, Morgan Guaranty Trust Company began to experiment with sales of CDs for forward delivery. The bank offered packages of forward CD contracts with sequential delivery dates. These packages were promptly labelled "roly-polies." See *The Wall Street Journal*, April 13, 1977, p. 38, col. 1.

[32] The risk of change in the spread between CD prices and Treasury bill prices is a manifestation of *basis risk*. Basis risk is the risk of imperfect correlation between changes in the price of the asset traded for future delivery and changes in the price of the asset being hedged. If the commercial bank were to hedge its loan commitment by taking a short position in Treasury bill futures, it would be hedged against the risk of change in the general level of interest rates, but it would be exposed to the risk of change in the yield spread between CDs and Treasury bills; i.e., it would bear basis risk.

[33] Ederington (1979) discusses a different type of imperfect hedge: hedging a long position in an asset by assuming a short position in a futures contract on the same asset with a settlement date more distant than the end of the hedging horizon.

assets are deliverable under the terms of a given contract, and it specifies how settlement prices on alternative deliverable assets shall be calculated. The exchange also specifies the available settlement dates. If an investor cannot satisfy his needs with one of the available settlement dates and contract specifications, he will have to arrange a forward transaction privately.

The future purchase price of an asset can be fixed exactly by assuming a long position in a futures contract on that asset. Conversely, the future sale price of an asset can be fixed exactly by assuming a short position in a futures contract on that asset. For these reasons, futures contracts can be used to eliminate risk. Futures contracts can also be used to reduce (but not eliminate) risk even when contracts for deferred delivery of an asset are not traded on a futures exchange. However, effective cross hedging requires a high correlation between changes in the spot market price of the asset being hedged and changes in the spot market price of the asset traded for deferred delivery.

FURTHER READING

Marcelle Arak and Christopher McCurdy, "Interest Rates Futures," Federal Reserve Bank of New York *Quarterly Review*, **4** (Winter 1979–80), 33–46.

Louis Ederington, "The Hedging Performance of the New Futures Markets," *Journal of Finance*, **34** (March 1979), 157–170.

Neil Stevens, "A Mortgage Futures Market: Its Development, Uses, Benefits, and Costs," Federal Reserve Bank of St. Louis *Review*, **58** (April 1976), 12–16.

Lester Telser and Harlow Higinbotham, "Organized Futures Markets: Costs and Benefits," *Journal of Political Economy*, **85** (October 1977), 969–1000.

APPENDIX: Mark-to-Market Settlement of Futures Contracts

This chapter has described the settlement price on a futures contract for some asset as the price which a buyer (or holder of a long position) agrees to pay for delivery of the asset on the settlement date, and as the price at which a seller (or holder of a short position) agrees to deliver that asset on the same date. This definition ignores an important component of settling futures contracts called *mark-to-market* settlement.

Exhibit A.1 shows the behavior of settlement prices on 90-day Treasury bill futures scheduled for June 19, 1980, settlement during the last 3 weeks of trading in that contract. Suppose an investor, "Buyer," assumed a long position in one contract on Monday, June 2, and agreed to a quoted settlement price of 92.23. In view of the quotation conventions for 90-day Treasury bill futures,[34] this would appear to imply that Buyer had the right to receive \$1 million face value of 90-day Treasury bills on Thursday, June 19, and the obligation to pay out a cash settlement price equal to 98.0575 percent of the face value of those bills, or \$980,575 [$98.0575 = 100 - (100 - P)(90/360)$ when $P = 92.23$]. What actually happened, however, is that the clearing corporation of the IMM changed the settlement price on Buyer's long position daily; i.e., it marked that

---

[34] See text at the reference to footnote 19 above.

EXHIBIT A.1

SETTLEMENT PRICES AND MARK-TO-MARKET SETTLEMENTS
ON 90-DAY TREASURY BILL FUTURES FOR JUNE 19, 1980,
SETTLEMENT

Date	Quoted settlement price	Implied dollar settlement price per contract*	Mark-to-market settlement on a long contract†
June 2	92.23	980,575	
3	92.73	981,825	$1250
4	92.83	982,075	250
5	93.06	982,650	575
6	93.07	982,675	25
9	93.48	983,700	1025
10	93.18	982,950	−750
11	93.32	983,300	350
12	93.59	983,975	675
13	93.84	984,600	625
16	93.71	984,275	−325
17	93.25	983,125	−1150
18	93.12	982,800	−325
		Cumulative mark-to-market settlement	$2225

*A contract is for $1 million face value of 90-day Treasury bills. The implied settlement price as a percent of the face value of the bills is $100 - (100 - P)(90/360)$, where P is the quoted settlement price.

†Equal to the increase in the implied dollar settlement price. Negative sign indicates cash call made on holder of a long position.

position to market, and it made an *immediate* cash settlement with Buyer for the amount of each of those daily changes in the settlement price.

The process of marking-to-market can be illustrated by examining the changing position of Buyer after June 2. At the close of trading on Tuesday, June 3, the settlement price for *new* positions in the June Treasury bill futures contract had changed to a quoted price of 92.73, or to an implied dollar price of $981,825 per contract. At that time the clearing corporation of the IMM changed the settlement price on Buyer's outstanding long futures contract from $980,575 to $981,825 and gave Buyer $1250 in cash. Buyer was then obligated to pay $1250 *more* for his Treasury bills on June 19 than his original contract price, that is, $981,825 instead of $980,575, but he also had $1250 in cash that he did not previously have.

On Wednesday, June 4, June Treasury bill futures closed at a quoted settlement price of 92.83, or at an implied dollar settlement price of $982,075 per contract. At that time the clearing corporation of the IMM again changed the settlement price on Buyer's long futures contract, from $981,825 to $982,075. To compensate him for the $250 increase in his settlement price, the IMM's clearing corporation gave him an additional $250 in cash.

As summarized in the last two columns of Exhibit A.1, the IMM's clearing corporation marked Buyer's long futures contract to market every day through the close of trading on Wednesday, June 18. As a result of those daily mark-to-markets, the settlement price on Buyer's contract changed from the original price of $980,575 to an ultimate price of $982,800. Thus, on the Thursday, June 19, settlement date, Buyer was required to pay $2225 more for $1 million face value of 90-day Treasury bills than he had originally agreed to pay. However, as a result of the daily mark-to-market cash settlements with Buyer by the IMM's clearing corporation, Buyer also had possession of $2225 in cash that he had not contracted for, and so the increased settlement price did not cause him any harm.

At this point one might wonder where the IMM's clearing corporation got the cash needed to compensate Buyer (and others with a long position in June Treasury bill futures). The answer is this: The cash came from those with a short position in the same contract. For example, suppose Seller took a short position in a June Treasury bill futures contract on June 2 at a quoted settlement price of 92.23, or at an implied dollar settlement price of $980,575 per contract. Seller was then in the position of being obligated to deliver, on June 19, $1 million face value of 90-day Treasury bills in return for $980,575 in cash. On June 3, the IMM's clearing corporation marked Seller's short futures contract to market (just as it marked Buyer's long contract to market) and raised the dollar settlement price on that contract to $981,825. This meant that Seller would get $981,825 (instead of $980,575) in return for delivering $1 million face value of 90-day Treasury bills on June 19. In return for this $1250 increase in the settlement price, the IMM's clearing corporation required Seller to pay $1250 *immediately*.

On Wednesday, June 4, the IMM's clearing corporation again marked Seller's short futures contract to market, by raising the settlement price on that contract to a quoted price of 92.83, or to an implied dollar price of $982,075 per contract. This $250 increase in the ultimate settlement price was offset by an immediate call on Seller for an additional $250 cash payment. By Wednesday, June 18, the IMM's clearing corporation had made a net increase in the cash settlement price on Seller's contract of $2225, from $980,575 to $982,800. In return for this increased settlement price, the IMM's clearing corporation had made an aggregate demand on Seller for $2225 in cash between June 3 and June 18.

The foregoing example illustrates the mechanics of mark-to-market adjustment of the settlement price of a futures contract. If subsequent trading in a particular contract results in a higher settlement price, all old contracts are marked to that higher price. Participants with a long position are then required to pay a greater amount on the settlement date (but receive an equal amount of cash immediately), and participants with a short position get to receive a greater amount on the settlement date (but have to pay out an equal amount of cash immediately). Conversely, if subsequent trading results in a lower settlement price, all old contracts are marked down to that lower price. Participants with a long position are then required to pay a smaller amount on the settlement date (but have to pay the amount of the decrease immediately), and participants with a short position get to receive a smaller amount on the settlement date (but receive the amount of the decrease immediately). This second type of mark-to-market settlement is illustrated in Exhibit A.1 by the change from June 9 to June 10. At the close of trading on June 10 the settlement price on a June futures contract was quoted at 93.18, or at $982,950 per contract. This was $750 lower than the settlement price at the close of trading on June 9. Because the settlement price fell, the holder of a long position in one contract had to pay $750 to the IMM's clearing corporation, and the holder of a short position in one contract got to receive $750 from that clearing corporation.

The convention of marking a futures position to market does not alter the aggregate amount of cash paid out to settle a long position, or received in settlement of a short position. As shown in Exhibit A.1, a market participant who assumed a long position in

June Treasury bill futures on June 2, 1980, agreed to pay $980,575 for $1 million face value of 90-day bills on June 19. He ultimately had to pay $982,800 for those bills, but he also received $2225 in cash prior to the June 19 settlement date. His net expenses were, therefore, just equal to his original settlement price ($980,575 = $982,800 paid out on the final settlement date, less $2225 received from cumulative mark-to-market settlements between June 3 and June 18). However, it should be noted that mark-to-market settlements do change the timing of the cash flows resulting from a futures position. As shown in Exhibit A.1, the holder of a long position in June Treasury bill futures received cash payments on 8 of the 12 days between June 3 and June 18 and had to pay out cash on 4 of those 12 days.[35]

Liquidation of a Futures Position prior to Final Settlement

The practice of marking futures contracts to market on a daily basis makes it easy to liquidate a futures position before the final settlement date. Suppose, for example, Buyer decided on Tuesday, June 10, that he did not want to take actual delivery of 90-day Treasury bills on his long futures contract. Following the close of the market on the preceding day, the IMM's clearing corporation had marked Buyer's contract to a dollar settlement price of $983,700. If Buyer opened a matching short position in June Treasury bill futures on June 10 at a quoted price of 93.18, he would be obligated to deliver $1 million face value of 90-day Treasury bills in return for $982,950 in cash on June 19. However, this short position would just offset his long position in the same contract. The IMM's clearing corporation would make a call on Buyer for the $750 difference and then cancel Buyer's matching positions. At this point Buyer has no remaining obligation to deliver cash or securities to the IMM's clearing corporation, and he will not be subject to any further mark-to-market settlement.

[35] Black (1976) shows that as a result of mark-to-market settlements, the *value* of a long or short position in a futures contract is always identically zero. He also shows that forward contracts can have positive or negative value, because those contracts are not marked-to-market.

CHAPTER 16

EQUILIBRIUM SETTLEMENT PRICES ON FUTURES CONTRACTS

The settlement price on a futures contract is the price at which market participants can contract for purchase and sale of the underlying asset on a deferred
delivery and deferred payment basis. For example, if the settlement price in
March on a GNMA pass-through for September settlement is 93, then an investor can contract in March to sell $100,000 of 8 percent GNMA pass-
throughs the following September at a price of $93,000. When the settlement
month arrives, the investor would be obligated to deliver the GNMA securities
and would receive the settlement price in cash.[1]

Settlement prices in futures markets are like prices in other financial
markets: they move to bring demand into equilibrium with supply. In examining equilibrium prices for common stock (see Chapters 11 and 12) and debt (see
Chapter 14), we assumed there was a fixed supply of securities, and then asked
what prices were required to raise or lower aggregate demand to the level of
that fixed supply. The analysis of equilibrium settlement prices on futures contracts cannot follow the same pattern, because the supply of futures contracts
cannot reasonably be asumed to be fixed. A futures contract is not a security
like stock or debt, but is a contract for the exchange of some underlying asset
on a deferred delivery and deferred payment basis. There is no reason to view
the supply of such contracts as fixed, even in the short run. Thus, in analyzing
equilibrium settlement prices on futures contracts, we must examine the nature
of both the demand for and the supply of those contracts.[2]

---

[1] The analyses in this chapter ignore daily mark-to-market settlements of futures contracts and
assume there is only a single lump-sum settlement on the settlement date. Mark-to-market settlements are described in the appendix to Chapter 15.

[2] See Working (1977) and Peck (1977) for compilations of articles on futures markets and the
behavior of settlement prices.

321

There are three categories of participants in a futures market who play a role in the determination of equilibrium settlement prices. *Hedgers* are market participants who can reduce their risk exposure by entering into contracts for the deferred purchase or deferred sale of an asset. For these participants, the desire to avoid risk creates an incentive to supply or demand long positions in futures contracts. Because it is important to understand clearly the economic motivations of hedgers, Section 16.1 describes a futures market in equilibrium when participation in that market is limited to hedgers.

Speculators are the second important class of participants in a futures market. Speculators are participants who incur risk when they assume positions in futures contracts. Speculators in futures markets are like most other types of investors: they bear risk in anticipation of making a profit. Section 16.2 broadens the analysis of Section 16.1 by examining the economic motivations of speculators and their effect on equilibrium settlement prices.

In many cases, the analysis of equilibrium settlement prices is complete when the activities of hedgers and speculators have been described. This is true when a futures market can reasonably be considered in isolation from other markets. However, in some cases an asset which is traded for deferred delivery and deferred payment in a futures market is simultaneously traded for immediate delivery and immediate payment in a spot market. For example, Treasury bonds can be bought and sold in a spot market, and can also be bought and sold for future delivery on the chicago Board of Trade.[3] In such cases it may be possible to make a riskless profit by buying (or selling) an asset in the spot market and simultaneously contracting to sell (or buy) that same asset in the futures market. This is known as *riskless arbitrage*. The possibility of arbitrage between a futures market and a spot market means we cannot examine that futures market without simultaneously examining the spot market for the same asset. More particularly, we cannot view the equilibrium settlement price on a futures contract as being determined solely by hedgers and speculators in the futures market. That settlement price will also depend on the nature of supply and demand in the spot market. The converse is also true: the equilibrium price in the spot market for an asset will depend on the activities of hedgers and speculators in the futures market for the same asset.

Arbitrageurs are the integrating link between spot markets and futures markets, and are the third important class of participants in a futures market. Section 16.3 describes the economic motivations of arbitrageurs and examines the implications of arbitrage for the relation between settlement prices in a futures market and spot market prices.

The analysis of Section 16.3 is called a *partial equilibrium anlaysis*. That is, it is an analysis of the determinants of the equilibrium relation *between* spot prices and futures prices. A partial equilibrium analysis does not address the determinants of the equilibrium *level* of either spot market prices or futures market settlement prices.

---

[3] See Exhibit 15.3.

Section 16.4 completes our analysis of equilibrium settlement prices on futures contracts by examining the collective influences of hedgers, speculators, and arbitrageurs in determining the equilibrium level of settlement prices. We will see that when arbitrage between a spot market and a futures market is possible, equilibrium prices in the two markets are determined simultaneously, rather than independently of each other. This implies that a market for immediate exchange and a market for deferred exchange are two parts of the same whole when arbitrage between those markets is possible.[4]

16.1 EQUILIBRIUM SETTLEMENT PRICES WHEN ONLY HEDGERS PARTICIPATE IN A FUTURES MARKET

Consider an asset, such as Treasury bills, which can be bought and sold for future delivery. Let $P_t(k)$ be the settlement price at time t on a futures contract due to be settled at time $t + k$, or k periods in the future.[5] If a market participant takes a long position in a futures contract at time t, he agrees to accept delivery of the asset and to pay a price of $P_t(k)$ at time $t + k$. If a market participant takes a short position in a futures contract at time t, he agrees to deliver out the asset against payment of $P_t(k)$ at time $t + k$.

A hedger is a market participant who can *reduce* his risk exposure by assuming a position in a futures contract. Hedgers can be divided into two categories: *long hedgers* and *short hedgers*. Long hedgers can reduce their exposure to risk by entering into a long position in a futures contract.[6] The pension fund described in Section 15.3 is an example of a long hedger. Short hedgers can reduce their exposure to risk by assuming a short position in a futures contract.[7] The mortgage banker described in Section 15.3 and the commerical banker described in Section 15.4 are two examples of short hedgers.

The desire of risk-averse hedgers to reduce their exposure to risk leads to a demand for long futures positions by long hedgers and to a supply of long futures positions from short hedgers. If there are only hedgers in the market, the equilibrium settlement price on a futures contract will be that price which equates the demand for long futures positions (by long hedgers) to the supply of those positions (from short hedgers). Thus, to describe the equilib-

---

[4] An important issue (which is not considered in this book) is whether the existence of a futures market for an asset tends to stabilize or destabilize the spot market price of that asset. See Powers (1970), Taylor and Leuthold (1974), and Froewiss (1978).

[5] The length of a period is arbitrary and could be a day, a week, a month, or a quarter of a year.

[6] A long hedger is defined as a market participant whose assets and liabilities are such that, prior to taking any position in the futures market, his net worth is inversely related to the settlement price on the futures contract; i.e., a higher settlement price is associated with a lower net worth. Taking a long position in the futures contract will, therefore, reduce the sensitivity of his net worth to changes in that settlement price. If the settlement price rises after he has assumed a long position, his gains on that long position will offset the other losses which he experiences.

[7] A short hedger is defined as a market participant whose assets and liabilities are such that, prior to taking any position in the futures market, his net worth is directly related to the settlement price on the futures contract; i.e., a higher settlement price is associated with a higher net worth, and a lower settlement price is associated with a lower net worth.

rium settlement price in a futures market composed of risk-averse hedgers, we need to investigate the supply of and demand for futures contracts by hedgers.

Demand for Long Positions by Long Hedgers

Consider a long hedger who has to decide at time t whether (1) to take a long position in a futures contract which will be settled at time $t+k$ or (2) to wait and buy the asset in the spot market at time $t + k$.[8] Let $P_t(k)$ be the settlement price at time t on a futures contract which will be settled k periods later (at time $t + k$), let P_{t+k} be the spot market price prevailing at time $t + k$, and let $\text{Exp}_t [P_{t+k}]$ be the value of P_{t+k} which market participants expect as of time t.[9]

If the settlement price on the futures contract is less than the expected future spot price, a long hedger would clearly be better off taking a long position in the futures contract rather than waiting to buy in the spot market. For example, suppose the settlement price is $P_t(k) = \$90$ and the expected future spot price is $\text{Exp}_t [P_{t+k}] = \$100$. By taking a long position in the futures contract, the long hedger can eliminate all uncertainty about his future purchase price *and* can contract now to buy at a price of $90, which is lower than the $100 price he expects he would have to pay if he waited and bought in the spot market at time $t + k$. Thus, if $P_t(k) < \text{Exp}_t [P_{t+k}]$, a long hedger would want to eliminate *all* his risk exposure by taking a sufficiently large long position in the futures contract.[10]

If the settlement price on the futures contract exceeds the expected future spot price, a long hedger can reduce his risk exposure only by contracting now to buy at a price greater than the expected future spot price. For example, if $P_t(k) = \$110$ and $\text{Exp}_t [P_{t+k}] = \$100$, then a long hedger must expect to pay $10 to eliminate his risk exposure. That is, to eliminate uncertainty about the cost of the asset to be purchased at time $t + k$, the long hedger must agree at time t to pay $110, which is more than the $100 he expects he would have to pay if he waited until time $t + k$ to fix the terms of his purchase. In general, the larger the premium of the settlement price $P_t(k)$ over the expected future spot price,

---

[8] For expositional simplicity we assume long hedgers have a direct demand for the asset traded for future delivery. It could also be the case that a long hedger has a direct demand for asset A, for example, but that a long position in a futures contract on asset B is useful for cross hedging part of his risk exposure. In that case he would have a choice between (1) taking a long position in a futures contract on asset B or (2) waiting to buy asset A in the spot market at time $t + k$. If he chooses (1), then at time $t + k$ he will take delivery of asset B on his futures contract, sell that asset, and buy asset A (which is what he wanted in the first place) with the proceeds. This will be an imperfect hedge if the spot market prices of asset A and asset B are not perfectly correlated, and the long hedger will bear basis risk. See footnote 30 in Chapter 15.

[9] The analysis of this chapter assumes homogeneous expectations of future spot market prices which are invariant with respect to changes in current settlement prices on futures contracts. Cox (1976) has investigated whether settlement prices might not contain information valuable to market participants, and hence affect expectations. See also Grossman (1976) and Grossman and Stiglitz (1976) for an analysis of the effect of current prices on future expectations.

[10] This is similar to the result from term structure theory that an investor with a two-period horizon would have no reason to buy one-period debt if the risk premium L_1 were positive. See Section 14.4. If he contracted the maturity of his investments, he would expect to earn a lower return and would bear risk.

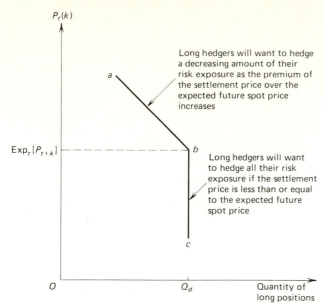

FIGURE 16.1
Demand for long positions in a futures contract from long hedgers.

the greater the "cost" of hedging and the smaller the demand by long hedgers for long positions in the futures contract.[11]

Figure 16.1 shows the demand for long positions in a futures contract by long hedgers as a function of the settlement price. Q_d is the number of futures contracts which would eliminate all of the risk borne by the long hedgers. If $P_t(k)$ is less than or equal to the expected future spot price $\text{Exp}_t [P_{t+k}]$, then long hedgers will want to hedge all of their risk. This is shown in Figure 16.1 as segment bc of the demand schedule. As $P_t(k)$ rises above $\text{Exp}_t [P_{t+k}]$, long hedgers will progressively reduce their demand for long futures positions. This is shown in Figure 16.1 as segment ab of the demand schedule. Segment ab of that schedule will be more nearly vertical the greater the risk aversion of long hedgers. This follows because more risk-averse long hedgers will be willing to pay a greater price, in terms of foregone expectations of profit, to hedge a given amount of risk, or to enter into a given number of long futures contracts.

Supply of Long Positions from Short Hedgers

The supply of long positions in a futures contract can be derived by examining the economic incentives of short hedgers. At time t, a short hedger has to

---

[11] This implies that hedgers are not completely risk-averse. They are willing to bear some risk if they can thereby expect to make more than they would make if they were fully hedged. This is similar to the result from term-structure theory that an investor with a two-period horizon may be willing to buy one-period debt if the risk premium L_1 is negative. See Section 14.4.

decide whether (1) to reduce his risk exposure by taking a short position in a futures contract which will be settled at time $t + k$ or (2) to wait and sell the asset in the spot market at time $t + k$.[12]

If the futures market settlement price $P_t(k)$ is greater than the expected future spot price, a short hedger would clearly be better off taking a short futures position rather than waiting to sell in the spot market. He can then eliminate all of his risk exposure, and he can contract now to sell at a price greater than he expects to get if he waited to sell in the spot market at time $t + k$. Thus, if $P_t(k) > \text{Exp}_t [P_{t+k}]$, a short hedger would want to hedge all of his risk.

If the settlement price on the futures contract is less than the expected future spot price, a short hedger can reduce his risk exposure only by contracting now to sell at a price less than the expected future spot price. The larger the discount of the settlement price below the expected future spot price, the greater the cost of reducing risk for a short hedger and the smaller his demand for short futures positions.

Figure 16.2 shows the supply of long positions in a futures contract from short hedgers as a function of the settlement price on that contract. (The supply of long positions from short hedgers is identical to their demand for short positions. Demand for a short position is demand for a forward commitment to sell. This is equivalent to a supply of a forward commitment to buy.) In Figure 16.2, Q_s is the number of futures contracts which would eliminate all of the risk borne by short hedgers. If $P_t(k)$ is greater than or equal to the expected future spot price $\text{Exp}_t [P_{t+k}]$, short hedgers will want to hedge all of their risk. This is shown in Figure 16.2 as segment de of the supply schedule. As $P_t(k)$ falls below $\text{Exp}_t [P_{t+k}]$, short hedgers will progressively reduce their supply of long positions. This is shown in Figure 16.2 as segment ef of the supply schedule.

Equilibrium in the Futures Market

The market in a futures contract will be in equilibrium when the settlement price on that contract is such that the supply of long positions just equals the demand for long positions. Thus, we need to place the demand schedule of Figure 16.1 on top of the supply schedule of Figure 16.2 and examine where the two schedules intersect.

Figure 16.3 shows one way the futures market can come into equilibrium. In that figure the quantity of long positions which would eliminate all of the risk borne by long hedgers exceeds the quantity of short positions which would

---

[12] For expositional simplicity we assume short hedgers have a direct supply of the asset traded for future delivery. For example, the mortgage banker in Section 15.3 has a direct supply of GNMA pass-throughs as a result of his origination of mortgages to homeowners. It could also be the case that a short hedger has a direct supply of asset A, for example, but that a short position in a futures contract on asset B is useful for cross hedging part of his risk exposure. For example, the commercial bank in Section 15.4 has a direct supply of its own CDs but takes a short position in futures on Treasury bills to hedge its risk exposure on forward commitments in commercial lending.

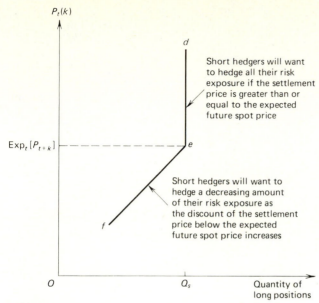

FIGURE 16.2
Supply of long positions in a futures contract from short hedgers.

FIGURE 16.3
Equilibrium in a futures market with a preponderance of long hedgers.

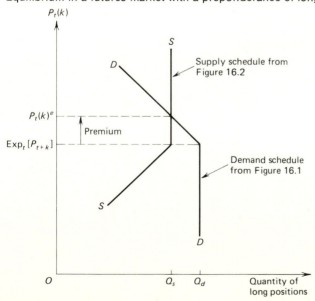

eliminate all of the risk borne by short hedgers, that is, $Q_d > Q_s$. This means that Figure 16.3 shows a futures market with a preponderance of long hedgers. In this case the equilibrium settlement price, denoted $P_t(k)^e$, exceeds the expected future spot price. The premium of the settlement price over the expected future spot price serves to ration the demand for long positions by long hedgers down to the supply of long positions forthcoming from fully hedged short hedgers.

Figure 16.4 shows a case opposite to that of Figure 16.3. Figure 16.4 shows a futures market with a preponderence of short hedgers, that is, $Q_d < Q_s$. In this case the equilibrium settlement price $P_t(k)^e$ is less than the expected future spot price. The discount on the settlement price serves to ration the supply of long positions forthcoming from short hedgers down to the demand for long positions by fully hedged long hedgers.

Comparing Figures 16.3 and 16.4 shows that if only risk-averse hedgers participate in a futures market, then the equilibrium settlement price on a futures contract can be either greater or less than the spot market price which is expected to prevail on the settlement date of that contract. If long hedgers predominate over short hedgers, the equilibrium settlement price will exceed the expected future spot price. (See Figure 16.3.) If short hedgers predominate over long hedgers, the equilibrium settlement price will be less than the expected future spot price. (See Figure 16.4.)

The Meaning of Open Interest in a Futures Market Limited to Hedgers The open interest in a futures contract is the number of outstanding contracts and

FIGURE 16.4
Equilibrium in a futures market with a preponderance of short hedgers.

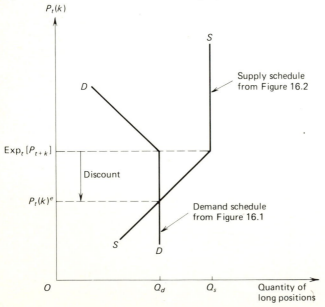

may be measured by the volume of long positions in the contract or by the volume of short positions in the contract. These two numbers must be identical, because for every buyer for deferred delivery there must be a seller for deferred delivery.

Open interest is an index of aggregate risk reduction in a futures market where only hedgers participate. Since long hedgers and short hedgers have congruent perceptions of the risk of not entering into a futures contract, a completed contract reduces the risk exposure of both of the parties to the contract.[13] The open interest in Figure 16.3 is Q_s. In this case short hedgers have eliminated all of their exposure to risk, and long hedgers have eliminated some, but not all, of their exposure. The open interest in Figure 16.4 is Q_d. In this case the opposite is true: long hedgers have eliminated all of their exposure to risk, and short hedgers have eliminated some, but not all, of their exposure.

16.2 EQUILIBRIUM SETTLEMENT PRICES IN A FUTURES MARKET WITH HEDGERS AND SPECULATORS

Speculators are market participants who bear risk if they are either long *or* short in a futures contract.[14] The difference between a hedger and a speculator is not one of more or less aversion to risk; a speculator may be just as risk-averse as a hedger. Rather, the difference is whether taking a position in a futures contract reduces risk or increases risk. A long position reduces the risk exposure of a long hedger. A short position reduces the risk exposure of a short hedger. Either a long position or a short position increases the risk exposure of a speculator.

Speculators, like other investors, will bear risk only if they can expect to profit. The expectation of profit leads to both a demand for and a supply of long futures positions from speculators. We first consider the characteristics of this speculative demand and supply, and then we add the demands and supplies of long positions from speculators to the demands and supplies from hedgers to determine the characteristics of a futures market in equilibrium when both hedgers and speculators participate in that market.

Demand for Long Positions by Speculators

In general, a speculator will acquire a long position in a futures contract if he can expect to make a profit reselling the asset in the spot market on the settle-

---

[13] See the discussion of the short hedging mortgage banker and the long hedging pension fund in Section 15.3.

[14] A speculator may be defined as a market participant whose assets and liabilities are such that, prior to taking any position in the futures market, his net worth is independent of changes in the settlement price on the futures contract; i.e., his net worth remains the same regardless of whether the settlement price rises or falls. Taking a long position in the futures contract would then make his net worth vary directly with the settlement price. Taking a short position would make his net worth vary inversely with the settlement price. It should be noted, however, that a futures position may not make *any* marginal contribution to the risk exposure of a speculator with a well-diversified portfolio of other assets. See Dusak (1973).

ment date.[15] The bigger the expected profit, the larger the long position he will want, i.e., the more risk he will be willing to bear.

If the settlement price on a futures contract is lower than the spot market price expected on the settlement date, a speculator can expect to profit by assuming a long position in that contract. Suppose, for example, the settlement price is $P_t(k) = \$90$ and the expected future spot price is $\text{Exp}_t [P_{t+k}] = \$100$. A speculator might acquire a long position in the futures contract, with the expectation of taking delivery of the asset on the settlement date and then reselling that asset in the spot market. The speculator knows he will have to pay out $90 at time $t + k$ to take delivery of the asset pursuant to his futures contract, because $P_t(k) = \$90$, and he currently expects to be able to sell the asset in the spot market at time $t \times k$ at a price of $100, because $\text{Exp}_t [P_{t+k}] = \$100$. Thus, the speculator expects to make $10 at time $t + k$. More generally, if $P_t(k) < \text{Exp}_t [P_{t+k}]$, long futures positions opened at time t are *expected* to yield a positive profit if they are held to settlement at time $t + k$.

There is, of course, no guarantee that the actual spot market price at time $t + k$ will equal its expected value; i.e., there is no guarantee that P_{t+k} will equal $\text{Exp}_t [P_{t+k}]$. The profits expected on a speculative futures position are uncertain, and the position is risky. This implies that the smaller the discount of $P_t(k)$ below $\text{Exp}_t [P_{t+k}]$, the smaller the demand for long positions by speculators.

If the settlement price on a futures contract exceeds the expected future spot market price, speculators will not want to hold any long position at all in that futures contract, because they cannot expect to profit from such a position.

Figure 16.5 shows the demand for long positions in a futures contract by speculators as a function of the settlement price. When the settlement price exceeds the expected future spot price, the speculative demand for long positions will be zero. This is shown as segment ab in Figure 16.5. As $P_t(k)$ falls to a discount below $\text{Exp}_t [P_{t+k}]$, speculators will be enticed into holding long positions (and bearing risk) because of an expectation of profit. The larger the discount, the larger the expected profit, and so the greater the willingness of speculators to bear risk. This is shown as segment bc in Figure 16.5.

The degree of risk aversion of speculators determines the slope of segment bc of the demand schedule in Figure 16.5. If speculators are highly risk-averse, they will be willing to bear a given amount of risk only if they expect large profits. In that case segment bc may be nearly vertical. If, on the other hand, speculators are largely indifferent to risk, they will demand large long positions at relatively small discounts of the settlement price below the expected future spot price. In that case line segment bc will be nearly horizontal.[16] In an ex-

---

[15] A speculator may also take a long position in a futures contract if he can expect to liquidate that position at a profit prior to settlement.

[16] Segment bc may also be horizontal if a long position does not make any marginal contribution to an individual speculator's total risk exposure, even if speculators are highly risk-averse. Dusak (1973) found that futures contracts on three commodities (wheat, corn, and soybeans) would not, in fact, add to the risk of a well-diversified stock portfolio. This result suggests that the speculative demand for long positions in future contracts on those commodities may be highly elastic with respect to increases in the discount of the settlement price below the expected future spot price.

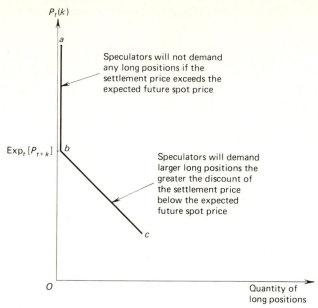

FIGURE 16.5
Demand for long positions in a futures contract from speculators.

treme case, if speculators were completely indifferent to risk, line segment bc would be completely horizontal.

Supply of Long Positions from Speculators

If the settlement price on a futures contract is greater than the spot market price expected on the settlement date, i.e., if $P_t(k) > \text{Exp}_t [P_{t+k}]$, then a speculator can expect to profit by assuming a short position in that contract. For example, suppose the settlement price is $P_t(k) = \$115$ and the expected future spot price is $\text{Exp}_t [P_{t+k}] = \$100$. If a speculator went short a futures contract at time t, with the expectation of buying the asset in the spot market on the settlement date to make delivery against his short futures contract, he would expect to make a profit. The speculator would expect to pay $100 at time $t + k$ to acquire the asset in the spot market, because $\text{Exp}_t [P_{t+k}] = \$100$, and he knows he will receive $115 when he delivers that asset against his short futures contract, because $P_t(k) = \$115$. Thus, he expects to make $15 at time $t + k$. More generally, when $P_t(k) > \text{Exp}_t [P_{t+k}]$, short futures positions opened at time t are expected to yield a positive profit if they are held to settlement at time $t + k$. The larger the premium of $P_t(k)$ over $\text{Exp}_t [P_{t+k}]$, the greater the expected profit and the greater the demand for short positions (or supply of long positions) by speculators. If the settlement price on a futures contract is less than the expected future spot price, speculators will be unwilling to hold short positions in the futures contract, because they could not expect to profit from those positions.

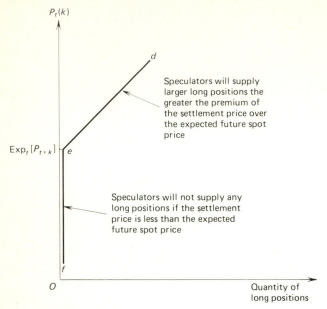

FIGURE 16.6
Supply of long positions in a futures contract from speculators.

Figure 16.6 shows the supply of long positions in a futures contract from speculators as a function of the settlement price. When $P_t(k)$ is less than the expected future spot price $\text{Exp}_t\,[P_{t+k}]$, the supply of long positions from speculators will be zero. This is shown as segment ef in Figure 16.6. As $P_t(k)$ rises to a premium above $\text{Exp}_t[P_{t+k}]$, speculators will be encouraged to hold short positions, i.e., to supply long positions, because of an expectation of profit. The larger the premium, the larger the expected profit, and so the greater the speculative supply of long futures positions. This is shown as segment de in Figure 16.6. The slope of segment de is determined by the risk aversion of the speculators: the lower their risk aversion, the more nearly horizontal that segment of the supply schedule.[17]

Comparing Figures 16.5 and 16.6 shows when speculators will demand long futures positions and when they will supply long futures positions. If the settlement price exceeds the expected future spot price, speculators will supply long futures positions (see segment de in Figure 16.6), but they will not demand any of those positions (see segment ab in Figure 16.5). If, on the other hand, the settlement price is less than the expected future spot price, speculators will have a positive demand for long futures positions (see segment bc in Figure 16.5), but they will not supply any of those positions (see segment ef in Figure 16.6). At any given settlement price, speculators may either demand or supply long futures positions—depending on whether that settlement price is below or

[17] Segment de may also be nearly horizontal if short positions in futures contracts do not make any substantial marginal contribution to an individual speculator's aggregate risk exposure. See footnote 16 above.

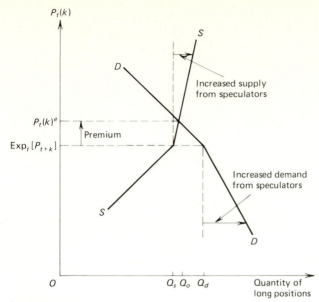

FIGURE 16.7
Equilibrium in a futures market with speculators and a preponderance of long hedgers.

above the expected future spot price—but they will not do both.[18] Thus, speculators make a net contribution to the demand for long positions in a futures contract when the settlement price is below the expected future spot price, and they make a net contribution to the supply of long positions when the settlement price exceeds the expected future spot price. This behavior has important consequences for the equilibrium settlement price in a futures market composed of both hedgers and speculators.

Equilibrium in the Futures Market

The market in futures contracts due to be settled at time $t + k$ will be in equilibrium when the settlement price on a contract is such that the aggregate demand for long positions (by both hedgers and speculators) equals the aggregate supply of long positions (from both hedgers and speculators).

Figure 16.7 shows an equilibrium in a futures market with a preponderance of long hedgers over short hedgers. The aggregate demand schedule in that figure, denoted DD, is the sum of the demand schedules shown in Figures 16.1 and 16.5.[19] The aggregate supply schedule, denoted SS, is the sum of the supply

[18] This statement will not be true if different speculators have different expectations about future spot market prices. Speculators who expect high spot market prices in the future might then demand long futures positions at the same time that speculators who expect low spot market prices in the future are supplying long futures positions.

[19] The demand schedules are aggregated by adding horizontally. That is, at any given settlement price the demand from long hedgers shown in Figure 16.1 is added to the demand from speculators shown in Figure 16.5 and the total is located on the horizontal axis of Figure 16.7.

schedules shown in Figures 16.2 and 16.6. Note how the presence of speculators leads to a greater aggregate supply of long positions when the settlement
price $P_t(k)$ exceeds the expected future spot price $\text{Exp}_t\ [P_{t+k}]$, and how the
presence of speculators leads to a greater aggregate demand for long positions
when $P_t(k)$ is less than $\text{Exp}_t\ [P_{t+k}]$.

As shown in Figure 16.7, the addition of speculators to a futures market with
a preponderance of long hedgers means that the equilibrium settlement price
will be at a smaller premium over the expected future spot price. A smaller
premium is adequate to bring the market into equilibrium, because it is no
longer necessary to ration the demand for long positions by long hedgers all the
way down the supply forthcoming from short hedgers. With speculators in the
market, long hedgers can contract to buy for deferred delivery from speculators
as well as from short hedgers.

Figure 16.8 shows an equilibrium in a futures market with a preponderance
of short hedgers over long hedgers. The existence of a demand for long positions from speculators when $P_t(k)$ is less than $\text{Exp}_t\ [P_{t+k}]$ implies that the
equilibrium settlement price will be at a smaller discount to the expected future
spot price than would be the case if there were no speculators. A smaller discount is adequate, because it is not necessary to ration the supply of long positions from short hedgers all the way down to the demand forthcoming from long
hedgers. With speculators in the market, short hedgers can make commitments
to sell for deferred delivery to speculators as well as to long hedgers.

The foregoing discussion shows that when risk-averse speculators participate in a futures market along with hedgers, the equilibrium settlement price
can be either above or below the expected future spot price. This qualitative
result is not different from the result reached in Section 16.1 for a futures
market composed only of hedgers. The effect of speculative activity in a futures
market is quantitative rather than qualitative: speculators narrow the difference
between the equilibrium settlement price and the expected future spot market
price.[20]

The Special Case of Speculators Who Are Indifferent to Risk In general, the
lower the risk aversion of speculators, the smaller the difference between the
settlement price on a futures contract and the expected future spot price. In an
extreme case, if speculators are completely indifferent to risk, the two prices
will be identical. This can be seen by imagining that segment *bc* of the speculative demand schedule shown in Figure 16.5 and segment *de* of the speculative
supply schedule shown in Figure 16.6 are horizontal at a settlement price equal
to the expected future spot price. In this case speculators demand arbitrarily
large long positions if $P_t(k)$ is less than $\text{Exp}_t\ [P_{t+k}]$ by any small amount, and
they supply arbitrarily large long positions if $P_t(k)$ exceeds $\text{Exp}_t\ [P_{t+k}]$ by any

---

[20] This may not be true if market participants have heterogeneous expectations. In that case
unusually optimistic speculators might pull the equilibrium settlement price above where it would
be if the market were limited to hedgers, or unusually pessimistic speculators might push the equilibrium settlement price below where it would be if the market were limited to hedgers.

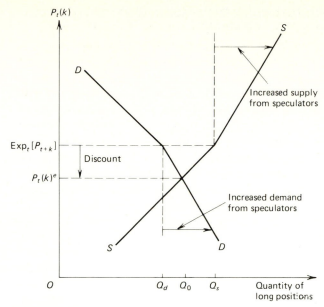

FIGURE 16.8
Equilibrium in a futures market with speculators and a preponderance of short hedgers.

small amount. In equilibrium, the settlement price must then be equal to the expected future spot price.[21]

The Meaning of Open Interest in a Futures Market Composed of Hedgers and Speculators   Open interest in a futures market which includes hedgers and speculators is an index of both aggregate risk reduction and risk transfer. In Figure 16.7 the open interest is Q_o. This open interest can be decomposed into an index of aggregate risk reduction and an index of risk transfer. Risk reduction occurs when short and long hedgers match their congruent perceptions of risk. This may be measured by Q_s in Figure 16.7. In addition, long hedgers in that figure are transferring to speculators some of their exposure to risk. This risk transfer may be measured by $Q_o - Q_s$. Note that Q_s does not depend on the presence or degree of risk aversion of speculators, but that $Q_o - Q_s$ will be greater the lower the risk aversion of those speculators.

Figure 16.8 shows an opposite situation. In that case short hedgers are matching and eliminating risk with long hedgers in an amount measured by Q_d, and they are transferring risk to speculators in an amount measured by $Q_o - Q_d$.

[21] Segment bc in Figure 16.5 and segment de in Figure 16.6 will be horizontal, and the settlement price will equal the expected future spot price, if futures positions do not make any marginal contribution to a speculator's risk exposure. In that case the expected change in settlement prices over some interval of time will be zero. Dusak (1973) presents evidence in support of this view for three commodities: wheat, corn, and soybeans. See also Black (1976) and Samuelson (1965).

16.3 RISKLESS ARBITRAGE BETWEEN A FUTURES MARKET AND THE SPOT MARKET FOR THE SAME ASSET

The preceding section examined the determinants of equilibrium settlement prices in a futures market composed of hedgers and speculators. The demand for and supply of long positions by those market participants was seen to depend on a comparision between (1) the price at which a participant can contract now to buy or sell later, i.e., the futures market settlement price, and (2) the price at which a participant *expects* he will be able to buy or sell later, i.e., the expected future spot market price. This particular price comparision is relevant for both hedgers and speculators, because they both view transactions in a futures market as substitutes for deferred transactions in a spot market. A long hedger, for example, has a choice between contracting now to buy later or waiting to buy later, and a short hedger has a choice between contracting now to sell later or waiting to sell later. It makes sense, therefore, that both hedgers and speculators should compare current settlement prices with expected future spot prices when deciding whether to assume positions in futures contracts.

When a long position in a futures contract is not more than a substitute for a deferred spot market purchase, it is reasonable to conclude the analysis of equilibrium settlement prices after examining the activities of hedgers and speculators. In some cases, however, a long position in a futures contract can also be a substitute for a *current* spot market purchase. In these cases it is unreasonable to suppose that settlement prices on futures contracts are determined solely by the activities of hedgers and speculators in the futures market. As described in this section and the following section, those settlement prices must also depend on the activities of arbitrageurs and on conditions of supply and demand in the spot market.

Arbitrage is a simultaneous purchase and sale of the same asset in two different markets that produces an immediately foreseeable net profit with no risk. One example of a riskless arbitrage is the purchase (or sale) of an asset in a spot market together with a matching sale (or purchase) of the same asset in a futures market.[22] The first part of this section describes circumstances sufficient to guarantee the existence of positive net profits with no risk on arbitrage transactions between a spot market and a futures market.

The settlement price on a futures contract cannot be an equilibrium price if it gives investors an opportunity to make a positive net profit with no risk. The second part of this section shows why this statement is true, and it derives a particular relation between spot market prices, futures market settlement prices, and the level of interest rates which must hold when a futures market is in equilibrium. This price relationship will be used in the following section to examine the determinants of the equilibrium settlement price on a futures contract when arbitrage with the spot market for the underlying asset is possible.

For the sake of expositional simplicity we will assume that an asset does not

---

[22] An appendix to this chapter describes more complicated arbitrage involving spread positions in futures contracts, i.e., matched long and short positions in futures contracts on the same asset with different settlement dates.

make any payments prior to the settlement date of a futures contract on that asset. This assumption is valid for Treasury bills but may not be valid for stocks (which usually pay dividends) or for Treasury bonds (which make semi-annual coupon payments). An appendix to this chapter shows how the results of the analysis should be altered for assets that make payments prior to the settlement of futures contracts.

Arbitrage between the Spot Market and the Futures Market

There are two ways of making riskless profits from arbitrage transactions involving a spot market and a futures market: buying an asset in the spot market and contracting to sell in the futures market, and short selling[23] the asset in the spot market and contracting to buy in the futures market. We examine below the conditions which will guarantee the existence of a riskless profit on either of these two pairs of transactions.

Spot Market Purchases and Short Positions in the Futures Market   If an asset deliverable against a futures contract can be purchased in a spot market transaction and can be costlessly inventoried[24] without spoiling, an arbitrageur could buy that asset in the spot market, carry it in his inventory for a period of time, and then deliver it in settlement of a short position in a maturing futures contract. Suppose, at time t, the price of an asset in the spot market is $P_t = \$80$, and the settlement price of a futures contract on that asset due to settle at time $t + k$ is $P_t(k) = \$100$. An arbitrageur could then purchase the asset in the spot market for $80 and simultaneously contract to sell the asset k periods later for $100 (by going short a futures contract). The *gross* profit on the spot purchase and deferred sale would be $20 ($100 proceeds received from settling the short futures position, less $80 purchase price).

This gross profit is riskless for the arbitrageur. His capital investment is fixed at time t at $P_t = \$80$, and his sale proceeds are also fixed at time t at $P_t(k) = \$100$. (He will not receive these proceeds until time $t + k$, but he knows at time t what they will be.) Since the arbitrageur has possession of the asset, he also knows he will be able to deliver that asset to settle his short futures position.

The foregoing transaction will present an opportunity for a riskless *net* profit if the arbitrageur can borrow for k periods the $80 needed to buy the asset and thereby obligate himself to repay something less than $100 at time $t + k$. Suppose, for example, the interval between time t and time $t + k$ is 1 year, and that an arbitrageur would have to promise to repay $90 in 1 year in order to borrow $80 now. The arbitrageur could then borrow $80, use that money to buy the asset in the spot market, and go short on a futures contract with a settlement price of $100. At the end of 1 year he would deliver the asset to settle his fu-

---

[23] Short sales of securities are described in Section 7.4.
[24] The most important inventory cost is warehousing fees, such as silo charges for grain. Warehousing (i.e., safekeeping) fees for securities are negligible and are ignored in this analysis.

tures contract, receive $100 payment, and pay off his loan by remitting $90 to his creditor. He would be left with a net profit of $10 on a riskless transaction.

The foregoing example can be generalized into a statement of a sufficient condition for a riskless net profit on arbitrage between a spot market and a futures market. Let $R_{k,t}$ be the continuously compounded yield per period on k-period debt at time t. This means that if an arbitrageur borrows $100 at time t, he will be obligated to pay back $100 \cdot \exp [k \cdot R_{k,t}]$ at time $t + k$.[25] There will be an opportunity for a riskless net arbitrage profit when

$$P_t(k) > P_t \cdot \exp [k \cdot R_{k,t}] \qquad (16.1)$$

If the inequality in Equation (16.1) holds, an arbitrageur could make a riskless profit by borrowing the amount P_t for k periods at the yield $R_{k,t}$, buying the asset in the spot market with the borrowed money, and simultaneously contracting to sell the same asset in the futures market for delivery and settlement at time $t + k$. On the settlement date of his futures contract he would receive $P_t(k)$ for delivering the asset, and he would have to repay $P_t \cdot \exp [k \cdot R_{k,t}]$ to his creditor. His net profit would be $P_t(k) - P_t \cdot \exp [k \cdot R_{k,t}]$, which, by Equation (16.1), is positive. Thus, the arbitrageur would have earned a positive profit with zero risk.

Spot Market Short Sales and Long Positions in the Futures Market   The preceding discussion described how an arbitrageur can make a riskless profit if the settlement price on a futures contract is "too high" relative to the contemporaneous spot market price of the asset, and if that asset can be costlessly inventoried without spoiling. An arbitrageur can also make a riskless profit if the settlement price on a futures contract is "too low" relative to the spot market price of the asset, and if that asset can be sold short in the spot market.

If an asset can be sold short in the spot market, an arbitrageur could short sell that asset and then cover his short position with a purchase of the same asset through settlement of a long position in a maturing futures contract. Suppose, at time t, the price of an asset in the spot market is $P_t = \$80$, and the settlement price on a futures contract due to be settled at time $t + k$ is $P_t(k) = \$85$. If an arbitrageur sold the asset short in the spot market for $80 and simultaneously contracted to buy it back k periods later for $85 (by going long on a futures contract), he would suffer a gross loss of $5 ($85 paid out to settle the long futures contract, less $80 received from the short sale of the asset in the spot market). However, the arbitrageur would have the use of $80 cash for k periods. If he can invest this $80 in debt securities that mature on the settlement date of the futures contract and that pay more than $5 interest, the whole transaction will yield a net profit.

The foregoing example can be generalized into a statement of a second sufficient condition for a riskless profit on an arbitrage transaction. Let $R_{k,t}$ be the

---

[25] The beginning of Section 14.2 describes the relation between present value and future value when yields are compounded continuously.

continuously compounded yield per period on k-period debt at time t. There will be an opportunity for a riskless net arbitrage profit if

$$P_t(k) < P_t \cdot \exp\ [k \cdot R_{k,t}] \qquad (16.2)$$

If the inequality in Equation (16.2) holds, an arbitrageur can make a riskless profit by short selling the asset in the spot market at a price of P_t, investing the proceeds in k-period debt, and simultaneously going long on a futures contract for settlement at time $t + k$. On the settlement date he would receive $P_t \cdot \exp\ [k \cdot R_{k,t}]$ from his maturing debt investment, and he would have to pay out $P_t(k)$ to settle his long futures contract. His net profit would be $P_t \cdot \exp\ [k \cdot R_{k,t}] - P_t(k)$, which, by Equation (16.2), is positive. The asset received from settling the long futures contract would be returned to the person who lent the arbitrageur that asset to deliver against the short sale made at time t.

It should be noted that the foregoing transaction is riskless. After entering into the short sale and long futures contract at time t, and after buying k-period debt at that time, the arbitrageur knows that he has an obligation to return the asset which he borrowed to deliver against the spot market short sale. However, he also knows he will be able to acquire that asset at time $t + k$, when his long futures position is settled at a price $P_t(k)$ fixed at time t. In addition, he knows he will have the funds needed to complete that purchase, because he knows that the maturity value of his debt investment, $P_t \cdot \exp\ [k \cdot R_{k,t}]$, will exceed the settlement price $P_t(k)$ on his futures contract [see Equation (16.2)].

Summary   The foregoing discussions described two types of arbitrage transactions between the spot and futures markets for an asset. The incentive to enter into either of the transactions is riskless profit. An arbitrageur can be quite indifferent about whether the asset is a Treasury bill or a jelly bean, and he can be completely ignorant about the forces that determine either the spot market price or the futures market settlement price of that asset. All he needs to know is that he can use the spot market to eliminate all of the risk associated with going long or short on a futures contract, and that he can make a positive profit net of his financing costs or interest earnings.

It should be noted that the foregoing analysis is *not* applicable to all futures markets. In particular, the analysis is applicable only if all of the following hold:

1 The asset *deliverable* on a futures contract can be bought and sold in a spot market.
2 The asset can be costlessly inventoried without spoiling.
3 The asset can be sold short in the spot market.

Not all assets traded for future delivery can be bought and sold in spot market transactions. For example, the International Monetary Market of the Chicago Mercantile Exchange sponsors trading in 3-month Treasury bill futures with a settlement date 1 year in the future. Bills deliverable against that contract do not exist, because such bills would have to have a maturity date 15 months in the future. [The maximum maturity of a Treasury bill at original issue is presently 52 weeks (see Section 1.1).][26]

Even when a deliverable asset can be bought and sold in spot market transactions, it may be impossible to inventory that asset at no cost without spoiling. Although inventory costs and spoilage are not a problem for securities, they are important for assets like grains and orange juice.

Finally, not all assets can be sold short in the spot market. For example, commercial paper and GNMA pass-throughs cannot be sold short in spot market transactions, because a short seller can never be sure that he will be able to locate and purchase a comparable security to return to the lender of the security sold short. Short sales are possible, however, with Treasury bills, Treasury notes, and Treasury bonds.

Partial Equilibrium between the Spot Market and the Futures Market

A market is in equilibrium when total demand is equal to aggregate supply. If the inequality of Equation (16.1), or the inequality of Equation (16.2), holds, the spot and futures markets for the asset cannot be in equilibrium, because there will be unlimited demand for, or supply of, the asset for immediate and deferred delivery arising out of arbitrage transactions. The only remaining possibility is that

$$P_t(k) = P_t \cdot \exp\left[k \cdot R_{k,t}\right] \tag{16.3}$$

As discussed below, Equation (16.3) is a condition of partial equilibrium *between* the spot market for an asset and the futures market for the same asset.

The Inequality $P_t(k) > P_t \cdot \exp\left[k \cdot R_{k,t}\right]$ Cannot Hold in an Equilibrium
Suppose the inequality of Equation (16.1) were true. We saw above that that inequality is a sufficient condition to make a riskless profit by:

1 Buying the asset in the spot market at price P_t
2 Contracting to sell the asset for deferred delivery in the futures market at settlement price $P_t(k)$
3 Borrowing funds for k periods at an interest rate of $R_{k,t}$ per period

Thus, if the inequaltiy of Equation (16.1) were true, there would be an unlimited demand for the asset in the spot market, there would be an unlimited supply of the asset in the futures market, and there would be an unlimited demand for credit with a k-period maturity. None of the three markets (spot market, futures market, and market for k-period credit) could be in equilibrium. More particularly, arbitrage transactions would put upward pressure on the spot market price of the asset and on the cost of k-period credit. The same arbitrage transac-

---

[26] Similarly, the bills deliverable on a futures contract in 1-year Treasury bills *never* exist prior to the settlement date on that contract, because the settlement date is fixed to coincide with the sale of those bills by the Treasury.

tions would also put downward pressure on the futures market settlement price. These pressures would cease only when

$$P_t(k) \leq P_t \cdot \exp [k \cdot R_{k,t}] \qquad (16.4)$$

Thus, the inequality of Equation (16.4) must hold in an equilibrium.

The Inequality $P_t(k) < P_t \cdot \exp [k \cdot R_{k,t}]$ Cannot Hold in an Equilibrium Suppose the inequality of Equation (16.2) were true. We saw above that that inequality is a sufficient condition to make a riskless profit by:

1 Short selling the asset in the spot market at price P_t
2 Contracting to buy the asset for deferred delivery in the futures market at settlement price $P_t(k)$
3 Lending funds for k periods at an interest rate of $R_{k,t}$ per period

Thus, if the inequality of Equation (16.2) were true, arbitrage transactions would place downward pressure on the spot market price P_t, because of short sales of the asset in the spot market. Similarly, arbitrage transactions would place upward pressure on the futures market settlement price $P_t(k)$, because of demand for long positions in futures contracts. Finally, arbitrage transactions would place downward pressure on the cost of k-period credit, because k-period loans would be forthcoming from the investment of the proceeds of spot market short sales. These pressures would cease only when

$$P_t(k) \geq P_t \cdot \exp [k \cdot R_{k,t}] \qquad (16.5)$$

Thus, the inequality of Equation (16.5) must also hold in an equilibrium.

The Equality $P_t(k) = P_t \cdot \exp [k \cdot R_{k,t}]$ Must Hold in an Equilibrium   The preceding discussions showed that the inequalities of Equations (16.4) and (16.5) must *both* hold in an equilibrium. However, those inequalities can be true simultaneously only if

$$P_t(k) = P_t \cdot \exp [k \cdot R_{k,t}] \qquad (16.6)$$

Thus, Equation (16.6) is a necessary condition for an equilibrium between the spot market for an asset, the futures market for the asset, and the market for k-period credit.[27] If Equation (16.6) is not satisfied, there will be an opportunity to profit from a riskless arbitrage and there will be upward or downward pressures on spot market prices, futures market settlement prices, and the cost of k-period credit.

[27] Equation (16.6) has a particularly important meaning when the asset is a debt security that matures one period after the settlement date of the futures contract, i.e., at time $t + k + 1$. The futures contract is then a commitment for a one-period forward loan. This special case is discussed in an appendix to this chapter.

Equation (16.6) implies that equilibrium settlement prices of futures con-tracts will be an increasing function of the futurity of the settlement dates of those contracts. For given values of the spot market price P_t and the levels of interest rates $R_{k,t}$ ($k = 1, 2, \ldots$), the settlement prices $P_t(k)$ will increase with the number of periods in the future that settlement is scheduled. For example, suppose that $P_t = \$100$ and that $R_{k,t} = .10$, or 10 percent per period, for $k = 1$, 2, 3. Then, in eqilibrium, we would have

$$P_t(1) = P_t \cdot \exp\,[1 \cdot R_{1,t}]$$
$$= \$100 \cdot \exp\,[.10]$$
$$= \$110.52$$
$$P_t(2) = P_t \cdot \exp\,[2 \cdot R_{2,t}]$$
$$= \$100 \cdot \exp\,[.20]$$
$$= \$122.14$$

and

$$P_t(3) = P_t \cdot \exp\,[3 \cdot R_{3,t}]$$
$$= \$100 \cdot \exp\,[.30]$$
$$= \$134.99$$

In general, the higher the level of interest rates, the more rapidly settlement prices rise as a function of the futurity of settlement.[28]

Interpretation of Equation (16.6) requires some care. That equation does *not* imply that settlement prices on futures contracts are "determined" by the spot market price of an asset and the term structure of interest rates. Equation (16.6) is only a statement of a *relative* price relationship necessary (but not sufficient) for the spot and futures markets, and the credit markets, to be in simultaneous equilibrium.

The preceding point can be illustrated with a simple example. Suppose that the markets are intially in equilibrium [so that Equation (16.6) holds] and that an increased demand for long futures positions suddenly develops. This increased demand will, in the first instance, force up the settlement price on fu-tures contracts, so that $P_t(k)$ rises above $P_t \cdot \exp\,[k \cdot R_{k,t}]$. We know from the discussion in the beginning of this section that this will encourage arbitrageurs to buy the asset in the spot market and simultaneously contract to sell the asset for deferred delivery in the futures market. This arbitrage activity will put upward pressure on the spot market price P_t. In this way the original increase in demand for the asset for *future* delivery may be transformed into an increase in demand for the asset for *immediate* delivery, and it may push up the *spot* market price of the asset. More generally, the price of the asset in the spot market will depend on conditions of supply and demand in the futures market.

The equilibrium condition described by Equation (16.6) is called a *partial*

---

[28] The difference between the settlement price and the spot market price is sometimes called the *basis* of the futures contract. See Ederington (1979, p. 159). Equation (16.6) shows that, to a first-order approximation, the basis is $P_t(k) - P_t = P_t \cdot k \cdot R_{k,t}$. Thus, the basis of more distant contracts (large k) will be more sensitive to changes in the level of interest rates than the basis of near con-tracts (small k).

equilibrium, because it only specifies a relation *between* spot market prices and futures market settlement prices. It does not say anything about the determinants of the *level* of either the spot market price or the futures market settlement price. This question is addressed in the next section, which examines the collective influences of hedgers, speculators, and arbitrageurs in determining the equilibrium level of the settlement price on a futures contract.

16.4 EQUILIBRIUM SETTLEMENT PRICES IN A FUTURES MARKET WITH HEDGERS, SPECULATORS, AND ARBITRAGEURS

An equilibrium price is a price which equates supply and demand. We used this definition in Section 16.2 for a futures market composed of hedgers and speculators, and concluded that an equilibrium settlement price equates the aggregate *demand* for futures contracts by long hedgers and speculators to the aggregate *supply* of those contracts from short hedgers and speculators. Similarly, the analyses of stock markets in Chapter 11 and 12 and debt markets in Chapter 14 described equilibrium spot market prices as those prices which equate the spot market demand for an asset to the available supply of that asset.

When an asset can be bought and sold for both immediate and deferred delivery, and when it can be costlessly inventoried without spoiling and sold short in the spot market, neither of the foregoing notions of an equilibrium price are quite accurate. This follows because, as shown in the preceding section, spot market prices and settlement prices on futures contracts will be linked by arbitrage. This intermarket arbitrage precludes the existence of independent equilibriums in the spot and futures markets.

To analyze the characteristics of equilibrium prices when arbitrage between a spot market and a futures market is possible, we will it find useful first to consider the characteristics of supply and demand in the futures market and the spot market separately, and then to consider the consequences of integrating the two markets by arbitrage.

The Schedule of "Excess Demand" in the Futures Market

In Section 16.2 we analyzed the equilibrium settlement price on a futures contract using the schedules of demand and supply from hedgers and speculators. (See Figures 16.7 and 16.8.) For present purposes, however, it will be more convenient to speak of a single "excess demand" schedule.

At any given settlement price, the excess demand for long positions in a futures contract is the amount by which the demand for long positions (from hedgers and speculators) exceeds the supply of long positions (from hedgers and speculators). An excess demand schedule is the schedule of gross demand for long positions, *less* gross supply of long positions in a futures contract from hedgers and speculators as a function of the settlement price on that contract.

Figure 16.9 shows an excess demand schedule. The settlement price $P_t(k)^f$ in that figure is the settlement price that would equate the demand for long positions in the futures contract by long hedgers and speculators with the supply of

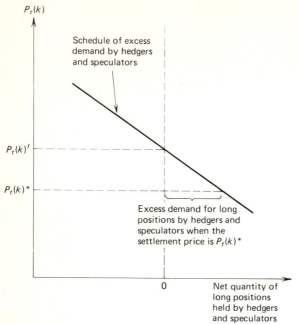

FIGURE 16.9
Equilibrium in the futures market.

long positions in that contract from short hedgers and speculators. More particularly, $P_t(k)^f$ would be the equilibrium settlement price if there were no
arbitrage activity with the spot market for the asset. We know from the results
of Section 16.2 that $P_t(k)^f$ will exceed the expected future spot market price if
the futures market has a preponderance of long hedgers over short hedgers.
(See Figure 16.7.) We also know that $P_t(k)^f$ will be less than the expected future
spot market price if the futures market has a preponderance of short hedgers
over long hedgers. (See Figure 16.8.)

Supply and Demand in the Spot Market

The next step in the analysis is to express the conditions of supply and demand in the spot market exclusive of arbitrage activity. Figure 16.10 assumes
that the total spot market supply of the asset is fixed at Q, and that the spot
market demand for the asset is a decreasing function of the price of that asset.[29]
The spot market price P_t^s in Figure 16.10 is the price which would equate the
aggregate spot market demand for the asset to the available supply of that asset
if there was no arbitrage with the futures market for the asset.

---

[29] The schedule of demand for the asset in the spot market can be expected to shift with changes
in the expected future price of the asset. See, for example, the analysis of the demand for stock in
Section 11.2.

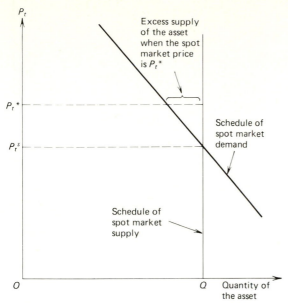

FIGURE 16.10
Equilibrium in the spot market.

Integrating the Spot and Futures Markets with Arbitrage

Thus far we have simply restated the determinants of equilibrium prices in *segmented* spot and futures markets. Suppose, however, that it is possible to arbitrage between those two markets, and suppose that $P_t(k)^f$ in Figure 16.9 is greater than $P_t^s \cdot \exp[k \cdot R_{k,t}]$ in Figure 16.10. We know from the analysis in Section 16.3 that this price relationship will trigger a *demand* for the asset in the spot market by arbitrageurs, and a *matching supply* of long positions in the futures market by the same arbitrageurs. [See the discussion at Equation (16.1).] This will have the effect of pushing the spot market price above P_t^s and pushing the futures market settlement price below $P_t(k)^f$.[30] These price pressures will continue as long as arbitrageurs can make a riskless profit by buying the asset in the spot market and simultaneously contracting to sell a matching amount of the same asset in the futures market.

Suppose arbitrage activity lowers the futures market settlement price to $P_t(k)^*$ in Figure 16.9 and raises the spot market price to P_t^* in Figure 16.10, and suppose those prices are such that $P_t(k)^* = P_t^* \cdot \exp[k \cdot R_{k,t}]$. At this point there is no incentive for further arbitrage activity, because the partial equilibrium condition of Equation (16.6) is satisfied.

Figure 16.9 shows that when the settlement price equals $P_t(k)^*$, there is a

---

[30] This arbitrage activity would also put upward pressure on the cost of k-period credit, but we ignore this effect for expositional simplicity.

positive excess demand from hedgers and speculators for long positions in the futures market, because $P_t(k)^* < P_t(k)^f$. That excess demand will be satisfied by arbitrageurs holding short positions in futures contracts.

Figure 16.10 shows that when the spot market price equals P_t^*, there is a deficient demand for the asset in the spot market by spot market investors, because $P_t^* > P_t^s$. Arbitrageurs holding the asset against short positions in futures contracts will make up this shortfall in spot market demand. Thus, if we consider the collective activities of hedgers, speculators, *and* arbitrageurs, there will be no excess demand for or supply of (1) the asset in the spot market or (2) long positions in the futures market, at the spot market price P_t^* and the futures market settlement price $P_t(k)^*$. Moreover, there will be no incentive for further arbitrage, because $P_t(k)^* = P_t^* \cdot \exp [k \cdot R_{k,t}]$.

The foregoing discussion showed that when $P_t(k)^f$ is greater than $P_t^* \cdot \exp [k \cdot R_{k,t}]$, arbitrage activity between the spot and futures markets will depress the settlement price in the futures market. This would likely result in a settlement price closer to the expected future spot market price if $P_t(k)^f$ exceeded that expected future spot price. However, if $P_t(k)^f$ were less than $\text{Exp}_t [P_{t+k}]$, that arbitrage activity would push the settlement price even further below the expected future spot price. Thus, there is no general result that arbitrage between a spot market and a futures market will necessarily narrow the difference between settlement prices and expected future spot prices. Arbitrage can make that difference either larger or smaller.

Summary

When an asset can be costlessly inventoried without spoiling and sold short in the spot market, the spot market and the futures market for that asset are two facets of the same entity; i.e., transactions in those markets are perfect substitutes. A demand for long futures positions can be risklessly satisfied by arbitrageurs who buy the asset in the spot market and assume matching positions in the futures market. This means that there is no meaningful distinction between demand for the asset for deferred delivery and demand for the asset for immediate delivery. One type of demand can be risklessly translated into the other type of demand. Similarly, a demand for short futures positions can be risklessly satisfied by arbitrageurs who short sell the asset in the spot market and assume matching long positions in the futures market, and so there is also no meaningful distinction between a supply of the asset for deferred delivery and a supply of the asset for immediate delivery.

The substitutability between spot market positions and futures contracts on the same asset means there is only one, integrated "market" for the asset. The only difference between spot market transactions and transactions in the futures market is that the latter provide for deferred payment. As a consequence of the deferred payment aspect of a futures contract, the futures market settlement price will exceed the spot market price as a function of the cost of credit. This is shown in Equation (16.6) and illustrated by the numerical example following that equation.

In light of the substitutability of spot market positions and futures contracts, and in light of the relationship which must prevail between spot market prices and futures market settlement prices, we can now state what constitutes an equilibrium spot market price and an equilibrium futures market settlement price when a deliverable asset can be bought and sold for spot delivery, costlessly inventoried without spoiling, and sold short. The equilibrium spot market price is that price which equates (1) the spot market demand for the asset *plus* the excess demand for long positions in futures contracts on that asset from hedgers and speculators in the futures market to (2) the available spot market supply of the asset.[31] This definition of an equilibrium spot market price implicitly translates the excess demand for long futures positions into a demand for the asset itself. In practice, this translation is accomplished by arbitrage. The contemporaneous equilibrium settlement price in the futures market will be related to the equilibrium spot market price by Equation (16.6).

CHAPTER SUMMARY

This chapter has examined the determinants of equilibrium settlement prices on futures contracts. The analysis focused on the distinctions between three classes of market participants: long hedgers and short hedgers, speculators, and arbitrageurs.

Long hedgers are market participants who can reduce their exposure to risk by assuming long positions in a futures contract. This means they have a "natural demand" for long positions. If the settlement price on a futures contract is less than the expected future spot market price, long hedgers will want to hedge completely their risk exposure. As the settlement price rises above the expected future spot price, the "cost" of hedging becomes increasingly high for long hedgers (in terms of foregone expectations of gain), and long hedgers will demand less than complete price protection and will reduce their demand for long futures positions commensurately.

Short hedgers are market participants who can reduce their exposure to risk by assuming short positions in a futures contract, and so they are "natural suppliers" of long positions. If the settlement price on a futures contract exceeds the expected future spot market price, short hedgers will want to hedge completely their risk exposure. As the settlement price falls below the expected future spot price, the supply of long futures contracts forthcoming from short hedgers will fall.

In general, the equilibrium settlement price in a futures market where only hedgers participate will exceed the expected future spot price if the market has a preponderance of long hedgers. Conversely, the equilibrium settlement price will be less than the expected future spot price if the market has a preponderance of short hedgers.

---

[31] The excess demand from the futures market could be negative, in which case arbitrageurs would be holding short spot market positions.

Speculators are market participants who bear risk when they are either long or short in a futures contact. The entry of speculators into a futures market previously composed only of hedgers will tend to narrow the difference between the settlement price and the expected future spot price. Speculators will have an incentive to supply long positions in a market with a preponderance of long hedgers, because the settlement price will then exceed the expected future spot price, and their supplies of long positions will push the settlement price down toward that expected future spot price. Similarly, speculators will have an incentive to demand long positions in a market with a preponderance of short hedgers, and their demands will push the settlement price up toward the expected future spot price.

Arbitrageurs are market participants who take matching long and short positions in the spot and futures markets for an asset on the basis of perceptions of riskless profit opportunities. This is different from speculation, which is the assumption of an unmatched long or short futures position on the basis of perceptions of expected (and not riskless) profit opportunities. Arbitrage between a spot market and a futures market tends to link together the spot market price and the futures market settlement price as a function of the cost of credit. This means that an imbalance between supply and demand in one market will be transmitted to the other market, and that equilibrium prices in the two markets cannot be independent of each other. Equilibrium prices will then be determined by balancing (1) the spot market demand for an asset and the excess demand for futures contracts on that asset from hedgers and speculators with (2) the spot market supply of the asset.

It should be noted that not all futures markets are linked to a spot market by arbitrage. Arbitrage cannot occur if the asset being traded for future delivery does not yet exist, or if it cannot be inventoried, or if it cannot be sold short. In these cases the futures market settlement price will depend only on the activities of hedgers and speculators in the futures market and not on the conditions of supply and demand in any spot market.

FURTHER READING

Fischer Black, "The Pricing of Commodity Contracts," *Journal of Financial Economics*, **3** (January–March 1976), 167–179.

Matherine Dusak, "Futures Trading and Investor Returns: An Investigation of Commodity Market Risk Premiums," *Journal of Political Economy*, **81** (November–December 1973), 1387–1406.

Kenneth Froewiss, "GNMA Futures: Stabilizing or Destabilizing?" Federal Reserve Bank of San Francisco *Economic Review* (Spring 1978), 20–29.

William Poole, "Using T-Bill Futures to Gauge Interest-Rate Expectations," Federal Reserve Bank of San Francisco *Economic Review* (Spring 1978), 7–19.

Richard Rendleman, and Christopher Carabini, "The Efficiency of the Treasury Bill Futures Market," *Journal of Finance*, **34** (September 1979), 895–914.

Paul Samuelson, "Proof that Properly Anticipated Prices Fluctuate Randomly," *Industrial Management Review*, **6** (Spring 1965), 41–49.

APPENDIX: Forward Loans and Spread Positions

Equation (16.6) in the text sets forth a partial equilibrium relation between the price P_t of an asset in the spot market at time t, the contemporaneous settlement price $P_t(k)$ of a futures contract on that asset which will be settled at time $t + k$, and the contemporaneous yield per period $R_{k,t}$ on k-period credit:

$$P_t(k) = P_t \cdot \exp\left[k \cdot R_{k,t}\right] \tag{A.1}$$

This relation must hold if the asset can be costlessly inventoried without spoiling, and if it can be sold short in the spot market.

Equation (A.1), and the arguments which led to that equation, can be used to identify what are called *forward loans*. This appendix defines a forward loan and the yield on such a loan, and then shows how a forward loan can be constructed implicitly from what are called *spread positions* in term debt securities and in futures contracts.

Forward Loans

Suppose an investor assumes a long position at time t in a futures contract on a discount debt security which will pay its face value FV when it matures at time $t + k + 1$, and suppose that futures contract will be settled at time $t + k$ at the settlement price $P_t(k)$. This long futures position is known as a *forward loan*. More specifically, it is a contract for a one-period loan which will start at time $t + k$ and which will mature at time $t + k + 1$. The forward loan will start at time $t + k$, because the investor will then be obligated to settle his long futures contract for the debt security by paying out the settlement price $P_t(k)$. Upon payment of the settlement price he will take possession of that debt security. The forward loan matures at time $t + k + 1$, because the debt security matures at that time. The investor will then receive the face value FV of the security. Thus, the long futures position is a commitment assumed at time t to lend money from time $t + k$ to time $t + k + 1$; that is, it is a forward loan commitment.

The yield on the foregoing forward loan can be computed readily. Let $f_{k,t}$ denote the yield at time t on a one-period loan which will start k periods in the future, or at time $t + k$. With this definition it follows that

$$P_t(k) = FV \cdot \exp\left[-f_{k,t}\right] \tag{A.2}$$

Equation (A.2) says that the maturity value FV of the debt security, discounted for one period at the yield $f_{k,t}$, equals the futures contract settlement price for that security. The yield on the forward loan is, therefore,

$$f_{k,t} = \ln\left[\frac{FV}{P_t(k)}\right] \tag{A.3}$$

For example, if the debt security pays $FV = \$1$ million at maturity, and if the settlement price of the futures contract for that security is $P_t(k) = \$.95$ million, then the yield on the forward loan is $f_{k,t} = .0513$, or 5.13 percent per period ($.0513 = \ln\left[\$1.0 \text{ million}/\$.95 \text{ million}\right]$).

The yield at time t on a forward loan can be related to the contemporaneous term structure of interest rates by Equation (A.1). A discount debt security which pays the amount FV at time $t + k + 1$ will, at time t, have a spot market price P_t equal to

$$P_t = FV \cdot \exp\left[-(k+1) \cdot R_{k+1,t}\right] \qquad \text{(A.4)}$$

That is, the spot market price P_t will equal the maturity value FV of the security, discounted for $k + 1$ periods at the contemporaneous yield $R_{k+1,t}$ on $(k + 1)$-period debt. Now replace, in Equation (A.1), the futures market settlement price $P_t(k)$ with its equivalent from Equation (A.2), and replace the spot market price P_t with its equivalent from Equation (A.4). Equation (A.1) then becomes

$$P_t(k) = P_t \cdot \exp\left[k \cdot R_{k,t}\right]$$
$$FV \cdot \exp\left[-f_{k,t}\right] = \{FV \cdot \exp\left[-(k+1) \cdot R_{k+1,t}\right]\} \cdot \exp\left[k \cdot R_{k,t}\right]$$
$$\exp\left[-f_{k,t}\right] = \exp\left[-(k+1) \cdot R_{k+1,t} + k \cdot R_{k,t}\right]$$

or
$$f_{k,t} = (k+1) \cdot R_{k+1,t} - k \cdot R_{k,t} \qquad \text{(A.5)}$$

Equation (A.5) shows how the yield on the forward loan is related to the yield per period on discount debt securities with k-period and $(k + 1)$-period maturities.[32]

Note that the expression in Equation (A.5) for the yield on a forward loan is identical to the expression defining a forward rate in Chapter 14. [See Equation (14.8).] This shows that that forward rate is actually the yield at time t on a commitment for a one-period loan which will begin at time $t + k$ and which will be paid off at time $t + k + 1$. Thus, we have identified the forward rate defined in Chapter 14 as the yield on a forward loan, and we have seen how to make a commitment for such a forward loan by assuming a long position in a futures contract on a discount debt security.

Forward Loans and Spread Positions in Term Debt Securities

The analysis which led to Equation (A.1) [or Equation (16.6)] rested on the equivalence between two positions:

1 Taking a long position at time t in a futures contract on some asset which will be settled at time $t + k$

2 Buying the same asset in the spot market at time t and financing that purchase with k-period credit

For the special case where the asset is a discount debt security which matures at time $t + k + 1$, these two positions are

1 Making a commitment for a forward loan which starts at time $t + k$ and which matures at time $t + k + 1$

2 Buying a $(k + 1)$-period debt security, and financing that purchase with k-period credit

The second position is known as a *spread position* in debt securities. That is, it is a position in a pair of debt securities, where one security is held long and the other security is

[32] The validity of the equilibrium condition of Equation (A.5) has been examined by Poole (1978), Lang and Rasche (1978), Rendleman and Carabini (1979), and Capozza and Cornell (1979) for the case of Treasury bill futures. See also Kane (1980).

held short. More precisely, a $(k + 1)$-period debt security is held long, and that security is financed with a borrowing for k periods, or with a short sale of a k-period debt security. This shows that a commitment for a one-period forward loan which starts in k periods is equivalent to a spread position in k-period and $(k + 1)$-period debt.[33] It is not, therefore, surprising that the forward rate $f_{k,t}$ on a forward loan should be related by Equation (A.5) to the spot market yields on k-period and $(k + 1)$-period debt securities.

Forward Loans and Spread Positions in Futures Contracts

We have defined a forward loan as a futures contract on a discount debt security, and we have seen that a forward loan can be constructed from a spread position in term debt securities. It turns out that a forward loan can also be constructed from a spread position in futures contracts on an arbitrary asset.

Suppose at time t an investor takes a long position in a futures contract on, e.g., gold that will be settled at time $t + k$, and the investor takes a matching short position in a futures contract on gold that will be settled at time $t + k + 1$. Denote the settlement prices on the two futures contracts as $P_t(k)$ and $P_t(k + 1)$, respectively. This spread position, or matched long and short positions, in gold futures is equivalent to a commitment to a forward loan which will start at time $t + k$ and which will mature at time $t + k + 1$. At time $t + k$ the investor will receive gold in settlement of his long futures position for which he will be obligated to pay $P_t(k)$. At time $t + k + 1$ the investor will be obligated to deliver the same amount of gold in settlement of his short futures position, for which he will receive $P_t(k + 1)$. Thus, the investor is commited to paying out the amount $P_t(k)$ at $t + k$ and receiving back the amount $P_t(k + 1)$ at time $t + k + 1$. This is equivalent to a commitment for a forward loan which starts at time $t + k$ and which matures at time $t + k + 1$.

The forward loan rate implicit in the foregoing spread position in gold futures is the value of $f_{k,t}^{\text{gold}}$ which solves the equation.

$$P_t(k) = P_t(k + 1) \cdot \exp\left[-f_{k,t}^{\text{gold}}\right] \tag{A.6}$$

Equation (A.6) says that the funds received by the investor at time $t + k + 1$, discounted for one period at the rate $f_{k,t}^{\text{gold}}$, is equal to the funds paid out by the investor at time $t + k$. The forward loan rate implicit in the spread position in gold futures is, therefore,

$$f_{k,t}^{\text{gold}} = \ln\left[\frac{P_t(k + 1)}{P_t(k)}\right] \tag{A.7}$$

In equilibrium, the forward loan rate $f_{k,t}^{\text{gold}}$ on the spread position in gold futures will equal the forward loan rate $f_{k,t}$ defined in Equation (A.3) for an ordinary forward loan. From Equation (A.1) we know that the settlement prices on the gold futures contracts must be related to the spot market price P_t of gold as

$$P_t(k) = P_t \cdot \exp\left[k \cdot R_{k,t}\right]$$
$$P_t(k + 1) = P_t \cdot \exp\left[(k + 1) \cdot R_{k+1,t}\right]$$

Substituting these values of $P_t(k)$ and $P_t(k + 1)$ into Equation (A.7) gives

---

[33] This means that, e.g., an arbitrageur may seek riskless profits by taking offsetting positions in (1) Treasury bill futures and (2) spread positions in Treasury debt. See Poole (1978), Lang and Rasche (1978), Rendleman and Carabini (1979), and Capozza and Cornell (1979)

$$f_{k,t}^{\text{gold}} = \ln \left[\frac{P_t(k+1)}{P_t(k)} \right]$$

$$= \ln \left[\frac{P_t \cdot \exp\left[(k+1) \cdot R_{k+1,t}\right]}{P_t \cdot \exp\left[k \cdot R_{k,t}\right]} \right]$$

$$= (k+1) R_{k+1,t} - k \cdot R_{k,t}$$

or, using Equation (A.5),

$$f_{k,t}^{\text{gold}} = f_{k,t} \tag{A.8}$$

Summary

This appendix has defined a forward loan which starts at time $t + k$ and which matures at time $t + k + 1$ as a futures contract that will be settled at time $t + k$ on a discount debt security that matures at time $t + k + 1$. This forward loan is equivalent to two different types of spread positions:

1 A long position in a $(k + 1)$-period discount debt security financed with a k-period borrowing, or matched with a short position in a k-period discount debt security.

2 A long position in a futures contract which will be settled at time $t + k$, matched with a short position in a futures contract on the same asset which will be settled at time $t + k + 1$. The identity of the asset being bought and sold for deferred delivery on these futures contracts is irrelevant.

Both of these spread positions are equivalent to the forward loan, because both are commitments for the payment of funds at time $t + k$ and the receipt of funds at $t + k + 1$.

In view of the equivalence between forward loans, spread positions in debt securities and spread positions in futures contracts for an arbitrary asset, it is possible to arbitrage between different combinations of these positions. For example, an arbitrageur might go long in a June gold futures contract, go short in a September gold futures contract (this would be equivalent to a commitment to a forward loan running from June to September), and then go short in a June contract in 90-day Treasury bills (this would be equivalent to a commitment for a forward borrowing running from June to September). This serves to point out that arbitrage in a futures market is not limited to matching transactions in the spot market for the same asset, and can involve matching transactions in futures market on other assets or in the spot market for debt securities.

APPENDIX: The Equilibrium Relationship between Spot Prices and Settlement Prices When an Asset Makes Payments to Holders

Equation (16.6) specifies a partial equilibrium condition between the spot market price of an asset and the settlement price of a futures contract on the same asset when that asset does not make payments to a holder prior to the settlement of the futures contract. Thus, Equation (16.6) is appropriate for the analysis of futures contracts on assets like precious metals and Treasury bills. However, not all assets satisfy the no payment prior to settlement assumption. For example, Treasury bonds make a coupon payment every 6 months, and most stocks pay quarterly dividends.

When an asset makes payments to a holder prior to the settlement of a futures contract on that asset, Equation (16.6) cannot be valid. Consider, for example, an arbitrageur who buys Treasury bonds to deliver against a short position in a futures contract on those bonds which is to be settled in 2 years. That arbitrageur would receive four semiannual coupon payments before surrendering his bonds. The value to the arbitrageur of these coupon payments is not recognized in Equation (16.6).

When an asset makes payments to a holder, the spot market price P_t in Equation (16.6) has to be replaced by the difference between that spot market price and the *present value* of any payments to be received prior to settlement of the futures contract. For example, if the arbitrageur in the example above knows he will receive four coupon payments *before* surrendering his bonds, then the current spot market value of the bonds *to be delivered* is the gross spot market price of those bonds, less the present value of the four coupon payments. This follows because the arbitrageur will not have to deliver those coupon payments along with the bonds; i.e., he will be delivering bonds with four fewer coupons than the bonds he is purchasing.

In general, if the present value of the payments to be received on an asset between time t and time $t + k$ is PV, then the partial equilibrium relation at time t between the settlement price of a futures contract on that asset to be settled at time $t + k$ and the spot market price of the asset will be

$$P_t(k) = (P_t - PV) \cdot \exp\ [k \cdot R_{k,t}] \tag{A.9}$$

The term $P_t - PV$ is the spot market price of the asset *net* of the present value of any pecuniary benefits derived from owning that asset up to the settlement date.

PART SIX

OPTIONS AND THE RISK STRUCTURE OF INTEREST RATES

The past decade has witnessed a remarkable growth in an important class of financial instruments: contracts for the *optional* purchase or sale of a designated asset at a fixed price. The most familiar members of this class of securities are call and put option contracts for the purchase and sale of common stock for cash. At the present time there is active trading on organized exchanges like the Chicago Board Options Exchange in call and put options on the common stock of more than 250 major American corporations.[1] The volume of option trading rivals, and sometimes surpasses, the volume of trading in underlying stocks.

Call and put options on common stock are not the only types of contracts for the optional purchase and sale of an underlying asset. A convertible debenture, for example, may be viewed as an ordinary debenture with the added feature of an optional right to acquire stock, where the acquisition price of the stock is denominated in units of the debenture (for example, 50 shares of stock can be acquired in exchange for 1 debenture). Similarly, the common stock of a corporation can be viewed as an option to acquire the assets of the corporation, where the price of exercising that option is the sum of money promised to the creditors of the corporation.[2] The stockholders keep control of the assets if they make the promised payments, but if they default and fail to make a payment, i.e., if they fail to exercise their option, the creditors take control of those assets. The recognition that securities like convertible debt and common stock are contracts for the optional purchase of other assets has had a profound impact on our understanding of those securities.

---

[1] The options market is exhaustively described in Securities and Exchange Commission (1978).

[2] The analysis of common stock as an option to acquire the assets of a corporation is pursued in Chapter 19.

The three chapters in this part describe various types of optional purchase and sale contracts, and explore the equilibrium valuation of those contracts. Chapter 17 describes the characteristics of simple call and put options on common stock and the markets for those options. It also describes the optional purchase or sale aspects of other securities, like convertible debt and callable debt. Chapter 18 develops a theory of the equilibrium price of a call option based on the possibility of arbitrage with the market for the underlying security. Chapter 19 applies the theory of equilibrium call option valuation to the problem of valuing risky debt securities and extends the theory of the term structure of interest rates for riskless debt (developed in Chapter 14) to a theory of the risk structure of interest rates.

CHAPTER 17

OPTIONS AND RELATED SECURITIES

This chapter describes call and put option contracts on common stock, the organization of the markets for those option contracts, and the characteristics of several related securities, including warrants, convertible debt, and callable debt. The primary purpose of the chapter is to specify carefully the nature of an option contract and to clarify the difference between an option and a futures contract. (It is quite common to confuse the two instruments when they are first encountered.) The secondary purpose of the chapter is to examine the characteristics of securities which have optional purchase or sale provisions more complex than simple call and put options on common stock. These more complex securities serve to illustrate that an option is nothing but a contract between the option writer and the option holder, and that contracts can be written with a wide variety of terms.

17.1 OPTIONS ON COMMON STOCK

Options are contracts for the *optional*, or discretionary, purchase or sale of an underlying asset. A *call* option is an option to buy, and a *put* option is an option to sell.

There are three major elements to the specification of both a call option contract and a put option contract:

1 Specification of the *underlying asset*, i.e., the asset which can be bought (if the option is a call) or sold (if the option is a put)

2 Specification of the *strike price*, or *exercise price*, of the option, i.e., the price at which the specified underlying asset can be bought or sold

3 Specification of the *expiration date* of the option, i.e., the last date on which the option to purchase or sell can be exercised[1]

The simplest options on common stock are fully described by specifying whether they are puts or calls, and by identifying the underlying asset, the exercise price, and the expiration date.[2]

Call Options

Consider a call option on 100 shares of IBM common stock with an exercise price of $60 per share optioned and an expiration date of January 15, 1981. This option allows the holder to buy 100 shares of IBM at a total cost of $6000 (that is, 100 shares optioned × $60 exercise price per share optioned) on or before January 15, 1981. If the holder chooses to exercise his option, he will tender the $6000 exercise price in cash and will receive 100 shares of IBM common stock. The holder of the option is not, however, obligated to exercise his option, and he is not under any obligation to purchase IBM stock at the $60 per share exercise price. He has the right, *but not the obligation*, to buy the optioned stock at the option exercise price.

If the holder of the foregoing option fails to exercise his purchase rights on or before January 15, 1981, those rights will expire. After that date he will not be able to acquire IBM stock by exercising his option. An option becomes a worthless piece of paper after its expiration date.

The Position of the Writer   As described above, the holder of an unexpired call option on IBM has the right to buy that stock at a fixed option exercise price. The person who granted him this right is called the *writer* of the option. A call option writer must be prepared to deliver stock in the event the holder of the option tenders payment of the option exercise price.[3] Thus, a call option writer is a potential seller of the optioned stock. There must be a call option writer for every call option holder, because somebody must stand ready to sell the stock which a call option holder has the right to buy.

Whether the writer of a call option will actually sell the stock which he has optioned is not within his control, and is entirely at the discretion of the holder of the call option. If the holder chooses to exercise his right to buy, the option writer will be obliged to sell him the optioned stock at the option exercise price. However, the call option writer cannot force the holder to accept the op-

---

[1] If an option can be exercised at any time up to and including its expiration date, it is called an *American-type* option. If it can only be exercised on its expiration date, it is called a *European-type* option. See Merton (1973b) for an extensive comparative analysis of the pricing of American and European put and call options.

[2] Snyder (1969) describes a more complex call option on common stock which has an "expiration price" as well as an expiration date. The option expires immediately if the underlying stock trades at or below the stated expiration price, and in any event expires on the stated expiration date.

[3] An investor can write a call option on stock he doesn't own, but he must then be prepared to assume a short position in the stock in order to effect delivery if his option is exercised. This is known as writing a *naked*, or *uncovered*, option.

tioned stock if the holder chooses not to exercise his purchase rights. Simply stated, a call option writer has the obligation, *but not the right*, to sell the optioned stock at the option exercise price.

If a call option is not exercised on or before the expiration date of the option, the obligation of the option writer to deliver stock against payment of the exercise price terminates. Thus, when the holder of a call option no longer has any right to buy the optioned stock, the writer of that option no longer has any obligation to sell the optioned stock.

Put Options

A put option is an option to sell stock at a fixed exercise price on or before a specified expiration date. Consider, for example, a put option on 100 shares of IBM common stock with an exercise price of $60 per share and an expiration date of January 15, 1981. This option allows the holder to sell 100 shares of IBM for an aggregate price of $6000 (that is, 100 shares optioned × $60 exercise price per share optioned) on or before January 15, 1981. If the holder chooses to exercise his option, he will tender 100 shares of IBM common stock to the put option writer and will receive the $6000 option exercise price in cash. The holder is not, however, obligated to exercise his sale rights; i.e., he has the right, but not the obligation, to sell the optioned stock at the option exercise price. If he fails to exercise his put option on or before the expiration date, his option to sell expires and becomes a worthless piece of paper.

The Position of the Writer   The writer of a put option has the obligation, but not the right, to buy stock. If the holder of a put option chooses to exercise his sale rights, the writer of that option must pay him the exercise price of the option in return for the optioned stock. If the holder of the put option chooses not to exercise his sale rights, however, the option writer cannot force him to sell the optioned stock.

The Difference between Holding Calls and Writing Puts

It is important to understand that holders of call options and writers of put options are both potential buyers of optioned stock but stand in very different positions. The holder of a call option has the right to buy stock at the option exercise price from the writer of that option, but nothing can force him to buy that stock. The writer of a put option, on the other hand, has the obligation to buy stock at the option exercise price if the optioned stock is tendered to him by the holder of his put, but he has no contractual right to buy that stock. Thus, the holder of a call option has the right (but not the obligation) to buy stock, while the writer of a put option has the obligation (but not the right) to buy stock.

Similar comments apply to the difference between holders of put options and writers of call options. Both are potential sellers of optioned stock. However, a put option holder has no obligation to sell the optioned stock if he doesn't want to, while a call option writer has no right to sell the optioned stock if the holder of the call option does not want to buy.

There are two important elements in the comparison of option contracts. First, is the option to buy or sell? Second, who has the right to exercise the option and who has the obligation to perform? These two elements are summarized in Table 17.1. As shown in that table, option holders always have the right to exercise, and option writers always have the obligation to perform.

The Difference between Option Contracts and Futures Contracts

It is also important to understand the difference between option contracts and futures contracts. Suppose, for example, an investor entered into a long position in a futures contract on IBM common stock with a settlement price of $60 per share and a January 15, 1981, settlement date. This futures position would give him *the right and the obligation* to buy IBM stock at a price of $60 per share on January 15, 1981. In contrast, if he held a call option on 100 shares of IBM with a $60 exercise price and a January 15, 1981, expiration date, he would have the right, but he would not have the obligation, to buy IBM stock at a price of $60 per share. Conversely, if he wrote a put option on IBM with the same terms, he would have the obligation, but he would not have the right, to buy IBM stock at a price of $60 per share.

The foregoing discussion suggests that options can be viewed as financial instruments which separate the rights from the obligations which are bundled together in futures contracts. Instead of taking a long position in a futures contract, an investor could buy a call option and thereby enjoy the right to buy the optioned stock without also bearing the obligation to buy that stock. On the other hand, he could sell (or write) a put option and thereby bear the obligation to buy the optioned stock without also enjoying the right to buy that stock. It is the separation of rights from obligations that distinguishes option contracts from futures contracts.

It is possible to reconstruct the rights and obligations of a futures contract by

TABLE 17.1
SUMMARY OF RIGHTS AND OBLIGATIONS OF OPTION
HOLDERS AND OPTION WRITERS

	Call option	Put option
Holder	Right to buy at the exercise price on or before the expiration date	Right to sell at the exercise price on or before the expiration date
Writer	Obligation to sell at the exercise price on or before the expiration date	Obligation to buy at the exercise price on or before the expiration date

taking appropriate positions in call and put option contracts. Suppose an investor bought a call option on 100 shares of IBM with a $60 exercise price and a January 15, 1981, expiration date, and suppose he also wrote a put option on 100 shares of the same stock with the same exercise price and the same expiration date. As a holder of the call he has the right to buy IBM stock at $60 per share, and as the writer of the put he has the obligation to buy IBM stock at $60 per share. Thus, holding a call *and* writing a put with common exercise prices and expiration dates is very similar to taking a long position in a futures contract on the optioned stock.[4]

17.2 OVER-THE-COUNTER OPTIONS AND EXCHANGE-TRADED OPTIONS

Until 1973, option contracts on common stock were written by individual or institutional investors and sold directly to other investors in over-the-counter transactions, i.e., in transactions not on the floor of a securities exchange. These options were called *over-the-counter options* or *OTC options*. The market in OTC options has largely (but not completely) disappeared as a result of the innovation of exchange-traded option contracts ("listed options") in April 1973. This section describes the institutional characteristics of both the OTC and listed options markets.

OTC Options

The OTC options market is an over-the-counter market in put and call option contracts which are written by individual investors and sold through securities dealers to other investors.[5] If an investor, "Buyer," wants to acquire an OTC call option on, for example, Potlatch Corporation common stock, he would go to a securities dealer who does a business in put and call options and ask him to locate another investor willing to write the desired call option contract on Potlatch stock. Assume that a second investor, "Seller," is willing to write the desired option in return for an immediate cash payment acceptable to Buyer. The securities dealer would then purchase the call option written by Seller and immediately resell that option to Buyer. If Buyer subsequently decided to exercise his purchase rights, he would tender the option exercise price to Seller and demand delivery of the optioned stock.

Most of the business in the OTC options market consists of the writing and sale of *new* option contracts. The exercise price of a new option is conventionally fixed at the current price of the underlying stock. Options written on a stock trading at $40 per share will carry an exercise price of $40 per share. If

---

[4] It is not identical, because an investor can exercise his long call option at *any* time on or before the expiration date, and he could be forced to honor an exercise of his short put option at *any* time on or before the expiration date. A futures contract cannot be settled before its scheduled settlement date.

[5] The structure of the OTC options market is described in Boness (1964), Stoll (1969), Snyder (1969), and Gates (1973). See also Gould and Galai (1974) and Black and Scholes (1972).

the stock price rises to $41.50 the following day, options written that next day will carry an exercise price of $41.50. The expiration date of a new OTC option is conventionally fixed at 1, 2, 3, 6, or 12 months from the date the option is written. Thus, a 3-month option written on January 15 would expire on April 15, while a 3-month option written the next day would expire on April 16. In all cases, however, the exercise price and expiration date of a new OTC option can be tailored to any special requirements of either the buyer or the writer.

OTC options are negotiable and can be sold by a current holder to another investor. As a practical matter, however, there is little trading in outstanding OTC option contracts. Most OTC options are held to expiration and either exercised by the original buyer or allowed to expire unexercised.

Listed Options

April 26, 1973, marked the beginning of a new era for options on common stock. On that date the Chicago Board Options Exchange (CBOE) began to sponsor public trading in standardized call option contracts. Four other exchanges (the American Stock Exchange, the Pacific Stock Exchange, the Philadelphia Stock Exchange, and the Midwest Stock Exchange) subsequently initiated their own programs of public trading in listed call options, and all five exchanges now sponsor trading in listed put options as well.[6]

At the present time the five options exchanges collectively sponsor trading in call and put option contracts on about 250 different issues of common stocks. For those stocks, trading in listed options has completely replaced trading in OTC options. However, if an investor wants to buy or write an option on a nonsponsored stock (like Potlatch), he will have to buy or write an OTC option through a securities dealer as described above. Thus, the OTC options market survives, on a reduced scale, for trading in options on nonsponsored stocks.

Listed options, like OTC options, are characterized by identifying their contract terms: the underlying asset, the exercise price, and the expiration date. However, the exercise price and expiration date of a listed option contract cannot be set at the mutual convenience of a buyer and seller. Instead, they must be selected from a limited set of combinations specified by an options exchange. Exhibit 17.1 shows that the CBOE-sponsored trading in eighteen different call option contracts on IBM common stock on July 7, 1980. Call options on IBM with combinations of exercise prices and expiration dates other than the eighteen sponsored combinations could not be traded on the CBOE on that day.

The expiration dates of listed options are spaced 3 months apart and occur in one of three regular cycles. Options in the January cycle, such as options on

---

[6] See Garbade and Kaicher (1978–79) for an expository overview of the market for listed options. Gates (1973) examines some of the early regulatory issues raised by the existence of a market for listed options. Securities and Exchange Commission (1978) provides an exhaustive review of the listed options market.

EXHIBIT 17.1
EXERCISE PRICE AND EXPIRATION DATE COMBINATIONS FOR CALL
OPTIONS ON IBM AVAILABLE ON THE CHICAGO BOARD OPTIONS
EXCHANGE ON JULY 7, 1980

Exercise price	Expiration date		
	July 19,1980	October 18, 1980	January 17, 1981
$45	X	X	X
$50	X	X	X
$55	X	X	X
$60	X	X	X
$65	X	X	N/A*
$70	X	X	N/A
$75	X	X	N/A

*N/A: Not available.

IBM or International Harvester, expire in January, April, July, or October. Options in the February cycle, such as options on National Semiconductor, expire in February, May, August, or November. Options in the March cycle, such as options on GM, expire in March, June, September, or December. The expiration date of a listed option is always the Saturday following the third Friday in the expiration month of that option. At any point in time an options exchange will sponsor trading in options which expire on the next three expiration dates for that option cycle. For example, Exhibit 17.1 shows trading in three expiration dates for IBM options. On Monday, July 21, 1980, the CBOE opened trading in IBM options expiring April 18, 1981, because the July 19, 1980, options on IBM had expired on the preceding Saturday.

When trading for a new expiration date first begins, at least two new call option contracts with that expiration date will be opened. The new contracts will have exercise prices which bracket the current price of the underlying stock. For example, on Friday, July 18, 1980, International Harvester stock closed at $32 per share. When trading for the April 18, 1981, expiration date began the following Monday, the new call option contracts had exercise prices of $30 and $35.[7]

If the price of a stock moves above the highest existing exercise price of an option on that stock, trading will be opened in a new option with an exercise price $5 or $10 higher than that highest existing exercise price. Conversely, if the price of a stock moves below the lowest existing exercise price of an option

---

[7] If the stock price is very close to one of the new exercise prices, a third exercise price may also be opened. For example, on July 18, 1980, IBM stock closed at $65.375 per share. On July 21, 1980, the CBOE opened trading in April 1981 options on IBM with exercise prices of $60, $65, and $70 per share.

on that stock, trading will be opened in a new option with an exercise price $5 or $10 lower than that lowest existing exercise price. As a result, there always exist listed options with exercise prices slightly higher and slightly lower than the current prices of underlying stocks.

Standardizing the expiration dates and exercise prices of listed options eliminated the heterogeneity of contract terms which characterized the OTC options market. Instead of hundreds of different call options on a particular stock, each with a different combination of exercise price and expiration date, there now exist only a dozen or two dozen different options. By limiting the number of different option contracts on a given stock, the options exchanges have fostered the development of a liquid secondary market in listed options. Contrary to the experience in the OTC options market, most investors do not hold listed options to expiration, and instead sell those options for cash before they expire.

The Options Clearing Corporation   An important feature of listed options is that all those options *held* by investors are written by a single institution, the Options Clearing Corporation (OCC), and that all those options *written* by investors are held by the OCC. The OCC plays a role in the listed options market identical to the role played by the clearing corporations of futures exchanges in the futures markets. When two investors agree to the purchase and sale of an option contract on the floor of an options exchange, the seller does not write an option directly to the buyer. Instead, the seller writes the agreed-upon option to the OCC, and the OCC writes an identical option to the buyer. Thus, the OCC is on the other side of every contract in listed options, just as a clearing corporation is on the other side of every futures contract.

If the holder of a listed call option decides to exercise his right to purchase the optioned stock, he will tender the exercise price in cash to the OCC. The OCC will immediately exercise an identical call option which it holds on some other investor to obtain the stock needed to complete the first investor's option exercise. Similar comments apply to the exercise of put options. As its name implies, the OCC acts as a clearing and settlement intermediary in the trading and exercise of listed options.

An investor who holds a listed option can liquidate that option by selling it to another investor through a transaction on an options exchange. The sale is completed by transferring the contractual obligation of the OCC from the former holder to the new holder. Similarly, an investor who has previously written an option to the OCC can cover his position by buying a listed option with the same exercise price and expiration date on an options exchange. His new purchase, combined with his earlier sale, leaves him with a net position of zero in that option contract on the books of the OCC. Unlike OTC options, listed options are fungible, because all holders buy from a common writer (the OCC) and all writers sell to a common holder (the OCC). Consequently, it has become more convenient to speak of being long or short (against the OCC) in a listed option rather than to speak of holders and writers of listed options.

17.3 RELATED SECURITIES

OTC and listed call and put options on common stock are not the only examples of purchase and sale contracts with an optional exercise feature. This section describes several other securities with the same feature.[8]

Warrants

Warrants are call option contracts issued (or written) by a corporation on which the underlying asset is usually one share of the common stock of the issuer of the warrant.[9] For example, in 1970 AT&T sold in excess of 31 million warrants on its common stock. The AT&T warrants carried an exercise price of $52 per share of AT&T stock and an expiration date of May 15, 1975. Investors exercised about 3 million of the AT&T warrants prior to May 16, 1975. The other 28 million warrants expired unexercised.[10]

Warrants are different from OTC and listed call options, because exercise of a warrant increases the outstanding supply of the underlying asset. The exercise of the 3 million AT&T warrants described in the preceding paragraph increased the outstanding supply of AT&T common stock by 3 million shares. OTC and listed call options are necessarily written against outstanding supplies of the underlying stock, because the writers of those options are not capable of increasing that supply. Exercise of an OTC or listed call option changes the identity of a holder of the underlying stock but does not increase the supply of that stock.

Debt Securities with Call and Put Features

A *callable debenture* is a debenture which carries a call option providing that the issuer can buy the debenture back from investors at specified exercise prices (or *call prices*) during specified intervals of time *prior* to the ultimate maturity date of the debenture. Exhibit 17.2 shows the call provisions on an April 1978 offering by Tenneco Inc. of $200 million of $8^7/_8$ percent 25-year debentures. Tenneco reserved to itself the right to buy back all or part of its debenture issue at exercise prices ranging from 108.63 percent of principal value in the first year after issue down to 100.00 percent of principal value after the twentieth year after issue.

In some cases a callable debenture will provide that the issuer does *not* have an option to buy back its debentures for some specified interval of time follow-

---

[8] In addition to the securities described in this section, Ingersoll (1976) has pointed out that the securities of dual-purpose closed-end managed investment companies are a form of option. Margrabe (1978) has examined margin accounts, exchange offers, and standby commitments as options to exchange one asset for another asset.

[9] Sometimes a company will issue warrants on the stock of another company. See Merton (1973b, fn. 6).

[10] The problem of valuing these warrants was examined in Schwartz (1977).

EXHIBIT 17.2

CALL PROVISIONS ON $8^7/_8$ PERCENT TENNECO INC. DEBENTURES ISSUED APRIL 20, 1978, AND MATURING APRIL 15, 2003

The Debentures will be redeemable at the option of the Company, at any time prior to maturity, as a whole or in part, on at least thirty days' notice given as provided in the Indenture, during the twelve-month periods ending April 14, in the years set forth below upon payment of the applicable percentage of the principal amount thereof set forth below, together in each case with accrued interest to the redemption date:

If redeemed during 12-month period ending April 14	If redeemed during 12-month period ending April 14	If redeemed during 12-month period ending April 14
1979 . . . . 108.63%	1986 . . . . 105.61%	1993 . . . . 102.59%
1980 . . . . 108.20%	1987 . . . . 105.18%	1994 . . . . 102.16%
1981 . . . . 107.77%	1988 . . . . 104.75%	1995 . . . . 101.73%
1982 . . . . 107.34%	1989 . . . . 104.32%	1996 . . . . 101.30%
1983 . . . . 106.90%	1990 . . . . 103.89%	1997 . . . . 100.87%
1984 . . . . 106.47%	1991 . . . . 103.45%	1998 . . . . 100.44%
1985 . . . . 106.04%	1992 . . . . 103.02%	

and thereafter at 100% of the principal amount thereof.

Source: Offering prospectus dated April 12, 1978; Morgan Stanley & Co. and White, Weld & Co., comanaging underwriters.

ing the date of issue. This interval is called the *call protection* period of the debenture. Exhibit 17.3 shows the call provisions on a November 1977 offering by South Central Bell Telephone Company of $250 million of $8^1/_4$ percent 38-year debentures. South Central Bell reserved to itself the right to buy back all or part of its debentures at exercise prices ranging from 107.00 percent of

EXHIBIT 17.3

CALL PROVISIONS ON $8^1/_4$ PERCENT SOUTH CENTRAL BELL TELEPHONE COMPANY DEBENTURES ISSUED NOVEMBER 17, 1977, AND MATURING NOVEMBER 1, 2015

The Company may, at its option, redeem all or from time to time any part of the Debentures on or after November 1, 1982 and prior to maturity, on at least 30 days' notice, at the following redemption prices (expressed in percentages of the principal amount) during the 12 months' periods ending October 31:

1983 . . . . 107.00%	1990 . . . . 105.25%	1997 . . . . 103.50%	2004 . . . . 101.75%
1984 . . . . 106.75%	1991 . . . . 105.00%	1998 . . . . 103.25%	2005 . . . . 101.50%
1985 . . . . 106.50%	1992 . . . . 104.75%	1999 . . . . 103.00%	2006 . . . . 101.25%
1986 . . . . 106.25%	1993 . . . . 104.50%	2000 . . . . 102.75%	2007 . . . . 101.00%
1987 . . . . 106.00%	1994 . . . . 104.25%	2001 . . . . 102.50%	2008 . . . . 100.75%
1988 . . . . 105.75%	1995 . . . . 104.00%	2002 . . . . 102.25%	2009 . . . . 100.50%
1989 . . . . 105.50%	1996 . . . . 103.75%	2003 . . . . 102.00%	2010 . . . . 100.25%

and thereafter at 100%, together in each case with accrued interest to the date fixed for redemption.

Source: Offering prospectus dated November 9, 1977; Morgan Stanley & Co., managing underwriter.

EXHIBIT 17.4
PUT PROVISIONS ON 8 PERCENT BENEFICIAL CORPORATION DEBENTURES ISSUED
JUNE 24, 1976, AND MATURING JUNE 15, 2001

The registered holder of each Debenture may for his convenience elect, during any year
beginning with 1983 and ending with 2000, to have the principal of his Debenture, or any portion thereof which is a multiple of $1,000, mature on June 15 of such year. Such election,
which is irrevocable when made, must be made within the period commencing February 15
and ending at the close of business on March 15 of such year, by surrender of the Debenture
at the office or agency of the Company to be maintained by the Company for that purpose in
the Borough of Manhattan, The City of New York, with the form of "Option to Elect Early Maturity Date" appearing on the reverse of the Debenture duly completed.

Source: Offering prospectus dated June 15, 1976; Blyth Eastman Dillon & Co., managing underwriter.

principal value during the sixth year after issue down to 100.00 percent of principal value after the thirty-third year after issue. However, South Central Bell
did not have any right to buy back its debentures at any time during the first 5
years after issue. Thus, the South Central Bell Telephone debentures carried a
5-year call protection period. A 5-year call protection period is common on the
callable debt of utility issuers. A 10-year call protection period is common on
the callable debt of industrial issuers.

Callable debentures may be viewed as ordinary debentures which carry a
bundle of call options written by holders of the debentures to the issuer. Those
options grant valuable purchase rights to the issuer and impose sale obligations
on investors. The issuer pays for the purchase rights by issuing the debentures
with a coupon rate higher than what would be required if the debentures were
not callable prior to maturity. In general, higher call prices require smaller compensating increases in coupon rates, because an issuer is less likely to find it advantageous to call an issue with higher call prices. Longer call protection also
requires smaller compensating increases in coupon rates, because an issuer
would then have a more limited set of purchase rights.[11]

Put options are a less common provision of corporate debentures. A *putable
debenture* is a debenture which carries a put option providing that an investor
can sell the debenture back to the issuer at specified exercise prices on
specified dates *prior* to the ultimate maturity date of the debenture. Exhibit
17.4 shows the put provisions on a June 1976 offering by Beneficial Corporation of $150 million of 8 percent 25-year debentures. Holders of those deben-
tures have the right to sell all or part of their debenture holdings back to
Beneficial on June 15 each year between 1983 and 2000, inclusive, at an exercise price of 100.00 percent of principal value.

A putable debenture may be viewed as an ordinary debenture which carries
a bundle of put options written by the issuer to investors who hold those debentures. Those options grant valuable sale rights to investors and impose

---

[11] Bodie and Friedman (1978) analyzed the increase in the required yield on new offerings of
debt resulting from the callability of that debt. The value of call options and call protection has also
been analyzed by Pye (1966, 1967), Jen and Wert (1967), and Elton and Gruber (1972).

purchase obligations on the issuer. Investors pay for for the sale rights by accepting a coupon rate on the debentures lower than what they would demand if the debentures were not putable.

It should be noted that holders of both callable and putable debentures are potential sellers of their debentures, and that issuers are potential buyers of both types of debentures. The difference between the two types of debentures is who has the right to exercise the option and who has the obligation to perform. In the case of callable debentures, issuers have the right to buy and investors have the obligation to sell if the issuers exercise their purchase rights. In the case of putable debentures, investors have the right to sell and issuers have the obligation to buy if investors exercise their sale rights.

Although putable corporate debentures are relatively uncommon, there is one type of putable debt security familiar to almost all Americans: United States Treasury saving bonds. Each savings bond specifies a redemption schedule of increasing prices at which a holder can sell the bond back to the Treasury at specified future dates. An investor can choose to exercise his sale rights at any time, or he can choose to continue to hold his bonds and exercise his sale rights at a later time.[12]

Convertible Debt Securities

A *convertible debenture* is a debenture which carries a call option providing that a holder of the debenture can purchase some underlying asset, usually the common stock of the issuer of the debenture, where the exercise price of the option is the debenture itself.[13] For example, in July 1979, Western Bancorporation sold $100 million of $7^1/_4$ percent 25-year convertible debentures. Each $1000 principal value debenture was convertible, at the option of the holder, into 27.211 shares of Western Bancorporation common stock at any time during the life of the debenture. This meant that a debenture holder had a call option to purchase 27.211 shares of Western Bancorporation stock, where the exercise price of that option was 1 debenture.

Most convertible debt specifies a simple exchange ratio of stock for debt. In some cases, however, a convertible debenture may provide a schedule of increasing or decreasing conversion ratios, with different ratios applicable for different intervals of time. In other cases a convertible debenture might specify an exercise price of both cash and the debenture, so that conversion would require payment of additional money as well as delivery of the debenture to the issuer.

---

[12] Brennan and Schwartz (1979) have examined the economics of savings bonds as putable debt instruments.

[13] Brennan and Schwartz (1977) derive the theoretical value of a convertible bond as a function of the terms of conversion and the value of the issuer's assets. See also Leibowitz (1974). A company will sometimes issue debentures convertible into the common stock of another company. See the offering by Textron Inc. of $85.42 million of $7^3/_4$ percent 25-year subordinated debentures convertible into the common stock of Allied Chemical Corporation at the rate of 16.949 shares per debenture (*The Wall Street Journal*, June 16, 1980, p. 33). See also Deborah Rankin, "Old Technique for Debentures," *The New York Times*, June 10, 1980, p. D2, col. 1.

A convertible debenture may be viewed as an ordinary debenture which carries a call option written by the issuer to the debenture holders. That option grants a valuable purchase right to the debenture holders and imposes a sale obligation on the issuer. Holders pay for the valuable purchase right by accepting a coupon rate on the debentures lower than what they would demand if the debentures were not convertible. In general, a higher conversion ratio, i.e., more shares of stock in return for each converted debenture, will result in a greater reduction in the coupon rate, because the more stock the investor will get upon conversion, the more likely he is to find it advantageous to convert his debentures, and he will therefore value the right to convert more highly.

CHAPTER SUMMARY

This chapter has described the institutional characteristics of several contracts for the *optional* purchase and sale of securities, including call and put options on common stock, warrants, callable and putable debt, and convertible debt.

Call options to buy common stock and put options to sell common stock are among the simplest option contracts in existence. These contracts are fully described by specifying the underlying asset, the exercise price of the option, and the expiration date of the option. A call option holder has the right (but not the obligation) to buy the underlying asset at the specified exercise price on or before the specified expiration date. A call option writer has the obligation (but not the right) to sell the underlying asset at the specified exercise price (if the holder of the option exercises his right to buy) on or before the specified expiration date. The first section of this chapter has made a distinction between puts and calls, and between the rights derived from holding an option and the obligations undertaken in writing an option.

Option contracts differ from futures contracts, because they separate the rights and obligations which are bundled together in a futures contract. For example, an investor with a short position in a futures contract has both the right and the obligation to sell the underlying asset on the settlement date at a specified settlement price. If, on the other hand, he held a long put option, he would enjoy the right, but would bear no obligation, to sell the underlying asset at a fixed exercise price. Conversely, if he wrote a call option, he would bear the obligation, but he would have no right, to sell the underlying asset at a fixed exercise price.

There are two options markets: the OTC options market and the exchange markets for listed options. Options in the former market are written by investors directly to other investors and bear the exercise prices and expiration dates which are agreeable to both parties. Options in the latter market are written by investors to the Options Clearing Corporation (OCC) and are written by the OCC to other investors, and bear one of the limited set of exercise price–expiration date combinations specified by an options exchange. The difference between OTC options and listed options is roughly equivalent to the difference between forward contracts and futures contracts.

The last section of this chapter has described some of the optional purchase and sale provisions which can be incorporated into corporate securities, including provisions for buying new issues of stock for cash, for calling and putting debt back to an issuer in exchange for cash, and for converting debt into stock. The range of these provisions suggests some of the wide variety of ways in which contracts for the optional purchase and sale of securities can be written.

FURTHER READING

Kenneth Garbade and Monica Kaicher, "Exchange-Traded Options on Common Stock," Federal Reserve Bank of New York *Quarterly Review*, **3** (Winter 1978–79), 26–40.

Securities and Exchange Commission, *Report of the Special Study of the Options Markets* (1978).

CHAPTER 18

EQUILIBRIUM CALL OPTION PRICES

Call option contracts on common stock are valuable securities, because they give purchase rights to holders and because they impose sale obligations on writers. More particularly, an investor will be willing to pay some positive price to acquire a call option, and he will demand some positive compensation to sell or write a call option.

This chapter examines the equilibrium pricing of call option contracts from two perspectives. Section 18.1 describes the consequences of alternative exercise prices and expiration dates for the price of a call option. This type of analysis is known as *cross-sectional* analysis, because it compares the prices of option contracts on the same stock at the same point in time. Section 18.2 takes a different perspective and examines the price of a call option contract with a fixed exercise price and a fixed expiration date as a function of the price of the underlying stock and the time remaining to the option's expiration date. This second mode of analysis is continued in Section 18.3, where the Black-Scholes model of call option pricing is developed.[1,2]

The analyses in this chapter are all partial equilibrium analyses, because they examine equilibrium relationships *between* the prices of different option contracts and *between* the prices of options and underlying stocks. The analy-

---

[1] The Black-Scholes model was first derived in Black and Scholes (1973). See also Merton (1973b) and Smith (1976) for surveys of option pricing. See Black (1975) for an expository article on the use of options for speculating and hedging. Merton, Scholes, and Gladstein (1978) examine how options can be used to modify the risk/return experience on a stock portfolio.

[2] Put option pricing is discussed in Black and Scholes (1973) and Merton (1973b). The relation between put and call option prices is discussed in the foregoing and in Stoll (1969), Merton (1973a), Stoll (1973), and Gould and Galai (1974).

TABLE 18.1
PRICES OF CALL OPTIONS ON IBM STOCK ON JUNE 8, 1979
(Per Share Optioned)

Exercise price	Expiration month		
	July 1979	**October 1979**	**January 1980**
$70	$8.25	$9.75	$11.00
75	4.00	6.00	7.63
80	1.38	3.38	4.88

ses do not examine the determinants of the *level* of call option prices. Some concluding comments in Section 18.3 sketch how a more general analysis of equilibrium call option pricing might be undertaken.

For expositional simplicity, the analyses in this chapter assume that an optioned stock does not make any dividend payments prior to the expiration date of an option on that stock.[3] The analyses also assume that there are no taxes on either ordinary income or capital gains.[4]

18.1 CROSS-SECTIONAL CHARACTERISTICS OF CALL OPTION PRICES

Table 18.1 shows the prices of nine different call option contracts on IBM stock at the close of trading on June 8, 1979. That table illustrates the cross-sectional characteristics of call option prices.[5] In particular, it shows the consequences, for the price of a call option, of higher vs. lower exercise prices and sooner vs. later expiration dates.

When discussing the pricing structure shown in Table 18.1, we will find it convenient to refer to an option by its expiration month and exercise price. For example, reference to the "October 75" option in Table 18.1 means the call option on IBM which had an exercise price of $75 per share optioned and which expired in October 1979.

As shown in Table 18.1, the price of an October 75 option was $6 per share optioned on June 8, 1979. This means that an investor would have had to pay $600 to buy an October 75 call option on 100 shares of IBM, and he would have received $600 if he sold or wrote the same option on the same number of shares. This section examines how and why the price of a call option on IBM differed when it had a later expiration date, for example, January 1980 instead

---

[3] Roll (1977b) and Geske (1979) derived an expression for the equilibrium value of a call option on a stock that pays a dividend before the option expires. See also Schwartz (1977). Galai (1978b) has examined the minimum value of an option on a stock that pays a dividend before the option expires.

[4] The effect of taxes on option pricing is discussed by Scholes (1976). See also Ingersoll (1976).

[5] The cross-sectional structure of option prices is examined in Merton (1973b) and Smith (1976).

of October 1979, or when it had a higher exercise price, for example, $80 per share optioned instead of $75 per share optioned.

Consequence of a More Distant Expiration Date

The price of a call option will be greater the more distant the expiration date of the option, everything else being the same. This can be illustrated by comparing the prices of the October 75 and January 75 call options on IBM shown in Table 18.1. The former options were priced at $6.00 per share optioned, and the latter (more distant) options were priced at $7.63 per share optioned.

It is reasonable that options with more distant expiration dates should be more valuable, because they give more rights to holders and because they impose more obligations on writers. The October 75 option on IBM shown in Table 18.1 could have been exercised at any time prior to October 21, 1979. The January 75 option could have been exercised at any time within that same interval, and could also have been exercised at any time during the following 3 months. Thus, a January 75 call gave a holder an additional 3 months to exercise his right to buy IBM stock at $75 per share, and was consequently more valuable than an October 75 call option.

There is another reason why options with more distant expiration dates have higher prices than options with closer expiration dates. Suppose the January 75 option on IBM shown in Table 18.1 was trading at $5.75 while the October 75 option was trading at $6.00. An arbitrageur could then have bought a January 75 option (for $5.75) and sold short (or written) an October 75 option (receiving $6.00) and made a net profit of at least $0.25 (that is, $6.00 received from short selling the October 75 option, less $5.75 cost of buying the January 75 option). This net profit would have been riskless, because the arbitrageur could not have lost money on the combined option position. As a writer of the October 75 option, the arbitrageur would have had a potential obligation to deliver IBM stock at $75 per share at any time up to and including October 20, 1979, when the October 75 option expired. However, as a holder of the January 75 option, he would have had the right to buy the same stock at the same price for at least as long an interval of time. Thus, if his short option was exercised, he could have acquired the underlying stock by exercising his long option at no loss to himself. If his short option expired unexercised on October 20, 1979, he could have sold his January 75 option for an additional profit. The existence of an opportunity for a riskless profit is inconsistent with the notion of a market in equilibrium. It follows that, in equilibrium, the price of an option must be greater the more distant the expiration date of that option, everything else being the same.

Options as "Wasting Assets" The foregoing analysis implies that, everything else remaining the same, the price of an option will fall as the option approaches its expiration date, or as the time remaining to expiration declines. This phenomenon is sometimes described with the phrase that an option is a "wasting asset" whose value declines over time. We will see in Section 18.3

that this decline in value through time plays an important role in the analysis of the equilibrium value of a call option contract.

Consequence of a Higher Exercise Price

The price of an option will be lower the greater the exercise price of that option, everything else being the same. This can be illustrated by comparing the prices of the October 75 and October 80 options on IBM shown in Table 18.1. The former option was priced at $6.00 per share optioned, and the latter option (with a greater exercise price) was priced at $3.38 per share optioned.

It is reasonable that a call option with a greater exercise price should be less valuable, because the cost to a holder of exercising such an option is greater. An investor could acquire IBM stock at a cost of $75 per share by exercising an October 75 call option, but he would have to pay $80 per share if he wanted to acquire the same stock by exercising an October 80 call option. It is reasonable that he would be willing to pay more for the former option than for the latter option, and it is similarly reasonable that he would be willing to sell or write the latter option for less than he would demand to sell or write the former option.

There is another reason why options with greater exercise prices must have lower prices. Suppose the October 80 option on IBM was trading at $6.50 while the October 75 option was trading at $6.00. An arbitrageur could then have bought an October 75 option (for $6.00) and sold short (or written) an October 80 option (receiving $6.50) and made a net profit of at least $0.50 (that is, $6.50 received from short selling the October 80 option, less $6.00 cost of the October 75 option). This net profit would have been riskless, because the arbitrageur could not have lost money on the combined option position. As a writer of the October 80 option the arbitrageur would have had a potential obligation to deliver IBM stock at a price of $80 per share at any time up to and including October 21, 1979. However, as a holder of the October 75 option he would have had the right to buy the same stock over the same interval of time at the lower price of $75 per share. If his short October 80 option was exercised, he could have acquired the underlying stock by exercising his long October 75 option at a price $5 less than the price he would receive from delivering that stock. If his October 80 option was not exercised, either he could have sold his long October 75 option immediately before its expiration date for an additional profit, or he could have allowed that option to expire unexercised. Since the existence of an opportunity for a riskless profit is inconsistent with the notion of a market in equilibrium, it follows that, in equilibrium, the price of an option must be less the greater the exercise price of that option.

18.2 THE PRICE OF A CALL OPTION AS A FUNCTION OF TIME AND THE PRICE OF THE UNDERLYING STOCK

This section and the following section examine the price of a call option contract with a given exercise price and expiration date as a function of time and the price of the underlying stock. In contrast to the previous section, we will

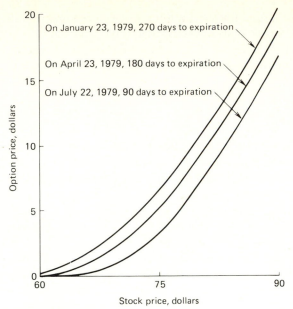

On January 23, 1979, 270 days to expiration

On April 23, 1979, 180 days to expiration

On July 22, 1979, 90 days to expiration

Option price, dollars

Stock price, dollars

FIGURE 18.1
Call option prices as a function of time and the price of the underlying stock. Option exercise
price = $75; option expiration date = October 20, 1979. Computed from Equation (18.11) with
$v^2 = .017885$ per annum and $R_f = .10$ per annum, or 10 percent per annum.

now examine the "longitudinal" structure of call option prices, or the behavior
of the price of a particular call option contract as time and the price of the underlying stock change.

Figure 18.1 illustrates the general characteristics of call option prices as a
function of time and the price of the underlying stock. The figure assumes the
call option has an exercise price of $75 per share optioned and an expiration
date of October 20, 1979. As shown in the figure, the price of the option is a
decreasing function of time, so that as the option gets closer to expiration, the
price of that option will fall (assuming the price of the underlying stock remains
unchanged). This phenomenon, that a call option is a wasting asset, was noted
in the previous section.

Figure 18.1 also shows that the price of the option is an increasing function
of the price of the underlying stock. The present analysis is primarily concerned with the relation between the price of a call option and the price of the
underlying stock at different points in time prior to and on the option's expiration date.

To establish some preliminary notation, let

S = stock price (for example, $77.25 per share)
E = option exercise price (for example, $75 per share optioned)
t^* = option expiration date (for example, October 20, 1979)
t = current date, where $t \leq t^*$ (for example, June 8, 1979)

Denote the price of an option, as a function of the stock price S and time t, as $C[S, t]$. The analysis of this section first describes the equilibrium price of an expiring option, or the form of the function $C[S, t^*]$. The analysis then goes on to examine the price of an unexpired call option, or the nature of the function $C[S, t]$ for $t < t^*$.

The Price of an Expiring Call Option

On its expiration date the price of a call option will be equal to the greater of (1) zero and (2) the excess of the price of the underlying stock over the exercise price of the option. This statement of the price of an expiring call option can be written as

$$C[S, t^*] = \max [0, S - E] \tag{18.1}$$

Figure 18.2 graphs the option price function set forth in Equation (18.1). As shown in the figure, if the price of the stock is less than the exercise price of the expiring option ($S < E$), the option will have no value ($C = 0$). This is reasonable, because the option is expiring and hence must be exercised immediately or be allowed to expire unexercised. However, it would be uneconomical to exercise the option if the stock price is less than the option's exercise price, because the stock could then be bought directly for less money than it would

FIGURE 18.2
Price of an expiring call option as a function of the price of the underlying stock. Option exercise price $E = \$75$.

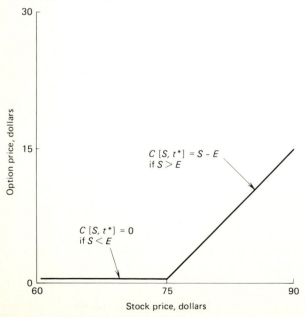

cost to exercise the option. The only other possibility is to allow the option to expire unexercised. Since nobody would pay anything for an option that, with certainty, will expire unexercised, it follows that the price of an option will be zero on its expiration date if the price of the underlying stock is less than the option's exercise price on that date.

Figure 18.2 also shows that if the price of the stock exceeds the exercise price of the expiring option ($S > E$), the option will be worth the amount of the excess ($C = S - E$). This follows because, as illustrated in Example 18.1, unless $C = S - E$ when $S > E$, there will exist an opportunity for a riskless profit by arbitraging between the expiring option and the underlying stock.

Intrinsic Value   The term max $[0, S - E]$ is commonly referred to as the

---

EXAMPLE 18.1
ARBITRAGE OPPORTUNITIES AT THE TIME OF A CALL OPTION'S EXPIRATION

Assume that a call option with an exercise price of $E = \$75$ per share is expiring, and that the contemporaneous price of the underlying stock is $S = \$78$ per share. Unless the price of the expiring option is $C = S - E = \$3$ per share optioned, there will be an opportunity to make a riskless profit by arbitraging between the stock and options markets.

Suppose, for example, the price of the option is $C = \$2$ per share optioned. An arbitrageur could then (1) buy the option, (2) short sell the underlying stock, and (3) exercise the option and deliver the stock obtained from the exercise to close out his short stock position. The net profit from these transactions would be

Proceeds from stock sale:	$S = \$78$
Cost of buying option:	$C = 2$
Cost of exercising option:	$E = 75$
Net profit:	$S - C - E = \$1$

Thus, if the price of an expiring option is less than $S - E$, the stock and options markets cannot be in equilibrium.

Suppose, on the other hand, that the price of the option is $C = \$5$ per share optioned. An arbitrageur could then (1) buy the stock and (2) short sell, or write, the option. Since the price of the stock ($S = \$78$) exceeds the exercise price of the expiring option ($E = \$75$), the buyer of the option is sure to exercise that option immediately. Thus, the arbitrageur can expect to have to (3) deliver the stock against an exercise of his short option. The net profit from these transactions would be

Proceeds from option sale:	$C = \$5$
Proceeds from option exercise:	$E = 75$
Cost of buying stock:	$S = 78$
Net profit:	$C + E - S = \$2$

Thus, if the price of an expiring option exceeds $S - E$, the stock and options markets cannot be in equilibrium.

The two foregoing examples show that, if $S > E$, then the price of an expiring option cannot, in equilibrium, be different than $S - E$.

intrinsic value of a call option, regardless of whether that option is expiring or not. If the stock price is less than a call option's exercise price, the option is said to be *out-of-the-money*, and it will have a zero intrinsic value; that is, max $[0, S - E] = 0$ when $S < E$. For example, IBM common stock was priced at $S = \$77.25$ per share at the close of trading on the NYSE on June 8, 1979. A call option on that stock with an exercise price of $E = \$80$ per share was, therefore, out-of-the-money and had zero intrinsic value on that date.

If the price of a stock is greater than the exercise price of a call option on that stock, the option is said to be *in-the-money*, and it will have a positive intrinsic value which is equal to the excess of the stock price over the option's exercise price; that is, max $[0, S - E] = S - E > 0$ if $S > E$. For example, a call option on IBM with a $70.00 exercise price would have had an intrinsic value of $7.25 on June 8, 1979 ($77.25 stock price, less $70.00 option exercise price).

Equation (18.1) says that the price of an expiring call option will just equal the intrinsic value of that option. Thus, whatever else may be true of the price of an option, we now know that it will converge to the option's intrinsic value as the option approaches expiration.

The Price of an Unexpired Call Option

We have just seen that, in equilibrium, the price of an expiring call option equals the intrinsic value of that option. If, however, an option is not going to expire for some interval of time, such as a few weeks or a few months, it may be worth substantially more than its intrinsic value. Some of the characteristics of the price of an unexpired call option can be analyzed by considering the minimum value of such an option.

The Minimum Value of an Unexpired Call Option The minimum value of an unexpired call option can be established by an arbitrage argument which involves an investment in riskless debt securities. Suppose R_f is the yield per unit time, compounded continuously, on riskless debt of all maturities.[6] A promise to pay $100 at time t^* would then be worth $100 \cdot \exp[-R_f \cdot (t^* - t)]$ at time $t < t^*$, because the promised future payment of $100 is discounted at the rate R_f over the interval $t^* - t$.[7]

In equilibrium, the price of an unexpired call option must satisfy two inequalities:

$$C[S, t] \geq 0 \tag{18.2a}$$

$$C[S, t] \geq S - E \cdot \exp[-R_f \cdot (t^* - t)] \tag{18.2b}$$

or

$$C[S, t] \geq \max[0, S - E \cdot \exp[-R_f \cdot (t^* - t)]] \tag{18.3}$$

---

[6] This assumes that investors can both borrow and lend at the rate R_f, and implies that the term structure of interest rates is flat at the rate R_f.

[7] Continuous compounding is described in the appendix to Chapter 1. See, especially, Equation (A.6b) in that appendix.

Equation (18.3) has two components. The first component, shown in Equation (18.2a), merely says that the price of the option must be nonnegative. The more interesting question is why the price of a call option also cannot be less than $S - E \cdot \exp \left[-R_f \cdot (t^* - t)\right]$, as stated in Equation (18.2b).

To see why the inequality of Equation (18.2b) must hold in equilibrium, suppose that the converse were true, so that

$$0 < C < S - E \cdot \exp \left[-R_f \cdot (t^* - t)\right] \qquad (18.4)$$

An arbitrageur could then buy the option (at a cost of C), short sell the underlying stock (receiving S), and make a riskless net profit of not less than $(S - C) \cdot \exp \left[R_f \cdot (t^* - t)\right] - E$ on the option's expiration date. The net proceeds from the option purchase and stock sale would be $S - C$ at time t. Invested in debt securities earning at the rate of R_f, these net proceeds would increase in value to $(S - C) \cdot \exp \left[R_f \cdot (t^* - t)\right]$ on the option's expiration date. On that expiration date the arbitrageur would do one of two things:

1 If the option is expiring in-the-money, he will exercise his option at a cost of E and use the stock which he receives from the exercise to close out his short stock position. His net profit will be the value of his maturing debt securities, less the cost of exercising the option, or $(S - C) \cdot \exp \left[R_f \cdot (t^* - t)\right] - E$.

2 If the option is out-of-the-money, he will allow his option to expire unexercised and will close out his short stock position by buying stock directly at a cost less than the option exercise price. His net profit will then exceed the net profit shown in item 1.

Note that the option exercise price sets the maximum amount of money the arbitrageur will have to pay to obtain the stock needed to close out his short stock position, and that the value of the arbitrageur's debt securities will exceed that exercise price on the expiration date,[8] so that the arbitrageur knows he will have sufficient funds to exercise his call option. Thus, the foregoing arbitrage is profitable and riskless. Example 18.2 gives a numerical example of the arbitrage.

Since opportunities for riskless arbitrage profits cannot exist in equilibrium, the inequality of Equation (18.4) cannot be true in equilibrium. Thus, the inequality of Equation (18.2b) must be true.[9]

---

[8] If, as stated in Equation (18.4), $C < S - E \cdot \exp \left[-R_f \cdot (t^* - t)\right]$, then it follows that $E < (S - C) \cdot \exp \left[R_f \cdot (t^* - t)\right]$, that is, that the value of the maturing debt securities exceeds the option exercise price.

[9] Galai (1978b) examined the validity of Equation (18.2b), and comparable inequalities for the case of an option on a stock that pays a dividend prior to expiration, using data from the CBOE. He found a surprising number of instances where an option was trading below its theoretical minimum value, but he also found that delay in the execution of an arbitrageur's stock sale and option purchase orders would change what appeared to be an opportunity for a large riskless profit into a much smaller risky profit opportunity. Galai did not consider whether transactions costs would eliminate the remaining expected profits, nor did he consider whether those expected profits were commensurate with the level of risk assumed in attempting to take advantage of the perceived profit opportunities.

EXAMPLE 18.2

THE ARBITRAGE OPPORTUNITY WHICH EXISTS WHEN THE PRICE OF A CALL OPTION IS LESS THAN ITS MINIMUM VALUE

Assume that a call option with $t^* - t = 180$ days to expiration and with an exercise price of $E = \$75$ per share has a price of $C = \$1$, that the contemporaneous price of the underlying stock is $S = \$74$ per share, and that the rate of interest on riskless debt securities is $R_f = .10$, or 10 percent per annum. We then have that

$$
\begin{aligned}
S - E \cdot \exp\ [-R_f \cdot (t^* - t)] &= 74 - 75 \cdot \exp\ [-.10(180/365)] \\
&= 74 - 75 \cdot \exp\ [-.04932] \\
&= 74 - 71.39 \\
&= \$2.61
\end{aligned}
$$

An opportunity for a riskless arbitrage profit exists, because the price of the option $(C = \$1.00)$ is less than its minimum value $S - E \cdot \exp\ [-R_f \cdot (t^* - t)] = \$2.61$. In particular, an arbitrageur could (1) buy the option, (2) short sell the stock, and (3) invest the net proceeds in debt securities. The net proceeds of the stock sale and option purchase would be

Proceeds from stock sale:	$S = \$74$
Cost of buying option:	$C = \underline{1}$
Net proceeds:	$S - C = \$73$

If $73 is invested at a rate of interest of $R_f = 10$ percent for $t^* - t = 180$ days, at maturity it will be worth

$$
\begin{aligned}
\$73 \cdot \exp\ [R_f \cdot (t^* - t)] &= \$73 \cdot \exp\ [.10(180/365)] \\
&= \$73 \cdot \exp\ [.04932] \\
&= \$76.69
\end{aligned}
$$

On the option expiration date the arbitrageur can do one of two things:

• If the price of the stock is then greater than $75 per share, he can exercise his option and use the stock obtained from the exercise to close out his stock position. His net profit will then be

Value of maturing debt securities:	$76.69
Cost of exercising option:	$\underline{75.00}$
Net profit:	$ 1.69

• If the price of the stock is less than $75 per share, he can close out his short stock position by buying the needed stock directly, at a price less than $75. His net profit will then exceed $1.69.

This shows that if $C < S - E \cdot \exp\ [-R_f \cdot (t^* - t)]$, then an arbitrageur can make a riskless profit of not less than $(S - C) \cdot \exp\ [R_f \cdot (t^* - t)] - E > 0$ by buying options and short selling the underlying stock and then closing out his position on the expiration date of the option.

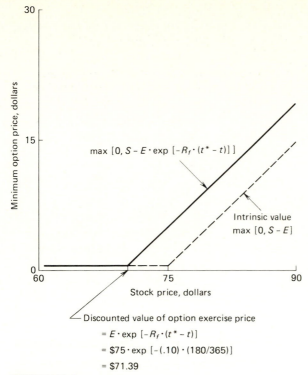

$$\text{max } [0, S - E \cdot \exp \, [-R_f \cdot (t^* - t)]\,]$$

Intrinsic value
max $[0, S - E]$

Discounted value of option exercise price
$$= E \cdot \exp \, [-R_f \cdot (t^* - t)]$$
$$= \$75 \cdot \exp \, [-(.10) \cdot (180/365)]$$
$$= \$71.39$$

FIGURE 18.3
Minimum price of an unexpired call option with 180 days remaining to expiration as a function of the price of the underlying stock. Option exercise price $E = \$75$; interest rate $R_f = 10$ percent per annum.

Figure 18.3 shows the minimum price of an unexpired call option with 180 days remaining to expiration as a function of the price of the underlying stock when the yield on riskless debt is $R_f = .10$, or 10% per annum. That figure shows that, if the stock price S exceeds the discounted value of the option's exercise price $E \cdot \exp \, [-R_f \cdot (t^* - t)]$, then the price of option must be strictly greater than the option's intrinsic value. In particular, the market price of an unexpired in-the-money call option must exceed its intrinsic value.

Early Exercise of a Call Option   We have thus far seen that it is never economical to exercise an out-of-the-money call option,[10] and that the market price of an unexpired in-the-money call option must exceed the option's intrinsic value. These two results have the important implication that only in-the-money options will be exercised, and that they will only be exercised on their expiration dates and not at any earlier date.[11]

---

[10] If a call option is out-of-the-money, the stock price is less than the option's exercise price, and so it is cheaper to buy the stock directly than to buy the stock by exercising the option.

[11] If a stock pays a dividend before a call option on that stock expires, it may be beneficial to exercise the option and acquire the stock shortly before the dividend is paid. See Roll (1977b) and Geske (1979).

This result may seem surprising, but it has a logical explanation. When an investor exercises an option, he destroys whatever value the option might have as a result of the time remaining to the option's expiration date. That is, he forces the economic value of the option to the option's intrinsic value. However, we have just seen that, in equilibrium, the market price of an unexpired in-the-money call option must be greater than the option's intrinsic value. Thus, the proceeds received from selling such an option to another investor must exceed the economic value of exercising that option, so that exercise is never more advantageous than sale. This phenomenon is sometimes described with the statement "A call option is never worth more dead than alive."

When the Price of an Unexpired Call Option Will Equal Its Minimum Value There are two circumstances in which the price of a call option will be equal to (or close to) the minimum value of that option. In the first instance, suppose the price of the underlying stock is much less than the option's exercise price, so that, for all practical purposes, it is certain that the option will remain out-of-the-money until its expiration date and hence will expire unexercised. Such an option is called a *deep-out-of-the-money* option. Because there is no chance the option will be exercised, the option will have no value, and so $C = 0$. Thus, the price of an option will equal the minimum price of that option when the stock price is far less than the option's exercise price.

Suppose, on the other hand, that the price of the underlying stock is much greater than an option's exercise price, so that, for all practical purposes, it is certain that the option will still be in-the-money on its expiration date. It is certain that such an option will not expire unexercised, and the option is called a *deep-in-the-money* option.[12] Because the option will not expire unexercised, the option is essentially a commitment to buy the optioned stock at the specified exercise price on the expiration date. A firm commitment to buy stock at price E at time t^* will cost $S - E \cdot \exp [-R_f \cdot (t^* - t)]$ at time t. That is, it will cost the difference between the stock price prevailing at time t and the present discounted value of the future payment. Thus, the price of an option will equal the minimum price of that option when the stock price far exceeds the option's exercise price.

When the Price of an Unexpired Call Option Will Exceed Its Minimum Value So far we have derived the minimum value of an unexpired call option [see Equation (18.3)], and we have examined two circumstances under which the price of an option will equal its minimum value: (1) when the option is deep-out-of-the-money and is certain to expire unexercised, and (2) when the option is deep-in-the-money and will not expire unexercised. When an option is neither deep-out-of-the-money nor deep-in-the-money, and when there are significant probabilities of both exercising and not exercising the option, the price of

---

[12] Note that it is not correct to say that a deep-in-the-money option is certain to be exercised. A holder of such an option could sell it back to the writer for cash instead of exercising. See Lipton (1971, pp. 14–15) for a discussion of deep-in-the-money call options as a leverage device.

the option will exceed its minimum value. This is illustrated in Figure 18.4. Point A in that figure shows the price of the option as $2.01 when the price of the underlying stock is $70.00. It is reasonable that this option should be worth more than its minimum value of zero, because there is some nonnegligible probability that the price of the stock will exceed the $75.00 exercise price of the option on the option's expiration date. That is, since it *might* be economical to exercise the option in the future, the option must have a positive price now.

The precise shape and position of the option price curve shown in Figure 18.4 cannot be fully specified on the basis of the analytical results obtained thus far. All we can say is that the price of the option should be near zero if the option is deep-out-of-the-money (as illustrated by point B in the figure), that the price of the option should be nearly equal to $S - E \cdot \exp[-R_f \cdot (t^* - t)]$ if the option is deep-in-the-money (as illustrated by point C), and that the price of the option should change smoothly with the price of the underlying stock between these two extremes. We also know that the option price curve shown in Figure 18.4 should converge to the intrinsic value price curve shown in Figure 18.2 as the option approaches expiration. Thus, while we have a notion of the general shape of the option price curve shown in Figure 18.4, we do not know the determinants of that price curve outside of three exceptional cases (deep-out-of-the-money options, deep-in-the-money options, and expiring options). The next section, on the Black-Scholes option pricing model, will fill the remaining gaps in our knowledge.

FIGURE 18.4
Price of a call option with 180 days remaining to expiration as a function of the price of the underlying stock. Option exercise price $E = \$75$; interest rate $R_f = 10$ percent per annum. Computed from Equation (18.11) with $v^2 = .017885$ per annum.

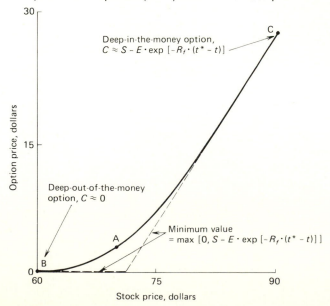

18.3   THE BLACK-SCHOLES OPTION PRICING MODEL

The objective of this section is to derive an explicit expression for the equilibrium price of a call option as a function of the price S of the underlying stock and time t. We assume that the option has an exercise price E and an expiration date t^*. One part of the function $C[S, t]$ is already known: when $t = t^*$, we have $C[S, t^*] = \max [0, S - E]$ [see Equation (18.1)]. The aim of the present section is to extend this expression for the price of an expiring call option "backward" in time, and to obtain option prices for values of t less than t^*.[13] This can be done by making use of the opportunities for hedging stock and options positions which are implicit in the option price curve shown in Figure 18.4.

Hedging a Long Stock Position with Short Call Options on that Stock

Although we do not know the precise position of the option price curve shown in Figure 18.4, the general shape of that curve implies that changes in the prices of the stock and the option will be positively correlated. More particularly, the price of the stock and the price of the option will increase and decrease together, because the option price curve has a positive slope. This implies that it is possible to short sell call options against stock held long in an amount sufficient to hedge, or insulate, the net worth of the aggregate position.[14]

In order to understand hedging, it is necessary first to define the hedge ratio of an option. The *hedge ratio* of an option, denoted by h, is the ratio of the *change* in the price of an option to a contemporaneous *change* in the price of the underlying stock. Graphically, the hedge ratio of an option is the slope of an option price curve, such as the curve shown in Figure 18.4, at a particular point along that curve. If the slope of the curve at point A in Figure 18.4 is .44, then the option has a hedge ratio of .44 when the price of the underlying stock is $70.00 per share and the price of the option is $2.01 per share optioned. If the stock price increases from $70.00 to $70.50 per share, the price of the option will increase from $2.01 to $2.23 per share optioned (.44 hedge ratio = $0.22 change in option price ÷ $0.50 change in stock price).

The hedge ratio of an option can change and is *not* a fixed number associated with that option. Figure 18.5 shows how the hedge ratio of the option illustrated in Figure 18.4 changes with the price of the underlying stock. At low stock prices the hedge ratio of the option will be near zero, because the slope of the option price curve will then be nearly flat. (Compare the slope of the option price curve at point B in Figure 18.4 with the value of the hedge ratio at point B in Figure 18.5.) At high stock prices, the hedge ratio of the option will be near unity—implying a dollar-for-dollar relation between changes in the stock price

---

[13] Valuing an option by starting at its known value on its expiration date and proceeding backward in chronological time is an explicit feature of numerical valuation procedures. See Schwartz (1977, n. 7). Brennan and Schwartz (1978) show the similarity between numerical valuation procedures and analytical valuation models.

[14] Hedging a stock position with options is described in Black (1975).

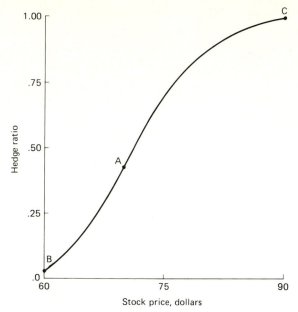

FIGURE 18.5
Hedge ratio of a call option with 180 days remaining to expiration as a function of the price of the underlying stock. Option exercise price $E = \$75$; interest rate $R_f = 10$ percent per annum.

and changes in the option price—because the slope of the option price curve will then be near unity. (Compare the slope of the option price curve at point C in Figure 18.4 with the value of the hedge ratio at point C in Figure 18.5.) The hedge ratio of an option will also change as a function of the time remaining to expiration and will be different for options with different exercise prices and expiration dates.[15] The notion of a hedge ratio is, nonetheless, a useful concept, as long as we keep in mind that it is not a fixed number.

Using a Hedge Ratio to Construct a Hedged Position in Stock and Options   Hedge ratios are important, because they can be used to compute the quantity of options that have to be sold short to hedge a given stock position. Suppose, for example, that an investor owns 1000 shares of stock and that a call option on that stock currently has a hedge ratio of .8. This hedge ratio means that the price of the option will increase (or decrease) by $0.80 if the price of the stock increases (or decreases) by $1.00 (.8 hedge ratio = $0.80 option price change ÷ $1.00 stock price change).

If the investor short sells call options on 1250 shares of stock, his net position will be hedged against the risk of small changes in the price of the underly-

---

[15] Footnote 27 later in this chapter describes how to compute the hedge ratio of an option as a function of the terms of the option contract, the price and volatility of the underlying stock, and the level of interest rates.

ing stock. If the price of the stock goes up by $1.00 per share, the investor will make $1000 on his long stock (1000 shares held long × $1.00 price increase per share) and he will lose $1000 on his short call options (1250 options held short × $0.80 price increase per share optioned). Conversely, if the price of the stock falls by $1.00 per share, he will lose $1000 on his long stock and he will make $1000 on his short options. In either case his gains on one security will offset his losses on the other security.

In general, an investor must short sell options on h^{-1} shares of stock to hedge one share of that stock. If the hedge ratio of an option is $h = .8$, he must short sell options on $h^{-1} = (.8)^{-1} = 1.25$ shares of stock for each share of stock which he holds long. If the hedge ratio is $h = .5$, he must short sell options on $h^{-1} = (.5)^{-1} = 2.00$ shares of stock for each share of stock which he holds long.

Rebalancing a Hedged Position   It should be noted that, because the hedge ratio of an option can change, an investor may have to "rebalance" his option position from time to time to maintain a hedge against stock held long. For example, Figure 18.5 shows that the hedge ratio of an option will rise when the price of the underlying stock increases. If the hedge ratio of the option was initially $h = .5$, the investor would have sold options on $h^{-1} = (.5)^{-1} = 2.00$ shares of stock for each share of stock held long. If the hedge ratio subsequently rose to $h = .8$, the investor would have needed to hold a short position in options on only $h^{-1} = (.8)^{-1} = 1.25$ shares of stock for each share of stock held long. Thus, as a result of the increase in the hedge ratio, the investor would have repurchased options on .75 shares of stock for each share of stock he was hedging.[16] The repurchase of options previously sold short as a result of an increase in an option's hedge ratio, or the short sale of additional options as a result of a decrease in an option's hedge ratio, is known as *rebalancing* a hedged position. An investor can maintain an effective hedge against stock held long by rebalancing his short option position from time to time.[17]

The Return on Wealth Committed to a Hedged Position in Stock and Options

A hedged position in stock and options consists of h^{-1} options held short for each share of stock held long. Imagine that an investor commits capital to a hedged position by buying one share of stock at a price of S and by short selling options on h^{-1} shares of that stock at a price of C per share optioned. The net amount of wealth committed to the hedged position would be

$$\text{Wealth committed} = S - h^{-1} \cdot C \qquad (18.5)$$

[16] That is, to bring his option position from short 2.00 options for each share of stock held long to short 1.25 options for each share of stock held long, he would have had to repurchase options on .75 shares of stock for each share of stock held long.

[17] Finnerty (1978) presents evidence suggesting that weekly rebalancing is sufficient to maintain a hedged position. See also, however, Garbade and Kaicher (1978–79, p. 35) for a discussion of why *large, sudden* stock price changes can expose an investor to risk even on a seemingly hedged position.

This commitment of wealth is equal to the cost of the one share of stock, less the proceeds received from short selling, or writing, call options on h^{-1} shares of the same stock.

Now suppose that over some short interval of time, denoted by Δt, the price of the stock changes by an amount ΔS and the price of the option changes by an amount ΔC. The change in the investor's wealth will then be

$$\text{Change in wealth} = \Delta S - h^{-1} \cdot \Delta C \qquad (18.6)$$

This change in wealth is equal to the change ΔS in the stock price, less the change ΔC in the option price times the number of options held short.

If we ignore the passage of time, the change in the investor's wealth given by Equation (18.6) will be negligible, because the change in the option price and the change in the stock price must be related as $h = \Delta C/\Delta S$, or $\Delta C = h \cdot \Delta S$. This implies that

$$\begin{aligned}
\text{Change in wealth} &= \Delta S - h^{-1} \cdot \Delta C \\
&= \Delta S - h^{-1}(h \cdot \Delta S) \\
&= 0 \qquad \text{when } \Delta t = 0 \qquad (18.7)
\end{aligned}$$

Thus, if the change in the stock price were to occur in an instant of time, the aggregate market value of the securities in the hedged position would neither increase nor decrease.

In most cases stock prices do not change in an instant of time, but change over some interval of time, and so it is not correct to ignore the passage of time when computing the change in the value of a hedged position. We have already established that options are wasting assets whose prices decline over time. This means that the value of a hedged position will change as the price of the options in the position declines over time. Since the options are held short, the value of a hedged position will increase over time.

The *rate* of return on the wealth committed to a hedged position is the change in that wealth, divided by the wealth originally committed to the position, divided by the amount of time over which the change in wealth occurs. Denoting the rate of return as R_h, we have

$$R_h = \frac{\text{change in wealth/wealth committed}}{\Delta t} \qquad (18.8)$$

Using Equations (18.5) and (18.6), this becomes

$$R_h = \frac{\Delta S - h^{-1} \cdot \Delta C}{(S - h^{-1} \cdot C) \cdot \Delta t} \qquad (18.9)$$

Since the value of a hedged position increases over time, we have $R_h > 0$.

Equation (18.9) defines the rate of return on wealth committed to a hedged position as a function of the change in the price of the stock and the change in the price of the option which occur over an interval of time Δt. This rate of return would be zero in the absence of the passage of time [see the discussion at Equation (18.7)] and therefore does not depend on the magnitude of the change in the price of the stock. More particularly, wealth committed to a hedged position in stock and options behaves as if it were invested in debt securities: it increases over time but does not vary with the price of the underlying stock. This implies that, in equilibrium, the rate of return on wealth committed to a hedged position in stock and options must equal the rate of return on wealth committed to riskless debt securities, that is, $R_h = R_f$. If $R_h > R_f$, arbitrageurs will borrow funds at the interest rate R_f to invest in hedged positions and will thereby earn a riskless net profit. If $R_h < R_f$, they will short sell stock, buy options to fully hedge their risk on that short stock, and invest the net proceeds in debt securities.[18]

The preceding argument shows that, in equilibrium, we must have $R_h = R_f$. If this equality does not hold, there will be flows of arbitrage capital between the stock market, the options market, and the debt market.[19] Using the definition of R_h from Equation (18.9), this implies the equilibrium relation

$$R_f = \frac{\Delta S - h^{-1} \cdot \Delta C}{(S - h^{-1} \cdot C) \cdot \Delta t} \tag{18.10}$$

Equation (18.10) is the equation that tells us how the price function of an expiring call option, $C[S, t^*] = \max [0, S - E]$, must be extended backward in time, for values of $t < t^*$, to obtain the price function of an unexpired call option.

The Black-Scholes Option Pricing Model

Deriving Equation (18.10) was the key conceptual step in the development of the option pricing model set forth by Fischer Black and Myron Scholes. Black and Scholes assumed that the logarithm of the price of a stock follows a random walk through time, where the change in the logarithm of the price is a normally distributed random variable.[20] (See Section 13.2 for a description of stock prices following a random walk.) With this assumption they were able to solve Equation (18.10) for the price of an unexpired call option. The details of their solution are shown in the appendix to this chapter. The solution is

$$C[S, t] = S \cdot N[d_1] - E \cdot N[d_2] \cdot \exp [-R_f \cdot (t^* - t)] \tag{18.11a}$$

---

[18] Black and Scholes (1972, p. 400) observe that the return on a hedged position could be more or less than the risk-free rate in the short run, but that the option price must converge to its equilibrium value in the long run, i.e., on the option's expiration date. Thus, arbitrage between risk-free debt and a hedged position in stock and options must ultimately be profitable, even if it is not immediately profitable.

[19] This argument is essentially the same argument used in Section 16.3 to derive the consequences of arbitrage between a futures market, a spot market, and a debt market.

[20] Option pricing models have been derived for other assumptions about the dynamic behavior of stock prices. See Merton (1976), Cox and Ross (1976), and Brennan and Schwartz (1978).

where
$$N[x] = (2\pi)^{-1/2} \int_{-\infty}^{x} \exp\left[-\tfrac{1}{2} u^2\right] du \qquad (18.11b)$$

$$d_1 = \frac{\ln[S/E] + (R_f + \tfrac{1}{2} v^2)(t^* - t)}{v(t^* - t)^{1/2}} \qquad (18.11c)$$

$$d_2 = d_1 - v(t^* - t)^{1/2} \qquad (18.11d)$$

and where v^2 is the variance per unit time of the logarithm of the price of the underlying stock.[21,22]

Equation (18.11) gives the equilibrium price of a call option as a function of five parameters:

S = the contemporaneous price of the underlying stock

E = the option's exercise price

v^2 = the volatility of the price of the underlying stock (expressed as the variance per unit time of the logarithm of the stock price[23]

R_f = the rate of interest on riskless debt securities (assumed to be the same for debt of all maturities)[24]

$t^* - t$ = the time remaining to the option's expiration date

Four of these parameters (S, E, R_f, and $t^* - t$) are directly observable. The volatility of the price of the underlying stock can be estimated from historical stock

[21] The term $N[x]$ is, as defined in Equation (18.11b), the probability that a normally distributed random variable with a mean of zero and a variance of unity will be less than or equal to the threshold value x.

[22] The option pricing model of Equation (18.11) can be derived in a simple way under the special assumption that all investors are indifferent to risk. Let S^* denote the (uncertain) price of the stock at the option's expiration at time t^*, and let S denote the price of the stock at time t. If the log of the stock price follows a gaussian random walk, we have $\ln[S^*] = \ln[S] + m(t^* - t) + v(t^* - t)^{1/2}z$, where z is a normally distributed random variable with a mean of zero and a variance of unity. This implies that the expected future stock price is $\text{Exp}[S^*] = S \cdot \exp\left[(m - \tfrac{1}{2} v^2) \cdot (t^* - t)\right]$ and that the expected value of the option on its expiration date is $\text{Exp}[\max[0, S^* - E]] = S \cdot \exp\left[(m + \tfrac{1}{2}v^2) \cdot (t^* - t)\right] \cdot N[f_1] - E \cdot N[f_2]$, where $f_1 = \{\ln[S/E] + (m+v^2)(t^*-t)\}/[v(t^*-t)^{1/2}]$ and $f_2 = f_1 - v(t^*-t)^{1/2}$. However, if investors are indifferent to risk, the current stock price must be equal to the present value of the expected future stock price discounted at the risk-free rate, that is, $S = \text{Exp}[S^*] \cdot \exp[-R_f \cdot (t^* - t)]$. This implies that m and v^2 must be such that $R_f = m + \tfrac{1}{2}v^2$. Similarly, the current option price must be equal to the present value of the expected future option value discounted at the risk-free rate; that is, $C = \text{Exp}[\max[0, S^* - E]] \cdot \exp[-R_f \cdot (t^* - t)]$. Equation (18.11) results when $m = R_f - \tfrac{1}{2}v^2$ is substituted in the expression for $\text{Exp}[\max[0, S^* - E]]$. [Note that d_1 in Equation (18.11c) will equal f_1 when $m = R_f - \tfrac{1}{2}v^2$, and that $d_2 = f_2$.] See Boness (1964) for the original derivation of this result, and see Smith (1976) and Galai (1978a) for a comparison of this derivation and the Black-Scholes derivation of the price of an option.

[23] The model of Equation (18.11) assumes that the volatility of the price of the stock is constant at the value v^2 at least until the option expires. Schmalensee and Trippi (1978) present evidence suggesting that the volatility of a stock moves inversely with its price. Merton (1973b) derives a call option pricing model for the more general case where the volatility of the price of the underlying stock and the interest rate on risk-free debt fluctuate as the option approaches expiration.

[24] This implies that the term structure of interest rates is flat at the yield R_f.

price fluctuations.[25] Thus, the Black-Scholes model can be readily used to compute the equilibrium price of a call option.[26] Example 18.3 illustrates the computational aspects of the Black-Scholes option pricing model.[27]

Implications of the Black-Scholes Model

The Black-Scholes model can be used to establish some important characteristics of the behavior of call option prices. First, the model shows that the price of a call option is an increasing function of the volatility of the price of the underlying stock.[28] Everything else being the same, options on more volatile stocks will have higher prices. This result is reasonable, because while a stock price in excess of the exercise price of an expiring option increases the value of that option, a stock price below the exercise price cannot depress the option's value below zero. Options on more volatile stocks are more likely to have positive values in excess of a given level at expiration, and hence have higher prices prior to expiration.

The Black-Scholes model also shows that the price of a call option is an increasing function of the rate of interest on riskless debt securities.[29] Everything else remaining the same, higher (or lower) interest rates will be associated with higher (or lower) call option prices. This result is also reasonable, because a right to buy stock in the future at a fixed exercise price becomes more valuable the greater the discount factor used to convert that future exercise price into a present value.

The Black-Scholes model also supports the conclusions derived in Sections 18.1 and 18.2:

- The price of a call option is an increasing function of the expiration date of the option and a decreasing function of the exercise price.[30]

---

[25] If historical data are used to estimate the volatility of a stock, errors in measurement may lead to overstating (or understating) the actual volatility of a stock with a high (or low) estimated volatility. This will, in turn, lead to an overestimate (or underestimate) of the value of an option on that stock. See Black and Scholes (1972). Latané and Rendleman (1976) have shown that the stock price volatilities implied by options prices are more highly correlated with the level of future price fluctuations than past price fluctuations. This implies that investors do not simply assume that the past level of fluctuations will continue in the future, and that they use information other than past price volatilities in forecasting future volatilities.

[26] Black and Scholes (1972) examined the validity of the option pricing model of Equation (18.11) using data from the OTC options market. They found that options on stocks with high historical volatilities tend to be undervalued, and that options on stocks with low historical volatilities tend to be overvalued, but that transactions costs eliminated any opportunities to derive a net profit from incorrectly priced options. Galai (1977) examined the validity of Equation (18.11) using data from the CBOE and found that while the model could be used to identify overvalued and undervalued options, the implied profit opportunities were (1) reduced if there were lags between identification of an incorrectly priced option and the execution of purchases and sales to take advantage of that incorrect pricing, and (2) eliminated by transactions costs.

[27] Note that the Black-Scholes model can also be used to compute the hedge ratio of an option. In particular, $h = \partial C/\partial S = N[d_1]$, where d_1 is defined in Equation (18.11c). Since d_1 depends on S, E, v^2, R_f, and $t^* - t$, the hedge ratio of an option will also depend on the values of those variables.

[28] That is, $\partial C/\partial v > 0$ in Equation (18.11).

[29] That is, $\partial C/\partial R_f > 0$ in Equation (18.11).

[30] That is, $\partial C/\partial t^* > 0$ and $\partial C/\partial E < 0$ in Equation (18.11).

EXAMPLE 18.3
CALCULATING THE PRICE OF A CALL OPTION WITH THE BLACK-SCHOLES OPTION
PRICING MODEL

The Black-Scholes model specifies the equilibrium value of a call option as a function
of five parameters. This example illustrates the steps required to obtain a numerical
option price. We begin by specifying hypothetical values for each of the five
parameters:

$$S = \$77.25 \quad \text{(price per share of the underlying stock)}$$
$$E = \$75.00 \quad \text{(exercise price of the option)}$$
$$t^* - t = 180 \text{ days}$$
$$= .4932 \text{ years} \quad \text{(time remaining to the option's expiration date)}$$
$$R_f = 10\% \text{ per annum}$$
$$= .10 \text{ per annum} \quad \text{(rate of interest on free risk debt securities)}$$
$$v^2 = (1\%)^2 \text{ per day}$$
$$= .0365 \text{ per year} \quad \text{(volatility of the price of the underlying stock)}$$

The only unusual parameter in the foregoing list is the volatility of the price of the underlying stock. If there is a 66 percent probability that the stock price will change by 1
percent or less in a single day, then, to a close approximation, the standard deviation of
the change in the logarithm of the stock price over a 1-day interval is 1 percent, and the
variance of the change in the logarithm of the stock price is $v^2 = (1 \text{ percent})^2$ per day, or
$v^2 = (.01)^2$ per day, or $v^2 = .0001$ per day, or $v^2 = .0365$ per year (that is, $.0001 \times 365$
days per year).

The first step in computing the price of an option with the Black-Scholes model is to
obtain the value of d_1:

$$d_1 = \frac{\ln [S/E] + (R_f + {}^1\!/_2 v^2)(t^* - t)}{v(t^* - t)^{1/2}}$$

$$= \frac{\ln [77.25/75.00] + [.1 + {}^1\!/_2 (.0365)](.4932)}{(.0365)^{1/2}(.4932)^{1/2}}$$

$$= .6550$$

The value of d_2 can then be computed:

$$d_2 = d_1 - v(t^* - t)^{1/2}$$
$$= .6550 - (.0365)^{1/2}(.4932)^{1/2}$$
$$= .5208$$

The values of $N[d_1]$ and $N[d_2]$ can be obtained from a table of standard normal probabilities:

$$N[d_1] = N[.6550] = .7437$$
$$N[d_2] = N[.5208] = .6988$$

With $N[d_1]$ and $N[d_2]$ available, the price of the call option can be computed as

$$C = S \cdot N[d_1] - E \cdot N[d_2] \cdot \exp [-R_f(t^* - t)]$$
$$= 77.25(.7437) - 75.0(.6988) \cdot \exp [-.10(.4932)]$$
$$= 57.45 - 52.41 \cdot \exp [-.04932]$$
$$= \$7.56$$

• The price of a call option is an increasing function of the price of the underlying stock. Moreover, at very low stock prices, when S is much less than E, ln $[S/E]$ will be a large negative number, so that d_1 and d_2 will also be large negative numbers. This implies that $N[d_1]$ and $N[d_2]$ will be near zero, and that C will be near zero. Conversely, when S is much larger than E, ln $[S/E]$, d_1 and d_2 will all be large positive numbers, so that $N[d_1]$ and $N[d_2]$ will be near unity. This implies that C will then be near $S - E \cdot \exp [-R_f \cdot (t^* - t)]$. Both these results on the price of a call option at extremely low and extremely high stock prices were derived in Section 18.2.

The Black-Scholes Model as a Partial Equilibrium Model of Call Option Prices

The Black-Scholes option pricing model follows from an analysis of the relation between the price of a call option and the contemporaneous price of the underlying stock. Given the assumptions of the model, if the price of an option is not equal to the price predicted by the model, there will be an opportunity for riskless arbitrage profits. For example, if the price of an option exceeds the price predicted by the model, arbitrageurs will enter the markets to (1) short sell the relatively overvalued option, (2) buy the relatively undervalued stock, and (3) borrow funds to finance their net cash outlays. Their transactions will put (1) downward pressure on the price of the option, (2) upward pressure on the price of the stock, and (3) upward pressure on the level of interest rates. The downward pressure on the option price will tend to push the price of the previously overvalued option down toward the price predicted by the model. At the same time, the upward pressures on the price of the underlying stock and on the level of interest rates will tend to push the price predicted by the model up toward the market price of the option. Thus, the net effect of the arbitrage transactions will be to push the stock, option, and debt markets back into relative equilibrium. These transactions will persist for as long as the markets remain out of relative equilibrium, i.e., for as long as the option price differs from the price predicted by the model.

The Black-Scholes model is a partial equilibrium model of option pricing which is similar to, but more complex than, the partial equilibrium model for the settlement price on a futures contract given by Equation (16.6). That is, the Black-Scholes model specifies an equilibrium relation *between* the price of a stock and the contemporaneous price of an option on that stock, just as Equation (16.6) specifies an equilibrium relation *between* the price of an asset and the contemporaneous settlement price of a futures contract for that asset. Both equations address the determinants of price relationships, but neither address the determinants of price levels.

A complete analysis of the determinants of the level of options prices would have to include the demand for and supply of options contracts by market participants other than arbitrageurs, the demand for and the supply of the underlying stock, and the role of arbitrage in intergrating the stock and options markets. Such an analysis would be quite similar to the analysis of spot and futures markets undertaken in Section 16.4.

CHAPTER SUMMARY

This chapter has analyzed the equilibrium characteristics of the price of a call option on common stock. The first section addressed the cross-sectional structure of call option prices, or the effect of alternative contract terms on the contemporaneous prices of call options on the same stock. The analysis concluded that, in equilibrium, a call option will be more valuable (1) the more distant the expiration date of the option and (2) the lower the exercise price of the option.

The second and third sections analyzed the longitudinal characteristics of the price of a call option, or the behavior of the price of a given option contract as a function of time and the price of the underlying stock. The analysis defined the intrinsic value of a call option as the excess, if any, of the price of the underlying stock over the option exercise price and showed that the equilibrium price of an expiring option is equal to its intrinsic value. The analysis also derived the minimum value of an unexpired call option and showed that the price of an unexpired option will equal its minimum value in two extreme circumstances: when the option is so deep-out-of-the-money that it is certain to expire unexercised, and when the option is so deep-in-the-money that it will not expire unexercised. Between these two extremes the price of an unexpired option will exceed its minimum value.

The last section of the chapter described how options can be used to hedge a position in stock, and why the notion of hedging implies a relationship between the behavior of stock prices and options prices and the return on risk-free debt securities. This relationship was expressed formally through the Black-Scholes option pricing model.

FURTHER READING

Fischer Black, "Fact and Fantasy in the Use of Options," *Financial Analysts Journal*, **31** (July–August 1975), 36.

Michael Brennan, and Eduardo Schwartz, "Finite Difference Methods and Jump Processes Arising in the Pricing of Contingent Claims: A Synthesis," *Journal of Financial and Quantitative Analysis*, **13** (September 1978), 461–474.

John Cox, Stephen Ross, and Mark Rubinstein, "Option Pricing: A Simplified Approach," *Journal of Financial Economics*, **7** (September 1979), 229–263.

Dan Galai, "Tests of Market Efficiency of the Chicago Board of Options Exchange," *Journal of Business*, **50** (April 1977), 167–197.

———, "Empirical Tests of Boundary Conditions for CBOE Options," *Journal of Financial Economics*, **6** (June/September 1978), 187–211.

Robert Geske, "A Note on an Analytical Valuation Formula for Unprotected American Call Options on Stocks with Known Dividends," *Journal of Financial Economics*, **7** (December 1979), 375–380.

Robert Merton, "Theory of Rational Option Pricing," *Bell Journal of Economics and Management Science*, **4** (Spring 1973), 141–183.

Clifford Smith, "Option Pricing: A Review," *Journal of Financial Economics*, **3** (January/March 1976), 3–51.

APPENDIX: The Black-Scholes Solution to Equation (18.10)

This appendix describes how Fischer Black and Myron Scholes derived an explicit equation for the price of a call option. Suppose there exists a function $C[S,t]$ giving the price of an option as a function of time and the price of the underlying stock. That function must satisfy two equations. First, as shown in Section 18.3, it must imply that the rate of return on a fully hedged position in stock and options is equal to the rate of return on risk-free debt securities:

$$R_f = \frac{\Delta S - h^{-1} \cdot \Delta C}{(S - h^{-1} \cdot C) \cdot \Delta t} \tag{A.1}$$

Second, at the expiration date t^* of the option the function must have the form

$$C[S, t^*] = \max [0, S - E] \tag{A.2}$$

The problem is to put Equation (A.1) in a useful form.

Since the hedge ratio h is the slope of the option's price curve, we have $h = \partial C / \partial S$. Multiplying the numerator and denominator of Equation (A.1) by h, and substituting $\partial C / \partial S$ for h, gives

$$R_f = \frac{\Delta S \cdot (\partial C / \partial S) - \Delta C}{[S \cdot (\partial C / \partial S) - C] \cdot \Delta t} \tag{A.3}$$

Now consider approximating the change ΔC in the option price which occurs when the stock price changes by an amount ΔS over an interval of time Δt with the first-order terms from a second-order expansion of the function $C[S, t]$.[31] The second-order expansion is

$$\Delta C = \frac{\partial C}{\partial S} \cdot \Delta S + \frac{\partial C}{\partial t} \cdot \Delta t + \frac{1}{2} \frac{\partial^2 C}{\partial S^2} \cdot (\Delta S)^2$$
$$+ \frac{1}{2} \frac{\partial^2 C}{\partial t^2} \cdot (\Delta t)^2 + \frac{\partial^2 C}{\partial t \cdot \partial S} \cdot \Delta S \cdot \Delta t \tag{A.4}$$

The term involving $(\Delta t)^2$ is clearly of second order and can be ignored, and the terms involving only ΔS and only Δt are clearly of first order and must be retained. However, we need to examine more carefully the terms involving $\Delta S \cdot \Delta t$ and $(\Delta S)^2$.

---

[31] The analysis of this approximation is taken from Figlewski (1977).

Black and Scholes assumed the logarithm of the price of the underlying stock follows a gaussian random walk through time. If the logarithm of the stock price has a mean change per unit time of m and a variance per unit time of v^2, we can write

$$\Delta S = \alpha \cdot S \cdot \Delta t + v \cdot S \cdot (\Delta t)^{1/2} z \tag{A.5}$$

where $\alpha = m + \frac{1}{2} v^2$ and where z is a normally distributed random variable with a mean of zero and a variance of unity. This implies

$$\Delta S \cdot \Delta t = \alpha \cdot S \cdot (\Delta t)^2 + v \cdot S \cdot (\Delta t)^{3/2} z \tag{A.6}$$

The product of ΔS and Δt is therefore of an order greater than first order in Δt and can be ignored in Equation (A.4).

Equation (A.5) also implies

$$(\Delta S)^2 = S^2 \cdot \alpha^2 \cdot (\Delta t)^2 + 2\alpha \cdot v \cdot S^2 \cdot z \cdot (\Delta t)^{3/2} + S^2 \cdot v^2 \cdot z^2 \cdot \Delta t \tag{A.7}$$

The only term in $(\Delta S)^2$ which is of first order in Δt is $S^2 \cdot v^2 \cdot z^2 \cdot \Delta t$. Since z is normally distributed with zero mean and unit variance, z^2 is chi-square-distributed with one degree of freedom, and we have[32]

$$\text{Exp } [S^2 \cdot v^2 \cdot z^2 \cdot \Delta t] = S^2 \cdot v^2 \cdot \Delta t \tag{A.8a}$$
$$\text{Var } [S^2 \cdot v^2 \cdot z^2 \cdot \Delta t] = 2S^4 \cdot v^4 \cdot (\Delta t)^2 \tag{A.8b}$$

Equation (A.8b) says that the variance of $S^2 \cdot v^2 \cdot z^2 \cdot \Delta t$ is small relative to its mean for small values of Δt,[33] and so we can approximate that random variable by its nonrandom expected value $S^2 \cdot v^2 \cdot \Delta t$ for small values of Δt. Thus we can approximate $(\Delta S)^2$ by $S^2 \cdot v^2 \cdot \Delta t$, which is first order in Δt.[34] Equation (A.4) then reduces to the first-order approximation

$$\Delta C = \frac{\partial C}{\partial S} \cdot \Delta S + \frac{\partial C}{\partial t} \cdot \Delta t + \frac{1}{2} \frac{\partial^2 C}{\partial S^2} \cdot S^2 \cdot v^2 \cdot \Delta t \tag{A.9}$$

Substituting the expression for ΔC given by Equation (A.9) in Equation (A.3) gives

$$R_f = \frac{- [(\partial C/\partial t) + \frac{1}{2}(\partial^2 C/\partial S^2) \cdot S^2 \cdot v^2] \cdot \Delta t}{[S \cdot (\partial C/\partial S) - C] \cdot \Delta t}$$

or

$$\frac{\partial C}{\partial t} = R_f \left(C - S \cdot \frac{\partial C}{\partial S} \right) - \frac{1}{2} \frac{\partial^2 C}{\partial S^2} \cdot S^2 \cdot v^2 \tag{A.10}$$

Equation (A.10) is a partial differential equation for the price of a call option as a func-

---

[32] If w has a chi-square distribution with n degrees of freedom, the expected value of w is n and the variance of w is $2n$. See Mood, Graybill, and Boes (1974, pp. 542–543).

[33] The ratio of the variance of $S^2 \cdot v^2 \cdot z^2 \cdot \Delta t$ to the mean of $S^2 \cdot v^2 \cdot z^2 \cdot \Delta t$ is $2S^2 \cdot v^2 \cdot \Delta t$ and hence is arbitrarily small for sufficiently small values of Δt.

[34] This approximation says that, although $(\Delta S)^2$ is of second order in ΔS, it is of first order in Δt, and must therefore be retained in a first-order approximation of ΔC.

tion of time t and the price S of the underlying stock. The solution to the equation depends on two constant parameters: the rate of interest R_f on riskless debt, and the variance v^2 per unit time of the logarithm of the price of the underlying stock.[35] The function $C[S, t]$ must satisfy Equation (A.10) and the boundary condition of Equation (A.2). The solution, derived by Black and Scholes, is given in Equation (18.11) in the chapter.

[35] These parameters are assumed to be fixed until the option expires. See footnote 24 earlier in this chapter.

CHAPTER 19

THE EQUILIBRIUM PRICE OF RISKY DEBT AND THE CREDIT RISK STRUCTURE OF INTEREST RATES

Chapter 14 analyzed yields on debt securities under the assumption that borrowers would not fail to make promised future payments to their creditors. The present chapter completes our examination of debt securities by analyzing (1) the equilibrium price of debt on which a borrower *could* fail to make promised payments, and (2) the resulting credit risk structure of interest rates.

It might seem odd that the topics considered in this chapter are grouped with chapters on option contracts, instead of with with the chapter on the term structure of interest rates. At first impression risky debt would seem to be more closely related to credit risk–free debt than to options. However, we will find that the theory of option pricing provides a powerful tool for investigating the value of risky debt.[1] This is only one manifestation of the revolution in financial theory that has been occurring during the past decade as a result of a more complete understanding of option valuation models, and as a result of a more extensive application of those models.

The presence of credit risk will have an obvious effect on the market price of debt securities. Consider, for example, the difference between a $1 million 13-week United States Treasury bill and $1 million of 13-week commercial paper issued by XYZ Corporation. The issuers of both securities promise to pay $1 million on the maturity date of the securities, but only the Treasury is absolutely certain to make good on its promise. The current market price of XYZ Corporation's commercial paper cannot, therefore, exceed the current

---

[1] The analysis of the value of risky debt using an option pricing model was first proposed by Black and Scholes (1973, pp. 649–652). The analyses of this chapter follow Merton (1974).

market price of the Treasury bill. The first section of this chapter examines the determinants of the price of risky debt and shows why the existence of credit risk will depress the price of such debt below the price of comparable Treasury debt.

It is commonplace when examining a debt security to examine its promised yield to maturity as well as its price. Suppose a security promises to pay its face value F at a maturity date t years in the future, but will not make any coupon payments prior to maturity, e.g., a Treasury bill or commercial paper. If that security has a present market price D, its *promised* yield to maturity is the value of R which solves the equation

$$D = F \cdot \exp\left[-R \cdot t\right] \tag{19.1}$$

Equation (19.1) says the present value D of the security is equal to the promised future payment F, discounted at the continuously compounded rate R for t years.[2] The value of R which solves Equation (19.1) is

$$R = \frac{\ln\left[F/D\right]}{t} \tag{19.2}$$

Thus, if an issue of commercial paper promises to pay its face value $F = \$1$ million at maturity in 182 days (so that $t = 182/365 = .4986$ years), and if it is currently priced at $D = \$925,000$, the promised yield on that paper would be

$$
\begin{aligned}
R &= \frac{\ln\left[F/D\right]}{t} \\
&= \frac{\ln\left[1,000,000/925,000\right]}{.4986} \\
&= \frac{\ln\left[1.081\right]}{.4986} \\
&= .1564, \text{ or } 15.64\% \text{ per annum}
\end{aligned}
$$

Note that an investor buying this paper would earn at the promised rate of 15.64 percent per annum only if the issuer made good on his promise to pay the $1 million face value of the paper at maturity. If the issuer paid any smaller amount, the investor's realized yield would be less than the promised yield.[3]

It is reasonable to anticipate that more risky issuers will have to promise to pay higher yields on their debt securities to compensate creditors for the greater risk of default. For example, assume that a Treasury bill and an issue of commercial paper both promise to pay the amount F in t years, that the

---

[2] Continuous compounding is described in the appendix to Chapter 1. See, especially, Equation (A.6b) in that appendix.

[3] Fraine and Mills (1961) compared the average promised yields with the average realized yields on corporate bonds from 1900 to 1943. See also the related study by Jen and Wert (1967) of the effect on bond yields of bond prepayments due to call options.

Treasury bill has a current price D_f and yield R_f, and that the commercial paper has a current price D and promised yield R. From Equation (19.2) we have

$$\text{Treasury bill yield: } R_f = \frac{\ln\ [F/D_f]}{t} \tag{19.3a}$$

$$\text{Commercial paper yield: } R = \frac{\ln\ [F/D]}{t} \tag{19.3b}$$

The commercial paper cannot be more valuable than the Treasury bill, and so $D \leq D_f$. From Equation (19.3) this implies that the promised yield on the commercial paper must not be less than the yield on the Treasury bill ($D \leq D_f$ implies $R \geq R_f$).

The credit risk structure of interest rates is the structure of the spreads between the promised yields on different issues of risky debt and the yield on comparable Treasury debt which is attributable to the risk of default by issuers of the risky debt.[4] The second section of this chapter examines the determinants of yield spreads which are attributable to credit risk.

Measuring the credit risk associated with a debt issue requires careful examination of the terms of the issue and the financial characteristics of the issuer. Such an examination can be expensive and time-consuming, and could reduce significantly the attractiveness of a given debt investment. On the other hand, the results of a completed examination can be communicated to other investors cheaply and quickly. These two aspects of evaluating credit risk—that the results of an examination are expensive to obtain but cheap to communicate—have fostered the growth of credit rating agencies, such as Moody's Investors Service, Inc., and Standard & Poor's Corporation. These agencies examine the terms of a debt issue and the financial position of the issuer, and announce to the general public a letter grade assigned to the issue, such as AA or Baa, which reflects the credit risk associated with that issue. The third section of this chapter describes the role of rating agencies as compilers and interpreters of information relating to credit risk on debt securities.

19.1 THE EQUILIBRIUM PRICE OF RISKY DEBT

A debt security is a contract between the issuer and investors, and can contain an enormous variety of terms in addition to promises to make specified payments of interest and principal. For example, to protect investors from the risk that the issuer will default, a debt security might carry covenants providing that the issuer will not pay out cash dividends to stockholders under specified conditions, or that the issuer will possess liquid assets in excess of a specified percentage of its short-term liabilities, or that the issuer will not make any substantial change in its business while the debt is outstanding.

---

[4] The yield on a debt security can exceed the yield on a comparable risk-free debt security if it is illiquid, or difficult to buy and sell quickly at a known price. "Illiquidity" yield premiums are not considered in this chapter. See Fisher (1959), Crane (1975, 1976), and Garbade and Hunt (1978).

If a debt security does go into default, investors will be concerned about the priority of their claims on the assets of the issuer. A debt security might, for example, be a general obligation of the issuer, e.g., commercial paper or debentures. Alternatively, it could carry a first lien on designated assets owned by the issuer which is superior to the claims of general creditors, in which case it is called a *mortgage bond*, or it could have a standing junior to the claims of general creditors, in which case it is called a *subordinated debenture*.

The equilibrium price of risky debt will, in general, depend on the covenants provided to protect holders of the debt against the risk of default by the issuer, on the priority in bankruptcy of the debt relative to other debt issued by the same corporation, and, of course, on the financial health of the corporation, as well as on the size of the promised payments of principal and interest. When analyzing the equilibrium price of risky debt, we will ignore most of these complexities and examine the debt of a corporation with an exceedingly simple capital structure.[5]

Suppose a corporation has assets with an aggregate market value A which have been financed by the issuance of two types of securities. The first security is debt which matures τ years in the future and which promises to pay the aggregate face amount F at maturity. The second security is common stock which does not pay dividends. Upon the maturity of the debt the stockholders can cause the corporation to do one of two things:

1 Pay the holders of the debt the promised amount F. The corporation can obtain the funds for this payment either by selling new debt or by liquidating some of the assets of the corporation. The stockholders keep control of the corporation if the corporation pays the creditors the promised amount F.

2 Default on the promise to pay the amount F to the creditors. If the corporation defaults, the creditors get control of the assets of the corporation and the stockholders get nothing.

The central question addressed in this section is this: What determines the value of the corporation's debt?

The Value of the Firm's Securities

Let D denote the aggregate value of the corporation's promise to pay the amount F in τ years, and let S denote the aggregate value of the firm's common stock. Since the firm has assets with market value A, we must have

$$A = D + S \qquad (19.4)$$

Equation (19.4) says that the market value of the firm's assets must equal the

---

[5] Black and Cox (1976) have analyzed the pricing of subordinated debt, and Brennan and Schwartz (1977) have analyzed the pricing of convertible debt, in the same spirit as the present analysis. Black and Cox (1976) also analyze the effect of restrictions on dividend payments on the price of risky debt. See Smith and Warner (1979) for an analysis of the purposes of bond covenants.

TABLE 19.1

AGGREGATE MARKET VALUES AND TERMS OF THE STOCK AND DEBT ISSUED BY A
CORPORATION

Debt:	Aggregate market value D. Promises to pay the amount F at a maturity date τ years in the future. At maturity creditors will receive (1) the amount F if the corporation pays according to its promise, or (2) the assets of the corporation if the corporation defaults on its promise.
Stock:	Aggregate market value S. At the maturity of the debt stockholders will receive (1) the assets of the corporation (net of any assets liquidated to pay the creditors the promised amount F) if the corporation pays according to its promise to its creditors, or (2) nothing if the corporation defaults on its promise.

market value of the firm's securities.[6] If A exceeds $D + S$, an arbitrageur could buy up all the firm's securities and liquidate the firm's assets at a net profit. If A is less than $D + S$, an arbitrageur could organize an identical firm by selling the same type of debt securities and buying the same assets, and could then sell the stock of the new firm at a net profit.

Table 19.1 summarizes the terms and aggregate values of the debt and stock of our hypothetical corporation. The key implication of that summary is that the corporation's common stock is a *call option on the assets of the corporation, with an exercise price of F and time to expiration of τ*. More particularly, when the debt matures, the stockholders can do one of two things:

1 Exercise their option to cause the corporation to pay the amount F to the creditors and thereby keep control of the assets of the corporation for themselves. They will do this only if the assets are worth more than F at the maturity date of the debt.

2 Decline to exercise that option, and let the creditors have the assets of the corporation. They will do this only if the assets are worth less than F at the maturity date of the debt.

Since the common stock of the corporation looks like a call option on assets currently worth A which has an exercise price of F and a time to expiration of τ years, we know from Equation (18.11) in the preceding chapter that the equilibrium market value of that stock must be

$$S = A \cdot N\,[d_1] - F \cdot N\,[d_2] \cdot \exp\,[-R_f \cdot \tau] \qquad (19.5a)$$

where

$$N\,[x] = (2\pi)^{-1/2} \int_{-\infty}^{x} \exp\,[-\tfrac{1}{2}\,u^2]\,du \qquad (19.5b)$$

$$d_1 = \frac{\ln\,[A/F] + (R_f + \tfrac{1}{2}v^2) \cdot \tau}{v \cdot \tau^{1/2}} \qquad (19.5c)$$

$$d_2 = d_1 - v \cdot \tau^{1/2} \qquad (19.5d)$$

---

[6] This equality was first demonstrated by Modigliani and Miller (1958), and asserts that the value of a firm is independent of its capital structure.

TABLE 19.2
DIFFERENCES AND SIMILARITIES BETWEEN EQUATION (18.11) ON THE VALUE
OF A CALL OPTION ON COMMON STOCK AND EQUATION (19.5) ON THE
AGGREGATE VALUE OF COMMON STOCK

	Equation (18.11)	Equation (19.5)
Underlying asset	Common stock priced at S	Assets of the corporation priced at A
Option exercise price	Price per share E	Aggregate face amount of debt securities F
Time to expiration	$t^* - t$	τ
Market value of the option	Call option priced at $\$C$ per share optioned	Common stock with aggregate market value S
Rate of interest on risk-free debt	R_f per annum, compounded continuously	R_f per annum, compounded continuously
Volatility of the logarithm of the value of the underlying asset	v^2 per annum	v^2 per annum

and where v^2 is the variance per unit time of the logarithm of the market value
of the firm's assets. Equation (19.5) is identical in form to Equation (18.11).
The only difference is what the symbols in the two equations mean. These differences are summarized in Table 19.2. Note that both equations denote the
rate of interest on risk-free debt of all maturities as R_f and that both equations
denote the volatility of the value of the underlying asset as v^2.

Equation (19.5a) gives an expression for the aggregate market value of
the stock of the corporation. Using that expression for S in Equation (19.4)
yields an expression for the aggregate market value of the debt of the corporation:

$$D = A - S$$
$$= A - \{A \cdot N[d_1] - F \cdot N[d_2] \cdot \exp\,[-R_f \cdot \tau]\}$$
$$= A \cdot (1 - N[d_1]) + F \cdot N[d_2] \cdot \exp\,[-R_f \cdot \tau]$$

or[7]
$$D = A \cdot N[-d_1] + F \cdot N[d_2] \cdot \exp\,[-R_f \cdot \tau] \qquad (19.6)$$

Equation (19.6) is an explicit expression for the aggregate market value of the

---

[7] Note that $1 - N[x] = 1 - (2\pi)^{-1/2} \int_{-\infty}^{x} \exp\,[-\frac{1}{2}\,u^2]\,du = (2\pi)^{-1/2} \int_{x}^{\infty} \exp\,[-\frac{1}{2}\,u^2]\,du$

$$= (2\pi)^{-1/2} \int_{-\infty}^{-x} \exp\,[-\frac{1}{2}\,u^2]\,du = N[-x].$$

debt of the corporation as a function of five parameters:

A = the current market value of the assets of the corporation
F = the face value of the debt
τ = the time remaining to the maturity of the debt
R_f = the rate of interest on risk-free debt
v^2 = the volatility of the value of the assets of the corporation

We want to examine how changes in these parameters affect the value of the corporation's debt.

The Determinants of the Value of the Firm's Debt

In our simple example a corporation has promised to pay an amount F to creditors in τ years. There are two elements to the market value of that promise: the value of a risk-free promise to pay the same amount at the same time, and the likelihood that the corporation will default on its promise.

The Value of Risk-Free Debt   Suppose there is no chance that a borrower will default on a promise to pay the amount F in τ years. The value of such a risk-free promise, denoted D_f, will be equal to the amount promised, discounted for τ years at the risk-free rate R_f:

$$D_f = F \cdot \exp\left[-R_f \cdot \tau\right] \tag{19.7}$$

Since the debt of our hypothetical corporation is not free of the risk of default, we can anticipate that the price of its debt will be less than D_f. It turns out that we can express the price D of the corporation's debt as a product of the price of comparable risk-free debt and a term which reflects the likelihood of default. That is, we can write D in the form

$$D = D_f \cdot G \qquad 0 \le G \le 1 \tag{19.8}$$

The term G is a price discount factor which reflects the risk of default. A higher risk of default will be associated with a lower value of G and a lower price on the risky debt relative to the price of comparable risk-free debt.

   An expression for the price of risky debt in the form of Equation (19.8) can be obtained by writing Equation (19.6) in a different way. Define the leverage ratio L as

$$L = \frac{F \cdot \exp\left[-R_f \cdot \tau\right]}{A} \tag{19.9a}$$

or

$$L = \frac{D_f}{A} \tag{19.9b}$$

L is the ratio of (1) the future promised payment F, discounted at the risk-free rate R_f for τ years, to (2) the current value A of the firm's assets, and it is a type of debt-to-total-asset-value ratio. Using this definition of L, Equation (19.6) can rewritten as

$$
\begin{aligned}
D &= A \cdot N[-d_1] + F \cdot N[d_2] \cdot \exp [-R_f \cdot \tau] \\
&= A \cdot N[-d_1] + D_f \cdot N[d_2] \\
&= D_f \cdot \left\{ \frac{A \cdot N[-d_1]}{D_f} + N[d_2] \right\}
\end{aligned}
$$

or

$$
D = D_f \cdot \{L^{-1} \cdot N[-d_1] + N[d_2]\} \tag{19.10a}
$$

where

$$
\begin{aligned}
d_1 &= \frac{\ln [A/F] + (R_f + {}^1\!/_2 v^2) \cdot \tau}{v \cdot \tau^{1/2}} \\
&= \frac{\ln [A/(F \cdot \exp [-R_f \cdot \tau])] + {}^1\!/_2 v^2 \cdot \tau}{v \cdot \tau^{1/2}}
\end{aligned}
$$

or

$$
d_1 = \frac{-\ln [L] + {}^1\!/_2 v^2 \cdot \tau}{v \cdot \tau^{1/2}} \tag{19.10b}
$$

$$
d_2 = d_1 - v \cdot \tau^{1/2} \tag{19.10c}
$$

Equation (19.10a) gives the price of risky debt as the product of the price D_f of comparable risk-free debt and a term which depends on the leverage L of the issuer, on the volatility v^2 of the value of the issuer's assets, and on the term to maturity of the debt. That is,

$$
D = D_f \cdot G[L, v^2, \tau] \tag{19.11a}
$$

where

$$
G[L, v^2, \tau] = L^{-1} \cdot N [-d_1] + N[d_2] \tag{19.11b}
$$

As shown in Equations (19.10a) and (19.11a), the value of risky debt will vary directly with the value of comparable risk-free debt; i.e., higher values of D_f will be associated with higher values of D, and lower values of D_f will be associated with lower values of D. This shows that the price of risky debt and the price of comparable risk-free debt will tend to go up and down together.

The Likelihood of Default   The second element influencing the price of risky debt is the likelihood of default by the borrower. Creditors will receive the promised amount F if the value of the corporation's assets equals or exceeds F when their debt matures, but they will receive a lesser amount if the value of the corporation's assets are less than F at the maturity date of their debt. This suggests that one important determinant of the current value of the corporation's debt is the current value of the corporation's assets. If the current value of those assets is small, there is a good chance the debt will not be paid as promised. Conversely, if the current value of the assets is large, there is virtually no chance the debt will not be paid as promised.

Figure 19.1 illustrates the variation in the aggregate value of the corporation's stock and debt as a function of the value of the firm's assets. Figure 19.1a

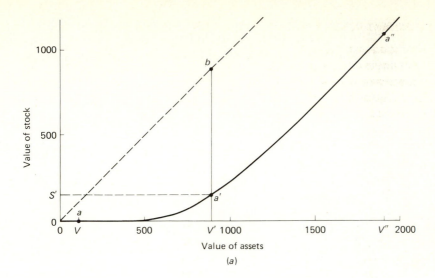

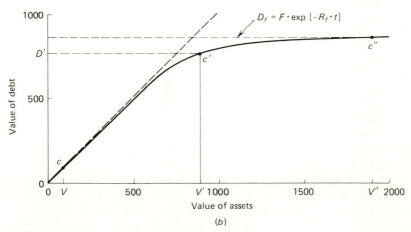

FIGURE 19.1
Aggregate market value of (a) stock and (b) debt issued by a corporation as a function of the market value of the corporation's assets. Computed from Equations (19.5) and (19.6) with $F = 1000$, $\tau = 2$ years, $R_f = .10$ per annum, and $v^2 = .0365$ per annum.

shows how the price of the stock changes with the value of the assets. (This figure looks like Figure 18.4, because the stock in the present example is a call option on the assets of the corporation.) As shown in Figure 19.1a, if the firm has assets of V', the value of the stock will be S'. The value of the firm's debt will then be the difference between V' and S', or the vertical distance between point b and point a' in Figure 19.1a. This difference is plotted as point c' in Figure 19.1b. As shown in Figure 19.1b, the value of the firm's debt will be D' when the value of the firm's assets is V'.

Two extreme cases for the value of the corporation's debt can be identified in Figure 19.1. If the firm has substantial assets, such as V''' in the figure, it will be virtually certain to pay off its debt as promised. In this case the value of the risky debt will be close to the value of risk-free debt, that is, $D = D_f = F \cdot \exp [-R_f \cdot \tau]$. More particularly, the risk of default is so small that moderate increases or decreases in the value of the firm's assets will not affect the value of the firm's debt. This is why the debt value curve in Figure 19.1*b* is virtually flat at point c''.

On the other hand, if the firm has inadequate assets, such as V in the figure, it will be virtually certain to default on its debt, so that creditors can expect to receive the assets of the corporation instead of the promised amount F in τ years. In this case the present value of the debt will be equal to the present value of the firm's assets (see point c in Figure 19.1*b*).

The foregoing suggests that the value of risky debt should be equal to the value of the corporation's assets when the value of those assets is relatively low, and should increase to the value of comparable risk-free debt as the value of those assets becomes large. This behavior of the price of debt is illustrated in Figure 19.1*b*. What is needed, however, is a standard against which the value of the assets can be compared in order to say whether that value is "high" or "low."

One important component of the relative size of the firm's assets is the current leverage of the firm, as defined by the leverage ratio or debt-to-asset ratio L shown in Equation (19.9). The lower the value of that leverage ratio, the smaller the debt of the firm relative to the firm's total assets. If L is near zero, the value of the corporation's risky debt will be close to the value of risk-free debt of the same maturity.[8] On the other hand, the higher the leverage ratio of the firm, the greater the debt of the firm relative to the firm's assets. If L is large, the value of the corporation's debt will be close to the value of its assets.[9]

Although the leverage ratio measures one important component of the risk of default, it is not a complete measure of that risk. Investors holding the corporation's debt are most concerned with whether the face value of their debt will be greater or less than the value of the corporation's assets on the maturity date of that debt. This *prospective* relationship depends in part on the current leverage ratio, but also depends on the volatility of the value of the firm's assets over the remaining term to the maturity date of the debt.

Equation (19.10) shows that the volatility of the corporation's assets over the interval remaining to the maturity of the corporation's debt, denoted by $v^2\tau$, has an effect on the price of that debt. It can be shown that the value of the dis-

---

[8] A value of L near zero implies that d_1 and d_2 in Equations (19.10*b*) and (19.10*c*) will be large positive numbers. This, in turn, implies that $N[-d_1]$ will be near zero and that $N[d_2]$ will be near unity, or that the term inside the braces in Equation (19.10*a*) will be near unity.

[9] A large value of L implies that d_1 and d_2 will be large negative numbers, and that $N[-d_1]$ will be near unity and that $N[d_2]$ will be near zero. In this case the term inside the braces in Equation (19.10*a*) will be close to L^{-1}, and D will be close to $D_f \cdot L^{-1} = D_f \cdot (D_f/A)^{-1} = A$.

count factor G will be lower the greater the volatility per unit time of the value of the assets and the longer the term to maturity of the debt. This result is reasonable, because (for any given current leverage ratio L) a corporation will be more likely to default on its debt the greater the unpredictability of the value of its assets on the maturity date of that debt. Greater unpredictability could result either from a longer term to maturity or from a greater likelihood of fluctuations in asset value over a given interval of time.

Summary

This section has examined the equilibrium value of risky debt by expressing the value of that debt in the form $D = D_f \cdot G[L, v^2, \tau]$ [see Equation (19.11)]. D_f is the value the debt would have if there were no chance that the issuer would default. The function G reflects the effect of the risk of default on the value of the debt. The size of this factor will be smaller, and the value of the risky debt will be lower, the greater the leverage of the issuer, the more volatile the value of the assets of the issuer, and the longer the maturity of the debt. Leverage, term to maturity, and volatility of asset value are issue and issuer characteristics that can be expected to increase the risk of ultimate default by an issuer, and hence that can be expected to depress the price of debt sold by that issuer below the price of risk-free debt of the same maturity.

19.2 THE CREDIT RISK STRUCTURE OF INTEREST RATES

The preceding section examined the *price* of risky debt as a function of the value of comparable risk-free debt and as a function of the risk of default by the issuer. However, it is more common when analyzing debt securities to examine *promised yields to maturity* than to examine prices. The credit risk structure of interest rates is the structure of yields on risky debt relative to the yield on comparable risk-free debt. This section draws on the results of the preceding section to analyze the determinants of the credit risk structure of interest rates.

The promised yield on risky debt is the value of R which solves the equation

$$D = F \cdot \exp\,[-R \cdot \tau] \tag{19.12}$$

or
$$R = \frac{\ln\,[F/D]}{\tau} \tag{19.13}$$

Using the expression for D given by Equation (19.10a), and recalling from Equation (19.7) that $D_f = F \cdot \exp\,[-R_f \cdot \tau]$, we have

$$R = R_f - \frac{\ln\,[L^{-1} \cdot N[-d_1] + N[d_2]]}{\tau}$$

or
$$R - R_f = \frac{-\ln\,[G[L, v^2, \tau]]}{\tau} \tag{19.14}$$

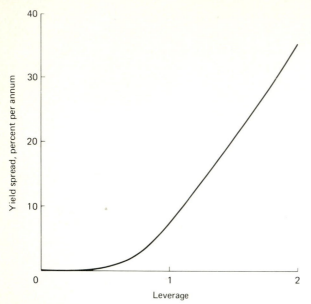

FIGURE 19.2
Yield spreads on risky debt as a function of the leverage of
the issuer. Computed from Equation (19.14) with $\tau = 2$ years
and $v^2 = .0365$ per annum.

Equation (19.14) is an expression for the spread between the promised yield on
risky debt and the yield on risk-free debt.[10] The function $-\ln[G]/\tau$ specifies directly the determinants of the credit risk structure of interest rates.

Equation (19.14) shows that the credit risk structure of interest rates is a
function of three variables: the current leverage of the issuer, the volatility of
the value of the issuer's assets, and the term to maturity of the debt. As shown
in Figure 19.2, the promised yield spread will be higher the greater the leverage
of the issuer. This means that more highly leveraged issuers have to promise to
pay greater yields to compensate investors for the greater risk that those investors will ultimately get less than they were promised.

Figure 19.3 shows that the promised yield spread will also be higher the
greater the volatility of the value of the issuer's assets. This means that issuers
engaged in more intrinsically volatile enterprises, such as manufacturers of ad-
vanced-technology electronics, also have to promise to pay greater yields to
compensate investors for the greater risk that those investors will ultimately get
less than they were promised.

Figure 19.4 shows the effect of term to maturity on the yield spread of risky
debt over risk-free debt. Unlike the effect of leverage and volatility, a longer

[10] Note that this equation assumes the yield on risk-free debt is R_f for debt of all maturities, i.e.,
that the term structure of interest rates is flat. Johnson (1967) has investigated the term structure of
interest rates for risky debt securities. In particular, he exhibits yield curves for debt with different
credit ratings.

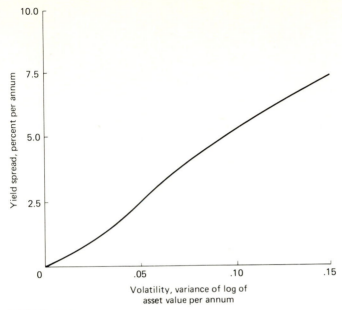

FIGURE 19.3
Yield spreads on risky debt as a function of the volatility of the
issuer's assets. Computed from Equation (19.14) with $L = .8$ and
$\tau = 2$ years.

term to maturity may imply either a decreasing or an increasing yield spread.
Two possibilities can be distinguished, depending on whether the issuer's leverage ratio is greater or less than unity.

A leverage ratio greater than unity means that the present value of the promise to pay the amount F (computed by discounting at the risk-free rate R_f)
exceeds the current value of the issuer's assets. [See the definition of L in
Equation (19.9a).] In this case a shorter term to maturity always implies a
greater yield spread. This illustrates the "maturity crisis" of a debt issuer that is
extremely likely to default on its maturing debt.[11] As that debt approaches maturity, its price will more closely reflect the value of the issuer's assets than the
(greater) value of comparable risk-free debt. As a result, the promised yield on
the issuer's debt will move to a substantial premium over the yield on risk-free
debt.

The case where the leverage ratio L is less than unity is a more common situation for actively traded and widely held debt. In this case the present value of
the promise to pay the amount F, when computed by discounting that promised
payment at the risk-free rate R_f, is less than the current value of the issuer's
assets. The yield premium on the issuer's debt, as a function of the term to maturity of that debt, will initially be an increasing function of maturity. This

---

[11] See Johnson (1967) for an empirical examination of maturity crises on risky debt securities.

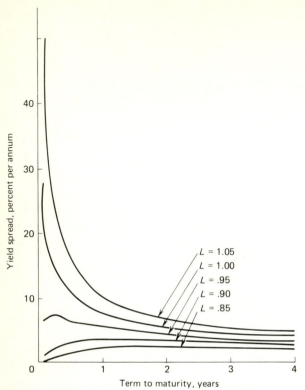

FIGURE 19.4
Yield spreads on risky debt as a function of the term to
maturity of that debt. Computed from Equation (19.14) with
$v^2 = .0365$ per annum.

reflects the increasing uncertainty that even a moderately leveraged issuer
might ultimately default if the maturity of that issuer's debt is increased. However, even for the case of a leverage ratio less than unity, Figure 19.4 shows
that, after an initial increase in yield spreads with increasing maturity, those
spreads will tend to decline with further increases in maturity. This reflects the
fact that yield is measured in units of return per unit time, and that a longer term
to maturity permits the amortization of a given risk-related price discount over
a longer interval of time [see Equation (19.14)]. Figure 19.4 shows that this
phenomenon of a declining yield spread with increasing maturity first appears
at relatively more distant maturities for issuers with lower leverage ratios; i.e.,
the "hump" in a yield-spread curve moves out with decreases in the issuer's leverage ratio.

Comparing the results of this section and the preceding section shows that
greater leverage and more volatile asset values will lead to both greater yield
spreads and greater risk-related price discounts on risky debt. Similarly, a more
distant maturity date will lead to a greater risk-related price discount on risky

debt. However, in some cases a more distant maturity date can lead to a smaller, rather than a larger, yield spread on risky debt. This suggests that yield spreads may not provide a valid way of comparing the relative risks on debt issues with different maturities.

19.3 BOND RATINGS

The preceding sections examined in some detail the determinants of the credit risk on a relatively simple debt security. The analysis suggested that the volatility of the value of the issuer's assets, the issuer's leverage, and the term to maturity of the debt all have an effect on the credit risk associated with that debt.

It is not difficult to imagine the markedly increased difficulty of evaluating the credit risk on debt issues with more complex terms sold by corporations with more complex capital structures. Debentures, for example, are more risky if a substantial part of the assets of the issuer is pledged against outstanding mortgage bonds, since the pledged assets may not be available to meet the claims of the debenture holders in the event of bankruptcy. Thus, the existence and size of senior debt are important in evaluating the financial risks inherent in the event of a default, and a bond analyst would want to look at measures of capitalization more sophisticated than a simple total-debt-to-total-asset-value leverage ratio. Similarly, a bond may be less risky if it is more likely to be retired before its stated maturity date through a sinking-fund redemption,[12] or if it can be sold back to the issuer at a fixed price by exercising a put option.[13]

In view of the multidimensional nature of credit risk, an interesting question arises as to what sets of issue and issuer characteristics lead to equivalent risk. Consider, for example, the risks associated with the debentures of two corporations with assets of equal aggregate value, one with no senior debt outstanding and the other with both mortgage bonds and somewhat more equity in its capital structure. If the only difference between the two firms was the mortgage bonds sold by the second firm, the debentures of the second issuer would be more risky. However, the greater equity of the second issuer reduces, to some degree, that risk difference. It may, in fact, mean that the debentures of the second issuer are less risky than those of the first.

The categorization of debt issues into classes of equivalent risk can clearly be a time-consuming and expensive process. Were it necessary for each investor to conduct his own credit investigations, the costs of those investigations would detract substantially from the attractiveness of debt investments. Each additional investment would burden the investor with the fixed costs of an additional investigation, regardless of the size of the investment. On the other hand, once an investigation is complete, the cost of communicating the results to other investors is negligible. Ideally, the results should be free to all since the marginal costs of communication are essentially zero.

---

[12] Sinking funds on corporate debt are described in Section 2.2.
[13] Put options on corporate debt are described in Section 17.3.

TABLE 19.3
CORPORATE BOND RATINGS

Moody's Investors Service, Inc.		Standard & Poor's Corporation	
Aaa	Bonds which are rated Aaa are judged to be of the best quality. They carry the smallest degree of investment risk and are generally referred to as *gilt edge*. Interest payments are protected by a large or by an exceptionally stable margin, and principal is secure. While the various protective elements are likely to change, such changes as can be visualized are most unlikely to impair the fundamentally strong position of such issues.	AAA	This is the highest rating assigned by Standard & Poor's to a debt obligation and indicates an extremely strong capacity to pay principal and interest.
Aa	Bonds which are rated Aa are judged to be of high quality by all standards. Together with the Aaa group they make up what are generally known as *high-grade* bonds. They are rated lower than the best bonds, because margins of protection may not be as large as in Aaa securities, fluctuation of protective elements may be of greater amplitude, or there may be other elements present which make the long-term risks appear somewhat larger than in Aaa securities.	AA	Bonds rated AA also qualify as high-quality debt obligations. Capacity to pay principal and interest is very strong, and in the majority of instances they differ from AAA issues only in small degree.
A	Bonds which are rated A possess many favorable investment attributes and are to be considered as *upper-medium-grade* obligations. Factors giving security to principal and interest are considered adequate, but elements may be present which suggest a susceptibility to impairment sometime in the future.	A	Bonds rated A have a strong capacity to pay principal and interest, although they are somewhat more susceptible to adverse effects of changes in circumstances and economic conditions.
Baa	Bonds which are rated Baa are considered *medium-grade* obligations, i.e., they are neither highly protected nor poorly secured. Interest payments and principal security appear adequate for the present, but certain protective elements may be lacking or may be characteristically unreliable over any great length of time. Such bonds lack outstanding investment characteristics and in fact have speculative characteristics as well.	BBB	Bonds rated BBB are regarded as having an adequate capacity to pay principal and interest. Whereas they normally exhibit adequate protection parameters, adverse economic conditions or changing circumstances are more likely to lead to a weakened capacity to pay principal and interest for bonds in this category than for bonds in the A category.

TABLE 19.3 *(Continued)*

Moody's Investors Service, Inc.	Standard & Poor's Corporation
Ba Bonds which are rated Ba are judged to have speculative elements; their future cannot be considered as well assured. Often the protection of the interest and principal payments may be very moderate and thereby not well safeguarded during both good and bad times over the future. Uncertainty of position characterizes bonds in this class.	BB Bonds rated BB, B, CCC, and CC B are regarded, on balance, as predomi- CCC nantly speculative with respect to the CC issuer's capacity to pay interest and repay principal in accordance with the terms of the obligation. BB indicates the lowest degree of speculation and CC the highest degree of speculation. While such bonds will likely have some quality and protective characteristics, these are outweighed by large undertainties or major risk exposures to adverse conditions.
B Bonds which are rated B generally lack characteristics of the desirable investment. Assurance of interest and principal payments or of maintenance of other terms of the contract over any long period of time may be small.	
Caa Bonds which are rated Caa are of poor standing. Such issues may be in default, or there may be present elements of danger with respect to principal or interest.	
Ca Bonds which are rated Ca represent obligations which are speculative in a high degree. Such issues are often in default or have marked shortcomings.	

Freely available credit evaluations are, in fact, quite common in the markets for corporate debt. Three private agencies (Moody's Investors Service, Inc., Fitch Investors Service, Inc., and Standard & Poor's Corporation) provide ratings on new debt issues. These ratings are undertaken by the agencies for a fee paid by the issuer. The agencies evaluate the earnings variability of the issuer, its capital structure, the indenture (or legal contract between the issuer and its creditors), and the quality of the management of the issuer.[14] The result is one of several possible letter grades used to denote the risk class of the issue.[15] Table 19.3 lists the grades and a brief description of their meaning as provided

[14] Sherwood (1976) discussed the procedures of Standard & Poor's in rating a variety of debt issues, including industrial and utility bonds, commercial paper, and municipal bonds. See also the description by I. Ross (1976) of Moody's and Standard & Poor's.

[15] Horrigan (1966), Pogue and Soldofsky (1969), West (1970), and Pinches and Mingo (1973, 1975) have studied the relation between corporate bond ratings and quantifiable characteristics of corporate debt issuers. Carleton and Lerner (1969) and Horton (1970) have done the same for ratings on municipal bonds. Fisher (1959) has related promised yield premiums directly to issuer characteristics, and Fraine and Mills (1961) and Johnson (1967) have related promised and realized yields to rating classes. See Ang and Patel (1975) for a comparison of Moody's ratings with ratings derived from statistical methods based on ability to predict future financial distress.

by two of the agencies. Note that, in every case, the description of the grades conveys at least a qualitative judgment about whether the issuer will be able to make good on its promises and whether, if default occurs, there are assets available to protect the debt holder.

Issues with similar ratings bear approximately the same level of risk, but the equivalence is not exact. If it were, all comparably rated issues would have the same promised yield. In fact, there are different yield levels within each rating category. This suggests that the market does not perceive equivalently rated issues as perfect substitutes. In addition, the rating agencies do not always agree among themselves as to the appropriate risk class for an issue. An issue might be rated AA by Standard & Poor's and A by Moody's. Differences in ratings by more than a single category, however, are rare.

CHAPTER SUMMARY

This chapter has analyzed the equilibrium valuation of risky debt securities using a call option pricing model. The key step in the analysis was recognizing that common stock is like a call option on the assets of a corporation: if the corporation pays off its creditors, the stockholders keep the assets, and if the corporation fails to pay off its creditors, the stockholders get nothing. The market value of the corporation's debt will then be equal to the difference between the value of the corporation's assets and the value of the call options, i.e., common stock, issued by the corporation.

Using the foregoing approach, the analysis demonstrated that the price of risky debt will be equal to the price of comparable risk-free debt, less a discount reflecting the risk of default. The discount due to default risk will increase as a function of three variables:

1 The leverage of the issuer
2 The volatility of the value of the issuer's assets
3 The term to maturity of the debt

The second section of the chapter reformulated the analysis of risky debt in terms of the spread between the promised yield on that debt and the yield on risk-free debt. This yield spread was shown to increase with the leverage of the issuer and with the volatility of the value of the issuer's assets. It was also shown that there is an ambiguous relation between yield spreads and the term to maturity of risky debt. Although the most common presumption is that yield spreads are a direct function of credit risk, it was shown that the opposite can be true for the debt of highly leveraged issuers or for long-term debt. In those cases longer maturities can imply smaller yield spreads rather than greater yield spreads, even though longer maturities also imply relatively larger price discounts as a result of greater credit risk.

The last section of the chapter described the role of credit rating agencies and attributed their existence to a demand by investors for expensive-to-produce but cheap-to-communicate credit evaluations.

FURTHER READING

Fischer Black and John Cox, "Valuing Corporate Securities: Some Effects of Bond Indenture Provisions," *Journal of Finance*, **31** (May 1976), 351–367.

Fischer Black and Myron Scholes, "The Pricing of Options and Corporate Liabilities," *Journal of Political Economy*, **81** (May/June 1973), 637–654.

M. J. Brennan and E. S. Schwartz, "Convertible Bonds: Valuation and Optimal Strategies for Call and Conversion," *Journal of Finance*, **32** (December 1977), 1699–1715.

Ramon Johnson, "Term Structure of Corporate Bond Yields as a Function of Risk of Default," *Journal of Finance*, **22** (May 1967), 313–345.

Robert Merton, "On the Pricing of Corporate Debt: The Risk Structure of Interest Rates," *Journal of Finance*, **29** (May 1974), 449–470.

Hugh Sherwood, *How Corporate and Municipal Debt Is Rated* (New York: John Wiley & Sons, Inc., 1976).

Clifford Smith and Jerold Warner, "On Financial Contracting: An Analysis of Bond Covenants," *Journal of Financial Economics*, **7** (June 1979), 115–161.

PART SEVEN

ORGANIZATION OF SECURITIES MARKETS

Until now the analyses in this book have viewed securities markets as loci for the equilibrium pricing of financial assets. but have not paid much attention to the role of markets as places for the actual purchase and sale of securities. In the four chapters of this part and the three chapters of the following part, we change our earlier focus and consider the institutional framework and transactional structure of securities markets.

Regardless of substantial differences in organization, all securities markets serve to bring together buyers and sellers. A perfect market might be defined as one where every investor knows, at all times, the best prices at which he can buy and sell securities. The gold fixings market described in Chapter 11 satisfied this definition, because all participants were continually aware of the prices announced by the auctioneer while he was seeking to establish an equilibrium.[1] In most markets, however, this level of perfection is not attained, because no investor finds it in his self-interest to acquire continuously such complete information. Although the absence of perfect information may have only minor implications for the general level of securities prices, it can have more substantial consequences for the prices of individual transactions.[2]

---

[1] As described in Section 11.1, the *only* price at which purchases and sales of gold can occur in the London fixings market is the price announced by the Rothschild auctioneer.

[2] Several conceptual analyses have, however, suggested that imperfect markets can degrade the "quality" of securities prices as signals for the efficient allocation of capital. These studies generally distinguish between the equilibrium prices that would clear a perfect market and the observed prices that clear imperfect markets. Goldman and Beja (1979) discuss the consequences of the slow and noisy adjustment of observed prices to equilibrium prices which results from an imperfect market. Beja and Goldman (1980) show that transient discrepancies between observed prices and equilibrium prices may attract speculation which can create oscillations and instability in the price adjustment process. Garbade and Silber (1979a) note that market imperfections can limit the number of traders actively involved in a market and can thereby reduce the liquidity of a security. See also Logue (1975) and Cohen, Hawawini, Maier, Schwartz, and Whitcomb (1980).

The four chapters in this part explore the institutional framework of secondary markets. Chapter 20 provides an introduction to the relation between market structure and different measures of market performance. As we will see, these measures are closely related to the speed of communication of quotation and transaction price information among market participants. The faster and more complete the communication, the closer the market will approach the ideal of a perfect market. The three following chapters describe some prominent examples of dealer, auction, and brokered markets. Our primary interest in those three chapters is to establish how the purchase and sale interests of ultimate investors come to affect the trading prices of securities in a wide variety of market structures.

CHAPTER 20

MARKET STRUCTURE

Markets facilitate the exchange of securities among investors. Not all assets trade in the same type of market, however, and different markets can be distinguished by the degree to which they facilitate the exchange process. This chapter presents a conceptual framework for analyzing the comparative structure of securities markets. The first section defines three commonly cited measures of market performance: depth, breadth, and resiliency. The definitions of these terms suggest some of the important attributes of markets which do not attain the ideal of one where all contemporaneous transactions occur at a common equilibrium price. The second section describes four market structures—direct search, broker, dealer, and auction markets—and explores the implications of these structures for market participants. The third section examines some of the determinants of market structure.

20.1 MEASURES OF MARKET PERFORMANCE

If every investor knew at zero cost the trading interests of every other investor, there would be a unique equilibrium price for a security at any instant of time.[1] Offerings of the security below that price would be taken quickly by willing investors, and bids for the security above the equilibrium price would rapidly attract willing sellers. It follows that only bids below the current equilibrium, and only offerings above that equilibrium, would go unfilled, and hence that the best (highest) bid would be less than the best (lowest) offer. Moreover, transactions

---

[1] As described in Section 11.1, the objective of the London gold fixings market is to locate, or fix, the unique equilibrium price of gold at a particular point in time.

would not occur at prices below the highest available bid (because that would imply the seller could have sold at a higher price) or above the lowest available offer (because that would imply the buyer could have bought at a lower price).

The standard of a market where complete information is free and fully disseminated is rarely attained in a world where information on the trading interests of other investors is expensive to acquire. Such a standard does, however, provide a norm against which actual markets may be compared.

The existence of bids at or above the lowest offering price on a security reflects an incompleteness of information characteristic of a *fragmented* market. Such market fragmentation will exist whenever transactors are unable to communicate with each other quickly and cheaply. The greater the costs of communication, and the longer the lags in communication, the more extensive will be the fragmentation of the market and the more likely it will be that transactions will take place away from the best available prices. Three qualitative measures of market performance underscore the importance of the speed at which information is disseminated to market participants.

Depth and Breadth of a Market

A market is said to have *depth* if there exists orders, either actual or easily uncovered, both above and below the price at which a security is currently trading. When a security trades in a deep market, temporary imbalances of purchase (or sale) orders that would otherwise create substantial price changes encounter offsetting, and hence stabilizing, sale (or purchase) orders.

A deep market requires that investors can learn of, and act upon, the bid and offer quotations of other investors promptly. The requirement of a deep market may also be satisfied if investors can leave their bids and offerings with a broker who keeps himself informed about the state of the market and who executes the limited price orders of his customers as soon as they become the most favorable quotations available.[2] Prompt communication of quotations and prompt execution of orders are preconditions for a deep market. Fragmented markets lack depth because, by definition, offsetting orders may go undiscovered for relatively long intervals of time.

A market is said to have *breadth* if the orders referred to in the previous paragraphs exist in substantial volume. The broader the market, the greater the potential for stabilization of transitory price changes which arise out of temporary order imbalances. The greater the number of investors who can learn promptly of changes in bid and offer quotations, the broader will be the market. For example, the substitution of electronic communication devices for print

---

[2] A *limited price* order is an order to buy at the stated price or any lower price, or to sell at the stated price or any higher price. Limited price orders must be distinguished from *market orders* to buy or sell at the best available price. Both types of orders are frequently used when investors engage agents to complete their transactions. The practice of leaving limited price orders with an agent is formalized on the New York Stock Exchange and other securities exchanges in the "book" of such limit orders kept by specialists or other floor brokers. See Section 22.2.

TABLE 20.1
ILLUSTRATIONS OF MARKET DEPTH AND BREADTH

	Size of existing or easily uncovered bids			
Bid price	(1) Thin and shallow	(2) Thin but deep	(3) Broad but shallow	(4) Broad and deep
$50	100	100	500	500
$49	200	200	500	500
$48	0	300	0	700
$47	0	300	0	900
$46	0	300	0	1500

media for the dissemination of quotes will likely broaden as well as deepen a market, since more investors can then keep in more timely touch with evolving securities prices.[3]

Although market depth and breadth are closely related in practice, they are not identical concepts. Table 20.1 shows four possible configurations of bid quotations in a market where the best existing bid is $50 per unit of the security. An investor can sell 100 units at that bid price in any of the four markets. To sell 300 units in either of the two thin markets, however, would require that the additional 200 units sold be priced at $49 per unit. In contrast, the investor could sell up to 500 units at the $50 bid price in either of the broader markets. In the two shallow markets there exist no bids below $49, but in the deeper markets there exist orders down to a $46 bid price.

In all four of the markets shown in Table 20.1, larger sale orders can only be accomplished at lower prices. However, the relation between the size of a sale order and the price at which the order can be executed is different in every market. Market 4, which is broad and deep, is clearly the best market. An investor in that market could sell 500 units at the $50 bid price, and he could sell an additional 3,600 units at prices down to $46. Market 1, which is thin and shallow, is clearly the worst market. An investor could sell only 100 units at the $50 bid price, and he could sell only another 200 units at $49. If he wanted to sell more than 300 units, he would have to make a special effect to find additional buyers. Market 2, which is thin but deep, will accommodate the sale of up to 1200 units, but only if the last 300 units are sold at a price of $46 per unit. Selling at such a deep discount may be more economical, in terms of speed of sale and price (net of search costs), than trying to find buyers outside the regular marketplace, in which case market 2 would be superior to market 1 for sales larger than 300 units. Market 3, which is broad but thin, will only accommodate the sale of 1000 units. However, those 1000 units can be sold in market 3 at a better average price than the price at which 1000 units could be sold in market

---

[3] See, for example, the discussion of NASDAQ in Section 21.3 and the superiority of NASDAQ to the "pink sheets" as a source of information on over-the-counter dealer quotations.

2. On the other hand, an investor can sell 1200 units quickly in market 2, but he could only sell 1000 units quickly in market 3. Thus, whether market 3 is better or worse than market 2 depends on the size of the sale order being executed.

Resiliency of a Market

A market is *resilient* if new orders pour in promptly in response to price changes that result from temporary order imbalances. A precondition of a resilient market is, of course, that investors can learn quickly when the trading price of a security has changed. The prompt dissemination of transaction prices is thus important to maintaining market resiliency.

Other things being equal, a market becomes deeper, broader, and more resilient the faster investors can acquire and act upon quotation and transaction price information. As the speed of communication increases, markets become relatively less fragmented and more integrated and approach the standard of a market where all participants have full information on the trading interests of all other participants.[4]

20.2   TYPES OF MARKET STRUCTURE

Securities markets may be characterized according to whether investors must seek out compatible trading partners by themselves (direct search markets), whether they typically choose to employ agents to conduct that search (brokered markets), whether they complete their transactions by trading with other participants who hold themselves out as always willing to buy and sell (dealer markets), or whether they transact directly against the orders of other investors by communicating through a single centralized intermediary (auction markets). Although none of these categories imply anything directly about the cost and speed of communication of price information, the structure of a securities market does have indirect implications for market integration.

Direct Search Markets

Perhaps the markets furthest from the ideal of complete price information are those where buyers and sellers must search each other out directly. Since the full cost of locating and bargaining with a compatible trading partner is borne

---

[4] Garbade and Silber (1978) explored the effects of the domestic telegraph, the transatlantic cable, and the consolidated ticker tape on the integration of geographically separated markets. Santomero (1974) and Hamilton (1978) investigated the effect of NASDAQ on price behavior in the over-the-counter market. Garbade (1978a) has addressed the consequences of electronic quotation systems for modern dealer markets. Among the oldest communications systems still in existence are the ticker tape of the NYSE and the private wire communication systems of members of the NYSE. The early ticker tapes are described by Hotchkiss (1905) and Meeker (1930, pp. 168–172). Some early private wires are described in *Commerce and Finance*, June 22, 1921, pp. 879–913; November 9, 1921, p. 1164; and April 15, 1925, pp. 695–713. Garbade and Silber (1979a) analyzed the impact of the ticker tape and broker's wires on the structure of the NYSE.

by an individual transactor, there is only a negligible incentive to conduct a thorough search among all possible partners for the best possible price. Failure to conduct a thorough search implies a high probability that, at the time a trade has been agreed upon by two participants, at least one of those participants could have gotten a better price were he in contact with some other undiscovered participant. Securities which trade in direct search markets are usually bought and sold so infrequently that no third party, such as a broker or dealer, has an incentive to provide any kind of service to facilitate trading. The common stocks of small companies, especially small rural banks, trade in fragmented direct search markets. Buyers and sellers of those issues must rely on word-of-mouth communication of their trading interests to attract compatible trading partners. Because there is no economical way of broadcasting either quotations or transaction prices, trades can occur at the same time at quite different prices, and transactions frequently occur away from the best possible price.

Brokered Markets

When trading in an issue becomes sufficiently heavy, brokers begin to offer specialized search services to market participants. For a fee, brokers undertake to find compatible trading partners and to negotiate acceptable transaction prices for their clients.

Brokers are most likely to appear when there are economies of scale in searching. If a broker can fill the orders of two customers at a cost less than twice the cost of the direct search which would otherwise be conducted by each of those customers, he can profitably acquire the business of both by charging a commission somewhat less than those costs of direct search.

Economies of scale in search can be divided into two categories. First, brokers may be able to make economical use of communication devices with high fixed costs but with a low marginal cost per contact. Where, for example, an individual investor might rely on ordinary telephone service to get in touch with potential trading partners, a broker may be able to use wide area telephone service or direct wires to place his calls.[5] Similarly, a broker may subscribe to specialized publications or electronic devices announcing bids or offerings in a wide variety of issues.[6] The marginal cost of acquiring information from such media may well be zero. An individual investor, on the other hand, would find a subscription uneconomical in view of his more infrequent transactions.

The second area of scale economies in brokerage is with respect to the value of information concerning the trading interests of other investors. A broker trying to find a buyer for one issue may not be able to attract the interest of a par-

---

[5] The importance of direct wires to facilitate trading was pointed out in *Silver v. New York Stock Exchange*, 196 F. Supp. 209 (S.D.N.Y. 1961). *Silver* concerned the refusal of the NYSE to allow several of its member firms to maintain direct wires to a nonmember firm for trading in municipal bonds and in equity issues not listed on the NYSE.

[6] See, for example, the description of the Blue List and the Kenny wire in Section 23.3.

ticular customer, but he may learn, in the course of speaking with him, that that customer is in the market for some other issue. To the seller of the first issue such information would be useless, but the broker may know a potential seller of the second issue and thus be able to arrange a transaction (and earn a commission) at little marginal expense to himself. One of the striking characteristics of some brokered markets is the willingness of brokers to provide free or low-cost portfolio advice to their clients. By giving such advice, brokers come to know intimately the purchase and sale interests of their clients.

Since a broker is frequently in contact with many market participants on a continuing basis, he is likely to know what constitutes a "fair" price for a transaction. A broker will usually know whether the offering price of a seller can easily be bettered by looking elsewhere or whether it is close to the lowest offer likely to be uncovered. Brokers not only provide search services at a cheaper price than an investor's own cost of search, they also arrange transactions closer to the best available prices than is possible in a direct search market. Their extensive contacts provide them with a pool of price information which individual transactors could not economically duplicate. By charging a commission less than the cost of direct search, they give transactors an incentive to make use of that information.

Dealer Markets

Whatever its advantages over direct search, brokerage has the disadvantage that it cannot guarantee that investor orders will be executed promptly. This uncertainty as to speed of execution creates price risk. During the time a broker is searching out a compatible trading partner for a client, securities prices may change and the client may suffer a loss. However, if trading in an issue is sufficiently active, some market participants may begin to maintain bid and offer quotations of their own. Such dealers buy for, and sell for, their own inventory at their quoted prices. Dealer markets eliminate the need for time-consuming searches for trading partners, because investors know they can buy or sell immediately at the quotes given by a dealer.

Dealers earn their revenues in part by selling securitites at an offer price greater than the bid price they pay for securities. Their bid-ask spread compensates them for providing to occasional market participants the liquidity of an immediately available market, and also for the risk the dealers incur when they position an issue in their inventory.[7]

Narrow spreads between the bid and offer quotations of dealers reduce the fragmentation of a market. Suppose, for the moment, all dealers quoted the same bid price and the same offer price on an issue. An investor seeking to buy that issue knows he cannot locate, outside the dealer community, an offering price lower than the common bid price of the dealers. (If there was such an offering, the investor making it would sell immediately at the better bid price.)

---

[7] Chapter 24 analyzes the determinants of bid-ask spreads.

This phenomenon bounds the lowest possible offer above the dealers' bid. The narrower the dealers' bid-ask spread, the less incentive a buyer has to seek out offering quotations lower than those of the dealers, because he can only hope to improve on the dealers' offer quote by the size of the spread; i.e., he knows he will not uncover an offer lower than the dealers' bid quotation. It follows that investors tend to complete more of their transactions with dealers, and less with other public investors, the narrower the spread quoted by the dealers. This, in turn, establishes the dealers' bid and offer quotations as the effective quotes for the whole market. Since those quotations are readily uncovered, market integration is enhanced.

In most cases dealers do not quote identical prices for an issue, because they disagree as to its value or because they have different inventory objectives.[8] Even in a dealer market it is therefore incumbent upon investors to search out the best prices for their trades. The expense of contacting several dealers to obtain comparative quotations is borne by investors. However, since dealers have an incentive to advertise their willingness to buy and sell, their identity will be well known and such contacts can usually be completed quite expeditiously. The ease of searching among dealers guarantees that those dealers quoting the best price (relative to other dealers) will be most likely to do business with public participants.

Auction Markets

Although dealer markets provide investors with the opportunity for an immediate execution of their orders, and although dealer markets can usually be searched more rapidly and cheaply than direct search or brokered markets, they do have several disadvantages. No one can guarantee that the quotation of a particular dealer could not be improved upon by contacting another dealer. This being the case, transactors in dealer markets have to bear some costs of searching out the best price.

A second factor in dealer trading is the expense of a dealer's bid-ask spread. Suppose one investor is willing to sell a particular bond at 99, and another is willing to buy at 101. If they could meet, they might agree to trade at 100, each doing better than his respective reservation price. Rather than incur the expense of searching each other out, however, they may both prefer to trade with a dealer bidding on the bond at $99^{1}/_{2}$ and offering the bond at $100^{1}/_{2}$. They would be giving up a half point each to the dealer's bid-ask spread to avoid the cost of search, even though they had an (undiscovered) coincidence of interests. Although dealers stand ready to trade even in the absence of such coincidences (otherwise they would be called brokers), it would be advantageous to investors if they could trade directly, inside a dealer's quotations, whenever possible.

[8] Garbade and Silber (1976), Garbade (1978a), Stoll (1978), Garbade, Pomrenze, and Silber (1979), and Amihud and Mendelson (1980) analyze the effect of dealer inventory objectives on dealer bid and offer prices.

Auction markets provide centralized procedures for the exposure of purchase and sale orders to all market participants simultaneously. By so doing they virtually eliminate the expense of locating compatible partners and bargaining for a favorable price. The communication of price information in an auction market may be oral if all participants are physically located in the same place, or electronic.[9]

When trading in an issue is sufficiently heavy, an auctioneer may simply record bids and offerings and notify participants whenever one investor bids at the offer price of another investor and thereby consumates a trade. When an auction is run as a repository of limited price orders, and if the list of such orders is kept large by the arrival of new orders, participants know they can execute immediately by bidding on the offer side of the auction (or offering on the bid side). Such continuous auction markets share with dealer markets the advantage of immediate execution but eliminate the cost implicit in dealer bid-ask spreads.

For less frequently traded issues an auctioneer might advertise explicitly for bids (when a participant is seeking to sell)[10] or offers (when he is seeking to buy). These so-called discrete auctions do not provide an opportunity for immediate execution. Even in this case, however, the price priority characterizing an integrated market is easily enforced, so that a better quote will get preference over a poorer quote.[11]

20.3 DETERMINANTS OF MARKET STRUCTURE

In the previous section we alluded to the importance of the volume of trading in determining whether a security will trade in a direct search, brokered, or dealer market. Brokers usually incur higher fixed costs but lower marginal costs of search than investors conducting their own search. Trading volume in a brokered market must be high enough to allow the brokers to cover their total costs. Similarly, dealers will not appear unless the rate of transactions is large enough to let them cover their costs and earn a return on their risky inventory positions by trading on their bid-ask spreads.

Another important determinant of market structure is the existence of

---

[9] The NYSE is the preeminent example of a physically centralized oral auction market (see Section 22.2). However, many of the issues listed on that exchange are also traded on regional exchanges and in the over-the-counter "third market." Thus, while the NYSE market in, for example, the common stock of Gulf Oil Corporation is an auction market, the national market in that stock more closely resembles a multiple-dealer market. The SEC has proposed the creation of a central market in major corporate securities, with competing exchanges and dealers linked together by electronics to form a true national auction market. See Peake (1978), Harman (1978), and Melton (1978–79).

[10] The Kenny wire for municipal bonds, described in Section 23.3, is a system for advertising for bids on municipal bonds which investors want to sell.

[11] The weekly auction of 91- and 182-day Treasury bills conducted by the district Federal Reserve banks for the United States Treasury is an example of a discrete auction. Buyers of bills do not obtain instant liquidity from such auctions, because they are conducted only once a week. Instant liquidity in bill purchases can be obtained from the dealer market in Treasury securities.

securities which are close substitutes for each other. Even if the volume of trading in a single security within a group is not large, there may be sufficient volume in the group as a whole to justify a brokered or dealer market. The convention of treating "New York names" in bank CDs as interchangeable illustrates the importance of close substitutes (see Section 4.1). As the fixed costs of dealing in CDs are spread over a larger trading volume, the opportunities for dealers to earn a spread become more frequent. Moreover, long and short positions are more easily balanced in securities which are close substitutes, thereby reducing the risk exposure of a dealer's aggregate inventory.[12]

A third important determinant of market structure is the size of a typical transaction relative to the frequency of those transactions. Suppose, for example, that three issues each have daily average trading volumes of $1 million, but that the first issue conventionally trades in $1000 pieces (1000 per day), that the second trades in $250,000 pieces (4 per day) and that the third trades in $10 million pieces (about once every 10 days). It might be quite feasible to establish a continuous auction market for the first issue. The number of trades is so large that bid and offer lists would be continually refilled, thereby offering the advantage of immediate execution without the need to pay a dealer's spread. For the second issue, however, trades are sufficiently infrequent that opportunities for immediate execution might be available only from a dealer. The third issue trades so infrequently that possibly no dealer would be willing to position it in his own inventory and bear the resulting risk of fluctuations in capital value while waiting for an offsetting order. That issue might trade in a brokered market.[13]

CHAPTER SUMMARY

This chapter has presented a broad overview of the structure of securities markets. Four different types of market structure were described, including direct search markets, brokered markets, dealer markets, and auction markets. Moving through this progression of structures, we saw that more highly organized markets are more likely to result in transactions at prices closer to the single equilibrium price which would prevail in a perfect market. Brokers provide search services at a price lower than the cost an investor would incur if he did his own search, and hence give him an incentive to make use of their greater knowledge of purchase and sale opportunities. Dealers provide opportunities for quick transactions at favorable prices, because they maintain continuous bids for and offerings of securities, and because dealers with better quotations (higher bids or lower offers) are easily distinguished from dealers with poorer quotations. Auction markets allow all investors to participate in a single

---

[12] See also the discussion in Section 26.4 on market thinness and substitutes among securities.

[13] Garbade and Silber (1979a) suggest that the number of participants in a market is an important determinant of both the structure of the market and the liquidity of the securities traded in the market.

price-setting process, and hence virtually eliminate the search for best price associated with brokered and dealer markets.

As the organization of a securities market becomes less fragmented and more integrated, that market can be expected to exhibit greater depth, breadth, and resiliency. Greater depth and breadth means the existence of larger immediately visible purchase and sale interests for a security. Such immediately visible interests tend to moderate the fluctuations in transaction prices which would otherwise result from temporary imbalances in orders to sell and buy. Greater resiliency means the appearance of a larger countervailing order flow whenever transactions prices change because of temporary order imbalances. Thus, if prices fall because of a temporary excess of sell orders, a resilient market will produce promptly a countervailing flow of purchase orders from investors seeking to acquire the security at temporarily "cheap" prices.

The structure of a market, be it direct search, brokered, dealer, or auction, is determined primarily by the relative profitability for market professionals of the alternative structures. No broker, dealer, or exchange will stay in business very long if it is unable to cover its costs and earn a competitive return on capital. In general, as the volume of trading in a security, or in a group of related securities, rises, market professionals have an incentive to begin to use trading technologies with higher fixed costs and lower marginal costs. This incentive will push the structure of a market towards more highly organized forms. For example, brokers might begin to provide search services in a market where trading was previously so infrequent that investors did their own search. Similarly, market professionals might organize an auction (either by providing a single geographic location for trading or by providing an electric communications system) in a market where investors previously traded with individual dealers.

The following three chapters describe in more detail the actual organization of a variety of securities markets. The reader should be attentive to the differences in the structures of those markets and to the economic reasons for those differences.

FURTHER READING

Avraham Beja and M. Barry Goldman, "On the Dynamic Behavior of Prices in Disequilibrium," *Journal of Finance*, **35** (May 1980), 235–248.

Kenneth Garbade and William Silber, "Technology, Communication and the Performance of Financial Markets: 1840–1975," *Journal of Finance*, **33** (June 1978), 819–832.

Kenneth Garbade and William Silber, "Structural Organization of Secondary Markets: Clearing Frequency, Dealer Activity and Liquidity Risk," *Journal of Finance*, **34** (June 1979), 577–593.

M. Barry Goldman and Avraham Beja, "Market Prices vs. Equilibrium Prices: Returns' Variance, Serial Correlation, and the Role of the Specialist," *Journal of Finance*, **34** (June 1979), 595–607.

CHAPTER 21

DEALER MARKETS

The distinguishing characteristic of a dealer market is the opportunity it provides for investors to sell and buy securities immediately at readily available bid and offer quotations. In offering to investors the *liquidity service* of an immediate execution of their orders, dealers bridge the time gaps between asynchronously arriving public purchases and sales.[1] Dealer inventories buffer transient fluctuations in net public demand for a security and thereby help to smooth out what might otherwise be volatile fluctuations in transaction prices.[2]

This chapter describes three quite distinct dealer markets: the market for United States Treasury issues, the market for corporate bonds, and the OTC market for common stock. While dealers in all three markets make bid and offer quotes and take inventory positions, differences among the securities have led to important differences in the way the dealers carry out their market-making functions. There exist only about 140 different Treasury securities (40 bill ma-

[1] Garman (1976) emphasizes the importance of dealers in bridging the gaps between asynchronously arriving purchases and sales, and distinguishes dealer markets with a "lumpy" order flow from the more abstract markets of economic theory with a "smooth" order flow.

[2] Garbade and Silber (1979a) analyze the role of dealer inventories in buffering transient fluctuations in public purchases and sales of securities and in dampening transient fluctuations in transactions prices. Stoll (1976) found that, on average, dealers in the over-the-counter market buy when prices are declining and sell when prices are rising. This would suggest that their transactions have a "stabilizing" influence on market prices. He also found that dealers are more likely to sell stock if they previously bought stock, and conversely. This suggests that they do not fully absorb shifts in public demand, but that they do "smooth out" the price consequences of those shifts. Amihud and Mendelson (1980) examined the relation between dealer inventories and transient price fluctuations at the level of individual transactions.

turities and 100 coupon issues), but the size of each issue is on the order of several billion dollars. There are, on the other hand, thousands of issues of corporate debt and stock, relatively few of which exceed $250 million in value. The homogeneity and large size of Treasury issues have fostered a classical dealer market in those securities, while the heterogeneity and relatively small size of corporate issues have produced some significant differences between the activities of corporate securities dealers and the usual definition of a dealer.

The structure of the dealer market in corporate bonds and the dealer market in OTC stocks can be distinguished by the nature of those securities and their investors. As debt securities with contractual payment obligations, most corporate bonds are close substitutes for each other, and the most sucessful bond dealers make markets in a full range of those issues. Indeed, transactional devices like swaps (see Section 21.2) virtually require that a dealer be willing to take almost any bond into his inventory. At the same time, bond investors typically trade relatively large blocks of bonds, and dealers require a substantial capital base to support their inventories. The high degree of interasset substitutability and large capital requirements have led to a corporate bond market dominated by a relatively few large firms, such as Salomon Brothers, Goldman, Sachs, and The First Boston Corporation. OTC stock issues, on the other hand, are not close substitutes for each other, and they do not typically trade in large blocks. The market in those securities consists of a large number of relatively small dealers, many of whom specialize in a narrow range of issues. The difference in the size of conventional transactions in corporate bonds (large) and OTC stocks (small) has also led to a difference in the relation between public investors and dealers in those issues. Corporate bonds investors trade directly with dealers, while OTC stock investors frequently trade through brokers. Some reasons for these differences are suggested below.

21.1 TREASURY DEALERS

The organization of the market in Treasury securities is like a wagon wheel.[3] At the hub of the wheel are some thirty-five primary dealer firms who stand ready to trade on demand with each other and with public investors.[4] Arrayed around the outside of this hub are hundreds of public investors, including banks, insurance companies, pension funds, and other institutional investors, who purchase and sell Treasury issues at irregular intervals according to their portfolio objectives and cash needs.

Transactions in the inside, or interdealer, Treasury market typically take place in conventional sizes like $0.5 million for a long-term bond, $1 million for

---

[3] Meltzer and von der Linde (1960) provide an excellent description of government securities dealers. R. Scott (1965), Hawk (1974), and McCurdy (1977–1978) also describe the market and its participants. Extensive material on the government securities market may be found in the *Report of the Joint Treasury-Federal Reserve Study of the Government Securities Market* (1969) and in three volumes of related staff studies. Additional data may be found in the *Treasury-Federal Reserve Study of the Government Securities Market* (1959).

[4] The primary dealers are identified in Exhibit 1.5.

a new note issue, and $5 million for a new Treasury bill. Dealers are expected to buy and sell, at their bid and offer quotations, at least one conventional unit when called upon by other dealers.

Transactions in the outside, or dealer-public, Treasury market are more heterogeneous in size and vary from tens of thousands to tens of millions of dollars. As a consequence of this heterogeneity, quotations vary as a function of the inventory risk a dealer assumes in completing an order. For example, a dealer seeking to expand his inventory may bid on a block of $25 million of an issue at the same price he would bid on a $1 million transaction in the same issue. On the other hand, if the dealer is seeking to reduce his inventory, he may quote a substantially lower bid on the larger block or refuse outright to bid on more than a $5 or $10 million piece of the block. Negotiations over the price and size of transactions are more common in the dealer-public Treasury market than in interdealer trading.

The Dealer-Public Treasury Market

In aggregate, dealer inventories of Treasury securities are small when compared with the holdings of public investors. The willingness of public investors to buy, hold, or sell Treasury issues at the prices quoted by dealers is, consequently, the primary determinant of the equilibrium values of those issues. If dealers are quoting too high a price, so that investors are net sellers and are transacting at a substantial rate, those dealers will find their inventories building up rapidly. The dealers will be forced to lower their bids toward an equilibrium price to stem further acquisitions. The critical role of public order flow in determining equilibrium values makes it important for dealers to have a sense of the trading interests of public investors.

Salesman are the primary link between dealer firms and public investors. These salesmen maintain contact between the public and the traders responsible for managing a dealer's position. An investor seeking to complete a transaction will normally contact a salesman and, through him, obtain the quotes of a trader. If those quotes are unattractive, the salesman may be able to offer suggestions about comparable issues on which the trader is able to offer better quotes. A stable sales force provides a regular basis of communication between investors and a dealer firm, even while trading interest may be shifting across different parts of the maturity spectrum.

Customer contacts provide important information to dealer firms. The more broadly a dealer can cover the public market with his salesmen, the more likely the dealer will learn of shifts in public preferences before they are reflected in either price movements or sharp changes in his inventory position. An extensive sales force also gives traders the opportunity to participate in more transactions with the public and thus to get a more informative picture of public interests. Such information is sufficiently important that a dealer with a small sales staff is typically unwilling to complete large transactions entirely at its own risk, and may be unwilling to make markets in longer-term issues with more volatile prices.

An extensive sales force also lets a dealer firm cover a short position, or liquidate a long position, quicker and without recourse to the interdealer market. The faster a dealer can shift his inventory to a desired level, the less unwanted risk he has to bear. To the extent he can complete such shifts without transacting with other dealers, he deprives those other dealers of useful information on changes in aggregate supply and demand.

If public investors always completed their transactions with a single favored dealer, and if the dealers never traded between themselves, there would be no reason to expect a close clustering of dealer quotes. In such a regime each dealer would stand alone as an independent market. In fact, however, the Treasury market is quite well integrated. Dealer quotations for conventional-size transactions rarely vary by more than a couple of 32nds of a percent of principal value on coupon issues or a few basis points on Treasury bills.

One reason why the Treasury market is not more fragmented is the low cost of search for the best price. Dealers advertise their willingness to make markets, and facilitate the exchange of information between investors and salesmen, to attract order flow. Investors are thus able to obtain comparative quotes quite readily. A dealer quoting away from the best available price on one or both sides of the market is quickly recognized as making a poor market. That dealer can expect to do little business until he improves his quotes. The low cost of searching for the best price reduces the likelihood that low bidders or high offerers will complete many transactions, and minimizes the fragmentation of the Treasury market.

The Interdealer Treasury Market

A second factor enhancing the integration of the Treasury market is the existence of an extremely well organized system of interdealer trading. A direct-wire telephone system links traders in different dealer firms. A trader who wants to move a position in the interdealer market, i.e., to trade with other dealers, can completely canvass the quotations of his competitors in a matter of minutes. The speed and low cost of search in the interdealer market force those dealers who want to do business to quote virtually identical prices. A high bidder is quickly discovered and hit, forcing him to lower his quotes to avoid acquiring an excessive inventory position. A low bidder is similarly easily discovered and can expect to do even less business with other dealers than with the public.

The speed and low cost of search in the interdealer market, and the convention among dealers of making reciprocal markets, mean that a trader does not, for example, have to raise his public bid substantially to cover a short position. He may, instead, bid only moderately aggressively in the interdealer market and probably complete his transactions quicker and at lower cost than if he had to rely on attracting infrequently arriving public orders. Interdealer trading smooths out random inventory imbalances among dealers and dampens quotations and transaction price fluctuations that might otherwise arise out of such imbalances. It makes the inventory experiences and price quotations of different dealers more homogenous and thereby enhances market integration.[5]

Interdealer Brokerage in Treasury Securities

Brokers have been active in facilitating interdealer trading in Treasury issues for almost as long as there have been dealers in those securities. These interdealer brokers, such as Fundamental Brokers Incorporated and Biggs & Coman, play the classical broker's role of bringing together compatible buyers and sellers. When a dealer decides to offer an issue in the so-called brokers' market, he contacts one of the brokers and states the issue, the offering size, and the price at which he is willing to sell. The broker then contacts other dealers to inform them of the offering. If one of the contacted dealers finds the offering attractive, he can buy the issue for the offering price plus a commission to the broker. After the offering is taken, the broker will generally recontact his dealer customers to inform them that a transaction occurred at the offering price. A similar process takes place when a dealer wants to buy an issue and places a bid with a broker.

An important reason why dealers place orders with brokers (rather than trading directly with other dealers) is because brokers conceal the identities of the ultimate transactors in a trade. Brokers in the Treasury market participate as principals on both sides of each trade which they broker. A selling dealer delivers his securities to, and receives payment from, the broker, and the buying dealer makes his payment to, and receives delivery of the securities from, the same broker. Neither dealer knows the identity of the other dealer. A trader selling an issue through a broker can maintain his interdealer and public offering prices even while having the broker show the issue to other dealers at a lower price. He can, therefore, complete a trade in the interdealer market without revealing that he is the dealer trying to establish a new inventory position.

The existence of an interdealer brokers' market in Treasury securities provides traders with a source of trading opportunities and information which supplements their direct contacts with customers and other dealer firms. A trader can transact as easily through a broker as he can with one of his competitors. Thus, it is useful for a trader to keep himself informed of the current purchase and sale orders in the brokers' market. During the business day a Treasury trader may contact repeatedly one or more of the interdealer brokers to see what bids and offerings are showing, and at what prices. In addition, the disclosure by brokers of transactions prices in their market conveys important information, since there is no other vehicle for reporting transactions in Treasury securities. Without the brokers' market a dealer would know the prices of only those trades in which he himself participated. The brokers' market gives him a window on the trading of other dealers.

---

[5] This point is explored in greater detail in Garbade (1978a). See also the similar point made in Hamilton (1978) and Ho and Stoll (1980).

Screen Brokers Until recently, brokers as well as dealers relied on direct-wire telephone communications. However, during the 1970s a more sophisticated type of electronic brokerage appeared in the interdealer Treasury market. This new type of brokerage was a direct result of an earlier partial fragmentation of the market. The rapid growth of trading in Treasury issues that resulted from large federal deficits and concomitant debt sales in the late 1960s and early 1970s, and an increase in the number of primary dealer firms active in the Treasury market, led to inefficiencies in the traditional mechanisms of bilateral dealer-to-dealer and broker-to-dealer telephone communication. Traders and brokers found it increasingly difficult to complete a thorough canvas of the quotes of other dealers in a sufficiently small interval of time. In rapidly moving markets, dealer quotes got out of line, and transactions took place away from the best available prices with increasing frequency.

In late 1974 a new broker named Garban, Limited, began to offer automated brokerage services to primary dealers in government securities. Each dealer has a video display screen in his office, provided by Garban, showing recent bids and offerings on actively traded issues. A trader interested in a particular bid or offering can call a broker at Garban and sell or buy the issue at the quoted price plus a commission.[6]

The brokers at Garban offered two incentives for traders to use their market. First, it was fast. New bids and offerings appeared on the screen of every dealer simultaneously. There was no need for a trader to wait after placing a purchase or sale order while a broker called individual dealers. Second, it was cheap. The usual brokerage commission on coupon issues was $1/_{64}$ of a percent of principal value (about \$150 per million dollars principal value) before Garban entered the brokers' market. Garban halved that commission rate. Within a year after its entry into interdealer brokerage, Garban had captured a substantial share of the order flow in the brokers' market. Shortly thereafter, Fundamental Brokers introduced its own competing electronic brokerage screens. Garban and Fundamental are now known collectively as *screen brokers*, in contrast to the older telephone brokers.[7] The latter still exist, primarily because of their ability to handle trades in inactive issues which are not listed by the screen brokers.

The brokerage services offered by Garban and Fundamental have had a substantial impact on the Treasury securities market.[8] Since only the best bids and offerings appear on the screens, executions take place on a strict price priority basis. Because the screens are available to every dealer, their presence has

---

[6] The use of electronic quotation devices in the goverment securities market is described by Garbade (1978b) and Platt (1979).

[7] The innovation of electronic trading by Garban is an example of market structure evolution fostered by the opportunity of profit to a market professional. As noted later in this section, the screen brokers have changed the structure of the Treasury securities market from a dealer market to something quite close to an auction market.

[8] Garbade (1978a) has explored the impact of electronic brokerage on competitive dealer markets through a series of simulation experiments. See also Garbade (1978b) and Platt (1979).

changed the interdealer market into a virtual continuous auction market. The bids and offerings on active issues appearing on the screens are continually refilled, and bid-ask spreads are extremely narrow. Traders no longer need to look to other dealer firms for an immediate market in an issue, but can look to the best quotes of the dealer community as a whole as those quotes are shown on their screens. They know they cannot hope to uncover a bid above the offering shown on a screen (or an offering below the bid), since every dealer sees, simultaneously, the same prices. The bid-ask spread on the screens is frequently so narrow that dealers also know it is unlikely they will be able to uncover somebody quoting inside that spread. The incentive to search for a better price away from the screens is thus negligible, and most interdealer trades in active issues go through the screen brokers.

The enhanced integration of the interdealer Treasury market has also had important effects on the public-dealer market, at least in transactions of a conventional size in active issues. Before the availability of the screens a public investor could get only the bid and offer quotations of a single dealer with one telephone call. It was up to the investor whether he wanted to spend additional time searching for a better price. With the advent of automated quotation systems, investors can call a dealer and learn not only his quotes but also the best quotes available in the interdealer market. Even though public investors cannot execute an order through Garban or Fundamental (those brokers serve only primary dealers), they can quickly decide if a dealer is quoting a price too far away from the price in the interdealer market. An investor is unlikely to sell to a dealer's bid if he knows the dealer can turn around and immediately resell the same issue through the brokers' market at a price one-sixteenth better and a profit of $625 per million dollars of principal value.[9] The availability of an extremely efficient brokers' market means that individual Treasury dealers are no longer offering an essential liquidity service in conventional-size transactions in active issues. Instead, the opportunity for immediate execution is offered by the market as a whole. Since individual dealers are not providing an essential liquidity service, competition has forced them to narrow their spreads substantially. The screen brokers have integrated not only interdealer trading but also the dealer-public market in active Treasury issues. They have, almost, brought public investors directly into their electronic auctions and have correspondingly reduced the need for individual dealers to provide independent markets for the immediate purchase and sale of conventional-size lots of actively traded Treasury issues.[10]

---

[9] For example, if a dealer bids at a price of 99 percent of principal value for an issue, and if there is a bid at $99\frac{1}{16}$ percent for the same issue on a screen, the dealer could make a riskless profit of $625 (that is, $\frac{1}{16}$ of 1 percent of $1 million) if he could buy $1 million of the issue at his own bid price of 99 percent and immediately resell it at the bid of $99\frac{1}{16}$ percent on the screen.

[10] This description suggests that Garban has created a centralized auction market in active Treasury issues not unlike that proposed by the SEC for equity issues. See footnote 9 in Chapter 20. It is interesting to observe that Garban was innovated privately, without government encouragement or regulation.

21.2   CORPORATE BOND DEALERS

The frequency of trading in individual corporate bonds is much lower than the frequency of trading in individual Treasury bonds, because of the relatively smaller size of corporate bond issues. Dealers in corporate bonds therefore charge a higher price for the liquidity service of a market for immediate execution; i.e., they quote bid-ask spreads on corporate bonds larger than the spreads quoted on Treasury issues.

The existence of relatively wide spreads and infrequent trading have created a less impersonal market in corporate bonds than in Treasury issues. An investor who repeatedly patronizes a single dealer for his corporate bond trading is more likely to get a better price quotation from that dealer than an infrequent customer, while both would likely get the same price if they were seeking to trade a Treasury issue. Corporate bond dealers recognize steady customers as a source of liquidity (in the sense of increasing inventory turnover), and they strive to keep those customers by quoting them prices more favorable than they might offer to infrequent customers. Treasury dealers, on the other hand, can vary their inventory positions through moment-to-moment price competition with other dealers and need not rely on long-term dealer-customer relations. Their quotes are, consequently, more homogeneous across customers than is the case with corporate bond holders.

Compared with the Treasury market, the interdealer market in corporate bonds is primitive. Dealers cannot afford to maintain a position at any particular time in more than a few dozen of the thousands of available issues, and so they are not likely to be able to accommodate another dealer seeking to buy a particular security. Unlike the case with Treasury issues, interdealer trading is not a significant source of liquidity to corporate bond dealers.

Liquidity in the corporate bond market is not derived by knowing what *is* available and what *is* being sought in the form of active bids and offerings, as in the Treasury market. Instead, it is derived by knowing what *may* be available from, or what *may* be sold to, public investors. A corporate bond dealer assumes much less risk in buying a particular issue if he knows a client is interested in that issue than if he buys the issue strictly for his own account. In the former case he may be able to turn over his purchase in a matter of hours or days, while in the latter case he may end up holding the issue for weeks. The corporate bond market is not an active market of "live" bids and offers known to most participants, but a market of purchase and sale interests which have only an uncertain potential for being converted into actual transactions. Knowledge of those interests is a critical determinant of dealer profits. This is a second reason why long-term customer relations are more important to a corporate bond dealer than to a Treasury dealer. A customer who reveals his portfolio objectives is much more valuable than a customer who calls only for occasional bids and offerings. Customers in the former category allow a dealer to enter into trades with other customers with less risk, while those in the latter category are useful only if the dealer has a (fortuitously) compatible inventory position and trading interest. In view of the importance of knowledge about investor trading interests, maintaining a competent sales staff is even more important to corporate bond dealers than to Treasury dealers.

The relatively high cost of trading corporate bonds, i.e., the wide bid-ask spreads on those issues, has stimulated the use of trading mechanisms other than cash purchases and sales. Many dealer-customer transactions in long-term bonds are arranged in pairs, where the dealer and customer *swap* two issues of comparable aggregate value, settling only the difference in cash.[11] Swaps let a customer alter his portfolio allocation in a single transaction and eliminate the need to first sell one issue and then, with the proceeds, buy another issue. From a customer's point of view, swaps completed inside the cash quotes of a dealer are economical. From a dealer's point of view, a swap lets a trader get out of one issue and acquire another which some third party may be seeking.[12] Moreover, if the two issues are close substitutes, the swap may not lead to a significant change in the risk exposure of the dealer's portfolio. The revenue from the swap may therefore be relatively cheap in terms of changes in dealer risk.

Although corporate bond dealers may appear to their customers to behave like classical dealers, in fact they are not wholly dissimilar from brokers. A corporate bond dealer will quote some bid price if a customer wants to sell an issue, but he is likely to quote a better price if he thinks he knows of the existence of another buyer to whom he can quickly resell the same issue. A broker may be characterized as one who bids a zero price unless he knows with certainty of the existence of another buyer of the same issue. This is simply an extreme case of the pricing behavior observed in corporate bond trading. Information on the purchase and sale interests of investors is nearly as important to bond dealers as it is to brokers. The difference between the two is that brokers trade only on the existence of such information, while a corporate bond dealer will trade on the probabilities of a more or less rapid appearance of a party on the other side of a transaction. A dealer's estimate of those probabilities will usually be reflected in his bid or offer quotation.

The ability to execute swaps gives a bond dealer a dimension of flexibility in his quasi-brokerage activities which is not available to an ordinary broker. A broker has to match cash buyers and cash sellers for specific issues. A bond dealer, however, can swap two issues with one investor and then swap out of his newly acquired position with some other investor. Thus, he can enter into purchase and sale transactions which are foreclosed to brokers, i.e., those where securities rather than cash serve as the medium of exchange.

---

[11] Homer and Leibowitz (1972) provide an extended discussion of various types of bond swaps.

[12] Swap transactions are especially useful to corporate bond dealers who have acquired a large position in a new issue through participation in an underwriting syndicate. By swapping out of the new issue the dealer brings his aggregate portfolio into better balance and acquires a diverse inventory of bonds attractive to investors who may not have been interested in the new issue. The secondarily acquired portfolio can then be unwound in cash transactions over a period of days or weeks. This may be more remunerative to the dealer than unwinding a large block of the new issue directly for cash. Some dealers, by overvaluing the securities acquired in a swap, have used swaps to undercut the fixed syndicate price of a new issue. See Bialkin et al. (1977, pp. 341–342) and the discussion of the offering of $100 million of 8 5/8 percent European Investment Bank notes in *The Wall Street Journal*, March 3, 1978, p. 18, col. 3.

Bond dealers may be characterized, in part, as maintaining complex barter markets for the exchange of corporate bonds. These barter markets arise out of the desire of investors to reduce their transactions costs, both pecuniary and nonpecuniary, below what they would be were all transactions for cash (as in a classical dealer market) and below what they would be if all transactions required matching of cash buyers and cash sellers (as in a classical brokered market).

21.3 OVER-THE-COUNTER TRADING IN UNLISTED STOCKS

In addition to the several thousand stocks listed and traded on organized stock exchanges, there exist perhaps 30,000 other stock issues which are not restricted from public trading but which are not listed on any exchange. These "unlisted" stocks trade in the OTC market. There are several reasons why a stock may not be listed on an exchange, including lack of widespread investor interest (typical for small companies with only a local or regional following), small issue size, or insufficient order flow. Most commercial bank, savings and loan, and insurance company stock issues trade in the OTC market.

The OTC stock market is primarily a dealer market. Since different OTC issues are not usually close substitutes for each other, a dealer with limited capital can make a successful market even in a relatively narrow range of stocks. As a result, there are a large number of relatively small OTC dealers. This is quite distinct from the corporate bond market, which is dominated by perhaps five dealer firms trading in a full line of corporate debt securities. OTC dealers do, however, concentrate their trading in particular industry groups or geographical areas. M. A. Shapiro, for example, has long been recognized as a leading OTC dealer in bank stocks.

Investors in both Treasury and corporate bonds almost always deal directly with the dealers who make markets in those securities. Investors in OTC stocks, however, typically complete their transactions through intermediary brokers. The existence of such intermediary brokers is attributable to scale economies of search available to those brokers. The nature of these scale economies can be readily appreciated from a description of the structure of the OTC market prior to 1971. Following that description this section will describe the dramatic change in OTC trading which resulted from the introduction, in February 1971, of an electronic quotation system called NASDAQ.

Pre-1971 OTC Market Structure

The structure of the OTC market, both before and after NASDAQ, parallels the structure of the market for Treasury securities. The focal point in the trading of any issue is the group of dealers who make a market in that issue. These dealers, who might number up to twenty or thirty in an active issue, are usually well known to each other. They actively check their competitors' markets to learn their prices and to balance their inventory positions through interdealer trading.

Public orders for purchase or sale are typically executed by brokers acting as agents for their customers. When handling a public order a broker will contact several dealers to search out the most favorable price. When a broker is satisfied with a dealer's quoted price, he will complete the transaction with that dealer and either charge his public customer the same price plus a commission for his brokerage services or charge the customer a markup over the dealer's price. Public investors use brokers to locate the most favorable dealer, because they are usually unfamiliar with the identities of the dealer firms making markets in specific issues and because brokers can contract dealers at lower cost. More generally, brokers can capitalize on economies of scale in search.

When handling a customer's order, a broker has to answer two basic questions. First, which dealers are active marketmakers? Second, which of those dealers is quoting the price most favorable to his customer? Prior to 1971 the first question was easily resolved by looking at the "pink sheets" of the National Quotation Bureau, Inc. (NQB).[13] These sheets, printed on paper with a pink tint, are distributed daily to subscribing brokers and list the bid and/or offer prices submitted by dealers to NQB the previous afternoon. There are three regional editions of the pink sheets (Eastern, Midwestern, and Pacific), and a dealer can enter quotes in any or all of them. An entry on a pink sheet includes the name of the security, the bid and offer quotation of the dealer, and the dealer's name. Exhibit 21.1 shows several examples of pink sheet quotations.

Because of the delay of nearly a day between the submission of a quote to NQB and the dissemination of the pink sheets to market participants, pink sheet quotes are always "stale" by the time a broker sees them. More generally, a dealer could not be expected to sell a stock on Tuesday morning at the offering price he quoted Monday afternoon. Thus, the pink sheets are more a vehicle for advertising interest in an issue than for disseminating firm price quotations. Indeed, dealers frequently show indications of interest such as OW (offerings wanted) or BW (bids wanted) instead of prices. The sheets are of real value, however, for identifying which dealers are active in a given issue.

After a broker has determined which firms are dealing in a security, he next has to locate the best price for his customer. Until 1971 this search process was conducted exclusively by telephone and teletype. A broker handling a public order typically called several dealers, incurring the direct costs of the telephone charges and the opportunity costs of alternative uses of his own time. These costs reduced the incentive of the broker to make a complete search of the OTC dealer market and resulted in executions away from better (but undiscovered) prices from time to time.[14]

The foregoing comments should not be interpreted as implying that investors would necessarily have been better off had they searched for the best dealer prices themselves. First, they could not easily identify dealers active in a

---

[13] The OTC market as it existed prior to NASDAQ is described by Friend et al. (1958), Bloomenthal (1960), Loomis and Rotberg (1964), Martin (1970), and Bloomenthal (1971).

[14] See, for example, Loomis and Rotberg (1964, p. 592, fn. 6).

EXHIBIT 21.1

"PINK SHEET" QUOTATIONS

Reproduced below are bid and offer quotations for eight securities as they appeared in the pink sheets of the National Quotation Bureau on June 5, 1978. The sheets note specifically that "offerings and wants are subject to previous sale or change in price."

Issue	Broker-dealer	Bid	Ask
ALRAC CORP	M RIMSON & CO	$1^{1}/_{2}$	$1^{3}/_{4}$
	FOSTER & MARSHALL	$1^{5}/_{8}$	2
	M H MEYERSON & CO	$1^{5}/_{8}$	2
ALPHANUMERIC	SAM B FRANKLIN & CO	$^{1}/_{2}$	$^{3}/_{4}$
	ROBERT M TANNEY	OW	
	M S WIEN & CO	$^{1}/_{2}$	$^{11}/_{16}$
ATLAS MINING CO	SPOKANE SECS CORP	.90	1.15
	MERRILL LUTHER	.95	1.10
BIRDSBORO CORP	EULER & CO	1	$2^{3}/_{8}$
	KAUFMANN ALSBERG & CO	$1^{7}/_{8}$	$2^{3}/_{8}$
	TWEEDY BRWNE	$1^{7}/_{8}$	$2^{3}/_{8}$
BOONTON ELECTRONICS	AMSWISS INTL	$7^{1}/_{2}$	$8^{1}/_{4}$
	STEVENS ROTHCHILD	7	8
CAMFLO MINES	CARL MARKS & CO	$13^{1}/_{8}$	$13^{1}/_{2}$
	LOEB RHOADS HRNBLWR	$12^{7}/_{8}$	$13^{3}/_{8}$
	MERRILL LYNCH	13	$13^{3}/_{8}$
CHATHAM CORP	HERZOG HEINE & CO	$1^{3}/_{4}$	$2^{1}/_{8}$
	F J MORRISSEY & CO	$1^{3}/_{4}$	$2^{1}/_{8}$
	TWEEDY BRWNE	$1^{5}/_{8}$	2
FUJITSU LTD	CARL MARKS & CO	$13^{3}/_{4}$	$14^{1}/_{4}$
	NOMURA SECS INTL	$13^{3}/_{4}$	$14^{1}/_{4}$
	MERRILL LYNCH	$12^{5}/_{8}$	$13^{1}/_{8}$

given issue. The pink sheets are generally available only to securities firms, and subscriptions to those sheets are expensive. Second, brokers usually had access to cheaper communication facilities such as direct wires to dealers and wide area telephone service (WATS) lines.[15] Thus, it made sense for a public investor to use a broker. The fact remains, however, that the OTC market prior to the introduction of NASDAQ was usually quite fragmented.

NASDAQ

In February 1971, the National Association of Securities Dealers[16] made available to dealers and brokers an automated quotation system called *NASDAQ*

---

[15] The superiority of direct wires over ordinary telephone service is pointed out in *Silver v. New York Stock Exchange*, 196 F. Supp. 209 (S.D.N.Y. 1961) at 212, 216, and 225.

[16] The National Association of Securities Dealers is a self-regulatory organization set up to police OTC trading practices. It is the only national securities association registered pursuant to the Maloney Act of 1938, which is incorporated into the Securities Exchange Act of 1934 as Section 15A.

(National Association of Securities Dealers' Automated Quotation system) to facilitate OTC trading.[17] NASDAQ is basically an electronic pink sheet, and as such was compatible with the preexisting structure of the OTC market. NASDAQ so accelerated the disclosure of price information, however, that it fundamentally altered the structure of that market.[18]

There are three levels of acess to the NASDAQ communication system. Level 3 terminals are available only to dealers and allow those dealers to enter bid and offer quotations on specific stocks into the system. These quotations, together with a legend identifying the stock and dealer, appear within seconds on video screens available to other dealers and brokers. Thus, unlike the prices shown on the pink sheets, NASDAQ quotations are hardly ever stale. Level 2 terminals display a montage of dealer bids and offerings on a given stock, arranged in order of decreasing bids and increasing offers, with the name of each dealer next to his quote. These terminals are available to brokers and institutional investors. Finally, level 1 terminals provide the best bid and offer price for each issue. These terminals are for use by customer representatives in brokerage firms.

NASDAQ's most important contribution to enhancing the integration of the OTC market was accelerating the disclosure of dealer quotations to brokers.[19] NASDAQ did little to increase the identifiability of dealers beyond what was possible with the pink sheets, but it greatly increased the efficiency of a broker's search for the best bid and offer prices. Thus, NASDAQ greatly reduced the occurrence of trading away from best available prices and provided a means for obtaining price priority in OTC trading. Quotes on NASDAQ are "soft," in the sense that a dealer is not contractually obligated to trade at his indicated price quotations. Quotations and transactions have to be confirmed by telephone contact between the broker and the dealer. Unlike the screen brokers in the Treasury market, the NASDAQ system has no capability for executing trades.

In addition to increasing the efficiency of a broker's search for best price, NASDAQ also facilitated interdealer trading. Prior to 1971 dealers kept in touch with each other by telephone, but with NASDAQ they could see the quotations of their competitors instantly and continuously throughout the day.

---

[17] For a description of the NASDAQ system, see Mendelson (1972, pp. 34–35), and Macklin (1973). Bleakley (1971) gives a detailed description of how traders used NASDAQ when it was first introduced.

[18] The innovation of NASDAQ is another example of market structure evolution fostered by an opportunity for profit. Unlike the brokers' screens in the Treasury securities market (which were innovated by private entrepreneurs), NASDAQ was innovated by the cooperative efforts of OTC dealers acting through the National Association of Securities Dealers (NASD). The dealers perceived that electronic dissemination of quotations would improve the efficiency and reduce the costs of OTC trading and attract more public trading. As noted later in this section, NASDAQ changed the structure of the OTC market from a dealer market to something quite close to an auction market.

[19] Hamilton (1978) found that the introduction of NASDAQ reduced bid-ask spreads in OTC trading by about 15 percent. Santomero (1974) similarly found that NASDAQ reduced spreads in the OTC market and enhanced the integration of OTC trading with trading in issues listed on a stock exchange.

Thus, NASDAQ has had an effect on the OTC market similar to the effect of screen brokers on the Treasury market. The fast and widespread disclosure of price information in both markets enhanced the integration of those markets and converted each into something quite close to an auction market.

At the present time there are about 2500 issues listed on the NASDAQ system. The remaining OTC issues trade very infrequently, and their markets continue to be based on the pink sheets and telephone communication. However, since there are generally only a limited number of dealers in any one of these non-NASDAQ OTC issues, the problem of market fragmentation is not severe.

CHAPTER SUMMARY

This chapter has described the organization of three important dealer markets: the Treasury securities market, the corporate bond market, and the OTC stock market. These markets are called dealer markets because, in each case, the focal point of trading can be located with a group of market professionals who provide the liquidity service of immediate execution by maintaining bid and offer prices at which they stand ready to buy and sell securities. The fact that these markets are dealer markets instead of brokered markets suggests that the volume of trading is sufficiently large that a dealer trading on his bid-ask spread can cover his costs and earn a competitive return on the capital committed to maintaining an inventory.

Although the three markets described in this chapter are all dealer markets, we saw that there are significant differences in their structures. For example, public investors in the OTC stock market use brokers to contact dealers, while public investors in Treasury and corporate debt go directly to the dealers in those securities. This difference can be attributed to differences in the number of dealers (relatively few in the Treasury and corporate debt markets, many in the OTC stock market) and to differences in investor characteristics (most investors in Treasury and corporate debt are institutions which can economically conduct their own search for the best price, while many investors in OTC stocks are individuals who find it cheaper to use brokers to conduct that search). We also saw that the volume of trading in Treasury debt and OTC stock is large enough to support electronic communication systems which have changed the markets in those securities into something quite close to an auction market. The only reason why those markets cannot yet be described as true auction markets is the fact that public investors cannot enter directly their own bids and offers into the electronic communication systems.

FURTHER READING

Fred Bleakley, "Is NASDAQ Really the Answer?" *Institutional Investor*, **5** (July 1971), 21.

Kenneth Garbade, "Electronic Quotation Systems and the Market for Goverment

Securities," Federal Reserve Bank of New York *Quarterly Review*, **3** (Summer 1978), 13–30.

Kenneth Garbade, "The Effect of Interdealer Brokerage on the Transactional Characteristics of Dealer Markets," *Journal of Business*, **51** (July 1978), 477–498.

M. B. Garman, "Market Microstructure," *Journal of Financial Economics*, **3** (June 1976), 257–275.

James Hamilton, "Marketplace Organization and Marketability: NASDAQ, the Stock Exchange, and the National Market System," *Journal of Finance*, **33** (May 1978), 487–503.

William Martin, chairman, *Joint Treasury-Federal Reserve Study of the U.S. Government Securities Market* (Washington, D.C.: Board of Governors of the Federal Reserve System, 1969).

Allan Meltzer and Gert von der Linde, *A Study of the Dealer Market for Federal Government Securities*, Joint Economic Committee Print, 86th Cong,, 2nd Sess. (United States Government Printing Office, 1960).

CHAPTER 22

AUCTION MARKETS

Brokered markets and dealer markets are two market processes which facilitate the purchase and sale of securities. The costs of transacting in either type of market, however, can be quite large. Those costs may be explicit, such as brokerage commissions and bid-ask spreads, or implicit, such as the cost of waiting while a broker searches for a compatible trading partner.

When the volume of trading in a security is sufficiently heavy, a third type of exchange process, an auction market, may become economically feasible. Auctions maximize the direct confrontation of buyers and sellers and in doing so reduce or eliminate the need for the search services of a broker and the liquidity services of a dealer. The crucial characteristics of an auction market are the exposure of all purchase and sale orders within a single market center and strict price priority in the execution of trades. Chapter 21 described one example of an auction market—electronic brokerage in interdealer trading in Treasury securities—and suggested that NASDAQ has an auctionlike function in the OTC market.[1] This chapter describes two additional auction markets: the national market in overnight loans of Federal funds and exchange trading of listed securities.

22.1 THE OVERNIGHT FEDERAL FUNDS MARKET

American banks borrow and lend tens of billions of dollars every day in the overnight Fed funds market.[2] About 100 banks actively participate in the na-

---

[1] See also the description of the London gold fixings auction in Section 11.1.
[2] Section 4.2 describes the mechanics of borrowing and lending in the Federal funds market.

tional market. This number is sufficiently large to make direct search for compatible trading partners uneconomical for individual banks. The reserve positions of participating banks typically fluctuate widely during the course of a business day. Borrowing and lending of overnight money can be undertaken alternately several times in a single day, and most banks want to complete their transactions expeditiously. The cost, in terms of time and money, of calling 99 other banks precludes direct search. In addition, because transactions in Federal funds are not based on a negotiable instrument, banks do not normally act like dealers trading an inventory position. The existence of line limitations[3] effectively precludes most banks from bidding for funds and offering funds simultaneously in the national market. A bank selling (or lending) funds to accomodate another bank cannot be perfectly confident that it will be able to replace those funds later in the day, and a bank buying (or borrowing) funds to accommodate a selling bank cannot be perfectly confident that it will be able to locate an acceptable buyer later in the day. (Some of the largest banks, such as Morgan Guaranty Trust, do, however, make a direct two-sided market to their correspondent banks. The correspondents are generally sellers of funds, and the buying banks run chronic reserve deficiencies to accommodate the offerings of the correspondents.)

As one might expect, Fed funds trade in an auction market.[4] Several firms, including Garvin-GuyButler and Mabon, Nugent, sponsor continuous auctions in Fed funds every business day. Communication between the auctioneers and the participating banks is entirely by telephone. The auctioneers at each of the firms maintain an order book of bids for funds and offerings of funds submitted by the banks. A bank entering the market as, say, a buyer at 11:30 A.M. either can take an outstanding offering tendered earlier by another bank or can enter a bid of its own on one of the auctioneer's books. If it chooses the latter strategy, it can either bid along with the current best bidders or get in front of those bidders by submitting a higher bid. The auctioneers ensure that transactors get the best available quote and thereby maintain price priority of execution.

The center of the market in Fed funds is the auctioneers' order books. Those books record the active bids and offerings, or immediately visible schedules of supply and demand, for funds in the national market. As long as there are orders on both sides of the market, an auctioneer can put any participating bank in touch with a compatible partner immediately at some price.

The interest rate on Fed funds changes when there is an excess supply or demand at the old rate. An increase in demand, for example, will be evidenced in the first instance by the sale of old offerings and by a drying up of new offerings. For a while buyers may be content to enter their demands at the old bid rate,

---

[3] Line limitations are the limits on the amount one bank will lend another bank on an unsecured basis. See Section 4.2.

[4] The foregoing paragraph suggested that a dealer market and a direct search market are both impractical for Federal funds, but did not rule out a brokered market. The reason overnight Federal funds trade in an auction market rather than a brokered market is the large volume of trading in overnight funds. As we will see in Section 23.1, term Federal funds trade in a brokered market. This is because trading in term funds is much thinner than trading in overnight funds.

hoping that more offerings will arrive later in the day. In the meantime, the auctioneers may temporarily behave like brokers and actively solicit offerings from individual banks.

In time, if no new offerings are forthcoming, some buyers will become impatient and will enter new bids at a higher rate. The auctioneers then call around to their clients a second time, announcing the new bids and trying to draw out an increased supply of loans. At this point the auctioneers are seeking to reintegrate what has become a temporarily fragmented market. There may well exist sellers of funds at the new bid, but their ignorance of that bid prevents them from having an immediate effect on the market. By communicating the new bid to other banks, the auctioneers disseminate valuable information and give those banks the opportunity to participate in trades at the new rate.

As long as orders are arriving reasonably frequently on both sides of the market, a Fed funds auctioneer can maintain his market simply by recording arriving orders and matching buyers and sellers. When an order book becomes unbalanced, however, the auctioneer plays a more active role by communicating that imbalance to market participants. The communication responsibilities of the auctioneer increase further when bid and offer rates begin to change. The auctioneer then has to find trading interests which do not appear on his book. The faster he can find such interests, the more accurately will the residual, unfilled orders on his book reflect actual market conditions.

22.2 EXCHANGE TRADING OF LISTED STOCKS

The facility with which market participants can confront each other, either directly or indirectly through brokers, is a major determinant of the cost of completing a transaction. Before the widespread use of the teletype, telephone, and computer-based communication systems, confrontation was possible only through physical proximity. Securities brokers and dealers found it beneficial to collectively support the expense of a securities exchange where they could easily meet with each other to complete transactions. The New York Stock Exchange (NYSE) is the preeminent securities exchange in the United States.[5] This section describes the trading structure of the NYSE as an example of an auction market in an exchange context.[6]

The Floor Market

All transactions in a stock listed on the NYSE and completed within the structure of that exchange's market occur at a unique place on the floor of the

---

[5] Zahorchak (1974) described the similar exchange auction markets on the American Stock Exchange. Schwert (1977) has studied the value of membership on the NYSE. Eiteman and Eiteman (1964) and Schmidt (1977) described the institutional structure of foreign stock exchanges, including those in London, Tokyo, Paris, Amsterdam, and Brussels. Silber (1975) describes trading on the Tel Aviv stock exchange. NYSE-listed issues are also traded in the OTC market [see Reilly and Slaughter (1973)] and on regional stock exchanges [see Garbade and Silber (1979b)].

[6] Option contracts and futures contracts are also traded on organized auction exchanges, including the Chicago Board Options Exchange and the Chicago Board of Trade.

exchange, at a so-called post. There are three major sources of the active bids and offerings in an issue available at a post: (1) floor brokers handling customer orders, (2) limited price orders left with the specialist for execution, and (3) the specialist in the issue buying and selling for his own account. (Each of these sources will be described in more detail in the following paragraphs.) Since trading is physically localized, the best available bid and offer quotes are easily uncovered. Competition and ease of communication among the market participants gathered at a post enforce price priority of execution[7] and guarantee the absence of bids above the lowest offer or offerings below the highest bid. The floor of the NYSE thus constitutes a perfectly integrated market.[8]

Floor Brokers   Orders from public investors are telephoned or telexed from brokerage houses to brokers located on the floor of the NYSE who bring the orders to the appropriate posts for execution. These orders can be either market orders or limited price orders.[9]

A market order is an order to buy or sell at the best price available at the time the order reaches a post. The broker bringing a market order to a post might execute all of the order immediately upon his arrival, or he might hold back all or part of the order for a short time to see if he can attract a price better than that which is currently available. He may also choose to quote a price on his transaction inside the current bid and ask price, thereby getting in front of other orders at the post and reducing the amount of time he anticipates he will have to wait until completing his trade.

A limited price order is an order to buy or sell at a designated price (the limit price stated on the order) or at any better price. Thus, a limit order is actually a bid for, or offering of, securities. A floor broker handling a limit order to buy at or below a stated price, or to sell at or above a stated price, will usually stand by the post with his order if the limit price on the order is near the current bid and ask prices.

Limit Order Books   When a limit order carries a price which is not close to current market prices, the broker handling the order knows it is unlikely the order will be executed any time soon. For example, a bid or purchase order at $50 on a stock currently trading at $55 may not be satisfied for days, and may never be satisfied. The broker representing the order wants to ensure the order is executed as soon as possible, but he does not want to stand around tendering the order for hours or days. As an alternative to maintaining a physical presence at the post, the broker can enter the limit order on an order book

---

[7] Rule 72 of the NYSE further provides that bids or offers at the same price have time priority in their order of execution, with the oldest order having the highest priority. Such conventions on time precedence are more difficult to enforce than price priority rules and are frequently ignored in other auction markets.

[8] Studies of the behavior of transactions prices on the NYSE, including Neiderhoffer and Osborne (1966), Simmons (1971), and Garbade and Lieber (1977), offer useful insights into the structure of the market on the floor of that exchange.

[9] Cohen, Maier, Schwartz, and Whitcomb (1978b) analyze the interaction of limit orders and market orders in determining the structure of returns on securities over time.

maintained by the specialist. Orders on the book are treated equally with other orders in terms of price priority. No trades can take place at a particular price unless all bids above, and all offerings below, that price have been cleared from the book. Entering a limit order on a specialist's book provides an economical alternative for a floor broker who would otherwise have to maintain a physical presence at a post to keep a limited price bid or offer active.

Specialists Specialists provide the third source of bids and offerings in listed securities. At least on the NYSE, specialists are members of the exchange who combine the attributes of both dealers and order clerks. Specialists have an affirmative obligation to maintain both bid and offer quotations at all times, good for at least one round lot (usually 100 shares) of the issues in which they specialize. In this respect a specialist acts as a dealer, trading for his own account and at his own risk. NYSE specialists also maintain the book of limit orders left by floor brokers, and in this respect they act as order clerks.[10]

Trading on the floor of the NYSE in a few dozen issues is sufficiently heavy that there are always active bids and offerings available from either floor brokers or the limit order book.[11] For these issues the dealer function of the specialist as a source of the liquidity service of immediate execution is relatively unimportant. In many issues, however, public trading interest is more sporadic and infrequent. In these cases the obligation of the specialist to provide the liquidity service of immediate execution can become quite important. Indeed, if the prices of the best purchase and sale orders on the specialist's book have a wide spread (which is common for infrequently traded stocks), the specialist may be the sole source of an economical market for immediate transactions.[12]

---

[10] The role of specialists on the NYSE has been a subject of dispute for over four decades. See Securities and Exchange Commission, *Report on the Feasibility and Advisability of the Complete Segregation of the Functions of Dealer and Broker* (1936), reprinted in part in Jennings and Marsh (1972, p. 690); Securities and Exchange Commision, *Report of Special Study of Securities Markets* (1963, chap. VI, pt. D); Securities Exchange Act Release No. 7432 on proposed Rule 11b-1 regulating specialists, reprinted in part in Jennings and Marsh (1972, p. 704); Fiske (1969); Wolfson and Russo (1970); Black (1971b); Smidt (1971); Bagehot (1971); and Note, "The Downstairs Insider:The Specialist and Rule 10b-5," *New York University Law Review*, **42** (1967), 695–715. Garbade and Silber (1979a) and Goldman and Beja (1979) both suggest that a specialist is best described as a substitute way of providing the breadth and depth which would be present in a perfect market. The role of the specialist in moderating fluctuations in stock prices has been examined empirically by Barnea (1974) and by Cohen, Maier, Ness, Okuda, Schwartz, and Whitcomb (1977).

[11] The possibility of floor brokers competing with a specialist in the execution of limited price orders is illustrated in White (1976).

[12] As a practical matter, this means the specialist in a thin issue is a monopoly supplier of liquidity services on the floor of the NYSE. Smidt (1971) argued that the absence of competition gives specialists an opportunity to extract monopoly profits by quoting wider bid-ask spreads, and by moving their quotations more aggressively in response to changes in inventory, than would be possible in a competitive dealer market. Barnea (1974) examined whether different specialists could be distinguished by the "quality" of their markets, where quality is measured in terms of bid-ask spreads and short-run price volatility.

The Tape Market

The price and size of almost all transactions completed on the floor of the NYSE are reported to the financial community over ticker tapes and desk-top recall devices like Quotron. The tape serves an important role in partially integrating investors located away from the floor into the floor market. Just as a Fed funds auctioneer calls around to participating banks when he wants to communicate new developments in his market, the tape announces changes in the order flow on the floor of the exchange.[13]

The tape almost always provides information only on past transactions; it is rarely used to broadcast bids or offerings.[14] However, since the prices at which sequential transactions take place are usually "near" each other, the tape does give some indication of the price at which subsequent trades might take place. Trades completed at successively lower prices, as the result of a temporary excess supply of securities on the floor, may attract an offsetting flow of purchase orders once they have been broadcast over the tape.[15] The tape clearly provides to investors a more timely source of price information than a printed list of transactions prices prepared after the close of the market. The existence of the tape improves the depth and breadth of the floor market, albeit with a time delay, since it serves to attract the interest of investors who have reservation purchase and sale prices but who may not have cared to enter active limit orders on a specialist's book. It is more important in improving the resiliency of the market, however, since its main function is to disseminate actual transactions prices.

The effect of the tape on market integration is probably most important for inactively traded issues. For active issues, where there is a continuous flow of purchases and sales on the floor, the time between observing the report of a transaction on the tape and entering an order is too long to allow participants located away from the floor to enter into the floor auction. By the time an off-floor order arrives at a post, the bids and offerings available in an active issue may have changed dramatically. For inactive issues, however, a specialist can use the tape to attract order flow on one side of the market or the other. Public investors, knowing that little will happen on the floor in the 5 or 10 minutes before their orders arrive, can more safely rely on the prices reported over the tape as a guide to where they will be able to transact.

CHAPTER SUMMARY

This chapter has described two important examples of auction markets: the overnight market in Federal funds and the market for common stocks listed on

---

[13] The origins of the ticker tape is described in Hotchkiss (1905).

[14] See, however, Rule 391 of the NYSE, providing for "special offerings."

[15] This suggests that it is as important to get orders onto the floor of the NYSE as it is to get reports of transactions prices off the floor. For a description of the early telegraphic order facilities maintained by brokers, see *Commerce and Finance*, June 22, 1921, pp. 879–913; November 9, 1921, p. 1164; and April 15, 1925, pp. 695–713.

the NYSE. There are two reasons why both of these markets are auction markets. First, both markets provide a device for the continuous exposure of the limited price orders of all market participants to all other participants. The auctioneers' order books serve this function in the Fed funds market. On the NYSE the same function is served by floor brokers who handle customer limit orders in person at a post and by the specialists' books.[16] These devices allow public participants to decide whether they want to provide liquidity services to others (by bidding for or offering loans or securities at limit prices) or whether they want to consume the liquidity services which others provide (by selling at stated bid prices and by buying at stated offer prices). Public participants in the dealer markets described in Chapter 21 do not have this choice; as a practical matter they must either trade at the bid or offer prices of a professional dealer or not trade at all. In particular, public participants in those dealer markets do not have an opportunity to show their own bid or offer prices to other public participants.

The second reason why the markets for overnight Federal funds and actively traded stocks listed on the NYSE are auction markets is that the volume of trading in both markets is so large that public participants can almost always obtain economical immediate execution of their market orders, i.e., of their orders to buy or sell at the best available price, from other public participants who entered limited price orders. More specifically, they do not usually need to buy liquidity services from a professional dealer or to engage a broker to search for a compatible trading partner. Not only does this imply that the Fed funds market and the NYSE provide devices to expose limited price orders continuously to all participants but also that those devices are used sufficiently heavily so that they offer an important source of liquidity to participants who want to trade immediately.

As was noted in the chapter, there are times when there are not enough public limited price orders to justify calling either the overnight Fed funds market or the NYSE auction markets. When this happens in Fed funds, the auctioneer changes to a broker and actively solicits borrowings or lendings of funds from banks; i.e., he begins to search for compatible trading partners for his clients. When the same phenomenon happens on the NYSE, the specialist starts to act like a dealer and trade actively for his own account to accommodate the demand for liquidity services from other participants. It was observed that, for many inactively traded stocks listed on the NYSE, specialist provision of the liquidity service of immediate execution is the norm rather than the exception, and that trading in those stocks therefore more closely resembles a dealer market than a true public auction market.

---

[16] An important component of the national market system for stocks presently being considered by the SEC is the need for an "electronic" limit order book. Such a book would allow brokerage firms to submit limit orders directly from their own offices, without having a floor broker bring the order to an exchange post. See Bloch and Sametz (1977) and Melton (1978–79). If an electronic book also has the ability to pair off bids and offers at the same price, it would become an electronic auction market. See the description of the Multiple Dealer Trading System in Melton (1978–79, p. 23).

FURTHER READING

Kalman Cohen, Steven Maier, Robert Schwartz, and David Whitcomb, "Limit Orders, Market Structure, and the Returns Generation Process," *Journal of Finance*, **33** (June 1978), 723–736.

Kenneth Garbade and Zvi Lieber, "On the Independence of Transactions on the New York Stock Exchange," *Journal of Banking and Finance*, **1** (October 1977), 151–172.

Note, "The Downstairs Insider: The Specialist and Rule 10b-5," *New York University Law Review*, **42** (1967), 695–715.

Harmut Schmidt, *Advantages and Disadvantages of an Integrated Market Compared with a Fragmented Market* (Brussels: Commission of the European Communities, 1977).

Nicholas Wolfson and Thomas Russo, "The Stock Exchange Specialist: An Economic and Legal Analysis," *Duke Law Journal,* **1970** (1970), 707–746.

CHAPTER 23

BROKERED MARKETS

When a security trades infrequently, dealers will quote a wide spread between the prices at which they are willing to buy and sell. That is, they place a high price on their provision of the liquidity service of immediate execution. If, however, an investor is willing to forgo speed in the execution of his order, and if he is willing to search for other investors with a compatible trading interest, he will typically be able to trade at a price more favorable than that quoted by a dealer. In a variety of thin markets, brokers facilitate such search efforts. This chapter describes three brokered markets: the term Federal funds market, the market in large blocks of common stock, and the retail market for municipal bonds.

Compatible trading partners are not readily identifiable in most brokered markets and a broker's principal resource is information, or access to information, on the identity of prospective buyers and sellers. Absent such information, he may have little advantage over his clients in consummating trades expeditiously. The quality of service which a broker can render is a direct function of how well he knows the state of the market and the trading interests of market participants.

While a broker may seek to keep himself informed about the trading interests of others primarily to better serve his clients, in the process he also keeps the entire market informed of new purchase and sale orders. In handling a customer's order, a broker disseminates information throughout the market, thereby giving the market more cohesion than it would otherwise have. The more efficiently brokers acquire and disseminate information, the more integrated their markets will be. In examining the institutional structure of brokered markets, it is important to appreciate the contribution of brokers to market integration as well as the value of the services which they render to their clients.

23.1   TERM LENDING OF FEDERAL FUNDS

As described in Section 4.2, term Federal funds are interbank loans with maturities greater than 1 day. The same firms which maintain the national auction market in overnight Federal funds, e.g., Garvin-GuyButler and Mabon, Nugent, also broker transactions in the term Fed funds market. The structure of the two markets are, however, quite distinct. Brokers of overnight funds rarely have to engage in any extensive search efforts for their client banks, because there is a steady flow of bids for and offerings of overnight funds throughout the day. As pointed out in Section 22.1, brokers of overnight funds generally run auction markets, only occasionally searching for trading partners for their clients or disseminating news of recent changes in market conditions. Term funds, on the other hand, trade in an exceedingly thin and almost classic brokers' market.

Brokers of term Fed funds open their market each morning by calling their client banks, advising the banks as to the level at which they believe the market will trade for different loan maturities, reporting existing bids and offerings already on their books, and soliciting additional purchase and sale interests. These calls serve to keep market participants informed of the state of the market and are an important service function provided by the brokers.

On any given day most of the banks solicited by a term funds broker will indicate that they do not have any immediate purchase or sale interests. Because of the thinness of the market, one of the most important functions of a broker of term funds is showing those bids and offerings which he does receive to other banks with a prospective trading interest. A skillful funds broker must have a reasonable idea of how much money can be enticed for a given maturity out of which banks, or, alternatively, which banks might be seeking to purchase funds of a particular maturity. The greater the number of client banks a broker covers, the more likely it is that he will locate two banks with compatible interests.

Although trading in term Fed funds is infrequent, and although brokers rarely have firm bids or offerings at more than a few maturities, there is relatively little uncertainty as to the equilibrium rate on a loan of any given maturity. From the point of view of both borrowers and lenders, there exists a wide variety of close substitutes for a term funds transaction, including CDs and short-maturity Treasury and federal agency issues. Because the markets in these instruments are far larger and more active than the term Fed funds market, their rates tend to establish upper and lower bounds on rates on term funds. For example, a bank would be unlikely to lend term funds at a rate below the CD rate offered by a borrower, and a borrower would be unlikely to buy funds at a rate substantially higher than the rate it is paying on its own CDs, after adjusting for reserve requirements. Brokers of term funds thus have little flexibility in negotiating a loan rate between a borrowing bank and a lending bank. Their primary function is identifying and bringing together buyers and sellers of term funds.

One of the more sensitive dimensions to brokering term funds is the exercise of discretion in disclosing the names of banks offering funds. A broker may show bank A offering 2-month money at an interest rate which bank B finds attractive. If the broker informs bank B of the identity of the offerer, and then calls bank A to confirm the transaction, he may find that bank A has no interest in lending money to bank B. This could be either because A perceives B as an unacceptable credit risk for an unsecured loan, or simply because A has already filled its loan lines to B.[1] The broker now has to inform bank B of bank A's disinterest, thereby souring B's relation with both the broker and bank A. Because line limitations are so important to term funds transactions, a good broker must be careful how he discloses the names of active bidders and offerers.

23.2 TRADING IN BLOCKS OF COMMON STOCK

Until the late 1950's the auction markets of the NYSE easily accommodated essentially all transactions in the common stock of corporations listed on that exchange.[2] Stock holdings were widely dispersed among many public investors, each of whom typically held a tiny fraction of the outstanding shares of any one company, and purchase and sale orders from those investors were usually for one or several round lots of 100 shares per lot.

The success of the auction market on the floor of the NYSE was predicated, in fact, on a large volume of relatively small orders. In maintaining trading markets with narrow transient price fluctuations, specialists stood ready to absorb or supply securities to offset short-run imbalances in supply and demand.[3] As long as they faced a large steady flow of small orders, they knew that most of those orders would be offsetting purchases and sales if transactions were occurring in a neighborhood of the current equilibrium price. Specialists did not have to assume undesirable inventory positions for more than a few hours or a few days. Over longer intervals their rates of purchases and sales approximately balanced.

During the 1950s, however, and at an accelerating rate in the 1960s, holdings of common stock became increasingly institutionalized.[4] Pension funds, open-end mutual funds, and other managed investment trusts were among the institutional investors assuming a growing importance in the market. The size of their portfolios was such that their shareholdings frequently exceeded several times the daily average trading volume of the stock of some corporations.

---

[1] Loan lines in the Federal funds are described in Section 4.2.

[2] The NYSE auction market is described in Section 22.2.

[3] Section 22.2 pointed out that the floor of the NYSE is an auction market for actively traded issues and a dealer market for inactive issues. The role of dealers in buffering short-run fluctuations in supply and demand is described in Garbade and Silber (1979a) and Amihud and Mendelson (1980). Stoll (1976) examined the inventory behavior of dealers in the OTC market. Smidt (1971) questioned whether NYSE specialists provided liquidity services as efficiently as competing dealers.

[4] Institutionalization of investments is discussed at length in the *Institutional Investor Study Report* of the Securities and Exchange Commission (1971).

Had institutional investors been content to make marginal adjustments in the allocation of their portfolios from time to time, they would have entered purchase and sale orders of a size comparable to those of retail investors and could have been accomodated within the framework of the existing dealer-auction market on the NYSE. For a variety of reasons, however, managers of institutional portfolios preferred to transact in large blocks of stock.

One of the principal reasons for the preference of institutional investors for block trading was that they often had early access to new information on the affairs of securities issuers.[5] When such information becomes available, the recipient has a clear incentive to sell off as much of his holdings as possible at the existing market price if the news is unfavorable, or to add to his holdings if it is favorable. That is, he has an incentive to trade large blocks of stock at prices which do not yet reflect information which is in the process of being disseminated.

Many institutional investors were also atypically aggressive in the management of their portfolios. Even in the absence of any new information they revised frequently their expectations of the future value of a security.[6] Having settled on their revised expectations, they wanted to buy or sell as rapidly as possible and in as large a size as possible.

The institutionalization of stock holdings and the implications of that institutionalization for the size of purchase and sale orders led to fundamental changes in the trading of common stock. Transactions in large blocks of stock simply could not be accommodated within the dealer-auction market found on the floor of the NYSE.[7] An order sent to the floor for the sale of 100,000 shares of stock which normally traded at an average rate of 10,000 shares per day might find buyers for perhaps 15,000 shares within a dollar of the last price at which a transaction took place. Beyond such initial interests close to the current price, floor markets were exceedingly thin. In most cases the seller of the block would have only the specialist to look to as a buyer in the size required to complete the sale. However, a specialist who bought 85,000 shares at a price close to the current market price would be open to enormous risk. The purchase would be so much larger than the normal trading volume of 10,000 shares per day that he would know there would be little likelihood of seeing a comparable volume of offsetting demand from public investors for a long time.

---

[5] In general, institutional investors have an incentive to acquire expensive but fast communications facilities, such as the Dow Jones and Reuters new wires, that would be uneconomical for retail investors. This gives institutions the ability to learn about and react to new developments and changing market conditions ahead of retail investors. In some cases the early access of institutional investors to new developments has been tantamount to fraud. See, for example, the fact situations described in *In the Matter of Investors Management Co., Inc., et al.* Fed. Sec. L. Rep. (CCH) ¶ 77,832 (1970) and *Faberge, Inc.* Fed. Sec. L. Rep. (CCH) ¶ 79,378 (1973).

[6] Aggressive institutional portfolio managers and stock analysts were called "gunslingers" during the 1960s. See Brooks (1973, p. 205).

[7] Fiske (1969), Levy (1971), and West (1971) discuss the implications of block trading for the auction markets of the NYSE. An interesting comparison of equity block trading with dealings in the Treasury markets may be found in the appendix "An Organized Exchange or a Dealer Market" to *Treasury-Federal Reserve Study of the Government Securities Market* (1959).

He would, therefore, have to position the 85,000 shares in his inventory for weeks, rather than for a few hours or days. During that time he would be exposed constantly to the risk of changes in the capital value of his position.[8]

Even more important than the risk of price changes due to ordinary market fluctuations was the possibility that an institutional investor was buying or selling on the basis of information not yet available to the market as a whole. A specialist bidding on a large block of stock at a price near the current market price could suffer enormous losses within a few hours as the information which led the seller to want to liquidate his position became more widely disseminated. Since institutional investors often have early access to new information, prudence would suggest care in bidding aggressively on their offerings.[9]

In blocks, as in any infrequently traded security, specialists were willing to provide the liquidity service of immediate execution by positioning securities in their own inventories only if they could buy (or sell) at substantial discounts (or premiums) or, equivalently, only if they could trade at a wide spread between their bid price and their offering price. The spread which a specialist required to position a block was so large that institutions sought alternative, more economical ways of completing their block transactions.

One alternative to dumping a block order into the auction market is to split the order into small trades over time. In fact, institutions frequently acquire stocks through a prolonged series of small purchases.[10] Such a procedure for block sales, however, is tantamount to the investor doing his own underwriting, i.e., holding the block beyond the time at which he has decided it should be sold.[11] By doing his own underwriting, an investor is avoiding the expense of the specialist's discount at the cost of bearing unwanted risk.

Another way for an institutional investor to complete a block transaction is to hire a broker to search out compatible trading partners and to negotiate an acceptable transaction price. About a dozen major broker-dealer firms provide such search and negotiation services, notably Salomon Brothers and Goldman Sachs & Co. Although these so-called block houses are members of the NYSE,

---

[8] Specialists on the NYSE had to work under the additional disadvantage that they were prohibited by Rule 113 of the NYSE from accepting orders directly from institutional investors for purchases and sales of the stocks in which they specialize. This rule insulated specialists from the block market. See Mendelson (1972, pp. 27–30) and Smidt (1971, p. 66).

[9] See Bagehot (1971). Cuneo and Wagner (1975) have explored how investors can obtain better executions by communicating the fact that they are not trading on the basis of incompletely disseminated information, but rather to rebalance their portfolio or to liquidate a position because of a need for cash. These trading techniques, known as *passive trading*, are described by Belliveau (1977).

[10] This observation is consistent with the empirical evidence presented in Section 13.3 suggesting that securities dealers do not typically provide liquidity services to buyers of large blocks of stock by selling stock short to accomodate their purchase interests.

[11] A steady stream of sell orders may also give the appearance of selling as a result of unfavorable information not yet fully disseminated in the market. This seems to have been the case when institutional investors sold large positions in Douglas stock in June 1964, on the basis of nonpublic information, and other investors, surprised at the ready availability of Douglas stock, surmised the presence of such information and withdrew from the market. See *In the Matter of Investors Management Co., Inc., et al.* Fed. Sec. L. Rep. (CCH) ¶ 77,832 (1970).

they do not look to the market on the floor of that exchange to complete block orders left in their care. Instead, they look directly to institutional investors and seek to interest those investors in participating on the other side of a block trade. The block houses are, as the phrase goes, "upstairs marketmakers," because they put together buyers and sellers away from the crowd on the floor of the exchange.[12] A block house may bring a completed block trade down to the floor and expose it on the floor, but this is incidental to its fundamental business of upstairs marketmaking.[13]

The brokered market in blocks is similar, in many ways, to the dealer market in corporate bonds. The critical ingredient to being successful in either market is knowing what institutions have an interest in buying and selling particular issues. Information is a major resource of both corporate bond dealers and block brokers. Absent an extensive sales force in contact with a wide variety of institutional investors, both would be ignorant of potential purchase and sale interests available in the market.

Brokering transactions in blocks of common stock is not, however, identical to making a dealer market in corporate bonds. There exists, for any given corporate bond, a large number of similar bonds which many investors would accept as nearly perfect substitutes. Bonds are distinguished primarily by their coupon rate, maturity, and credit rating. The exact identity of a particular issuer is not usually of great importance in completing bond transactions. Thus, a bond dealer who acquires a position in a bond can show that issue to a wide variety of potential buyers. For common stock, however, the identity of the issuer is of fundamental importance. A block broker therefore needs to know of trading interests in specific stocks, while a bond dealer needs to know only of trading interests in bonds that satisfy a given set of parameters. The specificity of information required in block brokerage is thus much greater than what is required for dealing in corporate bonds.

The Mechanics of a Block Sale

To understand the role of a block house in brokering block transactions, we will find it useful to describe in some detail the mechanics of a block sale.

Suppose XYZ Fund, an open-end mutual fund, decides to sell 175,000 shares of GM stock and approaches Salomon Brothers to broker the sale. Prior

[12] Some firms sell passive rather than active search services. These passive services allow investors to negotiate trades directly, without the intervention of firms normally identified as brokers. See Fredman (1974).

[13] NYSE Rule 390 provides that a member firm must complete a trade in most listed issues on the floor of the NYSE or some regional stock exchange if that firm is participating as principal or if it represents both buyer and seller. If a member firm brings a block transaction to the floor of the NYSE, it must execute that transaction in accordance with NYSE Rule 91 (when a member is trading for his own account, he first must offer any of his customer's stock which he is buying at the next highest price or bid for any stock which he is selling to his customer at the next lowest price) and NYSE Rule 127 (all public purchase and sale orders represented in the crowd or on the specialist's book at the same or better price must be executed at the price of the block trade).

to contacting any potential buyers, Salomon may give XYZ its own initial bid on the block, i.e., establish a price at which it would be willing to position the entire block in its own inventory. Such an intial bid is usually below the current trading price for round lots of stock. It is unlikely that Salomon will actually end up buying the entire block at its initial bid. The bid, however, protects XYZ in the event that news of the pending block sale becomes widely known and the price of GM stock in the round-lot market falls substantially. The bid is tantamount to a guarantee by Salomon Brothers that XYZ will be able to sell its 175,000 shares at no worse price, and hence the bid has the characteristics of a put option written by Salomon to XYZ.

Once the initial bid is made, Salomon has to decide how it will "shop" the block. Shopping the block is the process whereby Salomon contacts institutional investors and seeks to interest them in buying some of the offered stock. Although the offering price may not be specified immediately, both Salomon and its customers understand that it will be at or somewhat below the round-lot price appearing on the ticker tape at the time the sale is completed. The discount serves as an incentive to buy the offered stock.

In shopping the block, Salomon seeks out market participants who have a long-term investment interest in the security and who will not demand the price discount which a dealer would require as compensation for positioning services. Because Salomon has well-developed contacts with institutional investors, it will already have an idea who is interested in buying a large quantity of GM stock. Those customers are called first, as they are most likely to be willing to participate on the other side of the trade.

Working through its customer lists in order of decreasing probability of attracting a purchase interest, Salomon gradually begins to assemble a group of buyers. The more aggressively Salomon shops the block, the more institutions it must inform of the availability of the block. If a contacted institution has an interest in buying, no harm is done. If the institution has no immediate interest in the stock, however, it may begin to short sell modest amounts of that stock, anticipating that it will be able to cover its position later, after the block has traded, at a lower price.[14] When a block house shops a block, it must reveal valuable information to other market participants, i.e., the availability of the block. If that information becomes widely available, it may affect round-lot prices, leading to a poorer price to XYZ when the sale is completed. A good block broker knows the identity of potential buyers before he begins to shop the block. He can then go directly to those buyers and limit the access of other market participants to the information that he is shopping a block. It is in this sense that knowledge of the trading interests of institutional investors is a key resource of a block broker.

While it is shopping XYZ's block, Salomon faces a continuing decision whether to show the offering to more institutions or whether to stop shopping

---

[14] This anticipation is justified in view of the fact that prices on block sales are usually lower than prices on preceding round-lot transactions. See the discussion of block trading in Section 13.3.

and buy the unsold portion of the block for its own account.[15] The second choice has the advantage of limiting further disclosure, but requires purchase of the unsold stock for its own account. It will execute such a purchase only if it can buy the stock relatively cheaply. Like any other dealer, Salomon will provide XYZ with the liquidity service of immediate execution by positioning an issue in its inventory only if it is compensated for that service. From XYZ's point of view there is a similar trade-off between the possibility that further shopping of the block will force down the round-lot price and the certainty that the block broker will extract a fee for positioning the unsold portion of the block in his own inventory. The block should be shopped as long as the benefit of avoiding the liquidity costs of positioning services outweighs the consequences of further disclosure of the availability of the block.[16] Skillful block brokerage requires that the broker assemble as much institutional interest on the other side of the trade as possible, thereby minimizing his own participation, while at the same time limiting the effect of the block offering on prices in the round-lot market.

After Salomon has assembled sufficient buying interest for XYZ's 175,000 shares, it has to negotiate a transaction price on the block. Since the trade in our example was initiated by the seller, the price will probably be somewhat below the current round-lot price. Kraus and Stoll (1972, p. 575) found that blocks transactions initiated by sellers trade, on average, about 1.14 percent below the prices of immediately preceding round-lot transactions. This discount is the incentive offered by the seller to induce other investors, and possibly the block house, to take his stock.[17]

Relationship between the Block and Round-Lot Markets

The markets in blocks and round lots of the same stock are clearly different. While the dealer-auction market on the floor of the NYSE may be quite efficient for trading round lots, it does not offer enough depth or breadth for block trading. Block brokers must be employed to locate substantial purchase or sale interests not immediately visible on the floor.

While it might seem that prices on block transactions should be independent of prices in the round-lot market, this is not entirely the case. Participants in the

---

[15] This illustrates that a block broker is not a "pure" broker, as is a term Fed funds broker, but is a dealer as well. We have seen mixtures of functions before, such as in the overnight Fed funds market where the same person might act as an auctioneer and as a broker, and on the floor of the NYSE where the specialist might act as a dealer and as an auctioneer.

[16] It should be noted that, because NYSE Rule 113 prohibits a specialist from soliciting orders from institutional investors, specialists cannot offer the same "mix" of block brokerage and block positioning services that an upstairs marketmaker can offer. As a practical matter a specialist can only offer block positioning services. This means that as long as a mix of services is more economical to customers than positioning services alone, specialists are effectively precluded from the market for blocks of stock.

[17] Radcliffe (1973) discusses some qualitative and quantitative determinants of discounts on block sales.

block market need the smaller, but more frequently trading, round-lot market for information on the prices at which marginal changes in securities holdings are taking place. The process of negotiating an acceptable transaction price on a block would be far more difficult were there no round-lot market. We saw, in Section 13.3, that the prices at which blocks trade are generally in line with subsequent round-lot prices, except for transient liquidity discounts at the time of a block sale. These discounts have been found to disappear within a few minutes.[18] This suggests that the block and round-lot markets are much better integrated than one might suspect, a phenomenon attributable largely to the efforts of block brokers to locate trading partners with genuine investment interests.

23.3   THE RETAIL MARKET FOR MUNICIPAL BONDS

The market for municipal bonds can be described reasonably accurately as a two-part market, consisting of an institutional component and a retail component. The institutional part of the market consists of investors like commercial banks and fire, property, and casualty insurance companies. These institutional investors buy and sell bonds of states and large local issuers in blocks of between $250,000 principal value and $1 million principal value. The structure of this institutional market is quite similar to the dealer market in corporate bonds. In particular, a relatively small number of well-capitalized dealers bid on blocks of bonds which institutional investors want to sell, and then offer those bonds for sale out of their own inventories to other institutional investors.

The retail market for municipal bonds is very different from the institutional market and is characterized by a large number of brokers seeking to execute purchases and sales for individual investors. Transactions in the retail market typically involve blocks of bonds of less than $100,000 principal value and most commonly are for blocks of between $5000 and $75,000 principal value.

There are two primary determinants of the structure of the retail market for municipal bonds. The first is the fact that the exemption of the interest on municipal debt from federal income taxes makes that debt especially attractive to individuals in high tax brackets, many of whom are not professional investors. The demand by these investors for personalized advice about suitable municipal bond investments means that small municipal bond firms can compete effectively with much larger firms for retail business. In particular, the economies of scale in advising individuals investing between $100,000 and $5 million in municipal debt are far smaller than those available from dealing with professionally managed institutions investing between $10 million and $1 billion in municipal debt. This has fostered the continuing viability of a large number of relatively small retail municipal bond firms, each with its own group of regular retail clients.

---

[18] See Section 13.3, and see especially Kraus and Stoll (1972); Dann, Mayers, and Raab (1977); and Carey (1977) for analyses of the speed of "recovery" of subsequent round-lot transactions prices.

The second determinant of the structure of the retail municipal bond market is the existence of a large number of small municipal debt issues. These are in excess of 1 million different municipal issues outstanding, the vast majority of which have a total principal value smaller than $25 million. Small issue size can be attributed to two factors. First, a municipal bond might be sold by, for example, a country or school district with a limited need for credit. Second, even when an issuer needs a substantial amount of credit, it might choose to sell a strip of bonds with serial maturity dates rather than a single issue with a single maturity date. For example, on June 22, 1977, the state of Oregon sold $150 million of general obligation bonds: $10 million of those bonds bore a maturity date in 1989, and $20 million matured each year from 1990 to 1996, inclusive. Thus, Oregon sold eight different and distinct relatively small issues of municipal debt, rather than a single large issue.

As a general proposition, institutional investors prefer to invest in large municipal debt issues, because those issues can be more readily bought and sold in the large block sizes attractive to institutions. Small municipal debt issues tend to be held in small block sizes by retail investors.

The retail municipal bond market is primarily a brokered market rather than a dealer market. There are two reasons for the difference between the structures of the institutional and retail markets. First, many of the bonds traded in the retail market trade extremely infrequently, because they are parts of relatively small issues. Were a securities firm to bid on offerings of such bonds for its own account, it would have to anticipate holding the bonds for a relatively long period of time, and so its bid price might be quite low. Consequently, a customer is likely to get a better price by selling (through a broker) to another investor rather than to a dealer. Exacerbating this problem is the fact that retail trading is spread over a large number of small securities firms with small customer lists. Any single firm is unlikely to be able to match a buyer with a seller from its own client list, whereas if trading were concentrated in a smaller number of larger firms, such matches would be more likely.

When an individual investor wants to sell a small block of municipal bonds in the retail market, he will usually instruct the municipal bond firm with which he does business to act as a broker and to locate a compatible trading partner. The resulting search can take several forms. In the simplest case the broker might call several other brokers, inform them of his client's interest, and give them an opportunity to contact their own customers to see if those customers would be willing to enter into the desired transaction. This procedure is economical and adequate if the current equilibrium value of the bonds can be estimated at least approximately on the basis of recent transactions. A canvas of more than a small subset of the hundreds of municipal bond firms in existence would probably not improve the customer's ultimate transaction price.

However, if a customer's bonds are not well known, and if they trade extremely infrequently, such as bonds issued by a town or school district, the equilibrium value of the bonds might be highly uncertain and the seller's broker cannot be sure that a limited number of direct inquiries will produce a price close to the best available price. In this case the broker might be able to secure

EXHIBIT 23.1

"BLUE LIST" OFFERINGS

Reproduced below are offered yields and quantities for two New York State bonds as they appeared in the Blue List of Standard & Poor's Corporation on August 2, 1977. The Blue List notes that "The bonds set forth in this list were offered at the close of business on the day before the date of this issue by the houses mentioned, subject to prior sale and change in price."

Amount	Issuer	Coupon	Maturity	Yield	Offered by
130	NEW YORK STATE	6.50	6/30/87	5.25	ALTGELT & CO.
20	NEW YORK STATE	6.50	6/30/87	5.25	COOGAN, GILBERT
100	NEW YORK STATE	6.50	6/30/87	5.25	DOUGLAS & CO.
15	NEW YORK STATE	6.50	6/30/87	5.10	GIBRALTAR SEC.
25	NEW YORK STATE	6.50	6/30/87	5.20	NATIONAL INVEST CO.
25	NEW YORK STATE	6.50	6/30/87	5.10	A. E. PEARSON
175	NEW YORK STATE	6.50	6/30/87	5.20	SOGEN-SWISS
50	NEW YORK STATE	6.50	6/30/81	4.50	ADVEST
50	NEW YORK STATE	6.50	6/30/81	4.45	BAKER, WATTS & CO.
50	NEW YORK STATE	6.50	6/30/81	4.35	BANCO CREDITO
50	NEW YORK STATE	6.50	6/30/81	4.25	MCDONALD & CO.
10	NEW YORK STATE	6.50	6/30/81	4.40	MERRILL LYNCH
430	NEW YORK STATE	6.50	6/30/81	4.50	SOGEN-SWISS

a significantly better price by using communication devices that broadcast his customer's selling interest to a much wider group of brokers than he could reach economically on a direct basis. The two most important instruments for contacting a large number of municipal bond brokers are the Blue List and the Kenny wire.

The Blue List

The *Blue List* of municipal bonds, published daily by Standard & Poor's Corporation (S&P), is similar to the pink sheets of OTC stock quotations published by the National Quotation Bureau.[19] Each afternoon municipal bond firms prepare lists of bonds which they want advertised for sale in the Blue List, and submit those lists to S&P. S&P arranges the offerings by state of issuer, by issuer, and by specific bond, and prints and distributes the entire array before the opening of business the next business day. The publication is called the Blue List, because it is printed on paper with a blue tint.

Exhibit 23.1 shows a sample of the Blue List offerings of two New York State bonds. Each line shows the quantity of bonds offered (in thousands of dollars of principal value), the identity of the bonds (issuer, coupon, and maturity), the yield to maturity at which the bonds are being offered for sale, and the

---

[19] The pink sheets are described in Section 21.3.

EXHIBIT 23.2
"KENNY WIRE" OFFERINGS
Reproduced below are teletype advices of requests for bids on municipal bonds as they appeared on the Kenny wire on April 12, 1977.

Identification	Amount	Issuer	Coupon	Maturity
$345.WA	50	WASHINGTON PUB PWR SUP SYS REV	6.90	7-1-10
Y346.OM	50	OMAHA NEBRASKA PPD ELEC REV	4.125	2-1-82
P347.PE	40	PENNSYLVANIA	5.50	5-1-85
P348.PE	60	PENNSYLVANIA	5.60	6-15-85
Y349.BU	75	BUFFALO N.Y.	4.40	5-1-81
Y350.BU	50	BUFFALO N.Y.	4.90	5-1-84

broker making the offering. If a buyer is interested in a specific offering, he calls the offering broker directly, confirms that the bonds have not yet been sold, and tries to negotiate a transaction price.

As with the pink sheets, the value of the Blue List as a price communication device is impaired by its lack of timeliness. The offering yield on a municipal bond can change substantially between the time that yield is submitted for listing in the Blue List and the time the Blue List is distributed the next morning. The fact that one broker shows a bond in the Blue List at a higher yield than that quoted by another broker does not necessarily mean that he will still be offering that bond at a higher yield the next morning. Thus, the Blue List may have limited value for uncovering the best offer price on a municipal bond.[20] It does, however, show who has an interest in selling specified bonds, and is extremely valuable for that reason. A broker with the Blue List can use his time more efficiently by calling only those brokers with a clear interest in a particular transaction.

The Kenny Wire

The *Kenny wire* is an electronic auction of offerings of municipal bonds sponsored by J. J. Kenny and Company, a New York broker-dealer in municipal bonds. A broker who decides to offer municipal bonds on the Kenny wire calls J. J. Kenny and tells them the identity and size of the offering. J. J. Kenny logs the offering onto a computer which drives a network of teletype terminals in the offices of more than 600 banks and municipal bond firms across the country. The details of each offering are printed out on these terminals.

Exhibit 23.2 shows an example of the teletype advices of bonds offered on

---

[20] S&P has recently introduced a Blue List "ticker" which is a video screen showing offerings of municipal bonds as they are received by S&P each afternoon. This system is much more timely than the printed Blue List. Unusually cheap bonds shown on the Blue List ticker tend to be sold before the printed Blue List appears the following morning.

the Kenny wire. Each line shows a number identifying the offering (as assigned by J. J. Kenny's computer), the quantity of bonds offered (in thousand of dollars of principal value), and the identity of the bonds (issuer, coupon, and maturity).

A participant in the Kenny wire auction has the opportunity to bid before 4 P.M. each day on any offering of bonds shown in the system.[21] When he settles on a bid price, he calls J. J. Kenny and tells them the price he is willing to pay for the indicated bonds. At 4 P.M., J. J. Kenny identifies the highest bid on an offering and calls the original offerer to see if that bid is acceptable. If it is, the bidder is sold the bonds at his bid price. If the offerer declines the bid, he keeps his bonds and the bidder gets nothing and pays nothing.

There are important differences between the Kenny wire and the Blue List. The Blue List has no facility for completing a transaction. It only provides a means for brokers to advertise offerings of bonds. Any actual transaction must be negotiated directly between the buyer and the seller. This is why the Blue List identifies the broker who submitted a quotation (see Exhibit 26.1). The Kenny wire, on the other hand, is an anonymous auction. Bids submitted to J. J. Kenny are considered "firm" or "real."[22] Once an offerer has decided to sell to a bid, the only remaining step is to tell the bidder that he bought the bonds at his bid price. The bidder cannot retract his bid or otherwise negotiate with the offerer.

There are also important differences between the Kenny wire and electronic quotation systems like Garban in the Treasury securities market. Garban shows Treasury securities offered at firm prices. Participants other than an offerer can only do one of two things: buy at an offering price or decline to buy. If a participant chooses to buy, the offerer must sell at his offering price. The Kenny wire, on the other hand, shows offerings without any offering price and invites firm bids on the offered bonds.

The differences between Garban and the Kenny wire can be attributed to the liquidity of the Treasury market compared to the thinness of the municipal bond market. A Treasury dealer would be unwilling to submit a firm bid on an offering of Treasury bonds at what he believes to be the current market price if he has to wait several hours to find out if that bid has been accepted. If prices fall during the waiting period, he would suffer from being unable to revise his bid and buy at a lower price. If prices rise during the waiting period, the bidder would not enjoy an offsetting gain, because the offerer would decline the bid and reauction his bonds. Thus, to protect himself, the bidder would submit a bid below the current market price. The offerer, on the other hand, would be unwilling to accept such a low bid unless the market happened to fall during the interval since the bid was submitted. The net effect is that the volume of trading in Treasury securities on a system like the Kenny wire would be extremely small, and the system would be uneconomical.

---

[21] An offerer of bonds can specify an earlier cutoff time, but 4 P.M. is the norm.

[22] In some cases a bidder may specify that his quote is not firm, and request that he be informed of whether the seller is prepared to accept his bid before agreeing to buy the offered bonds. The usual case, however, is to give Kenny a firm bid.

In the municipal bond market, on the other hand, trading in a particular bond is often so infrequent that neither buyers nor sellers have a very precise idea about its current equilibrium value. Consequently, their estimates of that value will be quite disperse.[23] A seller of bonds on the Kenny wire has the advantage of being able to identify the highest of perhaps twenty to forty bids for his bonds. Even if each bidder bids at a discount from his own estimate of the equilibrium value of the bonds (to protect himself from market fluctuations while his bid is firm), the seller may gain more from being able to select the highest of a large group of disperse bids than he will lose from selling at a discount to the successful bidder's estimate of the equilibrium price. More generally, the seller may gain more from being able to examine a consolidated set of discounted but disperse bids submitted over a relatively long interval of time than he could gain from a smaller set of bids at smaller discounts uncovered by direct contacts over a much shorter interval of time. Compared with the process of contacting other brokers directly, the Kenny wire offers the benefit of exposing an offering to a large number of potential buyers at the cost of receiving individually weaker bids because buyers have to wait to find out if their bids were accepted.

CHAPTER SUMMARY

This chapter has described the search efforts of brokers in three thin markets: the market for term Federal funds, the market for large blocks of common stock, and the retail municipal bond market. In each case trading is sufficiently thin that the cost of the liquidity service of immediate execution which might be provided by a professional dealer is deemed excessive by market participants, who therefore prefer to search out compatible trading partners. Participants use brokers to conduct that search, because brokers are cheaper than searching directly.

The cost advantage of brokered search over direct search in the three markets examined in this chapter can be attributed to economies of scale in brokerage. Brokers of term Fed Funds and blocks of common stock maintain regular contact with a wide number of market participants and keep informed about the changing purchase and sale interests of those participants. When they receive a customer's order to buy or sell, they are more fully informed than the customer about where the customer's order might be completed. They can, consequently, obtain an execution of that order for a commission lower than what the customer would expend if he tried to execute his own order by searching directly. Similarly, brokers in the municipal bond market have access to communication systems, like the Blue List and the Kenny wire, with high fixed costs but relatively low marginal costs. As long as a broker can complete a sufficient number of trades through these systems, he can cover his fixed

---

[23] Price dispersion is examined in detail in Chapter 25.

costs and earn a profit even while he is charging a commission on each trade which is less the cost of a customer's direct search.

It should be remembered that the three markets described in this chapter are brokered markets because of economics, and not because of law or regulation. More generally, their character can, and does, change from time to time. For example, we saw that a block broker will sometimes buy stock for its own inventory to facilitate a block sale, and hence may act like a dealer. This behavior is especially likely in heavily traded issues (where the risk of positioning even a large block of stock is relatively smaller), in smaller block trades, and on days when trading volume generally is especially heavy. It occurs when the volume of trading, or the size of a trade, makes dealer liquidity services at least temporarily cheaper than broker search services. Similarly, the larger and more actively traded a municipal bond issue, the more likely it becomes that a broker will buy a customer's offering of that issue directly, and then seek to resell it himself, rather than act as a pure broker of the customer's offering. This means that the categorization of a market as a brokered market, a dealer market, or an auction market is not immutable, and can be expected to change from time to time. Such changes are a function of the relative costs of supplying broker search services, the liquidity services of immediate executions by dealers, and the liquidity services of an auction market, and of public demand for those services.

FURTHER READING

Kenneth Carey, "Nonrandom Price Changes in Association with Trading in Large Blocks: Evidence of Market Efficiency in Behavior of Investor Returns," *Journal of Business*, **50** (October 1977), 407–414.

Heidi Fiske, "Can the Specialist Cope with the Age of Block Trading?" *Institutional Investor*, **3** (August 1969), 29.

Securities and Exchange Commission, *Institutional Investor Study Report*, (1971).

Richard West, "Institutional Trading and the Changing Stock Market," *Financial Analysts Journal*, **27** (May–June 1971), 17.

PART EIGHT

THE TRANSACTIONAL STRUCTURE OF SECURITIES MARKETS

In developing an answer to the question of how securities prices are determined, we made extensive use of a competitive auction market model in Chapter 11. That model assumed away many of the structural characteristics of real trading markets. In particular, transactions in such competitive auction markets are costless, and information on the trading interests of individual transactors is unimportant. In real markets, however, investors incur costs when they buy and sell financial assets, and information on the identity of compatible trading partners is both necessary and expensive to acquire.

The chapters in this part explore three important characteristics of real securities markets: bid-ask spreads, price dispersion, and thinness. The origins of these characteristics lie within the institutional structures of the markets described in Part Seven. In particular, they stem from a lack of complete information about available trading opportunities. None of the characteristics are likely to affect the equilibrium values of securities substantially, but they do have consequences for the behavior of transactions prices in relation to equilibrium values.[1]

Our interest here is not to expand the equilibrium models of asset pricing developed in Parts Four through Six, but rather to consider in greater detail the pricing of individual transactions. To recall the comment made in the introduction of Part Four, we seek to put back some of the detail which we previously stripped from our description of a securities market.

---

[1] See, however, the conjecture of Beja and Goldman (1980) that if market prices do not adjust rapidly to equilibrium prices, speculators will have an incentive to enter the market. Those speculators could increase price fluctuations or "destabilize" prices. See also Goldman and Beja (1979) and Cohen, Hawawini, Maier, Schwartz, and Whitcomb (1980).

CHAPTER 24

BID-ASK SPREADS

The description in Chapter 11 of a competitive auction market paid little attention to the process by which buyers and sellers come to exchange their holdings of securities. The principal objective of the auction model was specification of how an auctioneer can arrive at a set of equilibrium prices at which supply equals demand for every security simultaneously. The model of a competitve auction is probably adequate for analyzing the cross-sectional structure of equilibrium prices in real markets. It does not, however, provide an adequate description of a mechanism for the exchange of securities and, as a result, is not especially useful for analyzing transaction prices.

In real markets, transactions take place only when compatible buyers and sellers know of each other's existence. No matter how primitive or sophisticated the communications devices used to bring together buyers and sellers, the basic feature of bilateral exchange is present in almost all secondary markets. If public investors were the only participants in a market, a buyer of a particular security might be unable to locate, in a given interval of time, another investor willing to sell that security at a price identified as the equilibrium price. Chapter 11 finessed this problem by assuming transactions took place, after a market had come into equilibrium, in a timeless, undefined transactional structure. In real markets, however, exchange could be quite costly and time-consuming if investors had to search extensively to locate compatible trading partners.

In many markets there exists a second category of market participants, called *inventory specialists* or *securities dealers*, who facilitate the exchange of securities among investors.[1] These dealers offer to public investors opportuni-

---

[1] See, for example, the descriptions of the dealer markets in Treasury securities, corporate bonds, and OTC stock in Chapter 21, and the description of the NYSE specialist in Section 22.2.

ties for immediate execution of their orders. By quoting bid and offer prices at which they are willing to buy and sell securities upon request, marketmakers bridge the gaps created by temporary imbalances between public purchase and sale orders.[2] The existence of dealers eliminates the need for a seller of securities to search out another investor with a compatible purchase interest, and enhances the liquidity of financial assets.[3] The spread between dealer bid and offer quotes is the price of the liquidity service which they provide. From an investor's viewpoint, such spreads are a cost of completing transactions expeditiously.

This chapter considers the nature and determinants of bid-ask spreads. We assume public investors can learn the quotes of competing dealers costlessly, so that all active dealers quote the same bid price and the same offering price. In the next chapter we relax this assumption of free search costs.

24.1   THE ORIGINS OF BID-ASK SPREADS[4]

The trading interests of public investors in a given security can be represented by intersecting supply and demand schedules, as shown by the curves labeled SS and DD in Figure 24.1. The horizontal scale of the diagram is denominated in the rate of arrival per unit time of public purchase and sale orders. Were we to continue to ignore the problem of matching a buyer with a seller in each trade, we would conclude that transactions will occur at the equilibrium price P^e. At price P^e the average rate at which purchase orders arrive in the market just equals the average rate of arrival of sale orders.

The demand schedule DD and the supply schedule SS in Figure 24.1 are predicated on the assumption that a transactor can obtain immediate execution of his order at the prevailing market price. However, nothing in the model guarantees such immediacy of execution. An order to purchase securities at price P^e may arrive in the market at a time when there are no compatible orders to sell. The model is, consequently, inconsistent. A more complete model has to recognize that each transaction involves a buyer and a seller.[5] If the transactors represented by the schedules SS and DD are to obtain immediate executions of their orders, then there must exist other market participants willing to supply that immediacy.

To identify suppliers of the liquidity service of immediate execution in our model, we must add the supply and demand schedules of dealers who are willing to transact upon the arrival of the purchase and sale orders of other investors. Suppose, as above, that P^e is the equilibrium price of a security, in the

---

[2] This role of dealers in bridging the time gaps between asychronously arriving public purchase and sale orders has been studied explicitly by Garman (1976), Amihud and Mendelson (1980), and Garbade and Silber (1979a).

[3] Garbade and Silber (1979a) analyzed the relation between dealer participation in a market and the liquidity of the asset traded in that market.

[4] This analysis of bid-ask spreads is based on the original work of Demsetz (1968).

[5] Garman (1976) first made the distinction between a market where purchase and sale orders arrive in a smooth, continuous stream through time and a market where orders arrive in discrete lumps.

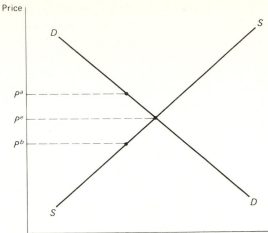

Price

P^a

P^e

P^b

Rate of arrival of public orders to buy or sell

FIGURE 24.1
Public supply and demand
schedules and dealer bid and
offer prices.

sense that the rates of arrival of public purchase and sale orders are equal at that price. Since dealers purchase securities only upon the arrival of public sale orders, they will be willing buyers at a bid price less than P^e, say price P^b shown in Figure 24.1. Waitng for a public order imposes an implicit cost on a dealer, and he is willing to bear this cost only if he can buy at a discount from the current equilibrium price P^e. Similarly, dealers will be willing to accommodate the arriving purchase orders of public investors only if they can sell at a premium over the equilibrium price. Thus, the dealers' asking price P^a shown in Figure 24.1 is greater than P^e. The premium on a dealer's asking price compensates the dealer for his willingness to forego immediacy in the execution of his sales and for his willingness to provide immediacy to other market participants who wish to buy the security.

In our extended model there will be two equilibrium prices. The equilibrium asking price P^a is that price at which dealers are willing to accommodate immediately the arriving purchase orders of public investors. The rate of arrival of those purchase orders depends on where the price P^a intersects the public demand schedule DD in Figure 24.1. The equilibrium bid price P^b is that price at which dealers are willing to accommodate immediately the arriving sale orders of public investors.[6] The rate of arrival of those sale orders depends on the intersection of P^b with the public supply schedule SS. Although Figure 24.1 shows an equality between the rates of dealer purchases and sales at the prices P^b and P^a, this need not be the case in all circumstances. Dealers may be net buyers or net sellers from time to time, although we expect their purchases and sales to balance over long intervals of time.[7]

---

[6] Different equilibrium purchase and sale prices imply that changes in transactions prices will be negatively serially correlated even when changes in the underlying equilibrium price are uncorrelated through time. See Niederhoffer and Osborne (1966), Simmons (1971), Garbade and Lieber (1977), and Cohen, Maier, Schwartz, and Whitcomb (1978b).

[7] See, for example, the effect of dealer inventory on dealer pricing as analyzed in Amihud and Mendelson (1980).

The level of dealer bid and offer prices is clearly dependent upon the location of the contemporaneous market equilibrium price P^e. In the present analysis we assume that dealers know P^e exactly and that they can therefore bid below and offer above that price with no uncertainty. The assumption of a known equilibrium price is an important simplification to the analysis of the dealer function. The consequences of relaxing the assumption are considered in Chapters 25 and 26.

The spread between dealer bid and offer prices, $P^a - P^b$, is the revenue earned by a dealer who completes a "round trip" transaction, or matching purchase and sale, with public investors. This bid-ask spread is the revenue accruing to a market participant who provides to other investors the opportunity to complete transactions immediately. Alternately, one-half of the spread is the transactions cost borne by a public investor trading with a dealer. This may be seen by noting that an investor who buys an issue and then turns around and sells that issue back to a dealer has completed two transactions, at a total cost equal to the spread between the dealer's bid and offer prices. In the next section we consider several securities characteristics which might be expected to influence the bid-ask spread of a dealer.

Distinguishing between Dealers and Nondealers

In the preceding discussion we treated dealers and public investors as readily distinguishable market participants. Although there do exist identifiable dealer institutions in many markets, e.g., specialists on stock exchanges and primary dealer firms in the Treasury securities market, the real distinction between a dealer and a nondealer is the type of order placed by each.[8] Dealers place limited price orders to buy or sell at a stated price. Nondealers enter market orders to buy at the lowest available offering price or to sell at the highest available bid. Limit orders supply liquidity services, because they provide to others an opportunity for immediate execution. Market orders consume liquidity services, because they are orders which demand immediate execution.

In most markets, participants identified as dealers can enter market orders as well as limit orders and in so doing can consume as well as provide liquidity services. For example, dealers in the Treasury markets are free to buy at the offering prices or to sell at the bid prices of their competitors.[9] In some cases the reverse is also possible, and participants usually identified as nondealers may choose to enter limit orders from time to time.[10]

---

[8] See, however, the study by Tinic and West (1974) suggesting that the cost of liquidity services is significantly greater in a market where professional dealers are not encouraged to participate (the Toronto Stock Exchange) than in markets where they are encouraged (the NYSE and the OTC markets). Their study implies that professional dealers do more in providing liquidity services than simply submitting limited price orders from time to time.

[9] Ho and Stoll (1980) analyzed the conceptual issues underlying dealer bid-ask spreads in a multiple-dealer market. Tinic and West (1972) examined the empirical relation between bid-ask spreads and dealer competition in the OTC market, and found that greater competition leads to lower spreads. Reilly and Slaughter (1973) examined whether the inclusion of NYSE-listed issues on NASDAQ had any effect on the NYSE market for those issues, and concluded that it had little, if any, effect on either NYSE trading volumes or bid-ask spreads.

[10] See the discussion of a Federal funds auctioneer's book in Section 22.1.

The facility with which investors can supply liquidity services varies according to the organization of individual markets. Nonmember transactors on the NYSE can enter limit orders as easily as market orders (see Section 22.2). Although they do not enjoy direct access to the floor, and hence cannot compete with specialists on a continuing basis, they can compete with those dealers on a selective basis. An off-floor transactor may choose to buy securities by bidding slightly above the best currently available bid rather than by buying at the lowest available offering price. If the bid-ask spread of a specialist is too large, public transactors will have an incentive to enter limit orders rather than market orders, and in so doing will force the specialist to quote closer prices. At some sufficiently small spread the gains from entering limit orders will be outweighed by the advantages of securing immediate executions, and public competition with professional marketmakers would diminish.[11]

In most OTC markets, public investors cannot compete so easily with professional dealers. For example, until recently there was no way for private investors to maintain bid or offer quotations continuously in the Treasury securities market. Investors could call individual dealer firms, but they were essentially restricted to selling at dealer bid prices or buying at dealer offering prices.

In some cases technological advances have opened the way for public competition with dealers in the provision of liquidity services. With the advent of screen brokers in the Treasury securities market, for example, investors acquired indirect access to an interdealer limit order system (see Section 21.1). They can now call a dealer and ask him to show a bid or offering on a broker's screen for their own account. This type of order uses the dealer as an agent to place the order rather than as a supplier of liquidity services.

24.2 DETERMINANTS OF BID-ASK SPREADS

Spreads between bid and offer prices are not the same on all securities. They range from quite narrow spreads on recently issued Treasury bills (in some cases as low as .0025 percent of the maturity value of a bill) to quite large spreads (up to 50 percent or more of the mean quote) on low-priced, infrequently traded stocks.[12] This heterogeneity of spreads reflects differences in the implicit costs of trading different securities and is a function of issue characteristics and the structure of trading patterns in individual issues. In this section we review the effect on spreads of the time rate of transactions in an issue, the price of an issue, the size of a transaction, and the presence in a market of investors trading on inside information.[13]

[11] Cohen, Maier, Schwartz, and Whitcomb (1979, 1981) examine the determinants of the bid-ask spread in a market where all participants, including professional dealers and public investors, compete on an equal basis, and conclude that, as long as orders do not arrive continuously, the market bid-ask spread will not vanish.

[12] Most studies of bid-ask spreads have analyzed spreads on common stock. See also the related studies by Tanner and Kochin (1971) on spreads on Canadian bonds, and by Garbade and Silber (1976) and Garbade and Rosey (1977) on spreads on United States Treasury bonds.

[13] Several studies of dealer bid-ask spreads have examined the characteristics of the dealers selling liquidity services as well as the characteristics of the securities being traded. Tinic (1972) examined the effect of specialist capital and diversification on NYSE spreads. Stoll (1978) analyzed the effect of dealer inventories, dealer capital, and risk aversion on dealer spreads.

Time Rate of Transactions

A bid-ask spread is the price of the liquidity service provided by a dealer who bridges the time gaps between asynchronously arriving public purchase and sale orders. If there is a large time interval separating the arrival of public orders, the liquidity service provided by a dealer is more valuable than if the time between arriving orders is small. Thus, investors should be willing to trade on relatively larger spreads for issues which are less active. Conversely, dealers will fill their bids and offers more rapidly in an issue for which the volume of trading is large, and so the implicit costs of waiting are smaller for such issues. Thus, dealers should be willing to quote narrower spreads on active securities.

Since the waiting cost for a dealer and the liquidity value of an immediate execution for an investor are both smaller on issues which trade actively, the bid-ask spread on a security should be inversely related to the time rate of transactions in that security. Issues which trade actively should have smaller spreads, *ceteris paribus*, than less active issues.

We can anticipate that competition will enforce an inverse relation between bid-ask spreads and trading volumes. Suppose that the bid-ask spread on a security was at a competitive level for some volume of trading, and that the trading volume suddenly doubled. If a dealer tried to maintain his spread at the level which prevailed prior to the increase in trading, he would give other dealers and public investors an incentive to outbid or underoffer his market by entering more favorable limit orders. In view of the increased trading volume, public investors would be unwilling to buy the now less valuable liquidity services at the old price of those services, i.e., at the old spread, and would perceive an advantage to entering limit orders of their own. Other dealers would be willing to supply the now less costly liquidity services at a lower price, i.e., at a smaller spread, and would narrow the spread between their bid and offer quotations. The resulting loss of order flow would force the first dealer to narrow his spread.

The effect of changes in trading volume on dealer spreads is evident from the recent history of several financial assets. Between 1974 and 1977 the volume of trading in GNMA pass-throughs increased dramatically.[14] Over the same period the typical spread on GNMAs decreased from about .50 percent of the principal value of a pass-through to about .125 percent of principal value. The recent experience in New York City bonds provides a similar example of the effect on spreads of a change in trading volume. Prior to mid-1974 New York City debt issues were among the most actively traded of all municipal securities, and spreads of less than .50 percent of principal value were not uncommon. After the financial plight of the city became evident in the spring of 1975, the trading volume in city issues fell sharply and spreads widened to as much as 10 percent of principal value on some issues. The inverse relation between

---

[14] GNMA pass-throughs are described in Section 1.3 and in Black, Garbade, and Silber (1981).

trading volume and spreads has been verified in every empirical study of the de-terminants of spreads.[15]

Price of a Security

The second major determinant of a bid-ask spread is the price of the security. Suppose, for example, a share of stock was quoted at $99 bid and $101 offered, and hence had a $2 spread. If the stock were to split 2 for 1, two shares of the new stock would equal one share of the old stock. Thus, two new shares would also be quoted at $99 bid and $101 offered, implying a single new share would be $49.50 bid and $50.50 offered, for a $1 spread.[16] Other things being equal, the bid-ask spread on an issue should be proportional to the price of the issue.

Several empirical studies of bid-ask spreads on common stock have in-dicated that spreads are less than proportional to the prices of those issues. Demsetz (1968) and Benston and Hagerman (1974) have suggested that this departure from strict proportionality is due to the size of the commission costs incurred in trading a given dollar amount of a stock: low-priced stocks incur greater costs than high-priced stocks. Even if the bid-ask spread costs per dollar value of all stocks were identical, investors would prefer to trade higher-priced issues to minimize their total transactions costs. The resulting relative concentration of trading in high-priced issues leads to lower relative spreads on those issues, so that spreads do not increase in strict proportion with price.

Size of a Trade

A third determinant of bid-ask spreads is the size of particular transactions. As a matter of convention in well-developed markets, dealers quote bid and offer prices for transactions in standard-size blocks. Specialists on the flooor of the NYSE must quote bid and offer prices good for at least one round lot (usually 100 shares) of the issues in which they specialize. Traders in the Treasury debt markets usually quote on $1 million principal value blocks of short-term issues and on $250,000 to $500,000 blocks of longer-term issues. Bid and offer prices for standard-size transactions may not apply, however, to significantly larger or smaller transactions.

A specialist quoting a round lot of some stock at $30 bid and $31 offered may not be willing to buy at $30 per share or to sell at $31 per share in a trans-action for 100 or 1000 round lots. A large purchase would leave him with a sub-stantial long position to sell off, and a large sale would force him to cover a short position. Neither of these inventory adjustments could be completed quickly,

[15] See Demsetz (1968), Tinic (1972), Tinic and West (1972), Tinic and West (1974), Benston and Hagerman (1974), Garbade and Silber (1976), and Stoll (1978).

[16] However, a study by Copeland (1979) has shown that bid-ask spreads widen relative to stock prices after stock splits. This may be attributable to a decline in trading volume.

because they require the execution of multiple conventional-size transactions on the other side of the market. In positioning a large block of securities in his inventory (either long or short), the dealer is bridging an unusually large transient imbalance in public purchase and sale orders. If asked for his market on a large transaction, he might quote $28 bid and $33 offered for the entire block, or he might quote different prices for successive pieces of the block. Either of these responses implies a larger spread per unit security in the block.

The spread between bid and offer prices for abnormally large transactions can be substantially wider than the spread on standard-size transactions. The liquidity service provided by a dealer participating in an abnormally large transaction is more valuable than that provided in ordinary transactions, since the time rate of transactions in large blocks is smaller than that of transactions in standard-size blocks. The more valuable service commands a commensurately higher price.

Dealers may also quote wider spreads on transactions that are smaller than a conventional size. Suppose, for example, a particular stock typically trades in blocks of 100 shares, and a dealer is asked to bid on an odd lot of 5 shares. If odd-lot trading is infrequent, the dealer knows he will not see any offsetting demand for the 5 shares for some time, nor will he be able to accumulate quickly enough additional odd lots to fill out a round lot. Since he anticipates having to hold the 5 shares in his inventory for a substantially longer interval of time than he would have to hold a round lot of 100 shares, he will demand a higher price for providing the liquidity service of an immediate market in those 5 shares and will quote a bid price lower than what he would show on a round lot. A similar argument applies to the offer side of the market, implying that spreads on odd lots may be greater than spreads on standard-size transactions.

Insider Trading

In our development of a competitive auction in Chapter 11, and in our analysis of the cross-sectional structure of equilibrium expected returns in Chapter 12, we assumed all investors had access to the same information about issuers of securities. Tests of the strong-form efficiency of the markets with respect to insider trading, presented in Section 13.4, showed this assumption is unjustified. Insiders appear to be able to time their purchases and sales significantly better than the average investor. The presence in a market of unusually well informed transactors imposes a unique type of risk on dealers and has consequences for the size of the bid-ask spreads quoted by those dealers.

Bagehot (1971) has pointed out that dealers always lose in transactions with insiders.[17] Insiders are willing to buy at the offering price of a dealer because they have information, not yet available to others, which will lead to an increase in the price of the security when it is ultimately disclosed. Dealers,

---

[17] See Jaffe and Winkler (1976) for why this is so, and Stoll (1976) for empirical evidence on the phenomenon.

therefore, always sell to insiders at prices below what may be interpreted as the "true" equilibrium value of a security. Conversely, dealers buy from insiders at bid prices above "true" equilibrium values. The special information available to insiders allows them to extract gains from, and transfer losses to, dealers. Their trading consequently reduces the net profits earned by dealers.

Because dealers always lose in transactions with insiders, they have to earn relatively more from their transactions with ordinary investors to stay in business. Were there no insiders trading a given security, dealers would set their spreads at a level determined by the factors mentioned earlier in this section. In the presence of potential insider trading, dealers must widen their spreads to earn enough from trading with ordinary investors to offset the losses incurred in trading with insiders. The bid-ask spread on a security should, therefore, increase as a direct function of the likelihood of a dealer trading with insiders.

Benston and Hagerman (1974) and Barnea and Logue (1975) have suggested that the risk borne by a dealer trading with investors in possession of inside information depends upon the importance of such information for the price of a security. Corporate stock prices, for example, are substantially more sensitive to adverse disclosures by issuers than are corporate bond prices. Similarly, one might expect that a stock with a large component of diversifiable, unsystematic risk relative to its systematic risk is more likely to be traded by insiders. The prices of securities whose risks are primarily systematic are more heavily influenced by well-known general market conditions than by firm-specific information. Benston and Hagerman (1974) have suggested this as a reason why spreads seem to be an increasing function of the diversifiable risk on individual securities.

Although we have thus far spoken of insiders as if they were readily identifiable, in fact they do not sport capital letter I's on their shirts. The difficulty of identifying investors trading on the basis of inside information leads dealers to widen the spreads quoted to all transactors. In some cases, however, insiders can be identified from their trading behavior.

Black (1971b) and Black and Scholes (1974a) have pointed out that insiders are likely to be more heavily represented in large block transactions than in transactions of a more ordinary size, and that they are likely to be more heavily represented among block transactors in a rush to trade. This follows because insiders have an incentive to "beat the market," and to do so in transactions of substantial size. This explains why there are transient discounts in the prices on block trades initiated by sellers, and why block positioners generally quote substantial discounts in the absence of specific knowledge of potential buyers.[18] The seller of the block is trading in an unusual size, and he is unwilling to sell his holdings in small pieces over a longer interval of time. Other transactors, consequently, are justified in believing that he is more likely to be trading on inside information than an ordinary investor, and to lower their bid prices accordingly.

---

[18] See Section 13.3 and Section 23.2.

As a corollary to the foregoing analysis of block traders, Black and Scholes (1974a) proposed several trading strategies designed to reduce transactions costs for those trading without any inside information.[19] These include giving a dealer a list of securities offered for sale and letting him choose which to buy, giving a dealer time to work out an order with other investors (essentially using the dealer as a broker), and not trading in large blocks. Each of these strategies is designed to signal to a dealer that a sale is not motivated by access to inside information, and that the dealer can safely quote prices which do not include an insider risk premium.

CHAPTER SUMMARY

This chapter has examined the difference between (1) the single equilibrium price at which all investors can buy and sell a security in a perfect auction market and (2) the bid and offer prices at which investors actually trade in real markets. The appearance of paired bid and offer prices in place of a single equilibrium price was traced to the cost of supplying the liquidity service of immediate execution.

The liquidity service of immediate execution cannot be supplied at zero cost in real markets, because supplying immediacy exposes the supplier to risk. In particular, it exposes his capital to the risk of unanticipated fluctuations in value for as long as he continues to hold the securities positions which he acquired when he supplied liquidity services to others. This means that, in general, securities cannot be sold quickly except at a discount to their current "equilibrium" price, and that they cannot be bought quickly except at a premium to their current "equilibrium" price. The sizes of the discount and the premium reflect the cost of supplying immediacy in sales and purchases, respectively, and so the size of the bid-ask spread reflects the cost of supplying liquidity services.

The size of the bid-ask spread for a security is a function of the frequency of trading in that security. More active securities trade on smaller spreads, because liquidity services are both less valuable and less costly to provide for such issues. In addition, the size of the spread on transactions of a particular size varies with the frequency of trading in transactions of that size. Odd lots and large blocks trade on larger spreads, because the frequency of trading in very small and very large orders is smaller (by definition) than the frequency of trading in standard-size blocks of securities.

The relation between the price of liquidity services and the cost of those services is enforced by competition. If a dealer is quoting a bid-ask spread on a security which is excessive in light of the cost of supplying liquidity services for that security, other dealers will have an incentive to capture trading business by quoting higher bid prices and lower offer prices, i.e., by quoting narrower spreads. In some markets public investors can also compete directly with pro-

---

[19] See also Cuneo and Wagner (1975).

fessional dealers by entering limited price orders to buy and sell, or by supplying liquidity services to other public investors.

FURTHER READING

Fischer Black and Myron Scholes, "From Theory to a New Financial Product," *Journal of Finance*, **29** (May 1974), 399–412.

Kalman Cohen, Steven Maier, Robert Schwartz, and David Whitcomb, "Transaction Costs, Order Placement Strategy, and Existence of the Bid-Ask Spread," *Journal of Political Economy*, **89** (April 1981), 287–305.

Larry Cuneo and Wayne Wagner, "Reducing the Cost of Stock Trading," *Financial Analysts Journal*, **31** (November–December 1975), 35–44.

Harold Demsetz, "The Cost of Transacting," *Quarterly Journal of Economics*, **82** (February 1968), 33–53.

James Hamilton, "Marketplace Organization and Marketability: NASDAQ, the Stock Exchange, and the National Market System," *Journal of Finance*, **33** (May 1978), 487–503.

Seha Tinic and Richard West, "Marketability of Common Stocks in Canada and the U.S.A.: A Comparison of Agent versus Dealer Dominated Markets," *Journal of Finance*, **29** (June 1974), 729–746.

CHAPTER 25

PRICE DISPERSION

The preceding chapter examined the liquidity service supplied by securities dealers who quote bid and offer prices. In a market where transactors can obtain the quotations of competing dealers instantly and costlessly, there is only one effective bid and one effective offer at each moment of time. These are, of course, the highest bid and the lowest offer.[1] In many financial markets, however, dealer quotations cannot be obtained costlessly. For example, if an investor has alternative productive uses for his time, he incurs an opportunity cost calling different dealers to check their quotations.

The existence of positive search costs can have an important effect on the transactional structure of a market. When information on dealer quotations is not free, investors may be willing to transact at prices less favorable than the best quotation. For example, an investor may believe some dealer is bidding $101 for an issue, but if he has located another dealer bidding $100.75, he may not consider the quarter-point gain worth the expense of searching to find the better bidder. When investors are willing to transact at prices other than the best prices, dealers can maintain bids and offerings away from what they know to be the best quotations and still do business. In the presence of positive search costs, rational investor search will not eliminate dispersion of bid and offer prices and can result in transactions away from the best bid and offer prices.

---

[1] See, for example, the auction markets described in Chapter 22, the screen brokers in the interdealer Treasury securities market described in Section 21.1, and the NASDAQ system described in Section 21.3. See also the analyses of markets with many competing suppliers of liquidity services by Cohen, Maier, Schwartz, and Whitcomb (1979, 1981) and Ho and Stoll (1980).

This chapter examines the relationships between dispersion of dealer price quotations, search costs, and transaction prices.[2] The first section suggests several reasons why dealers might choose to quote different prices. The second section analyzes rational investor behavior in searching among dealers quoting different prices and develops the concept of a reservation price. The third section extends transactions costs to include the costs of search. We will see in that section that dealer bid-ask spreads are not the full cost of transacting when there is price dispersion. The last section considers the simultaneous determination of investor search efforts and dealer price dispersion in an equilibrium context.

25.1 WHY DEALERS QUOTE DIFFERENT PRICES

Bid and offer prices quoted by one dealer can differ from those quoted by other dealers by choice or by chance. In the former case a dealer may be consciously quoting the best bid or offer to complete expeditiously transactions which will bring his inventory position to a desired level. By bidding above other dealers, he will have a greater chance of increasing his position. Conversely, by offering securities below the asking prices of other dealers, he will be able to reduce his inventory more rapidly. On the other hand, dealers sometimes quote different prices simply because they don't know the quotations of their competitors. Even if every dealer is satisfied with his current inventory, it could be that one dealer will be quoting different prices out of ignorance. This section discusses each of these causes of dispersion in dealer quotes.

Inventory Objectives

Differences in the purchase and sale interests of different dealers are probably the most important reason for dispersion of quotation prices in a dealer market. These differences arise out of discrepancies between the desired levels and the actual levels of dealer inventories, so that a dealer will wish to increase or decrease his current position towards a more optimal level. Factors which lead dealers to differ in their opinions of what constitues an optimal inventory position, and factors which leave dealers with different current inventory positions, can lead to dispersion of quotation prices.[3]

---

[2] The seminal article on search and price dispersion is Stigler (1961). Garbade and Silber (1976) analyzed the empirical characteristics of price dispersion in the Treasury securities market and the consequences of that dispersion for transactions costs. Garbade (1978a, b) considered the effect of improvements in interdealer communications on price dispersion. Other studies of imperfectly integrated markets include Santomero (1974) and Hamilton (1978) on the OTC market, Reilly and Slaughter (1973) on OTC/NYSE dual trading, Garbade and Silber (1978) on nineteenth-century markets in foreign exchange and government bonds, and Garbade and Silber (1979b) on NYSE/regional stock exchange dual trading. See also the analysis by Kessel (1971) suggesting that the reduction in reoffer yields when more than one syndicate bids on a municipal bond issue is due to the implicit improvement in the issuer's knowledge of the most interested buyers.

[3] The effect of dealer purchase and sale interests on dealer price quotations was demonstrated empirically in Garbade, Pomrenze, and Silber (1979). See also Stoll (1978) and Amihud and Mendelson (1980).

Expectations of future price movements are a key determinant of a dealer's desired inventory. A dealer who believes prices will rise in the near future will want to hold a larger position than a dealer who is neutral or bearish. The more firmly such beliefs are held, the more pronounced will be their effect on desired positions. To the extent that dealers differ in their expectations of future price movements, they will have different notions of what constitutes an optimal inventory position.

The volume of trading in a security is a second factor determining the optimal level of dealer inventories. Delivery of securities sold to customers is cheaper if the securities are sold out of a long position than if a dealer sells short. To deliver securities sold short, a dealer has to locate an existing holder willing to lend securities, and he has to pay the lender a fee for the use of his securities.[4] Other things being equal, dealer positions generally increase with trading volume. Different dealers may wish to hold different inventories because they engage in more or less transactions than other dealers.

The existence of some target inventory position does not, by itself, determine whether a dealer wants to be a buyer or a seller at any moment of time. The other side of the coin is the actual inventory position of the dealer. Even if all dealers share the same ideas on an optimal inventory, some may be buyers and some sellers because their current inventories are below or above that optimal level.

Dealer inventories fluctuate as a result of transactions with public investors. A dealer who quotes with the expectation of executing purchases and sales with equal probability may nonetheless find himself making several successive purchases as a consequence of randomly arriving public sale orders. The resulting accumulation of inventory may eventually lead him to offer the issue below the prices of other dealers to restore his inventory to its desired level. Different "market experiences" can, therefore, lead dealers to differ in their purchase and sale interests and hence to quote different prices.

Ignorance of Other Dealer Quotes

Dispersion of dealer quotation prices will occur if some dealers quote the highest bids and others quote the lowest offers to achieve desired changes in their inventory positions. This argument presumes that dealers actually know what constitutes a high bid or a low offer. Dealers sometimes quote different prices simply because they don't know what other dealers are quoting, i.e., because they do not have complete knowledge of the outstanding quotes in a market.

As one might expect, a dealer's ignorance of his competitors' quotations is a

---

[4] In the Treasury market, for example, borrowers of securities pay a premium of one-half of 1 percent per annum on the principal value of borrowed issues. Borrowers of common stock give a lender cash equal to the market value of the borrowed securities and accept interest on that cash at below-market rates. The cost of borrowing the stock is the difference between the market rate of interest and the interest actually earned on the cash delivered to the lender of the stock.

function of the speed of communication between dealers and of the number of dealers active in the market. The more dealers there are, the more likely it will be that some dealers will be bidding above or offering below any given price. Since checking the markets of other dealers takes time, and since quotes may change frequently, a dealer can rarely assert that his quote is, in fact, a high bid or low offer. The faster he can check other prices, however, the greater will be the likelihood that he is quoting where he wants to relative to other dealers. Dispersion of quotation prices due to ignorance of other dealer quotes is a decreasing function of the speed of interdealer communications. Technological innovations like electronic quotation devices can be expected to reduce price dispersion, because they facilitate the dissemination of dealer quotations.[5]

25.2 INVESTOR SEARCH AND RESERVATION PRICES

Based on the foregoing section we assume here that market participants know that dealers may be quoting different bid and offer prices. In the face of this possible dispersion of dealer quotations, an investor has to make a rational decision on how thoroughly he should search for the best possible price. This section presents the solution to the investor's search problem.

In solving the search problem we will assume that dealers make their quotations good for an arbitrarily long interval of time. This means an investor can always return to some previously contacted dealer and trade at that dealers' original quotation price. As we will see, this assumption of "durable quotes" does not really matter, because once an investor finds an acceptable price, he will stop searching and will trade immediately at that price.

To illustrate the nature of search, we analyze the behavior of an investor who is seeking to buy N units of a security and who is therefore checking the offer side of the market. Similar results can be derived for an investor seeking to sell an issue.

Suppose an investor might obtain from a dealer any of K possible offering prices: P_1 to P_K, with $P_1 < P_2 < \cdots < P_{K-1} < P_K$. Denote the probability of obtaining offer price P_k as f_k, where

$$\sum_{k=1}^{K} f_k = 1 \tag{25.1}$$

The probability distribution $f_1, \ldots, f_K$ of offering prices reflects the investor's perception of the dispersion of dealer quotations. We assume that the investor views all dealers as perfect substitutes, and that he does not believe any dealer is likely to be either a high or low offerer. The dollar cost of contacting a single

---

[5] See the discussion of screen brokers in the interdealer Treasury market (Section 21.1) and NASDAQ in the OTC market (Section 21.3). The effect of electronic quotation systems on price dispersion was studied in Garbade (1978a). See also Garbade and Silber (1978) for an analysis of the effect of the domestic telegraph and the transatlantic cable on price dispersion in nineteenth-century markets.

dealer is denoted by C. This cost includes both direct charges (such as telephone tolls) and implicit opportunity costs.

Suppose, after contacting a number of dealers, an investor has discovered price P_j as the best offering price for the desired security. If he looks no further, he could complete his purchase of N units at a cost of $N \cdot P_j$. If the investor contacts one additional dealer and is offered the security at price P_k, the best discovered offer will then be the lesser of P_j and P_k, denoted min $[P_j, P_k]$. He will actually receive the quoted price P_k with probability f_k. The additional contact, however, will cost the investor the amount C. If the investor chooses to make the contact, he will expect to be able to buy his N securities at the total expected cost TEC $[P_j]$, where

$$\text{TEC } [P_j] = C + N \sum_{k=1}^{K} \min [P_k, P_j] f_k \qquad (25.2)$$

This total expected cost is the sum of two terms: the cost of contacting another dealer, and the expected best offering price available to him after making that contact times the number of securities purchased.

The decision of an investor to stop searching depends on a balancing of the cost of checking another dealer's offering price against the expected improvement in the best available offering price. That improvement depends on the distribution of possible quotes and on the current best available quote. The investor should make the additional contact if the value of TEC $[P_j]$ in Equation (25.2) is less than his current known cost $N \cdot P_j$. He should stop searching if $N \cdot P_j$ is less than the value of TEC $[P_j]$.

In general, the average expected gain from contacting one more dealer, given that offer price P_j has already been uncovered, is

$$\text{AEG } [P_j] = P_j - \frac{\text{TEC } [P_j]}{N} \qquad (25.3)$$

This gain is the difference between the price at which he can currently buy and the price per unit he expects to pay after contacting one more dealer, including the cost of making that contact. AEG $[P_j]$ can be shown to be equal to[6]

$$\text{AEG } [P_j] = \sum_{k=1}^{j-1} (P_j - P_k) f_k - \frac{C}{N} \qquad (25.4)$$

This average expected gain is an increasing function of the current best available quote P_j. The higher (or lower) the value of P_j, the higher (or lower) will be

---

[6] From equation (25.2), TEC $[P_j]$ is $N \sum_{k=1}^{j-1} P_k f_k + N \sum_{k=j}^{K} P_j f_k + C$, because $P_k < P_j$ if $k < j$. From Equation (25.1), P_j can be written as $\sum_{k=1}^{K} P_j f_k$. These two results imply that AEG $[P_j]$, as defined in Equation (25.3), can be written as $\sum_{k=1}^{K} P_j f_k - \sum_{k=1}^{j-1} P_k f_k - \sum_{k=j}^{K} P_j f_k - C/N$, or as $\sum_{k=1}^{j-1} (P_j - P_k) f_k - C/N$.

the expected gain from further search.[7] The gain from search also depends on the ratio of C to N. The higher the cost of contacting a dealer, the lower the expected gain. Conversely, the greater the size of the contemplated transaction, the greater the expected gain.

For some offering price P_J, the expected gain from further search will be zero or negative, but if P_{J+1} is the best available offering price, the expected gain will be positive. P_J therefore satisfies the inequalities

$$\text{AEG } [P_J] \leq 0 < \text{AEG } [P_{J+1}] \tag{25.5}$$

P_J is the *reservation purchase price* of the investor. Once he discovers a dealer quoting price P_J or any lower price, he cannot expect to reduce further his total execution costs by contacting another dealer. An investor will, therefore, accept any quote less than or equal to P_J as soon as it is discovered.[8] More particularly, even though dealer quotes are assumed to be durable, an investor will stop searching *as soon as* he has found an acceptable offering quotation and will buy *immediately* at that price.

The foregoing analysis implies that it will be efficient for the investor to buy at *any* price between the lowest offering price P_1 and his reservation purchase price P_J. In particular, it may be efficient to buy securities at a price greater than the lowest price.

In general, the reservation purchase price of an investor will be greater the higher his costs of search. This means that an investor who incurs high search costs will be more likely to buy securities at a price greater than the lowest price than an investor who incurs low search costs and who therefore has a lower reservation purchase price. The reservation purchase price of an investor will also be greater the smaller the size of his trade.

The concept of a reservation price has a central importance in the analysis of transaction prices in markets with positive search costs. Since any dealer quotation between the lowest offering price and an investor's reservation purchase price will be acceptable to the investor, dealers can sell securities at prices greater than the lowest offering price. Suppose, for example, a dealer is asked to offer an issue to a customer who incurs high costs in contacting dealers.

---

[7] Observe, from Equation (25.4), that $\text{AEG } [P_{j+1}] - \text{AEG } [P_j] = \sum_{k=1}^{j} (P_{j+1} - P_k)f_k -$

$\sum_{k=1}^{j-1} (P_j - P_k)f_k = \sum_{k=1}^{j-1} (P_{j+1} - P_k)f_k + (P_{j+1} - P_j)f_j - \sum_{k=1}^{j-1} (P_j - P_k)f_k = (P_{j+1} - P_j)f_j -$

$\sum_{k=1}^{j-1} (P_{j+1} - P_k - P_j + P_k)f_k = (P_{j+1} - P_j) \sum_{k=1}^{j} f_k > 0.$ This shows that $\text{AEG } [P_{j+1}] > \text{AEG } [P_j]$,

or that the average expected gain from further search is an increasing function of P_j.

[8] Note that if $\text{AEG } [P_2] > 0$, then the investor will search until he uncovers the lowest offering price P_1. [Equation (25.4) shows that $\text{AEG } [P_1] = -C/N < 0$, and so it never makes sense to search after P_1 has been uncovered.] If $\text{AEG } [P_K] < 0$, then the investor will accept *any* price, because there is no positive expected gain from further search even if the best available price is the highest price P_K. It is possible to have $\text{AEG } [P_K] < 0$ if C is large enough or if N is small enough. See Equation (25.4).

Since the dealer knows the customer must have a relatively high reservation price (in view of the customer's high cost of search), the dealer might ask more of that customer than he would of customers who can search more cheaply. A similar argument shows the importance of transaction size for dealer quotations. Customers seeking quotes on small transactions will have relatively higher reservation purchase prices than customers trading in standard-size blocks. Dealers can therefore increase their offering prices to odd-lot customers and still quote inside the reservation prices of those customers.

We saw in Section 21.3 that retail investors use intermediary brokers to execute their purchases and sales of stock in the OTC market. In view of the foregoing analysis, this behavior is seen to be quite rational. Since many brokers in the OTC market maintain direct wires to dealer firms, their cost of contacting a dealer is lower than the cost which an investor would incur. Even before the advent of NASDAQ, an investor could expect to secure better execution of an order by using a broker to search out the best price. After NASDAQ, of course, the cost to a broker of obtaining a dealer's quotations fell to virtually zero, and the superiority of brokerage over direct search became even more pronounced.

25.3 THE EFFECT OF PRICE DISPERSION ON TRANSACTION COSTS

The cost of completing a purchase in a dealer market characterized by price dispersion can be divided into two components. The first is the offering price paid to the selling dealer, and the second is the expense of the search conducted by the buyer. In this section we derive expressions for the expected values of these two components and relate those expressions to the cost of executing a round-trip transaction.

The Expected Cost of Completing a Purchase

Suppose an investor wishes to purchase N units of a security and has computed his reservation purchase price as P_J for some J between 1 and K. Since he will accept any offering price less than or equal to P_J, the probability of obtaining an acceptable price from any dealer is

$$PS = \sum_{k=1}^{J} f_k \qquad (25.6)$$

Note that $0 < PS \leq 1$ for all possible reservation prices. From Equation (25.6), the probability of seeing an acceptable offering price is greater the higher the investor's reservation purchase price; that is, PS is an increasing function of J and hence of P_J.

The investor will only accept offering prices in the set $(P_1, ..., P_J)$. Given that he obtains an acceptable offer, the probability that the offer is at price P_k is

$$\tilde{f}_k = \frac{f_k}{PS} \qquad k = 1, \ldots, J \qquad (25.7)$$

The expected value of an *acceptable* offering price is

$$\tilde{P} = \sum_{k=1}^{J} P_k \tilde{f}_k \tag{25.8}$$

$\tilde{P}$ is also an increasing function of the investor's reservation purchase price P_J.[9] If an investor is willing to accept higher offering quotations, he must also expect to pay more to a dealer to complete his purchase.

The expected total cost of completing a purchase is

$$\text{Total expected cost} = PS \ (C + \tilde{P} \cdot N)$$
$$+ (1 - PS)PS(2C + \tilde{P} \cdot N)$$
$$+ (1 + PS)^2 PS(3C + \tilde{P} \cdot N)$$
$$+ \cdots \tag{25.9}$$

The first term in Equation (25.9) is the probability PS of seeing an acceptable offer on the first contact times the sum of the cost C of one contact and the expected purchase price $\tilde{P} \cdot N$. The second term is the probability $(1 - PS)$ of failing to obtain an acceptable offer on the first contact times the probability PS of success on the second contact times the sum of the cost $2C$ of two contacts and the expected purchase price on the second contact $\tilde{P} \cdot N$. The successive terms are similarly derived. Rearranging terms in (25.9), we have

$$\text{Total expected cost} = PS \cdot \tilde{P} \cdot N[1 + (1 - PS) + (1 - PS)^2 + \cdots]$$
$$+ PS \cdot C[1 + 2(1 - PS) + 3(1 - PS)^2 + \cdots]$$

It can be shown[10] that the first term in brackets reduces to $1/PS$ and that the second term in brackets reduces to $1/PS^2$, and so we have

$$\text{Total expected cost} = \tilde{P} \cdot N + \frac{C}{PS}$$

The expected cost per security is the total expected cost divided by N:

$$\text{Expected unit cost} = \tilde{P} + \frac{C}{N \cdot PS} \tag{25.10}$$

The expected cost per security of buying N securities, as shown in (25.10),

---

[9] Using the definition of $\tilde{f}_k$ from Equation (25.7) and the definition of PS from Equation (25.6), $\tilde{P}$ in Equation (25.8) can be written as $\tilde{P} = \sum_{k=1}^{J} P_k f_k \Big/ \sum_{k=1}^{J} f_k$. This shows that $\tilde{P}$ is a weighted average combination of the first J terms in the increasing sequence $P_1, ..., P_K$, and so it must be an increasing function of J and hence of P_J.

[10] If $V = 1 + x + x^2 + x^3 + \cdots$, then $xV = x + x^2 + x^3 + \cdots$, and $V - xV = 1$, so that $V = (1 - x)^{-1}$. $dV/dx = 1 + 2x + 3x^2 + \cdots = (1 - x)^{-2}$. Substituting $1 - PS$ for x gives the desired results.

consists of two elements. The first element is the expected payment $\tilde{P}$ to the selling dealer. The second element is the cost per security purchased of contacting a dealer C/N times the expected number of dealer contacts $1/PS$. A lower reservation price reduces the expected payment $\tilde{P}$ since fewer dealer offering prices will be acceptable. A lower reservation price also raises the number of contacts which the investor expects to have to make before completing his purchase, because it lowers the probability of seeing an acceptable offer on any given contact. As was discussed in the previous section, the reservation price increases with C and decreases with N. Investors seeking to execute large trades or who can search at little cost will complete their transactions at more favorable prices than other investors, but they must also expect to search more extensively.

The Cost of Round-Trip Transactions

We have analyzed the cost of purchasing securities when dealer offering prices are dispersed and investors have to search to find an acceptable purchase price. A similar result holds for investors searching among dealer bid quotations when they want to sell a security. Specializing the notation of (25.10), we have the expected cost per unit to purchase a security as $\tilde{P}_a + C/(N \cdot PS_a)$, where the subscript a refers to the asking side of the dealer market. The expected revenue per unit in selling a security is $\tilde{P}_b - C/(N \cdot PS_b)$, where P_b is the expected gross receipts from selling to an acceptable dealer bid and PS_b is the probability of obtaining an acceptable bid on any given contact. The expected cost of completing a round-trip transaction is the difference between these two terms:

$$\tilde{P}_a - \tilde{P}_b + \frac{C}{N}\left(\frac{1}{PS_a} + \frac{1}{PS_b}\right) \tag{25.11}$$

In a market where dealer quotations can be uncovered costlessly, the cost of a round-trip transaction is the spread between the lowest offer and the highest bid in the market.[11] Equation (25.11) shows that when investors incur search costs, the cost of a round-trip consists of two components. The first part is the spread between the expected offering price of an acceptable seller and the expected bid price of an acceptable buyer. Unless an investor's reservation price is equal to the best price, the term $\tilde{P}_a - \tilde{P}_b$ will exceed the spread between the best offer and best bid. The second part is the total expected search cost of uncovering an acceptable buyer and an acceptable seller. An investor will expect to incur search costs unless he is willing to accept any bid and any offer. The absence of free search and the existence of dispersion in dealer quotations thus

---

[11] This is because if C is zero, only the lowest offer and the higher bid will be acceptable (see footnote 8 in this chapter), and because the cost of searching until those quotations are uncovered is zero by hypothesis, that is, $C = 0$.

increases transaction costs in two ways: (1) it widens the spread between expected transaction prices beyond the spread between the best quotations, and (2) it burdens investors with the expense of search. The former cost is relatively more important for investors with high reservation purchase prices and low reservation sale prices. The second effect is more important for investors with reservation prices closer to the best quotations.

25.4 THE JOINT DETERMINATION OF DEALER PRICE DISPERSION AND INVESTOR SEARCH EFFORTS

The extent of investor search for an acceptable price depends on the dispersion of dealer quotations. The more widely dispersed the quotes, the more it will pay investors to search the market carefully. It is also the case, however, that price dispersion is a function of investor search efforts. In markets where investors search extensively, dealers are unlikely to quote widely dispersed prices. Search efforts and price dispersion are jointly determined in a simultaneous context.

To illustrate the simultaneous determination of price dispersion and investor search, consider a market where all trades are for one unit of a security (or for one conventional unit, like a round lot) and where all investors have the same search cost parameter C. It follows from the earlier sections of this chapter that all investors will have the same reservation purchase price and the same reservation sale price relative to the best available offer and bid prices.

Suppose that, because of some technological innovation in communications such as NASDAQ, the cost of contacting a dealer falls to one-half of the earlier level, i.e., to $\frac{1}{2}C$. The first consequence of this exogenous change in the market environment will be a reduction in the reservation purchase price and an increase in the reservation sale price of every investor. As the spread between investor reservation prices narrows, some dealer quotations which would have been acceptable before the reduction of search costs become unacceptable.

The desire to achieve an optimal inventory position is one of the main reasons why dealers bid above or offer below other dealers. In the context of the current example, high bidders will be able to complete their purchases faster following an increase in the reservation sale price of public investors because they will capture the business lost by weak bidders. Similarly, low offerers will be able to deplete their inventories more rapidly. As a dealer completes his desired purchase or sale program, he will restore his quotes to the level of the average quotes of other dealers. Since dealers can complete their inventory adjustments more rapidly when the spread between investor reservation prices narrows, those dealers will spend less time quoting inside the average market quotes. This in turn implies that dealers will quote comparable prices more of the time or, equivalently, that the dispersion of dealer prices will fall.

As the dispersion of dealer quotes declines, investors will have less incentive to search and will widen slightly the spread between their reservation prices. They will not increase the spread to the level which existed prior to the introduction of cheaper communication, however, since that spread was predicated on contact costs higher than investors now incur. A new equilibrium will be established with a narrower dispersion of dealer quotations, a smaller spread between reservation sale and purchase prices, and a lower expected cost to complete round-trip transactions.[12]

CHAPTER SUMMARY

This chapter has examined the consequences of search costs for transaction prices in a market where dealers might quote different bid prices and different offer prices in order to execute desired transactions more expeditiously. Rational search policies in such a market imply that buyers will accept offer prices that exceed the lowest offering price quoted by any dealer, and that sellers will accept bid prices that are less than the highest bid price quoted by any dealer. In general, investors will be more willing to accept less favorable prices the greater their costs of search and the smaller the size of their transactions.

As long as investors have an economic incentive to trade at prices which are less favorable than the best prices (to economize on costly search efforts), dealers will be able to buy and sell securities at bid and offer quotations away from the best quotations. This implies that dispersion of dealer quotations can persist through time and that transactions at unfavorable prices will not be a transient phenomenon.

When search is costly, the net cost of transacting will be the sum of two terms. The first term is the spread between the expected value of an acceptable offer price and the expected value of an acceptable bid price. This spread will exceed the spread between the highest bid price and the lowest offer price. The "extra" spread is a cost of trading on incomplete information in a fragmented market. The second term is the expected cost of searching until an acceptable bid price or an acceptable offer price has been located, and is the cost of acquiring information about trading interests in a fragmented market. It will usually be beneficial for an investor to incur the costs of acquiring more complete information about trading interests the larger the size of his transaction and the lower his cost of search.

Dispersion of dealer quotation prices will fall as the cost of investor search falls. This means that centralization of trading, or the introduction of more sophisticated communications, can be expected to increase the incidence of trading at the best prices and to reduce market fragmentation. In the limiting case where information on price quotations is free, only the best bids and offers will be acceptable and the market will not be fragmented.

---

[12] Garbade and Silber (1978) examined the effect of the telegraph on price dispersion in the nineteenth-century foreign exchange market and the effect of the transatlantic cable on price dispersion in the nineteenth-century Treasury bond market. Garbade (1978a) examined the effect of electronic quotation systems on price dispersion in the twentieth-century Treasury bond market.

FURTHER READING

Kenneth Garbade, "Electronic Quotation Systems and the Market for Government Securities," Federal Reserve Bank of New York *Quarterly Review*, **3** (Summer 1978), 13–20.

———, "The Effect of Interdealer Brokerage on the Transactional Characteristics of Dealer Markets," *Journal of Business*, **51** (July 1978), 477–498.

——— and William Silber, "Price Dispersion in the Government Securities Market," *Journal of Political Economy*, **84** (August 1976), 721–740.

———, "Technology, Communication and the Performance of Financial Markets: 1840–1975," *Journal of Finance*, **33** (June 1978), 819–832.

Philip Loomis and Eugene Rotberg, "Over-the-Counter Market Quotations," *Michigan Law Review*, **62** (1964), 589–606.

George Stigler, "The Economics of Information,"*Journal of Political Economy*, **69** (June 1961), 213–225.

CHAPTER 26

THINNESS

Chapter 11 defined equilibrium prices as prices which balance supply with demand for all financial assets simultaneously in a competitive auction market. Such prices have several intuitively appealing attributes. Competitive auction markets are perfectly integrated, and all market participants are always fully informed of the latest prices announced by the auctioneer while he is bringing the market to equilibrium. Each participant treats the announced prices as parameters upon which he conditions his demand for securities. Thus, the state of the market at any point in time is completely summarized by those prices. No investor needs to look further than the announced prices in determining his optimal portfolio allocation. Moreover, since all investors are assumed to participate in an auction, market clearing equilibrium prices necessarily reflect all trading interests. The institutional structure of a competitive auction leads, by definition, to the impounding of all purchase and sale interests into equilibrium prices. Thus, transactions which take place after an auction has come into equilibrium occur at prices which completely characterize the contemporaneous state of the market and which reflect the trading interests of all investors.

Real markets may be distinguished from the benchmark standard of a competitive auction by a lack of complete information on trading interests. Real markets are not perfectly integrated, and not all purchase and sale interests are continuously represented. It is not surprising, therefore, that real transaction prices do not share the attributes of the prices at which transactions occur following a competitive auction. We have already seen, in Chapter 24, that dealers provide market participants with the liquidity service of immediate executions only at the expense of a spread between their bid and offer quotations. The analysis of Chapter 25 suggested that transactions can occur at prices other than the best available bid or offer quotations when search is costly and time-consuming. The consequences, for the structure of transaction prices, of incomplete information on trading interests are not, however, limited to bid-ask spreads and price dispersion. A third consequence is a set of phenomena associated with "thin" markets.

The market for a security is thin if there are few buyers and sellers at any particular moment and if the frequency of transactions is low.[1] At the extreme, trading may be so infrequent as not to give a dealer sufficient incentive to provide liquidity services at a price which transactors find attractive, so that buyers and sellers choose to meet through the intermediary efforts of a broker, or to search each other out directly. A time series of transaction prices in an extremely thin market is likely to exhibit substantial discontinuities. The expense of identifying potentially compatible trading partners deters transactors (or their agents) from making a thorough search of the market. Transactions will take place among pairs of investors at prices which may not reflect the trading interests of other, unidentified (and hence uninformed) investors.

The most interesting aspects of thinness, however, occur in markets which are not so thin as to preclude the provision of liquidity services by dealers. These aspects stem from the requirements that dealers have to estimate the equilibrium price of a security as it evolves through time.[2] When trading in an issue is heavy, or when there exist many easily contacted potential purchasers and sellers, dealers can estimate an equilibrium price with reasonable accuracy. The ability of dealers to make accurate estimates is important for the behavior of transactions prices. In Chapter 24, for example, we assumed that dealers knew the location of the equilibrium price. With this knowledge they quoted bid prices somewhat below the equilibrium price and quoted offer prices somewhat above the equilibrium price. In thin markets, however, the equilibrium price of a security may be quite uncertain. This chapter explores the characteristics of thin dealer markets and the effects of dealer uncertainty about equilibrium values on the structure of transaction prices.

26.1 THINNESS AND UNCERTAINTY

Dealers have two basic sources from which they can derive information about the equilibrium value of a security: the trading interests of potential buyers and sellers, and the flow of transactions which they observe. The first source is more informative (although more expensive to exploit), because it provides a dealer with an idea of the characteristics of the demand and supply schedules of public investors. Block trading in common stock is infrequent. Block houses nonetheless have a good idea of the prices at which blocks of stock may be

---

[1] Several studies have used the term "thin" in the sense of an inelastic demand for a security, so that small changes in demand can lead to large *permanent* changes in price. See Silber (1975); Cohen, Maier, Ness, Okuda, Schwartz, and Whitcomb (1977); and Cohen, Maier, Schwartz, and Whitcomb (1978a). This chapter uses the term "thin" in the sense that small changes in demand lead to large, but not necessarily permanent, changes in price. See Garbade and Silber (1979a).

[2] This aspect of market making was pointed out by Bagehot (1971).

bought and sold, because they explore directly the trading interests of their institutional investor clients. The sizes of block transactions justify the expense of acquiring such information.

For many issues dealers cannot explore potential trading interests at an economically justifiable cost. If, for example, an issue is held in small amounts by many investors, it would be extremely expensive to keep informed directly of the trading interests of those investors.[3] In these cases the flow of actual transactions is a major source of information about equilibrium values.

When a security trades frequently, dealers observe a continuous flow of new information. If they are pricing the issue too high, they will quickly recognize that they are acquiring undesirably large inventory positions. The converse is true if they are pricing the issue too low. The structure of arriving orders provides dealers with information on shifts in the net demand schedule of public investors or, equivalently, on changes in the equilibrium value of the security.

When an issue trades infrequently, the quality of information which can be extracted from observation of arriving orders is low, and dealers will not be certain of the current location of the equilibrium price. Suppose, for example, a dealer knows with perfect certainty that the equilibrium value of an issue is $100 at 10 A.M. on some morning and quotes a market in that issue at $99.50 bid and $100.50 offered. (We ignore whether such confidence is justified, and assume it is). If the dealer does not see any purchase or sale interest in the issue until noon, at which time an investor sells at the dealer's bid quotation, the dealer will be uncertain whether the arriving order is purely random or whether the equilibrium value of the issue has declined below $99.50, so that his bid is now above the contemporaneous equilibrium. If, on the other hand, the dealer had participated in a half dozen transactions between 10 A.M. and noon, he would have had a much better idea of whether $100 was still the equilibrium value of the issue. A larger order flow would have given him more opportunity to perceive the evolution of the equilibrium price through time. The greater the frequency of transactions in an issue, the more informed a dealer will be at any point in time on the current equilibrium value of the issue. Conversely, the thinner the market, the greater the ignorance of the dealer.

Consequences of Uncertainty—The Case of a Monopoly Dealer

Uncertainty in the estimation of equilibrium values may be expected to have three consequences for the willingness of a monopoly supplier of liquidity services to enter into purchase and sale transactions.[4] First, the greater his uncer-

---

[3] See, for example, the description of the retail market in municipal bonds in Section 23.3. That market is often so thin that brokered search is a more economical way of completing sales than consuming liquidity services provided by a dealer.

[4] Smidt (1971) was the first to suggest some of the characteristics of a thin market in which liquidity is supplied by a monopoly dealer. See also Barnea and Logue (1975). Bloomenthal (1960) discusses the problems which can arise when a single dealer dominates the market for a security traded over-the-counter. See also the analysis of OTC dealer markets in *Norris & Hirshberg, Inc.*, 21 S.E.C. 865 (1946).

tainty, the more a dealer will try to protect himself by widening the spread between his bid and offer quotations. We have already established that bid-ask spreads are inversely related to the time rate of transactions in an issue, because liquidity services are more valuable and more costly to provide in securities with low transactions rates. Another reason for the same relation is the unwillingness of a dealer to quote a narrow bid-ask spread when he is uncertain about the equilibrium price. The greater his uncertainty, the more likely he is to unknowingly bid above the current equilibrium or to offer below that equilibrium for any given spread. Widening his spread reduces the likelihood of such perverse behavior.

It should be noted that the direct dependence of a dealer's spread on trading volume is conceptually different from the indirect dependence which stems from uncertainty about the equilibrium price. Suppose that two securities trade at the same rate, but that a dealer has sources of information on changes in the equilibrium value of the first security in addition to arriving orders; e.g., he may have direct contacts with investors who hold that issue. The dealer might then be willing to quote a narrower bid-ask spread on the first security than he would quote on the second security.

Uncertainty in the estimation of equilibrium value may also lead a dealer to reduce the breadth of his market. Bid and offer quotes refer to purchases and sales of a conventional size. If a dealer is well-informed on the equilibrium value of a security, he may be willing to make his quotes good for, say, ten conventional units on either side of the market. If he is less certain of the equilibrium value, he may be willing to buy or sell only five units at his bid or offer. A customer demanding liquidity services for transactions of a larger size would receive from the dealer a lower bid or a greater offering price on that portion of his order in excess of the five units. The effect of uncertainty on the bid-ask spread and breadth of a dealer's market is illustrated in Figure 26.1.

The third consequence of equilibrium price uncertainty for dealer pricing behavior is the effect of recent transactions on a dealer's estimate of the equilibrium price. If a dealer is confident in his current estimate, he will not be led to lower substantially that estimate just because he happens to execute a sequence of purchases from public investors, or if he happens to execute a sequence of sales. If, on the other hand, he is highly uncertain, executing a single purchase may lead him to lower his estimate on the grounds that he might have been bidding above the equilibrium. Executing a sequence of purchases will almost certainly lead him to lower his estimate of the equilibrium price.

Recent transactions in a thinly traded security can be expected to carry more weight in a dealer's mind than recent transactions in an active issue, because the former transactions convey relatively more information. Thus, the location of a dealer's bid and offer quotations for a thinly traded issue will be more heavily dependent on whether he has recently completed purchases or sales. The dealer's quotations will exhibit greater transient volatility than they would had he been better informed. Because of the sparsity of transactions in thin markets, dealers have greater difficulty distinguishing between permanent and temporary trading imbalances at any given price level. They are more

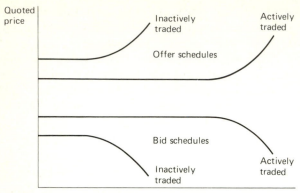

FIGURE 26.1
Bid and offer schedules on actively and inactively traded securities.

likely to mistake a temporary imbalance for a permanent imbalance and to shift the level of their quotations accordingly.

Transient volatility of a dealer's quotations is a characteristic of thinness conceptually different from wider bid-ask spreads or reduced breadth. Transient volatility occurs because the dealer is unable to estimate the current equilibrium price with great accuracy and, in using the information available to him, may tend to overestimate the equilibrium (when he has observed a random sequence of purchases by investors) or underestimate the equilibrium (when he has observed a sequence of sales by investors). His sources of information on equilibrium values are limited to the transactions which he observes. These transactions will, from time to time, give an incorrect impression of the direction of purchase and sale interests in the market as a whole. Over time his errors will balance out, but at any point in time he can be quoting prices which do not reflect the trading interests of all investors.

Having recognized that a dealer will quote a broader and more stable market the more accurately he can estimate the equilibrium value of a security, we also have to address the effect of his inventory position on his quotations.[5] Speculative price expectations withstanding, a dealer with a substantial long position in a security will be more interested in selling than in buying. He may, consequently, offer the issue at a price close to what he believes is the current equilibrium price, but bid relatively far below his estimate of that price. The extent to which a dealer shifts his quotes to achieve a specific change in his inventory is likely a function of his ignorance of the equilibrium price. Just as a well-informed dealer will make a broader market, i.e., be willing to acquire more of an issue at a price close to his bid price or to sell more of an issue at a price

---

[5] That dealers cannot set prices independently of their inventory positions is clear from the analyses of Garman (1976) and Amihud and Mendelson (1980). See also Garbade and Silber (1979a) and Stoll (1978).

close to his offer price, so will he be more willing to hold a given long or short position at his current quotations. This is not to say that well-informed dealers do not change their quotations so as to be better buyers or better sellers from time to time, only that they perceive less risk in holding a given position because they are more confident of their estimates of equilibrium prices, and therefore change their quotes less aggressively.

Shifts in a dealer's quotations resulting from his desire to achieve a given change in his inventory can introduce transient fluctuations in transactions prices which are unrelated to changes in equilibrium value.[6] If the dealer wants to increase his position, his bid will be closer to his perception of the equilibrium price than will his offer. Once he has acquired the desired securities, however, he will lower his bid and offer quotations to straddle, approximately, his estimate of the current equilibrium price. During the interval of time over which the dealer had a strong buying interest, selling investors would receive a better price (relative to the equilibrium price) than buying investors. This transient disparity in the treatment of buyers and sellers disappears as soon as the dealer has accomplished his inventory objective. If dealers in thin markets shift their quotations more aggressively than dealers in heavily traded securities, transient price fluctuations will be greater in thin markets.

Transactors in thin markets may expect to pay greater bid-ask spreads on standard-size orders, and especially on larger orders (because of the reduced breadth of a dealer's market in a thin issue). In addition, transactors bear the risk of buying at a time when the dealer is also a buyer, and thus of receiving poor offering quotes for their purchase orders. Similarly, if an investor happens to want to sell a security immediately after a dealer in that security has executed an unrelated purchase from some other investor, he will likely receive a lower bid. The greater the transient price fluctuations stemming from dealer inventory policies and learning behavior, the greater the risk of such adverse dealings. The price quotations of a dealer in a thinly traded issue may not, therefore, completely characterize the contemporaneous state of the market.[7] The dealer's quotes may be unusually high or low because of a transient inventory objective or because of the purchase or sale pattern of his most recent transactions.

26.2 COMPETITION AMONG DEALERS IN THIN MARKETS

The preceding section identified several consequences of uncertainty about equilibrium values for the structure of transaction prices in a monopoly dealer market, including wider bid-ask spreads, reduced breadth, and greater transi-

---

[6] This dimension of the process by which dealers quote bid and offer prices was first advanced by Smidt (1971), and is referenced in Barnea (1974), Barnea and Logue (1975), Logue (1975), and Stoll (1976).

[7] The effect of inventory positions and transaction sizes on dealer quotations, as well as the ability of dealers to distinguish between permanent and transitory price changes, has been considered by Stoll (1976) for OTC dealers.

tory price volatility. Some of these consequences may be mitigated if several dealers compete in the provision of liquidity services.

Competition among dealers in thinly traded issues is not rare. Many common stocks traded in the OTC market trade infrequently yet attract several competing marketmakers.[8] In discussing the effects of dealer competition we will assume an investor can contact all competing dealers at zero cost. Securities listed on NASDAQ come close to satisfying this assumption. The assumption eliminates from the analysis the complications of price dispersion and search.

When dealers compete in the provision of liquidity services, a customer faces their *aggregate* purchase and sale schedules rather than the schedules of a single dealer. These aggregate schedules may be expected to exhibit a narrower bid-ask spread, smaller transitory fluctuations around the equilibrium price, and greater breadth than the schedules of a single dealer.

Unless the competitor dealers are all quoting identical bid and identical offer prices, there will be a best bid and a best offer. Since, by assumption, search costs are zero, the effective bid-ask spread of the market will be at least as small as the spread quoted by any individual dealer. Even though each dealer may be quoting a wide spread to protect himself against buying at too high a price or selling at too low a price, the effective market spread to public transactors may be relatively narrow.

Unless all the dealers are simultaneously buyers or sellers, transient shifts in quotations due to idiosyncratic inventory objectives of individual dealers will not induce transient fluctuations in transactions prices. An investor can choose the dealer with whom he trades. If he is looking for a bid, he will avoid relatively poor bidders in favor of more eager buyers. Dealers trying to reduce their inventories will be unlikely to buy securities, and dealers trying to increase their inventories will be unlikely to sell securities. When there are competing dealers, investors can take advantage of whatever heterogeneity may exist among the quotations of the competitors and are not subject to the transient inventory objectives of a single dealer.

The aggregate breadth of a competitive dealer market is likely to be greater than the breadth of the market of a monopoly dealer. When there are competing dealers, investors have the option of trading in smaller-size lots with several dealers instead of placing a larger order with a single dealer. The risk of positioning an issue may then be spread among several dealers, none of whom are required to accept a large change in their inventory while providing an investor with an immediate execution of his order.

---

[8] Until recently the NYSE did not encourage competing specialists, and from the mid-1960s until 1976 every NYSE specialist enjoyed a monopoly franchise. Rather than competition, the NYSE relied on regulation to encourage specialists to make "good" markets. See Stigler (1964) for comments on the difficulties of such an approach. As an alternative to regulation, Smidt (1971) and Feuerstein (1972) have argued that the NYSE should encourage more competition. This view was endorsed in New York Stock Exchange (1976) and by a number of major securities firms (*New York Times*, June 2, 1977, p. 2, col. 3) and has been adopted by the NYSE. See White (1976) for a description of such competition and Hamilton (1976) for a study of the potential gains from specialist competition.

Competition and the Disclosure of Trading Information

The analysis of this section suggests that dealer competition in the provision of liquidity services is an unalloyed benefit to investors trading in thin markets. While this conclusion is justified within the context of the analysis, it does not necessarily remain true for all modes of competitive market making. Specifically, we implicitly assumed that no dealer suffers a loss of information as a result of the activities of his competitors. This requires that all transactions are reported to all dealers as they occur, and that no dealer can limit disclosure of the prices and quantities of his purchases and sales.[9]

If competing dealers can avoid reporting their transactions to their competitors, they will deprive those competitors of valuable information. This is especially true in thin markets where individual transactions convey relatively more information than transactions in heavily traded issues. Although privacy in a transaction is clearly to the advantage of the participating dealer, it is less clear that his gain outweighs the loss to his competitors and to investors generally. When dealers conceal their transactions, each dealer perceives the market as being thinner than is actually the case; i.e., each receives only a fraction of the total available information on public order flow. In response to this perception of greater thinness, each dealer individually may widen his bid-ask spread, reduce the breadth of his market, and shift his quotes more aggressively to achieve his inventory objectives. Thus, unless competition is accompanied by a mechanism for disclosure of transactions, investors will not necessarily benefit from that competition.

The innovation of consolidated ticker tape reporting of all transactions in common stocks listed on the NYSE provides an excellent example of a mechanism for disclosure of transactions. Many issues traded on the NYSE also trade on regional exchanges, such as the Midwest and Pacific stock exchanges, and in the OTC market. Until 1975, transactions in these other markets were not reported on the NYSE's ticker tape and were essentially unknown outside of the particular markets where they occurred. At the behest of the SEC those other markets have, since June 16, 1975, reported their transactions in NYSE-listed issues, whereupon the price and size of the trade are displayed on a consolidated ticker tape.[10] Several commentators observed that composite reporting provided specialists on the floor of the NYSE with valuable information which they did not receive before the innovation of the consolidated tape.[11]

26.3 THINNESS AND SUBSTITUTES AMONG SECURITIES

According to the definition of thinness given in the introduction to this chapter, the market for a security is thin if trading occurs infrequently. Our interest,

---

[9] The introduction of search costs and price dispersion will also reduce the relative advantages of a competitive dealer market. See the discussion in Chapter 25.

[10] Garbade and Silber (1979b) analyzed the effect of the consolidated ticker tape on stock prices.

[11] In a similar vein, the SEC has been encouraging the adoption of communication devices which would facilitate search for the best available price. See Harman (1978) and Melton (1978–1979).

however, is not in thinness per se, but rather in the implications of thinness for the ability of a dealer to estimate an equilibrium price, and in the effects of his uncertainty about that price on his behavior. Transient price volatility and other consequences of uncertainty are not necessarily associated with thinness. The assertion that uncertainty follows from thinness presumes that the only source of information on equilibrium prices is the market for the security of interest, which is not always the case.

Equilibrium prices are not determined for individual securities in isolation from each other but rather in a general or simultaneous equilibrium.[12] There exist, for many securities, a large number of close substitutes. Changes in the equilibrium value of one security can frequently be inferred from the prices at which transactions are occurring in its substitutes.

Many investors, for example, view Treasury bills, short-term federal agency issues, bank CDs, and commercial paper as close substitutes. That they are not perfect substitutes is evident from the presence of yield premiums on commercial paper, agency debt, and CDs. However, those yield premiums are fairly stable over short intervals of time, such as a few days and sometimes even weeks. Even though the markets in commercial paper, agency debt, and bank CDs are thinner than the market in Treasury bills, dealers in commercial paper, agency debt, and bank CDs do not suffer from a severe inability to estimate changes in equilibrium prices in their markets. Because yield premiums over bills are stable, knowledge of the price at which bills are trading conveys valuable information to commercial-paper, agency, and CD traders. An agency trader may go for hours without completing a trade yet have a fairly good idea of the equilibrium values of his issues, because he can observe the direction of activity in the Treasury bill market.

Even if the market for a security is thin in the sense of minimal investor interest in that security, dealers may nonetheless be able to estimate accurately the equilibrium value of the issue by observing activity in markets for close substitutes. The phenomena which we associated with thinness, such as reduced breadth and transient price volatility, may not be present, or may be mitigated, if a dealer can acquire information from other markets. The important question is not the thinness of the market in a single security, but the thinness of markets in groups of related securities.

The ability of a dealer to derive information on equilibrium prices from observation of the markets for substitute instruments depends on how closely the prices of those substitutes move with the price of the security of original interest. In the foregoing example, Treasury bills, agency debt, and CDs are all close substitutes. For other groups of securities the degree of substitutability may be smaller. Prices on long-term corporate debt may be expected to move synchronously when the reasons for their movement are related to variations in the demand for such debt by long-term investors. However, if a change in investor perceptions of the risk of default is responsible for the price variation,

---

[12] See the analysis of equilibrium pricing in Chapter 11.

price changes on different bonds may be quite unrelated. Observation of the Treasury bond market is unlikely to provide as much information to a corporate bond dealer on changes in the equilibrium level of yields in his own market as is the case for a CD dealer observing the Treasury bill market. Different issues of common stock provide an even better example of limited substitutability. While stock prices generally move up and down together in response to the arrival of new information which affects the values of all equity issues, each stock has a significant element of uniqueness which leads to price changes not reflected in variations in the prices of other stocks. For example, changes in the value of IBM stock may not provide important information to a dealer making a market in the stock of U.S. Steel.

Because dealers can derive information on equilibrium price levels by observing the markets of substitute securities, many dealer firms make markets in a variety of closely related securities instead of specializing in only one or two issues. Dealers trading one type of short-term debt instrument have a clear incentive to trade the entire spectrum of such instruments, because information derived from one market is useful to the dealer in his other markets. Similarly, since there is no sharp demarcation between short-, intermediate-, and long-term debt, dealers have an incentive to trade a full maturity range of debt instruments. The potential profit from acquiring as much information as possible, and in using that information as extensively as possible, impels dealers to broaden the range of securities in which they offer liquidity services.

In those cases where a security does not have close substitutes, it is less important for a dealer to keep in contact with a large number of markets. Fluctuations in the prices of some stock issues, such as those of high-technology firms, depend far more on changes in the fortunes of the issuers than on changes in general market conditions. Dealers can specialize in such issues without suffering a significant disadvantage relative to larger dealers making markets in a wider spectrum of stock issues.

CHAPTER SUMMARY

This chapter has examined the consequences of thinness for the prices of securities transactions. When a dealer is unable to estimate with much accuracy the equilibrium price of a security, he will be led to quote a wider bid-ask spread and will reduce the breadth of his market for that security. Both these consequences of thinness increase the cost of liquidity services in the security. In addition, if a dealer is uncertain about the equilibrium price of a security, he will shift the level of his bid and offer quotations more aggressively in response to his inventory position and in response to the structure of recent transactions, i.e., whether those transactions were purchases or sales. These consequences imply that a dealer's quotations may not accurately reflect the contemporaneous state of aggregate purchase and sale interests in the security.

Some of the costs to investors of trading in a thin market can be reduced by competition among dealers. However, the gains normally associated with competition may be offset, in whole or in part, by fragmenting information over several competing dealers and by introducing price dispersion into a market.

The last section of the chapter has pointed out that uncertainty about equilibrium prices, rather than thinness per se, is the proper focus of concern with thin markets. A security may be traded infrequently yet not exhibit any of the undesirable characteristics associated with thinness if it is a close substitute for an actively traded security. Information about the equilibrium price of the inactively traded security can then be extracted from observation of the market for the actively traded security.

FURTHER READING

Amir Barnea, and Dennis Logue, "The Effect of Risk on the Market Maker's Spread," *Financial Analysts Journal*, **31** (November–December 1975), 45–49.

Kalman Cohen, Steven Maier, Robert Schwartz, and David Whitcomb, "The Returns Generation Process, Returns Variance and the Effect of Thinness in Securities Markets," *Journal of Finance*, **33** (March 1978), 149–167.

Kenneth Garbade and William Silber, "Structural Organization of Secondary Markets: Clearing Frequency, Dealer Activity and Liquidity Risk," *Journal of Finance*, **34** (June 1979), 577–593.

———, "Dominant and Satellite Markets: A Study of Dually-Traded Securities," *Review of Economics and Statistics*, **61** (August 1979), 455–460.

Seymour Smidt, "Which Road to an Efficient Stock Market, Implications of the SEC Institutional Investor Study," *Financial Analysts Journal*, **27** (September–October 1971), 18.

REFERENCES

Aitchison, John, and J. A. Brown, *The Lognormal Distribution* (Cambridge: Cambridge University Press, 1957).

Alexander, Sidney, "Price Movements in Speculative Markets: Trends or Random Walks," *Industrial Management Review*, **2** (May 1961), 7.

Alexander, Sidney, "Price Movements in Speculative Markets: Trends or Random Walks, No. 2," *Industrial Management Review*, **5** (Spring 1964), 25.

Amihud, Yakov, and Haim Mendelson, "Dealership Market, Market-Making with Inventory," *Journal of Financial Economics*, **8** (March 1980), 31.

Andersen, Leonall, and Jerry Jordan, "The Monetary Base—Explanation and Analytical Use," Federal Reserve Bank of St. Louis *Review*, **50** (August 1968), 7.

Anderson, Alison, "The Disclosure Process in Federal Securities Regulation: A Brief Review," *Hastings Law Journal*, **25** (1974), 311.

Ang, James, and Kiritkumar Patel, "Bond Rating Methods: Comparison and Validation," *Journal of Finance*, **30** (May 1975), 631.

Arak, Marcelle, and Christopher McCurdy, "Interest Rate Futures," Federal Reserve Bank of New York *Quarterly Review*, **4** (Winter 1979–80), 33.

Arrow, Kenneth, "Limited Knowledge and Economic Analysis," *American Economic Review*, **64** (March 1974), 1.

Astrom, K., *Introduction to Stochastic Control Theory* (New York: Academic Press, 1970).

Bagehot, Walter, "The Only Game in Town," *Financial Analysts Journal*, **27** (March–April 1971), 12.

Balbach, Anatol, and Albert Burger, "Derivation of the Monetary Base," Federal Reserve Bank of St. Louis *Review*, **58** (November 1976), 2.

Ball, Ray, and Philip Brown, "An Empirical Evaluation of Accounting Income Numbers," *Journal of Accounting Research*, **6** (Autumn 1968), 159.

Banks, Lois, "The Market for Agency Securities," *Federal Reserve Bank of New York Quarterly Review*, **3** (Spring 1978), 7.

Barnea, Amir, "Performance Evaluation of New York Stock Exchange Specialists," *Journal of Financial and Quantitative Analysis*, **9** (September 1974), 511.

Barnea, Amir, and David Downes, "A Reexamination of the Empirical Distribution of Stock Price Changes," *Journal of the American Statistical Association*, **68** (June 1973), 348.

Barnea, Amir, and Dennis Logue, "The Effect of Risk on the Market Maker's Spread," *Financial Analysts Journal*, **31** (November–December 1975), 45.

Bar-Yosef, Sasson, and Lawrence Brown, "A Reexamination of Stock Splits Using Moving Betas," *Journal of Finance*, **32** (September 1977), 1069.

Basu, S., "Investment Performance of Common Stocks in Relation to Their Price-Earnings Ratios: A Test of the Efficient Market Hypothesis," *Journal of Finance*, **32** (June 1977), 663.

Beaver, William, "The Information Content of Annual Earnings Announcements," *Journal of Accounting Research*, **6** (Supplement 1968), 67.

Beaver, William, "Current Trends in Corporate Disclosure," *Journal of Accountancy*, (January 1978), 44.

Beaver, William, Paul Kettler, and Myron Scholes, "The Association between Market Determined and Accounting Determined Risk Measures," *Accounting Review*, **45** (October 1970), 654.

Beja, Avraham, "On Systematic and Unsystematic Components of Financial Risk," *Journal of Finance*, **27** (March 1972), 37.

Beja, Avraham, and M. Barry Goldman, "On the Dynamic Behavior of Prices in Disequilibrium," *Journal of Finance*, **35** (May 1980), 235.

Beja, Avraham, and Nils Hakansson, "Dynamic Market Processes and the Rewards to Up-to-Date Information," *The Journal of Finance*, **32** (May 1977), 291.

Bell, Geoffrey, *The Euro-Dollar Market and The International Financial System* (New York: John Wiley & Sons, Inc., 1973).

Bellemore, Douglas, and Lillian Blucher, "A Study of Stock Splits in the Postwar Years," *Financial Analysts Journal*, **15** (November 1956), 19.

Belliveau, Nancy, "Will Pension Officers Stop Trying to Beat the Market?," *Institutional Investor*, **10** (February 1976), 18.

Belliveau, Nancy, "Passive Trading Gets Active," *Institutional Investor*, **11** (April 1977), 56.

Benston, George, "The Effectiveness and Effects of SEC's Accounting Disclosure Requirements," in *Economic Policy and the Regulation of Corporate Securities*, H. Manne, ed. (Washington: American Enterprise Institute, 1969).

Benston, George, "Required Disclosure and the Stock Market: An Evaluation of the Securities Exchange Act of 1934," *American Economic Review*, **63** (March 1973), 132.

Benston, George, and Robert Hagerman, "Determinants of Bid-Ask Spreads in the Over-the-Counter Market," *Journal of Financial Economics*, **1** (December 1974), 353.

Ben-Zion, Uri, and Sol Shalit, "Size, Leverage, and Dividend Record as Determinants of Equity Risk," *Journal of Finance*, **30** (September 1975), 1015.

Bernstein, Leopold, "In Defense of Fundamental Investment Analysis," *Financial Analysts Journal*, **31** (January–February 1975), 57.

Bialkin, Kenneth, et al., "Current Issues and Developments in the Duties and Liabilities of Underwriters and Securities Dealers," *Business Lawyer*, **33** (November 1977), 335.

Bierwag, G. O., "Immunization, Duration, and the Term Structure of Interest Rates," *Journal of Financial and Quantitative Analysis*, **12** (December 1977), 725.

Bierwag, G. O., and M. A. Grove, "Slutsky Equations for Assets," *Journal of Political Economy*, **76** (February 1968), 114.

Bierwag, G. O., and George Kaufman, "Coping with the Risk of Interest Rate Fluctuations: A Note," *Journal of Business*, **50** (July 1977), 364.

Bierwag, G. O., and George Kaufman, "Bond Portfolio Strategy Simulations: A Critique," *Journal of Financial and Quantitative Analysis*, **13** (September 1978), 519.

Black, Deborah, Kenneth Garbade, and William Silber, "The Impact of the GNMA Pass-Through Program on FHA Mortgage Costs," *Journal of Finance*, **36** (May 1981), 457.

Black, Ficher, "Implications of the Random Walk Hypothesis for Portfolio Management," *Financial Analysts Journal*, **27** (March–April 1971a), 16.

Black, Fischer, "Toward a Fully Automated Exchange," *Financial Analysts Journal*, **27** (July–August 1971b), 29, and **27** (November–December 1971b), 25.

Black, Fischer, "Capital Market Equilibrium with Restricted Borrowing," *Journal of Business*, **45** (July 1972), 444.

Black, Fischer, "Yes Virginia, There Is Hope: Tests of the Value Line System," *Financial Analysts Journal*, **29** (September–October 1973), 10.

Black, Fischer, "Fact and Fantasy in the Use of Options," *Financial Analysts Journal*, **31** (July–August 1975), 36.

Black, Fischer, "The Pricing of Commodity Contracts," *Journal of Financial Economics*, **3** (January–March 1976), 167.

Black, Fischer, and John Cox, "Valuing Corporate Securities: Some Effects of Bond Indenture Provisions," *Journal of Finance*, **31** (May 1976), 351.

Black, Fischer, Michael Jensen, and Myron Scholes, "The Capital Asset Pricing Model: Some Empirical Tests," in *Studes in the Theory of Capital Markets*, Michael Jensen, ed. (New York: Frederick A. Praeger, Inc., 1972).

Black, Fischer, and Myron Scholes, "The Valuation of Option Contracts and a Test of Market Efficiency," *Journal of Finance*, **27** (May 1972), 399.

Black, Fischer, and Myron Scholes, "The Pricing of Options and Corporate Liabilities," *Journal of Political Economy*, **81** (May–June 1973), 637.

Black, Fischer, and Myron Scholes, "From Theory to a New Financial Product," *Journal of Finance*, **29** (May 1974a), 399.

Black, Fischer, and Myron Scholes, "The Effects of Dividend Yield and Dividend Policy on Common Stock Prices and Returns," *Journal of Financial Economics*, **1** (May 1974b), 1.

Black, Stanley, "An Econometric Study of Euro-Dollar Borrowing by New York Banks and the Rate of Interest on Euro-Dollars," *Journal of Finance*, **26** (March 1971), 83.

Blattberg, Robert, and Nicholas Gonedes, "A Comparison of the Stable and Student Distributions as Statistical Models for Stock Prices," *Journal of Business*, **47** (April 1974), 244.

Bleakley, Fred, "Is NASDAQ Really the Answer?" *Institutional Investor*, **5** (July 1971), 21.

Bloch, Ernest, and Arnold Sametz, *A Modest Proposal for a National Securities Market System and Its Governance* (New York: New York University, 1977).

Bloomenthal, Harold, "The Case of the Subtle Motive and the Delicate Art—Control and Domination in Over-the-Counter Securities Markets," *Duke Law Journal,* **1960** (1960), 196.

Bloomenthal, Harold, "Market-Makers, Manipulators and Shell Games," *St. John's Law Review,* **45** (1971), 597.

Blume, Marshall, "Portfolio Theory: A Step Toward Its Practical Application," *Journal of Business,* **43** (April 1970), 152.

Blume, Marshall, "Betas and Their Regression Tendencies," *Journal of Finance,* **30** (June 1975), 785.

Board of Governors of the Federal Reserve System, *Treasury-Federal Study of the Government Securities Market* (1959).

Board of Governors of the Federal Reserve System, *Joint Treasury-Federal Reserve Study of the U.S. Government Securities Market* (1969).

Board of Governors of the Federal Reserve System, *Reappraisal of the Federal Reserve Discount Mechanism* (1971).

Boatler, Robert, "Variation in the Price Elasticity of Demand for Treasury Bills," *Southern Economic Journal,* **42** (July 1975), 44.

Bodie, Zvi, and Benjamin Friedman, "Interest Rate Uncertainty and the Value of Bond Call Protection," *Journal of Political Economy,* **86** (February 1978), 19.

Boness, A. James, "Elements of a Theory of Stock-Option Value," *Journal of Political Economy,* **72** (April 1964), 163.

Borch, Karl, "Indifference Curves and Uncertainty," *Swedish Journal of Economics,* **70** (March 1968), 19.

Borch, Karl, "A Note on Uncertainty and Indifference Curves," *Review of Economic Studies,* **36** (January 1969), 1.

Breen, William, and Eugene Lerner, "Corporate Financial Strategies and Market Measures of Risk and Return," *Journal of Finance,* **28** (May 1973), 339.

Brennan, Michael, "Taxes, Market Valuation and Corporate Financial Policy," *National Tax Journal,* **23** (December 1970), 417.

Brennan, Michael, "Capital Market Equilibrium with Divergent Borrowing and Lending Rates," *Journal of Financial and Quantitative Analysis,* **6** (December 1971), 1197.

Brennan, Michael, and Eduardo Schwartz, "Convertible Bonds: Valuation and Optimal Strategies for Call and Conversion," *Journal of Finance,* **32** (December 1977), 1699.

Brennan, Michael, and Eduardo Schwartz, "Finite Difference Methods and Jump Processes Arising in the Pricing of Contingent Claims: A Synthesis," *Journal of Financial and Quantitative Analysis,* **13** (September 1978), 461.

Brennan, Michael, and Eduardo Schwartz, *Savings Bonds: Theory and Empirical Evidence* (New York: New York University, 1979).

Brimmer, Andrew, "Price Determination in the United States Treasury Bill Market," *Review of Economics and Statistics,* **44** (May 1962), 178.

Brooks, John, *The Go-Go Years* (New York: Weybright and Talley, 1973).

Brown, Philip, and John Kennelly, "The Information Content of Quarterly Earnings: An Extension and Some Further Evidence," *Journal of Business,* **45** (July 1972), 403.

Brown, Philip, and Victor Niederhoffer, "The Predictive Content of Quarterly Earnings," *Journal of Business,* **41** (October 1968), 488.

Brudney, Victor, and Marvin Chirelstein, *Corporate Finance* (Mineola, N.Y.: The Foundation Press, 1972).

Burger, Albert, "The Relationship between Monetary Base and Money: How Close?" Federal Reserve Bank of St. Louis *Review,* **57** (October 1975), 3.

Burger, Albert, Richard Lang, and Robert Rasche, "The Treasury Bill Futures Market and Market Expectations of Interest Rates," Federal Reserve Bank of St. Louis *Review*, **59** (June 1977), 2.

Buse, A., "Interest Rates, The Meiselman Model and Random Numbers," *Journal of Political Economy,* **75** (February 1967), 49.

Cagan, Phillip, and Anna Schwartz, "Has the Growth of Money Substitutes Hindered Monetary Policy?" *Journal of Money, Credit and Banking*, **7** (May 1975), 137.

Campanella, Frank, *The Measurement of Portfolio Risk Exposure* (Lexington, Mass.: Lexington Books, 1972).

Capozza, Dennis, and Bradford Cornell, "Treasury Bill Pricing in the Spot and Futures Markets," *Review of Economics and Statistics*, **61** (November 1979), 513.

Carey, Kenneth, "Nonrandom Price Changes in Association with Trading in Large Blocks: Evidence of Market Efficiency in Behavior of Investor Returns," *Journal of Business*, **50** (October 1977), 407.

Carleton, Willard, and Eugene Lerner, "Statistical Credit Scoring of Municipal Bonds," *Journal of Money, Credit and Banking*, **1** (November 1969), 750.

Carr, J. L., P. J. Halpern, and J. S. McCallum, "Correcting the Yield Curve: A Re-Interpretation of the Duration Problem," *Journal of Finance*, **29** (September 1974), 1287.

Carson, Ralph, "Some Abuses of Antitrust Prosecution: The Investment Bankers Case," *Michigan Law Review*, **54** (1956), 363.

Clark, Peter, "A Subordinated Stochastic Process Model with Finite Variance for Speculative Prices," *Econometrica*, **41** (January 1973), 135.

Clendenning, E. Wayne, *The Euro-Dollar Market* (London: Oxford University Press, 1970).

Cloos, George, "A Larger Role for Commercial Paper," *Journal of Commercial Bank Lending*, **51** (April 1969), 2.

Close, Nicholas, "Price Reaction to Large Transactions in the Canadian Equity Markets," *Financial Analysts Journal*, **31** (November–December 1975), 50.

Coats, Warren, "Regulation D and the Vault Cash Game," *Journal of Finance*, **28** (June 1973), 601.

Coats, Warren, "Lagged Reserve Accounting and the Money Supply Mechanism," *Journal of Money, Credit and Banking*, **8** (May 1976), 167.

Cohen, Jacob, "Federal Reserve Margin Requirements and the Stock Market," *Journal of Financial and Quantitative Analysis*, **1** (September 1966), 30.

Cohen, Kalman, Gabriel Hawawini, Steven Maier, Robert Schwartz, and David Whitcomb, "Implications of Microstructure Theory for Empirical Research on Stock Price Behavior," *Journal of Finance*, **35** (May 1980), 249.

Cohen, Kalman, Steven Maier, Walter Ness, Hitoshi Okuda, Robert Schwartz, and David Whitcomb, "The Impact of Designated Market Makers on Security Prices," *Journal of Banking and Finance*, **1** (November 1977), 219.

Cohen, Kalman, Steven Maier, Robert Schwartz, and David Whitcomb, "The Returns Generation Process, Returns Variance, and the Effect of Thinness in Securities Markets," *Journal of Finance*, **33** (March 1978a), 149.

Cohen, Kalman, Steven Maier, Robert Schwartz, and David Whitcomb, "Limit Orders, Market Structure, and the Returns Generation Process," *Journal of Finance*, **33** (June 1978b), 723.

Cohen, Kalman, Steven Maier, Robert Schwartz, and David Whitcomb, "Market Makers and the Market Spread: A Review of Recent Literature," *Journal of Financial and Quantitative Analysis*, **14** (November 1979), 813.

Cohen, Kalman, Steven Maier, Robert Schwartz, and David Whitcomb, "Transaction Costs, Order Placement Strategy, and Existence of the Bid-Ask Spread," *Journal of Political Economy,* **89** (April 1981), 287.

Cohen, Kalman, and Jerry Pogue, "An Empirical Evaluation of Alternative Portfolio-Selection Models," *Journal of Business*, **40** (April 1967), 166.

Cohen, Milton, "'Truth in Securities,' Revisited," *Harvard Law Review*, **79** (1966), 1340.

Collins, Daniel, "SEC Product-Line Reporting and Market Efficiency," *Journal of Financial Economics*, **2** (June 1975), 125.

Connelly, Julie, "The Irrepressible Growth of Commercial Paper," *Institutional Investor*, **12** (March 1978), 25.

Cooper, Ian, "Asset Values, Interest-Rate Changes, and Duration," *Journal of Financial and Quantitative Analysis*, **12** (December 1977), 701.

Cootner, Paul, ed., *The Random Character of Stock Market Prices* (Cambridge, Mass.: The M.I.T. Press, 1964).

Copeland, Thomas, "A Model of Asset Trading under the Assumption of Sequential Information Arrival," *Journal of Finance*, **31** (September 1976), 1149.

Copeland, Thomas, "A Probability Model of Asset Trading," *Journal of Financial and Quantitative Analysis*, **12** (November 1977), 563.

Copeland, Thomas, "Liquidity Changes Following Stock Splits," *Journal of Finance*, **34** (March 1979), 115.

Cox, Charles, "Futures Trading and Market Information," *Journal of Political Economy*, **84** (December 1976), 1215.

Cox, John, and Stephen Ross, "The Valuation of Options for Alternative Stochastic Processes," *Journal of Financial Economics*, **3** (January–March, 1976), 145.

Cox, John, Stephen Ross, and Mark Rubinstein, "Option Pricing: A Simplified Approach," *Journal of Financial Economics,* **7** (September 1979), 229.

Crane, Dwight, "Lessons from the 1974 CD Market," *Harvard Business Review*, **53** (November–December 1975), 73.

Crane, Dwight, "A Study of Interest Rate Spreads in the 1974 CD Market," *Journal of Bank Research*, **7** (Autumn 1976), 213.

Crowell, Richard, "Risk Measurement: Five Applications," *Financial Analysts Journal*, **29** (July–August 1973), 81.

Culbertson, John, "The Term Structure of Interest Rates," *Quarterly Journal of Economics*, **71** (November 1957), 485.

Cuneo, Larry, and Wayne Wagner, "Reducing the Cost of Stock Trading," *Financial Analysts Journal*, **31** (November–December 1975), 35.

Curley, Anthony, and Jack Guttenberg, "The Yield on Insured Residential Mortgages," *Explorations in Economic Research*, **1** (Summer 1974), 114.

Dann, Larry, David Mayers, and Robert Raab, "Trading Rules, Large Blocks and the Speed of Price Adjustment," *Journal of Financial Economics*, **4** (January 1977), 3.

Demsetz, Harold, "The Cost of Transacting," *Quarterly Journal of Economics*, **82** (February 1968), 33.

Demsetz, Harold, "Information and Efficiency: Another Viewpoint," *Journal of Law and Economics*, **12** (April 1969), 1.

Demsetz, Harold, "The Private Production of Public Goods," *Journal of Law and Economics*, **13** (October 1970), 293.

Doty, Robert, and John Petersen, "The Federal Securities Laws and Transactions in Municipal Securities," *Northwestern University Law Review*, **71** (July–August 1976), 283.

Duncan, Wallace, "Treasury Bill Futures—Opportunities and Pitfalls," Federal Reserve Bank of Dallas *Review* (July 1977), 1.

Dusak, Katherine, "Futures Trading and Investor Returns: An Investigation of Commodity Market Risk Premiums," *Journal of Political Economy*, **81** (November–December 1973), 1387.

Eckardt, Walter, and Donald Rogoff, "100% Margins Revisited," *Journal of Finance*, **31** (June 1976), 995.

Ederington, Louis, "The Yield Spread on New Issues of Corporate Bonds," *Journal of Finance*, **29** (December 1974), 1531.

Ederington, Louis, "Uncertainty, Competition and Costs in the Underwriting of Corporate Bonds," *Journal of Financial Economics*, **2** (March 1975), 71.

Ederington, Louis, "Negotiated versus Competitive Underwritings of Corporate Bonds," *Journal of Finance*, **31** (March 1976), 17.

Ederington, Louis, "The Hedging Performance of the New Futures Markets," *Journal of Finance*, **34** (March 1979), 157.

Ehrbar, A. F., "Technical Analysis Refuses to Die," *Fortune*, **92** (August 1975), 99.

Ehrbar, A. F. "Index Funds—An Idea Whose Time Is Coming," *Fortune*, **93** (June 1976), 145

Eiteman, Wilford, and David Eiteman, *Leading World Stock Exchanges: Trading Practices and Organization* (Ann Arbor, Mich.: University of Michigan, 1964).

Elliot, J. W., and M. E. Echols, "Market Segmentation, Speculative Behavior, and the Term Structure of Interest Rates," *Review of Economics and Statistics*, **58** (February 1976), 40.

Elton, Edwin, and Martin Gruber, "Marginal Stockholder Tax Rates and the Clientele Effect," *Review of Economics and Statistics*, **53** (February 1970), 68.

Elton, Edwin, and Martin Gruber, "The Economic Value of the Call Option," *Journal of Finance*, **27** (September 1972), 891.

Elton, Edwin, and Martin Gruber, "Estimating the Dependence Structure of Share Prices—Implications for Portfolio Selection," *Journal of Finance*, **28** (December 1973), 1203.

Elton, Edwin, and Martin Gruber, "Portfolio Theory When Investment Relatives Are Lognormally Distributed," *Journal of Finance*, **29** (September 1974), 1265.

Epps, Thomas, and Mary Epps, "The Stochastic Dependence of Security Price Changes and Transaction Volumes: Implications for the Mixture-of-Distributions Hypothesis," *Econometrica*, **44** (March 1976), 305.

Evans, John, "An Analysis of Portfolio Maintenance Strategies," *Journal of Finance*, **25** (June 1970), 561.

Fabozzi, Frank, and Jack Francis, "Stability Tests for Alphas and Betas over Bull and Bear Market Conditions," *Journal of Finance*, **32** (September 1977), 1093.

Fama, Eugene, "Mandelbrot and the Stable Paretian Hypothesis," *Journal of Business*, **36** (October 1963), 420.

Fama, Eugene, "The Behavior of Stock-Market Prices," *Journal of Business*, **38** (January 1965a), 34.

Fama, Eugene, "Portfolio Analysis in a Stable Paretian Market," *Management Science*, series A, **11** (January 1965b), 404.

Fama, Eugene, "Risk, Return and Equilibrium: Some Clarifying Comments," *Journal of Finance*, **23** (March 1968), 29.

Fama, Eugene, "Efficient Capital Markets: A Review of Theory and Empirical Work," *Journal of Finance*, **25** (May 1970), 383.

Fama, Eugene, "Risk, Return, and Equilibrium," *Journal of Political Economy*, **79** (January–February 1971), 30.

Fama, Eugene, "A Note on the Market Model and the Two-Parameter Model," *Journal of Finance*, **28** (December 1973), 1181.

Fama, Eugene, "Short-Term Interest Rates as Predictors of Inflation," *American Economic Review*, **65** (June 1975), 269.

Fama, Eugene, "Reply," *Journal of Finance*, **31** (March 1976a), 143.

Fama, Eugene, "Forward Rates as Predictors of Future Spot Rates," *Journal of Financial Economics*, **3** (October 1976b), 361.

Fama, Eugene, and Marshall Blume, "Filter Rules and Stock-Market Trading," *Journal of Business*, **39** (Supplement, January 1966), 226.

Fama, Eugene, Lawrence Fisher, Michael Jensen, and Richard Roll, "The Adjustment of Stock Prices to New Information," *International Economic Review*, **10** (February 1969), 1.

Fama, Eugene, and Arthur Laffer, "Information and Capital Markets," *Journal of Business*, **44** (July 1971), 289.

Fama, Eugene, and James MacBeth, "Risk, Return and Equilibrium: Empirical Tests," *Journal of Political Economy*, **81** (May–June 1973), 607.

Fama, Eugene, and Richard Roll, "Some Properties of Symmetric Stable Distributions," *Journal of the American Statistical Association*, **63** (September 1968), 817.

Fama, Eugene, and Richard Roll, "Parameter Estimates for Symmetric Stable Distributions," *Journal of the American Statistical Association*, **66** (June 1971), 331.

Feige, Edgar, and Robert McGee, "Money Supply Control and Lagged Reserve Accounting," *Journal of Money, Credit and Banking*, **9** (November 1977), 536.

Feldstein, Martin, "Mean-Variance Analysis in the Theory of Liquidity Preference and Portfolio Selection," *Review of Economic Studies*, **36** (January 1969), 5.

Ferber, Robert, "Short-Run Effects of Stock Market Services on Stock Prices," *Journal of Finance*, **13** (March 1958), 80.

Feuerstein, Donald, "Toward a National System of Securities Exchanges," *Financial Analysts Journal*, **28** (May–June 1972), 28, and **28** (July–August 1972), 57.

Figlewski, Stephen, "A Layman's Introduction to Stochastic Processes in Continuous Time," Salomon Brothers Center Working Paper No. 118, Graduate School of Business Administration, New York University (May 1977).

Figlewski, Stephen, "'Market Efficiency' in a Market with Heterogeneous Information," *Journal of Political Economy*, **86** (August 1978), 581.

Figlewski, Stephen, "Subjective Information and Market Efficiency in a Betting Market," *Journal of Political Economy*, **87** (February 1979), 75.

Figlewski, Stephen, "Futures Trading and Volatility in the GNMA Market," *Journal of Finance*, **36** (May 1981), 445.

Findlay, M. Chapman, and Elko Kleinschmidt, "Error-Learning in the Eurodollar Market," *Journal of Financial and Quantitative Analysis*, **10** (September 1975), 429.

Finnerty, Joseph, "Insiders and Market Efficiency," *Journal of Finance*, **31** (September 1976), 1141.

Finnerty, Joseph, "The Chicago Board Options Exchange and Market Efficiency," *Journal of Financial and Quantitative Analysis*, **13** (March 1978), 29.

Fisher, Irving, *The Theory of Interest* (New York: The Macmillan Company, 1930).

Fisher, Lawrence, "Determinants of Risk Premiums on Corporate Bonds," *Journal of Political Economy*, **67** (June 1959), 217.

Fisher, Lawrence, "Some New Stock-Market Indexes," *Journal of Business*, **39** (Supplement, January 1966), 191.

Fisher, Lawrence, and James Lorie, "Rates of Return on Investments In Common Stocks," *Journal of Business*, **37** (January 1964), 1.

Fisher, Lawrence, and James Lorie, "Rates of Return on Investments in Common Stock: The Year-by-Year Record, 1926–65," *Journal of Business,* **41** (July 1968), 291.

Fisher, Lawrence, and James Lorie, "Some Studies of Variability of Returns on Investments in Common Stocks," *Journal of Business*, **43** (April 1970), 99.

Fisher, Lawrence, and Roman Weil, "Coping with the Risk of Interest-Rate Fluctuations: Returns to Bondholders from Naive and Optimal Strategies," *Journal of Business*, **44** (October 1971), 408.

Fiske, Heidi, "Can the Specialist System Cope with the Age of Block Trading?" *Institutional Investor*, **3** (August 1969), 29.

Fleischer, Arthur, Robert Mundheim, and John Murphy, "An Initial Inquiry into the Responsibility to Disclose Market Information," *University of Pennsylvania Law Review*, **121** (1973), 798.

Fleuriet, Michel, *Public and Private Offerings of Public Debt* (New York: New York University, 1975).

Fraine, Harold, and Robert Mills, "Effect of Defaults and Credit Deterioration on Yields of Corporate Bonds," *Journal of Finance*, **16** (September 1961), 423.

Fredman, Albert, "The 'Fourth Market' Is Real," *The Commercial and Financial Chronical* (August 5, 1974).

Friedman, Milton, *A Program for Monetary Stability* (New York: Fordham University Press, 1959).

Friedman, Milton, "Price Determination in the United States Treasury Bill Market: A Comment," *Review of Economics and Statistics*, **45** (August 1963), 318.

Friedman, Milton, "Comment on Collusion in the Auction Market for Treasury Bills," *Journal of Political Economy*, **72** (October 1964), 513.

Friedman, Milton, "The Euro-Dollar Market: Some First Principles," *Morgan Guaranty Survey* (October 1969), 4.

Friedman, Milton, "Controls on Interest Rates Paid by Banks," *Journal of Money, Credit and Banking*, **2** (February 1970), 15.

Friend, Irwin, and Marshall Blume, "Measurement of Portfolio Performance under Uncertainty," *American Economic Review*, **60** (September 1970), 561.

Friend, Irwin, G. Wright Hoffman, Willis Winn, Morris Hamburg, and Stanley Schor, *The Over-the-Counter Securities Markets* (New York: McGraw-Hill Book Company, 1958).

Froewiss, Kenneth, "GNMA Futures: Stabilizing or Destabilizing?" Federal Reserve Bank of San Francisco *Economic Review* (Spring 1978), 20.

Galai, Dan, "Tests of Market Efficiency of the Chicago Board Options Exchange," *Journal of Business*, **50** (April 1977), 167.

Galai, Dan, "On the Boness and Black-Scholes Models for Valuation of Call Options," *Journal of Financial and Quantitative Analysis*, **13** (March 1978a), 15.

Galai, Dan, "Empirical Tests of Boundary Conditions for CBOE Options," *Journal of Financial Economics*, **6** (June–September 1978b), 187.

Galston, Arthur, *Security Syndicate Operations*, rev. ed. (New York: The Ronald Press Company, 1928).

Garbade, Kenneth, "Two Methods for Examining the Stability of Regression Coefficients," *Journal of the American Statistical Association*, **72** (March 1977), 54.

Garbade, Kenneth, "The Effect of Interdealer Brokerage on the Transactional Characteristics of Dealer Markets," *Journal of Business*, **51** (July 1978a), 477.

Garbade, Kenneth, "Electronic Quotation Systems and the Market for Government Securities," Federal Reserve Bank of New York *Quarterly Review*, **3** (Summer 1978b), 13.

Garbade, Kenneth, and Joseph Hunt, "Risk Premiums on Federal Agency Debt," *Journal of Finance*, **33** (March 1978), 105.

Garbade, Kenneth, and Monica Kaicher, "Exchange-Traded Options on Common Stock," Federal Reserve Bank of New York *Quarterly Review*, **3** (Winter 1978–79), 26.

Garbade, Kenneth, and Zvi Lieber, "On the Independence of Transactions on the New York Stock Exchange," *Journal of Banking and Finance*, **1** (October 1977), 151.

Garbade, Kenneth, Jay Pomrenze, and William Silber, "On the Information Content of Prices," *American Economic Review*, **69** (March 1979), 50.

Garbade, Kenneth, and Irene Rosey, "Secular Variation in the Spread between Bid and Offer Prices on U.S. Treasury Coupon Issues," *Business Economics*, **12** (September 1977), 45.

Garbade, Kenneth, and William Silber, "Price Dispersion in the Government Securities Market," *Journal of Political Economy*, **84** (August 1976), 721.

Garbade, Kenneth, and William Silber, "Technology, Communication and the Performance of Financial Markets: 1840–1975," *Journal of Finance,* **33** (June 1978), 819.

Garbade, Kenneth, and William Silber, "Structural Organization of Secondary Markets: Clearing Frequency, Dealer Activity and Liquidity Risk," *Journal of Finance*, **34** (June 1979a), 577.

Garbade, Kenneth, and William Silber, "Dominant and Satellite Markets: A Study of Dually-Traded Securities," *Review of Economics and Statistics*, **61** (August 1979b), 455.

Garbade, Kenneth, and Paul Wachtel, "Time Variation in the Relationship between Inflation and Interest Rates," *Journal of Monetary Economics*, **4** (November 1978), 755.

Garman, M. B., "Market Microstructure," *Journal of Financial Economics*, **3** (June 1976), 257.

Garvy, George, "The Discount Mechanism in Leading Industrial Countries Since World War II," in *Reappraisal of the Federal Reserve Discount Mechanism*, vol. 1 (Washington, D.C.: Board of Governors of the Federal Reserve System, 1971).

Gates, Stephen, "The Developing Option Market: Regulatory Issues and New Investor Interest," *University of Florida Law Review*, **25** (1973), 421.

Geelan, John, and Vincent Fay, *Option Margin Handbook* (New York: New York Institute of Finance, 1977).

Geske, Robert, "A Note on an Analytical Valuation Formula for Unprotected American Call Options on Stocks with Known Dividends," *Journal of Financial Economics*, **7** (December 1979), 375.

Gnedenko, B. V., and Z. N. Kolmogorov, *Limit Distributions for Sums of Independent Random Variables* (Cambridge, Mass.: Addison-Wesley Publishing Company, Inc., 1954).

GNMA Mortgage-Backed Securities Dealers Association, *The Ginnie Mae Manual* (Homewood, Ill.: Dow Jones-Irwin, Inc., 1978).

Goldman, M. Barry, and Avraham Beja, "Market Prices vs. Equilibrium Prices: Returns' Variance, Serial Correlation, and the Role of the Specialist," *Journal of Finance*, **34** (June 1979), 595.

Goldstein, Henry, "Should the Treasury Auction Long-Term Securities?" *Journal of Finance*, **17** (September 1962a), 444.

Goldstein, Henry, "The Friedman Proposal for Auctioning Treasury Bills," *Journal of Political Economy*, **70** (October 1962b), 386.

Gonedes, Nicholas, "Information-Production and Capital Market Equilibrium," *Journal of Finance,* **30** (June 1975), 841.

Gonedes, Nicholas, "Capital Market Equilibrium for a Class of Heterogeneous Expectations in a Two-Parameter World," *Journal of Finance,* **31** (March 1976), 1.

Gonedes, Nicholas, Nicholas Dopouch, and Stephen Penman, "Disclosure Rules, Information-Production, and Capital Market Equilibrium: The Case of Forecast Disclosure Rules," *Journal of Accounting Research*, **14** (Spring 1976), 89.

Gould, J. P., and Dan Galai, "Transactions Costs and the Relationship between Put and Call Prices," *Journal of Financial Economics*, **1** (July 1974), 105.

Gray, William, "Index Funds & Market Timing: Harris Trust's Approach," *Trusts & Estates*, **115** (May 1976), 314.

Greef, Albert, *The Commercial Paper House in the United States*, (Cambridge, Mass.: Harvard University Press, 1938).

Grier, Paul, "Reply to Robert Reback's Comment," *Journal of Business*, **47** (October 1974), 566.

Grier, Paul, and Peter Albin, "Nonrandom Price Changes in Association with Trading in Large Blocks," *Journal of Business*, **46** (July 1973), 425.

Grossman, Sanford, "On the Efficiency of Competitive Stock Markets Where Trades Have Diverse Information," *Journal of Finance*, **31** (May 1976), 573.

Grossman, Sanford, and Joseph Stiglitz, "Information and Competitive Price Systems," *American Economic Review*, **66** (May 1976), 246.

Grube, R. Corwin, O. Maurice Joy, and Don Panton, "Market Responses to Federal Reserve Changes in the Initial Margin Requirement," *Journal of Finance*, **34** (June 1979), 659.

Hackley, Howard, *Lending Functions of the Federal Reserve Banks: A History* (Washington, D.C.: Board of Governors of the Federal Reserve System, 1973).

Hamada, Robert, "The Effect of the Firm's Capital Structure on the Systematic Risk of Common Stocks," *Journal of Finance*, **27** (May 1972), 435.

Hamburger, Michael, and William Silber, "Debt Management and Interest Rates: A Re-Examination of the Evidence," *The Manchester School*, **39** (December 1971), 261.

Hamilton, James, "Competition, Scale Economies, and Transaction Cost in the Stock Market," *Journal of Financial and Quantitative Analysis*, **11** (December 1976), 779.

Hamilton, James, "Marketplace Organization and Marketability: NASDAQ, the Stock Exchange, and the National Market System," *Journal of Finance*, **33** (May 1978), 487.

Handal, Kenneth, "The Commercial Paper Market and the Securities Acts," *The University of Chicago Law Review*, **39** (1972), 362.

Harman, William, "The Evolution of the National Market System—An Overview," *The Business Lawyer*, **33** (July 1978), 2275.

Hart, Janet, and Laura Homer, "Some Credit Aspects of Unconventional Securities," *Mercer Law Review*, **25** (1974), 395.

Haugen, Robert, and Dean Wichern, "The Elasticity of Financial Assets," *Journal of Finance*, **29** (September 1974), 1229.

Hausman, W. H., R. R. West, and J. A. Largay, "Stock Splits, Price Changes, and Trading Profits: A Synthesis," *Journal of Business*, **44** (January 1971), 69.

Hawk, William, *The U.S. Government Securities Market* (Chicago: Harris Trust and Savings Bank, 1974).

Hayes, Samuel, "Investment Banking: Power Structure in Flux," *Harvard Business Review*, **49** (March–April 1971), 136.

Heller, Harry, "Disclosure Requirements under Federal Securities Regulation," *Business Lawyer*, **16** (January 1961), 300.

Henderson, James, and Richard Quandt, *Microeconomic Theory* (New York: McGraw-Hill Book Company, 1971).

Hewson, John, and Eisuke Sakakibara, "The Effect of U.S. Controls on U.S. Commercial Bank Borrowing in the Euro-Dollar Market," *Journal of Finance*, **30** (September 1975), 1101.

Hicks, John, *Value and Capital*, 2d ed. (Oxford: Clarendon Press, 1946).

Hillhouse, Albert, *Municipal Bonds, A Century of Experience* (New York: Prentice-Hall, Inc., 1936).

Hirshleifer, Jack, "The Private and Social Value of Information and the Reward to Inventive Activity" *American Economic Review*, **51** (September 1971), 561.

Hirshleifer, Jack, "Where Are We in the Theory of Information?" *American Economic Review*, **63** (May 1973), 31.

Ho, Thomas, and Hans Stoll, "On Dealer Markets under Competition," *Journal of Finance*, **35** (May 1980), 259.

Hodges, John, "'NASDAQ'—Heartbeat of the OTC Market," *Financial World* (October 25, 1972), 46.

Hoel, Arline, "A Primer on Federal Reserve Float," Federal Reserve Bank of New York *Monthly Review*, **57** (October 1975), 245.

Homer, Sidney, and Leibowitz, Martin, *Inside the Yield Book* (New York: Prentice-Hall, Inc., and New York Institute of Finance, 1972).

Hopewell, Michael, and George Kaufman, "Bond Price Volatility and Term to Maturity: A Generalized Respecification," *American Economic Review*, **63** (September 1973), 749.

Hopewell, Michael, and George Kaufman, "Costs to Municipalities of Selling Bonds by NIC," *National Tax Journal*, **27** (December 1974), 531.

Hopewell, Michael, and George Kaufman, "Commercial Bank Bidding on Municipal Revenue Bonds: New Evidence," *Journal of Finance,* **32** (December 1977), 1647.

Horrigan, James, "The Determination of Long-Term Credit Standing with Financial Ratios," *Journal of Accounting Research*, **4** (Supplement, 1966), 44.

Horton, Joseph, "Statistical Classification of Municipal Bonds," *Journal of Bank Research*, **1** (Autumn 1970), 29.

Horwitz, Bertrand, and Richard Kolodny, "Line of Business Reporting and Security Prices: An Analysis of an SEC Disclosure Rule," *Bell Journal of Economics*, **8** (Spring 1977), 234.

Hotchkiss, Horace, "The Stock Ticker," in *The New York Stock Exchange*, Edmund Stedman, ed. (New York: Greenwood Press, 1905).

Hsu, Der-Ann, Robert Miller, and Dean Wichern, "On the Stable Paretian Behavior of Stock-Market Prices," *Journal of the American Statistical Association*, **69** (March 1974), 108.

Hurley, Evelyn, "The Commercial Paper Market," *Federal Reserve Bulletin*, **63** (June 1977), 525.

Ibbotson, Roger, "Price Performance of Common Stock New Issues," *Journal of Financial Economics*, **2** (September 1975), 235.

Ibbotson, Roger, and Jeffrey Jaffe, "'Hot Issue' Markets," *Journal of Finance*, **30** (September 1975), 1027.

Ibbotson, Roger, and Rex Sinquefield, "Stocks, Bonds, Bills, and Inflation: Year-by-Year Historical Returns (1926–1974)," *Journal of Business*, **49** (January 1976), 11.

Ingersoll, Jonathan, "A Theoretical and Empirical Investigation of the Dual Purpose Funds," *Journal of Financial Economics*, **3** (January–March 1976), 83.

Jacobs, Arnold, "The Impact of Securities Exchange Act Rule 10b-5 on Broker-Dealers," *Cornell Law Review*, **57** (1972), 869.

Jaffe, Jeffrey, "The Effect of Regulation Changes on Insider Trading," *Bell Journal of Economics and Management Science,* **5** (Spring 1974a), 93.

Jaffe, Jeffrey, "Special Information and Insider Trading," *Journal of Business,* **47** (July 1974b), 410.

Jaffe, Jeffrey, and Robert Winkler, "Optimal Speculation against an Efficient Market," *Journal of Finance*, **31** (March 1976), 49.

Jarecki, Henry, "Bullion Dealing, Commodity Exchange Trading and the London Gold Fixing: Three Forms of Commodity Auctions," in *Bidding and Auctioning for Procurement and Allocation*, Yakov Amihud, ed. (New York: New York University Press, 1976).

Jen, Frank, and James Wert, "The Effect of Call Risk on Corporate Bond Yields," *Journal of Finance*, **22** (December 1967), 637.

Jennergren, L. Peter, "Filter Tests of Swedish Share Prices," in *International Capital Markets*, E. Elton and M. Gruber, eds. (Amsterdam: North-Holland Publishing Company, 1975).

Jennergren, L. Peter and Paul Korsvold, "The Non-Random Character of Norwegian and Swedish Stock Market Prices," in *International Capital Markets*, E. Elton and M. Gruber, eds. (Amsterdam: North-Holland Publishing Company, 1975).

Jennings, Richard, and Harold Marsh, *Securities Regulation*, 3d ed. (Mineola, New York: The Foundation Press, 1972).

Jensen, Michael, "The Performance of Mutual Funds in the Period 1945–1964," *Journal of Finance*, **23** (May 1968), 389.

Jensen, Michael, "Risk, The Pricing of Capital Assets, and the Evaluation of Investment Portfolios," *Journal of Business,* **42** (April 1969), 167.

Jensen, Michael, "Capital Markets, Theory and Evidence," *Bell Journal of Economics and Management Science*, **3** (Autumn 1972), 357.

Jensen, Michael, and George Benington, "Random Walks and Technical Theories: Some Additional Evidence," *Journal of Finance*, **25** (May 1970), 469.

Johnson, Ramon, "Term Structures of Corporate Bond Yields as a Function of Risk of Default," *Journal of Finance*, **22** (May 1967), 313.

Johnston, Robert, "Commercial Paper: 1970," Federal Reserve Bank of San Francisco *Monthly Review* (March 1971), 57.

Kane, Edward, "Short-Changing the Small Saver: Federal Government Discrimination against Small Savers during the Viet-Nam War," *Journal of Money, Credit and Banking*, **2** (November 1970), 513.

Kane, Edward, "Market Incompleteness and Divergences between Forward and Futures Interest Rates," *Journal of Finance*, **35** (May 1980), 221.

Kane, Edward, and Burton Malkiel, "The Term Structure of Interest Rates: An Analysis of a Survey of Interest-Rate Expectations," *Review of Economics and Statistics*, **49** (August 1967), 343.

Kantor, Michael, "Market Sensitivities," *Financial Analysts Journal*, **27** (January–February 1971), 64.

Kaplan, Robert, and Richard Roll, "Investor Evaluation of Accounting Information: Some Expirical Evidence," *Journal of Business*, **45** (April 1972), 225.

Karmel, Roberta, "The Investment Banker and the Credit Regulations," *New York University Law Review*, **45** (1970), 59.

Kelly, Paul, and John Webb, "Credit and Securities: The Margin Requirements," *Business Lawyer*, **24** (1969), 1153.

Kendall, Maurice, "The Analysis of Economic Time Series," *Journal of the Royal Statistical Society*, series A, **96** (1953), 11.

Kerekes, Gabriel, "Principles of Margin Trading," in *The Stock Market Handbook*, Frank Zarb and Gabriel Kerekes, eds. (Homewood, Ill.: Dow Jones-Irwin, Inc., 1970).

Kessel, Reuben, *The Cyclical Behavior of the Term Structure of Interest Rates* (New York: National Bureau of Economic Research, 1965).

Kessel, Reuben, "A Study of the Effects of Competition in the Tax-Exempt Bond Market," *Journal of Political Economy*, **79** (July–August 1971), 706.

Keynes, John, *A Treatise on Money* (New York: Harcourt, Brace and Company, Inc., 1930).

Kim, Tye, "An Assessment of the Performance of Mutual Fund Management: 1969–1975," *Journal of Financial and Quantitative Analysis*, **13** (September 1978), 385.

King, Benjamin, "Market and Industry Factors in Stock Price Behavior," *Journal of Business*, **39** (Supplement, January 1966), 139.

King, Joseph, *History of the San Francisco Stock and Exchange Board* (San Francisco: Jos. L. King, 1910).

Klemkosky, Robert, "The Impact of Option Expirations on Stock Prices," *Journal of Financial and Quantitative Analysis*, **13** (September 1978), 507.

Klemkosky, Robert, and John Martin, "The Adjustment of Beta Forecasts," *Journal of Finance,* **30** (September 1975), 1123.

Koo, Delia, *Elements of Optimization* (New York: Springer-Verlag New York Inc., 1977).

Kraus, Alan, and Hans Stoll, "Price Impacts of Block Trading on the New York Stock Exchange," *Journal of Finance*, **27** (June 1972), 569.

Kripke, Homer, "The SEC, the Accountants, Some Myths and Some Realities," *New York University Law Review*, **45** (1970), 1151.

Kripke, Homer, "The Myth of the Informed Layman," *Business Lawyer*, **28** (1973), 631.

Kripke, Homer, "A Search for a Meaningful Securities Disclosure Policy," *Business Lawyer*, **31** (November 1975), 293.

Kripke, Homer, "An Opportunity for Fundamental Thinking—The SEC's Advisory Committee on Corporate Disclosure," *New York Law Journal* (December 13, 1976).

Kripke, Homer, "Where Are We on Securities Disclosure after the Advisory Committee Report?" *Journal of Accounting, Auditing and Finance*, **2** (Fall 1978), 4.

Kripke, Homer, *The SEC and Corporate Disclosure: Regulation in Search of a Purpose* (New York: Law and Business, Inc./Harcourt, Brace Jovanovich, 1979).

Kryzanowski, Lawrence, "Misinformation and Security Markets," *McGill Law Journal,* **24** (1978a), 123.

Kryzanowski, Lawrence, "Misinformation and Regulatory Actions in the Canadian Capital Markets: Some Empirical Evidence," *Bell Journal of Economics,* **9** (Autumn 1978b), 355.

Kryzanowski, Lawrence, "The Efficiency of Trading Suspensions: A Regulatory Action Designed to Prevent the Exploitation of Monopoly Information," *Journal of Finance*, **34** (December 1979), 1187.

Kubarych, Roger, *Foreign Exchange Markets in The United States* (New York: Federal Reserve Bank of New York, 1978).

Lang, Richard, "The FOMC in 1979: Introducing Reserve Targeting," Federal Reserve Bank of St. Louis *Review*, **62** (March 1980), 2.

Lang, Richard, and Robert Rasche, "Debt-Management Policy and the Own Price Elasticity of Demand for U.S. Government Notes and Bonds," Federal Reserve Bank of St. Louis *Review*, **59** (September 1977), 8.

Lang, Richard, and Robert Rasche, "A Comparison of Yields on Futures Contracts and Implied Forward Rates," Federal Reserve Bank of St. Louis *Review,* **60** (December 1978), 21.

Langbein, John, and Richard Posner, "Market Funds and Trust-Investment Law," *American Bar Association Research Journal* (1976), 1.

Largay, James, "100% Margins: Combating Speculation in Individual Security Issues," *Journal of Finance*, **28** (September 1973), 973.

Largay, James, and Richard West, "Margin Changes and Stock Price Behavior," *Journal of Political Economy*, **81** (March–April 1973), 328.

Latané, Henry, O. Maurice Joy, and Charles Jones, "Quarterly Data, Sort-Rank Routines, and Security Evaluation," *Journal of Business*, **43** (October 1970), 427.

Latané, Henry, and Richard Rendleman, "Standard Deviations of Stock Price Ratios Implied in Option Prices," *Journal of Finance*, **31** (May 1976), 369.

Laufenberg, Daniel, "Contemporaneous versus Lagged Reserve Accounting," *Journal of Money, Credit and Banking*, **8** (May 1976), 239.

Laurent, Robert, "Reserve Requirements: Are They Lagged in the Wrong Direction?" *Journal of Money, Credit and Banking,* **11** (August 1979), 301.

Lee, Wayne, Terry Maness, and Donald Tuttle, "Nonspeculative Behavior and the Term Structure," *Journal of Financial and Quantitative Analysis*, **15** (March 1980), 53.

Leibowitz, Martin, "Convertible Securities," *Financial Analysts Journal*, **30** (November–December 1974), 57.

Levy, William, "Innovations in Block Trading," *Trusts & Estates* (September 1971), 763.

Lintner, John, "The Valuation of Risk Assets and the Selection of Risky Investments in Stock Portfolios and Capital Budgets," *Review of Economics and Statistics*, **47** (February 1965a), 13.

Lintner, John, "Security Prices, Risk, and Maximal Gains from Diversification," *Journal of Finance*, **20** (December 1965b), 587.

Lintner, John, "The Aggregation of Investor's Diverse Judgments and Preferences in Purely Competitive Security Markets," *Journal of Financial and Quantitative Analysis*, **4** (December 1969), 347.

Lipton, Martin, "Some Recent Innovations to Avoid the Margin Regulations," *New York University Law Review*, **46** (1971), 1.

Lipton, Martin, "Market Information," *Institute on Securities Regulation*, **5** (1974), 287.

Lipton, Martin, and Erica Steinberger, *Takeovers and Freezeouts,* (New York: Law Journal Seminars-Press, 1978).

Litzenberger, Robert, and Krishna Ramaswamy, "The Effect of Personal Taxes and Dividends on Capital Asset Prices," *Journal of Financial Economics*, **7** (June 1979), 163.

Lloyd-Davies, Peter, and Michael Canes, "Stock Prices and the Publication of Second-Hand Information," *Journal of Business*, **51** (January 1978), 43.

Logue, Dennis, "On the Pricing of Unseasoned Equity Issues: 1965–1969," *Journal of Financial and Quantitative Analysis*, **8** (January 1973), 91.

Logue, Dennis, "Market-Making and the Assessment of Market Efficiency," *Journal of Finance*, **30** (March 1975), 115.

Long, John, "Efficient Portfolio Choice with Differential Taxation of Dividends and Capital Gains," *Journal of Financial Economics*, **5** (August 1977), 25.

Loomis, Carol, "Paulette Papilsky's Deadly Threat to Wall Street," *Fortune*, **99** (April 23, 1979), 90.

Loomis, Philip, and Eugene Rotberg, "Over-the-Counter Market Quotations," *Michigan Law Review*, **62** (1964), 589.

Lorie, James, and Victor Niederhoffer, "Predictive and Statistical Properties of Insider Trading," *Journal of Law and Economics*, **11** (April 1968), 35.

Lucas, Charles, Marcos Jones, and Thom Thurston, "Federal Funds and Repurchase Agreements," Federal Reserve Bank of New York *Quarterly Review*, **2** (Summer 1977), 33.

McCallum, John, "The Expected Holding Period Return, Uncertainty and the Term Structure of Interest Rates," *Journal of Finance*, **30** (May 1975), 307.

McCulloch, J. Huston, "An Estimate of the Liquidity Premium," *Journal of Political Economy*, **83** (February 1975a), 95.

McCulloch, J. Huston, "The Tax-Adjusted Yield Curve," *Journal of Finance*, **30** (June 1975b), 811.

McCurdy, Christopher, "The Dealer Market for United States Government Securities," Federal Reserve Bank of New York *Quarterly Review*, **2** (Winter 1977–78), 35.

McDonald, John, "French Mutual Fund Performance: Evaluation of Internationally-Diversified Portfolios," *Journal of Finance*, **28** (December 1973), 1161.

McDonald, John, "Objectives and Performance of Mutual Funds, 1960–1969," *Journal of Financial and Quantitative Analysis*, **9** (June 1974), 311.

McDonald, John, and A. K. Fisher, "New Issue Stock Price Behavior," *Journal of Finance*, **27** (March 1972), 97.

McDonald, John, and Bertrand Jacquillat, "Pricing of Initial Equity Issues: The French Sealed-Bid Auction," *Journal of Business*, **47** (January 1974), 37.

Machlup, Fritz, "The Magicians and Their Rabbits," *Morgan Guaranty Survey* (May 1971), 3.

Macklin, Gordon, "Market for a New Age," *Financial World* (March 28, 1973), 6.

Malkiel, Burton, *The Term Structure of Interest Rates* (Princeton: Princeton University Press, 1966).

Malkiel, Burton, "The Valuation of Closed-End Investment-Company Shares," *Journal of Finance*, **32** (June 1977), 847.

Mandelbrot, Benoit, "The Variation of Certain Speculative Prices," *Journal of Business*, **36** (October 1963), 394.

Mandelbrot, Benoit, "Forecasts of Future Prices, Unbiased Markets, and 'Martingale' Models," *Journal of Business*, **39** (Supplement, January 1966), 242.

Mandelbrot, Benoit, and Howard Taylor, "On the Distribution of Stock Price Differences," *Operations Research*, **15** (November–December 1967), 1057.

Mann, Bruce, "Prospectuses: Unreadable or Just Unread?—A Proposal to Reexamine Policies against Permitting Projections," *George Washington Law Review*, **40** (1971), 222.

Manne, Henry, "Mergers and the Market for Corporate Control," *Journal of Political Economy*, **73** (April 1965), 110.

Margrabe, William, "The Value of an Option to Exchange One Asset for Another," *Journal of Finance*, **33** (March 1978), 177.

Markowitz, Harry, *Portfolio Selection* (New York: John Wiley & Sons, Inc., 1959).

Martin, Robert, "Broker-Dealer Manipulation of the Over the Counter Market," *Business Lawyer*, **25** (1970), 1463.

Mayers, David, "Nonmarketable Assets and Capital Market Equilibrium under Uncertainty," in *Studies in the Theory of Capital Markets*, Michael Jensen, ed. (New York: Frederick A. Praeger, Inc., 1972).

Meek, Paul, *Open Market Operations* (New York: Federal Reserve Bank of New York, 1978).

Meeker, James, *The Work of the Stock Exchange*, rev. ed. (New York: The Ronald Press Company, 1930).

Meeker, James, *Short Selling* (New York: Harper & Brothers, 1932).

Meiselman, David, *The Term Structure of Interest Rates* (New York: Prentice-Hall, Inc., 1962).

Melton, William, "The Market for Large Negotiable CDs," Federal Reserve Bank of New York *Quarterly Review*, **2** (Winter 1977–78), 22.

Melton, William "Corporate Equities and the National Market System" Federal Reserve Bank of New York *Quarterly Review*, **3** (Winter 1978–79), 13.

Meltzer, Allan, and Gert von der Linde, *A Study of the Dealer Market for Federal Government Securities*, Joint Economic Committee Print, 86th Cong., 2d Sess. (1960).

Mendelson, Morris, *From Automated Quotes to Automated Trading: Restructuring the Stock Market in the U.S.* (New York: New York University, 1972).

Merton, Robert, "The Relationship between Put and Call Option Prices: Comment," *Journal of Finance*, **28** (March 1973a), 183.

Merton, Robert, "Theory of Rational Option Pricing," *Bell Journal of Economics and Management Science*, **4** (Spring 1973b), 141.

Merton, Robert, "On the Pricing of Corporate Debt: The Risk Structure of Interest Rates," *Journal of Finance*, **29** (May 1974), 449.

Merton, Robert, "Option Pricing When Underlying Stock Returns Are Discontinuous," *Journal of Financial Economics*, **3** (January–March 1976), 125.

Merton, Robert, Myron Scholes, and Mathew Gladstein, "The Returns and Risk of Alternative Call Option Portfolio Investment Strategies," *Journal of Business,* **51** (April 1978), 183.

Miller, Edward, "Risk, Uncertainty, and Divergence of Opinion," *Journal of Finance*, **32** (September 1977), 1151.

Miller, Merton and Myron Scholes, "Rates of Return in Relation to Risk: A Re-Examination of Some Recent Findings," in *Studies in the Theory of Capital Markets*, Michael Jensen, ed. (New York: Frederick A. Praeger, Inc., 1972).

Modigliani, Franco, and Merton Miller, "The Cost of Capital, Corporation Finance, and the Theory of Investment," *American Economic Review*, **48** (June 1958), 261.

Modigliani, Franco, and Richard Sutch, "Innovations in Interest Rate Policy," *American Economic Review*, **56** (May 1966), 178.

Modigliani, Franco, and Richard Sutch, "Debt Management and the Term Structure of Interest Rates: An Empirical Analysis of Recent Experience," *Journal of Political Economy*, **75** (Supplement, August 1967), 569.

Monhollon, Jimmie, "Dealer Loans and Repurchase Agreements," in *Instruments of the Money Market*, 4th ed., Timothy Cook, ed. (Richmond, Va.: Federal Reserve Bank of Richmond, 1977).

Mood, Alexander, Franklin Graybill, and Duane Boes, *Introduction to the Theory of Statistics*, 3rd ed. (New York: McGraw-Hill Book Company, 1974).

Moore, Arnold, "A Statistical Analysis of Common Stock Prices," Ph.D. dissertation,

Graduate School of Business, University of Chicago (1962). An abstract appears as "Some Characteristics of Changes in Common Stock Prices," in *The Random Character of Stock Market Prices*, Paul Cootner, ed. (Cambridge, Mass.: The M.I.T. Press, 1964).

Moore, Thomas, "Stock Market Margin Requirements," *Journal of Political Economy*, **74** (April 1966), 158.

Morgan, I. G., "Stock Prices and Heteroscedasticity," *Journal of Business*, **49** (October 1976), 496.

Mossin, Jan, "Equilibrium in a Capital Asset Market," *Econometrica*, **34** (October 1966), 768.

Mossin, Jan, "Optimal Multiperiod Portfolio Policies," *Journal of Business*, **41** (April 1968), 215.

Mullineaux, Donald, "Deposit-Rate Ceilings and Noncompetitive Bidding for U.S. Treasury Bills," *Journal of Money, Credit and Banking*, **5** (February 1973a), 201.

Mullineaux, Donald, "Interest Rate Ceilings and the Treasury-Bill Market: Disintermediation and the Small Saver," Federal Reserve Bank of Boston *New England Economic Review* (July–August 1973b), 19.

Nelson, Charles, *The Term Structure of Interest Rates* (New York: Basic Books, Inc., Publishers, 1972a).

Nelson, Charles, "Estimation of Term Premiums from Average Yield Differentials in the Term Structure of Interest Rates," *Econometrica*, **40** (March 1972b), 277.

Nelson, Charles, "Testing a Model of the Term Structure of Interest Rates in an Error-Learning Framework," *Journal of Political Economy*, **80** (November–December 1972c), 1259.

New York Stock Exchange, *Report of the Committee to Study the Stock Allocation System* (1976).

Nichols, Dorothy, *Trading in Federal Funds* (Washington, D.C.: Board of Governors of the Federal Reserve System, 1965).

Niederhoffer, Victor, and M. F. Osborne, "Market Making and Reversal on the Stock Exchange," *Journal of the American Statistical Association*, **61** (December 1966), 897.

Officer, R. R., "The Distribution of Stock Returns," *Journal of the American Statistical Association*, **67** (December 1972), 807.

Osborne, M. F., "Brownian Motion in the Stock Market," *Operations Research*, **7** (March–April 1959), 145.

Peake, Junius, "The National Market System," *Financial Analysts Journal*, **34** (July–August 1978), 25.

Peck, Anne, ed., *Selected Writings on Futures Markets* (Chicago: Board of Trade of the City of Chicago, 1977).

Percus, Jerome, and Leon Quinto, "The Application of Linear Programming to Competitive Bond Bidding," *Econometrica*, **24** (October 1956), 413.

Peskin, Janice, "Federal Agency Debt and Its Secondary Market," in *Joint Treasury-Federal Reserve Study of the U.S. Government Securities Market*, Staff Studies, Part 2 (Washington, D.C.: Board of Governors of the Federal Reserve System, 1971).

Pinches, George, and Kent Mingo, "A Multivariate Analysis of Industrial Bond Ratings," *Journal of Finance*, **28** (March 1973), 1.

Pinches, George, and Kent Mingo, "The Role of Subordination and Industrial Bond Ratings," *Journal of Finance*, **30** (March 1975), 201.

Platt, Gordon, "Video Display Screens Cut Dealers' Spreads, Increase Volatility of Treasury Market," *The Money Manager* (April 9, 1979), 1.

Pogue, Thomas, and Robert Soldofsky, "What's in a Bond Rating?" *Journal of Financial and Quantitative Analysis*, **4** (June 1969), 201.

Poole, William, "A Proposal for Reforming Bank Reserve Requirements in the United States," *Journal of Money, Credit and Banking*, **8** (May 1976), 137.

Poole, William, "Using T-Bill Futures to Gauge Interest-Rate Expectations," Federal Reserve Bank of San Francisco *Economic Review* (Spring 1978), 7.

Posner, Richard, *Economic Analysis of Law* (Boston: Little, Brown and Company, 1972).

Powers, Mark, "Does Futures Trading Reduce Price Fluctuations in the Cash Markets?" *American Economic Review*, **60** (June 1970), 460.

Pozen, Robert, "Money Managers and Securities Research," *New York University Law Review*, **51** (1976), 923.

Praetz, Peter, "The Distribution of Share Price Changes," *Journal of Business*, **45** (January 1972), 49.

Praetz, Peter, "Rates of Return on Filter Tests," *Journal of Finance*, **31** (March 1976), 71.

Press, S. James, "A Compound Events Model for Security Prices," *Journal of Business*, **40** (July 1967), 317.

Pye, Gordon, "The Value of the Call Option on a Bond," *Journal of Political Economy*, **74** (April 1966), 200.

Pye, Gordon, "The Value of Call Deferment on a Bond: Some Empirical Results," *Journal of Finance*, **22** (December 1967), 623.

Pye, Gordon, "On the Tax Structure of Interest Rates," *Quarterly Journal of Economics*, **83** (November 1969), 562.

Radcliffe, Robert, "Liquidity Costs and Block Trading," *Financial Analysts Journal*, **29** (July–August 1973), 73.

Rattner, R. Lillian, "Another Look at Hedging in the GNMA Futures Market," *Savings Bank Journal*, **58** (April 1977), 35.

Reback, Robert, "Nonrandom Price Changes in Association with Trading in Large Blocks: A Comment," *Journal of Business*, **47** (October 1974), 564.

Reilly, Frank, and William Slaughter, "The Effect of Dual Markets on Common Stock Market Making," *Journal of Financial and Quantitative Analysis*, **8** (March 1973), 167.

Rendleman, Richard, and Christopher Carabini, "The Efficiency of the Treasury Bill Futures Market," *Journal of Finance*, **34** (September 1979), 895.

Rich, Georg, "A Theoretical and Empirical Analysis of the Eurodollar Market," *Journal of Money, Credit and Banking*, **4** (August 1972), 616.

Rieber, Michael, "Collusion in the Auction Market for Treasury Bills," *Journal of Political Economy*, **72** (October 1964), 509.

Rieber, Michael, "Some Characteristics of Treasury Bill Dealers in the Auction Market," *Journal of Finance*, **20** (March 1965), 49.

Rieber, Michael, "Bids, Bid Patterns and Collusion in the Auction Market for Treasury Bills," *Journal of Law and Economics*, **10** (October 1967), 149.

Ritter, Lawrence, and William Silber, *Principles of Money, Banking, and Financial Markets*, 3rd ed. (New York: Basic Books, Inc., Publishers, 1980).

Rittereiser, Robert, *Margin Regulations and Practice* (New York: New York Institute of Finance, 1977).

Robards, Terry, "How 5 Men 'Fix' Bullion Levels," *The New York Times* (December 24, 1974), 25.

Robertson, Wyndham, "The Underwriters Have to Offer Even More," *Fortune*, **87** (January 1973), 116.

Robertson, Wyndham, "Future Shock at Morgan Stanley," *Fortune*, **97** (February 27, 1978), 82.

Robichek, Alexander, and W. David Niebuhr, "Tax-Induced Bias in Reported Treasury Yields," *Journal of Finance*, **25** (December 1970), 1081.

Roll, Richard, "Bias in Fitting the Sharpe Model to Time Series Data." *Journal of Financial and Quantitative Analysis*, **4** (September 1969), 271.

Roll, Richard, *The Behavior of Interest Rates* (New York: Basic Books, Inc., Publisher, 1970).

Roll, Richard, "Investment Diversification and Bond Maturity," *Journal of Finance*, **26** (March 1971), 51.

Roll, Richard, "A Critique of the Asset Pricing Theory's Tests; Part I: On Past and Potential Testability of the Theory,," *Journal of Financial Economics,* **4** (March 1977a), 129.

Roll, Richard, "An Analytic Valuation Formula for Unprotected American Call Options on Stocks with Known Dividends," *Journal of Financial Economics*, **5** (November 1977b), 251.

Roll, Richard, and Stephen Ross, "An Empirical Investigation of the Arbitrage Pricing Theory," *Journal of Finance*, **35** (December 1980), 1073.

Rosenberg, Barr, and Walt McKibben, "The Prediction of Systematic and Specific Risk in Common Stocks," *Journal of Financial and Quantitative Analysis*, **8** (March 1973), 317.

Rosenberg, Barr, and James Ohlson, "The Stationary Distribution of Returns and Portfolio Separation in Capital Markets: A Fundamental Contradiction," *Journal of Financial and Quantitative Analysis*, **11** (September 1976), 393.

Ross, Irwin, "Higher Stakes in the Bond-Rating Game," *Fortune,* **93** (April 1976), 132.

Ross, Stephen, "The Arbitrage Theory of Capital Asset Pricing," *Journal of Economic Theory*, **13** (December 1976), 341.

Ross, Stephen, "The Current Status of the Capital Asset Pricing Model (CAPM)," *Journal of Finance*, **33** (June 1978), 885.

Royama, Shoichi, and Koichi Hamada, "Substitution and Complementarity in the Choice of Risky Assets," in *Risk Aversion and Portfolio Choice,* D. Hester and J. Tobin, eds. (New York: John Wiley & Sons, Inc., 1966).

Ruder, David, "Federal Restrictions on the Sale of Securities," *Northwestern University Law Review*, **67** (Supplement, 1972), 1.

Ruebling, Charlotte, "The Administration of Regulation Q," Federal Reserve Bank of St. Louis *Review*, **52** (February 1970), 29.

Ruff, Raymond, "Effect of a Selection and Recommendation of a 'Stock of the Month,'" *Financial Analysts Journal*, **19** (March–April 1963), 41.

Salmanowitz, John, "Broker Investment Recommendations and the Efficient Capital Market Hypothesis: A Proposed Cautionary Legend," *Stanford Law Review*, **29** (1977), 1077.

Samuelson, Paul, "Proof That Properly Anticipated Prices Fluctuate Randomly," *Industrial Management Review*, **6** (Spring 1965), 41.

Samuelson, Paul, "Efficient Portfolio Selection for Pareto-Lévy Investments," *Journal of Financial and Quantitative Analysis*, **2** (June 1967), 107.

Samuelson, Paul, "The Fundamental Approximation Theorem of Portfolio Analysis in Terms of Means, Variances and Higher Moments," *Review of Economic Studies*, **33** (October 1970), 537.

Sandor, Richard, "Innovation by an Exchange: A Case Study of the Development of the Plywood Futures Contract," *Journal of Law and Economics*, **16** (April 1973), 119.

Sandor, Richard, "Trading Mortgage Interest Rate Futures," Federal Home Loan Bank Board *Journal*, **8** (September 1975), 2.

Santomero, Anthony, "The Economic Effects of NASDAQ: Some Preliminary Results," *Journal of Financial and Quantitative Analysis*, **9** (January 1974), 13.

Sarri, Christopher, "The Efficient Capital Market Hypothesis, Economic Theory and the Regulation of the Securities Industry," *Stanford Law Review*, **29** (1977), 1031.

Schadrack, Frederick, "Demand and Supply in the Commercial Paper Market," *Journal of Finance*, **25** (September 1970), 837.

Schaefer, Stephen, Richard Brealey, Stewart Hodges, and Howard Thomas, "Alternative Models of Systematic Risk," in *International Capital Markets*, E. Elton and M. Gruber, eds. (Amsterdam: North-Holland Publishing Company, 1975).

Schmalensee, Richard, and Robert Trippi, "Common Stock Volatility Expectations Implied by Option Premia," *Journal of Finance*, **33** (March 1978), 129.

Schmidt, Harmut, *Advantages and Disadvantages of an Integrated Market Compared with a Fragmented Market* (Brussels: Commission of the European Communities, 1977).

Schneider, Carl, "Nits, Grits, and Soft Information in SEC Filings," *University of Pennsylvania Law Review*, **121** (1972), 254.

Scholes, Myron, "The Market for Securities: Substitution versus Price Pressure and the Effects of Information on Share Prices," *Journal of Business*, **45** (April 1972), 179.

Scholes, Myron, "Taxes and the Pricing of Options," *Journal of Finance*, **31** (May 1976), 319.

Schwartz, Eduardo, "The Valuation of Warrants: Implementing a New Approach," *Journal of Financial Economics*, **4** (January 1977), 79.

Schweitzer, John, "Commercial Paper and the Securities Act of 1933: A Role for Registration," *Georgetown Law Journal*, **63** (1975), 1245.

Schwert, G. W., "Stock Exchange Seats as Capital Assets," *Journal of Financial Economics*, **4** (January 1977), 51.

Scott, Ira, "Liquidity and the Term Structure of Interest Rates," *Quarterly Journal of Economics*, **79** (February 1965), 135.

Scott, Robert, *Government Securities Market* (New York: McGraw-Hill Book Company, 1965).

Securities and Exchange Commission, *Report of Special Study of Securites Markets* (1963).

Securities and Exchange Commission, *Institutional Investor Study Report* (1971).

Securities and Exchange Commission, *Report of the Advisory Committee on Corporate Disclosure* (1977a).

Securities and Exchange Commission, *Staff Report on Transactions in Securities of the City of New York* (1977b).

Securities and Exchange Commission, *Report of the Special Study of the Options Markets* (1978).

Senft, Dexter, *Inside Pass-Through Securities* (New York: First Boston Corporation, 1978).

Shapiro, Harvey, "How Do You Really Run One of Those Index Funds?" *Institutional Investor*, **10** (February 1976), 24.

Sharpe, William, "A Simplified Model for Portfolio Analysis," *Management Science*, **9** (January 1963), 277.

Sharpe, William, "Capital Asset Prices: A Theory of Market Equilibrium under Conditions of Risk," *Journal of Finance*, **19** (September 1964), 425.

Sharpe, William, "Mutual Fund Performance," *Journal of Business*, **39** (Supplement, January 1966), 119.

Sharpe, William, *Portfolio Theory and Capital Markets*, (New York: McGraw-Hill Book Company, 1970).

Shaw, David, "The Performance of Primary Common Stock Offerings: A Canadian Comparison," *Journal of Finance*, **26** (December 1971), 1103.

Sherwood, Hugh, *How Corporate and Municipal Debt is Rated* (New York: John Wiley & Sons, Inc., 1976).

Shull, Bernard, "Rationale and Objectives of the 1955 Revision of Regulation A," in *Reappraisal of the Federal Reserve Discount Mechanism*, vol. 1 (Washington, D.C.: Board of Governors of the Federal Reserve System, 1971).

Silber, William, "The Market for Federal Agency Securities: Is There an Optimum Size of Issue?" *Review of Economics and Statistics*, **56** (February 1974), 14.

Silber, William, "Thinness in Capital Markets: The Case of the Tel Aviv Stock Exchange," *Journal of Financial and Quantitative Analysis*, **10** (March 1975), 129.

Silber, William, *Municipal Revenue Bond Costs and Bank Underwriting: A Survey of the Evidence* (New York: New York University, 1979).

Simmons, Donald, "Common-Stock Transaction Sequences and the Random-Walk Model," *Operations Research*, **19** (July–August 1971), 845.

Sivesind, Charles, "Mortgage-Backed Securities: The Revolution in Real Estate Finance," Federal Reserve Bank of New York *Quarterly Review*, **4** (Autumn 1979), 1.

Smidt, Seymour, "Which Road to an Efficient Stock Market? Implications of the SEC Institutional Investor Study" *Financial Analysts Journal*, **27** (September–October 1971), 18.

Smith, Clifford, "Option Pricing: A Review," *Journal of Financial Economics*, **3** (January–March 1976), 3.

Smith, Clifford, and Jerold Warner, "On Financial Contracting: An Analysis of Bond Covenants," *Journal of Financial Economics*, **7** (June 1979), 115.

Smith, Vernon, "Bidding Theory and the Treasury Bill Auction: Does Price Discrimination Increase Bill Prices?" *Review of Economics and Statistics*, **48** (May 1966), 141.

Smith, Vernon, "Experimental Studies of Discrimination versus Competition in Sealed-Bid Auction Markets," *Journal of Business*, **40** (January 1967), 56.

Smith, Wayne, "Repurchase Agreements and Federal Funds," *Federal Reserve Bulletin*, **64** (May 1978), 353.

Snyder, Gerard, "Alternative Forms of Options," *Financial Analysts Journal*, **25** (September–October 1969), 93.

Solmssen, Arthur, *The Comfort Letter* (Boston: Little, Brown and Company, 1975).

Solomon, Frederic, and Janet Hart, "Recent Developments in the Regulation of Securities Credit," *Journal of Public Law*, **20** (1971), 167.

Solomon, Frederic, and Janet Hart, "Simplicity v. Effectiveness: Trade-Offs in Regulating Credit to 'Carry' Securities," *Mercer Law Review*, **25** (1974), 415.

Stapleton, Richard, and Marti Subrahmanyam, "Multi-Period Equilibrium Asset Pricing Model," *Econometrica,* **46** (September 1978), 1077.

Steffen, Roscoe, "The Investment Bankers' Case: Some Observations," *Yale Law Journal*, **64** (1954), 169.

Steffen, Roscoe, "The Investment Bankers' Case: Observations in Rejoinder," *Yale Law Journal*, **64** (1955), 863.

Stevens, Neil, "The Futures Market for Farm Commodities—What It Can Mean to Farmers," Federal Reserve Bank of St. Louis *Review*, **56** (August 1974), 10.

Stevens, Neil, "A Mortgage Futures Market: Its Development, Uses, Benefits, and Costs," Federal Reserve Bank of St. Louis *Review*, **58** (April 1976), 12.

Stigler, George, "The Economics of Information," *Journal of Political Economy*, **69** (June 1961), 213.

Stigler, George, "Public Regulation of the Securities Markets," *Journal of Business*, **37** (April 1964), 117.

Stoll, Hans, "The Relationship between Put and Call Option Prices," *Journal of Finance*, **24** (December 1969), 801.

Stoll, Hans, "Reply" *Journal of Finance*, **28** (March 1973), 185.

Stoll, Hans, "Dealer Inventory Behavior: An Empirical Investigation of NASDAQ Stocks," *Journal of Financial and Quantitative Analysis*, **11** (September 1976), 359.

Stoll, Hans, "The Supply of Dealer Services in Securities Markets," *Journal of Finance*, **33** (September 1978), 1133.

Subrahmanyam, Marti, "International Capital Market Equilibrium and Investor Welfare with Unequal Interest Rates," in *International Capital Markets*, E. Elton and M. Gruber, eds. (Amsterdam: North-Holland Publishing Company, 1975a).

Subrahmanyam, Marti, "On the Optimality of International Capital Market Integration," *Journal of Financial Economics*, **2** (March 1975b), 3.

Sunder, Shyam, "Relationship between Accounting Changes and Stock Prices: Problems of Measurement and Some Empirical Evidence," *Journal of Accounting Research*, **11** (Supplement, 1973), 1.

Sunder, Shyam, "Stock Price and Risk Related to Accounting Changes in Inventory Valuation," *The Accounting Review*, **50** (April 1975), 305.

Szeto, Michael, "Estimation of the Volatility of Securities in the Stock Market by Kalman Filtering Techniques," *Proceedings* 1973 *Joint Automatic Control Conference*, 302.

Tanner, J. Ernest, and Levis Kochin, "The Determinants of the Difference between Bid and Ask Prices on Government Bonds," *Journal of Business*, **44** (October 1971), 375.

Taylor, Gregory, and Raymond Leuthold, "The Influence of Futures Trading on Cash Cattle Price Variations," *Food Research Institute Studies*, **13** (1974), 29.

Telser, Lester, "A Critique of Some Recent Empirical Research on the Explanation of the Term Structure of Interest Rates," *Journal of Political Economy*, **75** (Supplement, August 1967), 546.

Telser, Lester, and Harlow Higinbotham, "Organized Futures Markets: Costs and Benefits," *Journal of Political Economy*, **85** (October 1977), 969.

Thackray, John, "The Launching of Floating Rates," *Institutional Investor*, **8** (September 1974), 43.

Tinic, Seha, "The Economics of Liquidity Services," *Quarterly Journal of Economics*, **86** (February 1972), 79.

Tinic, Seha, and Richard West, "Competition and the Pricing of Dealer Service in the Over-the-Counter Stock Market," *Journal of Financial and Quantitative Analysis*, **7** (June 1972), 1707.

Tinic, Seha, and Richard West, "Marketability of Common Stocks in Canada and the

U.S.A.: A Comparison of Agent versus Dealer Dominated Markets," *Journal of Finance*, **29** (June 1974), 729.

Tobin, James, "Liquidity Preference as Behavior Towards Risk," *Review of Economic Studies*, **25** (February 1958), 65.

Tobin, James, "Comment on Borch and Feldstein," *Review of Economic Studies*, **36** (January 1969), 13.

Tobin, James, "Deposit Interest Ceilings as a Monetary Control," *Journal of Money, Credit and Banking*, **2** (February 1970), 4.

Treynor, Jack, "How to Rate Management of Investment Funds," *Harvard Business Review*, **43** (January–February 1965), 63.

Treynor, Jack, "Efficient Markets and Fundamental Analysis," *Financial Analysts Journal*, **30** (March–April 1974), 14.

Turner, Bernice, *The Federal Fund Market* (New York: Prentice-Hall, Inc., 1931).

Vasicek, Oldrich, "Capital Asset Pricing Model with No Riskless Borrowing," unpublished manuscript, Wells Fargo Bank (March 1971).

Vasicek, Oldrich, "A Note on Using Cross-Sectional Information in Bayesian Estimation of Security Betas," *Journal of Finance*, **28** (December 1973), 1233.

Vasicek, Oldrich, and John McQuown, "The Efficient Market Model," *Financial Analysts Journal*, **28** (September–October 1972), 71.

Vickrey, William, "Counterspeculation, Auctions, and Competitive Sealed Tenders," *Journal of Finance*, **16** (March 1961), 8.

Von Neumann, John, and Oscar Morgenstern, *Theory of Games and Economic Behavior*, 2nd ed. (Princeton, N.J.: Princeton University Press, 1947).

Wallace, Neil, "The Term Structure of Interest Rates and the Maturity Composition of the Federal Debt," *Journal of Finance*, **22** (May 1967), 301.

Wallace, Neil, "Buse on Meiselman—A Comment," *Journal of Political Economy*, **77** (July–August 1969), 524.

Wallich, Henry, and Peter Keir, "The Role of Operating Guides in U.S. Monetary Policy: A Historical Review," *Federal Reserve Bulletin*, **65** (September 1979), 679.

Waud, Roger, "Public Interpretation of Federal Reserve Discount Rate Changes: Evidence on the 'Announcement Effect,' " *Econometrica*, **38** (March 1970), 231.

Webb, Kerry, "The Farm Credit System," Federal Reserve Bank of Kansas City *Economic Review*, **65** (June 1980), 16.

Weil, Roman, "Macaulay's Duration: An Appreciation," *Journal of Business*, **46** (October 1973), 589.

Welles, Chris, "The Beta Revolution: Learning to Live with Risk," *Institutional Investor*, **5** (September 1971), 21.

Welles, Chris, "Reprogramming the Money Manager," *Institutional Investor*, **11** (April 1977), 35.

West, Richard, "New Issue Concessions on Municipal Bonds: A Case of Monopsony Pricing," *Journal of Business*, **38** (April 1965a), 135.

West, Richard, "Bidding Competition for Municipal Bonds: The William Morris Episode," *Financial Analysts Journal,* **21** (July–August 1965b), 119.

West, Richard, "More on the Effects of Municipal Bond Monopsony," *Journal of Business*, **39** (April 1966), 305.

West, Richard, "Determinants of Underwriters' Spreads on Tax-Exempt Bond Issues," *Journal of Financial and Quantitative Analysis*, **2** (September 1967), 241.

West, Richard, "An Alternative Approach to Predicting Corporate Bond Ratings," *Journal of Accounting Research*, **8** (Spring 1970), 118.

West, Richard, "Institutional Trading and the Changing Stock Market," *Financial Analysts Journal*, **27** (May–June 1971), 17.

Westerfield, Randolph, "The Distribution of Common Stock Price Changes: An Application of Transactions Time and Subordinated Stochastic Models," *Journal of Financial and Quantitative Analysis*, **12** (December 1977), 743.

White, Shelby, "Showdown at Post 21," *Institutional Investor*, **10** (October 1976), 135.

Whitney, William, "The Investment Bankers' Case—Including a Reply to Professor Steffen," *Yale Law Journal*, **64** (1955a), 319.

Whitney, William, "The Investment Bankers' Case: A Surrejoinder," *Yale Law Journal*, **64** (1955b), 873.

Williamson, J. Peter, "Measurement and Forecasting of Mutual Fund Performance: Choosing an Investment Strategy," *Financial Analysts Journal*, **28** (November–December 1972), 78.

Willis, Parker, "The Secondary Market for Negotiable Certificates of Deposit," in *Reappraisal of the Federal Reserve Discount Mechanism*, vol. 3 (Washington, D.C.: Board of Governors of the Federal Reserve System, 1972a).

Willis, Parker, *The Federal Funds Market—Its Origin and Development*, 5th ed. (Boston: Federal Reserve Bank of Boston, 1972b).

Wolfson, Nicholas, Richard Phillips, and Thomas Russo, *Regulation of Brokers, Dealers and Securities Markets* (Boston: Warren, Gorham & Larmont, 1977).

Wolfson, Nicholas, and Thomas Russo, "The Stock Exchange Specialist: An Economic and Legal Analysis," *Duke Law Journal*, **1970** (1970), 707.

Wood, John, "Expectations, Errors, and the Term Structure of Interest Rates," *Journal of Political Economy*, **71** (April 1963), 160.

Working, Holbrook, "Whose Markets? Evidence on Some Aspects of Futures Trading," *Journal of Marketing*, **19** (July 1954), 1.

Working, Holbrook, *Selected Writings of Holbrook Working* (Chicago: Board of Trade of the City of Chicago, 1977).

Yawitz, Jess, "The Relative Importance of Duration and Yield Volatility on Bond Price Volatility," *Journal of Money, Credit and Banking,* **9** (February 1977), 97.

Ying, Louis, Wilbur Lewellen, Gary Schlarbaum, and Ronald Lease, "Stock Exchange Listings and Securities Returns," *Journal of Financial and Quantitative Analysis*, **12** (September 1977), 415.

Zahorchak, Michael, *Favorable Executions, The Wall Street Specialist and the Auction Market* (New York: Van Nostrand Reinhold, 1974).